Essays in Population History

Essays in Population History : *Mexico and the Caribbean*

Sherburne F. Cook and Woodrow Borah

Volume Two

University of California Press
Berkeley • Los Angeles • London

University of California Press
Berkeley and Los Angeles, California

University of California Press, Ltd.
London, England

Copyright © 1974, by
The Regents of the University of California

ISBN : 0–520–02272–6
Library of Congress Catalog Card Number : 75–123626

Photoset at Thomson Press (India) Limited
Printed in the United States of America

Preface

IN THIS SECOND VOLUME we present eight new essays. Like the essays of Volume I, they are extensions of a central core of inquiry carried out over a lengthening number of years. Since we explain the concerns and development of that inquiry in the preface to Volume I, we now merely remind the reader that our underlying interest has been the impact of European conquest and subsequent domination upon the aboriginal population of the Western Hemisphere. Our studies, initially limited for monographic focus to central Mexico, later extended to an examination of other regions and of the vital characteristics of the post-Conquest Mexican population down to the present. We have tried to rework highly diverse sources into comparable form in order to examine vital phenomena over a number of centuries, the longest span possible covering from the early or middle sixteenth century to the present. These eight new essays continue both extensions of interest.

Our first essay in this volume examines the population Yucatan in terms of numbers and settlement over a period of four and a half centuries: at the time of the coming of the Spaniards, during the initial decades of operation of lethal factors unleashed by that coming, and in subsequent centuries until the Mexican national census of 1960. The essay thus parallels the study of west-central Mexico in Volume I and our monograph on the population of the Mixteca Alta published in Ibero-Americana. It also parallels the chapters on Hispaniola and Colombia in Volume I and our previous work on the coasts of central Mexico. Yucatan is a low-lying peninsula which both resembles central Mexico in having humid, tropical areas and differs from it in having a high proportion of semi-arid land of low annual precipitation, high temperatures, and effectively lesser possible utilization of rainfall by plant life. A dominant karst formation increases the effective aridity. Culturally, the Yucatec Maya belong to southern Meso-America. Our inquiry began with the question whether or not we should find the same

general patterns we had found in central Mexico of massive destruction of native population upon the introduction of lethal factors by the Europeans but with variations in that destruction according to humidity and temperature. We quickly ran into unexpected problems arising from the fact that two essentially different groups of scholars have studied northern and southern Meso-America, each group with different interests and questions. The ethnohistorical sources show a similar difference in the information they furnish. Accordingly, an inquiry like ours that must rely upon the substructure provided by ethnohistorical sources and later scholarly studies could be carried across the divide of the Isthmus of Tehuantepec only with considerable difficulty. There is no need to repeat the rather complex findings of the chapter, but it is worth mentioning that our plotting of population as reported in the Mexican national censuses has also left us with the surprising discovery that the War of the Castes may not be entirely extinguished even in our day.

Our second essay in this volume examines the miscellaneous but substantial body of data available to us on racial groups in the Mexican population since the landing of Cortés on the Veracruz coast began the introduction of European and African genetic stock into a vast Amerindian reservoir. Mexico today is generally described as a mestizo country, but that term is both general and ambiguous. We have been interested in the progress of interbreeding, in determining regions of high and low occurrence, and in attempting on the basis of the relatively good data of the later eighteenth century to project trends across the far less satisfactory data of the ninteenth and twentieth centuries. We were already aware of the extent of Negro and part-Negro participation in the repopulation of the coasts; we were less prepared for the finding that there has been substantial participation by Negro and part-Negro genetic stock in the settlement of the North. The population of the Mexican North, with its often-reported vigor, derives from the thorough mixing of three racial stocks and within those stocks from the equally thorough mixing of substocks.

Six of our chapters are linked in that they deal with phenomena usually termed vital characteristics. Chapter III concerns itself with such data as we have been able to collect on age of marriage : samples from the parish records of the Mixteca Alta, ranging in date from the seventeenth century to perhaps

1850; samples from the Civil Register for the past century for a group of ex-districts in Oaxaca centering around the Mixteca Alta, again essentially a rural environment; and samples from the Civil Register for the city of Guadalajara. All marriage data since 1850 suffer from the major flaw that a large part of the population forms its reproductive units without civil or religious ceremony and so cannot be traced. Nevertheless, even with the limitation that formal marriage has been to some extent a class phenomenon, our data show a steady rise in the age at which Mexicans marry.

Chapters IV and V continue inquiry into the basic question underlying interest in age of marriage, namely, repro-ductivity. Chapter IV analyzes data available to us on baptismal and birth rates. For baptisms we had material from the parish registers of the Mixteca Alta and some more general reporting via diocesan authorities for the last decades of the colonial period. For recorded births, we had material from the Civil Register for the Mixteca Alta and adjacent regions and Mexican federal summaries of reporting from the entire network of the Civil Register. In our examination we have had to balance the deficiencies of baptisms as a record of births against failure to record births in the Civil Register. Our conclusions differ from those of demographers who have studied recent fluctuations in recorded and reconstructed Mexican birth rates.

Another approach to the study of reproductivity is through fertility and similar ratios, which on the whole are better adapted to make use of data from earlier centuries and from underdeveloped countries in this century. Our data permit study from the later eighteenth century to the census of 1960. We find no detectable change over that span of time, a conclusion congruent with our findings from baptismal and birth rates.

Our last three chapters deal with mortality. Chapter VI examines such data as we have been able to assemble on mortality prior to 1850. The available materials force us to examine death data in relation to recorded numbers of births or baptisms rather than to follow the more conventional procedure of calculating death rates. For comparison, we have calculated in parallel form data for Mexico in 1959–1960. We are led to the tentative conclusion that there was no change in mortality status in colonial and republican Mexico before the middle of the nineteenth century.

That there has been sweeping change in age and cause

of death in Mexico at some time since 1850 is easily apparent to any student. Chapters VII and VIII address themselves to an examination of change in mean age at death and in cause of death, respectively, searching for differences between two such dissimilar states as Oaxaca and Jalisco, selected as samples, and between subregions within these states such as coast and plateau or countryside and city. Our data consist of samplings of death certificates from the Civil Register for selected districts in those two states. Over a period of ten years we were able to have data extracted from perhaps 600,000 death certificates. Processing the data turned out to be unexpectedly difficult both in technique and expense; we were helped by an able research assistant trained in computer methods and by the generosity of the computer center on the Berkeley campus, which donated computer time in off-hours. Our examination of change in mean age and cause of death show substantial differences between Oaxaca and Jalisco despite similarity of general trend and substantial differences between subregions within those states.

In the years we have been engaged in these studies we have had help from many entities and people, whose kindness we should not want to forget. The acknowledgment in Volume I records many of our debts, which extend equally to Volume II. For Volume II we should mention further Professor France V. Scholes and Peter Gerhard, who generously furnished materials they had collected on Yucatan; Dr. Gloria Grajales of the Biblioteca Nacional in Mexico, who secured copies of rare materials for us; and Professor Hardin B. Jones, who introduced us to the possibilities of probability theory for the analysis of racial mixture. We have mentioned our debt to the computer center on the Berkeley campus; the research assistant trained in computer methods is Antonio Seward. Other research assistants in Mexico and the United States, too many to name, have helped us by taking off our shoulders the almost interminable chores of copying, transcribing, and initial tabulating.

Contents

	Abbreviations	xv
I	The Population of Yucatan, 1517–1960	1
II	Racial Groups in the Mexican Population Since 1519	180
III	Age at Marriage, 1690–1960	270
IV	Crude Birth Rates in Mexico, 1700–1965	286
V	Fertility and Similar Ratios in Mexico, 1777–1960	322
VI	Mortality in Mexico Prior to 1850	338
VII	Mortality Patterns in Mexico Since 1860 : Age at Death	358
VIII	Mortality Patterns in Mexico Since 1860 : Cause of Death	409
	Appendices :	
	A. Individual Parishes Used from the Census of 1777	436
	B. Towns in Jalisco and Ex-Districts in Oaxaca Whose Death Records were used	447
	C. Numbering System Used for Coding Causes of Death	449
	Works Cited	452
	Glossary	463
	Index	465

List of Maps

1.	Yucatan : Distribution of Population, 1600	132
2.	Yucatan : Distribution of Population, 1794	140
3.	Yucatan : Distribution of Population, 1910	170
4.	Yucatan : Distribution of Population, 1960	172

List of Figures

1.1. The non-Indian population of Yucatan between 1549 and 1795. 96
1.2. Total population of Yucatan, 1549–1960. 122
7.1. Distribution of deaths according to age in rural Jalisco. 369
7.2. Distribution of deaths according to age in Oaxaca. 370
7.3. Distribution of deaths according to age in Guadalajara. 371
7.4. Value of q_x for Oaxaca. The upper graph shows the recorded points for the age group 55–64; the lower for the age group 15–24. 375
7.5. Values of q_x for rural Jalisco plotted against age on paper with direct rectangular coordinates. 376
7.6. Values of q_x for rural Jalisco. The same points as in Figure 7.5 but plotted on semilog paper. 377
7.7. Values of e_x at 5 years of age for rural Jalisco, Guadalajara, and Oaxaca throughout the time span covered by our samples. The lines represent trends as estimated by eye. 398
8.1. Percentage of total deaths ascribed to each of the two major causes, adjusted for removal of unidentified causes, groups 800 and 900. 417
8.2. Ratio of numbers dying from cause 000 to those dying from consolidated causes 100, 200, 300, 600. 420
8.3. Rural Jalisco: Percentage of total deaths, adjusted for removal of unidentified causes, groups 800 and 900. 428
8.4. Oaxaca: Percentage of total deaths, adjusted for removal of unidentified causes, groups 800 and 900. 430
8.5. Rural Jalisco: Ratio of numbers dying from cause 000 to those dying from consolidated causes 100, 200, 300, 600. 431
8.6. Oaxaca: Ratio of numbers dying from cause 000 to those dying from consolidated causes 100, 200, 300, 600. 434

List of Tables

1.1 Tributaries according to 1549 assessments 41
1.2 Tributaries of 1579–1581 56
1.3 Statements by encomenderos on population reduction from the Conquest to 1579–1581 62
1.4 Convents listed in the Memorias of 1580, 1582, and 1586 66
1.5 Population of encomiendas in Mérida and Campeche in 1549 and 1606 71
1.6 Numerical relationship between fanegas of maize assessed against a series of encomiendas in 1606, and the money, in pesos, donated by the corresponding localities 73
1.7 Naborías in Yucatan, 1580–1650 78
1.8 Indians and non-Indians, expressed as heads of families, from "Expediente formada para el establecimiento de escuelas en Yucatan y Campeche, 1782–1805" 87
1.9 Number of non-Indians in Yucatan, calculated from the census of 1794–1795 94
1.10 Population of encomiendas which occur identically in both the 1606 and 1688 lists 98
1.11 Population of encomiendas which were in private hands according to the list of 1688 but which were vacant during the period 1645–1650 100
1.12 Population of encomiendas which occur identically in both the 1688 and 1785 lists 101
1.13 Adjusted populations and their ratios from certain parishes 104
1.14 Territorial entities of Yucatan and their Indian population 108
1.15 Condensation and summary of Table 1.14 112
1.16 Population of Yucatan, 1789–1970 123
1.17 Population density in restricted convent areas, 1583–1610 134
1.18 Population density in restricted parish areas, 1794 142
1.19 Concordance of partidos, or their equivalents, parishes, and municipios from 1794 to the present 146

1.20 Partidos, or equivalents, in 1794, 1910 and 1960   151
1.21 States, or equivalents, in 1794, 1910, and 1960   153
1.22 Populations and densities in eight partidos in the
      state of Yucatan, 1794, 1910, and 1960   155
1.23 Inhabited places according to their size, arranged by pre-
      sent federal entities and late colonial partidos, 1910 157
1.24 Inhabited places according to their size and population
      according to size of locality, arranged by present
      federal entities and late colonial partidos, 1960   161
1.25 Inhabited places according to their size and population
      according to size of locality, summarized, 1910 and 1960 166
1.26 Absolute and relative change in population of rural
      and urban localities between 1910 and 1960   175
2.1   Distribution of racial groups in New Spain,
      1568–1570, and 1646   197
2.2   Absolute and relative values for population of racial
      groups, from the census of 1742–1746   201
2.3   Absolute and relative values for population of racial
      groups, summarized from the original reports of
      individual parishes for the census of 1777   208
2.4   Absolute and relative values for the population of
      racial groups, 1789–1793   214
2.5   Percentage composition of population by racial
      group, 1789–1793   222
2.6   Comparison of identical or closely similar localities
      which appear both in the Matrícula of 1805 and in the
      censuses of 1793, 1777, and 1742, with respect to the
      percentage of pardos in the combined population of
      pardos and Indians   224
2.7   Tributary populations of 1701, 1735, 1805   227
2.8   Basic data for types of marital union, organized in
      4×4 and 3×3 subtables   242
2.9   Relative occurrence of types of racial union   250
2.10 Comparisons among four racial groups in four areas
      (1777) and among three racial groups in nine areas
      (1777–1793)   256
2.11 Rates of racial fusion   263
3.1   Age at marriage : Oaxaca and Guadalajara   278
4.1   Baptisms or births per 1,000 population in the Mixteca
      Alta, 17th century to 1882   289
4.2   Summary of birth rate data for the Mixteca Alta,
      17th century to 1950   296

4.3   Births per thousand population, 1820–1860   298
4.4   Births per thousand population, 1860–1890   304
4.5   Births per thousand population, 1895, 1900 and 1905 317
4.6   Births per thousand population, 1924–1929 inclusive 319
4.7   Births per thousand population, 1940, 1950, and 1960 320
4.8   Births per thousand population, in a series of years between 1938 and 1965   321
5.1   Fertility ratios from parishes reported in the 1777 census   324
5.2   Ratio of 72 percent children under 7 years of age to women aged 16 to 50; data from the census of 1793, summarized in the ramo de Historia   327
5.3   Ratio of children 0–4 years of age to reproductive women from the census of 1900 to 1960   328
5.4   Ratio of children to adult women, expressed as number of children per 1,000 women, for various racial groups, as found in documents of the late eighteenth century 333
5.5   Ratio of children to adult women as found in seven present-day censuses   337
6.1   Ratios of births (baptisms) and deaths in ten parishes of the Mixteca Alta between 1651 and 1850   341
6.2   Ratios of births and deaths as reported for 21 localities in the ramo de Padrones from the census of 1739   343
6.3   Ratios of births and deaths as reported in state censuses and other documents for the period 1810–1850   345
6.4   Ratios of births and deaths in the state of Jalisco from 1801 to 1855 as reported by Longinos Banda 349
6.5   Critical ratios (t) of pairs of means shown in Tables 6.1 to 6.4 for the ratios of births to marriages and for births to deaths   355
6.6   Ratio of births to deaths in 32 states of Mexico for the years 1959–1960   356
7.1   Number of deaths for various age groups and dates from 1880 to 1960, Jalisco and Oaxaca   365
7.2   Rural Jalisco and western Oaxaca: Mean value of log q_x and value of b 378
7.3   Rural Jalisco and western Oaxaca: Mean value of q_x 381
7.4   Rural Jalisco and western Oaxaca: Value of b 383
7.5   Rural Jalisco and western Oaxaca: Mean value of e_x 384
7.6   Rural Jalisco and Guadalajara: Mean value of log q_x and value of b 385

7.7   Rural Jalisco and Guadalajara : Mean value of q_x 386
7.8   Rural Jalisco and Guadalajara : Value of b 387
7.9   Rural Jalisco and Guadalajara : Mean value of e_x 388
7.10 Jalisco : Coast versus plateau : Mean value of log q_x and value of b 390
7.11 Jalisco : Coast versus plateau : Mean value of q_x 391
7.12 Jalisco : Coast versus plateau : Value of b 392
7.13 Jalisco : Coast versus plateau : Mean value of e_x 393
7.14 Oaxaca : Coast versus Mixteca Alta : Mean value of log q_x and value of b 395
7.15 Oaxaca : Coast versus Mixteca Alta : Mean value of q_x 396
7.16 Oaxaca : Coast versus Mixteca Alta : Value of b 396
7.17 Oaxaca : Coast versus Mixteca Alta : Mean value of e_x 397
7.18 Rural Jalisco, Oaxaca, and Guadalajara : Value of b, pre-1910 and post-1919   400
7.19 Deaths occurring in seven Jalisco parishes as given by Longinos Banda   403
7.20 Comparative values of expectation of life (e_x) at ages 10 and 20 years in Jalisco, 1800 to 1880   405
7.21 Mean age at death of those who died at the age of 10 years and older   406
8.1   Percentage of each major cause of death with all age groups   415
8.2   Ratio of deaths in group 000 to that in consolidated group 100, 200, 300, 600   419
8.3   Values of b for short time intervals based upon the percentage of each cause group at all ages, adjusted for the removal of group 800, 900   421
8.4   Percentage of all reported deaths from specific diseases of the infective, febrile type : Jalisco, Oaxaca, Guadalajara   422
8.5   Percentage of each major cause of death with all age groups   426
8.6   Ratio of deaths in group 000 to those in consolidated group 100, 200, 300, 600 as in Table 8.2   429
8.7   Percentage of all reported deaths from specific diseases of the infective, febrile type : Jalisco and Oaxaca, coast vs. plateau   432

Abbreviations

The following abbrevations appear in the text and in the notes :

AGI   Archivo General de Indias, Seville.
AGN   Archivo General de la Nación, Mexico City
AHN   Archivo Histórico Nacional, Madrid
DII   *Colección de documentos inéditos relativos al des-
        cubrimiento, conquista y organización de las anti-
        guas posesiones españolas de América y Oceanía,
        sacados de los archivos del reino, y muy especialmente
        del de Indias.* Madrid, 1864–1884. 42 vols.
DIU   *Colección de documentos inéditos relativos al descubri-
        miento, conquista y organización de las antiguas
        posesiones españolas de Ultramar.* Madrid, 1885–
        1932. 25 vols.
ENE   Paso y Troncoso, Francisco del, compiler. *Epistolario
        de Nueva España, 1505–1818.* Mexico City, 1939–
        1942. 16 vols.
IA   Ibero-Americana
Landa-Tozzer
        Landa, Diego de. *Landa's Relación de las Cosas de
        Yucatan. A Translation Edited with notes by Alfred
        M. Tozzer.* (Harvard University, Peabody Museum
        of American Archaelogy and Ethnology, Papers,
        XVIII.) Cambridge, Mass., 1941; reprinted New
        York, 1966.
SMGEB   Sociedad Mexicana de Geografía y Estadística.
        Boletín. Mexico City, 1839–1964. 97 vols.

Chapter I

The Population
of Yucatan, 1517–1960

I. INTRODUCTION

In this essay we turn to the study of the population of Yucatan from about 1517, the year of the first Spanish expedition to the coast of the peninsula, until the Mexican national census of 1960, in all a span of four-and-a-half centuries. Yucatan was a part of the general cultural region of Meso-America during pre-Conquest times. After the Conquest, for all but the first years of the colonial period, it lay within the jurisdiction of the Audiencia of Mexico. Since the end of Spanish rule it has been within the Mexican federation. Nevertheless, it was sharply differentiated culturally and linguistically from central Mexico, or the Nahuatl zone, by the fact that it was Maya, with the unusual and distinctive developments of lowland Maya culture in writing, calendar, and in social and political organization. Although influenced by the Toltec conquest in the tenth century A.D., it was neither conquered nor at war with the Triple Alliance in the fourteenth and fifteenth centuries but carried on peaceful interchange at the Campeche-Tabasco border. During the colonial period Yucatan held special status within the viceroyalty of New Spain as a province with a large degree of autonomy and with a very different history of settlement. Under the Mexican Republic, Yucatan has had a history of secession, reluctant adherence to federation, and a continued sentiment of particularism although one that no longer seeks expression in political separation.

For the purposes of our study, we shall define Yucatan as the territory of the present Mexican federal entities of Yucatan, Campeche, and Quintana Roo—the first two, states in the Mexican federation; the third, a federal territory. Their joint area is 141, 523 square kilometers,[1] distributed as follows :

[1]Mexico. Dirección General de Estadística, *VIII Censo general de población*, 1960, vols. Yucatán, p. viii; Campeche, p. 8, and Quintana Roo, p. viii.

Yucatan   43,379
Campeche   56,114
Quintana Roo   42,030

The three entities comprise what in the colonial period was the province of Yucatan, not including Tabasco (which we have placed in central Mexico in our studies) or British Honduras or Belize, the latter a largely uninhabited wilderness after the first decades of the sixteenth century until its occupation by British logwood cutters. Yucatan, as we define it, comprises what was the territory of eighteen autonomous Mayan states or autonomous areas at the time of the coming of the Spaniards, all of which spoke Yucatec dialects of Maya save for the Chontal-speaking state of Acalán in the drainage of the Candelaria River of southern and western Campeche. The fit is not exact, for the state of Chetumal included much of what is today Belize, and Acalán included some territory within the borders of Tabasco[2]; we also exclude Xicalango, which in the sixteenth century was within Tabasco but is now in Campeche. But these differences are unimportant for our purposes. Yucatan, as we define it, is equally not the whole of the peninsula of Yucatan; it is Mexican Yucatan, encompassing approximately two-thirds the total area of the peninsula. Mexican Yucatan, it should also be noted, is considerably smaller than the territory of the lowland Maya, for the latter were settled also in what is now the Department of Petén in Guatemala, in the eastern portions of Tabasco and Chiapas, in Belize, and along the Atlantic coastal plain of Guatemala and part of that of Honduras.[3]

Geographically, Mexican Yucatan is low-lying, either flat or rolling country, with low hills in the south on the border with the Petén and with a low range, called the Puuc, running irregularly eastward from Champotón on the Gulf of Mexico to the Caribbean. The climate is hot and humid. Rainfall is heaviest in the south and decreases to the north and especially in the central parts of the north. The only rivers are in the south, for the northern half of the peninsula is a limestone plain with subterranean percolation and drainage, a classical example of a karst formation. Accordingly, the rainfall disappears quickly and the water supply is precarious. The central part of the

[2]Roys, *The Political Geography of the Yucatan Maya, passim*, but especially Map 1 on p. 2; Scholes and Roys, *The Maya Chontal Indians of Acalan-Tixchel*, map between pp. 2–3. Jakeman, *The Maya States of Yucatan, 1441–1554*, pp. 77–126, finds a larger number of political units by subdividing some of Roy's entities or areas.
[3]Morley, *The Ancient Maya*, pp. 3–16.

northern coast is a region of scrub vegetation. One may distinguish three climatic zones : the east coast, essentially the territory
of Quintana Roo, of greater humidity and higher bush; the
central part of the north, comprising the state of Yucatan and
the northern part of Campeche, a region of summer rainfall and
low bush; and the southeast, with increasing rainfall and more
luxuriant growth, merging on the east with the tropical rainforest of Tabasco.[4]

In the centuries and even millennia before the Conquest,
the Maya of Yucatan are thought by almost all scholars to have
lived in small, scattered settlements and to have practiced a shifting cultivation of maize and other crops, clearing fields for a
term of years and then moving to new fields when the fertility
of the old was exhausted. The large clusters of buildings that
form imposing sites are thought to have been ceremonial centers
rather than the residences of an urbanized population. Whether
or not around such ceremonial centers, there were nuclei or
relatively dense clusters of dwellings interspersed with fields,
with populations that reached urban densities, is a moot point.[5]
The first descriptions by the Spanish use the term "cities" and
estimate large numbers of people in them.[6] At least one scholar
has argued that there was a considerable amount of permanent
cultivation[7]; another has uncovered in what was the state of
Acalán some evidence of ridged fields, thus indicating more

[4]*Ibid.*, pp. 13–16; Thompson, *The Rise and Fall of Maya Civilization*, pp. 26–27.
[5]Thompson, *The Rise and Fall, passim*; Morley, *passim*; Gordon R. Willey and William R. Bullard, Jr., "Prehistoric Settlement Patterns in the Maya Lowlands," in *Handbook of Middle American Indians*, II, 360–377; Sanders, "Cultural Ecology of the Maya Lowlands," in *Estudios de cultura maya*, II, 79–121; III, 203–241 (1962–1963). Each of these works gives a select bibliography of what is now an enormous literature. More recent studies that advance new points of view should also be looked at : Ruben E. Reina, "Milpas and Milperos: Implications for Prehistoric Times," in *American Anthropologist*, LXIX, 1–20 (1967); William A. Haviland, "A New Population Estimate for Tikal, Guatemala," in *American Antiquity*, XXXIV, 429–433 (1969); Bennett Bronson, "Roots and Subsistence of the Ancient Maya," in *Southwestern Journal of Anthropology*, XXII, 251–279 (1966); Frederick W. Lange, "Una reevaluación de la población del norte de Yucatán en el tiempo del contacto español: 1528," in *América indígena*, XXXI, 117–139 (1971); Lange, "Marine Resources: A Viable Subsistence Alternative for the Prehistoric Lowland Maya," in *American Anthropology*, LXXIII (1971), 619–639, and Gene C. Wilken, "Food-Producing Systems Available to the Ancient Maya," *American Antiquity*, XXXVI (1971), 432–448. Reina challenges the idea of great surpluses of peasant time for building monuments; Haviland reports that further exploration of the site of Tikal has disclosed the existence of a genuine urban core. The other writers point to far greater food supplies through use of root crops, marine resources, and techniques of land use other than simple slash-and-burn, shifting cultivation.
[6]See our discussion of the evidence on the size of the Indian population of Yucatan *ca.* 1517 in part III of this chapter.
[7]Wagner, "Subsistence Potential and Population Density of the Maya on the Yucatan Peninsula and Causes for the Decline in Population in the

intensive use of land than shifting cultivation.[8] The rest of Yucatan has not been surveyed to determine the presence or absence of such fields or the possible use of other means for more intensive cultivation.

Whatever the forms of cultivation and settlement, the Maya of the peninsula had a relatively tightly structured society, with classes and a high degree of political organization.[9] The great ceremonial sites of the Classical Period are in themselves evidence of such structure. In the later Post-Classic Period, after 1200 A.D., the Maya of the peninsula were organized in a confederation under the leadership of the rulers of Mayapán. This fell apart in the quarrels leading to the fall of Mayapán in 1441. Thereafter, a continuing series of wars and other calamities devastated the peninsula. During the anarchy and wars there emerged from the ruins of the League of Mayapán the eighteen states or autonomous areas that existed at the time of the coming of the Europeans.[10]

The pattern of European discovery and conquest differed considerably on the peninsula from that in central Mexico. Just when Europeans first discovered the peninsula cannot be certain since the hostility of the natives to the first-recorded expeditions suggests previous experience with the white men, perhaps with Spanish slaving ships hunting Indians for Hispaniola or Cuba.[11] The first recorded contact was through the wreck of a Spanish vessel bound from Darien to Santo Domingo that struck a reef near Jamaica in 1511. Twelve survivors fell into the hands of the Maya, probably of the state of Ecab, who promptly sacrificed five of them. Seven escaped and became slaves elsewhere, of whom two were still alive when Cortés landed in the peninsula. The first-recorded expeditions to Yucatan, those of Franciso Hernández de Córdoba, Juan de Grijalva, and Hernán Cortés (the last one continuing on to the conquest of central Mexico), took place in the years from 1517 to 1519. All three met with

Fifteenth Century," in International Congress of Americanists, XXXVIII session, Stuttgart-Munich, 1968, *Verhandlungen*, I, 179–196. See also the paper by Wilken, cited in footnote 5.
[8]Denevan, "Aboriginal Drained-Field Cultivation in the Americas," in *Science*, CLXIX (14 August 1970), 650.
[9]Thompson, *The Rise and Fall, passim*; Morley, *passim*; Ralph L. Roys, "Lowland Maya Native Society at Spanish Contact," in *Handbook of Middle American Indians*, II, 659–678.
[10]Morley, pp. 79–99, 143–144. Notice especially the quotations and discussion of native traditions of calamities as recorded by Landa, in Morley's account, pp. 96–97; Thompson, *The Rise and Fall*, pp. 97–127.
[11]The suggestion is that of Carl O. Sauer, who points out that Indians seeing Europeans for the first time rarely met them with the massive hostility that the Maya showed toward the first recorded landings. *The Early Spanish Main*, p. 215.

immediate hostility and were forced to leave.[12]

The Spanish conquest of Yucatan came about through a series of expeditions independent of the conquest of central Mexico. It was the work of Francisco de Montejo under royal concession. Subjugation of the Indians was a slow, bloody, difficult affair, characterized by stubborn native resistance that lasted from 1527 to 1547. Montejo's first attempt was an expedition that landed on the east coast of the peninsula but was forced to evacuate Yucatan in 1529. Montejo's second attempt came in 1531 in the form of an expedition from the west, from Tabasco, but after a series of bitter wars, Montejo and his men were again forced to abandon the peninsula in 1534 and 1535. The third but, this time, successful attempt began in 1540, also through entry from the west. Despite stiff and continuous resistance from some of the Indian states, including a determined revolt in the region around the new Spanish *villa* of Valladolid in 1545, Yucatan was under Spanish control by 1547. An important factor was assistance from the rulers of the state of Maní, the Xiu family,[13] whose testimony supplied much of the information in the *Relaciones Geográficas* of 1579–1582,[14] one of our major sources. The prolonged and difficult wars of Spanish conquest must be taken into account in assessing the demographic impact of the first years of European contact.

During the colonial period, Yucatan was an isolated area, relatively unattractive to Spanish settlement. It remained, therefore, essentially Indian.[15] The barrier of swamps and tropical rainforest and the feeble extent of commercial intercourse with central Mexico or with any other area contributed to its isolation. The basic support of the Spanish population was tribute and service from the Indians via encomiendas; the lack of exportable commodities and other economic opportunity was such that the Spanish Crown was forced to agree to the regranting of encomiendas at the discretion of the provincial governor until nearly the end of Spanish rule.[16]

[12]Morley, pp. 100–103; Rubio Mañé, *Archivo de la historia de Yucatan, Campeche y Tabasco,* I, xix–xxxii; Itinerario de la armada del rey católico á la isla de Yucatan, en la India, el año 1518, en la que fué por comandante y capitán general Juan de Grijalva, in García Icazbalceta, I, 281–308; Díaz del Castillo, I, 40–106 (Chaps. I–XX); Primera carta-relación de la justicia y regimiento de la Rica Villa de la Vera Cruz a la reina Doña Juana y al emperador Carlos V, su hijo, Veracruz, 10 July 1519, in Cortés, pp. 3–15.
[13]Chamberlain, *The Conquest and Colonization of Yucatan,* a detailed study and easily the best; Morley, pp. 103–113; Rubio Mañé, *Archivo,* I, xxxiv–xl. Dating of the expedition differs by months or a year.
[14]Relaciones de Yucatan, *DIU,* IX and XI, *passim.*
[15]See the estimates for the various racial components of the population later in this essay.
[16]As may be seen from the Cuentas de real hacienda . . . de Yucatan, 1540–

Administratively, the peninsula comprised a province under an alcalde mayor, later called governor and captain-general, who had extensive autonomy. The province had its own royal treasury, the Caja de Mérida, with branches in Campeche and also in Tabasco since the latter district also lay within the province. After the creation of the Audiencia of Guatemala in 1543, Yucatan was placed for some years within its jurisdiction, but in 1560 was transferred back to the jurisdiction of the Audiencia of Mexico, which thereafter audited accounts and served as a court of appeal.[17] Yucatan remained within the Audiencia of Mexico until the end of the colonial period.

In the last decades of the colonial period, the Bourbon reorganization of colonial government brought Yucatan much more closely under the control of the viceroy in Mexico City, for the governor as Intendant of Mérida reported directly and in detail to the viceroy. Nearly two decades before the change to the system of intendants, Yucatan began to benefit from a quickening of trade that diminished the isolation of the peninsula. In 1770 the province was given permission freely to load in its ports products of the peninsula for shipment to any port in Spain. This permission for what was called free trade antedated the granting of similar permission to the rest of the viceroyalty of New Spain in 1786. With the freeing of trade from the restrictions of the fleet system, Yucatan's trade increased rapidly and haciendas began to form.[18] There remained, however, the problem of products for profitable export. That problem was solved in the nineteenth century through the development first of sugar raising and then of henequen production, but the resulting commerce linked the peninsula to New Orleans, Havana, New York, and the ports of Europe rather than to Veracruz and Mexico. Thus, the development of trade in the nineteenth century furthered Yucatecan particularism. In the middle of the nineteenth century, the peninsula seceded for a time from the Mexican federation and was devastated by the

---

1650, MS, AGI, Contaduría, legajos 911A–911B. See also "Incorporacion a la Real Corona de las encomiendas de la provincia de Yucatan. Distritos de las Reales Cajas de Merida y Campeche," 1785–1786, in AGN, *Boletín,* ser. 1, IX, 456–569, 591–675 (1938).

[17]See the Cuentas de real hacienda . . . de Yucatan, 1540–1650, MS, AGI, Contaduría, legajos 911A–911B; Chamberlain, *The Conquest and Colonization of Yucatan,* pp. 281–307.

[18]Molina Solis, *Historia de Yucatan durante la dominación española,* III, 494 *et seq.* See also the information on the development of groups of laboríos living on haciendas later in this study.

bitter War of the Castes. It is only in recent decades that railroads, roads, and coastwise shipping have bound the region firmly into the Mexican federation and have ended much of its isolation from the rest of Mexico.

For the study of the population of Yucatan, the years from 1517 to 1960 fall into three major divisions : the size of the population when the Europeans first coasted the peninsula, the course of the population during the colonial period (1548–1813), and changes in the population during the period of the Mexican Republic (1821–1960). These divisions are dictated as much by the nature and availability of sources as by the forms of political administration. Our discussion will follow the basically chronological pattern of these three periods, but because our information on the size of the population at the time of the coming of the Europeans is found in early colonial sources, we combine our discussion of the sources for the first two of these periods. As a matter of convenience, we further, divide the colonial period into two subperiods, 1548–1609 and 1600–1813. The changes in the gathering of information on population after 1820 and the events peculiar to the century-and-a-half of Yucatan's inclusion in the Mexican Republic make it especially desirable to combine examination of sources and analysis for the study of that period in a discussion separate from that of the other periods.

II. THE SOURCES FOR THE PRE-CONQUEST PERIOD AND THE COLONIAL PERIOD

Our information on the population of Yucatan at the time of the Spanish exploration and conquest comes mainly from reports of the explorers and conquerors and from testimony gathered in the decades immediately after the Conquest by the Spanish. Much of it was reported in correspondence, in the Relaciones Geográficas of 1579–1582, and in historical writing. Our information for the colonial period comes mainly from four kinds of sources : tribute lists; ecclesiastical reports; answers to royal inquiries on the nature of the land and its people, most notably the Relaciones Geográficas; and the civil counts of the last years of Spanish rule. Among these sources, the ecclesiastical reports and tribute lists require a detailed knowledge of administrative practice in order to interpret them accurately. The ecclesiastical reports require as a necessary basis for using them,

first, a detailed knowledge of convent jurisdictions and parish
boundaries as they existed at the time of each report, and,
second, a knowledge of the age groups falling within the category
of *confesantes* and the other categories in which such reports
give numbers of people. The problems here are simple enough
so that they can be handled in the later analysis of the documents
and discussion of the proportions of various groups in the
population. The one category which requires extended discussion
at this point is that of the tribute lists with their statements
either of number of tributaries in towns or of amounts of tribute
assessed, for the definitions of tributary and the quotas assessed
per tributary changed at various times. The lists must be examined with a knowledge of the system and the definitions
prevailing in the year when each count was made. Accordingly,
before listing sources, we sketch a history of the Spanish levy of
tribute on the Indians of Yucatan.

Unlike the first Spanish tribute system in central Mexico,
that imposed in Yucatan represented a considerable departure
from the native arrangements for support of the nobility and
priesthood before the Conquest.[19] Montejo assigned Indian
towns to Spanish encomenderos who exacted tribute in commodities and service from their new charges. In the earliest
years of the encomiendas, there were no official schedules for
the tribute. Such schedules were set in 1548 for almost all
towns after a series of investigations carried out on royal
instruction and conducted jointly by Francisco de Montejo as
adelantado and by representatives of the Franciscan missionaries. The few towns that were omitted, such as Acalán, were
assessed in the next years. For some reason that is not clear from
the available documents, the Franciscans objected to the
assessments made and appealed the matter to the Audiencia of
Guatemala, in whose jurisdiction Yucatan then lay. That body,
after consideration, ratified the tribute schedules as they had
been made in a series of decisions in February 1549.

The assessments of 1548–1549 were based upon the
number of married males after exemptions of the aged, infirm,
and holders of posts in town government. Each married male
constituted a tributary. The tribute was levied in cotton *mantas,*
wax, maize, frijoles, chickens and turkeys, salt, other items in

---

[19]Chamberlain, *The Pre-Conquest Tribute and Service System of the Maya as
Preparation for the Spanish Repartimiento-Encomienda in Yucatan,* examines
the matter at some length.

small amounts, and personal service, the whole payable in three installments at four-month intervals. The annual quota per tributary is hard to determine with exactness because many of the commodities were stated in terms of plantings, the yield of which was delivered to the encomendero, but the quota consisted invariably of one manta, usually one pound of wax, from one-quarter to one-half a *fanega* of maize, from five-eights to two-thirds of a fowl, small amounts of other commodities, and personal service.[20] For our purpose the important item is the invariable ratio of one manta to one tributary, the manta being defined as four *piernas,* or strips of cotton cloth woven on a native loom, each strip three-quarters of a Spanish *vara* wide by four varas long. The whole came to twelve square varas and weighed five-and-one-half Castilian pounds.[21]

The first changes in the system came quickly. In 1552–1553 Lic. Tomás López Medel, who was sent by the Audiencia of Guatemala, *inter alia* to review tributes, ordered personal service deleted from the assessments in accordance with a provision of the New Laws of 1542–1543.[22] López Medel further issued a series of ordinances regulating Indian affairs, which, among other matters, ordered the caciques and principales to keep lists of the Indians in their towns and subordinate villages by marital status and age group, the lists to be revised steadily so that Spanish missionaries and justices could know the exact number of Indians in each category. It was also López Medel who began the wholesale relocation of the Indians in compact settlements on new sites for easier civil and religious administration.[23] The effect was to reorder towns and change boundaries so greatly that tracing pre-Conquest and pre-1552

[20]Chamberlain, *The Conquest and Colonization of Yucatan,* pp. 283–287; Scholes and Roys, *The Maya Chontal Indians,* pp. 150–153; Tasaciones de los pueblos de la provincia de Yucatan hechas por la Audiencia de Santiago de Guatemala en el mes de febrero de 1549, in Paso y Troncoso, *Epistolario,* V, 103–181.
[21]The specifications are set forth in the instructions of the Audiencia of Mexico to Gaspar Juárez de Avila, Mexico City, 22 August 1550, in Rubio Mañé, *Archivo,* I, 95. See also Cogolludo, *Historia de Yucatan, lib.* VII, *cap.* VI (I, 385–386). Twelve square varas would come to about ten square yards of standard U.S. measure.
[22]Provisiones para que el Licdo. Tomás López administre Justicia en las provincias de Campeche, Guatemala City, 9 January 1552, in Rubio Mañé, *Archivo,* I, 126–127; Chamberlain, *The Conquest and Colonization of Yucatan,* pp. 336–337.
[23]Ordinances of López Medel, in Cogolludo, *lib.* V, *caps.* XVI–XIX (I, 292–305). Further to ensure the accuracy of the lists of Indians, the Audiencia of Guatemala on 5 January 1560 ordered that the parish registers of marriages be examined to ascertain the true number of tributaries and that the parish priests, secular and regular, exhibit them when tribute counts were being made. *Ibid., lib.* VI, *cap.* VIII (I, 331–332).

towns is difficult.[24] A further change in the annual quota at this time was the work of the Franciscans, who in October 1553 got the encomenderos of the district of Mérida to agree to a reduction in the tribute in cloth from four piernas per tributary to three.[25] That change was then adopted in the other districts. The definition of a tributary remained unchanged.

The first change in the definition of a tributary came later. Available materials do not permit tracing the adoption of the change with precision. According to three distinguished and knowledgeable students of Maya history, it began in the recounts and reassessments of some towns in 1561–1562. In those reassessments the *gente menuda*—widows, widowers, unmarried adult men and women—were each counted as a half tributary and added to the tribute rolls.[26] If this view is right, the change began at the same time that the Audiencia of Mexico was implementing a similar change within New Spain proper. According to another version, the adoption of the change in definition came in the recounts and reassessments begun in 1583–1584 by Dr. Diego García de Palacio, an *oidor* of the Audiencia of Mexico, sent as inspector to Yucatan.[27] Our own examination of the documents of the *visita* and the internal coherence of the tribute counts leads us to accept the second version, which is given added backing by the fact that the inspector abolished exemptions for Indians employed in the churches and convents, implementing in Yucatan another feature of the tribute reform of 1557–1572 in New Spain.[28]

The visita of García de Palacio also brought a further reduction in the annual quota per tributary. The inspector set an annual quota of two piernas of manta, one fanega of maize, two chickens, and one turkey, the cloth and fowls payable in

[24]Roys, *Political Geography*, p. 10 *et passim*.
[25]Traslado del concierto que se hizo entre la ciudad de Mérida y los franciscanos de Yucatán sobre varios asuntos tocantes a los indios, Mérida, 27 October 1553, in Scholes and Adams, *Don Diego Quijada*, II, 102–105; Molina Solís, *Historia de Yucatan durante la dominación española*, I, p. 45.
[26]Roys, Scholes, and Adams, "Census and Inspection of the Town of Pencuyut," in *Ethnohistory*, VI (1959), 206–207. The authors also add : "A spinster was considered an adult at 16 and a bachelor, at 18."
[27]Molina Solís, *Historia de Yucatan durante la dominación española*, I, 202–203, declares that the change came during the visita of Dr. Diego García de Palacio in 1583–1584, citing as his source an unpublished letter of Francisco Palomino, Defender of the Indians, of 12 April 1585.
[28]See especially the analysis of the declarations of number of tributaries by encomenderos in the Relaciones Geográficas. It is obvious that they are thinking in terms of married males. For the abolition of exemptions in Yucatan, Memorial que el Provincial y Definidores de la Provincia de San Joseph de Yucatán envían al Real Consejo, 1586, in Scholes, ed., *Documentos*, II, 97.

two installments, the maize delivered in the installment due at Christmas.[29] The quota as set by García de Palacio and the new definition of tributary, including half-tributaries in the count, lasted without further change for the *indios de pueblo* on whom it was levied at least until the end of the seventeenth century.[30] The one innovation, beginning in the middle of the seventeenth century, was commutation to payment in coin for towns that lay twenty leagues or more from the nearest Spanish town, the payment being set at the prevailing wholesale price brought by the tribute items in public auction.[31]

What has been said thus far applied to the indios de pueblo, the Maya living in Indian towns under native local government. Under Spanish rule, there came into existence additional groups within the population who could not qualify for exemption as Spanish or mestizos but at first were not held to tribute: Indian laborers in Spanish service *(naboríos)*, who settled near the Spanish towns in suburbs; Mexican Indians and their descendants, the original Mexican Indians in Yucatan having been brought there by the Spanish in the Conquest for service as auxiliary troops and settled in special suburbs; and freed Negro slaves, their descendants, and various free people of part-Negro ancestry (the *negros y mulatos horros*). In 1563 Diego Quijada, the governor of Yucatan, urged Philip II to order that the Mexican Indians and the naboríor pay tribute.[32] It was pleasant advice to a monarch chronically in need of funds, although it was acted upon rather slowly, perhaps because of opposition by the Franciscans, perhaps because of plans for application to all of the Indies. In a series of general royal cédulas issued in the middle 1570s, the Crown ordered that Indian naboríos and wage laborers who were not members of Indian towns and all free people, male and female, of whole

[29]Molina Solís, *Historia de Yucatan durante la dominación española*, I, 202–203, who states that the tribute quota called for only one chicken a year rather than two. Cogolludo, *lib.* VII, *cap.* VI (I, pp. 385–386), indicates that the standard annual quota in his time (the middle of the seventeenth century) included two chickens. The royal treasury accounts for the later 1580s, and succeeding years agree with Cogolludo. (MS, AGI, Contaduría, legajos 911A–911B.)

[30]Summary of the reply from the Governor of Yucatan on Indian tributes of 1 May 1689, MS, in AGI, Audiencia de Méjico, legajo 471.

[31]Cuentas de real hacienda . . . de Yucatan, MS, AGI, Contaduría, legajó 911B.

[32]Diego Quijada to Philip II, Mérida, 15 March 1563, in Spain. Ministerio de Fomento, *Cartas de Indias,* pp. 388–390; Cogolludo, *lib.* VII, *cap.* IV (I, 376–377). Cogolludo states that the Mexican Indians were held to tribute during the administration of Quijada, but the royal treasury accounts show no such collections for those years.

or part-Negro stock be held to tribute.[33] These cédulas were
implemented in Yucatan in 1576–1577, the Indians not in
Indian towns and the free people of Negro and part-Negro
descent being counted and held to pay tribute in coin. The first
tribute from all groups was collected in 1577. For Indians the
quota per full tributary was one peso a year, payable in three
installments, the standard definition of tributary and half
tributary being used. For the negros y mulatos horros, the
quota was two pesos in coin a year, and both adult men and
women were held to payment.

The imposition of tribute on the Mexican Indian led to
their appeal to the Audiencia of Mexico on the ground that they
should be exempt for services in the Conquest. After five years
of litigation, the Audiencia ruled in favor of the Mexican
Indians, and, accordingly, in the summer of 1582, upon presentation of the formal document of judgment in Mérida and
Campeche, they were freed from payment, the tribute assessment of the suburbs where they lived being reduced appropria-
tely. With this adjustment, the levy of tribute from Indians
living outside Indian towns and from *pardos* continued into the
later seventeenth century. In the middle years of the seventeenth
century, the quotas remained unchanged.[34]

From the end of the seventeenth century until the second
half of the eighteenth century, we do not have at our disposal
information on changes in the tribute system. That is particularly unfortunate because there were sweeping changes. Our
fullest information is in the proceedings that attended the
expropriation of the encomiendas by the Crown in 1785.[35]
At that time all Indian women were exempt from levy under a

[33] *Recopilación de leyes de los reynos de las Indias,* for Indians not living in
Indian towns, *lib.* VI, *tít.* V, *ley* ix, excerpting a real cédula of Philip II signed in
Madrid, 15 February 1575; for free Negroes, mulattoes, and people of part
Negro descent, *ibid., ley* viii, and *lib.* VII, *tít.* V, *ley* ii. both the same
clause excerpting reales cédulas of Philip II, signed at Madrid, 18 May 1572
and 28 May 1573, requiring levy of tribute on children of Negroes and Indian
women, and *lib.* VII, *tít.* V, *ley* i, excerpting reales cédulas signed at Madrid
27 April 1574 and 5 August 1577, requiring tribute from free Negroes and
mulattoes, both men and women. (We omit mention of reales cédulas later
than 1577; some of these injunctions were reissued in 1592–1593.)
[34] Cuentas de real hacienda . . . de Yucatan, 1540–1650, MS, AGI, Contaduría, legajos 911A–911B.
[35] "Incorporacion a la Real Corona de las encomiendas de la provincia de
Yucatan. Distritos de las Reales Cajas de Merida y Campeche," 1785–1786,
in AGN, *Boletin,* ser. i, IX, 456–569, 591–675 (1938); see especially pp. 598–
602. A report to José de Galvez by a commission sent to Yucatan includes
some information on the tribute system. Their comments indicate that in
1766 the situation was the same as in 1785–1786. Discurso sobre la constitucion
de las provincias de Yucatan y Campeche, Merida, 12 July 1766, in Scholes,
Documentos, III, 10–16.

royal cédula issued at Buen Retiro on 2 February 1760, which extended to Yucatan the exemption already decreed for Indian women in New Spain. By 1785 all men, whether married or single, were classified as full tributaries and the ages of liability to levy were set at fourteen to sixty inclusive, a far wider range and different classification from those prevailing in New Spain proper. The inclusion of the unmarried men as full tributaries probably was instituted to make up for the exemption of women. The age range for liability to tribute, from fourteen to sixty inclusive, however, represented a traditional usage that probably dated from the beginnings of the Spanish tribute system in the middle of the sixteenth century.[36] By 1785 tribute was also paid in coin except for the occasional delivery of maize when the Indians judged it more convenient. The annual quota per tributary was defined as one-eighth of a cotton manta. For purposes of commutation the manta was valued at 14 pesos, the annual quota of a tributary being then 14 reales. Elements of an earlier levy remained in the statement of quota since it was also defined as commutation of cotton cloth at 10 reales, maize at 2, and a fowl at 2, for collection of tithe from the encomenderos and the Crown. Those values suggest that the prevailing quota of the later sixteenth and the entire seventeenth century was reduced early in the eighteenth century to one pierna, one-half fanega of maize, and one fowl, for in the middle seventeenth century the manta of four piernas sold at auction for prices varying from 4 to 5 1/2 pesos; 2 reales for maize also accords better with the price of a half fanega than a full one.[37] At the end of the eighteenth century, the effective quota per tributary was 14 reales in coin, plus additional levies for the community, the Church, and for special legal services for Indians.

Indian naboríos and the increasing group of employees living on haciendas without any connection with Indian towns (the *laboríos*) were held in 1785 to tribute under the same classification as the indios de pueblo, that is, each male of

[36]Cogolludo states that in the middle of the seventeenth century the ages for religious instruction were up to fourteen for males and twelve for females, these being the ages "quando luego se trata de casarlos . . . " (when they are married off as quickly as possible . . .), *lib*. IV, *cap*. XVIII (I, p. 229). Upon marriage the new couple would become tributaries, that is, the usual age for the males would be fourteen. The arrangement apparently was old custom by the time of Cogolludo. There is no reason to believe that in the sixteenth century, the arrangement was different. See the statement of Landa that in his time Indians married at ages 12–13 whereas earlier they had done so at 20. P. 42; Landa-Tozzer, p. 100.
[37]Cuentas de real hacienda . . . de Yucatan, MS, AGI, Contaduria, legajó 911 B.

appropriate age was considered a full tributary, but the annual quota was six reales against the one peso of eight reales of the later sixteenth and the seventeenth centuries. Obviously, there had been a reduction in quota. Indian employees on haciendas, incidentally, were likely to escape count and levy.

The most unusual change was in the treatment of free Negroes, mulattoes, and other pardos. Our information is of 1805. By then, as a matter of custom, all were exempt from tribute although the royal treasury officials in Mexico City, who prepared the *Matrícula de Tributarios* of that year, were unable to find out why.[38] It was probably in exchange for militia duty and, together with the reduction in the annual quota levied on naboríos and laboríos, probably took place in the 1670s, when the province of Yucatan, enduring an unsual vexatious series of raids by English and French corsairs, was forced to expand its militia very greatly through the enrollment of Spanish and mestizos into militia companies and the raising of companies of Indian bowmen and pardo pikemen.[39]

By 1785 tribute counts and reassessments were being made every five years. Fiscal practice had been tightened very considerably and made far more regular in the later eighteenth century. Except for the difficulty in locating and counting the laboríos, the counts of the last decades of the colonial regime were carefully made and among the best information on population that we have for the entire span of four-and-a-half centuries covered in the study.

We turn now to the sources we shall use for studying the population of Yucatan at the time of the coming of the Spaniards and during the colonial period. For convenience we list them in roughly chronological order and give them numbers, but we shall refer to them thereafter by author and abbreviated title.

(1) Pietro Martire d'Anghiera, *Decadas del Nuevo Mundo* (newly translated again from the Latin by Agustin

[38]Estado general del número de individuos de clase contribuyente que incluyen las últimas matrículas de tributarios del Reyno de Nueva España, Mexico City, 5 December 1805, and Estado general de los tributos y Medios Reales de Ministros y Hospital que segun las Matriculas corrientes deben contribuir cada año los Indios, Negros y Mulatos libres, y las demas castas tributarios del Reyno de Nueva-España . . . , Mexico City, 5 December 1805, MSS, in AGN, Tributos, XLIII, last expediente.
[39]Molina Solís, *Historia de Yucatan durante la dominación española*, II, 276–278, 292–297, 426–429. There had been a militia earlier, but service in it did not bring reduction of tribute for the naborías. The absence of tribute payments by free Negroes and mulattoes of Mérida in the royal treasury records for the 1640s and 1650s might be the beginning of such exemption. On the militia of Mérida in 1654–1655, see Cogolludo, *lib.* IV, *cap.* X (I, 204).

Millares Carlo, 2 vols., Mexico City, 1964–1965). Peter Martyr, as he is usually called in English, was an Italian prelate at the court of the Catholic kings and their successors. He reported news to correspondents in Italy in a series of letters and, afterwards, collected those on America into eight decades. His fourth decade is largely devoted to the Spanish expeditions to Yucatan and the early events of the Cortés expedition to Mexico. It was prepared as a decade in 1520 and first published in short form in Basel in 1521.[40] Peter Martyr does not give his sources, but he had access to many of the reports sent to the royal court and was able to interview Spaniards who had just returned from America.

(2) Gonzalo Fernández de Oviedo y Valdés, *Historia general y natural de las Indias* (2nd ed., 5 vols., Biblioteca de Autores Españoles, vols. 117–121, Madrid, 1959). Oviedo, a contemporary of the discovery and conquest of Yucatan, did not himself visit the peninsula or take part in the events there but knew some of the people who took part in the expeditions and as official chronicler had access to government documents. His principal source for the descriptions of Indian towns and the events of the conquest of Yucatan was Alonso de Luján, a member of the first two Montejo expeditions, who came in 1541 to Santo Domingo, where Oviedo knew him.[41]

(3) Carta de Fray Lorenzo de Bienvenida á S.A. el Principe Don Felipe, dándole cuenta de varios asuntos referentes á la provincia de Yucatán, 10 de febrero de 1548, in Spain. Ministerio de Fomento, *Cartas de Indias* (Madrid, 1877), pp. 71–81. This letter by Fray Lorenzo de Bienvenida has much information on the earliest economiendas, conditions before and after the revolt of 1545–1547, Indian customs, and forms of settlement. The letter is primarily a denunciation of the government of the Montejo family.

(4) Fray Francisco Ximénez, *Historia de la provincia de San Vincente de Chiapa y Guatemala* (3 vols., Guatemala City, 1929–1931; Biblioteca "Goathemala" de la Sociedad de Geografia e Historia, I–III). Fray Francisco's history reproduces the text of a report on the coming to Campeche in January 1545 of Las Casas, Fray Tomás Casillas, and a party of Dominicans bound for Guatemala and Chiapas. The report gives us one of our scarce estimates of the size of Yucatecan towns,

[40]I, pp. 43, 51.
[41]III, 397 (*lib.* 32, *cap.* II).

namely, that the Indian town of Campeche had about 500 houses and the Spanish villa 13 vecinos.[42]

(5) Cuentas de real hacienda dadas por los oficiales reales de Yucatán, 1540–1650, MS, AGI, Contaduria, legajos 911A–911B. These are the surviving records of the annual and biennial accounting by the royal treasury officials in Mérida and the *subcajas* of Campeche and Victoria (Tabasco). Records remain for a substantial number of years and give information on the assessments and payments of the towns of the encomiendas of Montejo, which were taken over by the Crown; of those of other towns that lapsed to the Crown for the period before they were regranted in encomienda; and, in the seventeenth century, of the tributes of towns paid to the Crown for a term of years in return for the right to continue the encomienda in the same family for another life. The records also contain summaries of the assessments and tribute payments of Mexican Indians, naboríos, and free Negroes and mulattoes. They give much information on the occurrence of epidemics, famines, and other natural disasters.

(6) The tribute assessments of 1549. As has already been stated, the tribute assessments made provisionally by Francisco de Montejo and the Franciscans in 1548 and confirmed by the Audiencia of Guatemala in February 1549 were the first systematic and general ones in Yucatan. Although there were some variations in the quota per tributary, it always contained one manta per tributary. The list does not cover all towns in Yucatan, for a few not in it were counted and assessed tribute in following years. The assessments are part of the Tassaciones de los naturales de las provincias de Guathemala y nicaragua y yucatan e pueblos de la villa de Comaiayua q̃ se sacaron por mandado de los señores presidents e oidores del audiencia y chancilleria real de los conffines, MS, 413ff., AGI, Audiencia de Guatemala, legajó 128. The sections on Yucatan and Tabasco have been published by Paso y Troncoso (*Epistolario,* V, 103–181, VI, 73–112) in a transcription marred by some misreading of names of towns. Ralph Roys, in *The Political Geography of the Yucatan Maya,* has traced the relation of the towns in the assessments of 1548–1549 to earlier and later

[42]I, 297 (*lib.* II, *cap.* XXXIV). We use Ximénez, who wrote his history in the early decades of the eighteenth century because he transcribes verbatim the report of the journey written by one of the Dominicans designated historian of the group. I, 249 (*lib.* II, *cap.* XXIII). The information is in Remesal, but as a summary of the same document. (I, 352; *lib.* V, *cap.* VI.)

Maya settlements. Because of the moving and disappearance of towns, his study is an especially important guide.

(7) Relacion de los conquistadores y pobladores que habia en la provincia de Yucatan, en la ciudad de Mérida, 25 July 1551, in *DII,* XIV, 191–220. This list contained in a report of Juan de Paredes and Julián Donzel to Lic. Cerrato, President of the Audiencia of Guatemala, reproduces information in the tribute assessments of 1549 but has some additional data on the changes in encomiendas and on assessments made after 1549.

(8) Fray Diego de Landa, *Relación de las cosas de Yucatan* (8th ed., Mexico City, 1959). Undated but written about 1566, Landa's *Relación* is important for information on Indian population before the Spanish Conquest as well as for conditions in the first decades of the colonial period. We have also consulted the English translation by Alfred M. Tozzer (*Landa's Relación de las cosas de Yucatan, a Translation,* Papers of the Peabody Museum of American Archaeology and Ethnology, Harvard University, XVIII, Cambridge, Mass., 1941) because of its remarkable and informative notes.

(9) Juan López de Velasco, *Geografía y descriptión universal de las Indias... desde al año de* 1571 *al* 1574 (ed. Justo Zaragoza, Madrid, 1894), pp. 247–258. Included within the description of Yucatan by López de Velasco is information on the number of Spanish *vecinos* and a list of Indian towns, for most of which the number of tributaries is given. Although López de Velasco made his compilation in the early 1570s, the information on the Indian towns of Yucatan demonstrably has as its ultimate source the assessment lists of 1549 but is less complete. The material on Yucatan in López de Velasco, incidentally, indicates the danger of assuming that all of his information represents counts taken in the late 1560s or early 1570s.

(10) Ralph L. Roys, France V. Scholes, and Eleanor B. Adams, "Report and Census of the Indians of Cozumel, 1570," in *Contributions to American Anthropology and History,* VI (Carnegie Institution of Washington, Publication no. 523, Washington, D.C., 1940), pp. 5–30. This article presents and analyzes the information gathered by Father Cristóbal de Asensio in an inspection of the Indian population of the Island of Cozumel. The report is in AGI, Indiferente General, legajo 1381, MS.

(11) The Relaciones Geográficas for Yucatan, 1579–1581, published in *DIU*, XI and XIII, together with the relación of Landa; the original manuscripts of the Relaciones Geográficas of Yucatan are in the AGI. These are the answers for towns of Yucatan to the famous questionnaire of Philip II of 1577. Unlike the practice in central Mexico, where Indians and local residents were questioned at length for the material given in the answers, the Relaciones for Yucatan were answers by the encomenderos, much of the material on the Maya past being supplied by Diego Xiu of the Xiu family. Accordingly, the Relaciones are considerably less informative than those for central Mexico. Those for Yucatan do, however, give information on current tribute assessments and for some towns on the yield in mantas when the encomienda was first held by the respondent.

(12) Carta de Fray Hernando de Sopuerta con una memoria de los frailes franciscanos que sirven en la provincia de Yucatán, 1580, in Scholes, *Documentos,* II, pp. 48–50. The list of Franciscans, arranged in two groups by knowledge or lack of knowledge of Maya, gives the convents, the number of Indian towns, and the total number of *casados* administered by each convent. The manuscript is in AGI, Audiencia de Guatemala, legajo 170.

(13) Memoria de los conuentos, vicarias y pu°s que ay en esta gouernacion de yucatan, coçumel y tauasco, a list of Franciscan convents and the towns assigned to each for religious administration. The list is an appendix to a letter of Guillén de las Casas, Governor of Yucatan, to the Crown, Mérida, 25 March 1582, in Scholes, *Documentos,* II, pp. 57–65. The MS of 4 ff is in AHN, section of Cartas de Indias, caja 2a, no. 21. Although the memoria does not give direct data on population, it is invaluable for determining parish boundaries in 1582.

(14) Ralph L. Roys, France V. Scholes, and Eleanor B. Adams, "Census and Inspection of the Town of Pencuyut, Yucatan, in 1583 by Dr. Diego García de Palacio, Oidor of the Audiencia of [Mexico]," in *Ethnohistory,* VI (1959), 195–225. This article presents and analyzes the information on the Indian town of Pencuyut in the series of inspections and recounts made by Dr. García de Palacio in 1583–1584. The manuscript is in AGN, Tierras, vol. 2809, legajo 20; it has been badly damaged by water so that the authors' reading of it is a feat in itself.

(15) "Yucatan. Papeles relativos a la visita del oidor

Dr. Diego García de Palacio. Año de 1583," in AGN *Boletín*, ser, I, XI, 385–482 (1940), publishing the official record of the inspection and count of the towns of Tizimín-Boxchen, Dzonotchuil, Tecay, and Tixcacauche by García de Palacio. The manuscript is in AGN, Civil, vol. 661. This document and the preceding one on Pencuyut are part of the general review of tribute assessments begun by Dr. García de Palacio but not completed by him. The documents are particularly valuable because they list the age groups. Unfortunately, no other records of this inspection have yet been found. The royal treasury accounts give the new assessments for the towns in the Crown and for the tributary classes of naboríos and free Negroes and mulattoes.

(16) List of Franciscan convents and the ánimas de confesión administered by each, Mérida, 3 May 1586, at the end of the Memorial que el Provincial y Definidores de la Provincia de San Joseph de Yucatán envían al Real Consejo de las Indias en la Corte del Rey don Felipe Nuestro Señor, 1586, in Scholes, *Documentos,* II, pp. 95–101, the list being on pp. 98–101. The manuscript is in AGI, Audiencia de Méjico, legajo 3167.

(17) Testim^o del donativo con que los yndios destas Prouincias siruieron a su mag^d, 1599, MS, 10ff., in AGI, Audiencia de Méjico, legaj^o 359. This is a summary of the amounts collected from the Indian towns of Yucatan for a *donativo gracioso* to the King. Technically a voluntary offering to help the monarch in his financial needs, it was actually a general, one-time levy upon the Indian towns.

(18) List of secular parishes in Yucatan, the number of Indian towns and total number of Indios or tributaries administered by each secular priest, in Carta del obispo de Yucatán, Fray Juan Izquierdo, a Su Majestad, sobre las prebendas y beneficios de la iglesia de Yucatán, Mérida, 15 June 1599, published in Scholes, *Documentos,* II, pp. 116–119.

(19) Minuta de los encomenderos desta provy^a y la rrenta que cada vno tiene, 1606, MS, 5 ff, in AGI, Audiencia Mejico, leg. 1841; published in Paso y Troncoso, *Epistolario,* XV, 26–41, but with errors. The *Minuta* is a summary of the prevailing tribute assessments as of 1606 for all towns in Yucatan held in encomienda. The assessments are given in terms of items due at a single delivery so that for an item such as maize given only once a year, the statement is for total amount, but for an

item paid in each of the semi-annual installments, like mantas, the statement is for half the total annual amount.

(20) Antonio Vázquez de Espinosa, *Compendio y descripción de las Indias Occidentales* (Smithsonian Miscellaneous Collections, vol. 108, Washington, D.C., 1948), pp. 112–120, reproduces two reports, one dated 1609 to the Viceroy of New Spain on the Franciscan convents in Yucatan, the number of Indian towns administered by each, and the *personas de confesión,* without counting niños, under the care of each convent; the other, probably of the same year 1609, giving the same information for the secular parishes of Yucatan.

(21) Francisco de Cárdenas Valencia, *Relacion historial eclesiastica de la Provincia de Yucatán de la Nueva España, escrita el año de* 1639 (Mexico City, 1937), pp. 98–110, lists the secular parishes and the Franciscan convents, each administering a parish or *doctrina,* the number of Indian towns in each parish, and the number of personas de confesión. In the description of each of thc Spanish towns, Cárdenas Valencia gives the number of vecinos and the number of personas de confesión under the care of the Franciscan convents in those towns.

(22) Diego López de Cogolludo, *Historia de Yucatan* (5th ed., 2 vols., Mexico City, 1957—a facsimile of the first edition of 1688). Cogolludo's chronicle is a major source for the history of Yucatan down to 1655. It gives much information on population and also describes the parish and doctrina structure of Yucatan as of the middle of the seventeenth century.

(23) Matrícula de los pueblos de la provincia de Yucatan con certificaciones de los vicarios: Comprehende no solo [los indios] encomendados si[no] tambien los Negros y Españoles, 1688, and Cuaderno de testimonios de certificaciones dadas por los oficiales de Yucatan y alcaldes mayores de sus partidos de las personas que poseían las encomiendas y su producto, 1688, MSS, AGI, Contaduría, legajo 920, *expedientes* 1 and 2.

(24) Matrícula y razon individual de el num⁰ fixo de los Indios Tributarios de Administracion y Doctrina, de cada Conuento y Guardianía, en esta Provinçia de San Joseph de Yucatan, assi de los que estan en cada Pueblo debaxo de Campana, como de los que Viuen en las estancias, Sitios y Ranchos ..., 28 June 1700, MS, 6ff., in AGI, Audiencia de Méjico, legajo 1035.

(25) Report of the pastoral inspection by the Bishop of

Yucatan, 1736–1737, MS, in AGI, Audiencia de Méjico, legajo 3168.

(26) "Incorporacion a la Real Corona de las encomiendas de la provincia de Yucatan. Distritos de la Reales Cajas de Merida y Campeche," 1785–1786, published in AGN, *Boletín,* ser. 1, IX, pp. 456–569, 591–675 (1938). The manuscript is in AGN, Civil vol. 1358. The report of 1786, prepared in compliance with a real cédula of 16 December 1785 ordering the incorporation of all encomiendas in Yucatan in the Crown, lists the prevailing assessments under the series of recounts and reassessments completed in 1784 and gives much information on the tribute system as of that date.

(27) "Expediente formado para el establecimiento de escuelas en Yucatan y Campeche, 1782–1805," in J. Ignacio Rubio Mañé, ed., *Archivo de la historia de Yucatan, Campeche y Tabasco,* III, pp. 159–303, publishing a manuscript in AGN, Historia, vol. 498. The document is important for giving proportions of racial and fiscal groups in the population.

(28) "Censos de poblacion de la intendencia de Yucatan, 1789–1795," in Rubio Mañé, *Archivo,* I, pp. 205–250, reproducing reports of two counts, one in 1789 and the other in 1794–1795. The manuscripts are in the Biblioteca Nacional, Mexico City (sección de manuscritos, est. 10, t. 3, tomo 379), and in AGN, Historia, vols. 522 and 523.

(29) Estado general del número de individuos de clase contribuyente que incluyen las últimas matrículas de tributarios del Reyno de Nueva España, Mexico City, 5 December 1805, and Estado general de los tributos y Medios Reales de Ministros y Hospital que segun las Matriculas corrientes deben contribuir cada año los Indios, Negros y Mulatos libres, y las demas castas tributarios del Reyno de Nueva-España..., Mexico City, 5 December 1805, MSS, in AGN, Tributos, XLIII, last expediente. The centralization of fiscal control in Mexico City under the Ordenanza de Intendentes and the inquiries into prevailing systems of tribute classification and the measures necessary to make them conform to the injunctions of the Ordenanza have given us these two excellent summaries of numbers of tributaries and of members of the tributary classes at the end of the colonial period. We shall use the short title of Matrícula de Tributarios.

(30) Fernando Navarro y Noriega, *Catalogo de los curatos y misiones de la Nueva España* (1st ed., Mexico City,

1813; here used in a new edition, Mexico City, 1943), a list of parishes and their location within the new subdelegaciones of the Ordenanza of Intendentes, organized by diocese.

(31) Policarpo Antonio Echánove, "Cuadro estadistico de Yucatan en 1814," a report dated Mérida, 20 March 1814, published in *El Fénix,* Campeche, 10 February to 20 March 1849, nos. 21–25 and 27–29; and "Resumen instructivo de los fondos de medio real de ministros y comunidades de indios de la provincia de Yucatan, en su tesorería principal de Mérida," a report dated Mérida, 22 April 1813, published in *El Fénix,* Campeche, 10 April 1849, no. 33.

III. THE POPULATION OF YUCATAN AT THE TIME OF THE SPANISH CONQUEST

For some decades scholars have attempted to estimate the population of Yucatan, or of larger Maya regions, either at the time of the coming of the Spaniards or in earlier centuries. Their estimates show a wide range, which time and further research have not brought nearer agreement. The difficulty of arriving at reasonably based estimates and perhaps the presence of an open-minded approach are apparent in the fact that scholars have changed their estimates and views in the course of their research. The range becomes quickly apparent if one reviews a sampling of the estimates. Spinden in 1929 thought that there were two peaks of population of all the Maya, one in the Classical Period at about the middle of the sixth century A.D. of perhaps eight million people, and one at the high point of the Toltec-dominated confederation, in the twelfth century, of perhaps even greater numbers. By the early sixteenth century, according to Spinden, there was substantial decline.[43] Yucatan, as we define it, would constitute perhaps one-third of the total Maya area, both lowlands and highlands included. Morley has agreed with this general pattern but estimated thirteen million for the peak Maya population. Thompson, on the other hand, thought two to three million a fair estimate for a peak population about 800 A.D.[44]

[43]"The Population of Ancient America," in Smithsonian Institution, *Annual Report,* 1929, pp. 462–463, 470–471.
[44]*The Rise and Fall,* p. 29. Thompson has taken a new look at the matter in the "Maya Central Area at the Spanish Conquest and Later: A Problem in Demography," in Royal Anthropological Institute of Britain and Ireland, *Proceedings,* 1966, pp. 23–37.

For the population of Yucatan, just before the Europeans appeared, the range of estimate is from eight million and upwards to under three hundred thousand. Helmuth O. Wagner, on the basis of his exploration of old water holes and kinds of soil in the peninsula, has recently indicated eight million as a reasonable estimate and suggests that the population may well have been ten million.[45] A new study by Frederick W. Lange, revising a study by Jakeman based upon a combination of analysis of subsistence factors, European reports of density of occupation, and patterns of political organization and settlement, arrives at a total of 2,285,800 as the population in 1528. Jakeman had estimated 1,375,000, or forty-five to the square mile of Yucatan and the Petén, an estimate well within the sixty to the square mile that he regarded as the limit of the carrying capacity of the land under shifting cultivation of maize. Morley, if one applies his average density of thirty per square mile to the area of Yucatan suggested a population of 1.6 million.[46] A lengthy study by Sanders arrives at an estimate of 535,000 to 592,000.[47] Kroeber, in an admittedly hasty guess first published in 1939, indicated an average that applied to the area of Yucatan would give a total population of about 280,000.[48] That is close to Roys' last estimate of 280,000, based upon the tribute count of 1549 without upward adjustment. However, Roys commented that since there had been flight, destruction, and losses through disease, the population might have been well over 300,000.[49]

Most of these estimates apply a theory of population density or an estimate of carrying power under then-prevailing technology, or a combination of both. Roys based his estimate firmly on the tribute lists of 1549; the estimate of Sanders is derived by adjusting the figures of the 1549 lists upward on the

[45]"Die Besiedlungsdichte Zentralamerikas vor 1492 und die Ursachen des Bevölkerungsschwundes in der frühen Kolonialzeit unter besonderer Berücksichtigung der Halbinsel Yucatan," in *Jahrbuch für Geschichte von Staat, Wirtschaft und Gesellschaft Lateinamerikas*, V, 78–79, 82; "Subsistence Potential and Population Density of the Maya on the Yucatan Peninsula and Causes for the Decline in Population in the Fifteenth Century," in International Congress of Americanists, XXXVIII, Stuttgart-Munich, 1968, *Verhandlungen*, I, 185–191.
[46]Lange, "Una reevaluación," in *América indigena*, XXXI, p. 127 *et passim* (1971); Jakeman, pp. 126–144; and tables published by Lange, *América indigena*, pp. 136–137; Morley, p. 47.
[47]"Cultural Ecology of the Maya Lowlands," in *Estudios de cultura maya*, II, pp. 92–94 (1962).
[48]*Cultural and Natural Areas of Native North America*, pp. 158–163.
[49]"Lowland Maya Native Society at Spanish Contact," in *Handbook of Middle American Indians*, III, p. 661.

theory of a population decline of approximately half during
the Spanish Conquest. Jakeman's study makes fullest use of
what we know about Indian political structure in 1528.

We shall turn to another method, partly used by Jakeman,
namely, to rely upon early Spanish reporting of size of towns
and numbers, on the theory that since the sixteenth century
Spanish whose reports we use were either directly on the spot
or transmitted testimony of people who were there, they were
in a position to know. We shall not list all the early Spanish
statements on numbers but refer readers to the summaries by
Chamberlain and Thompson.[50] In general, we rely upon the
statements in Oviedo, transmitting the testimony of Alonso
de Luján, who took part in virtually all the forays of the first
two Montejo expeditions.[51]

The most important problem in dealing with early
Spanish estimates is the size of the Maya household in Yucatan,
for most of the statements by early participants and writers are
in terms of *casas*. We are faced here with the fact that the Spanish
radically changed the organization of the Indian household and
did so rather quickly in the relocation and concentration of the
Indian population.[52] The situation in the later sixteenth century
is clearly set forth in the Relaciones Geográficas. The following
are sample accounts:

Motul:
Las casas de los naturales de este pueblo son de madera, cubiertas
de paja, y todas son de aposentos bajos, cubiertas a dos aguas, como
tejas, y en ellas biven mas sanos que no en las de piedra.... (The houses
of the Indians in this town are of wood, roofed with thatch. All are
one-story, with pitched roofs as for tiles, and in them the Indians
live in better health than in stone houses....)[53]

Hocaba:
Las casas que tienen en este pueblo y en toda la tierra son de madera....

[50]Chamberlain, *The Conquest and Colonization of Yucatan*, pp. 342–343;
Thompson, "The Maya Central Area at the Spanish Conquest and Later,"
in Royal Anthropological Institute of Great Britain and Ireland, *Proceedings*,
1966, pp. 23–37.
[51]The accuracy of Alonso de Luján, and of Oviedo's recording of his
account, may be tested by examining the longer account of the expedition
of Alonso Dávila to Chetumal, 1531–1533, prepared by Dávila and other
members of the expedition, Trujillo del Pinar, 18 March 1533, in *DII*, XIV,
97–113, with that in Oviedo, III, 414–424 (*lib. 32, caps.* VI–VIII).
[52]The ordinances of López Medel, in addition to ordering the concentration
of the Indians in compact settlements, decreed that each family live in a
single house, "cada vezino casa de por si...." Cogolludo, *lib.* V, *cap.* XVI
(I, 294).
[53]Relación de Mutul, Merida, 20 February 1581, by Martín de Palomar,
in *DIU*, XI, 87.

y duran quatro o zinco años que le rrenueban... y algunos caziques las tienen de cal y canto buenas. (The houses of the Indians in this town and all throughout the land are of wood.... They last four or five years, when they are rebuilt.... A few caciques have fine houses of masonry.)[54]

Sotuta and Tibolon:
Comunmente hazen sus casas los naturales de madera poniendo vnos horcones gruesos enyestos hincados en tierra, y encima arman la casa del ancho y largo que a de ser a manera de casa de teja y... los antiguos hazian sus casas de piedra y en algunas partes muy suntousas y... algunos caciques el dia de oy hazen sus casas como españoles, de cal y canto.... (The Indians usually build their houses of wood by setting in the earth great forked poles with the arms rising steeply, and on these they build their house of the desired size like a house of tiles.... Before the Europeans came, they built houses of stone, in some parts palatially.... Some caciques today build their houses of masonry like the Spaniards....)[55]

Chauaca:
Este pueblo de *Chuaca*... con sus casas de pieda de albañeria (sic) cubiertas de paja, donde hacian sus congregaciones y mercados, aunque no compasadas las calles, teniendo los vecinos de aquel pueblo sus casas grandes de madera muy fuerte, cubiertas de guano, *que es la hoja de un arbol a manera de palma*.... (This town of *Chauaca* ... with houses of masonry roofed with thatch, where the Indians assemble and hold markets. Although the streets are not regular, the residents have roomy houses strongly built of wood and thatched with *guano, which is the leaf of a tree, resembling palm*....)[56]

There are at least twenty other passages in the Relaciones Geográficas which might be quoted, but all are of the same tenor. The vastly predominant, if not the exclusive, house style in 1580 was a single family structure of wood and thatch.

In pre-Conquest times the Indian houses of Yucatan were different. The most comprehensive description of pre-Conquest house style is given by Landa:

Que la manera (que los indios tenían de) hacer sus casas era cubrirlas de paja, que tienen muy buena y mucha, o con hojas de palma, que es propia para esto; y que tenían muy grandes corrientes para que no se

[54]Relación de Hocaba, Hocabá, 1 January 1581, by Melchor Pacheco, in *DIU*, XI, 92.
[55]Relación de Çotuta y Tibolon, Sotuta, 1 January 1581, by Juan de Magaña, in *DIU*, XI, 100–101.
[56]Relación de la ciudad de Valladolid, Valladolid, 8 April 1579, by the town council, in *DIU*, XIII, 13–14.

lluevan, y que después echan una pared de por medio y a lo largo, que divide toda la casa y en esta pared dejan algunas puertas para la mitad que llaman las espaldas de la casa, donde tienen sus camas y la otra mitad blanquean de muy gentil encalado y los señores las tienen pintadas de muchas galanterías; y esta mitad es el recibimiento y aposento de los huéspedes y no tiene puerta sino toda es abierta conforme al largo de la casa y baja mucho la corriente delantera por temor de los soles y aguas, y dicen también para enseñorarse de los enemigos de la parte de dentro en tiempo de necesidad. El pueblo menudo hacía a su costa las casas de los señores; y que con no tener puertas tenían por grave delito hacer mal a casas ajenas. Tenían una portecilla atrás para el servicio necesario y unas camas de varillas y encima una esterilla donde duermen cubiertos por sus mantas de algodón; en verano duermen comunmente en los encalados con una de aquellas esterillas especialmente los hombres. "(The way that they built their houses was to cover them with straw which they have of very good quality and in great abundance, or with palm leaves, which is very well fitted for this, and they have very steep slopes, so that the rain water may not penetrate. And then they build a wall in the middle dividing the house lengthwise, leaving several doors in the wall into the half which they call the back of the house, where they have their beds; and the other half they whitened very nicely with lime. And the lords have their walls painted with great elegance; and this half is for the reception and lodging of their guests. And this room has no doors, but is open the whole length of the house; and the slope of the roof comes down very low in front on account of their love [more likely fear] of sun and rain. And they say that this is also for another object, to control their enemies from within in time of need. The common people built at their own expense the houses of the lords; and as (the houses) had no doors, they considered it a grave crime to do harm to the houses of others. They had a little door in the rear for the necessary service, and they have beds on small rods and on top a basket-work *servillo* mat on which they sleep covering themselves with their *mantas* of cotton. In summer they usually sleep in the whitened part of the house, on one of those mats, especially the men.")[57]

Landa clearly describes the wood and palm thatch construction and adds the fact that there was a partition that ran the length of the house. On one side of the partition lived the occupants; on the other, was the space for guests and entertainment. It is highly probable that such houses pertained to the upper class, that is, caciques, nobility, and the more prosperous commoners, rather than to the ordinary peasants.

[57]Pp. 34–35; Landa-Tozzer, pp. 85–87.

Although Landa does not say so, the household must have been multifamily. Only a relatively large group would set apart half its space for guests and ceremonial purposes. Furthermore, the fact that the men all slept together in a special place certainly argues that more than a man and his wife lived in the house. Landa, indeed, states explicitly that newly married couples lived for five or six years with the wife's parents or those of the bridegroom:

y de ahí en adelante (after the marriage) quedaba el yerno en casa del suegro, trabajando cinco o seis años para el mismo suegro; y si no lo hacía echábanle de la casa.... (and from this time forward the son-in-law stayed in the house of his father-in-law, working for his father-in-law for five or six years. And if he did not do this, they drove him out of the house.")[58]

[In the disastrous hurricane of the fifteenth century,] se vio que habían escapado quienes moraban en casas pequeñas, entre ellos los mozos recien casados que allá acostumbraban hacer unas casillas enfrente de las de sus padres o suegros donde moran los primeros años.... (and it was found that those had escaped who dwelt in the small houses and the newly married couples, who, in that land, are accustomed to build cabins opposite the houses of their fathers or their fathers-in-law, where they live during the first years....)[59]

The testimony of Landa is confirmed by that of Fray Lorenzo de Bienvenida:

Sabrá V.A. que en esta tierra apenas ay vna casa que tenga solo vn vezino, syno cada casa tiene dos, tres, quatro, seis y algunas á más, y entre ellos ay vn padrefamilias, que es el principal de la casa.... (Know Your Highness that in this land there is scarcely a house that has merely one head of a family, but rather each house has two, three, four, six, and some more. Among them is a paterfamilias, who is the chief of the house....)[60]

Roys, in discussing the prevalence of multifamily houses among the pre-Conquest Maya of Yucatan, points to this passage and to the passage in Landa quoted above that young married couples lived in small houses near those of the parents of the wife or husband. (This manner of housing newly-weds prior to the establishment of full-scale independent residence is

[58]P. 43; Landa-Tozzer, p. 101.
[59]P. 19; Landa-Tozzer, p. 41.
[60]Letter to Prince Philip, 10 February 1548, in Spain. Ministerio de Fomento, *Cartas de Indias*, p. 78.

a rather common feature of multifamily organization and has often been noted in ethnographic literature.) Roys comments further that such houses could still be found on the Island of Cozumel in 1570.[61]

On the other hand, Scholes and Roys, in their study *The Maya Chontal Indians of Acalan-Tixchel,* although conceding the existence of multifamily houses, estimate population on the basis of one-family households: "If Itzcamkanal had 900–1,000 houses, as Oviedo states, its total population would have been 4,000–4,500 on the basis of 4.5 persons per family and only one family to a house. If there were many multiple-family houses, the figure would have been considerably larger. It is impossible, however, to estimate the number of such houses...."[62]

There is, however, clear evidence for such an estimate, much of it because of the remarkable gathering of evidence on Yucatan by Roys and Scholes. Fray Lorenzo de Bienvenida stated that after the revolt of 1546 Cusama had 800 houses with four or five vecinos and their wives in each house.[63] In the Relaciones Geográficas, Juan Gutiérrez Picón declared that the town of Chauaca "hera de doszientas e cinquenta casas que abia como seiscientos ó setecientos vecinos...." (was of 250 houses with perhaps 600 or 700 heads of families....)[64]

The most convincing evidence is that in the surviving documents of the visita of Dr. García de Palacios as analyzed by Roys, Scholes, and Adams in their article on Pencuyut. The authors give the number of houses and the average number of inhabitants per house as reported in the García de Palacios counts of 1583 for the towns of Pencuyut, Tizimín-Boxchen, Dzonotchuil, Tecay, and Tixcacauche, all in the interior of Yucatan, and they add parallel data from the inspection of the Island of Cozumel in 1570. For the five mainland towns, the average number of inhabitants per house is 8.64; for Cozumel, it is 11.43. The authors regard Cozumel as nearer the pre-Conquest pattern:

[61]*The Indian Background of Colonial Yucatan,* p. 21. See also Roys, "Lowland Maya Native Society at Spanish Contact," in *Handbook of Middle American Indians,* III, 663.
[62]P. 160.
[63]Letter to Prince Philip, 10 February 1548, in Spain, Ministerio de Fomento, *Cartas de Indias,* p. 74.
[64]Relación extensa y general de la provincia de Valladolid y del pueblo de Tiquibalon, 4 March 1579, in *DIU,* XIII, 154.

Assuming that Cozumel in 1570, where there had been comparatively little Spanish supervision, represents the old residence pattern more than does our Pencuyut matrícula, it would appear that the smaller multiple-family household had begun to break down in the latter town. In Cozumel we find no house with less than two married couples, while in Pencuyut there are many.[65]

Cozumel in 1570 was remote from Spanish centers and only partly Christianized. It had no resident priest, and the encomendero hindered the inspection of that year by Father Asensio.[66]

If the average number of people per family was 4.5, as Roys and Scholes have postulated in their study *The Maya Chontal Indians of Acalan-Tixchel,* a household with two narried couples should have an average of nine persons. But the factor of 4.5 is too low. On the basis of all of our own work on Mexico, an average of from 5 to 6 persons per family can be safely assumed. Such a factor would give an average of 10 to 12 persons per household, the figure that Roys, Scholes, and Adams obtain for Cozumel. Such values also agree reasonably well with the value indicated by the testimony of Gutiérrez Picón on Chauaca, for 650 vecinos in 250 houses would mean an average of 2.6 vecinos and, in turn, 14.3 persons per house. The statement of Bienvenida on Cusama would be far above these values (4.5 vecinos per house and, accordingly, 24.8 persons), but Bienvenida wrote about Cusama as it was in 1548, when the population was decreasing and the average number of persons per family was less.

At this point it might be appropriate to embark upon a discussion of the average number of persons in a multifamily house in the New World. Data could be brought to bear from a great many sources, such as the chapter on family size in volume one of this work or the studies of Cook and Heizer on settlement size in California.[67] We shall not do so because it is not really necessary. The virtually universal value for the average number of persons per house in multifamily cultures is 12 to 18. There is nothing in the documentary material or

[65]"Census and Inspection of the Town of Pencuyut," in *Ethnohistory,* VI (Summer 1959), 204–205.
[66]Roys, Scholes, and Adams, "Report and Census of the Indians of Cozumel, 1570," in *Contributions to American Anthropology and History,* VI (1940), 7–8.
[67]*The Quantitative Approach to the Relation Between Population and Settlement Size,* and "Relationships Among Houses, Settlement Areas, and Population in Aboriginal California," in K.C. Chang, ed., *Settlement Archaeology,* pp. 79–116.

reports of archaeological excavations to indicate that Yucatan was different. We shall use the factor of twelve, understanding that it is a conservative choice.

We turn now to actual estimates of number, which are usually given in terms of casas or houses. We look first at some general statements and, at the same time, omit many which are completely vague as to exact numbers.

Writing in 1548, Fray Lorenzo de Bienvenida described the devastation wrought by the campaign of Gaspar and Alonso Pacheco in the Uaymil-Chetumal area in 1544 :

Y desto huyan los indios, y no senbraron, y todos murieron de hambre; digo todos, porque avia pueblos de á quinientas casas y de á mil, y el que agora tiene çiento, es mucho.... (The Indian fled from this and did not sow crops; all died of hunger. I say all, for there were towns of five hundred and a thousand houses, and the town that today has a hundred houses is large....)[68]

Oviedo, describing the Spanish expedition to the east coast in 1527–1528, states that after leaving Belma [Ecab?], the Spaniards advanced "por muchos pueblos de mill casas e de quinientas e mas e menos, e vieron muchos e buenos asientos donde pudieron poblar, si osaran, e dejáronlo de hacer por ser los españoles pocos e los indios muchos." (through many towns of a thousand and five hundred and houses, and ones of larger and smaller size. They saw many good sites for Spanish settlement if they dared, and they did not found settlements because the Spaniards were few and the Indians many).[69] These and other similar statements have been regarded as gross exaggerations with little, of any, foundation in fact. To them might be added the often quoted, rather poetic description of the Spanish entry into Chauaca in 1528 by Oviedo :

que a mediodía que comenzaron a entrar en él, no dejando de andar hasta que allegaron a la casa del cacique, donde el gobernador posó, era hora de vísperas, sin salir de la población. (They began to enter the town at midday without halting until they arrived at the house of the cacique, where the governor dwelled. They arrived there at the hour of vespers without having traveled outside the town.)[70]

This description cannot be casually dismissed as nonsense or

[68]Spain. Ministerio de Fomento, *Cartas de Indias,* pp. 80–81.
[69]III, 399–400 (*lib.* 32, *cap.* II).
[70]III, 402 (*lib.* 32, *cap.* III).

just plain prevarication. If Chauaca was a town of 10,000 to 15,000 people, if the Spaniards moved at the normal, rather slow pace of a mixed expedition entering new and interesting territory, and if Chauaca was like any other Yucatan town, with large milpas and other open spaces between the houses and with the nucleated distribution that has been disclosed by most excavations, the expedition could well have consumed three or four hours to cover the distance.

Two towns for which we have a good deal of evidence are Campeche and Champotón. Regarding Campeche, Oviedo states that in 1517 there were "hasta tres mil casas." (up to three thousand houses.)[71] The figure is also given by Peter Martyr,[72] who undoubtedly got it either from a report to the Crown or from testimony of a member of the expedition. In narrating the history of the 1528 expedition, Oviedo states of Campeche that "no es menor pueblo que Champotón." (It is as large a town as Champotón.)[73] Yet, the historian of the Dominican group which was in Campeche in January 1545 reported that there were 500 houses in the town.[74] According to Bienvenida, in 1547 the town had upwards of 200 houses.[75] It must be remembered that alongside the Indian town of Campeche there was a Spanish villa from which the Spaniards had every opportunity to evaluate the number of houses and the size of the population. The decline in thirty years was massive but consistent, and there is no reason to discredit these accounts.

Regarding Champotón, Oviedo makes three distinct statements: (1) In 1530–1531, when the Spaniards arrived there, 15,000 *hombres* (adult males) came out to meet them. (2) "Hay en Champotón hasta ocho mill casas de piedra e cubiertas de pajas...." (In Champotón there are up to eight thousand houses, of stone roofed with thatch.) (3) Ordinarily 2,000 *canoas* (dugouts) go out daily to fish.[76] If 15,000 adult males constituted most of the adult male population, the entire population would have amounted to close to 60,000 persons. If there actually were 8,000 houses of the multifamily type, the population would have been 96,000. This seems excessive, particularly since Campeche, for which the statement is

[71] II, 114 (*lib.* 17, *cap.* III).
[72] *Dec.* IV *lib.* (I, 401).
[73] III, 414 (*lib.* 32, *cap.* VI).
[74] Ximénez, I, 297 (*lib.* II, *cap.* XXXIV).
[75] Letter to Prince Philip, 10 February 1548, in Spain. Ministerio de Fomento, *Cartas de Indias*, p. 74.
[76] III, 413–414 (*lib.* 32, *cap.* V).

that it had 3,000 houses, was more or less equal in size to Champotón. If we reduce the figure of 8,000 to 5,000, we get a population of 60,000. As for the dugouts used for fishing, they certainly carried a complement of two men each and probably more. Thus, the services of at least 5,000 men were required. Even though fishing was a necessary and profitable pursuit, a town that could afford to supply 5,000 crew members and still leave ashore those who were physically unqualified or required for other occupations must have been of considerable size.

These three bits of evidence agree in suggesting a population for Champotón in 1517 of at least 50,000 to 60,000 people. It should also be noted that it would have been highly unlikely that Oviedo would have deliberately manufactured these three very specific items of information or that Alonso de Luján, his informant, would have done so.

If we now accept the figure of 3,000 houses for Campeche, we can ascribe to it a population of 36,000 in 1517 and earlier. These cities are about sixty kilometers apart airline distance. The regions between them and behind them in the interior must have comprised a substantial area of support and must have been at least moderately well populated. If so, we have to allow fully 50,000 persons in small towns and villages. Accordingly, the population of the coastal strip of what is now the northern part of the state of Campeche must have reached 150,000 before the Spaniards landed.

For the east coast of the mainland, in the former provinces of Ecab, Uaymil, and Chetumal, but excluding the Island of Cozumel, Roys has been able to assemble twenty five place names. Concerning sixteen of these, he has found no information whatever for the period of the Conquest. Reports of exact numbers are cited only from Oviedo and cover Mochi, Conil, Mazanahau, Yumpetén, and Chetumal in the year 1528 or 1531–1533. Cachi and Chable are noted as towns of some importance.[77] The earliest estimate for the island of Cozumel is 200 houses in the year 1547.[78]

Oviedo states that Mochi had up to 100 houses in 1528, and Conil had 5,000[79]; in 1531–1533 Mazanahau had 3,000 houses, and Chetumal had 2,000. Yumpetén was as large as

[77]Political Geography, pp. 146–162.
[78]Fray Lorenzo de Bienvenida to Prince Philip, 10 February 1548, in Spain. Ministerio de Fomento, Cartas de Indias, p. 74.
[79]III, 399–400 (lib. 32, cap. II).

Mazanahau,[80] that is, it had 3,000 houses. The total for the entire coast, as reported by Oviedo, is approximately 13,000 houses, plus the island of Cozumel. Thus, if Oviedo's figures are accepted, the population would have exceeded 150,000 persons.

Further points to consider are the following:

(1) The value for Conil—5,000 houses—is very large and may involve an error or exaggeration. Roys thought so.

(2) The Spaniards undoubtedly noted all the large towns but may have missed many of the smaller ones. This factor might tend to balance an overestimate of house numbers for the large places. Furthermore, it is possible that when Spaniards such as Oviedo or the actual members of the expedition state numbers of houses, they included not only the core of the town but also the entire peripheral area. If the latter were true, then the total number of houses would fairly represent the region as a whole.

(3) In arriving at an estimate of the population of the east coast at the time of the coming of the Spaniards, we should take into account evidence in the list of Franciscan convents and the towns of their districts, prepared in 1582. One section covers the east coast. Its heading reads: "En el curato de la Villa de Salamanca Bacalar ay los pueblos siguientes." Then follows a list of twenty three places, in addition to Bacalar. Included are Mazanahau, Yumpetén, and Chetumal, together with several other listed by Roys. At the end is the statement: "Las leguas destos pueblos a la villa corren desde dos hasta quarenta leguas por mar y tierra y esteros." (In the parish of the Spanish town of Salamanca [de Bacalar] there are the following Indian towns.... From these Indian towns to the Spanish one, the distances are from two to forty leagues by sea, land, and swamps.)

These twenty three towns, which were still viable in 1582, included three mentioned by Oviedo as having an aggregate of 8,000 houses nearly sixty years previously. If the remaining twenty fell within the range of 500–1,000 houses mentioned by Oviedo and Bienvenida, there would have been 10,000 additional houses, or 18,000 in all. This is a broad estimate, for it implies a population of 216,000 persons within the provinces of Uaymil and Chetumal. Yet it is not inconsistent with the impression left by all the Spaniards of a heavily populated region.

[80]III, 415 (*lib. 32, cap.* VI).

Roys has been able to locate ten towns in the province of Ecab and three on the island of Cozumel. These include Conil and Mochi.[81] At 500 houses per town, the total would be 6,500 houses. This figure is not too far from the 5,000 ascribed by Oviedo to Conil. It may be that Oviedo's estimate was really for the northeastern corner of the peninsula, that is, the entire province of Ecab, and thus there is no vast discrepancy. An estimate of 6,500 houses would mean 78,000 people.

We thus reach a tentative total of 294,000, or in round numbers, 300,000 as the population of the east coast in 1517.

Let us turn now to the north-central portion of the peninsula as delineated today by the boundary of the state of Yucatan. We have relatively little concrete information for this region. The single solid item is for the town of Chauaca. Aside from the description in Oviedo already quoted, we have the report of Blas González in the Relaciones Geográficas that on the expedition of 1527–1529, "ternia en aquel tiempo hasta tres mill yndios...." (it had at that time up to 3,000 Indian heads of families....)[82] At a family size of five, this means 15,000 people. According to Juan Gutiérrez Picón, whose statement has already been quoted, in 1543 there were 600–700 vecinos. According to another statement in the Relaciones Geográficas, in 1543, there were 1,000 vecinos, or 5,000 people.[83] In 1549, the town was assessed at 200 tributaries,[84] and by 1579 the number had falled to twenty indios, or vecinos.[85] This collapse is characteristic of all the sizeable towns of the pre-Conquest era and must be given due weight in estimating the aboriginal population.

According to Oviedo, the Montejo expedition of 1528 went beyond Chauaca to a town called Acu (or Aké, equivalent to Dzonotaké), which was as large as Chauaca. Four leagues beyond, the Spaniards came to Cicia (or Sisia), which was larger than "los que se han dicho...." (those that have been mentioned....) From there the Spaniards went four leagues farther to a town larger than Sisia, called Loche, and thence went down the coast to Salamanca.[86]

[81]*Political Geography*, pp. 143–156.
[82]Relación histórico descriptiva de los pueblos de Ixumul y de Tecuche, Valladolid, 12 May 1579, in *DIU*, XIII, 112.
[83]Relación de la ciudad de Valladolid, Valladolid, 8 April 1579, in *DIU*, XIII, 13.
[84]Relación de los pueblos de Chuaca y de Chechimila, by Juan de Urrutia, Valladolid, 4 May 1579, in *DIU*, XIII, 74.
[85]Relación de la ciudad de Valladolid, Valladolid, 8 April 1579, in *DIU*, XIII, 14.
[86]III, 402–403 (*lib.* 32, *cap.* III).

The listing of three large towns in this region has caused much confusion. Roys discusses the problems of location and indentification at some length without coming to a firm conclusion. The tribute list of 1549 gives only two towns, under the names of Cicia and Cenote, with 420 and 330 tributaries, respectively. Cenote is identified with Loche by Roys.[87] Nevertheless, the account in Oviedo is detailed and cannot be discarded lightly. Accordingly, we must consider that there probably were three towns, in addition to Chauaca, with approximately 3,000 vecinos in each.

The only other sixteenth century writer who gives population figures for the interior towns is Fray Lorenzo de Bienvenida. His data are for the period immediately subsequent to the savage fighting of the rebellion of 1546, that is, the year 1547 or close to it :

Cusama	800 houses
Ticul	1,000 plus houses
Maní	1,000 plus houses
Telchac	400–500 houses[88]

These were important places and came within the 500–1,000 house range even at a late date, perhaps because they were not in the center of the revolt of 1546. Together with the report for 1528 of the towns of the Tizimín area, they would furnish a quite decent sample of the interior population. What we lack, of course, is a count of the total number of such towns, of which the ones above would serve as a sample. It is just possible, however, that we can get an idea of this number.

The Franciscan convents in the list of 1582 were located in what were then, or had been, large, influential towns. Otherwise, they would not have been selected as administrative centers for religious purposes nor as suitable locations for convents. If we exclude the Spanish settlements at Mérida and Valladolid, we find the following centers :

Hunucmá	Tecaz
Concal	Sotuta
Tixcocob	Peto
Motul	Sisal
Dzidzantún	Tinum
Tecanto	Tizimín
Izamal	Chancenote
Hocabá	Ichmul

[87]*Political Geography*, pp. 107–108.
[88]Letter to Prince Philip, 10 February 1548, in Spain. Ministerio de Fomento, *Cartas de Indias*, p. 74.

Homún and Cusama   Hecelchacan
Maní   Calkiní
Otzcutzcab

Here are twenty-one towns, all of which would qualify for the range of 500–1,000 houses as their population prior to the arrival of the Spaniards. We are ignoring the dozens of smaller places which maintained an independent existence under the convents even after the relocations and concentrating of population in the 1550s were completed. Let us take the median of the range and allow 750 multifamily houses or their equivalent per *cabecera* (chief town). Then we get 15,750 houses, and at twelve persons per house, a population of 189,000, or in round numbers, 190,000.

A clue to the uncongregated towns and villages may also be obtained from the list of 1582. Such towns and villages are always indicated by the specification of the distance in leagues from the cabecera. There were 140 of them, including Ticul and Telchac, mentioned by Bienvenida. At the same time, there were approximately thirty five described as being located "en el mismo asiento" (in the same place) as the cabecera or some other town. By 1582 many of these towns and villages had been badly depleted of inhabitants, but at least those which were able to persist must have been reasonably well populated originally. We may ascribe fifty multifamily houses, or 600 persons, to each of the 140 which were independent in 1580. We get a total of 84,000. To account for the thirty five which had been congregated, and for the probably many unnamed localities, we may add 26,000 and consider the total to have been 110,000. The population of the interior, then, is estimated at 300,000.

The last area to examine within what we define as Yucatan is the province of Acalán, essentially the drainage of the Candelaria River. (We omit Xicalango, which lay in Spanish Tabasco.) The Cortés expedition of 1525 went through the province and stayed in the capital; Cortés described the region as rich and populous: "Esta provincia de Acalan es muy gran cosa, porque hay en ella muchos pueblos y de mucha gente." (This province of Acalan is very important, for there are many towns and many people in it.) The capital was "muy grande y de muchas mezquitas." (very large and with many temples.)[89]

---

[89]Quinta carta-relación... al emperador Carlos V, Mexico City, 3 September 1526, in *Cartas y documentos*, pp. 260–264.

The second Montejo expedition was in Acalán in 1530. Oviedo reports of the capital, Itzamkanac, that it had "hasta novecientas o mill casas muy buenas de piedra, e blancas, encaladas, cubiertas de pajas, las más dellas de hombres principales." (up to nine hundred or one thousand very good houses of stone, white or whitewashed, roofed with thatch, most of them belonging to upperclass people.) According to Oviedo, the Spaniards founded a town but abandoned it "como por allí cerca no había vecindad de otras poblaciones, sino sola esta provincia, e los indios eran pocos para los españoles...." (since there were no towns nearby except [those of] this province, and the Indians were few for the Spaniards....)[90] On the basis of this statement, Roys and Scholes estimate no more than 10,000 persons as the pre-Conquest population of the province.[91] It is far too low.

Roys and Scholes have located a listing of all towns and settlements in the province in the Paxbolon-Maldonado Papers; there were 76.[92] Bernal Díaz twice mentions the more than twenty pueblos or *poblezuelos* in the province.[93] Tuxakha, described by Cortés as a large town, and Tizatepelt (Cacchute), Chakam, and Tahçacab, which had two encomenderos in 1530, were larger towns.[94] At an average of twelve persons per house, the capital would have had 11,400 persons. Tuxakha, probably the second city in size, may be estimated at 500 houses and the three other larger settlements at 250 each; for the four towns: 1,250 houses and 15,000 persons. The sixteen other towns may be estimated at an average of 100 houses each, or 1,600 houses and 19,200 persons. The remaining settlements of the seventy-six were hamlets and may be estimated at an average of fifty persons each, or 2,750. The province of Acalán would have had, then, 48,350 persons, or in a round number, say, 50,000.

The Cortés expedition was in the province and capital city long enough so that European diseases had time to take hold. The second Montejo expedition five years later saw much altered population. We interpret Oviedo's comment on why the Spaniards abandoned the town they founded not to mean that the province was sparsely populated but that it was so distant from other provinces that Spaniards living there would

90III, 412–413 (*lib. 32, cap. V*).
91*The Maya Chontal Indians*, p. 160.
92*Ibid.*, pp. 8–10.
93II, 200, 204 (*cap. CLXXVI*).
94Scholes and Roys, *The Maya Chontal Indians*, p. 160; Cortés, *Cartas y documentos*, p. 260.

have to depend upon the Indians of Acalán province alone, and there were not enough of them to provide the kind of support the conquerors wanted. The native population dwindled so rapidly in the province that by 1553 the first tribute count found only 500 married men. There were fugitives in the back country from the Spanish concentration and transfer of the remaining population to Tixchel on the Campeche coast,[95] but even if they were as numerous as the settlement at Tixchel, the entire Indian population had shrunk by over 90 percent in less than three decades.

Our grand total for Yucatan about 1528 is 800,000, perhaps better written as 0.8 million. In view of known pre-Conquest history of the area, of the unanimous impressions of the first Spaniards, and of the bits of evidence which we can assemble, this estimate errs on the side of conservatism.

We should make a number of comments about our estimate. (Others doubtless will make even more.) First, our estimate does not really cover the Indian population of Yucatan before it began to suffer the effects of European contact. Native tradition recorded a devastating epidemic of smallpox in Katun 2 Ahau, which ran from June 1500 to February 1520. Landa, in describing this pestilence, mentions that it occurred more than fifty years before he wrote. Since he wrote in 1566, the epidemic must be placed as no later than 1516, that is, before the expedition of Hernández de Córdoba.[96] The records of the Maya tradition have caused some difficulty for scholars since the murderous outbreak of smallpox in central Mexico did not begin until 1520 when a Negro in one of the vessels of Pánfilo Narváez introduced the disease.[97] One must either postulate an error in the Maya dating, and so assume that from central Mexico the outbreak spread to Yucatan, or accept an independent outbreak in Yucatan. Tozzer has suggested an introduction by the expedition of Hernández de Córdoba[98];

[95]Scholes and Roys, *The Maya Chontal Indians*, pp. 160–161 *et passim*. Fray Lorenzo de Bienvenida in 1548 commented on the rapid depopulation of the province and declared that Itzkamanac had fallen to upwards of 200 houses. Spain. Ministerio de Fomento, *Cartas de Indias*, p. 75.
[96]Landa, p. 20; Landa-Tozzer, pp. 41–42 and notes; Roys, *The Book of Chilam Balam of Chumayel*, p. 138; Thompson, "The Maya Central Area at the Spanish Conquest and Later," in *Proceedings of the Royal Anthropological Institute of Great Britain and Ireland*, 1966, p. 24.
[97]Bancroft, I, pp. 541–543. Bancroft indicates that a "pioneer vessel" brought the epidemic to Cozumel at the time of Narváez' expedition to New Spain. This may be another attempt to reconcile the statement of Landa with the history of European expeditions to Yucatan and Mexico.
[98]Landa-Tozzer, p. 42, note 207.

Thompson wavers between the explanation of error and the introduction "from another locus of infection, perhaps Panama."[99] It is, of course, possible that native trade and intercourse could have carried smallpox from the Spanish settlements in Panama northward into the Maya area or that the disease might have been introduced by some Spanish vessel, perhaps a slaver, for the landing of which we have no record.

In addition to the ravages of smallpox, the reader must also bear in mind that our estimates are based upon reports by Spaniards and that many such reports were made after the European presence had begun to have an effect upon the population. Our estimate is for the year 1528 or even somewhat later; it is not of 1500 or 1492. We do not have available historical material, such as exists for central Mexico, in order to make an estimate for the population on the eve of the European Conquest but before any European influence had begun to affect numbers. We can only refer to the varying estimates already made on the basis of carrying capacity of land under the prevailing technology and patterns of settlement and political organization.

The second comment that we make is that a population of 0.8 million would mean an average density of 5.6 persons per square kilometer, or about 14.6 to the square mile. This is far less than the average density we have found for the population of central Mexico just before the coming of the Spaniards, that is 49 to the square kilometer or 125 to the square mile. The disparity is such that we are led to indicate two possible sets of explanations by no means mutually exclusive : (1) Contact with the Europeans probably unleashed lethal factors of such massive and rapid impact that our estimate covers a population that already had suffered massive loss, that is, the pattern we have found for Hispaniola and the coast of central Mexico applied also to Yucatan. Such an explanation would seem to have greatest validity for the more humid regions, especially the east coast and the southern and western areas; it would have lesser validity for the areas of dry bush in the north-central area of the peninsula. (2) There were significant differences between Yucatan and central Mexico at the beginning of the sixteenth century in density of settlement, manpower available, size and strength of state structures, and demographic

[99]"The Maya Central Area," in Royal Anthropological Institute of Great Britain and Ireland, *Proceedings*, 1966, p. 34.

vitality. In 1518 the population of central Mexico was probably the largest that it had even been to that date. The population of Yucatan, on the other hand, probably had been falling for nearly a century and perhaps longer. Native tradition, as recorded by Landa, reported a series of wars, famines, epidemics, and one immensely destructive hurricane in the years between the destruction of Mayapán and the coming of the Spaniards.[100] A population already in decline upon the coming of the Europeans, began, to suffer the additional devastation of foreign conquests and the introduction of new diseases.

IV. THE 1549 TRIBUTE ASSESSMENT

For estimating the population of Yucatan in the middle of the sixteenth century, the basic source is the tribute assessments confirmed by the Audiencia of Guatemala in 1549. The assessments cover towns held by encomenderos living in the Spanish villas of Mérida and Campeche, but unfortunately do not include towns held by encomenderos living in the Spanish villas of Valladolid and Salamanca de Bacalar. The territory omitted is essentially that of the old Maya states of Uaymil and Chetumal in southeastern Yucatan.

The formal assessment for each encomienda gives the tribute in detail, together with the name of the encomendero and other information. Since the tribute, except for one town, universally included one manta per tributary, we need only make a direct conversion of this commodity in order to obtain the number of tributaries. We present the information in the assessments of 1549 in condensed form in Table 1–1. The first column lists in alphabetical order the 178 towns of Yucatan which are in the assessments. The spelling of names, in general, is that of the document as transcribed and published in Paso y Troncoso, the most widely accessible form. Consequently, there are frequent and wide discrepancies in orthography due to some errors of transcription and to differences with forms favored by other writers and by present-day authority.

The second column of the table gives the name of the encomendero who held the town. For lack of space we show only the last name. The spelling here, in general, has been corrected to ordinary usage.

[100]Landa, pp. 19–20; Landa-Tozzer, pp. 41–42.

Table 1.1

Tributaries according to 1549 *Assessments*

Locality	Encomendero	Paso y Troncoso	López de Velasco	Roys	1551 Report
Acalaxan	Paredes	250	250	250	
Acumuchil	Ruiz	150	b	150	
Ahunacama	Montejo	180	b	180	
Alan	Montejo	580	580	580	
Amacalco	Montejo	860	c	860	
Ateque	González	140	a	140	
Atimzizibique	Tamayo	200	c	200	
Axaba	Cisneros	120	120	120	
Becal	Leal	100	c	100	
Bitancha	Núñez	60	60	a	
Boloncabil	Cano	210	210	210	
Boxchen	Burgos	210	210	210	
Boxchen	Triana	220	220	a	
Caba	Genovés	210	220	210	
Caba	Velasco	140	150	140	
Cacabachuc	Manrique	300	300	300	
Cacalchen	Burgos	50	50	50	
Cacalud	Pacheco	220	220	220	
Cacalut	Cano	180	180	180	
Calatamud	Álvarez	440	440	440	
Calkini	Barquero	70	c	70	
Cama	Baeza	88	88	88	
Campeche	Crown	630	630	630	
Cantemoy	Venio	310	310	310	
Canyzo	?	a	380	a	
Catanyque	Bellido	50	50	a	
Cauquel	Manrique	200	200	200	
Cax	Bracamonte	940	940	940	
Cazavaca	Campos	180	280	180	
Cenot	Ayala	330	330	330	
Cenput	Villanueva	190	190	190	
Cinanche	Villafrades	320	a	320	
Citipeche	Paredes	230	230	250	
Coaoyz	González	112	112	112	
Concal	Montejo	1,450	1,450	1,450	
Conil	Contreras	80	80	80	
Cozumel	Núñez	220	220	220	
Crincho	Sánchez	340	a	a	
Cueiual	?	a	480	a	
Culucumul	Osorio	140	140	140	
Cuytun	Baeza	160	160	160	
Cuzama	Crown	900	800	900	900
Chachetuniche	Cea	70	60	70	
Chalante	Quiros	700	700	700	
Chaltimohad	Hernández	550	550	500	
Chaltumbolio	Cetina	100	100	100	
Chaltun	Arzeo	130	130	130	
Champoton	Crown	420	420	420	

Table 1.1 (cont.)

Locality	Encomendero	Paso y Troncoso	López de Velasco	Roys	1551 Report
Chancenote	Rutia	600	c	600	
Chanzenot	González	230	230	a	
Chepez	Arévalo	300	330	300	
Chichimila	Rutia	160	c	160	
Chilulila	Cepeda	330	c	330	
Chilultel	Sánchez	350	350	350	
Choaca	Rutia	200	c	200	
Chomulna	Nieto	740	740	740	
Chuburna	Montejo	350	350	350	
Eautunil	Aguilar	380	380	380	
Eban	Martín	380	380	380	
Enpole	Núñez	17	17	17	
Entecud	Contreras	120	120	a	
Entixol	Medina	300	300	300	
Enzinzimato	Ciega	90	90	90	
Enzir	Ricalde	130	130	a	
Equimil	Rojo	180	180	180	
Guayacuz	García	270	270	270	
Guayma	Bellido	200	200	200	
Halacho	Pinos	200	c	200	
Hayan	Seguisamo	390	390	390	
Hayan	Rosado	360	360	360	
Hunycu	Gutierrez	550	550	550	
Ixcabche	Ricalde	370	c	a	
Ixconpiche	Sigüenza	230	c	230	
Ixil	Donzel	280	280	280	
Ixpocomucho	Jiménez	130	c	130	
Ixpona	Cisneros	250	250	250	
Ixtual	Julián	280	280	280	
Izona	Montejo	40	40	40	
Jozil	Ruíz	150	150	150	
Lobain	Martín	370	370	740	
Loucun	Galiano	370	370		
Macochi	Montejo	500	500	500	
Mama	Barrio	440	440	440	
Mani	Crown	970	971	970	970
Mape	González	28	28	a	
Mastunil	Vargas	500	500	500	
Maxcomul	Vizcaíno	260	c	260	
Mazabilco	Barajas	240	240	a	
Mona	Castilla	350	350	350	
Motul	Bracamonte	640	640	640	
Muca	1/2 Méndez				
	1/2 Magaña	250	b	a	
Nabolon	Contreras	320	320	320	
Nocacao	Martin	100	b	100	
Nolo	?	120	120	120	
Oache	González	60	60	a	

Table 1.1 (cont.)

Locality	Encomendero	Paso y Troncoso	López de Velasco	Roys	1551 Report
Ocova	Perálvarez	1,200	1,200	1,200	
Ovaca	Pacheco	1,200	1,200	1,200	
Ocu	Vela	250	b	250	
Pacat	Ocámpo	370	360	360	
Papacal	Juárez	680	680	680	
Pazaluchen	Osorio	200	200	a	
Pelzemy	Ciega	360	360	a	
Peucuinte	Donzel	250	250	250	
Pixila	Alonzo	260	260	260	
Pocobot	Carcía	250	c	250	
Popola	Cieza	430	430	430	
Quemanche	]?[	a	20	a	
Quibil	Crown	470	480	470	
Quimacana	Castilla	300	300	300	
Quimula	Alonzo	280	281	280	
Quinlacam	Cepeda	300	b	300	
Sahcabchen	Sánchez	350	c	350	
Sahumchen	Tamayo	380	380	380	
Suxbil	Bracamonte	620	620	620	
Tacul	Hernández	480	a	a	
Tacul	Crown	790	790	790	790
Tachay	Ayala	620	620	620	
Talinoli	Medina	290	290	290	
Tamoani	Perálvarez	160	b	160	
Taubcum	Julián	150	b	150	
Taxan	Crown	400	400	400	
Tebatun	Villanueva	220	220	220	
Tecal	Briceño	420	420	420	
Tecalt	Rey	310	310	310	
Tecon	Piloto	430	b	430	
Tecon	Triana	480	b	480	
Tecuxche	González	180	180	180	
Telchiqui	Crown	1,030	1,030	1,030	1,030
Telmut	Arevalo	330	330	a	
Temax	Sosa	580	580	580	
Temul	Rodríguez	460	460	460	
Tenabe	Llanos	330	c	330	
Tepaca	González	150	150	a	
Tepiche	Hernández	340	340	340	
Tequeat	Burgos	160	160	160	
Tequinavalon	Ponce	290	290	a	
Tequite	Contero	400	400	400	
Tetepot	Aguilar	120	130	a	
Tetic	Quirós	210	b	210	
Texan	P. Hernández	320	320	320	
Texcolumo	L. Hernández	60	60	60	
Texiol	Barajas	200	200	200	
Texip	Arevalo	310	310	a	

Table 1.1 (cont.)

Locality	Encomendero	Paso y Troncoso	López de Velasco	Roys	1551 Report
Texul	Zapata	730	630	630	
Tinchica	Pérez	360	c	360	
Tisbalatiun	Julián	220	220	220	
Tiscoco	Montejo	530	530	530	
Tispeche	Castañeda	350	350	a	
Tisueca	Yehues	160	160	160	
Tiscunchel	Méndez	220	220	220	
Tixbalatun	Diaz	170	170	170	
Tixconti	Medina	360	360	360	
Tixjocapai	Sánchez	700	700	700	
Tocauas	Burgos	370	360	370	
Totila	Velasco	210	210	210	
Vaca	Pacheco	480	480	480	480
Xenaba	Arceo	270	270	200	
Xocchen	González	110	110	110	
Xuchibila	Tablada	200	200	a	
Xuchibila	Tome	230	230	a	
Yahuaca	Portillo	130	b	130	
Yaxa	Camino	460	460	460	
Yaxocul	Crown	60	60	60	60
Yel	Pimentel	109	109	109	
Yocboz	Ayala	110	110	110	
Yocheo	Hernández	80	80	80	
Yotalain	López	160	160	160	
Zabanal	Crown	250	250	250	250
Zamiol	Cieza	160	160	160	
Zenote and Mopila	Martín	240	c	240	
Ziho	Triana	410	b	410	
Zihot	Íñiguez	210	a	a	
Zionop	González	110	110	110	
Zique	Gallego	340	340	a	
Zisnuache	Castillo	360	360	a	
Zitacacauche	Ruíz	160	160	a	
Zixmo	Mena	310	310	310	
Zizia	Ricalde	420	420	420	
Zizontun	Vaquiano	600	600	600	
Zozuta	1/2 Méndez				
	1/2 Magaña	720	620	720	
Zumaylco	Álvarez	400	b	400	
Total		57,644		51,246	

a not listed.
b mentioned, but no numerical values given.
c mentioned, with no numerical values, along with "con sus sugetos" (with their dependent villages).

The third column gives the actual number of mantas the town was assessed in annual tribute. There is only one exception, the town of Taubcum, for which there is no assessment in mantas. We have used the number of chickens as the best available substitute. It should be noted that we have ignored the figures given for the population of most, but not all, of the localities. In the majority of cases, the value for population coincides with that for mantas, but frequently there are minor deviations, and there is no way to evaluate the accuracy of the statement. The deviations are insignificant. As a measure of both consistency and safety, we adhere rigidly to the assessed number of mantas. As we have already indicated, we take this number as the direct number of tributaries.

The fourth column of the table gives the values stated as the population of towns in Yucatan by López de Velasco, who clearly got his figures directly or indirectly from the 1549 assessments. There are four towns that Paso y Troncoso listed that are missing from Velasco's list—Ateque, Cinanche, Crincho, and Tacul. The 1549 assessments as transcribed and published in Paso y Troncoso have three names which do not seem to appear in the list of López de Velasco—Canyzo, Cueiual, and Quemanche. The numbers of tributaries are identical for most towns and, in the exceptions, deviate usually by one digit.

López de Velasco, unfortunately, does not give numerical values for a number of towns. Twelve are listed by name with no further comment. Twenty-one others are listed by name together with the expression "con sus sugetos" (with their dependent villages). The absence of numerical values for these towns makes it useless to calculate a total for the statements in López de Velasco.

The fifth column of the table lists the number of tributaries given by Ralph Roys for towns corresponding to those listed in the assessments of 1549. *The Political Geography of Yucatan* is a brilliant survey of information on the location of towns in pre-Conquest Yucatan and goes a long way toward the reconciliation of the encomiendas as known from the 1549 assessments and the Relaciones Geográficas with the urban and village geography of Yucatan at the time of the Conquest. However, there are certain factors which make it difficult to obtain complete correspondence between Roys' values and those in the 1549 assessments or López de Velasco. Roys does not usually give the names of encomenderos, names which are always a clue to the identity of localities. Moreover, he usually gives the Maya or present-day forms of place names rather than the somewhat distorted forms found in the Spanish lists. Finally, he organizes his material according to the location and identity of the towns as such, with only secondary reference to their position in encomiendas. These procedures were entirely appropriate to his purpose but make it difficult to utilize his data for calculating the total number of tributaries.

Specifically, we find 151 places in the 1549 assessments for which recognizable equivalents are mentioned by Roys. Not all of them are on his maps. For these towns he has, without significant exception, copied the number of tributaries accurately. The other twenty-seven towns in the 1549 assessments are undoubtedly discussed by Roys or at least considered by him. They are not, however, given values for tributaries in a form which makes possible their inclusion in the table. As a result, the total we get from Roys is smaller by several thousand than that which we obtain from the 1549 assessments. Our total from those assessments is 57,644 tributaries. The corresponding total from Roys for 151 towns is 51,246. The means for the twenty seven missing towns is 237 tributaries per town. There is, therefore, no serious discrepancy. We should also state that Roys elsewhere gives approximately 57,000 tributaries as his estimate of the total for the 1549 assessments,[101] a value close to ours.

The table, as we have prepared it, requires some adjustment to arrive at an estimate of the total Indian population of Yucatan under Spanish control in 1549. One addition comes from the Relacion de los conquistadores y pobladores que habia en la provincia de Yucatan, en la ciudad de Mérida, 25 July 1551. In general, this 1551 report repeats the same values for seven towns, mostly held by the Crown. We have included those values for confirmation of the data. The exception is the villa of Valladolid, of which the report states: "otros indios están en la villa de Valladolid, pueden ser hasta trecientos casados, los quales están en cabeza de Su Magestad por muerte del encomendero, que se decía Gaspar de Torres...." (There are other Indians in the villa of Valladolid, perhaps up to 300 married men. They are held by the Crown because of the death of the encomendero, Gaspar de Torres....) Since that locality

[101]"Lowland Maya Native Society at Spanish Contact," in *Handbook of Middle American Indians*, III, 661.

and value are not in the 1549 assessments but these Indians clearly should be taken into account, we must add 300 tributaries to our total for the third column in Table 1–1.

Another adjustment is for the Indians of Acalán-Tixchel. This Indian province or state lay in the extreme western portion of Campeche. It is represented in the Memoria de los conventos of 1582 by the towns of Tixchel and Zapotitlán, administered by the convent of Campeche, and was the precursor of the eighteenth century parishes and present-day municipios of Carmen and Palizada. The earliest royal assessment, in 1553, set the number of tributaries for Acalán-Tixchel at 500.[102] These, too, must be added to our total.

With the adjustments for the Indians in Valladolid and those of Acalán-Tixchel, the total of the 1549 assessments and additions becomes 58,444 tributaries or married men. We use the conversion factor of 4.0 to arrive at 233,776 persons.

Our value, however, cannot be held to be the Indian population of Yucatan under Spanish control *ca.* 1549. There is still the area of Uaymil-Chetumal to be taken into account. Roys has estimated 21,000 persons for this area in 1549[103]; Sanders, 50,000 persons.[104] The first depends upon a static conception of movement of population, the second upon a somewhat more dynamic one. We have estimated the population of Uaymil-Chetumal at the time of the arrival of the Spaniards at 216,000. The area is high bush country, verging on tropical rainforest, and considerably more humid and with far more rainfall than north-central Yucatan. In climate it resembles Acalán, where a Contact population of approximately 50,000 persons fell to about 2,000 by 1553 (fugitives not included), a decrease of 96 percent in twenty-eight years. The Uaymil-Chetumal area, in contrast to Acalán, was the scene of prolonged and bitter warfare in all three of the Montejo expeditions. Landa, writing about 1566 commented on the provinces of Cochua and Chetumal, "siendo esas dos provincias las más pobladas y llenas de gente, quedaron las más deventuradas de toda aquella tierra." ("these provinces, which were formerly the thickest settled and the most populous, remained the most desolate of all the country.")[105] Accordingly, in allowance of

[102]Scholes and Roys, *The Maya Chontal Indians,* p. 152.
[103]"Lowland Maya Native Society at Spanish Contact," in *Handbook of Middle American Indians,* III, 661.
[104]"Cultural Ecology of the Maya Lowlands," in *Estudios de cultura maya,* II, 93.
[105]P. 27; Landa-Tozzer, pp. 60–61.

97 percent attrition or a survival of 6,500 would seem appropriate. Our estimate for the Indian population of Yucatan under Spanish control in 1549, then, is 240,276, or to stress the fact that this is an estimate, 240,000. This value should be compared with Roys' estimate of 280,000,[106] which includes an allowance of from 24,000 to 25,000 for the Petén, and with Sanders' estimate of 300,000.[107]

V. CONVERSION FACTORS, 1543–1813

Our documentary information on the Indian population of Yucatan during the sixteenth, seventeenth, and eighteenth centuries gives us counts in terms of certain categories of persons. In order to arrive at estimates of the total Indian population, we must employ a series of numerical factors. It is now time to discuss the derivation of the values we use for the two most important groups, counts of whom are our principal source of information, that is, tributaries and personas de confesión.

Let us start with tributaries. This is really a double category since the term tributary at first meant a married man and at a later time included widows, widowers, and unmarried adults (the half tributaries). In our previous work on central Mexico we have examined in detail the numerical relations among tributaries, married men, and the population. Through extensive examination of the records of the mid-sixteenth century, we have demonstrated that at the time and under the reorganized Spanish tribute system, implemented in 1557–1570, the stated number of tributaries should be multiplied by 2.8 in order to arrive at the total number of persons. During the same period, the factor for married men, or casados, was 3.3, and that factor should be applied to tributaries in counts made before the tribute reform when tributary meant a married man.[108]

Two centuries later, after the movement of the population had changed from a severe decline to a strong increase, these values showed substantial increases. Thus, the census of 1777 gave for sixty one rural parishes in the bishopric of Oaxaca

[106]"Lowland Maya Native Society at Spanish Contact," in *Handbook of Middle American Indians*, III, 661.
[107]"Cultural Ecology of the Maya Lowlands," in *Estudios de cultura maya*, II, 93.
[108]See especially IA : 43, pp. 75–103 and Chap. IV in Vol. I of these *Essays*.

a casado factor of 4.78 and the census of 1793, as summarized in the *ramo* of Historia in the Mexican National Archive gave for Yucatan a value of 4.96.[109] As to the factor for converting tributaries to total population, the information in the Matrícula de Tributarios of 1805 is decisive. For Mexico as a whole, but excluding the intendancy of Mérida, that is, Yucatan, the value is 4.42, and for the intendancy of Mérida alone, with a tributary population of 330,351, it is 4.07.[110]

The conversion factor for tributaries in Yucatan during the last years of the sixteenth century may be estimated with reasonable assurance from the information presented by Roys, Scholes, and Adams in their study of the census and inspection of Pencuyut (their Table 2). They summarize the data in the García de Palacio counts that have been found and add to it information from the count of Cozumel Island in 1570. They have combined the data for the two towns on Cozumel into a single item, which we leave as one item in order not to give undue weight to the small fraction of the population of Yucatan represented by the humid eastern coast. The three writers have also calculated tributaries for Cozumel under the reformed tribute system. Since the inspection and count were for church purposes, the records apparently did not state the number of tributaries. The García de Palacio counts, as already stated, applied the reformed definition of tributary. Because of its importance for our purposes, we reproduce the pertinent information here :

| | | | | Ratio : | |
Town	Casados	Tribs.	Pop.	P/C^a	P/T^b
Pencuyut	114	164	684	4.75	4.17
Tazimín-Boxchen	137	152	554	4.04	3.64
Dzonotchuil	165	188	659	3.99	3.50
Tecay	67	75	278	4.15	3.71
Tixcacauche	125	138	494	3.95	3.58
Cozumel Island	144	158	446	3.10	2.82
Mean				4.00	3.57

[a] Population to casados.
[b] Population to tributaries.

[109]See Chap. IV in Vol. I of these *Essays* and Table 20a there.
[110]*Ibid.* and Table 28a. For Mexico as a whole, the value is for tributary as defined in the Ordinance of Intendants and represents a change from the definition in use for over two centuries in central Mexico. The data for Yucatan are taken directly from the Matrícula de Tributarios, 1805.

These figures are very consistent and probably quite close to reality. For the tribute assessments of 1549, we may use 4.0 as the conversion factor to arrive at total population since at that time tributaries were equivalent to married men. For counts and assessments in the following years, we must still use it until the implementation of the reformed classification of tributary. By the time of the García de Palacio counts at the latest, and for counts during the remainder of the sixteenth century, we should use a conversion factor of 3.6.

The differences which appear between the conversion factors for tributaries and married men in Yucatan and those in central Mexico may be explained in part by the dissimilar historical experiences and cultural patterns of the two regions and in part by the fact that tribute was not assessed on exactly the same age groups. In Yucatan, for instance, according to the Matrícula de Tributarios of 1805, the tributary age ran from fourteen to sixty inclusive, and that was undoubtedly the range for a long time before probably to the beginning of the Spanish tribute system in the area. In central Mexico, the tributary age ran from sixteen to fifty. As a result, we have to note the rate of increase in both P/C and P/T as it was manifested in Yucatan itself and disregard central Mexico. Although the trend in both regions was in the same direction, the degree of change was not identical.

We have no intermediate points with which to determine the exact course of the increase in value of the conversion factor for tributaries in Yucatan. Hence, there is no alternative but to assume that it was linear. This means that the following values must be used at the corresponding dates:

3.6 at 1583
3.7 for the period 1600–1610
3.8 for the period 1690–1700
4.0 for the period 1785–1795
4.1 for 1813

We turn now to our second major category in which information on the Indian population is presented in the earlier colonial records, namely, personas de confesión. These were variously called as well *confesados* or confesantes. They were the persons who made regular confession, received communion, and were regarded as adult members of the community as compared with infant and with children receiving religious instruction prior to becoming adult members. If full advantage is to be taken of the important clerical documents giving population statements for Yucatan for the years between 1580 and 1800, it is essential to know what proportion of the population was considered full members of the Church.

The critical problem is the establishment of the lower age limit of this category. Once this line is drawn, we have enough data on age distribution to make a fair estimate of the proportion of personas de confesión in the population. The lower age limit seems to have been somewhat flexible but in general coincided with the beginning of puberty. Since ecclesiastical categories were introduced by the missionaries, it is worth looking first at the age limit for the similar category in central Mexico. There, the break between children being given doctrina and personas de confesión came at ages twelve to fourteen. In his exceptionally thorough study of the Augustinian reports on their parishes in the Archbishopric of Mexico, *ca.* 1570, Brinckmann establishes this point and quotes two statements. According to one, the personas de confesión are " 'de doze años arriba...' " (upwards of twelve years of age); according to the other, the ' "almas de confesión de las quales entran muchachos y muchachas de doze á catorze años...." ' " "(the people making confession into which group the boys and girls come at twelve to fourteen years of age....)"[111] Our own study of age category arrives at the same age limit.[112]

For Yucatan we have a series of scattered, direct statements that indicate that the practice in the peninsula was virtually identical with that of central Mexico and that it dates from the beginning of Christianization. Landa, writing *ca.* 1566, commented: "Que antiguamente se casaban de 20 años y ahora de 12 o 13...." " "(In olden times they married when they were 20 years old; but now they marry when they are 12 or 14 [*sic*].")[113] Cogolludo, writing in the middle of the seventeenth century, described the religious instruction of the young at some length:

Preuino el zelo de los Predidacores, y Maestros espirituales este

[111]*Die Augustinerrelationen Nueva España* 1571–1573, p. 121, citing the reports for Totolapan and Tlapa, respectively.
[112]See Chap. IV of Vol. I of these *Essays*.
[113]P. 42; Landa-Tozzer, p. 100. The Spanish texts in both the Garibay edition and that in *DIU*, XIII, p. 326, clearly state thirteen years of age; the text in *DIU* gives the ages in Roman numerals. The Spanish form of stating age, incidentally, is like ours so that these ages mean that the people had completed that number of years and were in the next year of life.

inconuinente con auer puesto en costumbre, que todos los niños, y
niñas de los Pueblos vayan los dias de entresemana a la Iglesia, donde
se les enseñan las Oraciones, y Doctrina Christiana, que para que
con menos trabajo llegue a la execution del deseo, está díspuesto
de esta forma.

Ya se dixo, como todos los Pueblos estàn diuisos en parcialidades. Cada vna, ò entre dos si son cortas, tiene vn Tupil, ò Alguazil
señalado, el qual por la mañana en saliendo el Sol recoge todos los de
su parcialidad de hasta catorze años ellos, y ellas de doze (que es
quando luego se trata de casarlos) y juntos à vn lado todos los varones,
y à otro las muchachas, hazen vna Procession, precediendo el Tupil
con vna Cruz mediana algo leuantada, y comencando en voz alta
con septimo tono las Oraciones por las calles, que salen derechas a la
Iglesia, donde entran con el mismo orden.... There follows a description of the order of religious instruction which continued through the
morning. (The preachers and religious teachers in their zeal avoided
this difficulty [the danger of lapses into heathendom if religious instruction were left to the parents] through instituting the custom that all
the boys and girls in the Indian towns go every weekday to the church,
where they are taught prayers and Christian doctrine. To carry out
religious instruction with less effort, it is ordered in this form :

It has already been stated that the Indian towns are divided into
sections. Each section, or two of them together if they have few people,
has a tupil, or constable, appointed, who in the morning when the sun
rises gathers all the children of his section, the boys up to fourteen
years of age and the girls up to twelve (the ages when the attempt is
made to marry them off immediately). They go in procession through
the streets that lead directly to the church, all the boys on one side and
the girls on the other, the tupil leading with a medium-sized cross held
in the air but not too high, and beginning to chant the prayers in a
loud voice in seventh liturgical mode. They enter the church in the
same manner.)[114]

In the Franciscan report on convents in Yucatan,
prepared in 1700, we read the following :

Está fiel, y legitimamente deducida de los padrones de confesiones
originales que los padres Guardianes... formaron de las confessiones
de este present año de sietecientos, salvo los Indizuelos e Indias
pequeñas, que no van puestas, y son los que por pequeños asisten
todos los días a la escuela, donde los Ministros les enseñan incesante-
mente la doctrina Christiana.... (This report is faithfully and accurately taken from the original lists of confessions that the reverend
guardians of the convents...prepared from confessions made in this
present year 1700. It does not include Indian boys and girls, namely,

[114]*Lib.* IV, *cap.* XVIII (I, 229-230).

those who as children go daily to school where instuctors continually teach them Christian doctrine. . . .)

In the "Expediente formado para el establecimiento de escuelas en Yucatan y Campeche, 1782–1805," we find statements defining the age of children who were suitable for education in school in the latter portion of the eighteenth century. These ages correspond to those accepted by the Church for the purpose of instruction in Christian doctrine :

Town of Tixcacaltuyu : "edad de seis a diez años" (age of six to nine years).

District of Valladolid : "Que los niños y niñas. . . están empadronados los varones desde la edad de cinco años hasta la de trece; y las hembras también desde los cinco hasta los once años." (Boys are put on the list from age five to thirteen and girls from five also until eleven.

Subdelegación of Campeche : the upper age limit for instruction is mentioned as, for males, "al cumplir los diez o doce años," (upon completing age ten or twelve; and for females, "cumplida la edad de los mismo diez o doce años. . . ." (upon completing the same age ten or twelve. . . .)[115]

It is clear from these statements that throughout the colonial period the lower age limit of personas de confesión, although somewhat variable, lay in the vicinity of the beginning of age thirteen, perhaps a year higher for boys and a year lower for girls. Furthermore, and here is a fact of importance, this limit conformed to the line drawn in most enumerations between niños and the adult categories. The overwhelming majority of Indians, upon reaching the end of the ages of religious instruction, married and thus became casados for the purpose of tribute counts.

Let us now examine certain numerical data. There are two possible methods. One is to make a segregation according to actual ages. This can be done if we have numerical values for adequate age categories. The other method is to divide the group described as niños from all other individuals. In both methods we may express the results initially as percentages of personas de confesión in the total population.

The values for the percentage of personas de confesión in the total population are remarkably consistent throughout and will require very powerful evidence to refute them. To

[115]Rubio Mañé, *Archivo*, III, 174, 197, 211, respectively.

(1) We use again the data from the García de Palacio counts and the Island of Cozumel as tabulated by Roys, Scholes, and Adams:

Town	Children	Total Pop.	% Personas de Confesión
Pencuyut	329	684	51.9
Tizimín-Boxchen	236	554	57.4
Dzonotchuil	280	659	57.5
Tecay	118	278	57.5
Tixcacauche	204	494	58.7
Cozumel	130	446	70.8
Mean			59.0

(2) Oaxaca, census of 1777.[116] We deduct from the total the age groups 0–4 and 5–9, together with one-half of that 10–14. Then we express the remainder not in these age groups as a percentage of the total population   62.5

(3) All Mexico, census of 1793,[117] the sum of the available figures, Indians only, percentage of all persons except niños   61.9

(4) Intendancy of Mérida less Tabasco (Yucatan), census of 1789,[118] all races, percentage of all except *niños*   57.6

(5) Subdelegación of Mérida (Yucatan), census of 1794,[119] all races, percentage of those in population after deducting all aged 0 to 7 and one-half of those aged 7–16   61.3

(6) Intendancy of Mérida, Matrícula de Tributarios of 1805, Indians only, percentage of all persons except niños   61.8

consider this segment as comprising 60 percent of the population from 1600 to 1800 will introduce such a small error as to be negligible. Although a much higher percentage for central Mexico is indicated in the decade 1560–1570 by our studies and that of Brinckmann,[120] it must be remembered that the value for Yucatan covers only the recovery after the great decline of the sixteenth century, whereas the values for central Mexico are derived from the period of continuing severe decline and those derived from Augustinian reports come from areas in central Mexico that suffered an even more severe decline. The one element in our data for Yucatan comparable with such values from central Mexico is the information for the island of Cozumel in 1570, in one of the areas of Yucatan where population decline was particularly rapid and severe. The island a few decades later became *despoblado*.

[116]See Chap. IV in Vol. I of these *Essays* and Table 16a there.
[117]*Ibid.*, and Table 26.
[118]MS, AGN, Historia, vol. 523, f. 9, published in Rubio Mañe, *Archivo*, I, 249–250.
[119]AGN, Historia, vol. 522, f. 257, published in Rubio Mañe, *Archivo*, I, 210–214.
[120]See Chap. IV in Vol. I of these *Essays*; Brinckmann, p. 120 *et seq.*

Rather than use 60 percent for the purposes of computation, it is preferable to convert it into a multiplicative factor. Therefore, to estimate the total Indian population from personas de confesión, we multiply the number of personas de confesión by 1.67.

VI. THE RELACIONES GEOGRAFICAS:
THE POPULATION IN 1580 AND IN 1543

The second major source, subsequent to the tribute assessments of 1549, which gives us an index to population change in the sixteenth century is the Relaciones Geográficas. Rather than include our discussion of them with other documents giving information on the population *ca.* 1580, we deal with them in a separate section because they also give information on the population as of approximately 1543, that is, before the great revolt of 1545–1547, and thus give us a further clue to the source of the decline in the Indian population before 1549.

The information contained in the Relaciones Geográficas is vast indeed and covers every aspect of life in Yucatan both post-Conquest up to the time of the preparation of the reports and pre-Conquest. Of special pertinence for our purposes are numerous statements of encomenderos about the number of Indians in their encomiendas. Such statements give the number found by the prevailing tribute count and assessment, that is, the last count taken before the report by each encomendero. Therefore, they have an average date somewhat earlier than the dates of the Relaciones Geográficas, which are 1579–1581. Since we have no way at this time to arrive at an accurate date, we shall use 1579 or *ca.* 1580.

Of the declarations by encomenderos of the number of Indians in their encomenderos at the time of the making of the report, we have been able to find forty-two that give information in usable form. They are set forth with pertinent data in Table 1.2. Under the heading 1579, we show for each town or small group of towns the number of Indians declared by the encomendero to be tributary to him at the time he made his report. In almost every instance the number is given as a rounded value, and the persons are designated as Indians, tributaries, or married males. Occasionally the number is expressed in terms of cotton mantas assessed or received annually.

The total Indian population at this date cannot be estimated

Table 1.2

Tributaries of 1579–1581, as given in the Relaciones Geográficas. These are compared with the number stated to have been living at the time of the conquest (i.e., about 1543), and with those given in the taxation list of 1549. Also shown are the ratios of the numbers present in 1543 and 1579 and those present in 1549 and 1579. For discussion and further explanation see text.

The encomenderos and documentary references are given for each town. For 1549 we use the taxation list (*ENE*, vols. V and VI), and for 1543 and 1579 the Relaciones Geográficas (*DIU*, vols. XI and XIII).

Town	1543	1549	1579	Ratio : 1579/1543	Ratio : 1579/1549
Mutul		640	500		0.78
1549 : *ENE* V : 121					
Francisco Braca-					
monte					
1579 : *DIU*-XI : 84					
Francisco Braca-					
monte					
Tecauto y Tepakan	600	700	500	0.83	0.72
1549 : *ENE* V : 132					
(Tixjocapai)					
sons Diego					
Sánchez					
1579 : *DIU*-XI : 117					
Cristóbal Sanchez					
Sahumchen		380	200		0.53
1549 : *ENE* V : 136					
Fco. Tamayo					
1579 : *DIU*-XI : 134					
Fco. Tamayo Pacheco					
Eban		380	300		0.79
1549 : *ENE* V : 135					
San Martin					
1579 : *DIU*-XI : 141					
Juan de la Cámara					
Tabi	400		150	0.38	
1549 : Not on list					
1579 : *DIU*-XI : 151					
Pedro García					
Chunhuhub	300		80	0.27	
1549 : Not on list					
1579 : *DIU*-XI : 151					
Pedro García					
Mama		440	380		0.86
1549 : *ENE* V : 152					
Berrio					
1579 : *DIU*-XI : 166					
Juan de Aguilar					
Cantemo		310	200		0.64
1549 : *ENE* V : 149					
Fco. Venio					
1579 : *DIU*-XI : 173					
Juan de Aguilar					

Table 1.2 (cont.)

Town	1543	1549	1579	Ratio : 1579/1543	Ratio : 1579/1549
Temax		580	500		0.86
1549 : *ENE* V : 125					
Hijos de Sosa					
1579 : *DIU*-XI : 175					
Juan de Sosa					
Zizantun		600	350		0.58
1549 : *ENE* V : 124					
Muñoz Vaquiano					
1579 : *DIU*-XI : 199					
Martín Sánchez					
Quizil y Sitipech	300	230	120	0.40	0.52
1549 : *ENE* V : 138					
Paredes					
1579 : *DIU*-XI : 211					
Juan de Paredes					
Pixila		260	200		0.77
1549 : *ENE* V : 129					
Rodríguez Alonso					
1579 : *DIU*-XI : 241					
Antón Corajo					
Xanaba		270	150		0.56
1549 : *ENE* V : 134					
Fco. Arzeo					
1579 : *DIU*-XI : 241					
Fco. Arzeo					
Quinicama	400	300	160	0.40	0.53
1549 : *ENE* V : 122					
Castilla					
1579 : *DIU*-XI : 252					
Pedro de Santillana					
Izamal y Sta. Maria	500	550	370	0.74	0.67
1549 : *ENE* V : 134					
García Hernandez					
1579 : *DIU*-XI : 266					
Juan Cueva Santillán					
Chubulna		350	260		0.74
1549 : *ENE* V : 109					
Montejo					
1579 : *DIU*-XI : 278					
Diego de Santillán					
Tixcocob		530	260		0.49
1549 : *ENE* V : 121					
Montejo					
1579 : *DIU*-XI : 280					
Diego de Santillán					
Nolo		120	130		1.08
1549 : *ENE* V : 120					
Montejo					
1579 : *DIU*-XI : 280					
Diego de Santillán					

Table 1.2 (cont.)

Town	1543	1549	1579	Ratio : 1579/1543	Ratio : 1579/1549
Macochi		500	319		0.64
1549 : *ENE* V : 116					
Montejo					
1579 : *DIU*-XI : 282					
Diego de Santillán					
Tetzal	400	220	90	0.23	0.41
1549 : *ENE* V : 139					
Antón Julián					
1579 : *DIU*-XI : 295					
Alonso Julián					
Ixtual	500	280	108	0.22	0.39
1549 : *ENE* V : 137					
Antón Julián					
1579 : *DIU*-XI : 296					
Alonso Julián					
Popola	900	430	400	0.44	0.93
1549 : *ENE* V : 176					
Fco. de Cieza					
1579 : *DIU*-XIII : 47					
Diego Sarmiento					
Sinsimato	600	90	8	0.01	0.09
1549 : *ENE* V : 177					
Fco. de Cieza					
1579 : *DIU*-XIII : 48					
Diego Sarmiento					
Zemul, Tixolopo, Tizmocul	900	160	150	0.17	0.94
1549 : *ENE* V : 178					
Fco. de Cieza					
1579 : *DIU*-XIII : 49					
Diego Sarmiento					
Chancenote		600	200		0.33
1549 : *ENE* V : 173					
Juan de Urrutia					
1579 : *DIU*-XIII : 68					
Juan de Urrutia					
Choaca	1,000	200	20	0.02	0.10
1549 : *ENE* V : 172					
Juan de Urrutia					
1579 : *DIU*-XIII : 13, 74;					
XIV : 13					
Juan de Urrutia					
Chichimila		160	228		1.42
1549 : *ENE* V : 171					
Juan de Urrutia					
1579 : *DIU*-XIII : 75					
Juan de Urrutia					

Table 1.2 (cont.)

Town	1543	1549	1579	Ratio : 1579/1543	Ratio : 1579/1549
Catanique	100	50	3	0.03	0.06
1549 : *ENE* VI : 96					
Juan Bellido					
1579 : *DIU*-XIII : 79					
Juan Bellido					
Guayma	300	200	120	0.40	0.60
1549 : *ENE* VI : 87					
Juan Bellido					
1579 : *DIU*-XIII : 79					
Juan Bellido					
Temul	500		80	0.16	
1549 : Not on list					
Benavides					
1579 : *DIU*-XIII : 122					
Juan de Benavides					
Xoquen	150	110	45	0.30	0.41
1549 : *ENE* VI : 103					
Alonso González					
1579 : *DIU*-XIII : 136					
Salvador Corzo					
Pixoy	300	112	100	0.33	0.89
1549 : *ENE* VI : 80					
Gaspar González					
1579 : *DIU*-XIII : 141					
Esteban González					
Cacalac		180	140		0.78
1549 : *ENE* VI : 83					
Juan Cano					
1579 : *DIU*-XIII : 145					
Pedro Valencia					
Tancuy		60	28		0.47
1549 : Not on list					
1579 : *DIU*-XIII : 146					
Pedro Valencia					
Tecemi	600	210	140	0.23	0.67
1549 : *ENE* VI : 86					
Burgos					
1579 : *DIU*-XIII : 167					
Diego de Burgos					
Atequeaque	400	160	28	0.07	0.17
1549 : *ENE* VI : 85					
Burgos					
1579 : *DIU*-XIII : 167					
Diego de Burgos					
Cacalchen	100	50	28	0.28	0.56
1549 : *ENE* VI : 187					
Burgos					
1579 : *DIU*-XIII : 167					
Diego de Burgos					

Table 1.2 (cont.)

Town	1543	1549	1579	Ratio : 1579/1543	Ratio : 1579/1549
Tecanxo y Tocauas 1549 : *ENE* V : 130 Hijos de Burgos 1579 : *DIU*-XIII : 167 Diego de Burgos	460	370	190	0.41	0.51
Yalcon 1549 : *ENE* VI : 79 Pimentel 1579 : *DIU*-XIII : 169 Juan Farfán	150	109	24	0.16	0.22
Zama 1549 : *ENE* VI : 93 Baeza 1579 : *DIU*-XIII : 197 Juan de Raygosa		88	50		0.57
Cicab 1549 : Cannot identify (probably Sisal) 1579 : *DIU*-XIII : 202 Alonso de Villanueva	500	300	240	0.48	0.80
Dohot 1549 : *ENE* VI : 104 (probably Tixbala- tun) Giraldo Díaz 1579 : *DIU*-XIII : 207 Giraldo Díaz	600	170	100	0.17	0.59

from the sum of these forty-two statements, for the aggregate number of encomiendas far exceeded forty-two. Therefore, we have to utilize the method of ratios. This procedure is possible because of the additional information provided in the reports and in the assessments of 1549. For 1549 there are thirty-nine towns listed in the assessments of that year which correspond clearly to localities reported in the Relaciones Geográficas or for which a reasonable interpretation of the two sets of documents suggests identity. In Table 1.2 the assessed number of tributaries as of 1549 is listed under the heading 1549 and the ratio of the number in 1579 to that in 1549 is shown in the last column, headed 1579/1549.

In certain instances the encomenderos, reporting in 1579–1581, made some statement with respect to the number of Indians who were alive at the time the Indians were first encountered or given in encomienda. The form varies widely and embraces such expressions as "solían ser," they used to be, "cuando me encomendaron este pueblo," (when this town was given to me in encomienda), "antes de la conquista" (before Conquest), etc. Some of the statements are ambiguous or inadequate and for that reason have been omitted. A few state the exact tribute which was first assessed, but since the assessment was in 1549, it cannot be ascribed to an earlier date. Nevertheless, there remain twenty-four towns for which the population level at the time of the first granting of the encomienda is indicated with fair certainty. These have been placed in the table under the heading 1543, the year in which the great majority of the encomenderos received their encomiendas and first became acquainted with their towns. The ratios of the number of Indian tributaries in 1579 to that in 1543 are shown in the column headed 1579/1543.

The samples are adequate as far as the number of items and the territorial distribution are concerned. There are possible sources of minor political or fiscal bias in the selection of the towns reported. They are too subjective for quantitative evaluation, but they are minor. On the whole, we judge that there is a reasonable balance of factors and that the ratios derived from these towns are not far from the truth.

We are able to test our mean derived ratio for 1579/1543 against the average of 6 personal estimates of encomenderos. See Table 1.3. Our mean derived ratio for 1579/1543, calculated from twenty-four localities, is 0.297. The average of the six personal estimates of encomenderos is 0.32. The correspondence is close.

The means of all available places for the two sets of ratios 1579/1543 and 1579/1549 are, respectively, 0.297 and 0.605. The value of t for the two means is 4.79, well beyond the 1 percent level of probability and definitely significant.

If we translate these ratios into other terms, we may say that if an hypothetical population of tributaries was 1,000 in 1549, then that population would have been 2,037 in 1543 and in 1579 it would have been 605. Our value for 1549 in terms of tributaries was 58,444 for Yucatan exclusive of Uaymil-Chetumal. The corresponding value for 1543 is 119,050, and for 1579 is 35,359. We omit Uaymil-Chetumal from these calculations because of the difficulties of estimate. In 1543 that area still had a large population; in 1579 it was virtually despoblado, so to remain for most of the colonial period. Our

Table 1.3

Statements by encomenderos on population reduction
from the Conquest to 1579–1581.

Source	Encomendero	Area and Statement	Ratio : 1579/1543
DIU 13 : 51	Diego de Contreras	Yucatan—"e entendido y sabido de los conquistadores antiguos que esta tierra hera de mucha cantidad de yndios, y al presente no ay la tercia parte..."	0.33
DIU 13 : 86	Francisco de Cárdenas	Quilquil—"de seis partes de los yndios que entonces avia no aya agora las tres..."	0.50
DIU 13 : 89	Diego Osorio	Tesoco and all Yucatan—testimony of conquerors—porqueste que decian tenia seiscientos tributarios y agora an quedado en doscientos..."	0.33
DIU 13 : 120	Juan de Benavides	Yucatan—"he oydo dezir a los conquistadores y a los mesmos naturales ... que esta tierra era de mucha cantidad de jente de yndios y que al presente no hay la tercia parte dellos..."	0.33
DIU 13 : 186–187	Juan Farfán el Viejo	Province of Valladolid of all Yucatan—"quando entramos los españoles en esta tierra avia grandisima multitude de gentes qual no hay agora porque se an muerto de ocho partes delas que avia entonces las seis."	0.25
DIU 13 : 208	Giraldo Díaz de Alpuche	Yucatan—"yo a quarenta años que entre en esta tierra e la ayude a conquistar toda y de diez partes de la gente que avia entonces faltan agora las ocho y mas..."	0.20
Mean			0.32

omission of Uaymil-Chetumal somewhat distorts the 1543
value, which should be even higher, but does not affect the
1579 value.

The estimate for total population depends upon the
conversion factor for tributaries. For 1549, when the tributary
was equivalent to a married man, we use the factor 4.0, and
thus reach the figure 233,776 for Yucatan exclusive of Uaymil-
Chetumal. For the era prior to 1549, the same factor is appropriate. Hence, for 1543, the total for Yucatan exclusive of

Uaymil-Chetumal would have been 476,200. With regard to the data for 1579–1581, a question arises which must be considered at some length. Should we use 4.0, or should we prefer 3.6, the factor which is appropriate for converting tributaries to total population after the change in the definition of tributary in the last decades of the sixteenth century, that is, after the inclusion of half tributaries and the abolition of many exemptions? If we apply 4.0, we arrive at 141,436 as the population in 1579; if we apply 3.6, we get 127,292.

The question is basically at what time was the changed definition of tributary implemented in Yucatan—at the time of the García de Palacio counts in 1583–1584 or earlier? The Relaciones Geográficas and the counts on which statements of tributaries in them were based antedate the García de Palacio inspection by some years. They are an excellent test case for settling the question. The Relaciones were written or dictated by the Spanish encomenderos themselves. Most of them were men who had been in the colony since the Conquest, particularly since Montejo's third expedition. They may have carried over certain ideas about the reporting of tributaries from earlier times. On the other hand, their support was overwhelmingly from Indian tribute, and they were keenly interested in definitions, counts, and yields. They must have known what types of individuals were included under the term tributaries, that is, whether certain categories such as widowers and unmarried men were half tributaries. Yet they repeatedly express numbers of tributaries in terms of householders or casados. In the Relaciones Geográficas we have found 41 passages in which an encomendero characterizes the people who pay him tribute. Of these passages, 13 use the word vecinos or householders; 3 use *vecinos tributarios*; 5 use indios; 6 use *indios tributarios*; 10 use *tributarios*; and 4 state the tribute in terms of mantas.

The following excerpts are especially pertinent:

Blas González, testifying on Ichmul: "ay en el dicho pueblo quatrocientos yndios casados los quales me dan de tributo..." (there are in the said town four hundreds married Indian men who give me as tribute....)[121]

Giraldo Díaz de Alpuche, testifying on Dohot: "solía ser pueblo grande que agora treynta años eran seiscientos casados sin los muchachos e solteros, a venido este a tanta dimynuicion que al presente no tiene cien yndios tributarios...." (the town

121*DIU*, XIII, 117.

used to be large. Thirty years ago, it had six hundred married males without counting the boys and bachelors. Population has decreased so much that the town does not have at present one hundred tributary Indians....)[122]

Juan de Urrutia, testifying on Chauaca : "por manera que avia en aquel tiempo en el dicho pueblo dozientos yndios casados tributarios sin biudos ni enfermos mocos y viejos que a estos *en ningun tiempo* les an mandado tributar...." (so that the said town had in those times 200 tributary married males without counting widowers or sick, young men, and the old, none of whom *at any time* has been held to pay tribute...) [italics ours].[123]

The diction is loose. Nevertheless, an examination of these statements creates a strong impression that the encomenderos were thinking of tributaries in terms of the original definition which depended upon the casado rather than upon a definition including widowers and unmarried men as half tributaries. Since, then, the encomenderos as a class were stating numbers of tributaries as a function of the casado, we must conclude that the change in definition occurred after the counts recorded as prevailing at the time of the preparation of the Relaciones Geográficas, and since there is no mention of a change anywhere in the Relaciones, that change took place after the years 1579–1581, we are thus led to the conclusion that the change of definition was put into effect in 1583–1584 through the inspection and recounts by Dr. García de Palacio. Accordingly, we apply the conversion factor of 4.0 to the estimated number of tributaries in Yucatan in 1579 and arrive at 141,436 persons for the population of indios de pueblo.

Apart from the problem of the conversion factor, we may make two brief comments. The decline in no more than six years from 1543 to 1549 was drastic. The successful occupation of Yucatan by the Spaniards on their third entry and the great rebellion of 1545–1547 may have been much more destructive of Indian life than the prolonged fighting of the first two entries and must have been much more devastating than is implied by the written records, except perhaps for such statements as that of Landa quoted previously.

The further decline to a very low value in 1579 appears excessive unless we assume that the destruction of the 1540s

[122]*Ibid.*, p. 207.
[123]*Ibid.*, p. 74.

had still to run its course, that the lethal factors introduced by the presence of the Europeans and the upset in Indian life through concentration and relocation of towns were still exerting downward pressure on the population, and further that not merely mortality but also flight into the higher bush and rainforest of the south and west brought the number of Indians remaining under Spanish control in Yucatan below the level at which it finally came to equilibrium.

VII. THE INDIOS DE PUEBLO, 1580–1610

Further information concerning the Indian population at or close to 1580 may be obtained from three church documents. The first is the Memoria de los conuentos, vicarias y pu^{o}s of 1582, of which we make much use in the discussions relating to the entire period 1580–1610. It is the most complete document of its kind, for it lists in detail the names and locations of all Franciscan convents or other religious entities, together with the dependent towns and villages within each parish attached to each convent, although it does not give the numbers of tributaries or communicants. The second document is the letter of Fray Hernando de Sopuerta and the attached Memoria de los frailes franciscanos que sirven en la provincia de Yucatan of 1580. This memoria lists Franciscan convents in existence in 1580 plus the number of Indian towns and casados administered by each. The third document is the list of Franciscan convents at the end of the Memorial que el Provincial y Definidores de la Provincia de... Yucatán... envían al Real Consejo de las Indias, 1586. The list also gives the number of Indian towns administered by each convent and the population, but the latter are stated as *animas de confesión,* equivalent to adults admitted to communion.

The data in the documents and the conversions to total population are summarized in Table 1.4. For converting to population, we use the factor 1.67 for personas de confesión in accordance with the decision made above. For casados we use the factor 4.0. This decision is based specifically upon the fragments of the García de Palacio counts and the census of Cozumel in 1570, taken from Roys, Scholes, and Adams, and presented above. There is no reason for modifying the factor derived from that data for counts of casados made in 1580.

Examination of Table 1.4 brings to attention certain

Table 1.4

Convents listed in the Memorias of 1580, 1582, and 1586. The number of named places or pueblos follow in parentheses. For total populations, casados are multiplied by 4.0, and confesantes by 1.67.

Memoria, 1582	Memoria, 1580			Memoria, 1586		
Convent	Convent	Casados	Pop.	Convent	Confesantes	Pop.
Mérida (14)	Mérida (11)	2,000	8,000	Mérida (6)	1,621	2,707
				Tahuman^d (4)	1,680	2,806
Hunacama (4)				Hunucmá (3)	1,878	3,136
Conkal (7)	Conkal (11)	2,500	10,000	Conkal (7)	4,746	7,926
Tixkokob (6)				Tixkokob (6)	2,755	4,601
Motul (8)	Motul (9)	2,000	8,000	Motul (8)	5,013	8,372
Dzidzantún (9)	Tzitzantún (7)	2,800	11,200	Dzidzantún (7)	6,743	11,260
Tekanto (8)	Tekanto (7)	1,800	7,200	Tekanto (7)	4,664	7,789
Izamal (16)	Izamal (10)	2,000	8,000	Izamal (10)	5,437	9,080
Hocabá (9)	Hocabá (8)	1,400	5,600	Hocabá (9)	3,463	5,783
Homún (6)	Homún (4)	1,000	4,000	Homún (5)	2,584	4,315
Maní (11)	Maní (11)	3,600	14,400	Maní (8)	7,591	12,677
Oxcutzkab (5)				Otzkutzkab (3)	2,257	3,769
Tekax (3)	Tekax (3)	1,000	4,000	Tekax (3)	2,503	4,180
Sotuta (10)	Zotuta (8)	2,000	8,000			
Peto^a (7)						
Sisal (15)				Dzidzal (14)	5,528	9,232
Valladolid^b (8)	Valladolid (18)	2,600	10,400			
Tinum (6)				Tinum (5)	1,646	2,749
Tizimín (23)	Tetzimín (10)	1,800	7,200	Tizimín (10)	5,888	9,833

Table 1.4 (cont.)

Memoria, 1582	*Memoria*, 1580			*Memoria*, 1586		
Convent	Convent	Casados	Pop.	Convent	Confesantes	Pop.
Chancenote (9)	Chancenote (9)	800	3,200	Ichmul (9)	2,831	4,728
Cuzamil (4)				Campeche (8)	1,918	3,203
Ichmul (8)	Ichmul (8)	1,000	4,000	Tixchel[a] (4)	685	1,144
Campeche (13)	Campeche (6)	1,000	4,000			
Xequechakán (5)	Xequelchakán (5)	1,500	6,000	Xecelchakán (6)	2,960	4,943
Calquiní (14)	Calquiní (5)	2,800	11,200	Calkiní (5)	6,292	10,508
[Bacalar[c] (24)]						
Total (228)	(150)	33,600	134,400	(147)	80,683	134,741

[a] A *vicaría*.
[b] A *visita de curas*.
[c] Omitted in the total of places.
[d] In the Memoria of 1582 Tahuman is listed under Mérida, and Tixchel is listed under Campeche.

significant points. The population totals derived from the 1580 and the 1586 documents are almost identical: 134,400 and 134,741. Both are close to the value derived from the Relaciones Geográficas, namely 141,436, but both are lower.

As to the accuracy of the two Franciscan reports of the number of Indians, there can be little question. The convents of the Franciscan province kept careful rolls of communicants, steadily revised as names had to be added or dropped. Cogolludo has given us a convincing report of the keeping of such lists in his day:

Grande fue la disposicion con que nuestros primeros Padres fundadores de esta Prouincia ordenaron el gouierno espiritual de estos Indios, y no ha sido, ni es menor la execucion de todo lo que conduze a su mayor Christianidad, y bien de sus almas.... La assistencia continua, assi de Clerigos, como de Religiosos, es en los lugares que se señalaron para cabeças, y Conuentos, de donde se reparten las visperas de las fiestas à los Pueblos de su administracion, y les es forcoso à los mas dezir aquel dia Missa en dos Pueblos, y à vezes en tres:...

Despues de auer dicho Missa se quentan por tablas, en que están escritas todos los vezinos de los Pueblos, segun las parcialidades que se han dicho, con que sabe el Docrinero los que han assistido à oirla. Esto se haze en los patios de fuera de las Iglesias.... Cada Principal (ò Chunthan, que ellos llaman) dà quenta de su parcialidad, cuya quenta està à su càrgo, y como ya se conocen en saliendo de la Iglesia se aparta cada vna à su sitio, donde con facilidad se sabe quien ha faltado de la Missa. Inquiere el Doctrinero la causa..... (The arrangement that our first priests, the founders of this province, enacted for the spiritual administration of these Indians was excellent, and the carrying out of all that leads to better Christianity and the good of their souls has not been nor is less.... Secular priests and friars are continually present in those places appointed to be the seats of parishes and convents. From these places they go out on the evenings before feast days to the towns under their care. Most of them have to say mass on such days in two towns and sometimes in three....

After the ministering priest has said mass, the Indians are counted in accordance with lists in which are inscribed all the residents of the towns by town sections as has been stated. Thus the priest knows who has been present at the mass. This is done in the courtyards outside the churches.... Each chief man (or Chunthan as they are called) gives the accounting for the section, with the count of which he is charged. As the Indians already know the system, each goes to the proper place on leaving the church, so that it is known with ease who has missed attendance at mass. The priest inquires into the reason. . . .)[124]

Such information was easily available to the provincial and other administrators of the Franciscan province.

There is, however, a problem of the completeness of coverage of the Franciscan reports of 1580 and 1586. The list of 1582, which gives no data on numbers of people, is the most complete. Even if we omit Bacalar, the list shows 228 inhabited places, including towns with convents in them. The other two give 150 and 147 pueblos for 1580 and 1586, respectively. Furthermore, the Memoria of 1580 lacks the following convents, with supporting areas, mentioned in the Memoria of 1582: Hunacama, Tixkokob, Otzkutzkab, Peto, Sisal (although part of Sisal may have been allocated to Valladolid), Tinum, and Cozumel. The Memorial of 1586 does not include Sotuta, Peto, Valladolid, Chancenote, and Cozumel. The reason for these gaps may be that only Franciscan establishments were included and that even at this early date some parishes had been turned over to seculars. Whatever the reason, both lists are clearly incomplete.

An additional factor which must be considered is the disturbance and confusion which attended the social reorganization of the period, especially the forced congregation of many small settlements. Not only did the natives thus removed to new environments die of starvation or disease,[125] but masses of them also absconded to the remote areas of the south and west.[126] Thus, there were fewer Indians to record at the same time that the mechanism for recording was as yet imperfectly developed. The final result would have been that both the Franciscan and fiscal counts would greatly underestimate the real number of Indians. That such a combination of circumstances existed is suggested by the great and sudden increase of reported Indians in Indian towns from approximately 140,000 in 1580–1585 to 185,000 in 1605. Such a rise in twenty years cannot easily be ascribed to a natural increase. Either the earlier figures must be too low or the later figures are too high. The later ones are internally consistent and fit very well into the long-term population pattern. Therefore, we must regard the

---

[124]*Lib.* IV, *cap.* XVII (I, 227–228).
[125]See the testimony of the Relaciones Geográficas in *DIU,* XI and XIII, *passim.*
[126]See the discussion of fugitivism in part X of this chapter.

earlier estimates for indios de pueblo in Yucatan, whether derived from fiscal or religious counts, as undervaluing the actual population.

After 1580, our next estimate is for the period 1599–1609, or *ca.* 1605. There are three documents which give data on population for these years: The Testim^o del donativo of 1599, the Minuta de los encomenderos of 1606, and the reports of 1609 on personas de confesión in parishes administered by Franciscans and by secular priests in Vázquez de Espinosa. The Memoria de los conuentos of 1582 is especially useful in establishing parish boundaries for the comparison and interpretation of the data. We shall analyze the data in each of the three documents.

The Minuta de los encomenderos of 1601 is an alphabetical listing of the encomenderos, the towns held by them, and the tribute due them under the prevailing assessments. A peculiarity in the listing is that the tribute is not given in terms of annual payment but in terms of items due at one delivery. Hence, for items such as mantas delivered in two installments, the listing gives only half the annual total. The relationship between the populations of encomiendas in 1606 and 1549 may be studied by comparison of the two sets of tribute assessments. For the encomiendas held by Spanish residents of Mérida and Campeche, we have found thirty-eight encomiendas which appear to be present in both documents without territorial alteration. Since there is not enough of such instances for encomiendas held by Spanish residents of Valladolid, we shall treat the district of Valladolid by another method.

With the former group, we first convert the stated number of tributaries, derived from number of mantas in 1549 and fanegas of maize in 1606, to the number of persons. Then we take the ratio of persons in 1606 to that in 1549 (that is, 1606/1549). For conversion to persons, we use the factor 4.0 for 1549 and 3.7 for 1606. The mean of the 38 ratios is 0.797, with the standard deviation (s.d.) equal to $\pm$ 0.284 and the standard error (s.e.) equal to $\pm$ 0.046. (See Table 1.5.)

In 1549 there was a total of 42,530 tributaries listed for all the encomiendas held by vecinos of Mérida and Campeche. At 4.0 per tributary, the population would have been 170,120 persons. If we apply the ratio just derived, we get a population in 1606 of 135,586 for Campeche and Mérida.

This result may be checked if we examine directly the

Table 1.5

Population of encomiendas in Mérida and Campeche in 1549 and 1606,
as calculated from the number of tributaries stated in the lists for the respective
dates. For 1549 the tributaries are multiplied by 4.0, and for 1606 by 3.7.

Encomienda	1549	1606	Ratio: 1606/1549
Chubulna	1,400	1,163	0.831
Mama, Peto	3,000	2,220	0.740
Temax	2,320	2,368	1.021
Tetiz, Dzudzal, Chalante, Uitzil	3,640	2,220	0.610
Concal, Cholul, Chable, Dzilan, Izona, Sitpach	8,280	3,404	0.411
Hocabá province	9,600	5,822	0.607
Cacalud	880	740	0.841
Pixila, Quinimila	2,160	2,220	1.028
Sotuta, Tibulón	2,880	1,776	0.617
Baca	1,920	1,480	0.771
Nolo	480	740	1.542
Cantunil	1,520	1,111	0.731
Motul, Tekax	6,320	5,920	0.937
Dzidzantún	2,400	2,370	0.988
Oxcutzcab	2,520	2,960	1.175
Ixtual, Tixhualatun, Taubcum	2,600	1,111	0.427
Sinanche	1,280	1,111	0.868
Tekit	1,600	1,036	0.647
Tecal	1,680	740	0.440
Ixil, Pencuyut	2,120	1,478	0.697
Izamal	2,200	1,850	0.841
Ekmul	720	440	0.611
Cauquel, Ocu, Yabocu	2,320	1,036	0.447
Mococha	2,000	1,850	0.925
Homún-Cuzama	3,600	2,220	0.617
Bolonpoxche, Sitilpech	2,000	1,184	0.592
Hunacama, Tixkoch	2,840	2,220	0.782
Tecoh	1,600	1,184	0.740
Tepaca, Tecanto	3,400	2,960	0.870
Dzan, Mona	2,840	2,960	1.042
Calotmud, Samahil	3,360	1,850	0.551
Muxuppipp	1,200	740	0.617
Royal Town			
Campeche	2,520	2,400	0.952
Champoton	1,680	666	0.396
Mani	3,880	5,420	1.397
Tacul	3,160	4,725	1.495
Telchac	4,120	2,350	0.570
Quini	1,880	1,538	0.818
Mean			0.797

S.D. = ± 0.284
S.E. = ±0.040

number of tributaries shown in the Minuta of 1606. We use the relationship one fanega of corn per tributary rather than mantas because of the peculiarity of the listing of tribute. In 1606 the total number of fanegas of maize due and hence the total number of tributaries was 37,874 in all those towns which fell within the districts of Mérida and Campeche. At a factor of 3.7 per tributary, the population would have been 140,134. This figure should be compared with the 135,586 obtained by application of the town-by-town ratio. The difference, 4,549, is approximately 2.1 percent of the 1549 value and is as consistent as can be expected with the data at hand. Nevertheless, since only thirty-eight encomiendas could be used out of eighty listed in the Minuta of 1606, it is preferable to base our estimate of the population upon the total number of tributaries rather than upon the mean ratio.

The area controlled by the villa of Valladolid likewise can be treated best by the use of total numbers. In 1549 there were 15,114 tributaries; in 1606 there were 9,780. When the established conversion factors are applied, the populations become 60,456 and 36,186, respectively. The ratio 1606/1549 is close to 0.60, much lower than that for the districts of Mérida and Campeche, and indicates that the Indian population in the latter districts was in a better position than in the district of Valladolid.

When we combine the totals for both portions of Yucatan, we get in 1549, 57,644 tributaries, and in 1606, 47,654 tributaries. When conversion to total population is made with the factor of 3.7 per tributary in 1606, we get for that year 176,320 as the number of indios de pueblo in all Yucatan.

The Testimonio del donativo of 1599 contains the names of 130 towns, almost all of which can be identified as to locality and administrative affiliation. Of them, forty-eight can be cross-compared with the corresponding encomiendas in the Minuta of 1606. The numerical units are, for the encomiendas the fanegas of maize in the prevailing assessments of 1606, and for the towns in the Testimonio del donativo the pesos donated to the King by each town. We can derive an estimate of population by calculating the ratio of fanegas of maize and hence of tributaries to pesos. These data for forty-eight towns are in Table 1.6, together with the mean of the ratios. The latter is 7.31; that is, on the average there were 7.31 tributaries to every peso donated by these towns. Since the 130 places donated a total of 5,217 pesos, this figure represents 38,136 tributaries.

Table 1.6

Numerical relationship between fanegas of maize assessed against a series of encomiendas in 1606, and the money, in pesos, donated by the corresponding localities, according to the Testimonio del donativo of 1599. The list is arranged according to encomienda. Each one includes all the localities mentioned in the 1606 list, and, where pertinent and where the record permits, the parts of split encomiendas have been consolidated to show the total assessment. Each monetary value represents the amount recorded for each locality, except that when any encomienda includes more than one town, the total is given for the pesos contributed by all the towns in the encomienda.

Locality	Pesos Donated	Fanegas Maize	Ratio: Fanegas Pesos
Mérida			
Chubulna	41/6	314	7.52
Teya	63/	512	8.13
Tetiz, Zuzal, Chalante, Uitzil	72/3	600	8.30
Caucel, Cholul, Sitpach, Chable, Izona, Dzilan	96/5	920	9.52
Uman	35/6	240	6.71
Pixila, Quinimila	67/3	600	8.91
Sotuta, Tibulón	88/	480	5.46
Baca	61/1	400	6.55
Nolo	20/	200	10.00
Cantunil	36/3	300	8.25
Motul, Tekax	229/	1,600	6.99
Dzidzantún	119/	640	5.38
Oxcutzcab	101/5	800	7.87
Tekit	50/4	280	5.55
Tecal	55/	200	3.64
Chicxulub	45/	400	7.89
Izamal	93/	500	5.38
Ekmul	15/	120	8.00
Timucuy	23/7	300	12.57
Ixil, Pencuyut	76/1	400	5.25
Quitilcum, Otolin	50/2	400	7.96
Teabo	86/	600	6.97
Mococha	59/	500	8.48
Bokoba, Suma	97/4	800	8.20
Bolonpoxche, Citipech	45/2	320	7.07
Mopila	30/	300	10.00
Tiscoco, Hunacama	76/1	600	7.88
Hocabá (entire prov.)	226/	1,600	7.08
Pustunich, Tixmeuac, Xanaba, Haztunich	208/1	880	4.23
Tecoh	43/4	320	7.35
Tecanto, Tepacan	87/6	800	9.12
Dzan, Mona	170/1	800	4.70
Tabi	19/	200	10.53
Muxuppipp	19/	200	10.53
Homún-Cuzama	90/7	600	6.60

Table 1.6 (cont.)

Locality	Pesos Donated	Fanegas Maize	Ratio: Fanegas Pesos
Campeche			
Maxcanul	150/	532	3.54
Becal	25/3	140	5.52
Tichel	69/5	320	4.60
Nohcabab	23/6	120	5.05
Valladolid			
Xoquén	20/7	200	9.58
Sisal	35/	440	12.57
Royal towns			
Maní	193/	1,460	7.56
Tacul	239/	1,248	5.22
Tixpeual	23/	208	9.04
Pomolche	43/2	380	8.78
Telchac	123/2	628	5.10
Temul	67/4	328	4.86
Quiní	68/	416	6.12
Mean			7.31
S.D.	2.125		
S.E.	0.307		

However, the list in the Testimonio del donativo is not complete. The Memoria de los conventos of 1582 mentions 227 places including convent towns and other towns in the parishes, but excluding the district of Bacalar. It is probable that many of the towns missing from the Testimonio del donativo had been congregated with and were included in those towns that were reported. Furthermore, the parish of Peto is reported for the donativo as a whole. On the other hand, the parishes of Xequelchakán, Cozumel, Chancenote, and Valladolid are not included at all, and those of Campeche and Tizimín only in small part.

In order to allow for the omissions, some type of estimate, even though it may be arbitrary, is both justified and required. We shall consider that 75 percent of the inhabited places are either reported by name or are otherwise included. Then we must increase the 38,136 tributaries by one-third to a total of 50,848. This value, when multiplied by the factor 3.7, gives a population of 188,138 for the indios de pueblo.

Our third source is the two lists of personas de confesión

in Vázquez de Espinosa. For the parishes under Franciscan control, the number of personas de confesión is 91,500; for parishes under control of secular priests, excluding the villa of Tabasco, the total is 25,700. (The document states 25,000.) The sum is 117,200 personas de confesión. If we apply the factor of 1.67 previously established, we get a population of 195,724.

The three quite different documentary sources, dating from a period embracing not more than ten years, independently give the following totals for the population of the Indian towns: 176,320, 188,138, and 195,724, respectively. The mean is 186,727. The range is 19,410 or ± 5.2 percent of the mean. We are certainly operating within a 10 percent error if we put the number of indios de pueblo in 1605 at 185,000.

VIII. THE NON-INDIANS, THE NABORIAS, AND THE MEXICAN INDIANS

Throughout the preceding discussion we have been dealing with the indios de pueblo, that is, the Indians of Yucatan settled in their own towns, which were organized as repúblicas de indios, but however modified by European reorganization of institutions and relocation, bore a direct relation to pre-Conquest towns. The tribute assessments, reports of encomenderos, and religious counts in so far as we have used them, all relate to the indios de pueblo and do not include other groups. There were, however, other groups coming into existence with the passage of time. Omitting them thus far creates little disturbance in the accuracy of our estimates of population because during the course of the sixteenth century, the new elements were numerically of trivial magnitude. By the year 1600, their proportion had increased to the point at which they require examination.

What we call other groups for want of a better term was a diverse series of racial and cultural categories that included both non-Indians and Indians. Among the non-Indians were Spaniards and other Europeans; mestizos, many reputed to be Spaniards but increasingly with the passage of time recognized as a separate group; Negroes, whether slave or free; and all mixtures with some proportion of Negro genetic stock. All of these groups were *gente de razón* as in central Mexico, and in the later colonial counts they were carefully segregated from the Indians as in central Mexico. There were,

in addition, Indian groups living in a status different from that of
the indios de pueblo: the naborías, who were local Indians
withdrawn from their towns and settled in suburbs of Spanish
cities or in the cities themselves for delivery of service to the
Europeans; the Mexican Indians, who were descendants of
Mexican-speaking Indians brought from central Mexico as
Spanish auxiliaries in the Conquest and settled in their own
towns, where both Nahuatl and Maya were spoken; and finally
the laboríos or workers on ranches and haciendas, who became
an increasingly numerous group in the eighteenth and early
nineteenth centuries, and, although like the naboríos, recruited
from the local Indians and removed from their towns of origin,
lived in the countryside. These groups also were segregated
from the indios de pueblo in most of the later colonial counts,
largely because they were liable to tribute at a different rate or
were exempt from it entirely.

In studying these other groups, it is very difficult to make
distinctions of a secondary ethnic character. Occasionally,
we find statements giving the numerical strength of Spaniards,
Negroes, naborías, or Mexican Indians, but these statements
permit no systematic analysis. Hence, since we are not attempting to make a detailed study of ethnic composition at this time,
it is preferable to consolidate the various component groups as
far as possible. Consequently, we focus attention upon two
principal categories: the indios de pueblo or the overwhelming
mass of the descendants of the original native inhabitants, who
were subject to full, normal tribute; and the other groups,
who either were not subject to tribute or paid it in some special
form. Wherever possible, we shall divide the category of other
groups into component elements.

The first step in the examination of population in the
two centuries preceding the Mexican War of Independence is
to outline what we know concerning the growth of the category
of other groups. For this purpose it is most convenient and
economical of time and space, even if it is tedious, to present
our information from the documents in conformity with a
series of key dates.

1549: In 1549 the Spanish population was negligible,
as was that of Mexican Indians and the rest of the other groups.
At most there were several hundred conquistadores, auxiliaries,
and camp followers. All else were indios de pueblo. When we
plot the graph of the population of other groups, we have to

take this date as the origin and put our first point very close to zero.

1580 : Although for this year an exact count of living encomenderos might be possible with considerable labor, we shall simply estimate their number at 200. To them should be added probably another 300 Spanish immigrants, merchants, military men, administrative officials, and clergy. Undoubtedly families had been established, fully Spanish or interracial; to account for them, a reasonable factor would be 4.0, especially in view of the relatively high proportion of clergy among the Spanish. Our total for Spaniards becomes 2,000.

Other elements had also come into existence by this time. There were sufficient naborías settled in suburbs of the Spanish towns and in the Spanish towns themselves for the assessment of tribute. They were liable at a special rate of one peso a year per adult male. The basic data that we possess on their tribute is presented in Table 1.7. Although the accounts as they have come down to us are fragmentary and confusing, some notion can be obtained of the number of naborías. In 1583 the aggregate of collections reached nearly 500 pesos. If we allow a few dependents and women, the occurrence of both of whom was inevitable, we may use a factor of 2.0 and consider the naborías throughout Yucatan to have been approximately 1,000 persons by 1580.

On another group, the Mexican Indians, we have but meager data. They were freed from tribute in 1582 by the Audiencia of Mexico because of their services in the Conquest. The implementation of that decision reduced the count of tributary naborías in two of the Indian suburbs of Mérida, San Cristóbal and Santiago, by twenty-one and twenty-three, respectively. The surviving treasury accounts sent to Spain give no other information except that San Román, a suburb of Campeche, had Mexican Indians resident who were to be released from tribute. The numbers are small, and, accordingly, we make no estimate for the Mexican Indians.

Negro slaves were also being imported; some were freed by their masters; and there was a good deal of interbreeding with Europeans, mestizos, and Indians. Unfortunately, we have no report on number. Free adults of Negro or part-Negro ancestry were held to tribute at a rate of two pesos a year, both men and women. The amount collected in 1580 was 75 pesos, but this amount represents a substantial underevaluation

Table 1.7

Naborías in Yucatan, 1580–1650. Data concerning taxation from AGI, Contaduria, legajos 911A-911B. The amounts recorded under each town name may be either assessments or actual payments for the year indicated. In certain instances, such as 1583 and 1644-1645, the numbers are clearly assessments. In other instances, they are probably payments. As an index to tributaries, therefore, these values must be regarded as approximations. For conversion to population, we use the factor 2.0.

Locality	1580	1583	1588	1590	1591	1592	1603	1605	1606	1644–1645
Mérida										
San Cristóbal	113/4	180/6	202/2	221/5	154/2	126/	301/6	52/4	45/	718/4
Santiago	83/	110/4	187/4	187/4	331/4	318/7	141/	459/	459/	319/4
Santa Lucía	55/4	104/6	102/1	111/	141/	141/	158/2	224/2	224/2	250/4
San Juan–San Sebastián			108/6	107/2	158/2	158/2		213/6	213/6	112/4
									52/4	
Campeche										
San Román	35/1		72/	92/2	88/4	104/2	54/	49/4	57/1	36/
Satna Ana Olca			89/	22/1	107/2	107/2	107/2	107/2	107/2	281/2
										52/4
Valladolid										
San Marcos	42/4	41/4	89/5	85/1	79/6	75/3	78/6	34/	53/3	201/5
Santa Ana of Valladolid		41/4	93/6	93/6	93/2	102/	93/6	93/6	93/6	206/6[a]
San Juan of Valladolid			102/	102/	102/		96/6	96/6	96/6	285/[a]
									36/	116/6[a]
Salamanca						34/4	34/1	39/	39/	
Manzanilla			30/1	31/7	31/7	78/2	43/	40/	52/4	
Total	329/5	479/	1,077/1	1,054/4	1,287/5	1,245/6	1,108/5	1,409/6	1,530/2	2,580/7

[a] Date of 1645.

of the true number, for the treasury accounts themselves indicate that assessment was much evaded and that the collection from those registered was difficult and erratic. To include children and dependents not held to tribute, we should multiply by 2.0, which yields 150 as the number covered by the tribute payment. As an adjustment for slaves and those evading assessment and collection, we double this value. Our estimate for Negroes and pardos, slave and free, in 1580 is 300.

According to these estimates, there must have been a minimum of 3,300 persons of what we call other groups in Yucatan in 1580. Of these, 2,300 were gente de razón and 1,000 were Indians. There were undoubtedly more people in these groups than this estimate. Nevertheless, the total of all such groups cannot have exceeded 2 percent of the total population of the peninsula.

1605: For this date we segregate the various groups that were not indios de pueblos as follows:

Spaniards and mestizos. We make an estimate intermediate between earlier and later values, namely, 600 vecinos. To compute persons, we apply a factor of 5.0 rather than a higher one that would be justified by the large families because of the relatively high proportion of clergy: 3,000.

Naborías. The mean of three years, 1603, 1605, 1606 (see Table 1.7), shows an annual tribute of 1,350 pesos. With a factor of 2.0, this means 2,700.

Free Negroes and mulattoes. The tribute collected in 1605 was 88 pesos. With a factor of 2.0, this would mean 176 persons, but we adjust for evasion in count and in payment to 350.

Mexican Indians, Negro slaves, and others. Here we make an outright guess of 1,000.

The total is 7,050, or close to 3.7 percent of the total population.

1639: For the year 1639 we rely almost exclusively upon the *Relacion historial eclesiastica* of Francisco de Cárdenas Valencia. The data on population are highly fragmented and are given in different places and in different forms. As a result, we have been obliged to gather the material and present it in detail according to locality and type of population reported. At best, we can achieve only an approximate total. In the following survey, the page numbers refer to the edition of Cárdenas Valencia printed in 1937.

Mérida

There were 400 Spanish vecinos (p. 79). These multiplied by 5.0 give 2,000.

Under the jurisdiction of the cathedral were the *indios criados* (Indians used as servants), etc., plus four other towns of naborías. In all, there were 600 persons *de administración* (p. 50). These were equivalent to personas de confesión, and we apply the factor 1.67, giving 1,000.

Under the jurisdiction of the monastery of San José were six towns of Indians, one of which was of naborías inside the limits of the Spanish city. The total of personas de confesión in all six towns was 1,968 (p. 55), of which one-sixth would have been 328. Multiplied by 1.67 this gives approximately 550.

The contributions and fees of the free Negroes and mulattoes to the special curate of the cathedral appointed for their administration amounted to 200 pesos (p. 50). This means perhaps 200 heads of families, or, at 5.0 per family, 1,000.

The total for Mérida is therefore 4,550.

Valladolid

There were 150 Spanish vecinos (p. 84). These multiplied by 5.0 give 750.

There were 215 mestizo, mulatto, and Negro vecinos (p. 84). These multiplied by 5.0 give 1,075.

There were 3,200 *"indios navorios y de otros siete pueblos que tiene sujetos a este beneficio..."* (naborías and the Indians of seven other towns administered within this parish...) (p. 84). The Memoria de los conventos of 1582 gives eight *sujetos* for the visita de curas of Valladolid. The inhabitants of the seven other towns were indios de pueblo. We may estimate one-eighth of the total as naborías. These 400 persons were probably personas de confesión rather than heads of families. Hence, we apply the factor of 1.67 and get approximately 670.

The Franciscan convent which is mentioned is that of Sisal (p. 86). In 1582, beside the cabecera, it had fourteen sujetos, all indios de pueblo. Hence, we do not include them.

Our total for Valladolid is 2,495.

Campeche

There were approximately 300 vecinos (p. 89) and about the same number of militiamen (p. 93). The three companies of militia included Spaniards, mestizos, and free Negroes and mulattoes. We use the factor of 5.0, giving 1,500.

The personas de confesión in the local parish amounted to 2,700 persons "así de españoles como de mestizos, mulatos, negros e indios navorios y de otros siete pueblos que tiene sujetos a su administración en su contorno y comarca. . ." (Spaniards, mestizos, mulattoes, Negroes, and Indian naborías and the Indians of seven other towns within the parish. . .) (p. 90). The Memoria de los conventos of 1582 shows six sujetos within six leagues of the Spanish town. If we allow 200 indios de confesión to each of the seven sujetos and subtract them as indios de pueblo, we have left 1,300 personas de confesión of all other groups. This value, multiplied by 1.67 gives 2,170.

We use this latter figure (2,170) since it certainly includes within it the figure above (1,500). Furthermore, we omit the Franciscan convent (p. 93) since its parishioners were entirely indios de pueblo.

Thus, our total for Campeche is 2,170.

Salamanca de Bacalar

There were 28 vecinos. This number, multiplied by 5.0 would give 140 persons. However, in the entire parish, there were 900 persons "así de españoles y de algunos pueblecillos que tiene de visita. . ." (Spaniards and [the Indians] of some small towns that are part of the parish. . .) (p. 95). Of the 900, we may estimate about a third to have been of groups other than indios de pueblo, including the 28 vecinos and their families. Then, 300 multiplied by 1.67 gives 500.

Our total for Salamanca de Bacalar is 500.

The sum of the estimates for the four towns and their districts is 9,715. This value does not include the gente de razón scattered throughout the countryside—clerics, ranchers, slaves—and the Indian laboríos then appearing as a small group. There must have been a considerable number in these groups. Consequently, we may round off the estimate to an even 10,000.

In addition to the above examination in detail, it is possible to make an alternative calculation. Although Cárdenas Valencia may have been inaccurate with respect to mestizos, Negroes, and Indians not in pueblos, his figures for Spaniards and others who occupied the social status of vecino appear to be relatively reliable. His total for this group in the entire province (Tabasco excluded) is 878 vecinos. At a factor of

5.0, this means 4,390 persons.

At this point we may leave Cárdenas Valencia entirely and consider the tribute assessments for 1644–1645 as found in the royal treasury accounts sent to Spain. The assessments are unusually complete and, furthermore, represent conditions as they existed some years previously or more or less at the time of the report by Cárdenas Valencia.

The total of assessments for naborías was 2,580/7 pesos. (See Table 1.7.) By this time, *ca.* 1640, we have to assume that the naborías, many of whom were living in organized, independent pueblos, called suburbs of the Spanish towns to distinguish them from the pueblos of the indios de pueblo, were supporting families. Therefore, we can no longer use the factor 2.0 but must use a higher value. For Spaniards and other groups with permanent residences and established social positions, we use the factor 5.0 for heads of families. Probably the naborías, even at this date, did not quite reach the same level of family number, but it would not be unreasonable to assign them a factor of 4.0. Then 2,580 multiplied by 4.0 would mean 10,320 persons.

The free Negroes and mulattoes were still paying tribute in the 1640s at the rate of one peso per year per adult man or woman, that is, a married couple paid two pesos. Hence, the total number of pesos paid should be multiplied by approximately 2.0 in order to estimate the number of persons. In 1644 the tribute assessed in Valladolid for this category was 19/6, and the same amount in Campeche. The assessments for Mérida and Salamanca are missing from the surviving treasury records but must at least have equaled those of the other two Spanish towns. The total then would be about 80 pesos, or 160 persons. This value makes no allowance for slaves or for evasion.

The sum of all the components is 14,870; if an adjustment were made for slaves and for free Negroes and mulattoes evading registration, it might be over 15,000. This value exceeds by a considerable margin the estimate of 10,000 obtained from the individual items in the report of Cárdenas Valencia. Very likely the factor of 4.0 for naborías and free Negroes and mulattoes is too high, but we have no clear evidence to support a more precise factor. On the whole, it is preferable to forego a precise estimate for the other groups at this date. In its place we can accept the range of 10,000 to 15,000 as representing the best we can achieve with the data at hand. This means that by

1639 non-Indians, naborías and Mexican Indians (the last of whom, although indistinguishable from their neighbors had a vested, fiscal interest in maintaining their identity until Indian tribute was abolished) constituted from 4 to 6 percent of the total population. If a single number becomes necessary, the midpoint of the range may be used, that is, 12,500 or approximately 5.5 percent of the total population.

1771: Subsequent to 1640 there are no documents available to us which distinguish clearly the gente de razón and Indian groups not included in indios de pueblo although there are several that give counts of the indios de pueblo. Our first clue at the end of this long gap is the comment in 1814 by Policarpo Antonio de Echánove, then a former employee of the royal treasury in Mérida, who wrote on the basis of royal treasury materials that in 1772 a count of the population showed a total of 214,974 persons and that the assessments for Indian tributaries showed a total of 35,848 tributaries, all males from fourteen to sixty years of age inclusive. This last group is probably the indios de pueblo with perhaps the naborías but excluding laboríos. We may apply to the value for tributaries the conversion factor of 4.0 appropriate for the last decades of the eighteenth century to reach a total number of persons, namely, 143,392, or almost exactly two-thirds of the population. The remaining third, that is, 70,582 persons, were the gente de razón, laboríos, and descendants of Mexican Indians. Unfortunately, we have no means of breaking down this figure and have only the total of the count.

1785–1795: For the decade 1785–1795, we are well provided with evidence on numbers. Between 1789 and 1795 a series of counts were made of the general population in an attempt to arrive at a fairly trustworthy count of the population. We have listed the two important ones. A second source of primary interest is the "Expediente formado para el establecimiento de escuelas en Yucatan y Campeche, 1782–1805," which we have also listed among our important sources. These sources distinguish all Indians as such, that is the indios de pueblo, naborías, laboríos, and Mexican Indians as a group, from the gente de razón or non-Indians, namely, Spaniards, mestizos, Negroes, and pardos. Accordingly, we are forced to segregate information in the form possible here and so move to the distinction Indian: non-Indian, joining the Indians previously discussed in other groups to the indios de pueblo. The naborías, laboríos and Mexican Indians were so small a fraction of the population down to the middle of the seventeenth century that the distortion is slight. We should keep in mind, however, that they, like the gente de razón, increased as a proportion of the total population.

The gross size of the non-Indian population may be learned immediately from the summary of the count of 1789. In the entire province of Yucatan, including Tabasco, there were 264,955 Indians and 99,067 persons of other ethnic affiliation. The total is 364,022, and the non-Indians constitute 27.2 percent of this number. We are unable to remove the data for Tabasco from the summary of ethnic groups, which is for the entire province.[127] Another report on Tabasco giving somewhat different totals indicates that non-Indians were a distinctly larger proportion of the population in Tabasco (46 percent) then they were in what we call Yucatan. If we had means of removing the data for Tabasco, it seems likely that the non-Indians as a proportion of total population for Yucatan would constitute perhaps 26 percent.[128] An item of supporting evidence comes from the study of Yucatan made in 1814 by Policarpo Antonio de Echánove, according to whom in 1814 there were in the peninsula of Yucatan, Tabasco not included, 125,000 non-Indians out of a total population of 500,000. Although this total may be inflated and is clearly a rounded estimate, the proportion is probably near to being correct, 25 percent.

If Yucatan at the close of the eighteenth century contained a population of whom fully one-quarter were non-Indians, there still remains the significant question how the gente de razón were distributed within the area and what was the pattern according to which the immigrants and their descendants settled throughout the territory. It is possible to obtain a clue to the answer by an analysis of the data in the "Expediente formado para el establecimiento de escuelas en Yucatan y Campeche, 1782–1805," which does not give aggregate populations but does give data for the determination of Indian and non-Indian fractions.

Before we examine the data in the expediente on the establishment of public schools in the peninsula, let us consider

[127]MS, AGN, Historia, vol. 523, f. 9, published in Rubio Mañé, *Archivo,* I, 249 250.
[128]"Informe del gobernador de Tabasco sobre dicha provincia y su poblacion," Tacotalpa, 24 June 1794, in Rubio Mañé, *Archivo,* I, 235–244, especially p. 237. The manuscript is in the Biblioteca Nacional, Mexico City.

the capital city, Mérida. We have available to us a rather careful count of 1794, the summary of which segregates the various ethnic groups in the jurisdiction of Mérida.[129] The jurisdiction of Mérida at that time included the city with its barrios and also some half dozen Indian towns in the vicinity. Consequently, the total is not strictly urban. On the other hand, the preponderance of Indians in the outlying villages would be balanced by the very heavy majority of non-Indians within the city itself, and something of a compromise achieved. In the jurisdiction of Mérida as a whole, there were 14,751 Indians and 13,078 non-Indians. The latter, therefore, amounted to 47 percent of the total number.

The relative proportion of non-Indians in the peninsula at large may be estimated from the reports from the *subdelegados* which constituted the supporting numerical data for the expediente on the establishment of public schools. Except for Mérida, each subdelegado stated, according to parish and town, either the number of heads of families or the number of school children who would be available for public instruction, or both. In all cases, whether children or parents, the non-Indians, who were designated vecinos, were clearly set apart from the Indians, who were designated as indios.

Although there is a wide disparity in the organization and format of the reports, it is possible with all but two of them to obtain a direct value for the heads of families in each town. Thus a ratio, or percentage, based upon totals or upon means of single ratios may be derived, which will then express the relation between Indians and non-Indians. As long as all the data are in terms of heads of families, it is not necessary to know the total population.

The actual numbers of heads of families are stated for the subdelegaciones of Campeche, Camino Real Bajo, Camino Real Alto, Beneficios Bajos, Beneficios Altos, La Sierra, and Tizimín. For the subdelegaciones of Valladolid and La Costa, the figures are given only for children of school age. Nevertheless, it is not difficult to develop an indirect metnod for estimating the number of adults in these two missing subdelegaciones. We determine the numerical ratio of heads of families to the children of school age in those families.

A preliminary note to this calculation is the fact that

[129]MS, AGN, Historia, vol. 522, f. 257, published in Rubio Mañé, *Archivo*, I, 210–212.

children of school age, according to these reports, were consistently taken as between the age of five or six years and that of eleven or twelve, depending upon sex and other factors. This is not a rigidly segregated age group, but, on the average and over the peninsula as a whole, it embraced essentially the same category of people.

There are 26 towns, 10 in Beneficios Bajos and 16 in Tizimín, which show both heads of families and children for non-Indians, and 27 towns in the same partidos which show both heads of families and children of school age for Indians. The non-Indians had 1,202 heads of families and 1,397 children of school age, or an adult/child ratio of 0.865. The Indians had 3,536 heads of families and 2,998 children, or ratio of 1.180. The difference in ratio must be ascribed to social and economic rather than genetic factors.

By the use of these ratios, we may calculate approximately the probable number of heads of families in the subdelegaciones of Valladolid and La Costa, as well as in several other individual towns for which the figures for heads of families are missing. The results for all localities are shown in detail in Table 1.8.

From the summary at the end of this table, it will be seen that with a total of over 50,000 heads of families, 31.2 percent of those living in cabeceras were non-Indian, as were 14.8 percent of those living in lesser Indian towns. If we treat the data in a somewhat different manner, we find that in 66 cabeceras the mean of the individual values of the percentage of non-Indians is 29.39, whereas that in 138 lesser towns is 14.51. The respective standard deviations are $\pm$ 17.57 and $\pm$ 16.41, which indicate a relatively high level of variability in each series. However, the standard errors are $\pm$ 2.16 and $\pm$ 1.40, with the value of t reaching 5.54. Consequently, a high degree of significance may be attributed to the difference between the means.

The figures from the jurisdiction of Mérida for the year 1794, discussed above, indicate that the truly urban centers contained an even greater proportion of non-Indians. Since the jurisdiction as a whole showed a population almost one-half non-Indians, the proportion of this group must have far exceeded the 50 percent level in the city itself, or the *casco*. It will not be unreasonable to consider that 75 percent of all the inhabitants were non-Indians. Similar considerations apply to the core areas of the Spanish cities of Campeche and Valladolid as well as on a

Table 1.8

Indians and non-Indians, expressed as heads of families, from "Expediente formado para el establecimiento de escuelas en Yucatan y Campeche, 1782–1805." The *cabeceras de curato* are in italics; the sujetos are not. There are two separate reports from Campeche.

Subdelegation and Town	Non-Indian	Indian	Total	% Non-Indian
Campeche I				
Sahcahchén	51	115	166	30.7
Holail		50	50	0.0
Champotón	208	58	266	78.2
Chicbul	76	113	189	40.2
La Ceiba	70	153	223	31.4
Xkeulil	25	81	106	23.6
Seiba Playa	182	150	332	54.8
Hool	133	60	193	68.9
Sihochac	30	81	111	27.0
Campeche II				
San Francisco				
Hampolol	70	12	82	85.4
Lerma	39	101	140	27.8
Samula	7	40	47	14.9
San Diego	8	73	81	9.9
Cholul	7	40	47	14.9
Poquiaxcum	52	64	116	44.8
Santa Rosa		56	56	0.0
China	29	58	87	33.3
Kulan		71	71	0.0
Pich	30	109	139	21.6
Tixmucuy	15	52	67	22.4
Bolonchencauich	9	62	71	12.6
Cauich	20	135	155	12.9
Total	1,061	1,734	2,795	
Camino Real Bajo				
Hunucmá	400	300	700	57.2
Tetiz	10	200	210	4.8
Kinchil		400	400	0.0
Uman	300	250	550	54.6
Bolonpoxche		100	100	0.0
Samahil	150	100	250	60.0
Kopoma	150	82	232	64.7
Chochola	78	116	194	40.2
Opichén	150	300	450	33.3
Maxcanú	400	624	1,024	39.1
Halacho	85	615	700	12.1
Total	1,723	3,087	4,810	

Table 1.8 (cont.)

Subdelegation and Town	Non-Indian	Indian	Total	% Non-Indian
Camino Real Alto				
Becal	50	350	400	12.5
Numkiní		500	500	0.0
Tepakan		120	120	0.0
Calkiní	200	400	600	33.3
Dzitbalche	40	500	540	7.4
Xequelchakan[a]	95	112	207	45.9
Pocboc [a]		142	142	0.0
Pokmuch[a]		89	89	0.0
Tenabo	150	93	243	61.7
Tinum	40	89	129	31.0
Bolonchén[a]	69	966	1,035	6.7
Hopelchén[a]	173	586	759	22.8
Dzitbalchén[a]	26	354	380	6.8
Total	843	4,301	5,144	
Beneficios Bajos				
Sotuta	110	55	165	66.7
Tabi	6	60	66	9.1
Yaxcabá[a]	49	239	288	17.0
Tixcacaltuyu	50	800	850	5.9
Tahchebichén	40	200	240	16.7
Hoctún	90	94	184	48.9
Tahmek	9	64	73	12.3
Seye	28	114	142	19.7
Xocchel	1	134	135	0.7
Hocabá	76	158	234	32.5
Tzanlahcat	21	118	139	15.1
Huhi	11	10	21	52.4
Sahcabá	10	43	53	18.9
Homún	43	121	164	26.2
Cuzama	9	113	122	7.4
Total	553	2,323	2,876	
Beneficios Altos				
Tihosuco	90	424	514	17.5
Tela		280	280	0.0
Tepich		222	222	0.0
Ichmul	191	272	463	41.3
Celul		90	90	0.0
Uaymax	18	208	226	8.0
Saban	7	300	307	2.3
Tinum	2	242	244	0.8
Tiholop	23	680	703	3.3
Sacalaca	38	200	238	16.0
Dzonotchel	39	194	233	16.8
Petul		75	75	0.0

Table 1.8 (cont.)

Subdelegation and Town	Non-Indian	Indian	Total	% Non-Indian
Chunhuhub	18	150	168	10.7
Polyuc	11	200	211	5.2
Tituc	8	192	200	4.0
Peto	180	388	568	31.7
Tzucacab (with hac.)	10	256	266	3.7
Chaksinkin	2	176	178	1.1
Tahdziu	80	420	500	16.0
Tixhualatún		162	162	0.0
Chikindzonot	42	304	346	12.1
Ekpetz		172	172	0.0
Total	795	5,607	6,366	
La Sierra				
Oxcutzcab	460	600	1,060	43.4
San Antonio Xul	40	130	170	23.5
Akil	39	269	308	12.7
Yotholín	22	105	127	17.3
Ticul	600	1,000	1,600	37.5
Nohcacab	110	630	740	14.9
Pustunich	12	125	137	8.8
Tekax	500	500	1,000	50.0
Tixmeuac	26	180	206	12.6
Tixcuytun	28	100	128	21.9
Ticum	28	150	178	15.7
Teabo	125	350	475	26.3
Chumayel	25	100	125	20.0
Pencuyut	30	350	380	7.9
Xaya	4	36	40	10.0
Maní	200	400	600	33.3
Chapab	23	79	102	22.5
Tipikal	4	120	124	3.2
Dzan	11	96	107	10.3
Mama	82	283	365	22.4
Tekit	150	152	302	49.7
Tecoh	70	400	470	14.9
Telchaquillo	5	105	110	4.5
Acanceh	54	75	129	41.8
Timucuy	4	85	89	4.5
Abala	10	87	97	10.3
Sacalum	60	250	310	19.3
Muna	400	600	1,000	40.0
Total	3,122	7,357	10,479	
Tizimin				
Tizimín	156	172	328	47.6
Sucopo	31	23	54	57.4
Dzonotake	4	47	51	7.8

Table 1.8 (cont.)

Subdelegation and Town	Non-Indian	Indian	Total	% Non-Indian
Kikil	60	49	109	55.1
Loche	41	65	106	38.7
Panaba	33	127	160	20.6
Sucila	157	128	285	58.7
Espita	156	551	707	22.1
Calotmul	65	157	222	29.3
Tacabo	8	128	136	5.9
Nabalam	26	103	129	20.2
Hunukú	15	39	54	27.8
Yalcoba	10	28	38	26.3
Sisbicchén		99	99	0.0
Chancenote	98	288	386	25.4
Tixcancal	28	91	119	23.5
Xcan	16	472	488	3.3
Total	904	2,567	3,471	
Valladolid [a]				
Santa Ana	68	166	234	29.0
San Juan	121	235	356	34.0
Laboríos	75	170	245	30.6
Yalcon		53	53	0.0
Tixhualatún		171	171	0.0
Kanxoc	6	35	41	14.6
Sisal	186	123	309	60.2
San Marcos		66	66	0.0
Pixoy		106	106	0.0
Popola		128	128	0.0
Temosón	3	85	88	3.5
Chemax	13	238	251	5.2
Chichimila	3	167	170	1.8
Xocen		180	180	0.0
Dzitnup		85	85	0.0
Ebtún		339	339	0.0
Uayma	11	76	87	12.7
Tinum	12	180	192	6.3
Piste	9	159	168	5.4
Kaua	19	120	139	13.7
Cuncunul	16	138	154	10.4
Cenotillo	42	143	185	22.7
Dzitas	11	143	154	7.1
Tunkas	74	145	219	33.8
Tixbakha	12	30	42	28.6
Xocenpich		27	27	0.0
Tixcacal	34	131	165	20.6
Tekom		133	133	0.0
Tekuche	3	66	69	4.1
Total	718	3,838	4,556	

Table 1.8 (cont.)

Subdelegation and Town	Non-Indian	Indian	Total	% Non-Indian
La Costa[a]				
Izamal	778	486	1,264	61.6
Sitilpech	1	80	81	1.1
Pixila		69	69	0.0
Sudzal		112	112	0.0
Xanaba		51	51	0.0
Kantunil	34	93	127	26.8
Cacalchén	78	201	279	27.9
Bokaba	18	136	154	11.7
Tixkokob	107	423	530	20.2
Ekmul	11	124	135	8.1
Euan		145	145	0.0
Nolo	7	146	153	4.6
Tixpeual		235	235	0.0
Yaxkukul		208	208	0.0
Conkal	44	292	336	13.1
Cholul		129	129	0.0
Zicpach		144	144	0.0
Chablekal	11	181	192	5.7
Ixil		380	380	0.0
Chicxulub	8	226	234	3.5
Mococha	12	295	307	3.9
Tixkunchel	6	154	160	3.8
Baca	50	510	560	8.9
Motul	112	556	668	16.8
Uci	11	97	108	10.2
Kini	10	79	89	11.2
Muxupip	15	63	78	19.2
Telchac	68	72	140	48.6
Dzemul	36	292	328	11.0
Zinanche	44	271	315	14.0
Dzidzantún	117	121	238	49.2
Yobain	65	197	262	24.8
Dzilam	43	86	129	33.1
Temax	228	206	434	52.5
Tekal	52	280	332	15.6
Dzonotcauich		66	66	0.0
Buctzotz	56	20	76	73.7
Cansahcab	57	194	251	22.7
Suma	20	68	88	22.7
Teya	33	34	67	49.3
Tepakan		119	119	0.0
Tekanto	38	183	221	17.2
Tixcocho		34	34	0.0
Sitilcum		23	23	0.0
Total	2,170	7,881	10,051	

Table 1.8 (cont.)

Subdelegation and Town	Non-Indian	Indian	Total	% Non-Indian
Campeche, I and II	1,061	1,734	2,795	38.1
Camino Real Bajo	1,723	3,087	4,810	35.8
Camino Real Alto	843	4,301	5,144	16.4
Beneficios Bajos	553	2,323	2,876	19.2
Beneficios Altos	759	5,607	6,366	11.9
La Sierra	3,122	7,357	10,479	29.8
Tizimín	904	2,567	3,471	26.0
Valladolid[a]	718	3,838	4,556	15.7
La Costa[a]	2,170	7,881	10,051	21.6
Total	11,853	38,695	50,548	23.45
Total all cabeceras	8,340	18,405	26,745	31.2
Total, all sujetos	3,513	20,290	23,803	14.8

[a]Values are calculated from the school children by the use of the factors discribed in the text.

smaller scale to Salamanca and the presidio at Carmen.

It is clear that the Spanish-speaking population, the gente de razón, or the Spaniards, mestizos, Negroes, and pardos were concentrated in the larger centers, particularly those of administrative importance. Even outside the Spanish cities, however, the sharp difference between the cabeceras and lesser towns emphasizes the persistence of this tendency. If we had adequate data, we could probably demonstrate a mathematical relationship between the size of a locality and the number of non-Indians living in it.

We now return briefly to consider the absolute size of the non-Indian population of the peninsula of Yucatan at approximately 1795. We have already presented the figures from the summary of the census of 1789 and those given by Echánove for 1814. We may check these statements by an independent calculation based upon the reports by locality and subdelegación of the census taken in 1794–1795.[130] We can readily do this, although the account sent to Mexico City gives only total

[130]Rubio Mañé, *Archivo,* I, 207–247. The manuscript is in the Biblioteca Nacional, Mexico City. We should note that this count of 1794–1795 represented a new attempt to achieve a fuller and more accurate census since the first attempts were held to be defective.

populations, by utilizing the multiplicative factors of percentages previously established.

The report of the census sent to Mexico City for use by the viceroy is organized according to subdelegaciones, or *partidos,* by parishes and by towns. By means of the reports of the subdelegates on the establishment of public schools and by the list of parishes published by Fernando de Noriega y Navarro in 1813, we can segregate the cabeceras from the lesser towns in each partido and get the totals for each. In addition, from the census itself, we can derive the values for the urban or military concentrations at Mérida, Campeche, Valladolid, Salamanca, and Carmen. The peninsula totals for all three types of habitat may then be multiplied by the appropriate factors, that is, those rounded off from the percentages found in Table 1.8. These operations have been carried out and the results placed in Table 1.9.

The number of non-Indians, in urban centers is 23,194; in cabeceras, 61,127; and in lesser towns, 18,541. The aggregate is 102,862 and is 28.7 percent of the population shown by the census for the province of Yucatan, less Tabasco. This value is slightly greater, but insignificantly so, than the percentage derived from our inspection of the count of 1789 and that given by Echánove for 1814. Clearly, the range of 25 to 30 percent will include the true value.

1805 : The one point in the later colonial period at which we can get a clue to the proportion of the other Indian groups, that is, Indians outside the category of indios de pueblo, is from the data in the Matrícula de Tributarios of 1805. For the intendancy of Mérida, less Tabasco, the Matrícula gives a population of the tributary class, including free Negroes and mulattoes, of 310,048. The free Negroes and mulattoes are 29,036 persons, and this value deducted from the total of the entire tributary class in the peninsula leaves as the total number of Indians of all categories 281,012. The Matrícula gives a count of 2,288 for *laboríos y vagos* (laborers attached to Spanish estates and Indians without affiliation to town or estate). This value is probably far too low since people in this group were notoriously difficult to locate and count. The officials who prepared the Matrícula of 1805 were also interested in the changes that implementation of the new tributary provisions of the Ordinance of Intendants of 1786 would mean and so calculated the difference in revenue from tributes of the *indios*

Table 1.9

Number of non-Indians in Yucatan, calculated from the census of 1794–1795 as published by Rubio Mañe, *Archivo de la historia de Yucatan,* I, 207–234, 235–247. We show first the stated numbers of all people in each partido : those who lived in the urban centers, in the cabeceras of the parishes, and in the lesser towns. The parishes were checked with the list published by Navarro y Noriega, which lists all the parishes of Mexico in 1813.[b]

	All People[a]			
Partido	*Total in Urban Center*	*Total in Cabeceras*	*Total in Lesser Towns*	*Grand Total*
Mérida (casco)	5,358	21,365	1,805	
La Costa		20,988	21,595	
Beneficios Bajos		16,269	9,417	
Beneficios Altos		12,125	18,399	
Salamanca (casco)	1,228	994		
Tizimín		11,444	4,894	
Valladolid (villa)	6,132	5,693	10,971	
La Sierra		77,941	28,528	
Camino Real Bajo		16,790	9,024	
Camino Real Alto		12,837	10,816	
Campeche (city)	16,940			
Sahcabchén		3,712	2,893	
Boloncauich		1,944	5,263	
Carmen (presidio)	1,267	1,655		
Total	30,925	203,757	123,605	358,287
	Non-Indians			
Total	23,194	61,127	18,541	102,862

Non-Indians in total population : 28.7%

[a]In Yucatan, minus Tabasco.
[b]The totals of those living in cabeceras and lesser towns were multiplied by 0.30 and 0.15, respectively, to get an estimate of non-Indians. These are the approximate values derived from the data in Table 1.8. The total for the urban centers is multiplied by 0.75, which is a fair estimate of the proportion of non-Indians.

de barrio of the Spanish cities of Mérida, Campeche, and Valladolid, that is, the naboría suburbs of those cities. Taxation of these naborías at the rate of 6 reales a tributary instead of the proposed uniform rate of 2 pesos (16 reales) meant a loss of revenue to the Crown of 3,827 pesos a year. Converted to reales (30,616) and divided by 10, the quota of additional tribute planned, the calculation of the royal treasury officials indicates 3,061 3/4 tributaries, or at the conversion factor of 4.1 per tributary, 12,550 persons. We should note again that the value for naborías is also low since it omits the Indians of that category attached to Salamanca de Bacalar, but the omission cannot be large. Similarly, the royal treasury officials in Mexico City, although aware of the exemption from tribute of the descendants of the Mexican Indians in Yucatan, made no attempt to determine their number since they could find no reason in their records for the exemption and planned to abolish it. The sum of the figures available to us is 14,482, or 5.3 percent of the Indian population. If we apply the proportion established earlier for Indians and non-Indians, that is, that the Indians constituted 71.3 percent of the total population in 1794–1795, then the Indians other than indios de pueblo represented 3.8 percent of the total population at that time. The value is low for the reasons just stated but cannot have been much higher than 6.0 percent. An interesting difference of Yucatan relative to most of central Mexico is the much slower growth as a component of the population of the peninsula of the Ladinoized or Hispanized Indians living outside of the traditional Indian towns.

The Matrícula de Tributarios also gives some information on the number of free Negroes and mulattoes in Yucatan. Net of Tabasco, there were 28,093, or since there are discrepancies in the Matrícula in this column, approximately 28,100. The figures does not agree and cannot easily be reconciled with that given by Echánove in 1814 that in the computations and counts of population for the formation of an electoral census in accordance with the Constitution of 1812, there were 55,000 non-citizens or pardos in the peninsula, even if one makes an adjustment for slaves, who were also noncitizens. The Matrícula is probably too low; since the free Negroes and mullatoes were not subject to tribute in Yucatan, there was less incentive to count them for fiscal purposes.

Let us return now to the non-Indians or gente de razón in general. If we survey the entire course of the growth of the non-Indian population in Yucatan, we cannot fail to deplore the lack of data between the middle of the seventeenth century and the later eighteenth century which might express directly or indirectly the magnitude of this demographic component. Nevertheless, a relatively close estimate is possible. In Figure 1.1, we have plotted consecutively points for the logarithms of the

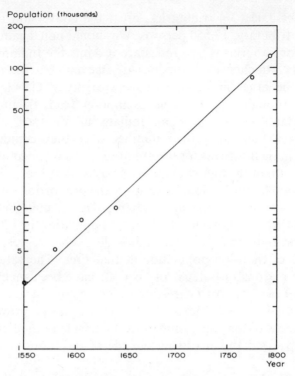

Population (thousands)

Figure 1.1   The non-Indian population of Yucatan between 1549 and 1795.

numbers of non-Indians which correspond to the years 1549, 1580, 1605, and 1639. Then we jump 133 years to 1772 for the logarithm of 103,000 as representing an acceptable value for 1795.

Rigid accuracy cannot be achieved, but the points on the graph appear to indicate very definitely a linear relationship. At the least, no other function will any better express the trend which associates these five points. Since this is true, we may, as a purely empirical procedure, interpolate on the logarithmic graph at any year of the time scale and read off the population. The error thus introduced may reach the order of ± 10 percent, but all our documentary sources down to modern times are subject to fully as great a range of tolerance. The range of magnitude will be substantially correct.

IX. THE INDIOS DE PEUBLO, TOTAL INDIAN POPULATION, AND TOTAL POPULATION OF THE PENINSULA, 1610–1813

For the study of the Indian population during the period 1610–1813 there are two distinct types of information. One consists of encomienda lists. The first is that of 1606 already discussed in detail; the second is that of 1688; and the third is that of 1785, prepared at the time of the incorporation of all private encomiendas in the Crown. It must be clearly noted and, indeed, emphasized that the encomienda lists include only tributaries and are therefore inadequate for the estimate of total populations. On the other hand, they are very useful for the determination of trends within the numerically dominant group, the indios de pueblo.

The second type of information comes from counts carried out by ecclesiastical authorities and the later civil and fiscal counts of the royal government. Of the counts carried out by ecclesiastical authorities, we have already discussed that of 1609 reported by Vázquez de Espinosa and have used information on groups other than indios de pueblo in the *Relación* of Cárdenas Valencia of 1639; the latter document contains the results of counts for virtually all parishes in Yucatan. The Franciscan report of 1700 and the Bishop's visita of 1736 also follow the population according to ecclesiastical jurisdiction. The Testimonio del donativo of 1599 is essentially a civil and fiscal document, organized by town; it is included here because of its versatility for our purposes and has already been discussed. The reorganized royal government of the later eighteenth and early nineteenth centuries has given us a number of very useful counts: the expediente on the formation of a public school system of 1782–1805, with data centered around 1790–1791; the census of 1794–1795, both in extenso and in summary; and the Matrícula de Tributarios of 1805, with its extensive information on all persons within the classes held liable to royal tribute. These clerical and civil counts are more versatile than the encomienda lists and not only can form the basis for the estimate of the total population of the peninsula but are also valuable for other purposes.

We consider first the data to be derived from the lists of encomiendas and the tributes which they were assessed. In Table 1.10 we have placed the figures pertaining to fifty-six encomiendas which appear territorially unchanged in both the 1606 list and that of 1688. The populations and ratios are calculated in the same manner as was employed for Table 1.5. Nearly half the encomiendas which existed at both dates are represented. The ratios show that in every one of those in our sample the population was lower in 1688 than in 1606. The

Table 1.10

Population of encomiendas which occur identically in both the 1606 and 1688 lists. The total populations (Indian) are calculated from the respective numbers of tributaries by applying the factor 3.7 in 1606 and 3.8 in 1688.

Encomienda	1606	1688	Ratio : 1688/1606
Chubulna	1,162	319	0.274
Muxuppipp in Motul	740	236	0.319
Ziho and Telchac	1,332	570	0.427
Cansahcab	1,924	487	0.253
Suma and Bokaba	2,960	666	0.225
Tekal	740	129	0.174
Teya	1,894	380	0.201
Tekanto and Tepakan	2,960	1,096	0.370
Pixila and Quinimila	2,220	570	0.257
Peto and Mama	2,220	1,038	0.467
Dzan and Mona	2,960	513	0.173
Uman	888	137	0.154
Nolo	740	342	0.462
Homun and Cuzama	2,220	765	0.344
Mopila in Yaxcaba	1,110	282	0.254
Tixhualatun in Valladolid	740	456	0.616
Xoquen	740	578	0.781
Baca and Yalcon	1,778	852	0.479
Izamal	1,850	282	0.153
Kantunil	1,110	190	0.171
Tzucacab	444	61	0.137
Xequelchakan	2,220	498	0.225
Pocoboco	592	236	0.399
Becal	518	259	0.500
Tenabo and Tinum	1,185	103	0.087
Pokmuch	740	312	0.422
Motul, Tekax, *et al.*	5,920	2,372	0.401
Halalcho	888	760	0.856
Yaxcaba in Sotuta	2,268	563	0.248
Yobain and Tixcacaltuyu	2,565	1,175	0.458
Uayma	740	304	0.411
Espita, Tzabcanul, 2/3 Tekom	1,850	731	0.395
Yalcoba	582	228	0.392
Samahil and Calatamud	1,850	472	0.255
Ixtual, Tixhualatun, Dzibikal, *et al.*	4,588	750	0.163
Tixcacal, Ecab, Yalsihon	888	673	0.758
Temax	2,268	319	0.141
Nohcacab in Becal	444	182	0.410
Dzitbalche	1,406	795	0.565
Chicxulub	1,480	532	0.359
Mopila in Calkiní	582	144	0.247
Uqui	1,776	201	0.113
Chancenote, Chichimila, Choaca	1,480	845	0.571
Tixkocho and part of Uitzil	1,110	148	0.133

Table 1.10 (cont.)

Encomienda	1606	1688	Ratio : 1688/1606
Xocchel, Tzanlahcat, Sacalum	2,220	719	0.324
Tzeme	740	122	0.165
Mococha	1,850	613	0.331
Senotchuil and Loche	1,258	205	0.163
Cauquel, Ucu, Yabocu	1,036	228	0.220
Pixoy	740	304	0.411
Kinlacam and Kulcab	2,220	760	0.342
San Luis and Santa Lucía Calkiní	370	91	0.246
Conkal et al. (Montejo encom.)	3,400	1,440	0.424
Quitilcum and Yotholin	1,480	357	0.241
Calotmul in Tizimín	888	380	0.428
Tzama and Pole	370	68	0.184
Total	87,244	27,838	
Mean			0.334
S.D. = ± 0.1414			
S.E. = ± 0.0189			

extent of the decrease is demonstrated by the range and the mean of the ratios. The mean of the ratios is 0.334, or, in other words, the population in 1688 was one-third of that existing in 1606. The standard deviation is ± 0.1414 and the standard error of the mean is ± 0.0189. There can be no question, therefore, concerning the veracity of the data as they stand in the documents.

A further step in the analysis is presented in Table 1.11. Here are data from sixteen encomiendas reported in the list of 1688 that are listed in the royal treasury accounting sent to Spain as having been vacant at some time during the years 1645–1650 and therefore paying their tributes to the Crown. The accounting gives the prevailing assessment for the period of Crown possession before the encomiendas were again granted to private holders. From the assessments we can calculate the number of tributaries and convert that value to the probable population in terms of persons. The table indicates a mean ratio of 0.326 between the population in 1688 and that in the years 1645–1650. This is essentially identical with the ratio obtained for the fifty-six encomiendas listed in table 1.10.

These data are of value in two respects. First, they confirm solidly the fact of the decline in population during the course of the seventeenth century. Second, they demonstrate

Table 1.11

Population of encomiendas which were in private hands according to the list of 1688 but which were vacant during the period 1645–1650 as recorded in AGI, *Contaduria,* legajo 911B. The tributaries for which the encomiendas were assessed from 1645 to 1650 have been adjusted for semi-annual payments and have been multiplied by the factor 3.7 to obtain the population.

Encomienda	1645–1650	1688	Ratio : 1688/ 1645–50
Chemax	1,140	456	0.400
Mopila	1,066	281	0.263
Tixcacal, Ecab, Yalsihon	1,472	673	0.457
Becal	814	258	0.317
Kikil and Tetzitz	732	220	0.301
Tinum and 1/2 Timoson	1,498	380	0.254
Tisunchel and 1/2 Tahmek	1,420	426	0.300
Cantunil	962	190	0.198
Bokaba and 1/2 Suma	1,856	357	0.192
Izamal	1,670	281	0.168
Xocchen	1,110	578	0.521
Tizimín	488	152	0.311
Chibxul and Hemal	1,132	380	0.336
1/2 Pokmuch	683	312	0.457
Chubulna	983	319	0.324
Tzama and Pole	163	68	0.417
Total	17,189	5,331	
Mean			0.326
s.d. = ±0.102			
s.e. = ±0.026			

that the sharp decrease in population occurred after the assessments which were in force at the beginning of the years 1645–1650 and were made in the 1630s and early 1640s.

The cause of the decline cannot be inferred from the raw figures in Table 1.10 and Table 1.11. However, we can think of two factors. The first is a food shortage to the point of famine and epidemics of an acute nature. The second is migration. Let us not forget that the values and ratios shown in the tables relate to the individual fortunes of long-established Indian towns. They do not show the total Indian population of Yucatan. Hence, internal redistribution could well affect adversely the number of inhabitants in a series of encomiendas.

In Table 1.12 we present data on forty-two encomiendas which appear in the lists of 1688 and 1785. The ratios are

Table 1.12

Population of encomiendas which occur identically in both the 1688 and 1785 lists. The total (Indian populations are calculated from the respective numbers of tributaries by applying the factor 3.8 in 1688 and 4.0 in 1785.

Encomienda	1688	1785	Ratio : 1785/1688
Mococha and Santa Catarina	612	2,568	4.20
Uqui	582	1,448	2.49
Cansahcab	486	1,180	2.42
Tekanto and Tepakan	1,095	2,360	2.16
Pixila and Quinimila	570	1,060	1.86
Mona	441	1,320	2.99
Uman	137	1,164	8.50
Nolo	342	1,107	3.25
Homun-Cuzama	764	2,600	3.40
Mopila in Yaxcaba	291	522	1.79
Chemax	456	1,500	3.29
Pixoy	304	396	1.30
Uayma	304	296	0.97
Xoquen	578	1,340	2.32
Xequelchakán	498	1,365	2.74
Pocoboco	236	512	2.17
Becal	259	1,509	5.83
Calkiní and Santa Lucía	91	164	1.80
Tzeme, Teya, and Tixculum	585	1,670	2.85
Baca and Yalcon	852	2,760	3.24
Bokaba, Suma, *et al.*	665	3,202	4.82
Motul, Tekax, Tzucacab, *et al.*	2,430	9,344	3.84
Halalcho	760	3,028	3.99
Popola (portion of Magana)	570	1,068	1.87
Yaxcaba and Kinchil	620	1,944	3.14
Hoctun	289	1,276	4.42
Espita, Tzabcanul, 2/3 Tekom	730	1,504	2.06
Yalcoba	228	484	2.12
Tixcacal, Yalsihon	673	924	1.37
Chicxulub	532	1,485	2.79
Mopila in Calkiní, Opilchen, *et al.*	395	1,696	4.30
Tunkas, Tixiol, Pokmuch	583	1,460	2.51
Peto, Mama, Chubulna, Muxuppipp, Tizimín	1,745	4,380	2.51
Xocchel, Sacalum, Tzanlahcat	715	3,348	4.68
Tahmek, Tixcunchel, Yaxakumche	813	2,242	2.76
Ichmul, Tiholop, Tecuche, Tinum	411	3,570	8.68
Cauquel, Ucu, Yabocu	357	668	1.87
Sucila, Tabi, Chunhuhub, Mexcitam	373	708	1.90
Tixhualatun in Valladolid	456	1,165	2.50
Siho and Telchac	570	748	1.31
Kinlacam and Kulcab	760	2,408	3.17
Conkal *et al.* (Montejo encom.)	1,440	4,265	2.96
Total	25,598	77,758	
Mean			3.07

S.D.= ±1.632

S.E. = ±0.252

startlingly different and show a recovery of population in these towns to a level at or above that of 1606. The mean of ratios of 1785 to 1688 is 3.07, with a standard deviation of 1.632 and a standard error of ± 0.252. Since the difference between the means of the ratios in Tables 1.10 and 1.12 is 2.74, and the square root of the sum of the squares of the standard errors is approximately 0.25, the critical ratio of the means, or t, must equal or exceed 10.0 and hence be highly significant.

Here, again, we have to remember that the recovery of the Indian tributary population during the eighteenth century pertains to the individual encomiendas and their constituent towns in the sample and not to the Indian population of Yucatan as a whole. The information on Indian tributaries, therefore, requires reinforcement from other sources. This support will be found in the ecclesiastical and civil reports to which we now turn.

In order to extract the maximum information from the Church and civil documents involved, a considerable amount of rather intricate treatment is necessary. We have used the Memoria de los conventos of 1582, Cogolludo, and the *Catálogo de los curatos* of 1813 for establishing parish boundaries and convent jurisdictions at various periods. The ecclesiastical counts in Vázquez de Espinosa (1609), Cárdenas Valencia (1639), the Franciscan report of 1700, and the bishop's report on his pastoral inspection (1736) all give inhabitants in terms of personas de confesión. In every instance, we have converted to total population by means of the factor 1.67, which, as previously explained, appears generally applicable over a wide range of places and time periods. The values in the Testimonio del donativo are in pesos and in some respects may not be completely reliable, although they are too useful to ignore. We have converted to total population by multiplying the stated number of pesos by 7.31, as we did previously, and then by the factor 3.7, the factor which is appropriate for converting tributaries to total population at that date.

For use of the data in the census of 1794–1795, an even more complicated procedure must be followed. The territorial totals are derived as we have previously described. The parish cabeceras are considered to have contained an average of 70 percent Indians since the non-Indians came to 30 percent. Their listed populations are therefore multiplied by 0.7. Similarly, the census values for the lesser towns in the parish are multiplied by 0.85. The Indian population of each parish is then estimated as the sum of the component town populations. In similar manner, we combine the Indian populations of the parishes to arrive at the Indian populations of the partidos or other larger territorial units.

The Indians in the Spanish cities must be treated in a somewhat more arbitrary manner. We omit the urban core of Mérida entirely, for it contained a relatively small but unknown number of Indians. On the other hand, we employ the usual factors with the peripheral parishes of San Cristóbal and Santiago. This method may yield too high a count of Indians, but no other procedure seems to be clearly preferable. For the city of Campeche we take 25 percent as the Indian component. For the parish of Santa Ana, which contains the villa of Valladolid, we take 25 percent of the number of persons in the villa plus 85 percent of those in the outlying towns. For the villa of Salamanca de Bacalar, we take 25 percent of the persons in the casco plus 85 percent of those in the single parish of Chichanha.

Once the methods for deriving populations have been established, we must select appropriate territorial units for comparison. These must be closely similar, if not identical, in extent from one period to another. It is frequently difficult to obtain a satisfactory series of such entities from the records because there occurred incessant movements of population, administrative reorganizations, and changes in procedures for recording numbers of persons. For working purposes, we have a hierarchy of three units: the town or village; the parish, the convent with its doctrina, or the beneficio; the partido, subdelegación, district, or jurisdiction. We have explored the suitability of all these by listing them according to their appearance and reorganization in the relevant documents.

The parochial organization may be outlined with considerable exactitude from the census of 1794–1795 and from the *Catalogo de los curatos* of 1813 so that the population may be ascertained for substantially all the parishes of Yucatan in 1794–1795. Moreover, by the use of the principal towns, the cabeceras, we can bring the later parishes into concordance with the convents and towns of the Franciscan report of 1700. A similar procedure is feasible for most, although not all, the parishes for the Testimonio del donativo of 1599. We may thus get a direct comparison of populations at the three dates mentioned. The relevant data will be found in Table 1.13, with

Table 1.13

Adjusted populations and their ratios from parishes for which there are reports in three documents : Testimonio del donativo, 1599; report of Franciscan province, 1700; census of 1794–1795. Adjustments of populations are described in the text, for each document. The figures given here are for the *Indian population only.*

Late Colonial Partido and Parish	Population 1599 (Donativo)	Population 1700 (Franciscan)	Population 1794 (Census)	Ratio: 1700/ 1599	Ratio: 1794/ 1700	Ratio: 1794/ 1599
Mérida (excluding town)						
San Cristóbal	5,062	3,026	11,351	0.60	3.75	2.24
Santiago	3,350	586	6,065	0.17	10.35	1.81
Camino Real Bajo						
Hunucmá	2,879		4,649			1.62
Uman	2,212		4,360			1.97
Kopoma	1,603	783	4,586	0.49	5.86	2.86
Maxcanú	4,060	722	3,780	0.18	5.24	0.93
Halacho		1,371	2,055		1.50	
Camino Real Alto						
Becal	2,546	2,647	3,595	1.04	1.36	1.41
Bolonchén		1,082	2,850		2.63	
Hopelchén		868	2,051		2.36	
Calkiní		3,782	4,888		1.29	
Campeche						
Campeche		712	4,235		5.95	
Bolonchencauich						
Pocyaxcum		262	3,541		13.51	
Pich		665	2,336		3.51	
Costa						
Mococha	4,306	2,639	2,110	0.61	0.80	0.49
Conkal	4,938	3,945	4,888	0.80	1.24	0.99
Tixkokob	2,839		2,211			0.78
Nolo	1,731		2,038			1.18
Telchac	3,335	2,552	2,343	0.77	0.92	0.70
Motul	4,788	3,792	3,594	0.79	0.95	0.75
Cacalchén	2,367	1,470	1,349	0.62	0.92	0.57
Dzidzantun		1,901	2,288		1.20	
Cansahcab	1,352	1,308	1,291	0.97	0.99	0.95
Temax	1,487	1,502	3,633	1.01	2.42	2.44
Teya	1,704	1,408	1,102	0.83	0.78	0.65
Tekanto	3,935	2,373	1,722	0.60	0.73	0.44
Izamal	10,707	2,257	4,483	0.21	1.98	0.42

Table 1.13 (cont.)

Late Colonial Partido and Parish	Population 1599 (Donativo)	Population 1700 (Franciscan)	Population 1794 (Census)	Ratio: 1700/ 1599	Ratio: 1794/ 1700	Ratio: 1794/ 1599
Beneficios Bajos						
Hoctun	2,192		3,300			1.50
Hocabá	3,300		2,486			0.75
Homun	2,455		1,662			0.68
Acanceh	1,687		3,720			2.20
Sotuta	2,892		2,537			0.88
Tixcacaltuyu	1,136		4,907			4.33
Yaxcabá	2,975		3,502			1.18
Beneficios Altos						
Chikindzonot	405		1,835			4.53
Sacalaca	663		1,867			2.82
Sierra Baja						
Abala		259	3,440		13.28	
Muna	3,141	981	3,790	0.31	3.86	1.24
Saculum	987	954	3,765	0.97	3.94	3.82
Teabo	3,171	3,450	6,479	1.09	1.88	2.04
Tecoh	1,860		4,620			2.48
Mama	3,487		7,228			2.07
Sierra Alta						
Ticul	10,790	4,080	12,458	0.38	3.06	1.15
Maní	6,680	3,884	8,381	0.58	2.16	1.25
Oxcutzcab	3,445	5,199	12,603	1.51	2.43	3.66
Tekax	4,663	4,989	12,329	1.07	2.47	2.64
Valladolid						
Santa Ana	406		3,113			7.66
Cenotillo		1,553	2,578		1.66	
Uayma		2,629	2,407		0.91	
Sisal	2,753	6,110	1,428	2.22	0.23	0.52
Chichimila	2,090	4,387	2,066	2.10	0.99	0.47
Tixcacal	1,444	2,283	998	1.58	0.44	0.69
Tizimín						
Kikil	324		2,174			6.50
Calotmul	866		4,263			3.23
Bacalar						
Chichanha		655	1,152		1.76	

Table 1.13 (cont.)

Summary

Mean of ratios for parishes in this table for
which we have population estimates:

Ratio: 1700/1599, 25 cases	0.86
Ratio: 1794/1700, 37 cases	2.95
Ratio: 1794/1599, 43 cases	1.90

Ratios of total population estimates for parishes
shown in this table:

Totals for those parishes used in calculating
the means shown above:

Ratio: 1700/1599, 25 parishes:		
Total population 1599:	94,704	
Total population 1700:	67,327	0.84
Ratio: 1794/1700, 37 parishes:		
Total population 1700:	83,076	
Total population 1794:	154,010	1.86
Ratio: 1794/1599, 43 parishes:		
Total population 1599:	129,013	
Total population 1794:	181,651	1.41

a total of fifty-five parishes represented.

On inspection of the table, it will be noted that data for
many parishes are not always available. The Franciscan report
of 1700 gives no information for parishes administered by the
secular clergy. Furthermore, ten parishes could not be satis-
factorily identified in the donativo list of 1599. Consequently,
the number of parishes which can be utilized for constructing
ratios between pairs of dates is limited and variable. Thus,
for the population ratio 1700/1599 we have 25 cases; for 1794/
1700 we have 37 cases, and for 1794/1599 we have 43 cases.

The results are summarized at the end of the table. For
the entire peninsula, the set of three ratios is calculated by the
usual two methods: the mean of the individual parish ratios,
and the ratio of the total Indian populations of the parishes for
each two dates. The two methods yield somewhat different
results, due to variations in the size of individual populations,
but the trend is clear. The population was lower in 1700 than in
1599 in the Franciscan parishes; from 1700 to 1794 there was
a strong increase. The overall change from 1599 to 1794, with
43 cases, was a pronounced increase.

We may now extend our restricted analysis by parish to one which embraces a much broader survey, including much more information on parishes administered by Franciscans and secular clergy for more points in time within the years 1609–1795, and combining the information into larger territorial units, namely, the partidos, jurisdictions, or subdelegaciones. With the exception of the donativo list of 1599, which is not pertinent here, all the data at our disposal are consolidated in a single large table, Table 1.14. A detailed explanation of this table is necessary.

Horizontally, Table 1.14, shows territorial units at a series of dates: 1582, convents; 1609, convents and secular parishes; 1639, the same; 1655, the same; 1700, Franciscan convents with their parishes only; 1736, convents and secular parishes; 1794–1795, parishes designated by cabeceras with lesser towns omitted; 1813, partidos or jurisdictions to which the parishes belonged. In each case, there is given the name, whether the entity was administered by Franciscans (F) or by secular clergy (S) and the estimated Indian population if the documents contain this information. The data, we should emphasise, are for Indians of all groups and not merely indios de pueblo.

Vertically, the partidos are set apart by lines extending across the table. Within each partido, the convents and parishes are arranged as far as possible in order of historical appearance. Nevertheless, there are some discrepancies in details because partido and convent lines did not always coincide. However, no serious error is thereby introduced. All populations are derived in the manner already described, except for a few in Table 1.14. These are outright estimates made necessary by gaps in the written record.

The extent and complexity of Table 1.14 makes difficult a rapid evaluation of the data. Consequently, we have condensed the figures and presented the significant results in Table 1.15. This table consists of three parts: Part A gives the total estimated Indian populations of the 31 Franciscan convent parishes in 1700, together with the populations of the same convent parishes or their equivalents in 1609, 1639, 1736, and 1794–1795. Part B gives the estimated Indian populations of the partidos or subdelegaciones as they existed in 1794, together with the populations of the same or equivalent territorial units in 1609, 1639, and 1736. Those of 1700 are omitted since they cannot be determined from the Franciscan report alone. The four partidos

Table 1.14

Territorial entities of Yucatan and their Indian population.

1582	1609		1639		1655
Mérida	Mérida (F)	4,342	Mérida	6,000[a]	Mérida-San Cristóbal (
	Mérida (S)	2,505			Mérida-Santiago (S)
Hunacama	Hunacama (F)	5,010	Hanucama (F)	3,809	Hunacama (F)
Mérida	Tahumán (F)	2,642	Tahumán (F)	3,173	Umán (F)
Calkiní	Maxcanú (F)	3,340	Maxcanú (F)	4,000	Maxcanú (F)
Xequelchakán	Xequelchakán (F)	4,175	Xequelchakán (F)	5,107	Xequelchakán (F)
Calkiní	Calquiní (F)	9,519	Calkiní (F)	8,464	Calkiní (F)
			Bolonchén (F)	817	Bolonchén (Vic.)
Campeche	Campeche (F)	3,340	Campeche (F)	3,617	Campeche (F)
	Campeche (S)	1,670	Campeche	1,130	Campeche (S)
			Bol-cauich (F)	902	
	Campotón (F)	3,008	Champotón (F)	3,617	Champotón (F)
			Sahcabchén (F)	1,318	Sahcabchén (F)
Conkal	Mococha (F)	4,339	Mococha (F)	4,791	Mococha (F)
	Conkal (F)	5,845	Conkal (F)	4,641	Conkal (F)
Tixkokob	Tixkokob (S)	4,676	Tixkokob (S)	5,244	Tixkokob (S)
	Telchac (F)	5,344	Telchac (F)	4,826	Telchac (F)
Motul	Motul (F)	7,682	Motul (F)	5,977	Motul (F)
	Cacalchén (F)	3,674	Cacalchén (F)	3,936	Calcalchén (F)
Dzidzantún	Dzidzantún	7,014	Dzidzantún (F)	5,080	Zizantún (F)
	Temax (F)	4,008	Temax (F)	2,578	Temax (F)
			Cansahcab (F)	4,643	Cansahcab (F)
Tekanto	Tekanto (F)	9,185	Tekanto (F)	5,875	Tekanto (F)
			Teya (F)	3,287	Teya (F)
Izamal	Izamal (F)	8,350	Izamal (F)	7,674	Izamal (F)
Hocabá	Hocabá (S)	6,012	Hocabá (S)	2,766	Hocabá (S)
			Hoctún (S)	2,555	Hoctún (S)
Homún	Homún (F)	2,839	Homún	2,520	Homún (F)
Sotuta	Sotuta (S)	3,340	Sotuta (S)	3,380	Sotuta (S)
	Yaxcabá (S)	3,340	Yaxcabá (S)	5,237	Yaxcabá (S)

1700		1736		1794–1795		1813 *(Partido)*
ɜrida (F)	3,602	San Cristóbal (F)	3,888	San Cristóbal	11,351	Mérida
		Santiago (S)	2,072	Santiago	6,065	
		Hunacama (S)	1,997	Hunucmá	4,649	Camino Real Bajo
		Umán (S)	1,964	Umán	4,360	
ıxcanú (F)	2,876	Maxcanú (F)	2,136	Maxcanú	3,780	
				Kopoma	4,586	
				Halacho	2,055	
		Xequelchakán (S)	2,706	Xequelchakán	4,259	Camino Real Alto
lkiní (F)	3,782	Calkiní (F)	2,404	Calkiní	4,888	
cal (F)	2,647	Becal (F)	1,562	Becal	3,595	
lonchén (F)	1,950	Bolonchén (F)	1,575	Bolonchén	2,850	
				Hopelchén	2,051	
ımpeche (F)	1,639	San Francisco (F)	1,710	Campeche (city)	4,235	Campeche
		Campechc (S)	4,008			
				Pocyaxcum	3,541	Bolonchencauich
				Pich	2,336	
		Seiba (S)	1,430	Champotón	837	Sahcabchen
				Seiba Playa	3,204	
				Sahcabchen	550	
				Chicbul	435	
				Palizada	1,589	Carmen
›cocha (F)	3,859	Mococha (F)	1,978	Mococha	2,110	Costa
ınkal (F)	3,859	Conkal (F)	2,886	Conkal	4,888	
		Tixkokob (S)	3,000	Tixkokob	2,211	
				Nolo	2,038	
hac (F)	2,552	Telchac (F)	1,442	Telchac	2,343	
›tul	3,792	Motul (F)	1,817	Motul	3,594	
·alchén	1,470	Cacalchén	935	Cacalchén	1,349	
antún (F)	1,901	Dzidzantún (F)	1,216	Dzidzantún	2,288	
nax (F)	1,502	Temax (F)	1,296	Temax	3,633	
ısahcab (F)	1,308	Cansahcab (F)	655	Cansahcab	1,291	
;anto (F)	2,373	Tekanto (F)	1,242	Tekanto	1,722	
·a (F)	1,408	Teya (F)	655	Teya	1,102	
ɪmal (F)	2,257	Izamal (F)	1,496	Izamal	4,483	
		Hocabá (S)	1,389	Hocabá	2,486	Beneficios Bajos
		Hoctún (S)	1,630	Hoctún	3,300	
		Homún (S)	1,216	Homún	1,662	
				Acanceh	3,720	
		Sotuta (S)	1,830	Sotuta	2,537	
		Yaxcabá (S)	2,271	Yaxcabá	3,502	
		Tixcacaltuyu (S)	2,271	Tixcacaltuyu	4,907	

Table 1.14 (cont.)

1582	1609		1639		1655
Peto	Peto (S)	3,006	Peto (S)	2,852	Peto
Ichmul	Ichmul (S)	4,676	Ichmul (S)	2,984	Ichmul (S)
			Tihosuco (S)	3,303	Tihosuco (S)
Homún	Tecoh (F)	3,674	Tecoh (F)	2,188	Tecoh (F)
Maní	Teabo (F)	3,674	Teabo (F)	4,572	Teabo (F)
			Mona (F)	3,677	Mona (F)
Ticul			Mama (F)	4,168	Mama (F)
Maní	Maní (F)	8,350	Maní (F)	7,597	Maní (F)
Oxcutzcab	Oxcutzcab (F)	4,676	Oxcutzcab	6,413	Oxcutzcab (F)
Ticul	Ticul (F)	10,020	Ticul (F)	7,607	Ticul (F)
Tekax	Tekax (F)	6,179	Tekax (F)	7,515	Tekax (F)
Valladolid	Valladolid (S)	5,010	Valladolid (S)	4,676	Valladolid (S)
Sisal	Sisal (F)	6,680	Sisal (F)	6,807	Sisal (F)
	Tichel (S)	1,336	Tichel (S)	2,856	Popola (S)
Chichimila	Chichimila (F)	5,100	Chichimila (F)	5,650	Chichimila (F)
					Tixcacal (Vic.)
Tinum	Tinum (F)	3,006	Tinum (F)	2,664	Uayma (F)
			Cenotillo (F)	1,565	Zonot (F)
Tizimín	Tizimín (F)	7,014	Tizimín (F)	4,286	Tizimín (F)
			Sucopo (F)	1,219	
			Calotmul (F)	3,387	Calotmul (F)
Chancenote	Chancenote (S)	5,010	Chancenote (S)	3,681	Chancenote (S)
					Nabalam (S)
Cozumel	Cozumel (S)	1,336	Cozumel (S)	832	Cozumel (S)
Bacalar	Salamanca (S)	1,002	Salamanca (S)	1,000[a]	

1700		1736		1794–1795		1813 *(Partido)*
		Peto (S)	3,086	Peto	3,003	Beneficios Altos
		Chunhuhub (S)	748	Chunhuhub	1,967	
		Sacalaca (S)	668	Sacalaca	1,867	
				Tahdziu	2,670	
		Ichmul (S)	2,739	Ichmul	9,122	
		Tihosuco (S)	1,937	Tihosuco	3,660	
		Chikindzonot (S)	868	Chikindzonot	1,835	
		Tecoh (S)	3,741	Tecoh	4,620	Sierra Baja
abo (F)	3,450	Teabo (F)	1,804	Teabo	6,479	
ona (F)	981	Mona (F)	2,472	Mona	3,790	
ala (F)	259			Abala	3,440	
culum (F)	954			Saculum	3,765	
		Mama (S)	1,456	Mama	7,228	
ani (F)	3,884	Manì (F)	2,672	Manì	8,381	Sierra Alta
cutzcab (F)	5,199	Oxcutzcab	4,810	Oxcutzcab	12,603	
ul (F)	4,080	Ticul (F)	3,781	Ticul	12,468	
kax (F)	4,989	Tekax (F)	2,939	Tekax	12,329	
		Valladolid (S)	4,248	Santa Ana	3,113	Valladolid
		Ticuch (S)	1,029	Ticuch	465	
		Chemax (S)	2,458	Chemax	1,750	
al (F)	6,110	Sisal (F)	3,019	Sisal	1,428	
ichimila (F)	4,387	Chichimila (F)	2,458	Chichimila	2,066	
cacal (F)	2,283	Tixcacal (F)	935	Tixcacal	998	
yma (F)	2,629	Uayma (F)	2,204	Uayma	2,407	
notillo (F)	1,553	Dzonotpip (F)	1,750	Cenotillo	2,578	
		Tzimin (S)	2,993	Tzimin	1,260	Tzimin
		Kikil (S)	2,391	Kikil	2,174	
		Calotmul (S)	4,192	Calotmul	1,098	
		Espita (S)	3,567	Espita	2,684	
		Chancenote (S)	1,870	Chancenote	1,449	
		Nabalam (S)	1,777	Nabalam	1,386	
		Xcam (S)	708	Xcambolon	1,710	
		Salamanca		300[a] Salamanca		307[a] Bacalar
ichanha (F)	655	Chichanha		600[a] Chichanha		845

[a] An estimate, see text.

Table 1.15

Condensation and summary of Table 1.14.

A. Total estimated Indian population of those parishes which were
Franciscan in 1700

	1609	1639	1700	1736	1794–1795
Population	123,577	128,273	84,190	58,307	127,344

B. Total for all entities, but omitting the Franciscan convents in 1700

Partido	1609	1639	1736	1794–1795
Mérida	6,847	6,000	5,960	17,416
Camino Real Bajo	10,992	10,982	6,097	19,430
Camino Real Alto	13,694	14,388	8,247	17,643
Campeche (group)	8,018	11,486	7,148	16,727
Costa	60,117	58,552	18,618	33,052
Beneficios Bajos	15,531	16,458	10,607	22,114
Beneficios Altos	7,682	9,139	10,046	24,124
Sierra Baja	7,348	14,605	9,473	29,322
Sierra Alta	29,225	29,132	14,202	45,781
Valladolid	21,042	24,218	18,101	14,805
Tizimín	12,024	12,573	17,498	12,121
Cozumel	1,336	832		
Bacalar	1,002	1,000	900	1,152
Total province	194,858	209,365	126,897	253,687

C. Percentage increase or decrease in population between 1639 and 1736,
and between 1639 and 1794/95, using 1639 as the point of reference

Partido	% Change 1639–1736	% Change 1639–1794/95
Mérida	− 00.7	+ 190.3
Camino Real Bajo	− 44.2	+ 77.0
Camino Real Alto	− 42.4	+ 22.6
Campeche (group)	− 37.8	+ 45.7
Costa	− 68.2	− 43.6
Beneficios Bajos	− 35.5	+ 34.3
Beneficios Altos	+ 09.9	+153.8
Sierra Baja	− 54.2	+100.8
Sierra Alta	− 51.2	+ 57.1
Valladolid	− 27.5	−39.0
Tizimín	+ 39.2	− 3.6
Cozumel		
Bacalar	0.0	0.0
Total province	− 39.3	+21.2

which originally were included in the area administered by the convent of Campeche have been consolidated for the sake of simplicity. They are Campeche, Bolonchencauich, Sahcabchén, and Carmen. The island of Cozumel disappears from the record after 1639. The partido of Bacalar contained close to 1,000 Indians throughout the two centuries, with no appreciable change. Part C expresses the changes in Indian population of each partido in relative terms. We take 1639 as the base and show the percentage of increase or decrease between 1639 and 1736. For example, in the partido of Camino Real Bajo, there was a decrease from 10,982 to 6,097. Then 10,982 minus 6,097 is 4,885 or −44.2 percent. A similar procedure is employed for the interval 1639 to 1794–1795.

An inspection of the three parts of Table 1.15 confirms what has already been found in Tables 1.10 to 1.13. Part A of Table 1.15 confirms and emphasizes the results seen in Table 1.13 with respect to the Franciscan parishes. We use here the convent lists of 1609 and 1639 in place of the donativo list of 1599 and find that there was a small increase from 1609 to 1639 and a sharp fall from 1639 to 1700. It is also apparent that this decrease continued until 1736 or close to that date. From 1736 to 1794 there was a very great increase.

Part B of Table 1.15 presents, in effect, the same findings as in part A, but with the inclusion of parishes under administration by secular clergy as well as those in Franciscan care. Part C gives an idea of the relative magnitude of the movement of Indian population. For the entire province of Yucatan (less Tabasco), the decrease from 1639 to 1736 was approximately 40 percent of the value in 1639. Then the Indian population recovered by 1794 to a level more than 20 percent above the value of 1639.

Part C also makes clear the regional or differential nature of the shifts in population. It is evident that the greatest increase from 1639–1794 came in the districts of Mérida, Beneficios Altos, and Sierra Baja. Mérida was urban and the other two partidos contained at that time much empty land which could be filled in by immigration from other partidos. The latter appear to have been principally the partido of La Costa in the north and those of Valladolid and Tizimín in the east. It is also notable that the population moved away from the coasts and toward the interior, which tended to become the area of greater population density. Much of the new settlement was in the Puuc, which has fertile pockets of land that are among the best in Yucatan.

In concluding this section, we may summarize both what has been stated previously and the data in our tables in order to estimate the total population of Yucatan for the period 1610–1813. We have already accepted 185,000 as a fair compromise among three estimates for the indios de pueblo at approximately the year 1600. As of 1605 we estimated all other groups to have been approximately 7,050 persons. For the year 1610 let us dispense with superfluous details and put the total population tentatively at 190,000. Then we may use the totals shown for Indians, that is, indios de pueblo, naborías and all others, in Table 1.15. For 1700 we estimate the total number of Indians by ratio from those in Franciscan parishes. We add estimates of the gente de razón, or non-Indians, where necessary, obtaining these by interpolation from the graph in Figure 1.1. Expressed in round numbers, we arrive at the following statement of the population of Yucatan 1610–1794:

Date	Indian	Non-Indian	Total Pop.
1660			190,000
1639	210,000	12,500	222,500
1700	182,500	20,000	202,500
1736	127,000	34,000	161,000
1794	254,000	103,000	357,000

X. CALAMITIES AND FUGITIVISM

The remarkable decline after the mid-seventeenth century of the Indian population within the area under Spanish control cannot be ascribed exclusively to the interaction of natality and mortality. Furthermore, although Yucatan in the colonial period had a long history of droughts, famines, and epidemics, there is no record of any as catastrophic and prolonged as would be required to explain in full both the initial decline of the population and its failure to recover during approximately a century. Consequently, we are obliged to consider very carefully internal migrations that could have carried masses of Indians out of the counting radius of treasury officials and priests from 1645 to 1736 and then have returned them to civil count by the time of the census of 1794–1795.

That there have been natural disasters is easily apparent. The records, chronicles, and histories of the colonial period are replete with accounts of them. North-central Yucatan is dry bush, short of rainfall, even in the better years, and so unusually subject to drought in years of lesser precipitation. The karst formation of northern and central Yucatan does not store water except at depths that make it available for drinking but hardly for irrigation without pumping facilities beyond the technology of the Maya during the colonial period. Accordingly, periods of lessened rainfall would be times of lessened crop yield or actual crop failure. The danger of drought was complicated by infestations of locusts, which tend to be present on the dry margins of climatic zones as in Yucatan. Fragmentary though they are, the royal treasury records contain a number of references to infestations of *langosta* (locusts) and to special officials appointed for mobilizing the Indians to destroy the the insects.[131] In addition, there were epidemics from time to time often adding to the ravages of drought.

As an illustration of the frequency of disasters, we may list those known for the century from 1560 to 1654:

1564	Drought[132]
1569–1570	Epidemic[133]
1571–1572	Drought and famine[134]
1575–1576	Epidemic, drought and famine[135]
1604	Famine[136]
1609	*Tabardillo* (typhus)[137]
1618	Locusts[138]
1627–1631	Smallpox and measles, four years of poor harvests, locusts, famine[139]
1648–1656	Yellow fever, famine, smallpox[140]

The years 1648–1656 are described by Cogolludo as ones of unusually severe and compounded calamities. In 1648 yellow fever appeared in Campeche; from there it spread to Mérida and to Valladolid. Although at first, it ravaged the

[131]Entries in the accounts for 1587–1588, 1590, 1592, and 1593. In 1587–1588, the royal treasury spent 303/4 for the eradication of locusts in the towns of Mococha, Telechaque, Quiní, and Espegual — the largest expenditure of this kind in the accounts.
[132]Royal treasury accounts for 1564.
[133]Molina Solís, *Historia de Yucatán durante la dominación española,* I, 114–115.
[134]Royal treasury accounts for 1571–1572; Cogolludo, *lib.* VI, *cap.* IX (I,335); Molina Solís, *Historia de Yucatan durante la dominación española,* I, 128–130.
[135]Royal treasury accounts for 1576; Molina Solís, *Historia de Yucatán durante la dominación española,* I, 166, but giving the date as 1575.
[136]Royal treasury accounts for 1604.
[137]Cogolludo, *lib.* IX, *cap.* I (I, 466).
[138]*Ibid., lib.* IV, *cap.* XV (I, 218).
[139]*Ibid., lib.* X, *cap.* XVII (I, 592–595).
[140]*Ibid., lib.* IV, *cap.* XVII; *lib.* VII, *cap.* VI, *lib.* XII; *cap.* XI–XVI, XXI, XXIII (I, 227–228, 385–386, 714–730, 742–745, 750–751, respectively).

Spanish cities, it soon moved into the Indian towns. The epidemic lasted two years, with great loss of life. In 1651, although the crop of 1650 had appeared to be ample, maize became scarce and remained so for two years of famine. In 1654 smallpox began to carry off many of the survivors. Cogolludo, writing in 1656, mentioned the calamities as continuing to that year:

see entiende auer faltado casi la mitad de los Indios cõ las mortandades de la peste, hambre, y viruelas, que desde el ano de mil y seiscientos y quarēta y ocho, hasta el presente de cinquenta y seis, en que voy trasladando esto, han fatigado tanto esta tierra. (it is thought that nearly half the Indians died in the epidemic, famine, and smallpox that from the year 1648 until the present one of 1656 in which I transcribe this, have so vexed this land.[141]

Elsewhere, describing the checking of attendance at mass against tablets, he comments:

Esto se haze en los patios fuera de las Iglesias, y aora veinte años auia Pueblos tan grandes, que era necessario para esta quenta salirse à la Plaça del Pueblo, que todas estan conjuntas a las Iglesias: oy faltan en ellos mas de la mitad de sus vezindades, que es lastima verlos. (This is done in the courtyards outside the churches. Twenty years ago there were towns with so many inhabitants that for this count it was necessary to go out to the town square; all squares are near the churches. Today more than half the inhabitants are missing; it is painful to see them.)[142]

The disasters of the years 1648–1656 were an unusual concatenation; those of the other years were probably no more than the recurrent crop failures, famines, and epidemics that characterized the lot of humanity until very recently in all but a very few favored portions of the globe.

The remarkable demographic occurrence in Yucatan was not the calamities but the failure of the recorded population to recover to the extent one might expect in the intervals between such disasters. Here we turn for an explanation to a characteristic response of the Maya to crop failures and epidemics in the regions under the control of the Spanish cities. To the east, south, and west, after the mid-sixteenth century, lay large areas of vacant land with greater rainfall, higher bush that on clearing and burning would give the humus for raising maize, and with no encomenderos, treasury officials, or priests to

[141]*Ibid., lib.* VII, *cap.* VI (I, 385–386).
[142]*Ibid., lib.* IV, *cap.* XVII (I, 227–228).

levy taxes and enforce rules of conduct. The Spanish sources are unanimous that in times of food shortage and epidemic—the two tended to go together whichever came first—substantial numbers of Indian peasants left their towns to settle on the vacant lands. As free peasant communities developed in the back country, with their own political institutions and religious observances that revived many heathen practices, they served as an attraction for a trickle of the hardy and dissatisfied even between the major expulsive movements of the calamities. In the later seventeenth century, there were added inducements for migration to the back country. Perhaps most important was the increasingly oppressive weight of the *repartimiento de mercancías*, a practice whereby Spanish civil administrators distributed animals and goods to the Indians in forced sales at artificial prices, burdening the Indians with unwanted things and reaping a substantial profit for the administrator. The raids of English and French corsairs may also have played a role in driving the population inland.[143]

The Spanish, both civil administrators and clergy, were aware of these flights into the interior and the building up of independent Maya communities there. They made repeated efforts to bring the inhabitants back to their former towns or to settle them in new towns under Spanish civil and religious control. In 1550 Francisco de Montejo led an expedition into the part of southern Yucatan called the Sierra in order to persuade the large number of fugitives believed to be there to return to their towns.[144] That same year Father Landa worked among fugitive Indian warriors in the country back of Maní, persuading them to settle mear Oxcutzcab under Franciscan religious administration.[145] In 1560–1561 Pablo Paxbolon, the young cacique of Tixchel, with permission of the provincial government, led an expedition into the interior in order to bring out fugitive families living there. A series of expeditions led finally to the settlement of many of the fugitives at Zapotitlán near Tixchel.[146] In 1571, according to Cogolludo, excessive export of maize from the peninsula led to so severe a shortage that many Indians died of hunger and most of them left their homes to seek food.[147] We do not know what efforts were made to per-

[143]See the excellent statement in Scholes and Roys, *The Maya Chontal Indians,* pp. 305–307 *et passim.*
[144]Cogolludo, *lib.* V, *cap.* XI (I, 273–274).
[145]*Ibid., lib.* V, *cap.* XIV (I, 286).
[146]Scholes and Roys, *The Maya Chontal Indians,* pp. 185–220.
[147]Cogolludo, *lib.* VI, *cap.* IX (I, 335).

suade the fugitives to return at this time; almost certainly there
were some. In the years 1595–1601 the Spaniards made attempts
to reduce fugitive Indians in two directions, those who had
fled to the Bahía de la Ascensión and those who had fled into
the Petén area of present-day Guatemala, the Itzáes with their
capital on an island in Lake Petén and fugitives joining them.[148]
By the beginning of the seventeenth century settlements of
fugitives in the central southern part of the peninsula had
reached sufficient size so that a report of 1604 by Pablo Paxbolon,
cacique of Tixchel, lists well over a dozen of them.[149]

The most sizeable effort at reduction in the earlier colonial
period came in 1612–1613 when Franciscan missionaries
succeeded in persuading fugitives in the Sahcabchén area of the
Puuc to accept Spanish rule and Franciscan spiritual administration. A series of new towns were founded—San Antonio de
Sahcabchén, San Lorenzo de Ulumal, Tzuctok, and Cauich—
paying tribute directly to the Crown and organized as a new
Franciscan parish under a convent at Sahcabchén.[150]

The difficulties of keeping the Maya peasants in their
towns, of persuading them to return, and of maintaining them
if they did return are well illustrated by the two major crises,
that of 1627–1631 and that of 1648–1656. In 1627–1631, four
years of poor crops, locusts, famine, and epidemics forced a
large part of the population to search for food in the back
country. Late in 1631, the new governor, Fernando Centeno
Maldonado, began a campaign to bring back the fugitives.
Emissaries, especially friars, were sent into the back country
and managed to persuade many thousands to return. According
to Cogolludo, 16,000 tributary persons were brought back to
the region of La Costa alone (approximately the later partido
of La Costa). The problem was to feed the returned fugitives
until they could support themselves and to protect them from
efforts of the caciques and *principales* to sell maize at extortionate
prices. In 1632 the governor forced disclosure of food stores
and a form of rationing by threatening to hang offenders.[151]
During the famine that began in 1651, thousands of Indians
again fled into the back country. Late in 1652 expeditions
were sent to bring them back from the interior regions to the

[148]*Ibid., lib.* VIII, *cap.* VIII (I, 441–444).
[149]Scholes and Roys, *The Maya Chontal Indians,* pp. 256–258, 503–507.
[150]Cogolludo, *lib.* IX, *cap.* III (I, 472); Scholes and Roys, *The Maya Chontal
Indians,* pp. 251–289; Cárdenas Valencia, p. 74; Royal treasury accounts
for 1645.
[151]Cogolludo, *lib.* X, *cap.* XVII (I, 592–595).

west, south, and east. Over 22,000 were returned to their towns; they were as Cogolludo grimly calls them "the residue left by famine." Each encomendero was assessed a half peso for the costs of the expeditions, but unfortunately

no se dispuso, que tuuiessen que comer en sus pueblos, ni aun siquiera que les ayudassen a hazer casas, con q̃ muchissimos se desaperecieron presto, y aun se llebarõ algunos de los q̃ con la hambre no se huyeron. Antes de dos meses acabada la reduccion fuy yo electo en la Congregaciõ Guardian de el Convento de Mani, y quãdo lleguè à èl ninguno halle de los reducidos, siendo el pueblo de la sierra donde mas se auian embiado, segun dixo el Capitan Pedro de Hercilla. (no arrangement had been made for them to be fed in their towns nor even for them to be given help in building houses. Accordingly, very many of them quickly disappeared and even took with them some of the Indians who had not fled despite the famine. Before the resettlement had been completed two months, I was elected Guardian of the Convent of Maní in the provincial meeting. When I arrived at the convent, I found none of the returned fugitives although Maní was the town in the Sierra where more had been sent than anywhere else according to Captain Pedro de Ercilla.)[152]

Ironically, a few years before the disasters of 1648–1656, in the years 1643–1644, the Spanish authorities mounted an extensive campaign to bring back fugitives, and according to Cogolludo succeeded in returning 9,423 persons.[153]

In the later seventeenth century the same factors that led to fugitivism continued to operate but were reinforced by flight from the repartimiento de mercancías, labor demands by Spaniards for logwood cutting, and the attacks of English and French corsairs along the coast.[154]

It is clear that the population counts of the century from 1645 to 1750 cover the population in the area under effective Spanish control but do not take into account a substantial number of Indians living in the bush, often in fairly sizable settlements.[155] We have no means of estimating what relation they bore to the indios de pueblo under Spanish administration.

In the second half of the eighteenth century, a large proportion of the fugitives were returned to Spanish control.

[152]*Ibid., lib.* XII, *cap.* XXIII (I, 750–751).
[153]*Lib.* XII, *cap.* I (I, 679).
[154]Scholes and Roys, *The Maya Chontal Indians,* pp. 305–307 *et passim.*
[155]Cogolludo gives a very interesting description of the population of the unreduced area and its political and religious organization and usages as of 1645. *Lib.* XII, *cap.* VIII (I, 698–701).

In part, the return reflects the impact of an invigorated and reorganized provincial administration under the Bourbons that extended Spanish control far deeper into the interior; in part, it probably meant the return of some of the fugitive population to the old Indian towns. As late as 1769–1770, however, prolonged famine led large parts of the Indian population to abandon its towns and flee sixty leagues and more.[156] Presumably the provincial government and the clergy in the end were able to bring almost all of the fugitives back to their towns at that time. The pattern of flight has continued into the nineteenth century when perhaps the most notable instance was the flight of a substantial proportion of the peasant population into the interior during the War of the Castes and the setting up of independent, neo-Indian states that lasted for a number of decades. The most powerful of them succumbed only to federal troops armed with up-to-date equipment in the 1890s and as late as 1901.[157] We still cannot be sure what there is in the back country of the peninsula, which continues to be carried in Mexican national censuses as having no inhabitants. One wonders whether the assertions are based upon inquiries in the actual area.

XI. POPULATION, 1813–1970

The coming of independence to Mexico in 1821 meant considerable changes in territorial organization and in the forms of data for study of the population of Yucatan. Upon the organization of the Mexican federation in 1824, Yucatan without Tabasco became a state, with its capital at Mérida. The upheavals of the middle of the nineteenth century, regional rivalries among the Hispanized population, and the desire of the national government to break up the strongly particularistic Yucatecan mass led in 1858–1861 to the splitting off of Campeche as a separate state. For a few years the Isla del Carmen was a separate federal territory. In 1902 the east coast of the peninsula was separated from the state of Yucatan as the federal territory of Quintana Roo.

For the years 1813–1970 virtually all of the data available to us are in published form. The methods and purposes of

[156]Echánove, "Cuadro estadístico de Yucatán en 1814"; Molina Solís, *Historia de Yucatán durante la dominanción española*, III, 252–253.
[157]Reed, *The Caste War of Yucatan, passim* but especially pp. 132–240. See also the discussion of the nineteenth century in part XI of this chapter.

counting show considerable differences from those of the colonial period. During the nineteenth century, counts were made by state or district authorities. with no supervision from outside of the peninsula. The careful control exercised by the Spanish viceregal and royal governments thus no longer operated, nor was it replaced in the nineteenth century by national supervision. Church counts based upon continued recording of communicants and children undergoing religious instruction were no longer made. Another major source of information for the colonial period, the tribute counts, went out of existence with the abolition of Indian tribute but was replaced until the middle of the nineteenth century by a new form of count for the *obvenciones,* a head tax on Indian males, paid in lieu of tithes for the support of the Church. It was levied in the 1840s at the rate of one real a month per male, or 1 1/2 pesos a year, so heavy a sum that bitter Indian resentment at the weight of the levy contributed greatly to the outbreak of the War of the Castes in 1847. The registers for collection of the obvenciones were prepared in each town without supervision by the authorities in Mérida. Since the village curates depended upon the tax for support, the registers were subject to inflation as well as evasion. Adjustments for both elements account for many of the differences in estimates of population, especially in the 1840s, for the registers for collection of the obvenciones are the major source for estimates of the Indian population. The non-Indian population was subject to a head tax that gives a paralled basis for an estimate.[158] From the abolition of obvenciones during the War of the Castes until the end of the nineteenth century, we are forced to depend upon partial counts and estimates by state governments and private writers; many simply copy or adapt previous statements. The first national census, a poor one, was taken in 1895. Beginning with 1900, there has been a series of decennial national counts of relatively good quality.

Another feature of the demographic data available to us for the period since independence has been the elimination of most evidence on race. Parish registers in Mexico ceased to record racial affiliation in entries for births, marriages, and deaths or to keep separate registers by race. For the peninsula, we

---

[158]For a history of the obvenciones, see Cline, pt. 2, pp. 603–609. For the problems in using them as a basis for estimate and information on the totals of persons registered for obvenciones and head tax, see Regil and Peón, pp. 287–291. See also González Navarro, pp. 25–28, 45–49, 63 *et seq.*

do not know when the village priests ceased to record information on race or to keep separate books.[159] The registers for the collection of obvenciones and those for head tax do give a gross division between Indians and non-Indians. That is paralleled by a question on race in the Mexican national census of 1921, the answers to which are probably of dubious reliability. In later censuses, attempts at ascertaining race have used indications of poverty and so measure the latter.

We have assembled the most important reports on population for the years 1813–1970 and have simply listed the stated numbers of inhabitants in Table 1.16. We also depict the data graphically in Figure 1.2, which covers the entire course of the population in the peninsula from 1549 to 1960.

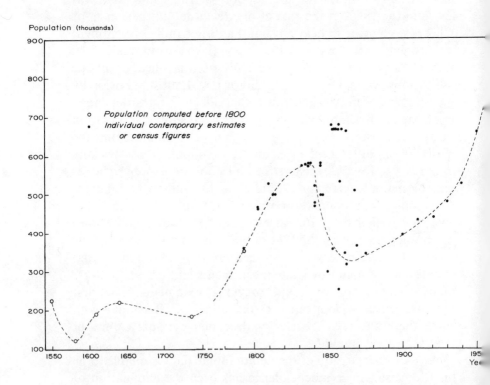

Figure 1.2.   Total population of Yucatan, 1549–1960.

[159]González Navarro, pp. 40–42. The information in González Navarro's discussion on Yucatan is based on an examination of some of the parish registers in Mérida and in Izamal.

Table 1.16

Population of Yucatan, 1789–1970.

A.   1789–1850

Date	Pop. of Peninsula	Sources and Comments
1789	333,382	AGN, Historia, vol. 523, f. 9; Rubio Mañe, *Archivo,* I, 249–250. The basic figure is 364,022 plus 599 clergy. Tabasco had 30,640 persons. We omit clergy since we do not know distributions.
1794	357,000	Our estimate. See text.
1803	465,800	Humboldt, *lib.* III, Chap. VIII (II, 91, 327–328, 335) *N.B.*: Does not include Tabasco.
1810	528,700	Navarro y Noriega, *Memoria,* table. *N.B.*: This estimate includes Tabasco. If Tabasco could be eliminated, the estimate would be close to Humboldt's.
1813–1814	500,000	Echánove, reporting estimates for assigning representation in the Spanish Cortes.
1832	574,496	Baqueiro, p. 81.
1835	578,939	J.M. Regil and A.M. Peón, "Estadistica," *SMGEB,* 1ª ép., III (1852), 287, citing *Tabla estadistica* of Hernández; Stephens, I, 272.
1837	574,496	Regil and Peón p. 287, citing departmental junta charged with making recommendations on setting boundaries of internal divisions.
	582,173	Cline, pt. 2, pp. 92, 686, citing *División territorial,* 24 May 1837, in Alonso Aznar Pérez, *Colección de leyes, decretos y órdenes o acuerdos de tendencia general del poder legislativo... de Yucatan* (3 vols., Mérida, 1849–1851), I, 260–264.
1838	580,984	R. Durán, "Memoria sobre el censo de la Republica Mexicana," and M. P[ayno?], "Artículo sobre la poblacion de la republica," *SMGEB,* 1ª, ép., IX (1862), 274 and VII, 139 resp., both citing José Gómez de la Cortina.
1841	481,400	Baqueiro, p. 81, citing the *memoria estadística* of the secretary-general of state government for 1841.
	472,876	Stephens, I, 273, citing a count made by order of the state government on 8 April 1841.
	525,000	Stephens, I, 273, result of 1841 count adjusted for evasion by P. de R. Cline, pt. 2, p. 92, prefers this value.
	600,000	Stephens, I, 273, result of 1841 count adjusted for evasion by J.B., Jr.
1842	575,361	Regil and Peón, p. 287, their own calculation on the basis of the registers for payment of church tax (obvenciones) for 1842. Non-Indians estimated at 25% of population.

Table 1.16 (cont.)

A.   1789–1850 (*cont.*)

Date	Pop. of Peninsula	Sources and Comments
1845	504,635	Regil and Peón, p. 287, citing the estimate that the secretary-general of state government, Joaquín García Rejón, appended to his memoria presented in 1846.
	580,329	Cline, pt. 2, p. 92, personal estimate.
	731,833	Regil and Peón, pp. 290–291, on basis of registers for head tax and church tax for 1845; Regil and Peón considered the estimate far too high.
1846	628,720	Regil and Peón, p. 287, citing the estimate that the secretary-general of state government, Joaquín García Rejón, appended to his memoria presented in 1846. The basis was the registers; all agreed the estimate to be too high.
1850	299,455	Regil and Peón, p. 291 and Table 3, citing the count of 1850 reported by the secretary-general of state government.

B.   Population by district, 1846 and 1850

	Population	
District	1846	1850
Mérida	118,839	91,229
Valladolid	97,468	23,066
Izamal	72,096	67,423
Tekax	134,000	35,505
Campeche	82,232	82,232
Total Yucatan	504,635	299,455

Source: Regil and Peón, p. 291 and Table 3.

C.   1852–1881

	Population			
Date	State of Yucatan	State of Campeche	Peninsula	Sources and Comments
1852			680,948[a]	José M. Garcia, "Ideas," in *SMGEB*, 1 ép., VII (1859), 128, citing Almonte, *Guia*.

Table 1.16 (cont.)

C. 1852–1881 (*cont.*)

	Population			
Date	State of Yucatan	State of Campeche	Peninsula	Sources and Comments
1853			360,855	*Ibid.*, citing *Anales* of Secretaría de Fomento, in turn citing estimate of departmental government.
1854			668,623[a]	*Ibid.*, citing *Anales* of Secretaría de Fomento.
			256,381	Cline, pt. 2, p. 92, citing "Censo de Yucatan en 1854," MS in Echániz Collection, total published under date 1857 by Baqueiro, *Reseña*, p. 108.
1856			668,623[a]	José M. García, p. 128, and Durán, p. 274, both citing table of Lerdo de Tejada.
1857			668,623[a]	Manuel Orozco y Berra, in app. no. 9 to Secretaría de Fomento, *Memoria*, 1853–1857, stating that War of the Castes precluded any information and so he based his estimate on J.M. Regil's information of 1853.
			680,325[a]	José M. García, p. 128, citing García Cubas.
1858		86,453		A. Garcia Cubas, "Materiales," *SMGEB*, 2[a] ép., II (1870), 353, citing Aznar Barbachano; Aznar Barbachano and Carbo, p. 153.
	450,000			M.P[ayno?], p. 145.
			680,948[a]	*Ibid.*, p. 142, citing Jesús Hermosa, *Manual de geografía y estadística de la República Mexicana*, published in Paris.
1861		86,455		Aznar Barbachano and Carbó, app. no. 44.
			350,000	Cline, pt. 2, p. 92, personal estimate.
1862			320,212	*Ibid.*
	248,156			Girerol, p. 81.
		87,895[b]		Durán, p. 266.
			576,647	*Ibid.*, p. 275.
1868	282,934[b]			Girerol, p. 81.

Table 1.16 (cont.)

C. 1852–1881 (*cont.*)

	Population			
Date	State of Yucatan	State of Campeche	Peninsula	Sources and Comments
	422,365			García Cubas, "Materiales," p. 366 : broken down as follows : 282,634 : official information of 1868 ; 139,731 : in rebellion.
1869		80,366[b]		García Cubas, "Materiales," p. 353, citing memoria of governor presented in 1869.
1874		85,799[b]		Salazar and Rosado, Table 4, but see statement pp. 4–5 that it is based on *datos imperfectos,* without a count.
1881	260,629			Baqueiro, p. 81.

D. 1900–1970, Data from Mexican national censuses

	Yucatan	Campeche	Quintana Roo	Peninsula
1900	309,652	86,542	(in Yucatan)	396,194
1910	339,631	86,661	9,109	435,401
1921	358,221	76,419	10,966	445,606
1930	386,096	84,630	10,620	481,346
1940	418,210	90,460	18,752	527,422
1950	516,899	122,098	26,967	665,964
1960	614,049	168,219	50,169	832,437
1970[c]	840,000	247,000	84,000	1,171,000

[a] These are fundamentally the same estimate. The figure of 668,623 probably omits the Island of Carmen, then separated from both Campeche and Yucatan. The estimate by Jesús Hermosa, listed by M.P[ayno?], assigns the island a population of 12,325, the estimate of the Secretaria de Fomento of 1857, gives it a population of 11,807, or a total population for the peninsula of 680,430. See M.P[ayno?], "Articulo," *SMGEB,* 1ª ép., VII (1859), 143.
[b] The figures for Campeche and Yucatan have been combined for 1862, 1968–1869, and 1874–1881 to get points on figure 1.2.
[c] Calculations of the Direction General de Estadistica, in González Navarro, p. 172.

During the period following independence from Spain, only one technical problem of significance emerges. This pertains to the great upheaval of the mid-nineteenth century known as the War of the Castes. It will be observed that from

1789 to 1838 a series of counts and estimates indicates that the population moved upward in a consistent manner from approximately 357,000 to 580,000. According to Figure 1.2, this rise began at some time near 1750 and continued without any perceptible interruption until approximately 1840. The War of Independence had virtually no demographic impact in Yucatan. Immediately after 1840 a profound disturbance occurred, associated in part with the War of the Castes. However, from the data at hand it appears that the break may really have come somewhat earlier, for the values shown in Table 1.16 for the years 1841 to 1846 indicate that the rise may already have begun to level off.

From 1846 to 1862 we note two widely disparate sets of estimates. One runs between 628,000 and 680,000. The other is erratic but centers around 300,000. Cline, who has studied this period in great detail, believes, and we agree, that the second set of values more closely reflects the facts. First, a population above 650,000 by 1850 is inherently improbable. Second, it is likely that those who published such values were simply extrapolating the previous rate of growth without reference to the actual situation. Third, it is undoubtedly true that the War of the Castes had a highly adverse effect upon the population. This effect was exerted in various ways: (1) An unknown number of persons were killed or died of starvation in what was a bloody social war. (2) An unknown number of persons emigrated to other parts of Mexico or to foreign countries. (3) A large number of persons merely moved into the relatively unoccupied territory to the south, east, and west and remained there either permanently or until they could come back. An area of close to 70,000 square kilometers became independent of state or national authority and filled up with a substantial population, some of it organized in independent native states.[160] Even with the occupation of Chan Santa Cruz by Mexican federal troops at the turn of the century, a relatively substantial population has continued to live in the interior although its number is dwindling and it is slowly coming under state and federal authority.[161]

We have no reliable information on the number of persons who fled to the interior. García Cubas, in his estimate for 1868, gave the state of Yucatan a population of 422,365

[160]Baqueiro, *Reseña*, 13. See Cline, *passim*, with his discussion of independent populations and areas outside of state and federal control.
[161]Cline, pt. 1, pp. 9–12, 41–43.

inhabitants. Of that number 282,634 lived in the area under control of state authorities and were counted in the attempt at a state census in that year, and 139,731 persons were living "sustraidos de la obedience del gobierno," that is, in a state of rebellion. Since the Mexican authorities had no means of counting fugitives and rebels, the statement by García Cubas must be regarded as a mere guess. Nevertheless, attempts at an estimate of the numbers of Maya living in the independent states and in other parts of the interior suggest that their number in the 1860s may have been around 100,000.[162] In 1868–1869, the combined populations of the states of Yucatan and Campeche in the area under control of the state authorities was approximately 363,000. Of the 580,000-odd persons in the peninsula in 1838, perhaps 120,000 had died or emigrated; perhaps as many as 100,000 still survived in the interior, and 363,000 lived in Mexican polity. The latter group has to be regarded, demographically, as constituting the population of Yucatan.

Not much comment is necessary on the remainder of the data. Recovery began in the 1870s and was well under way by the time of the census of 1900. Although the bulk of the increase has been by excess of births over deaths, some of it has come about through the extension of federal control into the interior, a process that still continues. Since 1900 the increase of the population in Yucatan in general has paralleled that of Mexico as a whole save that in Yucatan the effect of the Revolution of 1910–1917 was relatively slight. A preliminary calculation of 1970 indicates that the population in that year was nearly 1,200,000.

On the whole, we are dealing with some very interesting long-term fluctuations which probably transcend purely local events and which have ecological as well as demographic significance. Let us recall that prior to 1810 there were two distinct populations, the Indian and the non-Indian, the latter comprising immigrant Europeans, Negroes, and some admixture of Indian. In 1810 the non-Indians formed from 25 to 30 percent of the population. According to the data reported by Regil and Peón for 1845 from the registers for collection of obvenciones and the head tax, the non-Indians then formed approximately 30 percent of the population. In the later nineteenth century,

---

[162]*Ibid.*, pt. 1, pp. 13–15. According to Cline, Behrendt in 1867 estimated the population of the three independent Maya states at about 80,000. To this number would have to be added an estimate for peasants living in small settlements without affiliation to these states.

there has been Chinese, Japanese, and Korean immigration into the peninsula to add some thousands to the non-Indian group,[163] but essentially both Indians and non-Indians have risen in number through natural increase. According to the census of 1921, Indians by then were only 43 percent of total population of the three federal entities in the peninsula and the non-Indians formed 57 percent of the total population.[164] Obviously there has been substantial Hispanization as well as differential rates of natural increase.

Beginning at zero level at the time of the Conquest, the non-Indian component in the population underwent a steady, consistent increase, which was probably logarithmic in form, to the end of the colonial period. Meanwhile, the native population, which was declining even before the Conquest, underwent an extremely sharp reduction during the Conquest and the decline continued as late as 1600. There was then recovery and rise until about 1645; after that date a severe, prolonged collapse took place again. Equilibrium was not restored until perhaps 1740 but was then followed by a rapid increase, which was expressed in the total population and continued until approximately 1840. At that point another dramatic collapse brought the population to approximately half its previous value. Recovery did not begin for a generation, but during the past hundred years the increase has been enormous.

XII. DENSITY AND DISTRIBUTION

Thus far we have followed changes in total number. We can learn much about the population of the Yucatan peninsula by studying its distribution and density during the four centuries since the Spanish Conquest. This aspect of the demography of the region is of particular interest in view of the extensive discussions in archaeological literature on the political and economic history of Mayan civilization and on the amount of production and size of population that might account for its spectacular building of monuments. Accordingly, much has been written on population density and the carrying capacity of the land for periods when the number of inhabitants must have exceeded anything that has been seen in the peninsula

[163]González Navarro, pp. 211–214.
[164]González Navarro, p. 292, Table 13, based on the *resumen general* of the census of 1921, p. 62.

since the fifteenth century to the present day.

Our data on population density and distribution are most effectively summarized at four rather widely separated dates : 1600, 1794–1795, 1910, and 1960. The first date coincides with the full establishment of the Spanish regime in both political and religious aspects. We have civil as well as ecclesiastical documents which set forth the numbers of persons; the documents have already been used to give the totals arrived at and have been discussed previously in this essay.

It is possible to formulate estimates of the population at the middle of the sixteenth century, but these rely upon broad ratios and upon tribute lists for the colony as a whole. It is very difficult to achieve adequate segregation of local areas so as to make internal comparisons. To date the best effort to lay out the organization of local areas in the setting of native provinces or states is that by Ralph L. Roys in *The Political Geography of the Yucatan Maya,* 1957, a truly notable work that has been of great help to students ever since. Nevertheless, many of the villages described by Roys and even placed upon his maps were founded by the Spaniards long after 1550. Conversely, many towns mentioned by Roys as of pre-Conquest origin are not located on his maps. Our own examination has convinced us that it is not feasible, with the information available, to associate measured areas with population for more than a fraction of the peninsula. We prefer therefore to examine the population in 1550 and prior thereto in other terms, as we have already done earlier in this essay.

Subsequent to 1600, the next date for which we have a reasonably complete statement of both population and the area which contained it is 1794–1795. Thereafter it is necessary to jump to the twentieth century. During the nineteenth century, there were indeed several counts, but the period 1840–1870 was so disturbed by civil war that none of them is entirely suitable. From 1870 to 1895 attempts at counts were made, but the methods used were such that they are perhaps better called estimates. In 1895 the Mexican federal government took the first national census, including within it the peninsula. Since then it has taken decennial censuses. The census of 1895 was admittedly a trial run and faulty. That of 1910 is the most complete in local coverage of those taken prior to the Mexican Revolution. It has the additional advantage that it is the first that records Quintana Roo as a separate federal entity. Accordingly, we use the data of the census of 1910. Our final selection is the census of 1960, the latest for which there has been full publication of local data.

The general boundary of the peninsula for our purposes is relatively (one might almost say remarkably) stable : the three present-day federal entities of Yucatan, Campeche, and Quintana Roo, or their historical counterparts. Beyond their periphery we do not go, yet within the broad region they encompass, we may make inter-entity comparisons of considerable importance.

It will be desirable to describe our procedure in temporal sequence, together with the results obtained. Let us consider the data from approximately 1600. For examining the population at that date we have used the donativo list of 1599, the tribute list of 1606, and the ecclesiastical reports of 1609 in Vázquez de Espinosa. The populations are given in Tables 1.5, 1.6, 1.10, 1.13, and 1.14, to which reference may be made for details. The local territorial unit is the convent and the territory under its religious administration, technically a single parish or doctrina. No other choice is possible, for the encomiendas are nowhere defined as to boundary and frequently include towns widely separated spatially. Even the territories of the convents underwent constant modification, usually in the form of division into smaller territories and the building of new convents as needed. We therefore adhere to the organization which was in force in 1582 and is completely set forth in the memoria of that year.

Our first step was to plot the towns on an outline map, copied with scale 1 : 500,000 from the appropriate sheets of the official Mexican sectional map of the country, edition of 1958. The results are on our Map 1. The towns are represented by dots, the larger ones for the convent towns or the parish cabeceras, the smaller ones for other towns in the parish or the *sujetos de doctrina*. Most of the places, which also appear on the tribute list of 1606 and which, therefore, were held in encomienda, are shown by solid dots. Other places, which were not held in encomienda by private persons, are shown as circles.

By 1582 the policy of *congregación,* that is, of concentrating populations in larger settlements and moving towns to what the Spanish regarded as more convenient locations, had been carried out extensively and, indeed, was almost completed. In the Memoria of 1582, towns which had been moved near to

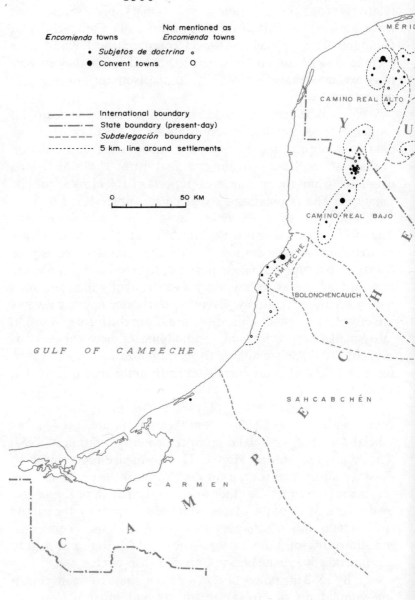

1600

Not mentioned as
Encomienda towns   *Encomienda* towns

• *Subjetos de doctrina*   ◦
● Convent towns   ○

— ·· — ·· — International boundary
— · — · — State boundary (present-day)
— — — — *Subdelegación* boundary
·········· 5 km. line around settlements

0   50 KM

MÉRID

CAMINO REAL ALTO

Y   U

CAMINO REAL BAJO

CAMPECHE

BOLONCHENCAUICH

C H E

GULF OF CAMPECHE

SAHCABCHÉN

P

E

C A R M E N

M

A

C

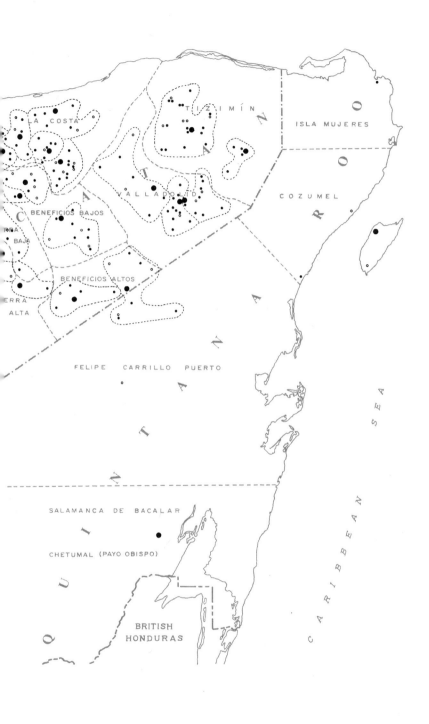

LA COSTA

TIZIMÍN

BENEFICIOS BAJOS

VALLADOLID

ISLA MUJERES

COZUMEL

BENEFICIOS ALTOS

ERRA
ALTA

BAJA

FELIPE CARRILLO PUERTO

SALAMANCA DE BACALAR

CHETUMAL (PAYO OBISPO)

BRITISH
HONDURAS

CARIBBEAN   SEA

or consolidated with another town are indicated as being *en el mismo asiento* (in the same place) as the recipient town. Since the distances were usually not very great and since we do not know the original location, we have placed the congregated towns next to or in contact with the central point representing the cabecera. The effect is to produce a group of clusters which may appear somewhat artificial but which actually do represent conditions as they existed at the time.

The next problem concerns areas, and here we are obliged to use a certain amount of intuition. If in 1600 the territories assigned to the convents possessed recognized measured boundaries beyond the assignment of towns to the jurisdiction of each convent, we have no record of such boundaries. As a substitute, we resort to a purely *ad hoc* approach. We establish an arbitrary limit or periphery around the group of towns in the jurisdiction of any convent. The limit is five kilometers, roughly one league, or about one hour's walking time. It represents the short-range, close-to-home operating radius of primitive farmers who live in small settlements. There is by no means the implication that the people never passed beyond this line in the course of their daily business but simply that most frequently they stayed within it. In those instances in which two or more convents lay too near each other for us to draw a five-kilometer peripheral limit, we have drawn the lines at approximately the half-way mark between the convents. As a final step, the territory of each convent as we delimited it was measured on the 1:500,000 map with a compensating polar planimeter and converted to square kilometers.

The results, including populations and areas expressed to the nearest square kilometer are given in Table 1.17. The

Table 1.17

Population density in restricted convent areas, 1583–1610. Convent areas calculated as based upon operating radii of 5 and 25 kilometers, respectively, with boundaries as indicated in the Memoria of 1582. Convent populations are based upon the Compendio (1609) of Vázquez de Espinosa, as given in Table 1.14.

Convent, 1582	Pop. 1609	Sq. km., 5–km. radius	Density, no./ sq. km.	Sq. km., 25–km. radius	Density, no./ sq. km.
Mérida	9,489	710	13.38	1,458	6.51
Hunacama	5,010	366	13.70	1,475	3.40

Table 1.17 (cont.)

Convent, 1582	Pop. 1609	Sq. km., 5–km. radius	Density, no./ sq. km.	Sq. km., 25–km. radius	Density, no./ sq. km.
Calkiní	12,859	566	23.14	2,387	5.39
Hecelchakán	4,175	471	8.86	2,798	1.58
Campeche	8,018	540	14.85	2,645	3.03
Conkal	10,184	282	36.05	895	11.38
Tixkokob	4,676	242	19.33	274	17.07
Mutul	16,700	452	37.00	677	24.70
Dzidzantún	11,022	871	11.75	2,088	5.28
Tekanto	9,185	376	24.46	376	24.46
Izamal	8,350	613	13.65	951	8.78
Hocabá	6,012	608	9.90	718	8.37
Homún	6,513	424	15.35	532	12.25
Sotuta	6,680	756	8.84	2,274	2.94
Maní	18,370	1,633	11.25	2.500	7.35
Oxcutzcab	4,676	258	18.11	863	5.42
Tekax	6,179	416	14.85	1,322	4.68
Peto	3,006	682	4.41	1,959	1.53
Ichmul	4,676	1,359	3.44	4,741	0.98
Valladolid	5,010	634	7.92	1,806	2.78
Sisal	13,026	589	22.13	1,324	9.84
Tinum	3,006	1,322	2.27	3,112	0.97
Tizimín	7,014	1,534	4.57	3,983	1.76
Chancenote [a]	5,010				
Cozumel [a]	1,336				
Bacalar [a]	1,002				
Total	197,697	15,704		41,158	
ave. density			12.59		4.80
Mean of convent densities			14.75		7.41
S.D.			9.17		6.77
S.E.			1.91		1.41

[a] The densities for the last three convent areas have not been estimated because there is no sound basis for the establishment of territorial limits. The convent of Chancenote administered a nucleus of towns some 50 kilometers northeast of Valladolid, but also had jurisdiction over Ecab, Conil, and Cachi, 15–20 leagues away on the coast of the province of Ecab. We cannot make adjustment for these places because we do not know their populations.
The convent of Cozumel held possession of the island plus the two villages of Pole and Tzama on the mainland. That of Bacalar had jurisdiction of the villa at Salamanca together with twenty-three places scattered at a distance of from 2 to 40 leagues "por mar y tierra y esteros." Clearly, no limits of 5 or 25 kilometers can be drawn for these convents.
[b] The total population, 197,697, *omits* the three convents mentioned above. Nevertheless, it still differs by approximately 1 percent from the total given for the Compendio of 1609 in Part VII. The discrepancy is due first to the fact that the previous total was for Indians only, whereas the convent area populations given in Table 1.14 are derived from Table 1.14, which, in turn, shows the values for all persons mentioned by the 1609 document. Second, the total given in Part VIII (195,724) was from the totals stated by Vázquez de Espinosa. That used here, (197,697) was obtained by calculating the population of each convent area separately. The two sets of figures are not identical and cannot be made so, but the difference is trivial.

corresponding densities are also given as persons per square kilometer.

A second arbitrary limit to the influence of the convent has been set at twenty-five kilometers. This distance coincides approximately with a full day's walk, or a moderate day's horseback ride. It is also equivalent to the maximum extent of practical administrative control and of ordinary economic and social activity in the Yucatan of 1600. To penetrate beyond this range into an uninhabited region, or into an area not under immediate Spanish supervision, would have required an expedition of military or missionary character. In order to avoid a confusion of lines, we have drawn the twenty-five-kilometer limits on our working maps only for the purpose of measuring areas, and do not show them on Map 1. It is understood that where the spheres of influence of two or more convents impinge upon each other, the intervening territory is allocated as nearly equally as possible to the convents concerned. The calculated population densities are included in Table 1.17.

For the 23 convents used, the average density upon assigning the total population within the five-kilometer limit is 12.59 persons per square kilometer, and upon assigning the total population within the twenty-five-kilometer limit is 4.80 persons per square kilometer. If for each limit the 23 individual convent values are averaged, the respective densities are 14.75 and 7.41 per square kilometer. The discrepancies between the two methods are due to differential weighting of territorially large and small convent jurisdictions. For the two sets of averages the standard deviations are ± 9.17 and ± 6.77, and the standard errors of the means are ± 1.91 and ± 1.41. The degree of dispersion is therefore considerable although the means may be taken as reasonably close approximations.

With the data available for 1600 the use of most larger units is not practicable. The parish populations of 1794–1795 and those of the municipios of the twentieth century fit very well into the scheme of the civil districts, or partidos, as they existed at the end of the colonial periods. Moreover, the latter entities delimit quite well variations of an environmental character. Nevertheless, although their boundaries have been shown on Map 1, they are not particularly well adapted to the analysis of convent areas, primarily because many of the convent jurisdictions overlapped the borders of the later partidos. So many such instances are involved that a satisfactory reconciliation of areas and populations becomes hopeless. Accordingly, we have abandoned the attempt. On the other hand, it is quite possible to establish large-scale distinctions in accordance with the boundaries of the present-day Mexican federal entities.

To this end the figures in Table 1.17 have been adjusted by counting all of Calkiní in Campeche, all of Chancenote in Quintana Roo, and all of Ichmul in Yucatan. Then, if we use for the present purposes, the areas given for the three federal entities in the Mexican census of 1960 (cited in the opening pages of this essay), we get these densities as of 1600 in persons per square kilometer :

Campeche	0.45
Yucatan	3.49
Quintana Roo	0.17

The highest density is in Yucatan, with almost no people recorded for Quintana Roo and those in Campeche confined to the northwestern coastal strip. This distribution is confirmed immediately by a glance at Map 1.

It must be remembered that this apparent concentration of inhabitants in the northern and northeastern extremity of the peninsula at the end of the sixteenth century reflects to some extent the fact that the Spaniards had accurate knowledge only of their own zone of occupation. Interior Campeche and most of Quintana Roo were only lightly held and probably contained a thin settlement of unconverted and unreduced natives who had escaped the net of the Conquest or had fled from it and hence were not recorded by either priests or royal fiscal agents. Furthermore, we know that the east coast had been thickly inhabited at or before the year 1500 and by 1600 had become almost completely depopulated. Thus the low densities and the peculiar distribution observed for *ca.* 1600 may represent in part a condition generated by the Conquest itself.

A further step will narrow the analysis to contrasting regions within the single state of Yucatan. Even superficial observation of the maps, from those of Roys to the present-day series issued by the Mexican federal government, gives the impression that the western portion of the state has been more densely settled than the eastern portion. For 1600 we can calculate the number of persons within the five-kilometer limits of fourteen western convents and of six eastern convents, all of which lie wholly or partially within the present state of

Yucatan. The eastern group consists of Peto, Ichmul, Valladolid, Sisal, Tinum, and Tizimín. The western group includes all other convents except Calkiní, Hecelchakán, and Campeche. The western group had a population of 123,046 in an area of 8,007 square kilometers; the eastern, a population of 35,738 in 6,120 square kilometers. The corresponding densities were 15.36 and 5.85 persons per square kilometer. If individual convent densities are used, the means are 17.70 and 7.46, respectively. The value of t for these means is 2.45, at the 2 percent level of probability. Hence, there appears a reasonable likelihood that the western portion of the present state of Yucatan was more densely populated than the eastern. If so, the question is pertinent whether this condition was referable to intrinsic environmental factors or to the historical effect of previous events.

By 1794 the large territories administered by the convents had been divided into smaller parishes, many more under secular control, and a new district organization into partidos had been instituted, the parishes serving as divisions within the partidos. The census of 1794–1795, in the version published by Rubio Mañé, lists seventy-five parishes and fourteen partidos. For our analysis we retain each parish total as given in the report but modify the arrangements in certain minor respects:

(1) We have separated the parishes in Sierra Baja from those in Sierra Alta; that is, we have divided what was then one partido.

(2) We have treated the three parishes in the partido of Carmen and the two in the partido of Bacalar as isolated pueblos for the purpose of drawing five and twenty-five-kilometer limits.

(3) In order to segregate the city of Campeche, we have to divide the parish of Poxyaxcum and have added 166.1 square kilometers with 2,662 inhabitants to the casco of Campeche. The balance of the parish of Pocyaxcum (1,632 persons and 112.9 square kilometers) is retained, with the parish of Pich, in the partido of Bolonchencauich.

(4) The parishes of Ichmul, Sacalaca, and Tihosuco extend in part into, and that of Chunhuhub lies entirely within, the territory of Quintana Roo. Hence, modifications have to be made in the boundary of the partido of Beneficios Altos; we shall discuss them subsequently.

Map 2 shows the parishes and partidos of 1794–1795,

including the adjustments we have outlined. The parish cabeceras are shown as larger, and the sujetos de doctrina or other towns within the parishes as smaller circles. Towns still in encomienda according to the list of 1786 are shown as solid dots; towns not on the list are shown as open circles. In order to conform to the system employed with the data of 1600, the approximate five-kilometer limit of each parish is drawn on the map. The data for densities are given in Table 1.18.

Drawing a twenty-five-kilometer limit for each parish is not appropriate because of the number of parishes and their closeness to each other in 1794–1795. As an alternative we have carried a line across the peninsula approximately twenty-five-kilometers distant from the constellation of parishes as a whole (the dotted line on Map 2). Thus the region of local Spanish administrative control can be separated from the essentially abandoned area to the south and east. In the demarkation of this territory, it is, of course, necessary to ignore the settlements at Palizada and Bacalar. The total area under effective Spanish administration, according to direct planimeter measurement was 67,490 square kilometers, and the average density of the zone covered by the census, excluding Palizada and Bacalar, was 5.26 persons per square kilometer.

We may compare the densities for 1600 and 1794–1795. When we use total populations, the average densities within the five-kilometer limit are 12.59 and 17.53, respectively (see Table 1.17 and 1.18). With the means of the convents and of the parishes, the values are 14.75 and 21.48, respectively. If the three cities are omitted from the totals for 1794–1795, the mean density is 19.68 persons per square kilometer. These figures suggest that there was some increase in the density of local populations from 1600 to 1794–1795. However, the variability was very great, and t for the two means 14.75 and 19.68 is 1.55, a value of little or no significance.

The areas embraced by the twenty-five-kilometer limits may be compared at the two dates with respect to total population only, for no means density can be calculated for the parishes of 1794–1795. According to Table 1.17, in 1609 there were 197,697 persons on 41,158 square kilometers, a density of 4.80 persons per square kilometer. In 1794–1795 the corresponding density was 5.26 persons. Here, also, the difference is negligible.

At this point, we may extend the comparison between

1794

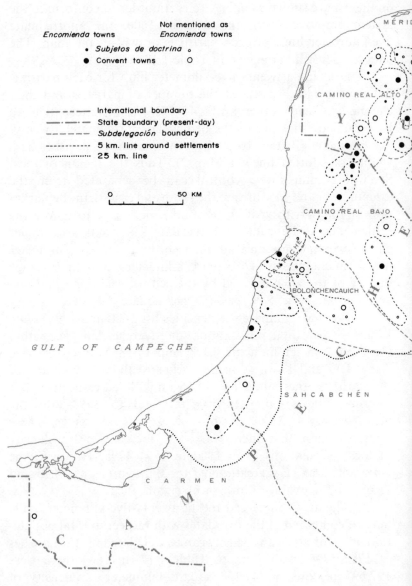

Encomienda towns | Not mentioned as Encomienda towns
- Subjetos de doctrina ∘
● Convent towns ○

————·——— International boundary
————·——— State boundary (present-day)
————————— Subdelegación boundary
------------ 5 km. line around settlements
··············· 25 km. line

0 |——|——|——|——|——| 50 KM

MÉRID

CAMINO REAL ALTO

Y

CAMINO REAL BAJO

E

BOLONCHENCAUICH

H

C

GULF OF CAMPECHE

SAHCABCHÉN

E

P

C

M

CARMEN

A

C

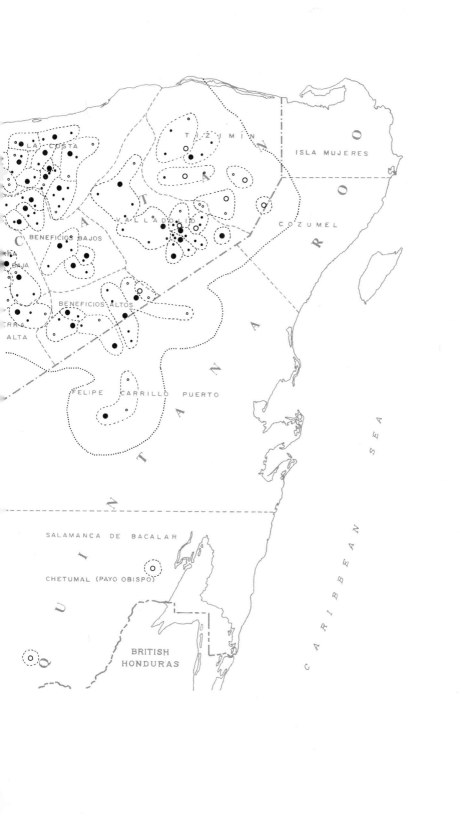

LA COSTA

T I Z I M I N

ISLA MUJERES

C O Z U M E L

V A L L A D O L I D

BENEFICIOS BAJOS

BENEFICIOS ALTOS

RRA
ALTA

FELIPE CARRILLO PUERTO

SALAMANCA DE BACALAR

CHETUMAL (PAYO OBISPO)

BRITISH
HONDURAS

CARIBBEAN SEA

Table 1.18

Population density in restricted parish areas, 1794. Density, in persons per square kilometer is for each parish area within a five-kilometer operating radius. Parishes and pueblos are arranged according to partido. See text for discussion.

Partido and Parish	Area, sq. km.	Total Pop.	Density, Persons per sq. km.
Carmen			
Casco del Presidio	78.6	1,627	16.35
Sabancuy (single pueblo)	78.6	548	6.97
Palizada (single pueblo)	78.6	1,107	14.10
Sahcabchén			
Sahcabchén ⎫ Chicbul ⎬	633.7	1,371	2.17
Champotón	80.6	1,239	15.50
Seiba Playa	535.4	3,995	7.46
Campeche			
Casco de la Ciudad	262.8	16,940	64.45
Pocyaxcum (in part)	166.1	2,662	16.10
Bolonchencauich			
Pocyaxcum (in part)	112.9	1,632	14.45
Pich	645.0	2,913	4.52
Camino Real Alto			
Bolonchén	166.1	4,071	24.50
Hopelchén	741.8	4,300	5.80
Hecelchakán	488.6	5,558	11.38
Calkiní	108.0	5,175	47.80
Becal	233.8	4,579	19.46
Camino Real Bajo			
Halalcho	120.9	2,938	24.30
Maxcanú	145.1	5,405	37.25
Kopoma	403.1	5,668	14.07
Umán	333.8	4,833	17.46
Hunacama	235.4	5,970	25.35
Mérida			
Caso de Mérida ⎫ San Cristóbal ⎬ Santiago ⎭	338.6	28,528	84.50
La Costa			
Conkal	282.2	6,037	21.37
Mococha	122.6	2,648	21.59
Tixkokob	158.0	2,979	18.85
Nolo	88.7	2,536	28.60
Telchac	211.2	2,870	13.59

Table 1.18 (cont.)

Partido and Parish	Area, sq. km.	Total Pop.	Density, Persons per sq. km.
Motul	209.6	4,815	23.00
Dzidzantún	306.4	2,905	9.48
Cacalchén	161.3	1,785	11.07
Cansahcab	156.4	1,733	11.10
Teya	48.4	884	18.25
Tekanto	185.4	2,483	15.35
Temax	503.1	4,607	9.16
Izamal	406.4	5,948	14.65
Beneficios Bajos			
Hoctún	311.2	4,118	13.21
Hocabá	220.9	3,160	14.31
Homún	153.2	2,228	14.55
Sotuta	676.3	4,527	6.69
Tixcacaltuyu	203.2	6,678	32.82
Yaxcobá	125.8	4,965	39.50
Sierra Baja			
Abala	120.9	4,908	40.60
Muna	129.0	5,418	41.98
Saculum	104.8	5,379	51.30
Acanceh	161.3	5,066	31.45
Tecoh	254.8	6,199	24.34
Mama	133.8	9,218	68.90
Teabo	414.4	8,621	20.98
Sierra Alta			
Ticul	306.4	16,583	54.10
Maní	238.7	10,954	45.85
Oxcutzcab	354.8	17,143	49.70
Tekax	395.1	16,970	42.95
Beneficios Altos			
Tahdziú	112.9	3,646	32.30
Peto	295.1	3,961	13.42
Sacalaca	504.7	2,373	4.71
Ichmul	574.1	10.988	19.12
Tihosuco	540.2	4,723	8.74
Chikindzonot	145.1	2,401	16.55
Chunhuhub	512.8	2,432	4.74
Valladolid			
Santa Ana (villa)	169.3	7,990	47.25
Cenotillo	859.5	3,175	3.70
Uayma	709.5	2,907	4.10
Sisal	185.4	1,779	9.60
Chichimila	153.2	2,568	15.77
Tixcacalcupul	153.2	1,302	8.50
Tecuch	150.0	577	3.85
Chemax	112.9	2,498	22.15

Table 1.18 (cont.)

Partido and Parish	Area, sq. km.	Total Pop.	Density, Persons per sq. km.
Tizimín			
Tizimín	254.8	2,255	8.85
Kikil	609.5	2,647	4.34
Calotmul	382.2	5,308	13.88
Chancenote	185.4	1,957	10.56
Nabalam	432.2	1,729	4.00
Xcambolon	112.9	2,442	21.63
Salamanca de Bacalar			
Casco de la villa	78.6	1,267	15.61
Chichanha	78.6	994	12.65
Total	20,443.9	358,284	
Ave. density			17.53
Mean of all parish densities			21.48
Mean of parish densities, minus Campeche, Mérida, and Santa Ana, and consolidating Pocyaxcum			19.68
S.D.			14.30
S.E.			1.71

densities of population at 1600 and 1794–1795 to larger territorial units. We have already suggested that such a comparison is feasible only at the level of the present-day Mexican federal entity, for data by partidos cannot easily be brought to comparability with data by convent jurisdictions. We have had to make some adjustments in order to fit convents and their jurisdictions within the boundaries of the Mexican federal entities. Similarly, some adjustments are necessary to fit the parishes of 1794–1795 into the boundaries of present-day federal entities.

Our most serious problem involves the parishes of Ichmul, Sacalaca, and Tihosuco, all of which cross the boundary of Yucatan into Quintana Roo, and the parish of Chunhuhub, which lay entirely within the present-day federal territory. It is very difficult to divide parish populations and areas. Hence, even at the risk of introducing a not inconsiderable error, we shall consider all the inhabitants of these parishes as having lived within the boundaries of the present state of Yucatan. In a similar manner we allocate the entire parish of Chancenote to the state of Yucatan.

For the comparison, we use the areas of the federal entities as given in the census of 1960. Our results are as follows :

Entity	Area sq.km.	Pop. 1794–1795	Density 1794–1795	Density 1600
Campeche	56,114	57,717	1.03	0.45
Yucatan	43,379	298,306	6.88	3.49
Quintana Roo	42,030	2,261	0.17	0.17

Although there was little change in local rural density, the gross density of Campeche and Yucatan increased substantially. That of Quintana Roo, extremely low in any event, remained constant or perhaps fell. Such a finding is in conformity with the rise in total population, which we have estimated as from approximately 195,000 to 360,000, or almost double. If the religious jurisdictions of the convents and their successors, the smaller doctrinas and secular parishes of 1794–1795, underwent no appreciable alteration in density within the ordinary, daily operating radius, then the increase can have come from only two sources : (1) the growth of cities, particularly Campeche and Mérida, and (2) the filling up of peripheral territory along the coasts, in interior Campeche, and on the Yucatan-Quintana Roo border.

Our examination of the data from *ca.* 1600 indicated a probable difference in population density between the western and eastern portions of the state of Yucatan when short range (five-kilometer) limits are considered. Let us see if this distinction persisted until 1794–1795. From Table 1.18 we derive the densities based upon totals as well as upon means of parishes. The western portion of the state includes thirty-five parishes which coincide geographically with the convents and their jurisdictions previously allocated to this fraction of the state, Mérida omitted. The eastern portion embraces twenty parishes, Valladolid omitted, and among them we place the four which wholly or in part extend into Quintana Roo. For the western and eastern portions, the densities are respectively, on totals, 23.32 and 8.82; on means, 26.50 and 8.83. The value of t for the means is 4.07, highly significant. There can be little doubt, therefore, that in 1794–1795 the two portions of the state still differed in average local density.

For the period since 1794–1795, it is necessary to dispense entirely with both the convent and encomienda listings. In their place, we may use the parish organization of 1794–1795

and the twentieth century system of civil division into municipios; in Quintana Roo, *delegaciones*. During the nineteenth
century there were no comprehensive and reliable counts which
could supply the requisite detail.[165] For the larger units, apart
from the three contemporary Mexican federal entities, we must
utilize the partidos which formed the basis of the 1794–1795
count and which persisted in modified form until the Mexican
Constitution of 1917 forbade administrative units intermediate
between the municipios and the states or federal territories.
Calculations based upon the partidos may be carried out
even to the present day by combining either the parishes of
1794–1795 or the municipios of recent years in groups which
follow quite closely the lines of the late colonial division into
districts. Thus, through the medium of the partidos, populations
of parishes in 1794–1795 may be compared with those of the
municipios of the present century. For the latter we use two
key dates, 1910, the best census of the Díaz regime, and the
most recent census available in detail, that of 1960.

The boundaries of the late colonial partidos, as determined from the 1794–1795 census, have been duplicated on all
maps (Maps 1–4). In order to correlate parishes and municipios
at various dates, we have formulated a concordance in Table
1.19, in which the corresponding local entities are assigned to

Table 1.19

Concordance of partidos, or their equivalents, parishes, and municipios
from 1794 to the present. Areas are also shown for partidos, as measured by
planimeter on a 1 : 500,000 map.

Partido, or Equivalent, with Area (sq. km.)	Includes Parishes in 1794	Includes Munici- pios in 1910	Includes Munici- pios in 1960
Carmen (19,900)	Presidio Sabancuy Palizada	Carmen Sabancuy Palizada	Carmen Palizada
Sahcabchén (19,100)	Sahcabchén Chicbul Champotón Seiba Playa	Champotón Seiba Playa Chan Laguna	Champotón
Campeche (693)	Casco of Campeche Pocyaxcum (in part)	Campeche China Lerma	Campeche (in part)

[165]González Navarro (Table 2, p. 172) has calculated average densities per
square kilometer for Campeche and Yucatan, the latter state including Quintana Roo for the middle years of the nineteenth century on the basis of estimates of the period.

Table 1.19 (cont.)

Partido, or Equivalent, with Area (sq. km.)	*Includes Parishes in 1794*	*Includes Municipios in 1910*	*Includes Municipios in 1960*
Bolonchencauich (3,447)	Pocyaxcum (in part)	Bolonchenticul	Campeche (in part)
	Pich	Pich	
		Tixmucuy	
		Xhanha	
		Dzitbalche	
Camino Real Alto (8,590)	Bolonchén	Hopelchén	Calkiní
	Hopelchén	Hecelchakán	Hopelchén
	Hecelchakán	Becal	Hecelchakán
	Calkiní	Calkiní	Tenabo
	Becal	Dzitbalchén	
		Numkiní	
		Pomuch	
		Tenabo	
Isla Mujeres (4,218) (census, 1960)	None	Isla Mujeres Holbox	Isla Mujeres
Cozumel (7,808) (census, 1960)	None	Cozumel	Cozumel
Felipe Carrillo Puerto Entire: (15,919) (census, 1960)	None	Santa Cruz Bravo	Felipe Carrillo Puerto
In part: 6,380, after excluding portion assigned to Beneficios Altos, B. (q.v.)	None	Santa Cruz Bravo (in part)	Felipe Carrillo Puerto (in part)
Chetumal (14,086) (census, 1960)	Casco of Bacalar Chichanha	Payo Obispo Xcalak Icaiki Bacalar	Chetumal
Valladolid (5,580)	Santa Ana	Valladolid	Valladolid
	Cenotillo	Chichimila	Chan Kom
	Uayma	Uayma	Kaua
	Sisal	Tinum	Quintana Roo
	Chichimila	Tixcacalcupul	Tunkas
	Tixcacalcupul	Dzitas	Cenotillo
	Tecuch	Tunkas	Dzitas
	Chemax	Cenotillo	Temoson
			Tinum
			Uayma
			Chichimila

Table 1.19 (cont.)

Partido, or Equivalent, with Area (sq. km.)	*Includes Parishes in 1794*	*Includes Municipios in 1910*	*Includes Municipios in 1960*
			Tekom
			Cuncunul
			Chemax
			Tixcacalcupul (in part) (excludes Ekpetz)
Tizimín (7,530)	Tizimín	Tizimín	Tizimín
	Kikil	Espita	Sucila
	Calotmul	Sucila	Espita
	Chancenote	Calotmul	San Felipe
	Nabalam	Panaba	Río Lagartos
	Xcambolón	Rio Lagartos	Panaba
			Calotmul
Beneficios Altos A. In Yucatan (2,483)	Tahdziú	Peto	Peto
	Peto	Tzucacab	Tzucacab
	Chikindzonot		Chikindzonot
	Ichmul (in part) (excludes Saban, Uaymax, Celul)		Tahdziú
			Tixcacalcupul (in part) (includes Ekpetz)
	Sacalaca (in part) (excludes Sacalaca)		Yaxcabá (in part) (includes Tiholop)
	Tihosuco (in part) (excludes Tepich)		
B. In Yucatan and Quintana Roo (12,022)	Tahdziú	Peto	Peto
	Peto	Tzucacab	Tzucacab
	Chikindzonot	Felipe Carillo Puerto (in part) (that portion west of Long. 88° 0′, and north of Lat. 19° 30′)	Chikindzonot
	Ichmul		Tahdziú
	Sacalaca		Tixcacalcupul (in part) (includes Ekpetz)
	Tihosuco		
	Chunhuhub		Yaxcabá (in part) (includes Tiholop)
			Felipe Carillo puerto (in part) (that portion designated in 1910)

Table 1.19 (cont.)

Partido, or Equivalent, with Area (sq. km.)	*Includes Parishes in 1794*	*Includes Municipios in 1910*	*Includes Municipios in 1960*
Beneficios Bajos (3,129)	Hoctún	Hoctún	Hoctún
	Hocabá	Hocabá	Hocabá
	Homún	Homún	Homún
	Sotuta	Huhi	Huhi
	Tixcacaltuyu	Tahmek	Sanhacat
	Yaxcobá	Xocchel	Seye
		Seye	Sotuta
		Cuzama	Tahmek
		Sotuta	Cuzama
			Cantamcyec
			Xocchel
			Yaxcaba (in part) (excludes Tiholop)
Sierra Baja (2,750)	Abala	Muna	Acanceh
	Muna	Tekit	Timucuy
	Saculum	Saculum	Tecoh
	Acanceh	Mama	Abala
	Tecoh	Acanceh	Muna
	Mama	Tecoh	Saculum
	Teabo	Abala	Mama
		Timucuy	Chumayel
		Chumayel	Tekit
		Teabo	Teabo
			Mayapán
Sierra Alta (4,447)	Ticul	Ticul	Ticul
	Maní	Santa Elena	Santa Elena
	Oxcutzcab	Maní	Maní
	Tekax	Chapab	Chapab
		Tekax	Dzan
		Oxcutzcab	Oxcutzcab
		Tixmeuac	Akil
			Tekax
			Tixmeuac
La Costa (5,858)	Conkal	Izamal	Baca
	Mococha	Tekanto	Bokabá
	Tixkokob	Tepakan	Buctzotz
	Nolo	Kantunil	Cacalchén
	Telchac	Motul	Cansahcab
	Motul	Baca	Conkal
	Dzidzantún	Telchac	Chicxulub
	Cacalchén	Dzemul	Dzidzantún
	Cansahcab	Sinanche	Dzilam Bravo
	Teya	Bocaba	Dzilam González
	Tekanto	Tixkokob	Dzemul

Table 1.19 (cont.)

Partido, or Equivalent, with Area (sq. km.)	Includes Parishes in 1794	Includes Municipios in 1910	Includes Municipios in 1960
	Temax	Conkal	Dzoncauich
	Izamal	Chicxulub	Ixil
		Cacalchén	Izamal
		Mococha	Kantunil
		Yaxkokul	Mococha
		Ixil	Motul
		Temax	Muxupipp
		Cansahcab	Sinanche
		Dzidzantún	Sudzal
		Teya	Suma
		Dzilam Gonzales	Tekal
		Yobain	Tekanto
		Buctzotz	Telchac
			Telchac Puerto
			Temax
			Tepakan
			Teya
			Tixkokob
			Tixpeual
			Yobain
			Yaxkokul
Camino Real Bajo (5,044)	Halacho	Hunacama	Hunacama
	Maxcanú	Umán	Umán
	Kopoma	Kinchil	Kinchil
	Umán	Tetiz	Tetiz
	Hunacama	Maxcanú	Maxcanú
		Halacho	Halacho
		Opichén	Opichén
		Chochola	Chochola
		Celestún	Celestún
			Kopoma
			Samahil
Mérida (1,210)	Casco of Mérida	Mérida	Mérida
	San Cristóbal	Kanasín	Kanasín
	Santiago	Progreso	Progreso
			Ucu

appropriate partidos. The calculated areas, populations, and densities for 1794–1795, 1910, and 1960 are shown in Table 1.20.

The partidos as listed conform to present-day boundaries in that, with one exception, the first five lie wholly in Campeche, the second nine in Yucatan, and the last four in Quintana Roo. The latter group, although included with the partidos, actually follow approximately the lines of the four present-day delegaciones. The exception is the partido of Beneficios Altos,

Table 1.20

Partidos, or equivalents, in 1794, 1910, and 1960; densities are in persons per square kilometer.

Partido, or equivalent, with area (sq. km.)	1794 Pop.	1794 Density	1910 Pop.	1910 Density	1960 Pop.	1960 Density
Carmen (19,900)	2,958	0.15	19,349	0.97	47,133	2.37
Sahcabchen (19,100)	6,605	0.35	11,294	0.59	17,036	0.89
Campeche (693)	19,602[a]	8.30	20,509	29.60	48,827	70.50[b]
Bolonchencauich (3,447)	4,545[c]	1.32	8,717	2.53	5,499	1.59[d]
Camino Real Alto (8,590)	23,653	2.76	27,297	3.18	49,654	5.77
Camino Real Bajo (5,044)	25,814	5.11	44,266	8.77	48,565	9.62
Mérida (1,210)	28,528	23.58	86,395	71.40	213,572	176.40
La Costa (5,858)	42,590	7.27	70,135	11.98	109,507	18.72
Beneficios Bajos (3,129)	25,676	8.21	24,978	7.98	37,790	12.07
Sierra Baja (2,750)	44,819	16.31	30,420	11.06	36,440	13.25
Sierra Alta (4,447)	61,650	13.86	29,349	6.60	45,051	10.13
Beneficios Altos (A. 2,483)	21,778[e]	8.76	7,450	3.00	18,850	7.60
Beneficios Altos (B. 12,022)	30,524[e]	2.54	8,670	0.72	27,879	2.32
Valladolid (5,580)	22,796	4.01	31,879	5.72	59,438	10.66
Tizimin (7,530)	16,338	2.17	15,541	2.06	44,001	5.85
Isla Mujeres (4,218)	100[f]	0.02	2,292	0.56	3,949	0.96
Cozumel (7,808)	100[f]	0.02	1,062	0.20	7,562	1.40
Felipe Carrillo Puerto (A. 15,919)	8,846[g]	0.55	2,447	0.15	19,900	1.25
Felipe Carrillo Puerto (B. 6,380)	100[f,g]	0.01	1,227	0.19	10,871	1.71
Chetumal (14,086)	2,222	0.13	3,313	0.20	18,758	1.12

[a] Estimated population. The figure from the 1794 census includes the Casco of Campeche and the towns of Lerma, China, and Kulam, which were in the parish of Pocyaxcum.

Notes to table 1.20 (cont.)

b Estimated population. The figure from the 1960 census includes the city of Campeche and as many of the suburban towns as can be located on the government maps. Populations for these towns are taken from *VIII Censo General de Poblacion,* 1960, *Localidades de la Republica por Entidades Federativas y Municipios,* I (1963), 52–53.

c Estimated population. The figure includes the partido of Bolonchencauich as given in the census of 1794, excluding the three towns mentioned in note a.

d Estimated population. The figure is that for the municipio of Campeche, after having excluded those suburban towns mentioned in note b.

e Two methods for handling the partido of Beneficios Altos, which overlapped the boundary between two contemporary states. That area which is called Beneficios Altos A is that portion of the partido (2,483 sq. km.) which was within the state of Yucatan (see Table 1.19). Beneficios Altos B is the entire partido (12,022 sq. km.). That portion within Quintana Roo (9,539 sq. km.) is here defined as the land (in the delegación of Felipe Carrillo Puerto) which lay west of long. 88° 0′, and north of lat. 19° 30′.

In 1794 the population of A is the sum of the number of persons reported in the census for the six parishes and parts thereof which are stated in Table 1.19. That of B included all seven parishes, entire.

In 1910 the population of A was that of the municipios of Peto and Tzucacab, in the state of Yucatan. The population of B was that of A plus approximately one-half the population (1,220) reported for the entire district of Payo Obispo in Quintana Roo. This is an estimate but is roughly accurate.

In 1960 the population of A is that of the municipios listed in Table 1.19. The population of B is that of A plus an estimated 9,029 for the delegación of Felipe Carrillo Puerto. This estimate was obtained by locating as many inhabited places as possible on the 1:500,000 map (Chetumal sheet) in the area assigned to Beneficios Altos (see above) and by pro-rating the remainder. Since a great many of the listed places are not to be found on the map, the error is likely to be considerable.

f The areas included in Isla Mujeres, Cozumel, and Felipe Carrillo Puerto (apart from that portion in Beneficios Altos B) are not reported in the census of 1794 as having any inhabitants. However, there must have been a few people scattered here and there. Hence, in order to make some allowance for these, we arbitrarily assign a value of 100 to each area.

g Felipe Carrillo Puerto A is the entire delegación as in 1960, or its equivalent. Felipe Carrillo Puerto B is the remainder after deducting the territory west of long. 88° 0′ and north of lat. 19° 30′, which was allocated to Beneficios Altos.

In 1794, B is assigned the arbitrary population of 100 (see note f). A includes both B and that portion of Beneficios Altos, the inhabitants of which lived in the present state of Quintana Roo. The number of these was 8,746. With B, the total is 8,846.

In 1910 the population of Felipe Carrillo Puerto A is that of the entire district of Payo Obispo as the latter is given by the census. In 1960 it is the entire delegación of Felipe Carrillo Puerto. At both dates the population of Felipe Carrillo Puerto B is the value of A minus the inhabitants of that portion which was included in Beneficios Altos B.

---

for which it was necessary to calculate densities by means of two alternative methods. One was to consider the partido as a territorial unit to be included within Yucatan. The other was to divide the partido and assign an estimated area and population to Yucatan and Quintana Roo. (For details see Table 1.19 and notes e and g to Table 1.20).

In Table 1.21 the data presented in Table 1.20 have been reorganized and consolidated according to the boundaries of the three federal entities and have been combined into totals for the entire peninsula. The densities have also been reformulated on a relative basis with the figures for 1960 taken as 100.0.

In both parts of Table 1.21 all magnitudes are displayed as (1) including and (2) excluding the cities and corresponding partidos of Campeche and Mérida. Table 1.22 segregates for the three given dates the western portion (five partidos) and the eastern portion (three partidos) of the state of Yucatan.

Table 1.21

States, or equivalents, in 1794, 1910, and 1960; densities are in persons per square kilometer; figures are taken from Table 1.20.

State, or equivalent with area (sq. km.)	1794		1910		1960	
	Popula-tion	*Density*	*Popula-tion*	*Density*	*Popula-tion*	*Density*
		Absolute Values				
Including city and partido of Campeche and Mérida						
Campeche (51,730)	57,363	1.11	87,166	1.69	168,149	3.25
Yucatan (47,570) Using Beneficios Altos B	298,735	6.28	341,633	7.18	622,243	13.08
Quintana Roo (32,492) Using Felipe Carrillo Puerto B	2,522	0.08	7,894	0.24	41,140	1.27
Entire Peninsula (131,792)	358,620	2.72	436,693	3.31	831,532	6.31
Excluding city and partido of Campeche and Mérida						
Campeche (51,037)	37,761	0.74	66,657	1.31	119,322	2.34
Yucatan (46,360) Using Beneficios Altos B	270,207	5.84	255,238	5.51	408,671	8.81
Quintana Roo (32,492) Using Felipe Carrillo Puerto B	2,522	0.08	7,894	0.24	41,140	1.27
Entire Peninsula (129,889)	310,490	2.39	329,789	2.54	569,133	4.38

Table 1.21 (cont.)

State, or equivalent, areas as above	1794	1910	1960
	Relative Values[a]		
Including Campeche and Mérida			
Campeche	34.2	52.0	100.0
Yucatan	47.3	54.8	100.0
Quintana Roo	6.3	18.9	100.0
Entire Peninsula	43.1	52.5	100.0
Excluding Campeche and Mérida			
Campeche	31.6	56.0	100.0
Yucatan	66.4	62.6	100.0
Quintana Roo	6.3	18.9	100.0
Entire Peninsula	54.6	58.0	100.0

[a] With 1960 taken as 100.0 in all cases.

The primary finding from the analysis of these tables is that which has been previously suggested. The total population, and the density of the peninsula as a whole, showed a moderate but not sensational increase between 1794–1795 and 1910. The vicissitudes of the intervening century have already been discussed, and we know that after passing a very low minimum in the mid-nineteenth century, the population began a steady rise. By 1910 it appears definitely to have exceeded its numbers of 1794–1795.

The rise continued with intensification during the following fifty years so that the population almost doubled by 1960. However, beneath the overall trend, there may be detected changes of a subordinate but significant character. Some of these may be mentioned.

(1) The increase in population and therefore of density was most marked in Quintana Roo, less so in Campeche, and least in Yucatan.

(2) The relative numbers were heavily weighted by the two cities, Campeche and Mérida, which have undergone extremely rapid growth during the past sixty years. Their effect is clearly evident (see Table 1.21) when they are deleted from the state and regional totals. Nevertheless, after removing the cities, the same relative order of increase is seen among the

Table 1.22

Populations and densities in eight partidos in the state of Yucatan, 1794, 1910, and 1960. The city and partido of Mérida are omitted. Partidos and areas as shown below. The division is between the western and the eastern portion of the state.

Date	Western Portion			Eastern Portion			Eastern Portion		
	Camino Real Bajo La Costa Beneficios Bajos Sierra Baja Sierra Alta			Valladclid Tizimin Beneficios Altos B			Valladolid Tizimin Beneficios Altos A		
	Area, sq.km.	*Population*	*Density*	*Area, sq.km.*	*Population*	*Density*	*Area, sq.km.*	*Population*	*Density*
1794	21,228	200,549	9.45	25,132	69,658	2.77	15,593	60,912	3.91
1910	"	199,148	9.37	"	56,090	2.23	"	54,870	3.52
1960	"	277,353	13.05	"	131,318	5.22	"	122,289	7.85

states : Quintana Roo maximal, Yucatan, minimal, Campeche intermediate.

(3) In the peninsula in 1910 several partidos (Beneficios Bajos, Sierra Baja, Sierra Alta, Beneficios Altos, and Tizimín) contained fewer inhabitants than they did in 1794–1795 although the deficit was more than compensated for by the growth of Mérida, Campeche, and the other western partidos. Thus a redistribution was in progress, with loss in the central portion and gain on the periphery. Between 1910 and 1960 the universal massive expansion of population produced an increase of density in all but one of the partidos. The exception is Bolonchencauich, in the interior of the state of Campeche, for which we have no immediate explanation.

(4) The distinction between the western and the eastern portions of the state of Yucatan, already noted for local densities in 1600 and 1794–1795, persists even to 1960 (see Table 1.22). If the metropolitan area of Mérida is omitted, one can see that the density in the western partido has remained consistently higher than that in the three eastern partidos. The explanation of such a difference, which has lasted for four centuries, must be sought in some inherent feature of the economy and ecology of the two regions.

XIII. SETTLEMENT SIZE

Together with an extension of occupied territory in Yucatan, there has occurred an increase in the average size of the community. We now describe briefly the extent of this process.

Our information concerning number and size of inhabited places is confined almost entirely to the present century. Prior to 1900 there are few data because all counts and estimates were based upon relatively large territorial units such as convent jurisdictions and parishes or encomienda holdings. Even for towns with the status of cabecera, there is no distinction made between the center of the town and the dispersed rural settlements, except a rather crude segregation to be found in the summaries by partido of the 1794–1795 census. This report is discussed subsequently.

For simplicity, we compare Yucatan at only two dates, 1910 and 1960, as we have done in the preceding section. Our sources for the data are the respective volumes for the three federal entities in the *division territorial* parts of the censuses :

Lista de las localidades, 1910 and *Localidades de la república,* 1960. Both list all places reported by the census takers together with the corresponding number of inhabitants. It is possible, therefore, to count and classify settlements according to geographical location, political linkage, and size of population. This we have done and have set forth the principal results in Tables 1.23 and 1.24. Table 1.23, which presents the data from the

Table 1.23

1910–I. Inhabited places according to their size, arranged by present federal entities and late colonial partidos.

A. Number of localities with population indicated				
Area	0–99	100–2,499	2,500 +	*Total no.*
Campeche				
Carmen	13	32	1	46
Sahcabchén	63	32	0	95
Campeche[a]	16	8	1	25
Bolonchencauich	93	29	0	122
Camino Real Alto	88	39	2	129
Total	273	140	4	417
Yucatan				
Camino Real Bajo	110	77	3	190
Mérida	47	60	2	109
Costa	421	145	2	568
Beneficios Bajos	181	53	0	234
Sierra Baja	111	59	1	171
Sierra Alta	145	42	2	189
Beneficios Altos[b]	61	8	1	70
Subtotal	1,076	444	11	1,531
Valladolid	387	54	1	442
Tizimín	161	33	0	194
Subtotal	548	87	1	636
Total	1,624	531	12	2,167
Quintana Roo				
Isla Mujeres	17	7	0	24
Cozumel	9	1	0	10
Felipe Carrillo Puerto	3	1	0	4
Payo Obispo	6	4	0	10
Total	35	13	0	48
GRAND TOTAL	1,932	684	16	2,632

Table 1.23 (cont.)

1910–II. Inhabited places according to their size, arranged by present federal entities and late colonial partidos.

B. Percentage of localities with population indicated

Area	0–99	100–2,499	2,500+	Total no.[a]
Campeche				
Carmen	28.26	69.57	2.17	
Sahcabchén	66.32	33.68	0.00	
Campeche[a]	64.00	32.00	4.00	
Bolonchencauich	76.23	23.77	0.00	
Camino Real Alto	68.22	30.23	1.55	
Total	65.47	33.57	0.96	
Yucatan				
Camino Real Bajo	57.89	40.53	1.58	
Mérida	43.12	55.05	1.83	
Costa	74.12	25.53	0.35	
Beneficios Bajos	77.35	22.65	0.00	
Sierra Baja	64.91	34.51	0.58	
Sierra Alta	76.72	22.22	1.06	
Beneficios Altos[b]	87.14	11.43	1.43	
Subtotal	70.28	29.00	0.72	
Valladolid	87.56	12.21	0.23	
Tizimín	82.99	17.01	0.00	
Subtotal	86.16	13.68	0.16	
Total	74.94	24.51	0.55	
Quintana Roo				
Isla Mujeres	70.83	29.17	0.00	
Cozumel	90.00	10.00	0.00	
Felipe Carrillo Puerto	75.00	25.00	0.00	
Payo Obispo	60.00	40.00	0.00	
Total	72.92	27.08	0.00	
GRAND TOTAL	73.40	25.99	0.61	

1910–III. Population according to size of locality, arranged by present federal entities and late colonial partidos.

A. Aggregate population in localities with indicated persons

Area	0–99	100–2,499	2,500	Total no.
Campeche				
Carmen	712	11,602	6,535	18,849
Sahcabchén	1,977	9,317	0	11,294

Table 1.23 (cont.)

A. Aggregate population in localities with indicated persons (*cont.*)

Area	0–99	100–2,499	2,500	Total no.
Campeche[a]	383	2,371	16,775	19,529
Bolonchencauich	3,046	6,646	0	9,692
Camino Real Alto	2,555	18,693	6,049	27,297
Total	8,673	48,629	29,359	86,661
Yucatan				
Camino Real Bajo	2,905	30,368	10,693	43,966
Mérida	2,004	16,435	67,956	86,395
Costa	10,991	51,054	7,590	69,635
Beneficios Bajos	4,632	20,346	0	24,978
Sierra Baja	3,314	24,051	3,055	30,420
Sierra Alta	3,556	15,812	9,981	29,347
Beneficios Altos[b]	1,562	2,758	3,130	7,450
Subtotal	28,964	160,824	102,405	292,192
Exclude Mérida	26,960	144,389	34,449	205,798
Valladolid	8,486	19,074	4,319	31,879
Tizimín	4,157	11,384	0	15,541
Subtotal	12,643	30,458	4,319	47,420
Total	41,607	191,282	106,724	339,613
Exclude Mérida	39,603	174,847	38,768	253,218
Quintana Roo[c]				
Isla Mujeres	273	2,019	0	2,292
Cozumel	240	822	0	1,062
Felipe Carrillo Puerto	189	2,258	0	2,447
Payo Obispo	170	3,138	0	3,308
Total	872	8,237	0	9,109
GRAND TOTAL	51,152	248,148	136,083	435,383
Exclude Mérida	49,148	231,713	68,127	348,988

1910–IV. Population according to size of locality, arranged by present federal entities and late colonial partidos.

B. Percentage of population in localities with indicated persons

Area	0–99	100–2,499	2,500+	Total no.[d]
Campeche				
Carmen	3.78	61.55	34.67	
Sahcabchén	17.50	82.50	0.00	

Table 1.23 (cont.)

B. Percentage of population in localities with indicated persons (*cont.*)

Area	0–99	100–2,499	2,500+	Total no.[d]
Campeche[a]	1.96	12.14	85.90	
Bolonchencauich	31.43	68.57	0.00	
Camino Real Alto	9.36	68.48	22.16	
Total	10.01	56.11	33.88	
Yucatan				
Camino Real Bajo	6.61	69.07	24.32	
Mérida	2.32	25.40	72.28	
Costa	15.78	73.32	10.90	
Beneficios Bajos	18.54	81.46	0.00	
Sierra Baja	10.89	79.07	10.04	
Sierra Alta	12.12	53.87	34.01	
Beneficios Altos[b]	20.97	37.02	42.01	
Subtotal	9.91	55.05	35.04	
Exclude Mérida	13.10	70.06	16.74	
Valladolid	26.62	59.83	13.55	
Tizimín	26.75	73.25	0.00	
Subtotal	26.66	64.23	9.11	
Total	12.25	56.32	31.43	
Exclude Mérida	15.64	69.05	15.31	
Quintana Roo[c]				
Isla Mujeres	11.91	88.09	0.00	
Cozumel	22.60	77.40	0.00	
Felipe Carrillo Puerto	7.72	92.28	0.00	
Payo Obispo	5.14	94.86	0.00	
Total	9.57	90.43	0.00	
GRAND TOTAL	11.75	56.99	31.26	
Exclude Mérida	14.08	66.40	19.52	

[a] In the *Tercer censo de poblacion de los Estados Unidos Mexicanos* (1910), p. 112–113, Campeche, China, and Lerma are listed as separate municipalidades. In the *Lista alfabetica de localidades,* p. 11–20, they are all placed under Campeche.

As in the census of 1960, we have set apart the city of Campeche plus adjacent territory, including China and Lerma, and have arbitrarily included one-half (sixteen) of the towns under 100 persons which appear in the minicipalidad of Campeche.

The remainder of the former partido of Bolonchencauich is retained under that name. It includes, from the municipalidad of Campeche, the other sixteen places under 100 persons, and three places of 100 to 499 persons. In addition,

Notes to Table 1.23 (cont.)

it contains the municipalidades of Pich, Tixmucuy, Dzibalchén, Bolonchenti-
cul, Hopelchén, and Xkanha. The last municipalidad, Xkanha, is placed for
1960 in Camino Real Alto.
[b] This partido was restricted to territory which was within the state of Yucatan
in 1910.
[c] Since, in colonial times, the present entity of Quintana Roo was not organized
in partidos, for the censuses of both 1910 and 1960 we utilize the boundaries
of the four existing delegaciones.
[d] In all cases, 100 percent.

Table 1.24

1960–I. Inhabited places according to their size, arranged by present
federal entities and late colonial partidos.

A. Number of localities with population indicated

Area	0–99	100–2,499	2,500 +	Total no.
Campeche				
Carmen	236	46	2	284
Sahcahchén	8	19	2	29
Campeche [a]	23	4	2	29
Bolonchencauich	22	14	0	36
Camino Real Alto [b]	71	41	7	119
Total	360	124	13	497
Yucatan				
Camino Real Bajo	43	50	4	97
Mérida	48	56	3	107
Costa	222	84	13	319
Beneficios Bajos [c]	116	35	4	155
Sierra Baja	125	33	4	162
Sierra Alta	132	29	3	164
Beneficios Altos [d]	60	22	2	84
Subtotal	746	309	33	1,088
Valladolid [e, f]	592	59	2	653
Tizimín	498	50	3	531
Subtotal	1,070	109	5	1,184
Total	1,816	418	38	2,272
Quintana Roo [g]				
Isla Mujeres	32	6	0	38
Cozumel	44	13	1	58
Felipe Carrillo Puerto	227	46	0	273
Payo Obispo	73	18	1	92
Total	376	83	2	461
GRAND TOTAL	2,552	625	53	3,230

Table 1.24 (cont.)

1960–II. Inhabited places according to their size, arranged by present federal entities and late colonial partidos.

B. Percentage of localities with population indicated

Area	0–99	100–2,499	2,500+	Total no.[h]
Campeche				
Carmen	83.10	16.20	0.70	
Sahcabchén	27.59	65.51	6.90	
Campeche[a]	79.31	13.79	6.90	
Bolonchencauich	61.12	38.88	0.00	
Camino Real Alto[b]	59.67	34.45	5.88	
Total	72.41	24.98	2.61	
Yucatan				
Camino Real Bajo	44.32	51.56	4.12	
Mérida	44.86	52.34	2.80	
Costa	69.59	26.33	4.08	
Beneficios Bajos[c]	74.83	22.59	2.58	
Sierra Baja	77.16	20.37	2.47	
Sierra Alta	80.48	17.69	1.83	
Beneficios Altos[d]	71.42	26.20	2.38	
Subtotal	68.57	28.40	3.03	
Valladolid[e, f]	90.65	9.04	0.31	
Tizimín	90.02	9.34	0.55	
Subtotal	90.37	9.21	0.42	
Total	79.93	18.40	1.67	
Quintana Roo[g]				
Isla Mujeres	84.21	15.79	0.00	
Cozumel	75.86	22.42	1.72	
Felipe Carrillo Puerto	83.15	16.85	0.00	
Payo Obispo	79.35	19.56	1.09	
Total	81.56	18.01	0.43	
GRAND TOTAL	79.01	19.35	1.64	

1960–III. Population according to size of locality, arranged by present federal entities and late colonial partidos.

A. Aggregate population in localities with indicated persons

Area	0–99	100–2,499	2,500+	Total no.
Campeche				
Carmen	4,245	17,881	25,057	47,183
Sahcabchén	338	8,652	8,046	17,036

Table 1.24 (cont.)

A. Aggregate population in localities with indicated persons (*cont.*)

Area	0–99	100–2,499	2,500+	Total no.
Campeche[a]	618	1,425	47,049	49,092
Bolonchencauich	617	4,637	0	5,254
Camino Real Alto[b]	1,768	21,754	26,132	49,654
Total	7,586	54,349	106,284	168,219
Yucatan				
Camino Real Bajo	785	24,992	22,793	48,570
Mérida	1,197	24,027	188,348	213,572
Costa	4,383	49,244	55,700	109,327
Beneficios Bajos[c]	2,462	22,334	13,044	37,840
Sierra Baja	1,609	19,824	15,007	36,440
Sierra Alta	1,931	18,128	24,992	45,051
Beneficios Altos[d]	2,186	6,628	10,999	19,813
Subtotal	14,553	165,177	330,883	510,613
Exclude Mérida	13,356	141,150	142,535	297,041
Valladolid[e,f]	8,903	28,560	12,520	49,983
Tizimín	8,390	21,326	23,740	53,456
Subtotal	17,293	49,886	36,260	103,439
Total	31,846	215,063	367,143	614,052
Exclude Mérida	30,649	191,036	178,795	400,480
Quintana Roo[g]				
Isla Mujeres	732	3,217	0	3,949
Cozumel	1,043	3,604	2,915	7,562
Felipe Carrillo Puerto	4,494	15,406	0	19,900
Payo Obispo	1,273	4,630	12,855	18,758
Total	7,542	26,857	15,770	50,169
GRAND TOTAL	46,974	296,269	489,197	832,440
Exclude Mérida	45,777	272,242	300,849	618,868

1960–IV. Population according to size of locality, arranged by present federal entities and late colonial partidos.

B. Percentage of population in localities with indicated persons

Area	0–99	100–2,499	2,500+	Total no.[h]
Campeche				
Carmen	9.00	37.89	53.11	
Sahcabchén	1.98	50.78	47.23	

Table 1.24 (cont.)

B. Percentage of population in localities with indicated persons (*cont.*)

Area	0–99	100–2,499	2,500+	Total no.[h]
Campeche[a]	1.26	2.90	95.84	
Bolonchencauich	11.74	88.26	0.00	
Camino Real Alto[b]	3.56	43.82	52.62	
Total	4.51	32.31	63.18	
Yucatan				
Camino Real Bajo	1.62	51.45	46.93	
Mérida	0.56	10.95	88.19	
Costa	4.01	45.07	50.93	
Beneficios Bajos[c]	6.51	59.02	34.47	
Sierra Baja	4.42	54.40	41.18	
Sierra Alta	4.29	40.24	55.47	
Beneficios Altos[d]	11.03	33.46	55.51	
Subtotal	2.85	32.35	64.80	
Exclude Mérida	4.50	47.52	47.98	
Valladolid[e,f]	17.81	57.15	25.04	
Tizimín	15.67	40.00	44.33	
Subtotal	16.72	48.23	35.05	
Total	5.19	35.02	59.79	
Exclude Mérida	7.65	47.70	44.65	
Quintana Roo[g]				
Isla Mujeres	18.54	81.46	0.00	
Cozumel	13.79	47.66	38.55	
Felipe Carrillo Puerto	22.58	77.42	0.00	
Payo Obispo	6.79	24.68	68.53	
Total	15.03	53.54	31.43	
GRAND TOTAL	5.64	35.60	58.76	
Exclude Mérida	7.40	43.99	48.61	

[a]The city of Campeche plus adjacent territory with the towns China and Lerma have been set apart as the partido of Campeche. The remainder of the former partido of Bolonchencauich has been retained under that name. The small places of less than 100 persons, which cannot be located on the map, have been allocated equally to the two areas.
[b]Includes Xkanha and Xmabén, which, according to the 1:500,000 map, were in Quintana Roo in 1910.
[c]Excludes the town of Tiholop, in the municipio of Yaxcabá, which falls in Beneficios Altos.
[d]Restricted to the territory within the state of Yucatan.

[e] Excludes the town of Ekpetz in the municipio of Tixcacaltuyu, which is in Beneficios Altos.
[f] The municipio of Chemax, which was in the partido of Valladolid in 1910 and could not be segregated, has been moved to Tizimin.
[g] See footnote c, Table 1.23.
[h] In all cases, 100 percent.

census of 1910, shows the number of inhabited places in Campeche, Yucatan, and Quintana Roo, grouped by size and arranged according to the partidos of the late colonial period. Table 1.24 does the same thing for the data from the census of 1960 and is identical in format to Table 1.23.

In the tables there are three categories of size. The first consists of those places which contained fewer than 100 persons. The second extends from 100 to 2,499 persons per locality. The third includes all towns and cities of 2,500 or more. The line is drawn at 2,500 in Mexico as it is elsewhere to separate the rural environment from the urban. For each category the tables show the number of places reported in the 1910 or 1960 census that fall within each federal entity and partido (I). We have also put these figures on a relative basis and have expressed each as a percentage of the total localities found in every territorial unit (II).

The tables further treat the populations in the same way as the number of inhabited localities. For each category of size within each partido and Mexican federal entity, the tables show the total number of people (III) and also the percentage of the population represented by the total number (IV).

Tables 1.23 and 1.24 are unavoidably extensive and cumbersome. Moreover, it is difficult to derive broad relationships from such a mass of numerical values. Consequently, in Table 1.25 we dispense with the partidos and retain only the totals for Mexican federal entities. The two exceptions are that we continue to segregate the western and eastern portions of the state of Yucatan and also continue to give values for populations with and without the inclusion of Mérida.

In order to obtain a different perspective, we have plotted on Maps 3 and 4 the same data as form the basis for Tables 1.23 and 1.24. Here we have placed for 1910 and 1960 those localities of over ninety-nine inhabitants which could be found on the published maps of the peninsula. This array includes the vast majority of the localities of the indicated size which are mentioned in the census lists for those dates. Places that could be

Table 1.25

1910–I. Inhabited places according to their size.
Summarized by Mexican federal entities.

A. Number of localities with population indicated

Area	0–99	100–2,499	2,500+	*Total no.*
Campeche	273	140	4	417
Yucatan west[a]	1,076	444	11	1,531
Yucatan east[b]	548	87	1	636
Yucatan, *total*	1,624	531	12	2,167
Quintana Roo	35	13	0	48
Total peninsula	1,932	684	16	2,632

Percentage of localities with population indicated

Area	0–99	100–2,499	2,500+	*Total No.[c]*
Campeche	65.47	33.57	0.96	
Yucatan west[a]	70.28	29.00	0.72	
Yucatan east[b]	86.16	13.68	0.16	
Yucatan, *total*	74.94	24.51	0.55	
Quintana Roo	72.92	27.08	0.00	
Total peninsula	73.40	25.99	0.61	

1910–II. Population according to size of locality.
Summarized by Mexican federal entities.

A. Aggregate population in localities with indicated persons

Area	0–99	100–2,499	2,500+	*Total No.*
Campeche	8,673	48,629	29,359	86,661
Yucatan, west[a]	28,964	160,824	102,405	292,193
Exclude Mérida[b]	26,960	144,389	34,449	205,798
Yucatan east	12,643	30,458	4,319	47,420
Yucatan, *total*	41,607	191,282	106,724	339,613
Exclude Mérida	39,603	174,847	38,768	253,218
Quintana Roo	872	8,237	0	9,109
Total penisula	51,152	248,148	136,083	435,383
Exclude Mérida	49,148	231,713	68,127	348,988

Table 1.25 (cont.)

Percentage of population in localities with indicated persons			
Area	0–99	100–2,499	2,500 +	*Total No.[c]*
Campeche	10.01	56.11	33.88	
Yucatan, west[a]	9.91	55.05	35.04	
Exclude Mérida	13.10	70.06	16.74	
Yucatan, east[b]	26.66	64.23	9.11	
Yucatan, *total*	12.25	56.32	31.43	
Exclude Mérida	15.64	69.05	15.31	
Quintana Roo	9.57	90.43	0.00	
Total peninsula	11.75	56.99	31.26	
Exclude Mérida	14.08	66.40	19.52	

1960–1. Inhabited places according to their size.
Summarized by Mexican federal entities.

A. Number of localities with population indicated			
Area	0–99	100–2,499	2,500 +	*Total No.*
Campeche	360	124	13	497
Yucatan, west[a]	746	309	33	1,088
Yucatan, east[b]	1,070	109	5	1,184
Yucatan, *Total*	1,816	418	38	2,272
Quintana Roo	376	83	2	461
Total peninsula	2,552	625	53	3,230

Percentage of localities with population indicated			
Area	0–99	100–2,499	2,500+	*Total No.[c]*
Campeche	72.41	24.98	2.61	
Yucatan, west[a]	68.57	28.40	3.03	
Yucatan, east[b]	90.37	9.21	0.42	
Yucatan, *Total*	79.93	18.40	1.67	
Quintana Roo	81.56	18.01	0.43	
Total peninsula	79.01	19.35	1.64	

Table 1.25 (cont.)

1960–II. Population according to size of locality.
  – Summarized by Mexican federal entities.

A. Aggregate population in localities with indicated persons

Area	0–99	100–2,499	2,500+	Total No.
Campeche	7,586	54,349	106,284	168,219
Yucatan, west[a]	14,553	165,177	330,883	510,613
Exclude Mérida	13,356	141,150	142,535	297,041
Yucatan, east[b]	17,293	49,886	36,260	103,439
Yucatan, *total*	31,846	215,063	367,143	614,052
Exclude Mérida	30,649	191,036	178,795	400,480
Quintana Roo	7,542	26,857	15,770	50,169
Total peninsula	46,974	296,269	489,197	832,440
Exclude Mérida	45,777	272,242	300,849	618,868

Percentage of population in localities with indicated persons

Area	0–99	100–2,499	2,500+	Total No.[c]
Campeche	4.51	32.31	63.18	
Yucatan, west[a]	2.85	32.35	64.80	
Exclude Mérida	4.50	47.52	47.98	
Yucatan, east[b]	16.72	48.23	35.05	
Yucatan, *Total*	5.19	35.02	59.79	
Exclude Mérida	7.65	47.70	44.65	
Quintana Roo	15.03	53.54	31.43	
Total peninsula	5.64	35.60	58.76	
Exclude Mérida	7.40	43.99	48.61	

[a] Includes these partidos: Camino Real Bajo, Mérida, Costa, Beneficios Bajos, Sierra Baja, Sierra Alta, and Beneficios Altos.
[b] Includes these partidos: Valladolid and Tizimin.
[c] In all cases, 100 percent.

thus located are shown by solid dots. For others we have used open circles and have placed them arbitrarily near the cabecera of the appropriate municipio. In order to give some idea of relative size, we have graded the dots and circles so that the diameter increases with size of population.

The census of 1794–1795 can be used in this section of our study for a single specific purpose. In the published version that we rely on, there is at the end of the report from each partido or jurisdiction a paragraph headed *"Contiene la jurisdicción"* (The district contains), followed by a list of the various kinds of territorial units existing in the district, together with the number of each. These include cities, villas, pueblos, ranchos, and many others.

The partidos, except in Quintana Roo, are those listed in Tables 1.23, 1.24, and 1.25. For Quintana Roo, the only district mentioned is the jurisdiction of Salamanca de Bacalar. Although the categories of settlement are listed separately in the census, we combined for convenience the cities with villas, and haciendas with ranchos and estancias. The latter three jointly correspond very approximately with our category of places with 0–99 persons. Similarly, the pueblos correspond to our category 100–2, 499 persons, and the cities and villas to that of 2,500 and over.

We may formulate the data in summary thus :

Federal Entity	Cities and Villas	Pueblos	Haciendas, Ranchos, Estancias	Total
Campeche	1	37	252	290
Yucatan, west	1	131	962	1,094
Yucatan, east	1	46	292	339
Quintana Roo	1	1	9	11
Total	4	215	1,515	1,734

If we accept these figures as being in some measure comparable with those in the later censuses, we see that over the peninsula as a whole and through two centuries, the total number of recognized settlements has more or less kept pace with the population. In 1794–1795 there were approximately 356,000 people and 1,734 settlements; in 1910 there were 435,000 people and 2,632 settlements; in 1960 there were 832,000 people and 3,230 settlements.

Although for the past two hundred years there has been a consistent increase in the number of settlements, the distribution of this increase has not been uniform throughout the region. We see this distinction most clearly in the smallest places. The state of Campeche and the western seven partidos in the state of Yucatan show little significant change in the number of localities under 100 persons. Thus, for Campeche in 1794–1795, 290

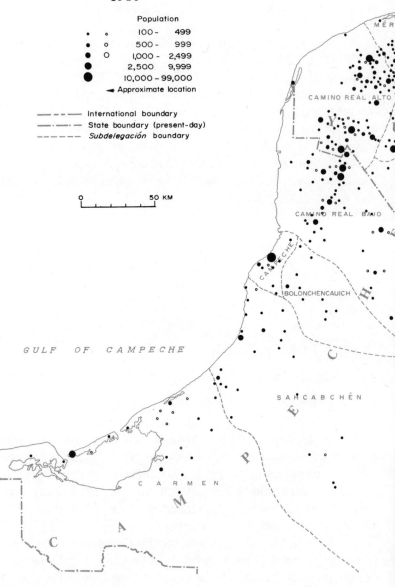

1910

Population

·	∘	100 - 499
•	∘	500 - 999
●	○	1,000 - 2,499
⬤		2,500 9,999
⬤		10,000 - 99,000

◂ Approximate location

International boundary
State boundary (present-day)
Subdelegación boundary

0   50 KM

MÉRID

CAMINO REAL ALTO

Y · U

CAMINO REAL BAJO

CAMPECHE

BOLONCHENCAUICH

C · H · E

GULF OF CAMPECHE

SAHCABCHÉN

C

P

E

CARMEN

C A M

C

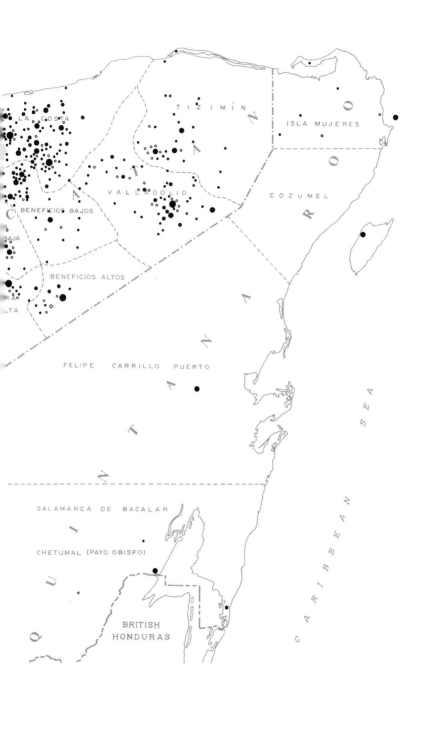

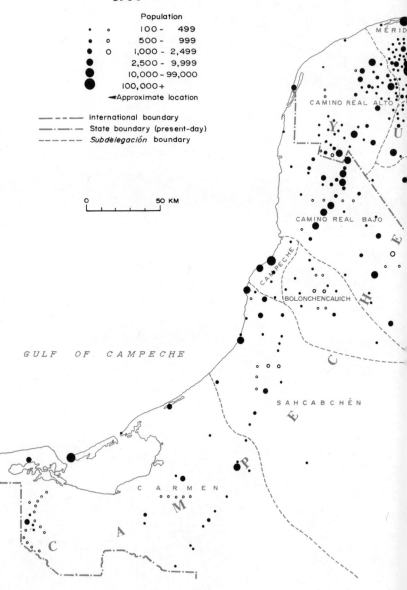

1960

Population

•	∘	100 - 499
•	∘	500 - 999
●	O	1,000 - 2,499
●		2,500 - 9,999
⬤		10,000 - 99,000
⬤		100,000 +

◂ Approximate location

—·—·— International boundary
—·—·— State boundary (present-day)
— — — *Subdelegación* boundary

0   50 KM

MÉRID

CAMINO REAL ALTO

Y   U

A

CAMINO REAL BAJO

CAMPECHE

BOLONCHENCAUICH

H

C

GULF   OF   CAMPECHE

SAHCABCHÉN

E

P

CARMEN

M

A

C

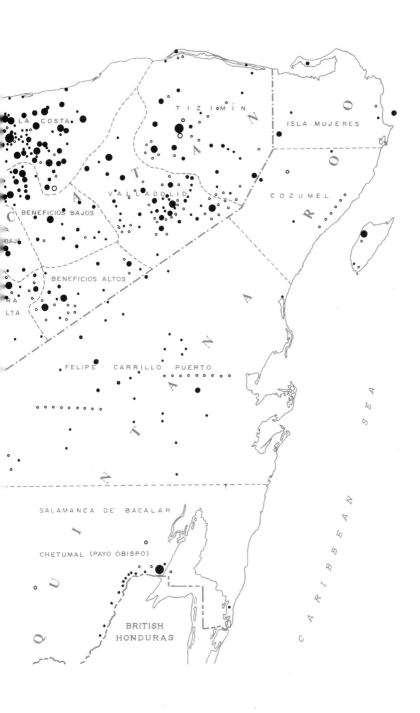

such places; in 1910, 273; in 1960, 360. In Yucatan, west, the analogous values are 962, 1,076, and 746. But in the two eastern partidos of the state of Yucatan we find, respectively, 292, 548, and 1,070; and in Quintana Roo, 9, 35, and 376. In the east and southeast, clearly, a new population has effected a very substantial occupation of many small, scattered settlements.

The changes in the number of settlements are in general reflected in the level of the populations which inhabited them. The populations can be examined most easily if we reduce the categories of size from three to two and separate all places with less than 2,500 inhabitants from all those with more than that number. In other words, we make a broad distinction between rural and urban environments. At the same time we may depict the extent of change by expressing for each of the two groupings the ratio of its 1960 to its 1910 population. For this purpose, of course, the 1794–1795 census cannot be used.

In Table 1.26 we show the absolute population values for the federal entities in 1910 and 1960, together with the ratios just mentioned. The rural population in some entities increased, but in Yucatan, west, an actual decline occurred, and the increase in Campeche was very moderate. On the other hand, in Yucatan, east, and particularly in Quintana Roo the increase has been impressive. This rise is undoubtedly correlated with the increase in the number of small towns previously noted.

Meanwhile, the urban population was augmented by a much greater amount. In Campeche and Yucatan, west, even if we leave Mérida out of consideration, the cities increased by a factor of nearly four. In Yucatan, east, the rise was double this value, and in Quintana Roo the city of Chetumal suddenly exploded as an urban entity.

From the data we present, it is clear that at least since the beginning of the present century, and probably for a long time previously, two forces have been operating in Yucatan. One is urbanization, a feature which has been common to the population of all Mexico. The other is the movement into the unoccupied lands to the east and south. In the latter areas these trends have to some extent neutralized each other, for the people who take up vacant land and establish new settlements in the countryside cannot at the same time contribute to the number of city dwellers. In most of Campeche and in the western two-thirds of the state of Yucatan, urbanization has proceeded in all types of community, with relative if not absolute

Table 1.26

Absolute and relative change in population of rural and urban localities
between 1910 and 1960.

Area	Absolute values of population			
	Localities 0–2,499		Localities 2,500+	
	1910	1960	1910	1960
Campeche	57,302	61,935	29,359	106,284
Yucatan, west[a]	189,788	179,730	102,405	330,883
Exclude Mérida	171,349	154,506	34,449	142,535
Yucatan, east[b]	43,101	67,179	4,319	36,260
Quintana Roo	9,109	34,399	0	15,770
Total peninsula	299,300	343,243	136,083	489,197
Exclude Mérida	280,861	318,019	68,127	300,849

Area	Ratio population 1960–1910	
	Localities 0–2,499	Localities 2,500+
Campeche	1.08	3.62
Yucatan, west[a]	0.95	3.09
Exclude Mérida	0.96	4.13
Yucatan, east[b]	1.56	8.39
Quintana Roo	3.74	
Total	1.15	3.60
Exclude Mérida	1.13	4.42

Area	Ratio of urban to rural population in 1910 and 1960	
	1910	1960
Campeche	0.51	1.72
Yucatan, west[a]	0.54	1.83
Exclude Mérida	0.20	0.92
Yucatan, east[b]	0.10	0.54
Quintana Roo		0.46
Total peninsula	0.45	1.43
Exclude Mérida	0.24	0.95

[a] Includes these partidos: Camino Real Bajo, Mérida, Costa, Beneficios
Bajos, Sierra Baja, Sierra Alta, and Beneficios Altos.
[b] Includes these partidos: Valladolid and Tizimin.

reduction in the rural population. It follows that the increase in gross density noted previously in all three federal entities is referable primarily to the growth in size of existing towns and only secondarily to the establishment of new settlements in unpopulated areas.

XIV. SOME COMMENTS

The changes in numbers and distribution of population in the peninsula of Yucatan from the early sixteenth century to the present show marked differences from those of central Mexico during the same length of time. Clearly, the massive barrier of the Isthmus of Tehuantepec and the swamps in lowland Tabasco and the adjacent sections of Campeche, as well as the long economic isolation of the peninsula because of lack of any major export product until the nineteenth century, have played an important role in giving these two areas of Meso-America different histories. Equally, the peninsula, although essentially low-lying and coastal, does not show the same relatively uniform pattern of very rapid and almost complete destruction upon the arrival of the Spaniards and relatively slow but steady recovery as do the lowlands and coasts of central Mexico.

At the time of the coming of the Spaniards central Mexico had reached a very high level of population, probably the highest until then, with heavy rural densities and very substantial urban agglomerations. The coming of the Spaniards unleashed a series of lethal factors that brought about a substantial contraction of population. That loss of population showed a marked relation to climate expressed in altitude, destruction being heaviest and most rapid on the humid, tropical coasts where the Indians virtually disappeared, and decreasing in rapidity and extent with rise in altitude, that is, colder climate. In general, the lethal factors lost much of their effect in the middle or later sixteenth century. By the early or middle seventeenth century, a recovery of population began that has continued, except for temporary setbacks by epidemics, famine, and the two massive civil wars of independence and the Mexican Revolution. On the coasts, with more rapid and thorough loss of population, recovery began by the last quarter of the sixteenth century but has been relatively slow though steady.

The population of Yucatan, on the other hand, probably reached a peak in the Toltec period and had been falling for perhaps a century or more at the time that the Spaniards arrived. Our initial estimate of 800,000 covers a population that already had undergone the impact of factors unleashed by the Europeans, but even if the population, as seems likely, was larger in, say, 1500, it probably did not reach anything like the average density of that of central Mexico, that is, forty-nine to the square kilometer. A population of 800,000 in Yucatan would give an average density of 5.6 per square kilometer; even if one considers the population as of 1500 to have been half again as large, double, or even triple, the average density was yet so far below that of central Mexico that the kind of settlement must have been considerably different. Social, political, and religious superstructures must have had proportionately far less production for their support.

The coming of the Spaniards to Yucatan unleashed lethal factors that, as in central Mexico, brought about a dramatic fall of population in the peninsula. The decline came to an end in the early years of the seventeenth century at somewhat less than 25 percent of the value of our initial estimate. During this sixteenth century period of loss of population, the Spaniards, under the aegis of the Franciscans, relocated the Indian population so thoroughly that it is difficult today to find the pre-Conquest sites. Congregación in the peninsula was far more thorough and involved far more drastic relocation of the population than did the similar policy implemented in central Mexico. The dominance in Yucatan of a single order, the Franciscans, may have been important in the more thorough implementation of the policy. We should notice also that the loss of population was virtually total in the areas of higher bush and tropical rainforest, that is, the east coast (Quintana Roo), the southern part of the state of Yucatan, and the southern and western parts of Campeche. The survival of the population occurred on the north coast and in the adjacent interior, that is, essentially in the areas of low bush.

Had the population of Yucatan followed the pattern of central Mexico after the early seventeenth century, it should have shown a relatively steady rise until the present, although with interruptions in 1810–1821 and 1913–1921. Instead, in the middle of the seventeenth century, the Indian population began to fall again in the areas under Spanish control, reaching a new nadir in the middle of the eighteenth century, and one probably lower than that of the first decline under Spanish impact. One element in the decline was undoubtedly the flight of substantial numbers of Indians into the relatively unoccupied lands of Quintana Roo, the south, and the west. This factor of flight into nearby unoccupied lands marks another important difference from central Mexico, where such lands were not available, and the largest zone of refuge lay in the north with its special conditions of distance, mining, frontier communities, and the pressure of hostile Indians upon the newcomers. The factor of flight, however, is not sufficient in itself to explain the decline in the population of the Spanish areas of Yucatan; there must have been an actual loss of numbers through excess of deaths over births as well.

After the middle of the eighteenth century, the population of Yucatan increased steadily until the early decades of the nineteenth century, a growth which was not disturbed by any turmoil attending the achievement of political independence from Spain. A major setback to growth came in the middle decades of the nineteenth century with the War of the Castes, and the same phenomena of flight into relatively empty lands, actual excess of deaths, as well as massive emigration from the peninsula. In the last decades of the nineteenth century, the population began again to increase, in substantial measure because of the development of a valuable export product, henequén, and that increase has continued with little variation. Unlike central Mexico, the upheaval of the Mexican Revolution has had little demographic impact in the peninsula.

We should like to call particular attention to three characteristics of the population history in the peninsula during the span of time that has interested us. First is the almost bellows-effect of fugitivism that we have already mentioned. Under pressure, the peasants of Yucatan disappear in substantial numbers into the bush in the east, south, and west, where living conditions are in some respects easier and the chances of crop failure considerably less. The remarkable thing is that very substantial numbers return to the areas of lower bush after a generation or so.

Second is the far smaller proportionate amount of immigration of Europeans and Negroes into the peninsula during the colonial period and most of the nineteenth century. Whereas racial mixture has been widespread in the peninsula, the number of non-Indians entering into it has been proportionately so much less than in central Mexico that Indian stock predominates to a far greater extent. Relative to central Mexico, Yucatan remains more Indian in its genetic base.

Third is the pattern of population destruction and recovery in Yucatan and its relation to the pattern of central Mexico. In terms of altitude, Yucatan would fall within the zone of lowlands and coasts of central Mexico; yet the history of its population as a whole does not show the virtually complete and very rapid destruction of population that do the coasts of central Mexico. If one divides Yucatan into subregions, the destruction of the population was least and recovery began earlier in the subregion of the low bush. The subregions of high bush and tropical rainforest had, when the Spanish arrived, substantial populations that largely disappeared by the middle of the sixteenth century. These subregions became waste that served to harbor fugitives. In the present century, there has been steady settlement of these more humid areas. In Yucatan then the presence or absence of rainfall and surface moisture has had a substantial role in conditioning the action of the factors unleashed by the Spaniards. The areas of high bush and tropical rainforest correspond to the central Veracruz coast and show roughly the same pattern of rapid, massive loss of population. The areas of low bush correspond approximately to the plateau of central Mexico and experienced slower and much less massive destruction of population. The comparison again points to the probable operation of disease as the major component among the lethal factors. Our essay thus points both to similarities and dissimilarities in pattern between Yucatan and central Mexico that other scholars may well want to consider in studying the Yucatec Maya in themselves and in relation to northern and western Meso-America.

Chapter II

Racial Groups in the Mexican Population Since 1519

I

In 1519 central Mexico, that is, Mexico west and north of the isthmus of Tehuantepec, was densely inhabited by Indians. Their number, as we have indicated in earlier studies, reached an aggregate of from 18 to 30 million. That year a few hundred Spanish males landed on the shore of Veracruz and began the permanent entry of Europeans and Africans into the region. By 1521 the Spaniards probably numbered between two and three thousand. Thereafter they increased very rapidly. Simultaneously, the native population underwent catastrophic decline. We have estimated that by 1568 the Indians had been reduced to between 2½ and 3 million. The Spaniards meanwhile had increased through births and immigration to over 60,000 persons.

During the same years two other processes were initiated which continue to the present day and which have carried profound socio-ethnic significance. The first of these was interbreeding between the European immigrants and the indigenous peoples. The bulk of the Spanish newcomers were males—administrators, clergy, soldiers, traders, and adventurers of all sorts. Very few brought families. Furthermore, relatively few unmarried Spanish females migrated. Since there was only limited objection to racial intermarriage, the major consideration being class, families of mixed origin came into being very rapidly. In addition, the popular Spanish mores of the time, with their emphasis upon sexual activity outside of marriage, encouraged a vast amount of racial interbreeding by Spanish men through the keeping of Indian mistresses and casual encounters that produced substantial numbers of illegitimate children of mixed race. Thus there arose a new racial category, the mestizo. If of legitimate birth or of upper class parentage, mestizos could consider themselves Spaniards and be so counted since in dress, education, and way of life they were indistinguishable from Europeans. The category of Europeans or Spaniards, therefore, included a substantial number of mestizos accepted by the Spaniards as part of their group. Some mestizos born into the Indian nobility or reared completely within Indian society merged into the Indian population. Nevertheless, there came into being a substantial number of people of mixed Indian-European racial origin who were recognized as a separate group called mestizos. With the passage of time they became an increasingly prominent group within the population.

The second process was set in motion by the introduction of thousands of Negro slaves from Africa. They were of especially great value as servants to the Spaniards, auxiliaries in their expeditions, foremen on their estates, laborers on sugar and cacao plantations in the hot country, and workers in the newly developed mines on the plateau. They became particularly important on the coasts, where the aboriginal population almost vanished, and in the north in the zone of new Spanish settlement beyond the line of occupation by sedentary Indian populations at the time of the Conquest. As one would anticipate, the Negroes very quickly began to interbreed freely with the Indians and to a considerable extent with the whites. Racial mixtures involving Negroes were greatly favored by the fact that slaves were imported in proportions that on the average brought in twice as many men as women and the additional fact that Negro and mulatto women were greatly favored as mistresses by the whites. There thus came into being a series of mixtures of Negro with European and with Indian (*jarocho, zambo,* etc.), which the Spanish grouped together under the general term pardo, the term including free Negroes as well. We shall use the term pardos to include all persons of full or part Negro ancestry, whatever the mixture. As in the instance of mestizos, some pardos were able to pass as Spaniards, although popular prejudice and royal legislation restricted the number to those who possessed wealth and education.

By the first decades of the seventeenth century, when the Indian population of central Mexico may have reached nadir with perhaps 1.1 million souls, the Europeans and Negroes were increasing very rapidly both by immigration and procreation. Conditions were thus unusually favorable for extensive racial mixture.[1]

For the middle and later sixteenth century, as we have already indicated, there is available a substantial amount of material on population, almost all of it on Indians and much of it fiscal. Our major sources of data on other racial groups in the population are the compendium prepared by López de Velasco in the early 1570s[2] and the fragmentary records on Negro slaves shipped to the New World or imported into New Spain. For the seventeenth century, data on racial groups in the population are far less satisfactory. At the end of the sixteenth century, comprehensive and relatively accurate primary sources of information on population come to a halt. It is not until the eighteenth century that there are others. Even the tribute records, which yield such a wealth of data concerning the Indians, fail us after 1600 or at best 1610. For an isolated town or parish or even a district, it is possible to get statements of local populations, but these items are widely scattered and highly erratic both in space and time.[3] For other than purely specialized interest, they are difficult to assemble and interpret. There are available two compendia, that of Vásquez de Espinosa for the early seventeenth century[4] and that of Diez de la Calle for the middle seventeenth century,[5] but they have the special problems of all such compendia: the data are of widely varying years and for mestizos and pardos so fragmentary as to be virtually useless. The statements on numbers of Indian tributaries in Diez de la Calle, for example, are based on the tribute counts of the 1590s and reflect the failure of the viceregal government to carry out extensive counts and reassessments between 1600 and 1670.

When we turn to the eighteenth century, sources on

[1]The preceding passages are a synthesis of a vast literature. Much of it is summarized in Mörner, *Race Mixture in the History of Latin America,* which has an extensive bibliography; in Instituto Panamericano de Geografía e Historia, Comisión de Historia, *El mestizaje en la historia de Ibero-América*; Rosenblat, II, pp. 54–66 *et passim*; Moreno Navarro, "Un aspecto del mestizaje americano: el problema de la terminología," in *Revista española de antropología americana* [*trabajos y conferencias*], IV (1969), pp. 201–227; Borah and Cook, "Marriage and Legitimacy in Mexican Culture: Mexico and California," in *California Law Review,* LIV, no. 2 (May 1966), pp. 948–966, 995. See also Moisés González Navarro, "Mestizaje in Mexico during the National Period," in Mörner, ed., *Race and Class in Latin America,* pp. 145–169. For Negroes and pardos, Aguirre Beltrán, *La poblacion negra de Mexico,* is indispensable.
[2]Pp. 182–282.
[3]See Chap. I in Vol. I of these essays.
[4]Pp. 120–188.
[5]Pp. 110–245.

numbers and racial elements in the population of Mexico become much better. Of greatest importance are the *Theatro americano* of Villaseñor y Sánchez and a battery of documents found in the Archivo General de Indias. Among the latter are extensive samples of the census of 1742–1746,[6] the Informe de Curatos for the diocese of Guadalajara in 1760,[7] and the very substantial remnants of the census of 1777 for the bishoprics of Oaxaca, Puebla, and Durango.[8] Finally, there are in the Archivo General de la Nación in Mexico City, the surviving records of the military census and general census of 1789–1793,[9] and the Matrícula de Tributarios of 1805.[10] These records make it feasible to carry out a much more searching examination of racial distribution than was possible in the pioneer and still indispensable study of Gonzalo Aguirre Beltrán, *La población negra de México,* 1519–1810, which, although devoted to the study of Negroes and mixtures with a Negro component, examines data on other racial groups in its chapters on numbers of persons at various points in time.

We have already listed and discussed the sources mentioned above in our discussion on the sources for the demographic history of Mexico. Nevertheless, we shall describe them at some length for the specific purposes of studying racial elements. The Fuenclara count of 1742–1746 was rather primitive as a census. Some of the reports are still extant in the Archivo General de Indias. The respondents were local authorities, usually the alcaldes mayores or district governors, more rarely parish priests, other civil officials, and military commanders. Each report contained a discussion of many matters but usually furnished a statement of the total number of inhabitants. Often there was a more detailed breakdown according to village or town, according to civil status, and according to racial group. Individuals were not often mentioned as such; on the contrary, the most common unit for expressing number was the family or, more accurately, the household.

The reports of the Fuenclara count formed the basis for the extensive compendium published by José Antonio Villaseñor as the two volumes of the *Theatro americano.* The *Theatro* is a well-organized, comprehensive digest of the reports. If we

[6]AGI, Indiferente General, legajos 107–108.
[7]AGI, Audiencia de Guadalajara, legajo 401.
[8]AGI, Audiencia de Méjico, legajos 2578–2581, 2589–2591; Indiferente General, legajos 102, 1736.
[9]In the ramos of Padrones and Historia.
[10]AGN, Tributos, XLIII, last expediente.

had the complete body of the district reports made in 1742–1746, those documents would serve as the primary basis for analysis. As matters stand, however, we have only a small fraction of the entire census. Furthermore, examination of extant reports and the corresponding sections of the book shows that while Villaseñor y Sánchez repeated a great deal verbatim, and in most instances transcribed the numerical data with fair fidelity, at the same time he did a considerable amount of editing and rearranging. Some of his alterations were drastic and departed greatly from the reports. To account for such deviations, which could scarcely have occurred through error but must reflect intent, we can only assume that Villaseñor y Sánchez had available further information which he incorporated in his text. Nevertheless, at this remove we cannot resolve such discrepancies. Hence we have been constrained to adopt a more or less mechanical procedure. Where we find usable population data in a report and these data are not given in the *Theatro americano,* we accept the figures. Where a contradiction exists between the report and the book, and the report appears to be consistent and reasonable, we use its data; otherwise, we rely upon the book. Our sample of nearly 200 places contains between forty and fifty for which the population totals are derived from the district reports.

We should comment here upon the summary of the *Theatro americano* which is in the Archivo General de la Nación.[11] Aguirre Beltrán secured most of his numerical data for the census for 1742–1746 from this document. On inspection it turns out to be a direct recapitulation of the book, which does not contain the additional information found in the district reports in the Archivo General de Indias and does not in any way amplify the presentation of Villaseñor y Sánchez. Hence we have confined our attention exclusively to the *Theatro americano* and to the surviving district reports.

Villaseñor y Sánchez, probably because of inadequacy in local reporting, fails to give populations for extensive portions of the north and west. His book is arranged in six parts by bishopric: Mexico, Puebla, Oaxaca, Valladolid (Michoacán), Guadalajara, and Durango. The data for populations in the diocese of Guadalajara are scanty since for most of the jurisdictions, numbers are replaced by semi-quantitative words, such as "few", "some", "many", and the like, which are useless

[11]Ramos of Reales Cédulas, LXXXV, expediente 142.

for computation. The descriptions for the diocese of Durango are even briefer and more generalized. Consequently, if the few numbers actually given are added to those from the other bishoprics so as to derive a total for Mexico, the final values for racial groups are distorted. The center and south are over-weighted, the north and west largely neglected. This bias, which was ignored by Aguirre Beltrán, is important in the light of the regional differences which we have found in racial composition.

Because there exists the lacuna represented by the lack of data for the two northern bishoprics, it is fortunate that we possess another document which partially fills the gap. This is the report by the Bishop of Guadalajara on his pastoral inspections carried out from 1755 to 1760, in the Informe de Curatos. The bishop, with extreme care, listed for each parish the numbers of families of Indians and of non-Indians, the latter grouped together as españoles. The discrepancy in time between the *Theatro americano* and the Informe de Curatos, about thirteenth years if one takes the average of the periods of gathering information, is of little significance. The areas do not overlap and the units of expression are identical in the two sources. Hence, our first reliable enumeration according to racial group, based upon the number of families throughout, is the joint record provided by the count of 1742–1746 and the Bishop of Guadalajara in his report of 1760.

The next comprehensive count was the census of 1777. The active enumerators were the parish priests, who submitted their reports to their bishops. The original manuscripts of approximately 200 of these parish reports are still extant in the Archivo General de Indias. They cover close to one-half of the parishes in three bishoprics—Oaxaca, Puebla, and Durango. Unlike the system employed in 1742–1746, the priest did not merely state totals. He listed his parishioners by name and, as a rule, showed for each individual the sex, age, family relationship, and race. Unfortunately, some of the reports are incomplete with respect to one or more of the categories mentioned. On the whole, notwithstanding, they present a very substantial body of data and constitute a well distributed and fully adequate sample of the three bishoprics. We can use them directly with only minor modifications.

In 1789–1793, during the administration of Viceroy Revillagigedo II, two more censuses were taken, both more elaborate than their predecessors and both supervised and carried out by the civil, not the ecclesiastical, authorities. Of the records that have come down to us, by far the more complete are those of the military census, which covered those parts of the population from which men could be drawn for military service, in effect, the non-Indians. The enumeration covered, however, not merely adult males but also women and children— all non-Indians of whatever age and sex. The surviving reports constitute the hundred-odd volumes of the ramo of Padrones in the Archivo General de la Nación. Roughly one-half deal with Mexico City, the other half with a wide sample of jurisdictions from the country at large.

The reports in Padrones are of particular interest in that the enumerations carefully specify race. Many, indeed, are arranged in solid blocks according to race. Thus there might be a complete census which included all the españoles and mestizos living in a certain town, a second embracing only mulattoes and Negroes, and so on. The totals immediately segregate the numerical values for the groups. One byproduct of this system is less fortunate. In many instances we can find the report for one group but not those for the others. Moreover, counts of Indians are entirely absent. For this reason the value of the census as a whole is seriously diminished.

The hand-written report sheets bound in the volumes of Padrones may be examined in detail and the individuals counted, classified, or otherwise treated statistically. In addition, there are summaries, each complied from the report sheets of a single enumeration by the recording agent or someone preparing the sheets for transmission to the central authority, and each placed at the end of the corresponding file of individual names. These summaries vary in form but usually show totals according to the customary categories, including racial groups.

To the summaries of the military census may be added a score or more of summaries of the general census of the same years, found in the ramo of Historia in the Archivo General de la Nación. The latter are usually compilations covering entire provinces or intendancies and were made usually by other persons than those responsible for the reports of the military census. These summaries may or may not include information on racial groups; if they do, they are of considerable value for the study of race and racial mixtures.

One more document merits attention, namely, the

Matrícula de Tributarios of 1805, tabulating the tributary population (not merely tributaries) for the entire country from counts made in the immediately preceding years. The category of tributary population included all Indians except a few who were declared gente de razón. Thus the Matrícula is a good index to the number of Indians. Also designated as tributaries and clearly segretaged from the Indians were numerous Negroes and people of part-Negro genetic stock, usually designated *negros y mulatos libres*. Some indication, therefore, of the relative number of Negro and part-Negro tributaries, on the one hand, and of Indian tributaries, on the other, as of approximately 1800–1805 may be secured from this document. Its importance lies primarily in showing the geographical distribution of these racial groups.

The censuses and counts of the eighteenth century, and indeed of the entire colonial period, carefully distinguished the race of the people enumerated. In 1810, however, the outbreak of the War of Independence began a series of political and social upheavals that drastically changed governmental policy. An immediate consequence of the upheavals and independence was that the few counts of population made were of districts or states and usually were poorly done. No serious attempt was made at a count of the population in the entire country until nearly the end of the nineteenth century. In that period, racial fusion proceeded so far that any refined determination of racial origin in individual cases was out of the question. Even more important was the universal repudiation of the colonial system of distinctions based on race. Minor and unsuccessful survivals have been the continued distinction between Indians and non-Indians in Yucatan until the middle of the nineteenth century and the attempted revival of identification of Indians through linguistic and economic criteria in censuses since the Revolution of 1910.[12]

The most serious difficulty encountered in the study of racial composition during the last years of colonial Mexico is that of determining the genetic origin of any particular person in a census. There are three primary racial stocks—white, black, and red—which we may designate as E, P, and I, respectively, symbols that we shall use throughout our discussion. As a model, let us assume that we start with equal numbers of each,

[12]González Navarro, "Mestizaje in Mexico During the National Period," in Mórner, ed, *Race and Class in Latin America,* pp. 145–169.

disregard all sex differences, and allow marriage to be governed by chance alone. Then, since we began with pure-line couples, we have EE, PP, and II. In the F_1 generation there are six possible combinations: EE, EP, EI, PP, PI, and II. The new derivatives, if we employ local terminology, are EP (mulatto), EI (mestizo), and PI (zambo). In the F_2 generation, if we still allow union to be by chance, there will be twenty-one combinations, and in the F_3 generation, 231. To recognize and name all of these combinations is an obvious impossibility in practice. Yet those who controlled the political, economic, and religious life of the colony attempted to find a solution. They did so by creating a series of categories (classes, castes, strata) based upon social as well as racial determinants. Hence, we depart significantly from rigid and accurate genetic criteria.

The first clear line of demarcation set apart the Indians from all other groups. They were of relatively homogeneous descent, retained much of their aboriginal culture, including language, and were distinguished politically and economically by their liability for tribute. Aguirre Beltrán found no difficulty in expressing their individuality by the term *indígenas* (natives), following a centuries-old practice.

All those not classed as Indians were consolidated for many purposes as the gente de razón or people of reason, essentially those held to full responsibility in terms of European law and religious responsibility. Despite the equivocal position of Negroes and pardos, to whom the term applied in a legal sense but not always in a social or fiscal sense, the term was useful in segregating Indians from non-Indians and in designating that fraction of the population not liable for payment of tribute.

Within the first century of Spanish rule, three principal subgroups of non-Indians came to be recognized. For their classification, Aguirre Beltrán develops a concept somewhat different from that which is usually encountered and to which we adhere. He emphasizes the extent of inter-breeding to the point of considering all inhabitants as mixed, that is, mestizo, except for the Indians and the immigrants from Europe *(europeos)*. The latter, he concedes to have been of pure white genetic stock. Aguirre Beltrán then divides the great mass of mixed bloods according to the predominant racial element into Euromestizos, Afromestizos, and Indomestizos.[13] If we look

[13]See pp. 212–213.

at the matter as a purely genetic problem, we must agree that Aguirre Beltrán has a good argument. The allocation of a person to a racial category in the eighteenth century, as has been pointed out previously, was determined by social as well as racial considerations, and there was a good deal of blurring of racial distinctions and passing. On the other hand, the custom of the period used a simpler terminology, and the authorities made their counts in fewer categories. It seems preferable to follow the custom of the period rather than resort to a new framework of terminology derived from a present-day assessment of an old situation. Accordingly, we return to the fourfold basic distinction of the colonial counts : the Indians and three non-Indian groups.

The first non-Indian category was that of the whites, who consisted of European immigrants and their descendants reputed to be of pure European stock. Since the immigrants were almost exclusively from Spain, the entire group was designated españoles. The second non-Indian category was that of the mestizos, a new group derived from the mixture of whites and Indians which proceeded with great rapidity from the time of the Conquest. Socially, the mestizo was immediately below the español and was clearly differentiated from the Indian. The third group comprised the African Negroes, who were imported as slaves, and their identifiable offspring, whether free or slave. The position of such offspring collectively was equivocal. Many intermarried with Indians and eventually were lost in the mass of the Indian population. Many, although mixed with both Indian and European genetic stock, retained their status as Negroes, mulattoes, or pardos, and if free, were part of the tributary class along with the Indians. A few remained slaves. Others, indeed a large proportion, did not pay tribute but were nevertheless recorded as pardos, *morenos,* negros, or mulattoes, although along with Spaniards and mestizos. For purposes of military duty, they were gente de razón, and indeed in many regions preferred as soldiers; for other purposes, they were sometimes segregated from the gente de razón as a separate group.[14]

We have to deal historically with the four groups as if they were clear biological entities; yet it is evident, as was emphasized by Aguirre, that they were ranges of intergrading

---

[14]See Aguirre Beltrán, pp. 153–196; see also our discussion on pardos in part VIII of our chapter on Yucatan, and Fonseca and Urrutia, I, 440–441.

types. Each represents a predominant but not rigidly distinct racial character. Furthermore, the allocation of a specific person to a given group was determined not only by his skin color and the conformation of his features, but also by his economic position, his social status in the community, and even by his own preference. These factors were all taken into consideration by the parish priest in making entries in the parish registers or counting his parishioners and by the compilers of civil counts.

This extreme fluidity in racial composition is reflected in the reports. Since each report was written by a different person and since there was no sure set of governing rules, the mode of presentation became the prerogative of the recorder himself. Some recorders examined carefully the origin of each person; some lumped great masses of people together under a single designation; some cited the racial group within which the head of a family fell and ignored the wife and children. Clearly an exact allocation of every individual to one of the four major racial groups is impossible. The best we can do is to follow the statements made in the documents and accept in each case the racial designation made by the author of the document.

If there is still doubt, we may adopt certain general guidelines, and recognize that the results are at best reasonable approximations.

(1) Where a source (census or report) states an explicit numerical total for families or persons belonging to españoles, mestizos, pardos, or indios, that figure is accepted without change.

(2) Where a list of persons is given under the common heading españoles, etc., the number of such persons is counted and used as the total.

(3) Where a list of persons is provided and each person is assigned to a racial group, a count is made of the total number within each group.

(4) Where the allocation of persons in a list is incomplete, a few quite arbitrary rules will govern:

(a) Where a family head and his wife are of the same racial group, the children are also assigned to it.
(b) Children follow the racial group of a widow.
(c) Where the husband and wife differ, the children are allocated as follows:

1 : E plus M gives M   4 : M plus P gives P
2 : E plus I gives M   5 : M plus I gives M
3 : E plus P gives P   6 : P plus I gives P

It will be noted that this system tends to reduce E and I and to increase M and P. However, in addition to the fact that we see no preferable alternative, we argue that this trend actually was in progress. At the beginning in the sixteenth century, the Indians constituted a large but limited reservoir of genetically pure stock. Whenever one of them crossed with a member of another race, the offspring were inevitably lost to the Indian fraction and went to increase some mixed group, except for the small proportion who were absorbed back into the Indian mass. Meanwhile, to be sure, Indians married Indians, but their relative, even if not their absolute, number steadily diminished. The same considerations applied in some but much less measure to the European component. Here, however, there was continuous replenishment through immigration throughout the colonial period.

(d) Where the race of only the head of the family is given, the other members are assigned to this group.

(5) In certain parishes and jurisdictions, no racial information whatever is given, or it is so meager as to be useless. Such reports have been omitted entirely from consideration.

An important aspect of socio-ethnic development in Mexico pertains to the regional differences which had become well established by the eighteenth century. These differences were generated by climatic, or edaphic, factors, such as the environments on the coasts and the upland; by economic accident, such as the discovery of important silver mines; by political and social pressures, such as the steady drive toward northward migration; and by the nature of the previously existing Indian settlement and the extent to which colonial Spanish society could adapt it to European purposes.

In order to demonstrate these distinctions and to utilize the available data of the later colonial period effectively, it is desirable to delineate a number of characteristic regions or areas. A similar procedure was adopted by us in describing the population changes of the sixteenth century, and we employ the system then developed, but with modifications. Some revision is necessary mainly because for discussion of the later colonial data we consider all of Mexico north and west of the isthmus of Tehuantepec, omitting Yucatan and Chiapas, whereas in the previous work we discussed a much more limited area.

The primary segregation embraces three broad regions in the Mexico of the later eighteenth century. We designate these according to their approximate position in the country as a whole as center, west, and north.

I. The center includes rather precisely the territory which in pre-Conquest times was subject to the Triple Alliance and various enclaves within that territory, such as Tlaxcala. It is thus nearly all the land extending from the Maya on the south and east to the Tarascan and Chichemec frontiers on the west and north. It may be subdivided for certain purposes as follows :

IA. The central plateau. This large expanse covers approximately the areas in our 1960 study designated as I, IIA, IV, and V. Its western portion includes most of the archbishopric of Mexico, that is, the present-day states of Mexico, Hidalgo, and Morelos, and the Federal District and northern Guerrero. The eastern portion embraces much of the bishopric of Tlaxcala or Puebla, with the state of Tlaxacala, most of Puebla, and central Veracruz almost to the coast. Here we have also placed the bishopric of Oaxaca except for the Pacific and Gulf coastal strips. The boundary of this area on the northeast runs approximately along the foot of the Atlantic escarpment and therefore retains those settlements which were at moderate to high elevation, including those above 200 to 300 meters. The only exception of any significance is in the jurisdictions of Orizaba and Córdoba, which reach close to the coast and in parts are relatively low. On the south and southwest we draw the line, perhaps arbitrarily, at the Balsas River and at the foot of the western escarpment so as to retain in the plateau region the jurisdictions of Tixtla, Chilapa, and Tlapa; the Mixteca Baja; and the Mije-Chontal section of Oaxaca. On the west the boundary coincides quite closely with that which separates the present-day state of Michoacán from the states of Mexico and Hidalgo.

IB. The central coasts. Here are our former areas II, III, VI, and VII. On the Atlantic side is the Huaxteca (or Pánuco), that is, as nearly as we can describe it, the jurisdictions of Tampico, Papantla, and Misantla north of Veracruz; and the remnants of Cosamaloapan and Coatzacoalcos to the south. For Tabasco we have no data whatever; most of it lay in the province of Yucatan once that was organized in the middle decades of the sixteenth century. It must be recognized that in the latter half of the eighteenth century the Gulf coast, which earlier had been thoroughly depopulated, was only sparsely settled. Hence the reports are uniformly scattered and fragmentary. On the Pacific side, the definition is clearer. To the southeast lie Tehuantepec and Huatulco, adjacent to Jicayán and the Costa Chica. Then there is a gap as far as Acapulco, a local Spanish settlement, beyond which lay what was left of Zacatula. Since both the ecology and the racial character of the two coastal strips are closely similar, we treat them jointly as a single territorial unit unless special circumstances, as in the data for 1739, dictate otherwise.

II. The west is set apart culturally and administratively from the center rather than ecologically since it embraces both plateau and coast. It is the territory which in 1960 we placed in areas VIII, X, and most of IX. In general, it was well populated in 1519 by the Tarascans of Michoacán and by a constellation of sedentary tribes in Colima, Jalisco, and Nayarit. The Spanish conquest had been substantially completed by 1530, and the western portion was soon organized under the Audiencia of Nueva Galicia. The ecclesiastical authority was vested in the bishoprics of Michoacán and Guadalajara. It is possible to separate a plateau and a coastal division of the west as we have previously done. However, the extreme paucity of data on race in the eighteenth century documents makes such a distinction futile. We have therefore considered the region only as a whole.

The northern boundary has been drawn only approximately. In principle it follows the somewhat irregular line of conquest which had been reached by 1530 and excludes settlements which were unreduced at that period. Hence, it includes coastal Nayarit, the land south of the Rio Santiago, and eastward through Tepatitlán in Jalisco, but leaves out the wild Indian country to the north and the new towns in northeastern Jalisco and in Aguascalientes and Zacatecas.

III. The north covers everything above the ancient Chichemec frontier as it existed in the decade 1520–1530. In other words, we place here all the territory which was entered and settled by the Spaniards and their Indian allies after the conquest of the Triple Alliance and the Tarascan state. It is this feature of new settlement by a stable but aggressive society which sets apart the entire north rather than geographical location, altitude, or climatic and biotic differences. The southern boundary runs roughly from the foot of the western mountains north of Lake Chapala along the state lines of Michoacán, Mexico, and Hidalgo to the Gulf.

Subordinate areas can, of course, be distinguished. We report some of them because of the manner in which population or census data are preserved in the documents. Otherwise, there is frequently little difference among them. For convenience, they may be designated by letters.

A. The sixteenth century settlements in the state of Querétaro.

B. The cities and ranches which were established early within the boundaries of the state of Guanajuato through extensive migration from the south.

C. The mountainous region of northeastern Jalisco and southwestern Zacatecas which even in the late eighteenth century was still close to its aboriginal condition. Since there was little immigration or settlement except for a few military bases and mining camps, and this was a pocket of prolonged Indian resistance that owed the success of the Indian resistance to the fact that it lay outside the main stream of northward movement, we have not included the few reports on districts within it with the remainder of area III. (See also subsequent comment.)

D. The region of sixteenth century settlement and mining operations which reached from Lagos and Teocaltiche in Jalisco through Aguascalientes to embrace most of the present state of Zacatecas.

E. Here will be found close to one-third of modern Mexico, the huge expanse once known as the Provincias Internas. Included are the present states of Sinaloa, Sonora, Durango, Chihuahua, San Luis Potosí, and parts of Tamaulipas, Nuevo León, and Baja California, together with the North American states of California, Arizona, New Mexico, and Texas. The extremely incomplete and fragmentary evidence precludes any further subdivision. Specific territory such as the bishoprics of Guadalajara and Durango will be indicated by name when pertinent in text and tables.

II

There are two types of data which permit us to study the extent, distribution, and fusion of ethnic categories in colonial Mexico. The first consists of statements of numbers according to race or caste in terms of families or persons. They are found in or may be calculated from all the documents previously mentioned. The second consists of information concerning marriages. In the original reports of the censuses of 1777 and 1793, where the population is listed person by person, the race of each married man or woman is usually stated. From these sheets, therefore, one may estimate the degree and character of interracial union.[15]

We consider now total populations. The initial step in the analysis of sources is to segregate the reports of numbers according to some simple system which conforms to the data and which can be carried through a long period with a minimum of exception and adjustment. The most satisfactory approach is to retain the four primary categories which were utilized by all administrative and clerical officials: españoles, mestizos, pardos or mulattoes, and indios. We do this with the full realization that these terms refer to subpopulations which were differentiated on the basis of social as well as purely racial criteria.

We have already mentioned the modifications introduced by Aguirre Beltrán. However reasonable these are for his purposes and for the restricted study of a single racial component, they cannot be profitably employed for the analysis of the detailed census reports of the later eighteenth century. Therefore, whenever we have drawn upon the tabulations of Aguirre Beltrán, it has been necessary to recast his categories. Our principal modifications are the combination of his europeos and Euromestizos as equivalent to españoles; the combination of his *africanos* and Afromestizos to form pardos in the wider sense of Negroes and racial mixtures with a Negro genetic component; and the substitution for his Indomestizos and indígenas of the words mestizos and indios or Indians, respectively.

[15]A further major source of information on marriages is, of course, the surviving registers of marriages in each parish; they are, however, local in character, and assembling countrywide data from them would be impossible for our purpose in this essay. Two studies of racial mixture and racial preference in marriage based on local parish records are Carmagnani, "Demografia e società. La struttura sociale di due centri minerari del Messico settentrionale (1600–1720)," in *Revista storica italiana*, LXXXII (1970), 560–591; and Love, "Marriage Patterns of Persons of African Descent in a Colonial Mexico City Parish," in *Hispanic American Historical Review*, LI (1971), 79–91.

In examining any of the sources, we immediately encounter the difficulty that many enumerations do not distinguish clearly among the four subpopulations but either give a combined figure for two or more of them or list the total for one, with the omission of the others. The result is that we must adopt a standard procedure which will be applicable to the maximum number of cases and which will permit as much comparison as possible.

With each document we first tabulate the data so as to isolate the largest and most stable category, the Indians. We can then proceed with two primary fractions of the total population : Indians and non-Indians. The latter, it will be remembered, form the compound group, the gente de razón. This group can then be split, insofar as the records permit, into its three components, españoles, pardos, and mestizos. For the purpose of comparing populations of greatly varying sizes, the absolute numbers may be converted to relative values, usually in the form of percentages. Thus we arrive at a routine formulation of the principal components.

Indios :   percentage in total population
Españoles ⎫
                             1. percentage of each in non-Indian
pardos   ⎬   population
                             2. percentage of each in total population
Mestizos ⎭

For the years extending from the Conquest to the middle of the eighteenth century, we do not analyze the numerous but widely dispersed sources of information concerning the non-Indian population. Indeed, an adequate treatment of racial history during these two centuries in Mexico would require a substantial volume. At the same time it is possible to show in very condensed form the major trends, as has been done by Aguirre Beltrán. For this purpose we have prepared Table 2.1 in two parts, the years 1568–1570 and 1646, respectively, in part using data assembled by Aguirre Beltrán, in part reworking his data or substituting new information which has become available in the quarter century since he wrote his study. In the table for 1570 we have substituted our own reworking of the data in López de Velasco on españoles and have used a factor of six for converting vecinos into persons. The higher factor is based upon the larger households of the Spaniards evident in

Table 2.1

A. Distribution of racial groups in New Spain, 1568–1570

Absolute Numbers

Area[a]		Non-Indians[b]				Indians	Total Pop.
		E	M	P	Total		
I		47,366	2,142	17,696	67,204	2,283,795	2,350,999
II		6,200	200	2,155	8,555	250,525	259,080
III		9,300	75	2,705	12,080	111,253	123,333
	Total	62,866	2,417	22,556	87,839	2,645,573	2,733,412

Relative Values

Area		As % of Non-Indians			As % of Total Pop.			
		E	M	P	E	M	P	I
I		70.5	3.2	26.3	2.0	0.1	0.8	97.1
II		72.5	2.3	25.2	2.4	0.1	0.8	96.7
III		77.0	0.6	22.4	7.5	0.1	2.2	90.2
	Total	71.5	2.8	25.7	2.3	0.1	0.8	96.8

[a] I = Dioceses of Mexico. Tlaxcala, and Antequera (Oaxaca); II = diocese of Michoacán; III = diocese of Guadalajara or Nueva Galicia
[b] E = Europeans or Spaniards; M = mestizos; P = pardos; I = Indians.
Sources and methods of estimate:
Europeans or Spaniards: López de Velasco's statements as tabulated in IA: 35, pp. 5–11, especially Table 4. The clergy are allocated 2,000 to area 1,200 to area II, and 300 to area III.
Mestizos and pardos: Aguirre Beltrán, pp. 203–213 especially *cuadro* VI. We use the estimate for Indomestizos directly as mestizos and combine those for Negroes and Afromestizos as pardos.
Indians: IA: 44, pp. 48 and 57–109 (Table 5 and appendix). The total for area I of this table has been reduced by 4,000 to adjust for the portion of Tabasco in the diocese of Mérida. The diocese of Michoacán is calculated as all of area VIII of IA: 44, one-half of area X, and one-sixth of area VII. The diocese of Nueva Galicia is calculated as all of area IX and one-half of area X.

B. Distribution of racial groups in New Spain, 1646

Absolute Numbers

Area[a]		Non-Indians				Indians	Total Pop.
		E	M	P	Total		
I		98,202	13,890	45,815	157,907	1,073,384	1,231,291
II		10,820	2,024	8,295	21,139	117,747	138,886
III		16,230	1,082	8,290	25,603	102,289	127,891
	Total	125,252	16,996	62,400	204,648	1,293,420	1,498,068

Table 2.1 (cont.)

B. Distribution of racial groups in New Spain, 1646 (*cont.*)

Relative Values

Area	As % of Non-Indians			As % of Total Pop.			
	E	M	P	E	M	P	I
I	62.2	8.8	29.0	8.0	1.1	3.7	87.2
II	51.2	9.6	39.2	7.8	1.5	6.0	84.7
III	63.4	4.2	32.4	12.7	0.8	6.5	80.0
Total	61.2	8.3	30.5	8.4	1.1	4.2	86.3

[a]As in part A save that area II, Michoacán, includes San Luis Potosí, and area III, Nueva Galicia, includes the bishoprics of Guadalajara and Durango but excludes New Mexico, then part of the diocese of Durango. The two areas are larger than in 1568–1570 through Spanish advance northward.

Sources and methods of estimate:
Europeans or Spaniards: Application of proportion between López de Velasco and Diez de la Calle (pp. 110–245), as in IA: 35, pp. 11–14. Mexico City and the clergy are calculated separately. Mexico City is taken from Diez de la Calle directly; the clergy are estimated at 6,500 and assigned 4,500 to area I; 800 to area II; and 1,200 to area III.
Mestizos and pardos: Basic data from Aguirre Beltrán, pp. 221–222, especially cuadro X; values for Indomestizos and for Negroes and mulattoes have been recalculated to allow for increase as an exponential process.
Indians: By proportion from estimates of 1568, with the addition of 50,000 for new Indians brought under Spanish control in the north.

our study of household and family in the first volume of these essays and upon a report of the 1560s which showed a substantial number of adult Spanish males in addition to vecinos.[16] We have further used our own estimates of numbers of Indians in central Mexico as of 1568 since they are based upon detailed examination of the fiscal and church material that has become available in recent years. We have used Aguirre Beltrán's

[16]Relacion de todos los pueblos de castellanos de Nueva España, n.d., but *ca.* 1560, in Latorre, *Relaciones geográficas de Indias,* pp. 103–111. The report gives numbers of Spaniards in terms of casas, vecinos, hombres, and españoles, with varying ratios for conversion to adult males. For Mexico City, the statement is 3,000 casas with up to 8,000 hombres in them; Guayangareo (Valladolid and, now, Morelia) had 30 casas with 40 españoles; Puebla had 500 casas with 800 españoles; Antequera, 200 casas with 350 españoles; and so on. For most towns the report gives merely españoles or vecinos. It also estimates for all of New Spain a floating population of 3,000 Spanish hombres, beyond its figures for populations in towns.

estimate for Indomestizos, Negroes, and Afromestizos without change but combined, as we have indicated, since our own examination of data at our disposal leads us to the conclusion that attempts at new estimates by us would not yield substantially different values. We have also modified Aguirre Beltrán's geographic regions, which are the sixteenth century dioceses, by combining them into areas the boundaries of which approximate but do not completely coincide with the areas we have established above. We have omitted the dioceses of Yucatan and Chiapas as outside central and northern Mexico.

The data in part A of Table 2.1 are estimates and should be read as such rather than as accurate to the last digit. Nevertheless, they show beyond a reasonable doubt that by 1570 the non-Indians had come to constitute approximately 3.2 percent of the entire population. The white component amounted to approximately two-thirds of the non-Indians, the African component (mostly slaves) amounted to approximately a quarter of the non-Indians. There were few mestizos.

Part B gives estimates of the four racial groups in the Mexican population as of 1646. For Spaniards we have used our own calculation based upon the proportion of change in population relative to 1570 of those urban centers for which Diez de la Calle gives data. For Indians we have used a new calculation that the audiencias of Mexico and Nueva Galicia, excluding Yucatan and New Mexico, had an Indian population of close to 1.3 million. It had reached a nadir at something between 1.1 and 1.2 million early in the seventeenth century and by the mid-century was definitely on the increase. In addition, the northward advance of Spanish settlements and missions had added perhaps another 50,000 Indians in 1646. Our figures for mestizos and pardos are based upon Aguirre Beltrán's estimates of those groups for 1646 but represent a revised calculation. His method, in the absence of sufficient data of the period, was to compute for each of his groups of mestizos the mean annual increase as shown by the values of 1570 and of 1742 and then multiply by seventy-five (that is, 1646 minus 1570). In other words, this is an interpolation based upon an assumed linear increase. But the increase during these 172 years must have been exponential rather than linear. Hence, his estimates for close to the half-way point, 1646, must be too high, causing both his calculated absolute values and percentages based on them to inflate the number of non-Indians. Accordingly, we have recalculated Aguirre Beltrán's estimates on the assumption of exponential increase. The table demonstrates a rapid rise in the relative proportion of the gente de razón in the total population; in 1646 they were approximately 14 percent of the total population. Although the españoles and pardos continued to be the largest group of non-Indians, the mestizos were increasing much more rapidly than either group. The table also demonstrates the tendency for non-Indians to concentrate in the west and north at the expense of the Indians.

We now consider the first group of the major sources of population statistics which were gathered in the eighteenth century. This is the book of Villaseñor y Sánchez (1746–1748), the material in whose *Theatro* is supplemented by figures from some of the original reports of the 1742–1746 census, those extant in the Archivo General de Indias, and from the Informe de Curatos for the bishopric of Guadalajara in 1760. We immediately encounter certain technical considerations which require comment and which pertain to all the eighteenth century documents.

The fact, already mentioned, that we are confronted with enumerations of many entities which do not distinguish clearly among the four racial categories means that we must resort to a process of selection which yields for each category a different sample from the complete array of localities. To use a hypothetical case, let us assume that a certain census reports the total population of 300 places. Of these, the Indians are segregated in 200. Therefore, the sample for percentage of non-Indians includes 200 items. Similarly, the percentage of españoles can be obtained for 100, pardos for 50, and mestizos for 10. Thus, each sample includes a different set of localities although all lie within the common set supplied by the census. Consequently, the percentage values will reflect the general features of the area although none will exactly equal the true value for the entire 300 entities.

Another problem arises with respect to the accuracy and reliability of the values obtained for populations of civil jurisdictions and parishes. The number of families or persons taken from the documents and the totals derived for areas and given in the tables are shown as running precisely to the last integer. For instance, in the 1742–1746 count, the jurisdiction of Chalco, in the central area, was found to have 4,148 families, of which 3,893 were Indian. The entire central area is shown in part A of Table 2.2 as containing 273,766 families. Clearly these numbers, as well as all others, can be but approximations, the limits of which we have no means of knowing. The intrinsic errors include faulty enumeration, poor judgment in allocation to racial group, mistakes in arithmetic, and slips of transcription by many hands. Since we cannot possibly arrive at the precise number in a population, our best recourse is to accept and utilize the values as they occur and concede freely that we are dealing with a very spurious exactitude.

Finally, beyond the error in conveying the information, error which although considerable may well be random, there exists a series of disturbing discrepancies in the relative number of specific categories living locally. This variability can strongly influence decisions concerning the distribution of racial groups. What is involved may be demonstrated by citing a few individual instances reported in the 1742–1746 census for the number of Indians as compared with non-Indians.

(1) Within the present-day states of Mexico, Hidalgo, and Morelos, the 1742–1746 census reports 27 jurisdictions, for each of which we can calculate the percentage of non-Indians

Table 2.2

Absolute and relative values for population of racial groups, from the census of 1742–1746. The figures represent families.

A. Non-Indians						
Area	*No. of Entities*	*Total Families*	*Indian*	*Non-Indian*	*% Non-Indian based on Total*	*% Non-Indian based on Mean*
Central Plateau	79	243,588	218,304	25,284	10.38	11.09
Central coasts	14	30,178	26,717	3,461	11.47	15.09
Center, total	93	273,766	245,021	28,745	10.50	11.69
West	68	63,277	39,902	23,375	36.94	40.14
North	39	78,131	22,219	55,912	71.56	60.34

Table 2.2 (cont.)

B. Españoles

Area	No. of Entities	Total Families	Non-Indian	Españoles	% Españoles in Total Families	% in Non-Indian Based on Total	% in Non-Indian Based on Mean
Central plateau	22	63,155	10,284	4,201	6.65	40.90	36.74
Central coasts	6	12,468	2,200	271	2.17	12.32	14.76
West	10	10,723	4,382	1,734	16.18	39.55	46.47
North	6	17,013	7,635	2,956	17.37	38.70	32.85

C. Mestizos

Area	No. of Entities	Total Families	Non-Indian	Mestizos	% Mestizos in Total Families	% in Non-Indian Based on Total	% in Non-Indian Based on Mean
Central plateau	14	34,154	5,886	2,330	6.82	39.60	45.65
Central coasts	2	5,299	746	54	1.02	7.24	5.84
West	7	8,717	3,361	1,068	12.25	31.75	22.90
North	4	13,680	7,003	2,601	19.03	37.10	38.15

D. Pardos

Area	No. of Entities	Total Families	Non-Indian	Pardos	% Pardos Total Families	% in Non-Indian Based on Total	% in Non-Indian Based on Mean
Central plateau	14	37,412	5,736	1,221	3.26	21.30	28.82
Central coasts	5	9,508	2,076	1,785	18.78	86.00	85.46
West	9	10,386	4,065	1,020	9.83	25.10	25.94
North	4	13,680	7,003	1,727	12.64	24.68	24.83

in the total population. If we then average the 27 values, the result is 14.65 percent. When we examine the individual percentages, we find 11 above the mean and 16 below it, a reasonable division. However, of the former group of percentages, the highest is 67.15 percent at Pachuca, and of the latter the lowest is 0.36 percent at Metztitlán, not 50 miles from Pachuca. The reasons for the wide disparity will be appreciated by anyone familiar with the history of the region and aware that Pachuca was an important mining center in 1742 and had been one for two centuries.

(2) If we calculate the corresponding percentages for the 21 parishes in that portion of the northern area which includes Zacatecas and northeastern Jalisco, we find 10 parishes with no Indians (100 percent non-Indian) and 4 parishes with all Indians (0 percent non-Indian). The intermediate values range from 41 to 93 percent. It is difficult to believe that such a situation actually existed, that in Fresnillo and Zacatecas City there was not a single Indian family. Yet how shall we revise the report submitted by a serious and competent bishop?

(3) In Table 2.2 the Colotlán-Bolaños area in the north (region III) is omitted, in part for the reasons already outlined. An additional factor is the unsatisfactory numerical material in the reports. One of the nineteen parishes mentioned in the Informe de Curatos as belonging to the area has no segregation of racial groups. Two are military and mining establishments with no Indians. The remainder are remote villages with no gente de razón of any description. These data simply cannot be treated in the usual manner.

Our procedure was to tabulate all the serviceable reports from the three sources listed above. The total number of localities was 200. The data were then reorganized and consolidated into the four parts of Table 2.2, which show, respectively, the values for Indians, españoles, mestizos, and pardos. In each part the numerical totals for families are given for the central plateau and central coasts (area I), the west (area II), and the north (area III). For each total the table specifies the number of entities out of the entire 200 which contributed to it. In part A, the population is divided between Indians, on the one hand, and the sum of non-Indians, on the other. In parts B, C, and D, the populations are given for the indicated number of entities, followed by division into total non-Indians and then into the number of españoles (B), mestizos (C), and pardos (D), respectively.

In addition to the absolute number of families, Table 2.2 shows the corresponding relative values in terms of percentages. Thus, part A contains the percentages of Indians in the total population; part B contains the percentage of españoles in the total population; parts C and D perform the same function for mestizos and pardos.

In part A the percentage of non-Indian families is derived according to two methods. The first is to divide the number of these families (x 100) shown for an entire area by the total families in that area. The second is to compute the percentage for each jurisdiction or parish individually and then take the average. The results for the same area necessarily diverge at least slightly because of the different weights accorded to large and to small entities. Of the two methods, the second is preferable for the purpose of comparing regions, although the first gives a quite satisfactory figure.

In parts B, C, and D, the relative value of the subpopulation in each case is calculated by both methods described only for the percentage within the non-Indian population. The percentage in the entire population (including Indians) is based upon total values alone.

Let us now consider the Indian population, the residue of the aboriginal inhabitants as it existed two-and-one-half centuries after the first entrance of the white and black races. The entire country north of Tehuantepec, as represented by approximately 415,000 families in 200 jurisdictions and parishes contained close to 74 percent Indians and 26 percent other stocks and mixtures. At the same time, part A of Table 2.2 demonstrates very substantial differences in the percentage of non-Indian (and reciprocally Indian) families reported from the three major regions into which we have divided viceregal New Spain.

In area I (the center), the percentage of non-Indian families calculated from total numbers is 10.50, and from the average, of entity values, 11.69 (with the standard deviation equal to $\pm$ 12.55 and the standard error equal to $\pm$ 1.30). Of the 93 entities 79 are located on the plateau, 14 on the coasts. The former show, according to the means of local values, 11.09 percent, the latter 15.09 percent. The difference is negligible ($t = 1.095$). However, the percentages for the west are much higher (36.94 on the total numbers, 40.14 by the means), and the north still greater (71.56 by totals, 60.34 by the means). The validity of these differences may be tested by analysis of variance. For the three primary areas, with the means of entities, the value of F (variance) is 57.6, extremely significant.

Within the primary regions it is possible to discover restricted or subordinate areas which vary among each other with respect to the relative importance of the Indian population and the gente de razón. For example, on the central plateau we may set apart the western portion (states of Mexico and Hidalgo), the northeastern portion (Puebla, Tlaxcala), and the southeastern portion (Oaxaca, including the Mixteca Alta, the Zapoteca, and the central valleys). These provide, respectively, 27, 20, 17 jurisdictions for which the average percentages of non-Indian population are 14.64, 12.91, and 1.24. Evidently, there is little difference between the first two, but highland Oaxaca has many fewer non-Indians than either of them. If it were worthwhile, a rather detailed analysis could be made, but these refined distinctions are of interest primarily for purely local or regional studies.

On the whole, the conclusion is warranted that the central region, the area formerly under Aztec authority, was still heavily Indian in character, that the Tarascan territory and Nueva Galicia were almost equally divided between Indian and non-Indian, and that the stretch of post-Conquest settlement to the north was inhabited by a racial conglomeration in which the Indians were thinly represented, and which had migrated from the center and south of Mexico. At the same time, throughout Mexico, there were distinct differences between geographical units of lower orders of magnitude, such as jurisdictions, parishes, and towns.

We may consolidate briefly the data for Mexico entire. For the full sample of each of the three racial subpopulations, we show the number of entities which contributed to the sample, the total non-Indian families, with the number and percentage of these families who were in the subpopulation named in the left-hand column.

Racial Group	No. of Entities	Non-Indian Families	No. of Families in Racial Group Indicated	% of Families in Racial Group Indicated
Españoles	44	24,501	9,162	37.00
Mestizos	27	16,996	6,053	35.60
Pardos	32	18,880	5,753	30.45
				103.05

From the sum of the percentages (103.05), it is clear that a sampling error is present of plus or minus several percent. Nevertheless, there is a remarkably even division among the three components throughout the country as a whole.

In the individual tables this same consistency is observed and, indeed, with one important exception, extends to the proportions of the components found in the four geographical regions : central plateau, central coasts, west, and north. The exception is the central coastal area, both Atlantic and Pacific, in which the relative number of pardos is very great (85 percent) and that of españoles and mestizos is correspondingly small.

An analysis of variance demonstrates the weight of this exception. One method is to calculate F for españoles, for mestizos, and for pardos as the percentage of each of these is distributed among the four regions. When we do this, we get F for the three racial groups equal to 3.53, 4.11, and 11.76, respectively. The third is highly significant, the other two moderately significant (between the 1 and 5 percent levels of probability). If, for pardos, the coastal region, with five entities participating, is omitted, F for the remaining three areas becomes completely without significance.

An alternative method is to use as a basis the distribution of percentages for the three racial types, as they occur within each of the four regions separately. The values of F then are found to be (in parentheses are the numbers of contributing entities) :

Central plateau	3.49	5 percent level	(50)
Central coasts	65.49	highly significant	(13)
West	5.25	1 percent level	(26)
North	0.17	non-significant	(14)

From the foregoing presentation of the data, three tentative statements may be made concerning the racial composition of the Mexican people at the mid-eighteenth century.

(1) The Indian (aboriginal) population was still overwhelmingly preponderant on the central plateau and along both coasts (85–90 percent).

(2) The Indian component was much smaller in the west-central region (Michoacán and Nueva Galicia had 60–65 percent) and was further reduced in the newer settlements to the north (30–40 percent). The white, black, and mixed groups were correspondingly augmented.

(3) Among the non-Indian fraction, the three components designated españoles, mestizos, and pardos constituted approximately equal numbers in all areas. The outstanding exception was the very high concentration of the black element along the central coasts (85 percent of the non-Indians).

Our second important body of data is supplied by the census reports of 1777. In most of these, the parish priests, according to their best judgment, stated directly the racial affiliation of each person. Thus we have been able to count with reasonable fidelity the number in each principal racial group, parish by parish.

We have tabulated the reports from a total of 202 parishes, within the bishoprics of Oaxaca, Puebla, and Durango, which contained a total population of very close to 600,000 persons. Of these, eleven did not differentiate racial affiliation and, consequently, had to be omitted from consideration. For the comparison of Indians with non-Indians we used the remaining 191 parishes. Of the latter, 179 showed a segregation of subpopulations among the non-Indians. In addition, we examined, but did not include in our calculation, the returns from 26 Indian missions in Durango. These missions were all in the territory of the Tepehuán and Tarahumara tribes in the Sierra Madre Occidental. They consisted of the Indian congregations which were administered by a few missionaries and were maintained as relatively independent units. For only 8 of them is there any report of non-Indian communities, and these were counted separately from the mission establishments. It is best to omit this series of reports entirely unless some special purpose can be served by their inclusion.

The coverage of Mexico as a whole is more restricted than with the 1742–1760 documents, for the bishoprics of Mexico, Michoacán, and Guadalajara are entirely lacking. Hence there are no data whatever for the western region (area II), and the north is limited to the bishopric of Durango, which fell entirely within the region designated IIIE. Not all the parishes in any of our three bishoprics are to be found in the records, but the representation is close to 50 percent and the sample is quite adequate, especially since the geographical distribution is very uniform. The numerical totals are in persons, not families. The results of our analyses are shown in Table 2.3, parts A to F.

First let us examine part A, which shows the relationship

Table 2.3

Absolute and relative values for population of racial groups. Summaries of the figures counted from microfilm of the orginal reports of individual parishes for the census of 1777. The numbers in these tables represent persons, not families. The regions are as in Table 2.2. All entities are parishes.

A. Non-Indians

Area	No. of Entities	Total Pop.	Indian	Non-Indian	% Non-Indian Based on Total	% Non-Indian Based on Mean of Parishes
Central plateau	139	424,877	358,992	65,885	15.51	12.86
Central coasts	22	62,013	44,917	17,096	27.57	30.69
West	*Absent*					
North (Durango)	30	84,665	20,839	63,826	75.39	71.07

B. Españoles[a]

(1)	(2)	(3)	(4)	(5)	(6)	(7)	(8)
Central plateau	127	395,828	63,191	17,403	4.40	27.54	30.65
Central coasts	22	63,013	17,096	1,491	2.37	8.72	13.83
West	*Absent*						
North (Durango)	30	84,665	63,826	15,593	18.42	24.43	26.74

C. Mestizos[a]

(1)	(2)	(3)	(4)	(5)	(6)	(7)	(8)
Central plateau	127	395,828	63,191	32,999	8.34	52.22	44.28
Central coasts	22	63,013	17,096	1,243	1.97	7.27	15.52
West	*Absent*						
North (Durango)	30	84,665	63,826	9,445	11.16	14.80	17.41

Table 2.3 (cont.)

D. Pardos[a]

(1)	(2)	(3)	(4)	(5)	(6)	(7)	(8)
Central plateau	127	395,828	63,191	12,789	3.23	20.24	25.07
Central coasts	22	63,013	17,096	14,362	22.79	84.01	70.65
West	Absent						
North (Durango)	30	84,665	63,826	38,788	45.81	60.77	55.85

[a] Column 1 represents the region, column 2 the number of entities contributing, column 3 the total population, column 4 the non-Indian population, column 5 the number in the racial group concerned, column 6 the percentage of the racial group in the total population, column 7 the percentage of the same group in the non-Indian population based upon total numbers, column 8 the same as column 7 but based upon the means of parish values.

E. Non-Indian Population

Area	No. of Entities	% of Each Racial Group in Each Area as the Mean of Parish Values			Variance (F) for Each Area with Respect to the Occurrence in It of the Three Racial Groups
		Españoles	Mestizos	Pardos	
Central plateau	127	30.65	44.28	25.07	22.445
Central coasts	22	13.83	15.52	70.65	47.103
West	Absent				
North (Durango)	30	26.74	17.41	55.85	28.690
Variance (F) for each racial group with respect to its occurrence in the three areas		6.838	25.811	42.401	

Table 2.3 (cont.)

F. Non-Indian Population

Subarea	No. of Entities	% of Each Racial Group in Each Subarea of the Central Plateau as the Mean of Parish Values			Variance (F) for Each Subarea, as in part E
		Españo-les	Mesti-zos	Pardos	
Eastern section	52	34.79	50.61	14.60	39.100
Central Veracruz	11	20.22	49.99	29.79	3.144
Highland Oaxaca	39	33.50	36.80	29.70	0.860
Mixteca Baja-Balsas	25	22.18	40.26	37.56	5.129
Variance (F) for each racial group, as in part E		3.206	2.878	6.698	

between Indians and non-Indians. The three areas to which the census is applicable are characterized by great differences in the relative proportion of the two racial components.

The central plateau gives, respectively, by totals and by means of parishes 15.51 and 12.86 percent of non-Indians; the central coasts 27.57 and 30.69 percent; the north (Durango) 75.39 and 71.07 percent. For the percentages by means of parishes in the three regions, the value of F is 121.3, extremely significant. The geographical trend of these percentages simulates that shown in part A of Table 2.2, but the spread is somewhat greater.

Of particular interest are the central coasts. The mean percentage of non-Indians in twenty-two parishes is 30.69. However, the variability is great. The standard deviation is $\pm$ 33.61 and the standard error is $+7.17$. If the individual parishes are examined, wide disparities are noted between areas of geographic propinquity and ecological similarity. For instance, Cosamaloapan showed 0.70 percent non-Indians but nearby Tlalixcoyan had 92.90 percent. It is very difficult to believe that these two neighboring parishes, in southern Veracruz differed so profoundly in racial composition. On the south coast of Oaxaca, the parish of Los Cortijos reported a population 100 percent non-Indian whereas Pinotepa de Don Luis, not far away, contained only 1.12 percent gente de razón.

In contrast to the coasts, the central plateau was much more consistently Indian in character. The mean of 139 parishes was 12.86 percent non-Indian, with a standard deviation of $\pm$ 14.58, but a standard error of ± 1.24. The value of t for the means of the two regions, plateau and coast, is 4.25, well beyond the 1 percent level of probability.

The bishopric of Durango, with thirty parishes, gives a mean value for non-Indian population of 71.07 percent, a figure which may be compared with 60.34 percent for the north in part A of Table 2.2. At the same time, the respective percentages based upon total population were 75.39 and 71.56. Clearly the same type of inhabitants were present in both cycles of enumeration, although different local areas are concerned. That the percentage figures for the bishopric of Durango in 1777 differed widely from those for Oaxaca and Puebla is shown by deriving the appropriate values of t. For the means of Durango and the central coasts, t is 5.12, and for those of Durango and the central plateau, t is 13.62. These values conform to that for F found by analysis of variance in the three regions collectively.

The remaining parts of Table 2.3 pertain specifically to the gente de razón. In parts B, C, and D are shown respectively the absolute and relative numbers of the españoles, mestizos, and pardos in the non-Indian population. The relative values for each group are expressed both as a percentage of the total population and as a percentage of the non-Indian population, the latter based upon the total numbers and the means of parish percentages. As in part A, there are three principal regions, the central plateau, the central coasts, and the bishopric of Durango (in area III E). The west, area II, is absent.

If we examine the racial groups in the three areas, the percentages of which are derived both from total numbers and from parish means, we find certain conclusion to be warranted.

(1) The relative strength of the pardos is very high on the central coasts, also very substantial in the north, and moderate to low on the plateau.

(2) The españoles are few on the coasts, moderate in

number on the plateau and in the north.

(3) The mestizos are few on the coasts and in the north but show a substantial number on the central plateau.

If these results are recast in terms of areas, we find that :

(4) On the plateau, the racial groups are rather evenly divided, but mestizos exceed españoles, with pardos the fewest.

(5) On the coasts, the pardos preponderate heavily.

(6) In Durango the pardos constitute one-half or more of the non-Indian population, with the mestizos the fewest.

Of these differences, the two which appear to be of salient consequence are the very heavy concentration of the pardos on the coasts and their surprising strength in the north. The demographic importance of the Negro and part-Negro element in these two regions can be appreciated if it is noted that this group comprised about 25 percent of the total population on the coasts and close to 45 percent in Durango.

The test of the validity of the percentages shown in parts B, C, and D is demonstrated in part E. The six values for F range from approximately 6 to 47, with from 22 to 127 individual items. The 1 percent level of probability for these numbers of cases and groups corresponds to F values of the order of 3 to 5. Consequently, our results would imply a high degree of significance. On the other hand, it must be remembered that we are using data which are subject to numerous sources of error before any analysis is undertaken and that the samples, although adequate, are by no means complete. Therefore, secondary differences, even though they possess great statistical significance, should not be regarded as necessarily important socially and racially.

That this point of view is justified is demonstrated by the percentages, and values for F, to be found in part F, where the central plateau region is split according to the four principal subordinate areas into which the bishoprics of Puebla and Oaxaca may be divided. The number of cases is smaller; the entire region is relatively homogeneous. The differences between percentages are still considerable; yet, of the seven values calculated for F, one is highly significant statistically, two are significant (at or above the 1 percent level of probability), and four possess little or no significance.

From this discussion it is apparent that the six semi-quantitative conclusions set forth above may be accorded reasonable confidence. On the other hand, the 1777 census as we have it, will not support much further refinement in treatment of the record.

The documents in which we encounter today the censuses of 1789–1793 have already been described. With these we possess the advantage that a very comprehensive series of population summaries have already been computed and are available in the ramos of Padrones and Historia at the Archivo General de la Nación in Mexico City. It is therefore unnecessary for the present purpose to utilize the extensive person-by-person enumerations recorded in the many volumes of the ramo of Padrones. Our figures are in Tables 2.4, parts A to E, the form of which follows that of Table 2.3, parts A to D for the census of 1777. Parts A, B, C, and D of Table 2.4 show, respectively, the total numbers and corresponding percentages for non-Indians in the total population and for españoles, mestizos, and pardos in both non-Indian and total populations.

The geographic segregation distinguishes the usual four major regions : the central plateau, the central coasts, the west, and the north. Under each, where they are available, are shown two types of data. The first consists of totals and percentages for jurisdictions (called also subdelegaciones) because the jurisdiction was the unit district for reporting and tabulation. It will be noted, to be sure, that relatively few of the more than 200 existing jurisdictions are represented in the summaries contained in Padrones and Historia. The second category of data embraces totals for large entities, particularly provinces, with the addition of two important jurisdictions, Puebla and Durango, and, as a separate item, Mexico City.

In order to show, insofar as possible, the exact body of knowledge at our disposal, we have included part E. Here are given the number of persons in each racial group for all localities summarized in the two ramos. The data for many localities are incomplete; frequently mestizos and pardos are combined as a single group. Hence the totals and percentages in parts A to D include only those entities for which the corresponding values can be found in part E. It is thus clear that with the censuses of 1789–1793, as with the pervious censuses, the tabulations bring to light serious gaps in the record—extending to whole regions. Moreover, here, as previously, the samples are unlike for each of the principal racial groups, and the results are subject to the same range of error.

The racial distributions demonstrated by the figures

Table 2.4

Absolute and relative values for the population of racial groups, 1789–1793. The values for the groups for jurisdictions, as well as for individual entities, are derived from the more detailed data in part E, which also shows where possible the documentary source of each numerical total, in all cases from the ramos of Padrones and Historia in the Archivo General de la Nación. All are from the censuses of 1789–1793, except the jurisdiction of Puebla, which is from that of 1777.

A. Non-Indians

Area and Entities	Total Pop.	Indian	Non-Indian	% Non-Indian Based on Total	% Non-Indian Based on Mean of Jurisdictions
Central plateau					
20 jurisdictions	371,253	344,740	26,513	7.14	8.44
Mexico City	104,760	25,603	79,157	75.60	
Province Mexico	1,043,223	742,186	301,047	28.87	
Province Tlaxcala	59,158	42,878	16,280	27.52	
Jurisdiction Puebla	71,366	24,039	47,327	66.38	
Province Oaxaca	411,336	363,080	48,256	11.75	
Central coasts					
3 jurisdictions	54,328	40,007	14,321	26.36	23.07
West	*Absent*				
North					
14 jurisdictions	444,825	213,549	231,276	52.00	52.40
Jurisdiction Durango	10,897	2,491	8,406	77.15	
Province Guanajuato	397,966	175,182	222,784	56.00	
Province Sonora	38,305	23,189	15,116	39.38	
Province Sinaloa	55,062	18,780	36,282	65.90	
Province New Mexico	30,953	10,664	20,289	65.55	
Province Ant. Calif.	4,076	3,234	842	20.60	

B. Españoles[a]

(1)	(2)	(3)	(4)	(5)	(6)	(7)
Central plateau						
20 jurisdictions	371,253		12,933	3.48		
51 jurisdictions		211,216	86,277		40.86	43.12
Mexico City	104,760	79,157	52,706	50.30	66.70	
Province Mexico	1,043,223	301,047	136,295	13.07	45.30	

Table 2.4 (cont.)

			B. Españoles[a] (cont.)			
(1)	(2)	(3)	(4)	(5)	(6)	(7)
Province Tlaxcala	59,158	16,280	8,074	13.66	49.65	
Jurisdiction Puebla	71,366	47,327	18,369	25.57	38.80	
Province Oaxaca	411,336	48,256	26.527	6.45	55.00	
Central coasts						
3 jurisdictions	54,328		5,250	9.57		
6 jurisdictions		28,977	5,943		20.50	21.26
West						
6 jurisdictions		21,174	8,605		40.65	40.02
North						
14 jurisdictions	444,825		105,533	23.75		
16 jurisdictions		253,580	119,205		47.05	45.75
Jurisdiction						
Durango	10,897	8,406	1,145	10.50	13.62	
Province						
Guanajuato	397,966	222,784	103,506	26.00	46.50	
Province Sonora	38,305	15,116	8,199	21.40	54.30	
Province Sinaloa	55,062	36,282	18,533	33.70	51.05	
Province New						
Mexico	30,953		14,553	47.00		
Province Ant.						
Calif.	4,076	842	241	5.92	28.65	

[a]Column 1 represents region and entities, column 2 the total population, column 3 the non-Indian population, column 4 the number in the racial group concerned (españoles), column 5 the percentage of the racial group in the total population, column 6 the percentage of the same group in the non-Indian population based upon total numbers, column 7 the same as column 6 but based upon the means of entity values.

			C. Mestizos[a]			
(1)	(2)	(3)	(4)	(5)	(6)	(7)
Central plateau						
34 jurisdictions		190,962	83,923		43.95	43.15
Mexico City	104,760	79,157	19,357	18.50	24.33	
Province Mexico	1,043,223	301,047	112,113	10.75	37.22	
Province Tlaxcala	59,158	16,280	7,509	12.70	46.07	
Central coasts						
5 jurisdictions		21,818	1,240		5.68	9.68

Table 2.4 (cont.)

C. Mestizos[a](*cont.*)

(1)	(2)	(3)	(4)	(5)	(6)	(7)
West						
5 jurisdictions		13,136	1,928		14.68	17.44
North						
6 jurisdictions[b]		119,649	35,545		29.70	29.08
Jurisdiction						
Durango	10,897	8,406	386	3.54	4.60	
Province						
Guanajuato	397,966	222,784	46,982	11.81	21.08	
Province Sonora	38,305	15,116	3,902	10.18	25.80	
Province Sinaloa	55,062	36,282	2,671	4.85	7.36	
Province Ant.						
Calif.	4,076	842	418	10.26	49.65	

D. Pardos[a]

(1)	(2)	(3)	(4)	(5)	(6)	(7)
Central plateau						
34 jurisdictions		190,962	30,933		16.20	18.48
Mexico City	104,760	79,157	7,094	6.77	8.97	
Province Mexico	1,043,223	301,047	52,639	5.05	17.48	
Province Tlaxcala	59,158	16,280	697	1.18	4.28	
Central coasts						
5 jurisdictions		21,818	19,193		87.90	83.60
West						
5 jurisdictions		13,136	5,983		45.55	47.00
North						
6 jurisdictions[b]		119,649	24,817		20.85	19.61
Jurisdiction						
Durango	10,897	8,406	6,875	63.10	81.75	
Province						
Guanajuato	397,966	222,784	72,276	18.15	32.42	
Province Sonora	38,305	15,116	3,015	7.87	19.95	
Province Sinaloa	55,062	36,282	15,078	27.35	41.55	
Province Ant.						
Calif.	4,076	842	183	4.49	21.75	

[a] Column headings as in part B.
[b] Includes 5 small cities.

Table 2.4 (cont.)

E. Basic data used for parts A to D

Here are given the numerical values taken from the summaries in Padrones (P) and Historia (H). Only the figures for the four racial groups are given here, as they occur in the documents mentioned. Where appropriate, the non-Indian population may be obtained by summing the values for españoles, mestizos, and pardos. Similarly the total population may be obtained by summing the values for all four racial groups. For lack of space these totals are omitted here. The sources P or H are followed by the volume number and folio number(s).

Area and Entity[a]	*Españo-les*	*Mesti-zos*	*Pardos*	*Indians*	*Source*
Central plateau					
Chalco	300	152			P : 3 ; 24
San Cristóbal	830	924			P : 6 ; 361
Texcoco	3,499	1,808			P : 43 ; 153
Zumpango	500	1,292			H : 72 ; 165
Cuautitlán	1,014	2,237	255		P : 4 ; 239
Coyoacán	2,198	1,211	522		P : 6 ; 115, 143
Tacuba	1,826	3,523	309		P : 6 ; 299, 314
Tulancingo	7,263	7,830	1,161		P : 1 ; 338, 375
Ixmiquilpan	1,471	2,422	54		P : 2 ; 90
Pachuca	2,755	3,821	3,039		P : 2 ; 211, 259
Actopan	1,474	2,291	43		P : 3 ; 95
Tula	2,003	1,843	251		P : 7 ; 406
Cuautla Amilpas	1,324	2.001	5,215		P : 8 : 107, 264
Otumba	1,118	935	130		P : 12 ; 202, 203
Lerma	821	283	87		P : 12 ; 244, 249
Tetepango	1,762	2,460	297		P : 18 ; 101
Teotihuacán	895	388	266		P : 18 ; 341, 351
Zempoala	315	638	749		P : 20 ; 33, 57
Toluca	3,994	2,858	165		P : 21 ; 260, 263
Xochimilco	1,145	643	75	18,049	P : 29 ; 3
Chilcuautla	183	647	65	4,607	H : 523 ; 228
Aculco	1,444	1,796	261	4,692	H : 523 ; 230
Huejutla	595	270	457		P : 3 ; 406
Chicontepec	239	576	380		P : 12 ; 25, 32
Tehuacán	1,821	2,199	1,436		P : 3 ; 318
Ápam	1,295	651	1,059		P : 4 ; 369, 398
S. Juan Llanos	3,496	4,637	165		P : 8 ; 229
Tochimilco	421	517	104		P : 12 ; 112
Tlaxcala (city)	8,329	6,050	282		P : 22 ; 403, 405
Atlixco	2,093	2,122	1,182		P : 25 ; 85, 87, 105

Table 2.4 (cont.)

E. Basic data used for parts A to D (cont.)

Area and entity[a]	Españo-les	Mesti-zos	Pardos	Indians	Source
Central plateau (cont'd)					
Huejotzingo	1,931	3,679	381		P:27; 141, 143, 149
Izúcar	1,028	2,121	3,850		P:28;84,86,135
Chietla	266	754	1,017		P:28;184,186
Tepeaca	8,691	13,199	1,245		P:38;541,569
Orizaba	4,903	3,457	759		P:19;325,425
Jalapa	5,673	3,095	2,009		P:20;245,337
Antequera	1,160	974		35,569	H:523;94
Cuatro Villas	339	152		17,249	„
Villa Alta	192	120		58,088	„
Nochixtlán	335	5		5,615	„
Teposcolula	4,433	184		38,974	„
Huitzo	181	123		5,281	„
Teotitlán del Valle	96	177		12,159	„
Teutila	37	44		23,825	„
Ixtepeji	89	85		5,469	„
Miahuatlán	330	928		14,745	„
Nejapa	225	950		12,885	„
Chontales	26	89		7,283	„
Teotitlán del Camino	460	401		18,506	„
Zimatlán	476	960		16,548	„
Teococuilco	71	85		12,782	„
Huajuapan	500	4,746		25,524	„
Juxtlahuaca	1,211	70		6,890	„
Tixtla	1,471	1,475	1,701		P:17;26,182
Tlapa	859	1,284	1,962		P:21;52,94
Central coasts					
Tamiahua	336	153	2,453		P:18;184,178
Acapulco	122	141	5,416		P:16;244,429
Igualapa	235	594	5,206		P:18;230,232
Huamelula	33	141	336		P:12;65,75
Jicayán (1777)	659	211	5,782		H:72;197
Jicayán (1793)	2,802	5,379		20,568	H:523;94
Huamelula	207	376		3,250	„
Tehuantepec	2,241	3,316		16,189	„
West					
Charo	94	28	124		P:12;43,53
Cuitzeo	1,636	653	1,423		P:16;66,106
Acámbaro[b]	1,650	1,045	1,385		P:23;217,341
Jiquilpan (1777)	3,380	5,106			H:73;137
Colima	4,376	1,133			P:11;668
Autlán	1,186	228			H:73;127

Table 2.4 (cont.)

E. Basic data used for parts A to D (*cont.*)

Area and entity[a]	Españo-les	Mesti-zos	Pardos	Indians	Source
Motines	436	110	540		P:21;321,364
Ahuacatlán	1,409	92	2,511		P:14;188
Amula	1,441	137			H:72;202
North					
Querétaro					
(juris.)	14,821	12,888	5,358	47,430	P:12;141
S. Juan del Río	5,014	3,021	1,011		P:35;587,671
Dolores	3,131		3,606	8,924	H:523;88
Celaya	15,176		18,119	34,506	,,
Silao	6,043		8,044	14,544	,,
San Miguel	3,410		5,247	13,930	,,
Irapuato	6,293		11,237	13,171	,,
Guanajuato	24,160		19,438	11,814	,,
Pénjamo	2,670		8,548	9,734	,,
Salamanca	8,509		5,380	13,345	,,
San Felipe	3,541		6,959	7,221	,,
Salvatierra	6,032		6,420	12,543	,,
San Luis de la					
Paz	4,315		6,899	19,531	,,
Yuriria	5,435		4,479	1,900	,,
Acámbaro[b]	1,997		3,121	4,956	,,
Aguascalientes	8,658	2,191	2,409		P:5;224, 286, 313
Dolores (city)	1,885	1,362			P:24;114
Silao (city)	3,318	1,741			P:42;327
San Miguel					
(city)	2,873	1,753			P:36;264
Irapuato (city)	3,439	2,157	1,968		P:37;448,601
Celaya (city)	9,790	3,890	3,338		P:26;926,1175
Guanajuato					
(city)	15,374	13,589	10,733		P:32;355
					P:33;672

[a] Jurisdiction unless otherwise stated.
[b] For convenience, one of the reports of Acámbaro is placed with the West, the other with the North. The jurisdiction is on the boundary between the two regions.

E. Basic data used for parts A to D (*cont.*)
Large entities and special cases

Central plateau					
Mexico City	52,706	19,357	7,094	25,603	
Mexico (prov.)	136,295	112,113	52,639	742,186	H:523;145
Tlaxcala					
(prov.)	8,074	7,509	697	42,878	H:523;113
Puebla (juris.)					
(1777)	18,369	28,958		24,039	H:73;122
Oaxaca (prov.)	26,527	21,729		363,080	H:523;94

Table 2.4 (cont.)

E. Basic data used for parts A to D (*cont.*)

Area and entity	Españo-les	Mesti-zos	Pardos	Indians	Source
North					
Durango					
(juris.)	1,145	386	6,875	2,491	H : 522; 268
Guanajuato					
(prov.)	103,526	46,982	72,276	175,182	H : 523; 76
Sonora (prov.)	8,199	3,902	3,015	23,189	H : 522; 274
Sinaloa (prov.)	18,533	2,671	15,078	18,780	H : 522; 275
New Mexico					
(prov.)	14,553	5,736		10,664	H : 522; 246
Ant. Calif.					
(prov.)	241	418	183	3,234	H : 522; 267

presented follow, in general, the lines laid down in prior enumerations. Briefly, we observe these conditions:

(1) The non-Indian population (gente de razón) is relatively small on the central plateau, assumes greater proportions on the coasts, and reaches a maximum in the north (data for the western region are wholly lacking). The means of jurisdictions (see Table 2.4, part A) provide a value for F of 62.26, highly significant. Furthermore, the larger, single entities manifest the same trend toward a relatively smaller Indian population in the north. This finding is supported by a comparison of percentages for three provinces in the center (Mexico, Tlaxcala, Oaxaca) with those for three in the north (Guanajuato, Sonora, Sinaloa). The value for t is 3.25, at the 2 to 5 percent level of probability.

It is interesting to observe with the regional percentages in the north that whereas the non-Indian component is relatively strong numerically in the provinces of Guanajuato, Sinaloa, and New Mexico, and strongest of all in the jurisdiction of Durango, it is comparatively weak in the farther northwest, Sonora and Antigua (Baja) California. This distinction arises from the fact that the former group of provinces were long settled and had been filled up by immigration from the south as the aboriginal inhabitants were decimated and dispersed. On the other hand, the northwest, at this time, was in essence either frontier or wild Indian country, populated predominantly by mission converts, and indeed the home of such powerful hostile tribes as the Apache. If we had the census reports for the ultimate frontier, Arizona and Upper California, we would find a vanishingly small percentage of non-Indians in the total population.

(2) In its distribution, the Negro and part-Negro component reaches relatively high levels along the central coasts and remains at a low level on the plateau, a condition which parallels that seen with the censuses of 1777 and 1742–1746. If the mean value from 4 small jurisdictions in Michoacán and one in Nayarit is to be credited, the level was relatively high in the west. For the north, the results are somewhat equivocal. In six jurisdictions, five of which contained cities (Querétaro, Irapuato, Celaya, Guanajuato, and Aguascalientes), the mean percentage of pardos among the non-Indians was 19.61. However, the jurisdiction of Durango, which also contained a city, had 81.75 percent; the province of Guanajuato had 32.42 percent; and the province of Sinaloa had 41.55 percent. In the frontier provinces of Sonora and Antigua California the level of the pardo fraction was again low. On the whole, we must consider that the longer-established areas in the west and north contained a relatively large proportion of persons designated as Negro and part-Negro among the non-Indian population.

(3) Both españoles and mestizos constitute a relatively small proportion of the non-Indians on the central coasts, a condition arising naturally as the result of the heavy concentration of the black component in these areas. There is a corresponding predominance of the white and mestizo elements on the plateau. Otherwise, apart from purely local variation, the distribution of the non-Indian, non-pardo component appears to have been rather uniform throughout the well settled portions of the country.

(4) A significant factor in the control of racial distribution may have been the composition of the urban, as opposed to the rural, population. In Table 2.5 we have assembled percentages of the various racial fractions as found in a group of cities, or jurisdictions primarily urban in character. Also we show the percentages for the predominantly rural provinces of Mexico, Tlaxcala, Oaxaca, Guanajuato, Sonora, Sinaloa, New Mexico, and Antigua California, together with those for a few jurisdictions.

The distribution of Indians is clear. For six cities the mean percentage of non-Indians is 75.62, for eight rural provin-

Table 2.5

Percentage composition of population by racial group, 1789–1793, approximately according to residence: urban versus rural.

Locality	% Non- Indian in Total Pop.	% Españoles in Non- Indian Pop.	% Mestizos in Non- Indian Pop.	% Pardos in Non- Indian Pop.	Source
Mexico (prov.)	28.87	45.30	37.22	17.48	H:523;145
Mexico City	75.60	66.70	24.33	8.97	
Puebla (juris.)					
(1777)	66.38	38.80			H:73;122
Tlaxcala (prov.)	27.52	49.65	46.07	4.28	H:523;113
Tlaxcala (city)		56.80	41.41	1.79	P:22;403
Oaxaca (prov.)	11.75	55.00			H:523;94
Antequera (juris.)	27.34	77.70	3.97	18.33	H:522;259
Oaxaca (city)	72.10	81.40	3.47	15.13	H:522;259
Guanajuato (prov.)	56.00	46.50	21.08	32.42	H:523;76
Guanajuato (juris.)	78.70	55.40			H:523;88
Guanajuato (city)[a]		42.80	38.44	18.76	P:30;839
Guanajuato (casco)[b]	86.40	65.20			H:523;88
Querétaro (juris)	41.05	44.80	39.01	16.19	P12;141
Querétaro (city)	76.05	47.80	34.78	17.42	P:12;141
Aguascalientes (juris.)		65.30	16.53	18.17	P:5;171
Aguascalientes (city)		77.20	18.94	3.86	P:5;313
Irapuato (juris.)	57.10	35.90			H:523;88
Irapuato (congreg.)		45.45	28.55	26,00	P:37;448
Celaya (juris.)	49.15	45.55			H:523;88
Celaya (city)		57.60	22.60	19.61	P:26;926
Durango (juris.)	77.15	13.62	4.63	81.75	H:522;268
Sonora (prov.)	39.38	54.30	25.80	19.95	H:522;274
Sinaloa (prov.)	65.90	51.05	7.36	41.55	H:522;275
New Mexico (prov.)	65.55				H:522;246
Ant. California (prov.)	20.60	28.65	49.65	21.75	H:522;267

[a] Excluding mines and haciendas.
[b] Urban core.

ces and jurisdictions it is 39.45. The critical ratio of these means is 4.07, beyond the 1 percent level of probability. Similar analysis for the proportion of españoles, mestizos, and pardos in the non-Indian population leads to no positive result. The most promising group in this respect is that of the españoles, who certainly constituted a large fraction of the inhabitants of the principal cities, particularly Mexico City. However, the mean of ten cities from Table 2.5 is 55.04 percent of the non-Indians whereas that for seven provinces is 47.21. The critical ratio of these means is 0.97, completely nonsignificant. Values for pardos and mestizos are even smaller. The conclusion, therefore, must be that although the gente de razón as a class tended to congregate in urban communities, there was little variation within the class, regardless of its type of residence.

In addition to the three formal censuses, which enumerated all four primary racial components of the population, we can utilize a series of documents which yield valuable evidence concerning two of them, pardos and Indians. Of these, the most complete and accurate is the Matrícula of 1805. Here will be found a very careful count of the tributary population as it existed during the decade of the 1790s. In it the distinction is clearly drawn between the pardo and the Indian portions. Moreover, in conjuction with earlier records of the tributaries, it becomes possible to make a rough assessment of the changes which may have occurred in the relative proportion of the two racial groups throughout the eighteenth century.

The fact that the Matrícula covers only the tributary class raises the question whether the racial groupings were identical with or parallel to those in the general population. We know that, with the exception of caciques and a few others, all Indians were subject to tribute. Hence we may regard their population as including the same social category in both the Matrícula and the censuses of 1742–1746 to 1793. With regard to the Negroid caste we cannot be so sure. A great many slaves, when freed, passed into the tributary class. Others, however, intermarried with whites and mestizos, and they or their offspring could become regarded as true gente de razón, not subject to tribute. Hence the numerical relationship between those designated Negroes, pardos, and mulattoes who were tributaries, and the Indians, may not have coincided exactly with that governing the two racial groups in the population as a whole.

For the late eighteenth century there are a few scanty

indications. We can find thirty-three entities, jurisdictions, or parishes for which we have figures from both the Matrícula and at least one of the censuses. For these cases we can calculate the percentage of pardos in the combined population of pardos and indios and thus get a direct comparison. These percentages are assembled in Table 2.6. Geographically they are widely scattered, and arithmetically they tell us only that their magnitude appears to run consistently in all the recorded sources. Rigid statistical analysis is not feasible. We have, however, calculated the mean difference in percentage values between the 1805 figures and those for 1742-1746, 1777, and 1793, using the earliest census for which a figure is available. Furthermore, we have selected the values for jurisdictions where they exist, otherwise those for parishes, with the realization that a parish is not coterminous with a jurisdiction, even if they both carry the same name.

For thirty-three pairs of percentages, the earlier figures exceed those of 1805 on the average by 1.86 percent. The standard error of this mean is ±1.05. The mean, therefore, is less than twice as great as its standard error and cannot be regarded as significant. An alternative method is to determine t for the means of the two sets of percentages. The value of t is 1.07, definitely nonsignificant.

At the end of Table 2.6, we have placed the percentages for the provinces and/or bishoprics of Mexico, Puebla, Oaxaca, Guanajuato, San Luis Potosí, Arizpe, and Durango for the

Table 2.6

Comparison of identical or closely similar localities which appear both in the Matrícula of 1805 and in the censuses of 1793, 1777, and 1742, with respect to the percentage of pardos in the combined population of pardos and Indians. The units were tributaries for 1805, families for 1742, and total persons for 1777 and 1793. Localities are jurisdictions unless otherwise noted. Parishes, found exclusively in 1777 are indicated by (p).

Area and Entity	% Pardos in Pardos plus Indians			
	1805	1793	1777	1740
Central plateau				
Cuautla Amilpas	25.00			7.95
Teotihuacán	1.79			0.67
Xochimilco	0.54	0.41		
Zumpango	5.29			1.49

Table 2.6 (cont.)

Area and Entity	%Pardos in Pardos plus Indians			
	1805	1793	1777	1740
Tlaxcala	0.71	1.60		
Amozoc	3.56		8.90(p)	
Tecali	0.09		2.76(p)	0.37
Tepeaca	0.58		4.28(p)	3.78
Teziutlán	0.00			7.36
Totomehuacán	0.92		4.73(p)	
Tochimilco	3.80			0.46
Acayucan	0.16		26.80(p)	5.07
Cosamaloapan	0.00		0.35(p)	11.77
Papantla	0.00			11.02
Tuxtla	0.00		4.90(p)	
Córdoba	8.43			11.52
Misantla	3.90		14.08(p)	
Orizaba	7.56		9.61(p)	9.93
Huajolotitlán	0.00		0.73(p)	
Miahuatlán	1.21		2.10(p)	
Nejapa	4.80			0.36
Nochixtlán	0.35		0.35(p)	
Villa de Oaxaca	4.48		1.73(p)	
Teotitlán del Camino	3.38		12.55(p)	
Teotitlán del Valle	1.54		0.51(p)	0.00
Chilapa	4.07			2.09
Tixtla	1.71		10.84(p)	
Chiautla	7.10		13.42(p)	
Central coasts				
Jicayán	15.50	22.10		10.00
West				
Jiquilpan	23.10	18.20		
North				
Querétaro	4.95	10.15		19.80 (city)
León	30.50			38.55
San Luis de la Paz	9.05			12.30
Large entities				
Mexico (prov.)	3.47	6.63		
Puebla (bishopric)			2.26	
Puebla (prov.)	2.41			
Oaxaca (bishopric)			6.70	
Oaxaca (prov.)	4.03			
Guanajuato (prov.)	20.75	29.20		
San Luis Potosí (prov.)	35.50			
Arizpe (prov.)	47.20			
Durango (bishopric)			65.05	

dates indicated. There is a strong similarity between the values for each region at different dates, although the correspondence in magnitude is by no means exact. We have to conclude as a result of these tests that for a specified geographical area, the numerical relationship between pardos and Indians as seen in the tributary population did not differ to a material extent from that obtaining in the population at large.

We may now direct attention exclusively to the racial composition as manifested in the tribute records and consider the changes which may have occurred during the eighteenth century as well as the geographical distribution of the Negroid component at the time of the Matrícula.

At the beginning, the tributary class consisted entirely of Indians, the survivors of the Conquest and the great population decline of the sixteenth century. Relatively soon, however, a few liberated slaves and free mulattoes were incorporated with the Indians, and their number increased both absolutely and relatively throughout the seventeenth century. We have a few occasional and widely dispersed items of record from the first century and a half of Spanish occupation, but without a search of prohibitive dimensions they cannot be consolidated so as to give a coherent picture of racial development.

Indeed, our best analysis of the racial status of New Spain between 1520 and 1700 is that of Aguirre Beltrán, which has already been discussed. From our revision of his data, as shown in Table 2.1, it may be ascertained that in 1570 the total of indios, africanos, and afromestizos was 2,733,412, of whom 22,556, or 0.8 percent were pardos. In 1664, the analogous results were for the total 1,498,068, and for the Negro and part-Negro portion 62,400, or 4.2 percent. It should be emphasized that these figures apply to all Mexico north of the isthmus of Tehuantepec and to the entire population thereof.

With respect to the tributary population as a distinct class, therefore, we find that 1701 is the date of the first acceptable compilation of numbers, in which the negros y mulatos libres (hereafter abbreviated to N&ML) are segregated as a group from the Indian component. This compilation is in a document dated June 1, 1701,[17] which consists of lists of towns with current tribute assessments. The manuscript has been damaged by fire and only a few of the districts can be deciphered. The data which are still legible have been presented in part A of Table 2.7.

[17]MS, AGI, Contaduría, legajo 809, ramo 35.

Table 2.7

Tributary populations

A. 1701

Number and percent of negros y mulatos libres (N&ML) in the tributary population according to tribute lists of 1701. For the source see the text. Note that the numerical units are tributaries.

Area and political entity : *district or jurisdiction*	*N&ML*	*Total Tribs.*	*% N&ML*
Central plateau			
Puebla and sujetos	134	4,933	2.71
Acapetlahuaca *et al.*	33	2,816	1.17
Cuautitlán *et al.*	13	1,844	0.70
Chiautla de la Sal	24	679	3.54
Chilapa	15	982	1.54
Sultepec	21	1,422	1.48
Cholula	5	3,555	0.14
Atlatlauca (Pue.) *et al.*	2	592	0.34
Huayacocotla *et al.*	21	2,105	1.00
Total	268	18,928	1.42
Mean percentage value			1.40
West			
Amula, Tuxcacuesco	6	483	1.24
Autlán *et al.*	11	499	2.20
Total	17	982	1.73
Mean percentage value			1.72
North			
Cuitzeo, Salvatierra	143	1,228	11.65

B. 1735

Central plateau			
Cuautla	125	1,979	6.32
Chalco	67	7,737	0.87
Temascaltepec	79	2,513	3.14
Tula	20	1,970	1.02
Yahualica	12	1,124	1.07
Ixmiquilpan	6	3,222	0.19
Tenango	27	1,095	2.46
Coatepec	15	899	1.67
Cuernavaca	179	7,164	2.50
Sultepec	2	1,754	0.11
Coyoacán	16	3,550	0.45
Ecatepec	1	1,476	0.07
Lerma	5	1,001	0.50

Table 2.7 (cont.)

B. 1735 (*cont.*)

Area and political entity : district or jurisdiction	*N&ML*	*Total Tribs.*	% *N&ML*
Atitalaquia	11	811	1.36
Metztitlán	5	4,960	0.11
Texcoco	23	5,928	0.39
Tetepango	23	1,168	1.97
Tacuba	7	5,300	0.13
Toluca	13	3,789	0.34
Tulancingo	9	3,685	0.24
Tepeaca	59	13,227	0.45
Chietla	28	456	8.34
Puebla	315	8,891	3.54
Atlixco	41	4,696	0.87
Tochimilco	2	1,193	0.17
Huatlatlauca	10	998	1.00
Apam	3	410	0.73
Huejotzingo	23	3,787	0.61
Teopantlán	8	339	2.36
Cholula	2	5,802	0.03
Tlaxcala	11	14,435	0.08
Tehuacán	82	6,473	1.27
Huayacocotla	64	3,345	1.91
Córdoba	82	3,774	2.17
Cuicatlán	8	433	1.85
Teotitlan del Camino	22	2,809	0.78
Zimatlán	12	1,338	0.90
Oaxaca	125	7,826	1.60
Cuatro Villas	8	4,598	0.17
Nejapa	27	4,553	0.59
Tixtla	6	2,557	0.23
Chilapa	15	2,472	0.61
Tonalá	23	1,918	1.20
Acatlán	10	1,826	0.55
Zacualpan	2	687	0.29
Ixcateopan	37	1,799	2.06
Chiautla	20	982	2.04
Tetela del Río	29	1,028	2.82
Total	1,719	163,777	1.05
Mean percentage value			1.50
Central coasts			
Pánuco	83	2,011	4.13
Tehuantepec	145	3,689	3.93
Zacatula	171	554	30.85
Total	399	6,254	6.38
Mean percentage value			12.97

Table 2.7 (cont.)

B. 1735 (*cont.*)

Area and political entity: district or jurisdiction	N&ML	Total Tribs.	% N&ML
West			
Tingüindín	9	584	1.54
Jiquilpan	83	1,567	5.30
Tancítaro	43	504	8.53
Maravatío	149	4,582	3.25
Zirándaro	22	740	2.98
Jacona	48	1,311	3.66
Pátzcuaro	386	6,590	5.86
Colima	51	747	6.83
Autlán	239	1,044	22.90
Ixtlán	71	559	12.70
Tuxpan	25	1,157	2.16
Amula	24	532	4.51
Total	1,150	19,917	5.78
Mean percentage value			6.69
North			
Cadereita	14	901	1.56
Querétaro	169	9,021	1.87
Celaya	502	18,597	2.70
León	393	3,695	10.63
Guanajuato	95	3,280	2.89
Total	1,173	35,494	3.31
Mean percentage value			3.93

C. 1805[a]

Area and partido	(1)	(2)	(3)	(4)	(5)	(6)
Central plateau						
Actopan	243	4,534	5.36	1,688	22,664	7.45
Ápam	42	1,101	3.82	285	5,348	5.33
Chalco	253	12,317	2.05	953	51,005	1.87
Chilapa	178	4,551	3.93	1,103	21,819	5.05
Coatepec	4	1,323	0.30	20	5,790	0.35
Cuautitlán	44	4,022	1.10	192	18,896	1.02
Cuautla Amilpas	814	3,253	25.03	2,816	13,134	21.42
Cuernavaca	1,654	11,007	15.02	4,318	36,835	11.71
Coyoacán	22	3,744	0.59	59	15,652	0.38
Ecatepec	33	2,606	1.27	193	12,961	1.49
Huejutla	57	1,820	3.24	292	6,425	4.55
Yahualica	33	3,385	0.98	149	13,275	1.12
Ixmiquilpan	7	4,321	0.16	43	22,534	0.19

Table 2.7 (cont.)

C. 1805ᵃ *(cont.)*

Area and partido	(1)	(2)	(3)	(4)	(5)	(6)
Ixtlahuaca	77	11,858	0.65	523	51,161	1.02
Lerma	10	800	1.25	60	2,815	2.13
Malinalco	74	4,237	1.75	358	18,785	1.91
Metepec	130	8,907	1.46	607	36,210	1.68
Metztitlán	607	7,920	7.67	1,780	31,808	5.60
Mexico City	418	10,090	4.14	1,453	35,769	4.06
Pachuca	6	1,053	0.57	20	5,503	0.36
Tacuba	49	6,610	0.74	224	33,767	0.66
Taxco	892	5,308	16.80	3,914	23,539	16.62
Temascaltepec	386	8,476	4.55	1,794	37,219	4.82
Tenango	194	10,945	1.77	1,025	44,794	2.29
Teotihuacán	33	1,846	1.79	175	10,681	1.64
Tetela del Río	1,086	4,195	25.90	4,505	15,172	29.70
Tetepango	111	4,651	2.39	487	21,612	2.25
Mexicalcingo	0	2,222	0.00	0	10,090	0.00
Texcoco	23	7,569	0.30	151	32,760	0.46
Tixtla	80	4,669	1.71	506	21,262	2.38
Tlaxcala	76	10,719	0.71	275	40,968	0.67
Toluca	13	4,618	0.28	76	16,298	0.47
Tula	28	2,162	1.33	181	10,912	1.66
Tulancingo	101	6,807	1.48	496	31,148	1.59
Jilotepec	256	16,107	1.59	1,111	65,808	1.69
Xochimilco	23	4,304	0.54	122	18,694	0.65
Zacualpan	474	7,591	6.25	2,584	32,282	8.01
Zempoala	8	904	0.89	43	4,590	0.94
Zumpango	72	1,434	5.02	291	6,847	4.25
Acatlán	193	3,795	5.09	1,198	17,581	6.81
Amozoc	49	1,374	3.57	223	6,679	3.30
Atlixco	132	6,284	2.10	541	26,453	2.05
Chiautla	194	2,732	7.10	1,087	12,689	8.57
Chietla	215	681	31.60	775	2,550	31.00
Cholula	21	4,917	0.43	85	25,249	0.34
Huauchinango	52	7,716	0.67	224	28,891	0.78
Huayacocotla	100	4,299	2.33	472	19,697	2.40
Huejotzingo	30	4,159	0.72	78	14,391	0.54
Izúcar	467	4,865	9.60	1,896	19,955	9.51
Llanos	10	8,323	0.12	45	36,998	0.12
Puebla	236	3,221	7.32	705	13,087	5.39
Tecali	2	2,138	0.09	6	12,024	0.05
Tehuacán	224	8,376	2.68	1,132	40,378	2.81
Tepeaca	67	11,498	0.58	437	50,446	0.87
Tepeji de la Seda	84	5,231	1.61	640	27,285	2.35
Totomehuacán	7	768	0.91	30	3,810	0.79
Otumba	0	1,362	0.00	0	6,842	0.00
Tlapa	457	8,106	5.64	2,823	38,609	7.32
Tochimilco	48	1,263	3.80	300	6,340	4.73
Zacatlán	2	8,230	0.24	2	39,495	0.05
Córdoba	218	2,562	8.51	546	11,846	4.61
Orizaba	616	8,148	7.56	2,529	36,089	7.01

Table 2.7 (cont.)

C. 1805ᵃ (*cont.*)

Area and partido	(1)	(2)	(3)	(4)	(5)	(6)
Jalacingo	20	2,372	0.84	98	10,939	0.90
Jalapa	433	4,942	8.76	2,263	24,982	9.05
Chichicapa	83	4,462	1.86	479	20,977	2.28
Chontales	3	1,625	0.18	19	8,026	0.24
Huajuapan	367	6,675	5.50	2,096	28,951	7.24
Miahuatlán	40	3,291	1.21	209	15,683	1.33
Nejapa	139	2,897	4.80	898	14,643	6.14
Nochixtlán	6	1,692	0.35	26	8,241	0.32
Oaxaca	351	8,191	4.29	1,908	38,080	5.01
Cuatro Villas	35	4,270	0.82	169	16,865	1.00
Teozacoalco	17	2,419	0.70	121	12,573	0.96
Teposcolula	58	11,681	0.50	339	60,021	0.57
Teutila	18	5,727	0.31	94	25,803	0.36
Teotitlán del Camino	162	4,795	3.38	955	22,064	4.33
Teotitlán del Valle	43	2,804	1.53	245	13,564	1.81
Villa Alta	8	10,683	0.08	64	53,962	0.12
Juxtlahuaca	10	1,710	0.58	35	6,380	0.55
Tetela	0	1,877	0.00	0	9,596	0.00
Teusistlan	0	1,978	0.00	0	8,459	0.00
Huajolotitlán	0	1,222	0.00	0	5,661	0.00
Ixtepeji	0	1,146	0.00	0	5,629	0.00
Total	13,830	410,487	3.369	60.664	1,815,345	3.342
Mean percentage value			3.522			3.651
*Central coasts, Atlantic*ᵇ						
Acayucan	5	3,105	0.16	15	14,398	0.10
Antigua Veracruz	0	334	0.00	0	1,800	0.00
Cosamaloapan	0	1,015	0.00	0	4,412	0.00
Papantla	0	2,268	0.00	0	10,804	0.00
Tampico	2	3,568	0.06	6	10,232	0.06
Tuxtla	0	2,468	0.00	0	10,213	0.00
Veracruz	12	557	2.15	46	2,079	2.22
Total	19	13,315	0.143	67	53,938	0.124
Mean percentage value			0.339			0.340
Central coasts, Pacific						
Acapulco	522	1,090	47.90	3,852	6,359	60.60
Zacatula	571	1,251	45.65	2,852	6,033	47.30
Igualapa	2	2,077	0.10	14	8,915	0.16
Huatulco	52	712	7.31	179	3,255	5.50
Tehuantepec	505	4,912	10.28	3,903	24,769	15.77
Jicayán	966	6,237	15.50	5,335	30,895	17.27
Total	2,618	16,279	16.082	16,135	80,226	30.111
Mean percentage value			21.113			24.433

Table 2.7 (cont.)

C. 1805ᵃ (*cont.*)

Area and partido	(1)	(2)	(3)	(4)	(5)	(6)
West						
Angamacutiro	355	1,367	25.95	1,550	5,139	30.20
Apatzingán	661	1,054	62.70	2,625	4,403	58.65
Ario	767	1,281	59.90	2,239	3,874	57.75
Carácuaro	161	250	60.40	517	875	59.10
Charo	40	462	8.66	207	2,032	10.18
Chucándiro	120	281	42.70	394	924	42.65
Cocupao	336	1,265	26.55	1,813	6,003	30.20
Cuitzeo	257	1,647	15.60	1,327	7,567	17.55
Erongarícuaro	60	916	6.55	197	2,556	7.71
Huango	173	366	47.30	784	1,512	51.85
Huaniqueo	200	753	26.55	972	2,913	33.35
Huimeo	990	2,849	34.70	4,134	11,653	35.50
Indaparapeo	245	1,081	22.65	994	4,243	23.42
Motines	164	690	23.80	554	2,134	25.95
Paracho	31	1,483	2.09	103	4,355	2.37
Pátzcuaro	160	1,335	12.00	481	4,503	10.70
Puruándiro	466	1,182	39.40	1,639	4,239	38.65
Santa Clara	147	603	24.40	608	2,116	28.75
Tacámbaro	230	589	39.05	690	1,799	38.35
Taretan	295	675	43.70	927	2,338	39.70
Tiripitío	232	1,030	22.50	1,100	4,108	26.80
Tlalpujahua	373	1,284	29.05	2,199	6,794	32.35
Tlazazalca	901	2,940	30.65	3,952	12,412	31.80
Valladolid	567	1,896	29.90	1,958	6,383	30.70
Urecho	260	312	83.30	865	1,027	84.20
Uruapan	157	1,382	11.36	446	4,972	8.97
Jiquilpan	950	4,110	23.10	3,187	14,138	22.55
Zamora	1,788	3,035	58.90	7,685	12,872	59.70
Zinapécuaro	161	1,807	8.90	851	7,356	11.58
Zitácuaro	1,203	7,047	17.05	4,513	25,920	17.40
Acaponeta	440	526	85.30	1,914	3,821	50.20
Ahuacatlán	257	836	30.75	1,255	4,037	31.10
Autlán	830	1,646	50.45	4,138	7,461	55.45
Barca	1,536	3,933	39.05	5,597	14,530	38.50
Barranca	130	844	15.40	533	3,567	14.95
Colima	1,221	2,305	53.00	4,549	9,048	50.30
Compostela	91	91	100.00	482	482	100.00
Cuquío	247	1,439	17.15	1,214	6,658	18.23
Etzatlán	946	1,729	54.70	4,123	7,913	52.10
Guadalajara	0	357	0.00	0	1,392	0.00
Huauchinango	476	1,134	42.00	2,465	5,722	43.10
Lagos	2,459	5,181	47.40	10,029	21,071	47.65
Ostotipaquillo	471	536	87.90	1,699	2,208	76.90
Tala	299	863	34.65	1,370	3,466	39.55
Tepatitlán	428	1,156	37.00	2,057	5,048	40.75
Tepic	855	1,256	68.10	3,479	5,437	64.00
Tequepexpan	201	715	28.10	768	2,596	29.60

Table 2.7 (cont.)

C. 1805ᵃ (cont.)

Area and partido	(1)	(2)	(3)	(4)	(5)	(6)
Tequila	301	832	36.20	1,210	3,593	33.65
Tlajomulco	223	1,644	13.57	845	6,158	13.95
Tomatlán	146	298	49.00	1,183	2,010	58.90
Tonalá	87	2,052	4.24	438	8,128	5.39
Tuxcacuesco	518	1,615	32.10	2,041	6,108	33.40
Jolapa	273	273	100.00	1,199	1,199	100.00
Zapotlán	788	3,246	24.25	3,811	13,413	28.40
Sayula	1,498	8,930	16.78	5,686	34,587	16.43
Sentispac	170	420	40.50	1,063	1,995	53.30
Total	27,341	88,829	30.779	112,659	352,777	31.934
Mean percentage value			36.624			36.864
North						
Dolores	473	2,689	17.60	2,465	11,232	21.95
Guanajuato	535	4,962	10.78	2,387	22,475	10.65
Irapuato	351	3,725	9.42	1,573	17,034	9.23
León	1,608	5,267	30.50	8,848	27,510	32.15
Marfil	157	964	16.30	816	4,480	18.20
San Luis de la Paz	375	4,136	9.06	2,061	22,688	9.10
San Miguel	1,118	5,324	21.00	6,326	23,598	26.80
Silao	155	3,411	4.55	897	16,757	5.36
Pénjamo	1,094	3,376	32.40	6,703	17,962	37.30
Piedra Gorda	594	1,414	42.00	3,318	7,297	45.90
Celaya	1,626	23,625	6.88	9,018	107,508	8.39
Cadereita	285	3,741	7.62	1,845	19,764	9.34
Querétaro	687	12,871	5.34	3,705	63,374	5.85
Zimapan	139	2,331	5.96	538	10,611	5.07
Charcas	3,660	6,027	60.70	16,763	27,530	60.90
Guadalcázar	814	2,117	38.45	4,709	9,575	49.20
S.L. Potosí	1,614	5,788	28.90	7,960	31,306	25.40
Santa María del Rio	1,639	4,168	39.35	8,280	21,041	39.35
Río Verde	749	2,131	35.15	3,857	9,408	41.00
Valles	1,369	8,300	16.50	6,190	32,662	18.95
Venado	367	1,339	27.40	1,935	7,025	27.55
Aguascalientes	1,777	2,293	77.50	6,928	9,816	70.50
Fresnillo	3,968	5,519	71.90	18,127	24,053	75.40
Mazapil	998	1,120	90.00	5,374	5,914	90.80
Nieves	896	1,009	88.70	4,585	5,204	88.00
Pinos	884	2,010	44.00	5,397	11,904	45.30
Sombrerete	261	1,248	20.90	999	5,123	19.50
Juchipila	1,517	4,421	34.35	6,668	19,026	35.05
Zacatecas	2,466	4,310	57.20	10,279	19,108	53.80
Álamos	153	256	59.80	578	1,083	53.40
Copala	801	1,190	67.30	3,131	4,753	65.90
Cosalá	159	366	43.40	774	1,959	49.70
Culiacán	360	1,082	33.90	1,774	5,387	32.95

Table 2.7 (cont.)

C. 1805*ᵃ* (*cont.*)

Area and partido	(1)	(2)	(3)	(4)	(5)	(6)
Moloya	202	345	58.60	759	1,460	51.30
Ostimuri	130	217	59.90	494	918	53.90
Rosario	563	617	91.30	2,586	2,872	90.00
Total	34,544	133,689	25.839	168,647	629,417	26.794
Mean percentage value			37.905			38.420

*ᵃ*Columns 1, 2, and 3 pertain to the tributaries as stated in the document. Column 1 gives the number of N&ML; column 2 the total number of tributaries as stated; column 3 shows the percentage of N&ML in the total. Columns 4, 5, and 6 pertain to the total tributary population. Column 4 gives the aggregate number of persons who fell within the category of negros y mulatos libres, as calculated by adding the separate components stated for each district in the document; column 5 gives the total tributary population as stated; column 6 shows the percentage of N&ML in the entire tributary population.
*ᵇ*Misantla is omitted. The record shows for N&ML 10 casados, 23 tributaries, but 222 niños and 65 *reservados*. Clearly there is a serious error.

D. Summary

The final results from the preceeding tables are here assembled and summarized for convenience in comparing dates and areas.

	Central Plateau	Central Coasts	West	North	All Areas
1701					
No. of entities	9		2	1	12
N&ML tribs.	268		17	143	328
Total tribs.	18,968		982	1,228	21,138
% N&ML (total)	1.42		1.73	11.65	1.85
% N&ML (means)	1.40		1.72	11.65	1.85
1735					
No. of entities	48	3	12	5	68
N&ML	1,719	399	1,150	1,173	4,441
Total tribs.	163,777	6,254	19,917	35,494	225,442
% N&ML (total)	1.05	6.38	5.78	3.31	1.97
% N&ML (means)	1.50	12.97	6.69	3.93	3.10
1805*ᵃ*					
No. of entities	83	13	56	36	188
N&ML tribs.	13,830	2,637	27,341	34,544	70,352
Total tribs.	410,487	29,594	88,829	133,689	662,599
% N&ML (total)	3.37	8.91	30.78	25.84	10.62
% N&ML (means)	3.52	9.93	36.62	37.91	20.41
No. of entities	83	13	56	36	188
N&ML trib. pop.	60,664	16,202	112,659	168,647	358,172
Total trib. pop.	1,815,345	134,164	352,777	629,417	2,931,703
% N&ML (total)	3.34	12.08	31.93	26.79	12.22
% N&ML (means)	3.65	11.46	36.86	38.42	20.74

*ᵃ*See part E.

Table 2.7 (cont.)

E. Data for the Atlantic and the Pacific divisions of the Central coasts
according to the Matrícula of 1805

1805	Atlantic	Pacific
No. of entities	7	6
N&ML tribs.	19	2,618
Total tribs.	13,315	16,279
% N&ML (total)	0.143	16.082
% N&ML (means)	0.339	21.123
No. of entities	7	6
N&ML trib. pop.	67	16,135
Total trib. pop.	53,938	80,226
% N&ML (total)	0.124	20.111
% N&ML (means)	0.340	24.433

There are twelve districts, nine on the central plateau, within the present states of Mexico and Puebla, two in southwestern Jalisco, and one in Michoacán-Guanajuato, territory which we have considered to be in the northern area. All but the last fall within the range ot 0.1 to 3.5 percent N&ML. The northern district has over 11 percent.

The tribute lists of 1735[18] are much more extensive. We find a total of 68 partidos or jurisdictions which report both Indian and Negro tributaries. Of these, 48 are on the central plateau, 3 on the central coasts, 12 in the west, and 5 in the north (Querétaro and Guanajuato). There are many others which mention no Negroes, but it is impossible to determine whether in these districts there were actually no Negroes or whether they were merely omitted by inadvertence or intent. The total numbers and percentage values for each district will be found in part B.

Part C contains the figures from the Matrícula of 1805. There are a total of 188 usable partidos from 10 provinces (excluding Mérida). These entities are arranged in four groups, as previously: central plateau (83), central coasts (13), west (56), and north (36). The Atlantic and Pacific coasts are shown separately in order to emphasize the great disparity in the reported number of N&ML.

For each partido is listed the stated number of *tributarios enteros* of each of the two racial stocks, together with the percentage of N&ML in the total (indios de pueblo and indios

[18]MS, AGI, Audiencia de Méjico, legajo 798.

laboríos y vagos are considered collectively as indios). The comparable data are also presented as based upon aggregate numbers, for the last column of the tabulation given in the Matrícula is devoted to the *"Total de Individuos de la Clase Tributaria."* The total population of N&ML is calculated by adding the values for the various categories and adjusting for the married women. The result is not absolutely accurate but is subject to an error of less than 1 percent. For each of the four geographical areas, we also show the total number of tributaries and of population, the percentage of N&ML according to totals, and the percentage as the mean of the individual district values.

In order to facilitate convenience of reference we have brought together in part D the consolidated finding for these four primary regions as calculated for the three critical dates of documentary evidence, 1701, 1735, and 1805. For 1805 the values are shown as obtained with both tributaries and with total tributary populations. For this date also the seven Atlantic and six Pacific coastal partidos are summarized separately in part E.

The tributary data for the central coasts present certain anomalies which merit brief attention. The sampling in 1701 is quite inadequate for all regions except the central plateau; there are no reports for the coasts. In 1735 only three coastal partidos are represented. The two larger of them (Pánuco and Tehuantepec) contain relatively few Negro tributaries; the third (Zacatula), a small partido, has very many. The result is an inflation of the mean percentage of N&ML tributaries as compared with that obtained from the totals. It may be noted here that a similar effect is seen, on a lesser scale, in almost every other period and region and is referable, as in the case just described, to high values obtained with numerically small territorial units. Consequently, one must infer that although the mean percentages of N&ML are useful and indeed essential for any statistical treatment of the data, the percentages derived from the total numbers may present a more accurate picture of racial distribution.

We return to the problem of the coasts. With the Matrícula of 1805, whereas the percentages of N&ML have been averaged for the 13 partidos, the results, as shown in part D of Table 2.7, obscure some very wide discrepancies. If the individual reports of partidos (part C) are examined, it is evident that on the Atlantic side in the province of Veracruz, four partidos reported no tributary Negro population at all, and for the other three it was negligible (see also part E). The tributary figures in the Matrícula run contrary to the well-recognized high level of black population in this area. Clearly the pardos either evaded classification as tributaries or gained exemption. The explanation is easily found in the exemption from tribute accorded to all pardos who served in the coastal militia and to their families.[19]

The six Pacific coastal partidos show many tributary pardos, but the values are very erratic: Acapulco and Zacatula had a tributary population at least one-half black; Tehuantepec, Jicayán, and Huatulco had numerous Negroes; but Igualapa in southeastern Guerrero had virtually none. The anomalies in reporting racial groups to be found on this coast in 1777 have already received comment. Here we can add only that much further investigation with local documentary sources is needed in order to clarify the mystery. In the meantime, we can accept the population figures for the tributary class on both central coasts only with great reservation.

If we now examine more broadly the geographical distribution of the two types of tributary, we may ignore the figures presented for the year 1701 because the only area in which the sample is in any way adequate is the central plateau (part A of Table 2.7).

In the reports dated 1735, the percentage of N&ML who were tributaries, as based upon total numbers, was 1.05 for the central plateau, 6.38 for the coasts (with only three partidos), 5.78 for the western provinces, and 3.31 for the north (with only five partidos, all from Querétaro and Guanajuato). The corresponding percentages, based upon means of partido values, were 1.50, 12.97, 6.69, 3.93 (see part B of Table 2.7). Despite the differences between the two sets of percentages, the regional distinctions are probably significant. With the second set of values for the four areas, an analysis of variance (F) gives 11.77. If we divide the entire 68 partidos into two groups, with 51 in the central portion of Mexico, and 17 in the west and north, the value of t for the difference between the respective means, 5.15, is well beyond the 1 percent level of probability. It may be concluded, therefore, that a stronger representation in the tributary class of the black component existed on the coasts and in the west and north than on the central plateau.

Our best data are those for 1805, where we have represent-

[19]Fonseca and Urrutia, I, 440–441.

ed nearly 700,000 tributaries and almost 3,000,000 people in 188 partidos. The reports for individual partidos are in part C of Table 2.7 and the summaries with respect to number of tributaries and to the total population are in part D. The central plateau displays minimal percentage values for the black group. The west and north consistently run very much higher, with the coasts occupying an intermediate position. Even using the suspect data from the coasts, an analysis of variance for tributaries in 188 partidos, with the mean percentages ot N&ML, yields a value for F of 50.74. In its distribution through the country, therefore, and in so far as the pardo and Indian components are concerned, the tributary population followed closely the lines laid down by the population at large. At all three dates, 1701, 1735, and 1805, the results show a distribution of the Negro tributary fraction consistent with the pattern provided by the censuses of the eighteenth century.

The secular trend of relative increase on the part of the pardos is evident in part D of Table 2.7. On the plateau a series of substantial samples indicate that this element doubled its strength during the century, although it never achieved great absolute magnitude. The value of F for 140 individual percentages at the three dates, is 3.96, moderately significant. In the west, if we may use the two partidos at 1701, the value of F for 70 items is 11.08, highly significant. The coasts and the north cannot be treated by the same method, owing to inadequate or dubious data, but there is no reason to believe that the trend in these areas was much different.

At the end of the colonial era, in all New Spain, outside of Yucatan, the total tributary population, in round numbers, amounted to 2,900,000 souls. Of these, 360,000 or 12.4 percent were N&ML. These findings confirm the results obtained with the general censuses of 1742 to 1793, and the tabulations for the earlier centuries adapted from Aguirre Beltrán. They emphasize once more the steady increase of that portion of the Mexican population which was ultimately derived from Africa.

III

At the beginning of the preceding section, it was suggested that the censuses of 1777 and 1793 might serve as a source of information concerning not only distribution of racial types but also marital behavior and rates of racial fusion. These phenomena and processes may be studied because many of the available reports from the two enumerations specify the socio-racial origin of each individual, including the two partners in every conjugal establishment. Thus we may tabulate and classify according to ethnic character all such unions existing in a particular locality.

Any appropriate population is divided into the four conventional groups, españoles, mestizos, pardos, and indios, which for convenience are abbreviated again to the initials E, M, P, and I. In any mixed population there are ten combinations, placed in parentheses to indicate that the sex is not involved : (EE), (EM), (EP), (EI), (MM), (MI), (MP), (PP), (PI), and (II). If it is desirable to segregate the sexes in mixed categories, this may be accomplished by using the first of two initials in a pair as the male and the second as the female, without the parentheses. We would then have, with four racial groups, sixteen types, EE, EM, ME, EP, PE,... etc. Thus EE will always represent a male and a female español, but EM will show a male español with a female mestizo, and ME the reverse. In any area, town, parish, or jurisdiction, it is possible to assign each married couple to the appropriate combination and obtain the total for each of these by simple addition.

The values may be written down the page as a list. However, the interrelations of the various combinations will be depicted much more clearly by using a 4 × 4 table. Thus we have sixteen squares. Each of the four columns is headed by E, M, P, or I and represents males. Each horizontal line denotes females. The method is illustrated thus :

		Males			
	E	*M*	*P*	*I*	
E	EE	ME	PE	IE	sum *E*
M	EM	MM	PM	IM	sum *M*
Females *P*	EP	MP	PP	IP	sum *P*
I	EI	MI	PI	II	sum *I*
	sum *E*	sum *M*	sum *P*	sum *I*	sum *Total*

Each column and row may be added to obtain the sum. Moreover two or more tables may be combined by adding the values in corresponding squares. It should be emphasized that the numbers entered in each square represent married *couples*. Hence the number of married *persons* will always be twice as great as the values shown.

Various complications arise with the actual censuses. In the first place it is evident that the race must be adequately stated for every persons. With any particular locality, if this information is lacking for more than a few persons, the entire enumeration must be discarded.

In the second place, many entities (towns, etc.) for which we have records contain a very small number of cases for certain racial combinations. As a result, the sampling error is likely to be serious. In order to minimize random dispersion we have attempted to establish a set of consolidated areas, each of which contains a sufficient number of couples. These areas, on the other hand, must be reasonably homogeneous with respect to racial character.

The census of 1777 contains four clearly defined regions :

(1) The city of Antequera is large enough and unique enough to be set apart from the bishopric of Oaxaca as a whole (3,151 couples).

(2) There are sixty rural parishes reported from the bishopric of Oaxaca, each too small to use independently. The total number, however, is sufficient enough to obliterate trivial individual differences (37,011 couples).

(3) There are similarly fifty rural parishes in the bishopric of Puebla (40,249 couples).

(4) In the bishopric of Durango there are fourteen parishes, including the city of Durango, for which the census supplies usable data (7,138 couples).

For the census of 1793, as found in the ramo de Padrones, that portion which we employ here constitutes an adequate and well-distributed sample of the records which are still preserved in the Archivo General de la Nación. Five areas have been segregated :

(1) The city of Querétaro (3,127 couples).

(2) The province of Puebla. Three towns, or jurisdictions, are included : Orizaba, Tehuacán, San Juan de los Llanos (4,024 couples).

(3) The province of Guanajuato. Four jurisdictions, are included : Guanajuato, Irapuato, Celaya, Aguascalientes (12,219 couples).

(4) Southern Hidalgo, in the province of Mexico. There are seven jurisdictions : Ápam, Tula, Tulancingo, Pachuca, Otumba, Actopan, Ixmiquilpan (6,367 couples).

(5) The Valley of Mexico, in the province of Mexico.

There are six jurisdictions : Huejutla (not in the valley), Xochi-milco, Cuautitlán, Tacuba, Coyoacán, Texcoco (3,796 couples).

The third problem relates to the representation of racial groups in the census. We have noted previously here and in other essays that the census of 1777 embraced the entire population without distinction of age, sex, or social origin. Hence all racial groups are fully recorded, and the division into sixteen categories described above is fully valid. However, in the military census of 1793, the detailed reports of which are found in Padrones, the Indians are omitted, save for a very few who might have married members of other groups. Consequently, any conclusions based upon these data which involved the participation of Indians would be utterly misleading and could not be accepted. As a result of this situation, all numerical operations which require information concerning Indians have to be confined to the census of 1777. On the other hand, it would be unfortunate as well as unnecessary to discard abruptly the mass of data provided by that of 1793. Some degree of reconciliation may be achieved if we consider the interracial relations only among the three groups which constituted the gente de razón : españoles, mestizos, and pardos. For this purposes we reduce the sixteen combinations to nine : EE, EM, ME, EP, PE, MM, MP, PM, PP, and consider, in effect, the reproductive interaction of the three non-Indian groups wholly apart from any influence exerted by the Indian component. The detailed procedure follows.

With both censuses we construct the 4 × 4 table for all racial groups. Then we delete the combinations which include Indians and recalculate the row and column totals. With the census of 1793 there is little change in the proportions of the three non-Indian groups, but with the 1777 census the reduction in total numbers, as well as the percentage composition, may be considerable. Nevertheless, if we wish to employ the two censuses in combination, no other approach is feasible.

The basic data are presented in Table 2.8. This table is divided into thirteen parts. Parts A to D inclusive give values for the marital combinations of four racial groups, from the census of 1777, as obtained for each of the four regions into which our sample from this census has been divided. Parts E to M inclusive show the corresponding figures for the three types of non-Indians, españoles, mestizos, and pardos. Parts E to H repeat the census of 1777, with the Indians omitted.

Table 2.8

Basic data for types of marital union, organized in 4x4 and 3x3 subtables. The racial groups are designated by letters : E, M, P, and I. Males are shown in the top row, females in the first (left-hand) column. the last column shows the total females in each row; the bottom row shows total males for each column.

In each square are three numbers. The first (top) is the observed number, as counted from the record, for the combination indicated. The second (in parenthesis) is the number expected under the hypothesis of random contact. The third is the ratio of the observed to the expected number. (For further discussion see text.) Sex is shown by (m)=male; (f) = female.

A. 1777 Antequera

	E(m)	M(m)	P(m)	I(m)	Total Female
E(f)	725	165	90	25	1,005
	(314)	(238)	(167)	(286)	
	2.308	0.693	0.540	0.087	
M(f)	142	307	104	81	634
	(199)	(150)	(105)	(180)	
	0.714	2.048	0.991	0.451	
P(f)	72	127	257	45	501
	(157)	(119)	(83)	(142)	
	0.457	1.068	3.096	0.317	
I(f)	47	148	72	744	1,011
	(316)	(240)	(168)	(287)	
	0.149	0.617	0.429	2.592	
Total male	986	747	523	895	3,151

B. 1777. Oaxaca, 60 rural parishes

	E(m)	M(m)	P(m)	I(m)	Total Female
E(f)	252	34	9	25	320
	(3.24)	(4.58)	(16.05)	(296.20)	
	7.800	7.423	0.561	0.084	
M(f)	49	356	40	47	492
	(5.00)	(7.03)	(24.68)	(455.50)	
	9.800	50.640	1.621	0.103	
P(f)	45	39	1,700	76	1,860
	(18.85)	(26.60)	(93.20)	(1,723.35)	
	2.287	1,427	18.235	0.044	

Table 2.8 (cont.)

B. 1777. Oaxaca, 60 rural parishes (cont.)

	E(m)	M(m)	P(m)	I(m)	Total Female
I(f)	29	100	107	34,103	34,339
	(347.63)	(490.38)	(1,720.51)	(31,780.68)	
	0.083	0.204	0.062	1.073	
Total male	375	529	1,856	34,251	37,011

C. 1777. Puebla, 50 rural parishes

	E(m)	M(m)	P(m)	I(m)	Total Female
E(f)	1,455	442	72	103	2,072
	(97.45)	(213.28)	(70.89)	(1,690.40)	
	14.920	2.073	1.016	0.061	
M(f)	327	3,136	177	383	4,023
	(181.21)	(414.10)	(137.63)	(3,282.02)	
	1.728	7.570	1.287	0.117	
P(f)	66	307	1,053	191	1,617
	(76.05)	(166.44)	(55.32)	(1,319.15)	
	0.868	1.846	19.130	0.145	
I(f)	45	258	75	32,159	32,537
	(1,530.28)	(3,349.16)	(1,113.15)	(26,544.29)	
	0.028	0.077	0.067	1.211	
Total male	1,893	4,143	1,377	32,836	40,249

D. 1777. Durango, city and 13 rural parishes

	E(m)	M(m)	P(m)	I(m)	Total Female
E(f)	986	136	130	43	1,295
	(235)	(202)	(544)	(314)	
	4.192	0.673	0.239	0.137	
M(f)	119	596	164	147	1,026
	(186)	(160)	(431)	(249)	
	0.64	3.726	0.380	0.591	

Table 2.8 (cont.)

D. 1777. Durango, city and 13 rural parishes (*cont.*)

	E(m)	M(m)	P(m)	I(m)	Total Female
P(f)	136 (565) 0.241	205 (485) 0.423	2,279 (1,308) 1.742	494 (756) 0.653	3,114
I(f)	53 (309) 0.172	175 (265) 0.660	426 (716) 0.595	1,049 (413) 2.540	1,703
Total male	1,294	1,112	2,999	1,733	7,138

E. 1777. Antequera, non-Indian population

	E(m)	M(m)	P(m)	Total Female
E(f)	725 (463) 1.566	165 (295) 0.559	90 (222) 0.405	980
M(f)	142 (261) 0.544	307 (167) 1.840	104 (125) 0.832	553
P(f)	72 (215) 0.335	127 (137) 0.927	257 (104) 2.470	456
Total male	939	599	451	1,989

F. 1777. Oaxaca, 60 rural parishes, non-Indian population

	E(m)	M(m)	P(m)	Total Female
E(f)	252 (40.5) 6.222	34 (50.1) 0.679	9 (204.4) 0.044	295
M(f)	49 (61.0) 0.803	356 (75.6) 4.710	40 (308.4) 0.130	445

Table 2.8 (cont.)

F. 1777. Oaxaca, 60 rural parishes, non-Indian population (*cont.*)

	E(m)	M(m)	P(m)	Total Female
P(f)	45	39	1,700	1,784
	(244.5)	(303.2)	(1,236.3)	
	0.184	0.129	1.375	
Total male	346	429	1,749	2,524

G. 1777. Puebla, 50 rural parishes, non-Indian population

	E(m)	M(m)	P(m)	Total Female
E(f)	1,455	442	72	1,969
	(517.26)	(1,087.41)	(364.43)	
	2.813	0.407	0.197	
M(f)	327	3,136	177	3,640
	(956.16)	(2,010.10)	(673.65)	
	0.342	1.561	0.263	
P(f)	66	307	1,053	1,426
	(374.59)	(789.49)	(263.92)	
	0.177	0.390	3.988	
Total male	1,848	3,885	1,302	7,035

H. 1777. Durango, city and 13 rural parishes, non-Indian population

	E(m)	M(m)	P(m)	Total Female
E(f)	986	136	130	1,252
	(327)	(247)	(678)	
	3.015	0.551	0.192	
M(f)	119	596	164	879
	(230)	(173)	(476)	
	0.517	3.445	0.345	
P(f)	136	205	2,279	2,620
	(684)	(517)	(1,419)	
	0.199	0.397	1.606	
Total male	1,241	937	2,573	4,751

Table 2.8 (cont.)

I. 1793. Querétaro, city, non-Indian population

	E(m)	M(m)	P(m)	Total Female
E(f)	1,433 (965) 1.484	261 (536) 0.431	28 (220) 0.127	1,722
M(f)	289 (544) 0.531	655 (302) 2.170	27 (124) 0.218	971
P(f)	31 (243) 0.128	58 (135) 0.430	345 (55.5) 6.215	434
Total male	1,753	974	400	3,127

J. 1793. Puebla, 3 jurisdictions, non-Indian population

	E(m)	M(m)	P(m)	Total Female
E(f)	1,237 (679) 1.822	371 (776) 0.478	55 (208) 0.265	1,663
M(f)	379 (757) 0.501	1,339 (910) 1.471	135 (232) 0.582	1,853
P(f)	27 (207) 0.130	167 (237) 0.705	314 (63.6) 4.938	508
Total male	1,643	1,877	504	4,024

K. 1793. Guanjuato, 4 jurisdictions, non-Indian population

	E(m)	M(m)	P(m)	Total Female
E(f)	5,186 (3,211) 1.615	838 (1,630) 0.514	135 (1,319) 0.102	6,159
M(f)	718 (1,423) 0.505	1,776 (723) 2.460	237 (585) 0.405	2,731

Table 2.8 (cont.)

K. 1793. Guanjuato, 4 jurisdictions, non-Indian population (*cont.*)

		E(m)	M(m)	P(m)	Total Female
P(f)		465 (1,735) 0.268	620 (881) 0.705	2,244 (713) 3.150	3,329
	Total male	6,369	3,234	2,616	12,219

L. 1793. Southern Hidalgo, 7 jurisdictions, non-Indian population

		E(m)	M(m)	P(m)	Total Female
E(f)		2,084 (1,121) 1.860	470 (1,208) 0.389	21 (249) 0.084	2,575
M(f)		565 (1,262) 0.448	2,319 (1,360) 1.705	15 (277) 0.054	2,899
P(f)		123 (389) 0.316	198 (419) 0.473	572 (85.3) 6.700	893
	Total male	2,772	2,987	608	6,367

M. 1793. Valley of Mexico, 6 jurisdictions, non-Indian population

		E(m)	M(m)	P(m)	Total Female
E(f)		1,556 (971) 1.602	388 (869) 0.447	5 (109) 0.046	1,949
M(f)		301 (782) 0.385	1,253 (699) 1.792	14 (87.6) 0.160	1,568
P(f)		35 (139) 0.252	51 (124) 0.411	193 (15.6) 12.380	279
	Total male	1,892	1,692	212	3,796

Parts I to M are derived from the census of 1793. In all parts, under each racial combination, are placed three numerical values. The first gives the number of marital unions as counted from the census reports. The others will be discussed shortly.

Meanwhile, an important preliminary problem concerns the participation of the two sexes. We may ask, Do the males differ from the females with respect to occurrence of marriage within the same group (intragroup) or outside of it (extragroup)?

The problem may be reduced to simple terms by using the data in Table 2.8 and by calculating two magnitudes. The first consists of the average proportion of males among total males as compared with that of females among total females, all of whom marry men or women within the same racial group (intragroup). There are two variants of this procedure. One is to employ the four areas and four racial groups reported in the 1777 census. The other is to omit Indians and use only the other three groups with the four areas in 1777 plus the five areas in 1793.

With the first variant, for each sex we have sixteen combinations, EE, MM, PP, and II, for each of the four areas. The average percentage of males who appear in this type of union is 72.93; that of females is 73.02. The difference is 0.09 percent, and the value of t for this difference is 0.06, totally insignificant. If we turn to the second variant and use the data for españoles, mestizos, and pardos, deleting Indians, there will be twenty-seven combinations, or items: EE, MM, and PP for each sex in the nine areas derived from both censuses. The mean for males is 76.71 and for females 74.82. The value of t for the difference is 0.65, again without significance. It is thus evident that in so far as marriage within the same socio-racial group is concerned, there is no appreciable difference in the behavior of males and females.

The second magnitude pertains to the proportion of males and females who marry persons of a different group (extragroup). The number of combinations is greater than in the previous calculation. For the data from the four groups and four areas in 1777 we have for españoles alone, EM-ME, EP-PE, EI-IE, or three sets of two pairs, for each of which the percentage of E males married to women of M, P, or I is calculated with reference to total E males in the area, and for which a comparable value is obtained for females. Hence with the four-area data from 1777, there are forty-eight such pairs of percentages. With this series, the mean percentage of males married extragroup is 9.047, and of females 9.029. The difference is completely without significance.

A similar operation performed with the three-group, nine-area data for the combined 1777 and 1793 censuses gives for males 11.47 percent, and for females 12.72 percent. The difference between the means is larger, 1.25 percent, but still without significance ($t = 0.80$).

The conclusion to be drawn from these calculations is that no obvious preference based upon sex was shown by any of the racial groups represented in the two censuses. To be sure, there are local distinctions which may become very pronounced. However, these are submerged when all the available information is consolidated, and thus no universal, consistent bais referable to sex appears to have existed. It follows, therefore, that with each racial combination the total number of unions may be substituted for the male and female separate values. For example, if in any locality there were 100 marriages involving a Spanish male and a mestizo female (EM), and 50 involving a Spanish female and a mestizo male (ME), the two numbers may be combined as 150 unions between Spanish and mestizo.

If now we wish to study the variations in type of union displayed by the four racial groups, within the setting of the region from which the sample was drawn, we may examine the values given in Table 2.8, parts A to M. Since, however, it is difficult and confusing to follow by eye so many numbers and since the sample areas differ so widely in absolute size, it is desirable to recast the data, and express the figures in a condensed, relative form. This has been done in Table 2.9. Here, the sexes have been consolidated: for example, (EM) refers to all unions of español and mestizo, regardless of which was male or female. In this manner, the possible combinations with four ethnic groups (part A) have been reduced from 16 to 10, and with three groups (part B) from 9 to 6.

The number of the marital unions in each ethnic combination, furthermore, has been recalculated as the percentage of all the unions which were recorded in the regional sample indicated. In part A, the four-group series from 1777, there were 175,098 persons involved (that is, 87,549 couples), of whom 139,305 were Indians. In part B, the three-groups series from 1777 and 1793, there were 91,664 persons (45,832 couples), none of whom were Indians. In part B, moreover, the percentage values for the

Table 2.9

Relative occurrence of types of racial union. Percentage of each type among the total unions in each area indicated. With mixed groups, the sexes are consolidated.

A. Four-group series, from census of 1777

Area	(EE)	(EM)	(EP)	(EI)	(MM)	(MP)	(MI)	(PP)	(PI)	(II)
Antequera	23.01	9.74	5.14	2.28	9.74	7.34	7.26	8.15	3.71	23.63
Oaxaca, 60 pars.	0.68	0.22	0.15	0.15	0.96	0.21	0.40	4.59	0.49	92.15
Puebla, 50 pars.	3.61	1.91	0.34	0.37	7.78	1.20	1.59	2.62	0.66	79.92
Durango, 14 pars.	13.81	3.58	3.73	1.35	8.36	5.20	4.51	31.91	12.90	14.65

B. Three-group series, from censuses of 1777 and 1793

Area	(EE)	(EM)	(EP)	(MM)	(MP)	(PP)
Antequera (1777)	36.50	15.45	8.15	15.45	11.62	12.83
Oaxaca (1777), 60 pars.	9.98	3.29	2.14	14.10 ·	3.13	67.36
Puebla (1777), 50 pars.	20.70	10.94	1.96	44.58	6.88	14.94
Durango (1777), 14 pars.	20.74	5.37	5.60	12.56	7.77	47.96
Querétaro (1793), city	45.81	17.58	1.89	20.96	2.72	11.04
Puebla (1793), 3 juris.	30.75	18.63	2.04	33.26	7.51	7.80
Guanajuato (1793), 4 juris.	42.46	12.73	4.91	14.54	7.01	18.35
South. Hid. (1793), 7 juris.	32.75	16.26	2.26	36.40	3.35	8.98
Valley Mex. (1793)	41.01	18.15	1.05	33.00	1.71	5.08
Mean of above values	31.19	13.16	3.33	24.87	5.74	21.59
% based upon total of 45,832 *unions*	32.55	13.08	3.37	25.63	5.99	19.52

nine areas have been averaged, and for comparison with these figures, the percentages have been computed for the total numbers in the entire series.

The most cursory inspection of Table 2.9 brings into prominence two important features. The first is the fact that with every racial group, the proportion of intragroup unions exceeds that of any single extragroup combination. Furthermore, in most individual areas, as well as in the totals for part B of the table, the proportion of intragroup union exceeds the sum of all extragroup combinations. Thus, the percentage of EE exceeds the percentage of EM plus the percentage of EP; MM exceeds EM plus MP, etc. The universal tendency, therefore, was for more men and women of every racial type to choose a spouse within the same group than to intermarry with another group.

The second feature is represented by the extreme to which this tendency was carried in Oaxaca and Puebla by the Indians. In sixty parishes of the former bishopric, 92 percent of all unions were between Indians, and in fifty parishes of Puebla, close to 80 percent. Meanwhile, in Durango, the analogous value was approximately 15 percent. Immediately it will be recalled that, according to all the eighteenth century enumerations, a great majority of the total population in the two southern bishoprics was Indian. Would it not be natural, therefore, that Indian-Indian unions should predominate? In addition, would it not be anticipated that the members of any racial group, whether a majority or a minority of the population would seek to marry their own type? If so, one might easily account for the very general excess of intragroup over extragroup marriages.

The data as presented in Tables 2.8 and 2.9 ask these questions but do not answer them. It is possible, nevertheless, to explore their implications in greater depth if we have recourse to certain assumptions or, perhaps we might say, models.

Let us state one hypothesis: *In late colonial Mexico, the sole factor which determined the ethnic character of a marital or reproductive union was random propinquity or contact between individuals in an unrestricted environment.* Clearly, since these conditions were rarely, if ever, satisfied, such an hypothesis can be attacked from all sides and on many grounds. On the contrary, it has the merit of being simple, neat, and nicely adapted to quantitative evaluation. In any formal test we anticipate wide deviations, but the nature and extent of the deviations provide a better understanding of the actual phenomena, even though the hypothesis or model has to be rejected.

The mechanics of application are relatively uncomplicated. Under the hypothesis of random contact, unions between sexes will occur in direct proportion to the relative numbers of each ethnic group present in the environment. The environment is considered here as the region or area which provides the sample of population, one of the four areas in 1777 or five areas in 1793, as given in the tables. The spatial extent of a region is irrelevant, if we adhere to the assumption of random selection.

Having assembled the *observed* (recorded and counted) numbers of unions for each racial pair (called x), and having placed these in 4×4 or 3×3 tables, as in Table 2.8, we total the males and females in columns and rows. We then calculate for each combination the *expected* number of unions (called m), given the stated total number of each sex and racial type, and the probability that the conjunctions will follow random contact alone. In all parts of Table 2.8, for each combination, the second number in each square is the expected value and is further distinguished by enclosure in a parenthesis. For example in Antequera, 1777 (part A), the observed number of unions of E males and E females was 725. The number expected under the hypothesis of random contact was (314).

A glance at the table shows that in every case the observed value differs from the expected, sometimes by a wide margin, and for this reason alone the hypothesis of random selection cannot be considered to hold with precision. However, at this point arises the question, How can we measure and assess the degree of deviation of the observed from the expected, in other words, the extent to which the reality departs from the model? This parameter—the degree of departure—is itself a valuable tool in the analysis.

The most direct and satisfactory method is merely to take the ratio of the two magnitudes, observed/expected. If the two estimates coincide, the hypothesis holds perfectly, and the ratio will equal 1.0. If the expected number is smaller than observed, the ratio exceeds 1.0, and if it is greater, the ratio is less than 1.0. In the case mentioned above (EE for Antequera) the ratio is 725/314, or 2.308. The ratios are placed in the tables as the third number in each square.

We may now revert to the question raised previously in connection with the percentages of racial groups, Are the consistently high values found for intragroup marriages referable to the mere propinquity of similar persons, or is some other factor involved? If we examine the ratios of observed to be expected in Table 2.8 for intragroup unions, we find them without exception to exceed 1.0. In other words, their number is always greater than would be predicted under the hypothesis of random selection. Hence, other considerations must have been partially responsible for the final result. Conversely, in most cases extragroup unions show ratios less than 1.0 and are, consequently, less frequent then would have been predicted.

Further examination of extragroup unions suggests that there may have existed in certain cases a bias toward marriage with one rather than another racial group. A test of this possibility may be carried out with the Indians reported in 1777 for the four areas shown in Table 2.8, parts A to D. The values of the ratio observed/expected (x/m) may be listed for each extragroup combination, (IE), (IM), and (IP). The respective mean values of x/m for these combinations are 0.101, 0.356, and 0.291. The value of F for the three types is 1,465, which, with three classes of four items each, is completely non-significant. We have to say, therefore, that when Indians married outside their own caste, they exercised no conspicuous choice.

The other three racial types are best examined in the three-group series taken from both censuses. When the sexes are consolidated, there are three possible extragroup categories, (EM), (EP), and (MP). The respective mean values of x/m are 0.506, 0.202, and 0.428. If we employ them in sets of two and compute t for each set, we get for (EM)-(EP), 7.10; for (EM)-(MP), 0.90; for (EP)-(MP), 2.78. Only the first of these values for t is significant beyond the 1 percent level of probability. If we calculate F for the three types jointly, we get 9.71, the high significance of which may be referred primarily to the succession of low values of x/m for (EP). In other words, españoles clearly tended to seek mestizos rather than pardos, but neither mestizos nor pardos appear to have manifested any marked selectivity in the choice of spouses native to other ethnic groups.

We may reconsider briefly the intragroup marriages. It has been noted that these consistently show higher observed values than would be expected. The cause of this difference cannot be ascertained from the data at hand, but it is possible to test the weight of one factor, the relative numerical importance in the population as a whole.

If we examine the Indians in the four-group series from 1777, we may list the four areal values for (II) and, in a parallel manner, list the percentage of Indian adults (married men and women) in the total married population of each area. Then a simple correlation tells whether there is any correspondence, arithmetically, between the two sets of magnitudes. When this operation is performed, the value of r is -0.990, highly significant even for only three degrees of freedom. This finding may be interpreted as indicating that the excess of the observed intragroup marriages over the expected number is greater, the smaller the proportion of Indians in the general population. This interpretation, however, must take account of the fact that two of the four pairs of magnitudes pertain to the rural parishes in Oaxaca and Puebla, where the mass of the Indians literally never came into physical contact with other socio-racial groups.

We then test in a similar manner the other three types, as they appear in the nine-area series from both censuses. For the three groups separately, the correlation coefficients of the ratio x/m with the percentage of total married persons in the area are españoles, -0.902; mestizos, -0.828; and pardos, -0.718. With 8 degrees of freedom, r at the 1 percent level of probability lies at 0.765, and at the 5 percent level at 0.632. Therefore, these values may be regarded as significant. Moreover, if we combine all three groups, to get twenty-seven pairs of figures, the value of r is -0.753, well beyond the 1 percent level of probability for 26 degrees of freedom. There can be little doubt, therefore, that a negative association existed between the relative proportion of any racial group in the population and the tendency of its members to marry within the group.

In several respects it has now been shown that the marital behavior of the principal racial groups in the population of colonial Mexico did not conform strictly to the hypothesis of random selection based upon propinquity. Other factors clearly influenced the kind and degree of selection. Of these one of the most obvious was the high probability that members of any group would marry within the same group. Another factor the presence of which can be detected in at least a few instances is that a person from a particular group would exercise conscious or unconscious choice between possible spouses from other and equally available groups. In order to encompass these and doubtless many unknown factors within a single term, we may refer to them all as demonstrating preference.

If we were to abandon completely the theory of random contact and resort to an hypothesis which recognized only preference as mediating choice of marital partner, we should encounter serious difficulty. Thus, if each person married only within his or her own racial domain, all of Table 2.8 would have to be altered by substituting new figures for the expected values. The number in each intragroup combination would be expected to equal approximately one-half the sum of the living males and females in the entire group. This number would always be greater than that actually observed. Hence the ratio x/m would always be less than 1.0. Furthermore, the expected extragroup unions would always be zero, and, therefore, in practice each such ratio would equal a finite integer divided by zero, or infinity. This result is absurd and shows that the hypothesis would have to be abandoned. If it is true that an hypothesis neither of random contact or of preference alone can satisfy the recorded data but that both appear to be involved, it may be possible to construct a model which will bring expectation closer to reality. If we can improve the relationship between observed and expected with but a single such model, this fact will be sufficient to demonstrate the validity of the premise that both propinquity and personal preference were factors participating in the control of racial mixture.

In order to accomplish this purpose, we may propose an hypothesis (designated II), based upon that of random contact (designated I) and modifying it : *The number in any ethnic union is a function of the number of persons in the population which participates, but with intragroup unions the expected number will be twice as great as is thereby demanded because of the added factor of preference, whereas with extragroup unions the expected number will be one-half as great.* Specifically, we would alter Table 2.8 by doubling each intragroup expected value and by halving each extragroup expected value. As a consequence, each intragroup ratio is divided by two and each extragroup ratio is multiplied by two.

The problem now becomes how to evaluate the effect of this change in such a way as to express hypothesis II and at the same time to determine whether it approaches more or less closely to the observed relationship than hypothesis I. We need some kind of quantitative index as a measure for comparison. We suggest the following procedure as one which is purely empirical and quite without theoretical significance.

Let us imagine a perfect model, in which the observed numbers throughout exactly equal those expected. Then, for each type of union, the ratio x/m will equal 1.0. The variance, in its usual expression $\Sigma d^2/n\text{-}1$ will be zero, and the ratio of the variance to the mean will likewise be zero. If, under the hypothesis being studied, the variance is not zero, the value of its ratio to the mean will indicate the extent of departure from the perfect model. Moreover, two hypotheses may be compared in that the one with the greater relative variance will depart the more widely from the ideal condition. See Table 2.10.

For each four-group and three-group area we recalculate the ratio x/m in accordance with the requirements of hypothesis II. Then, for convenience in carrying out the arithmetic, we multiply them all by 10^3. The next step is to write the logarithms

Table 2.10

Comparisons among four racial groups in four areas (1777) and among three racial groups in nine areas (1777–1793) according to hypotheses I and II (see text). Under each hypothesis, column 1 gives the mean of the logarithms of the individual ratios of observed to expected numbers (mean of log x/m x 10^3, expressed as the antilogarithms of the mean. Column 2 gives the variance of each mean ($\Sigma d^2/n\text{--}1$), also as the antilogarithm. Column 3 gives the ratio of column 2 x 10^3 to column 1. See the text for further discussion.

Area	*Hypothesis I*			*Hypothesis II*		
	(1)	(2)	(3)	(1)	(2)	(3)
	Four-group series					
Antequera (1777)	682.3	1.465	2.15	933.3	1.205	1.29
Oaxaca (1777)	843.3	29.240	34.67	1,593.0	6.720	4.22
Puebla (1777)	693.4	6.058	8.73	1,511.0	3.669	2.43
Durango (1777)	704.8	1.537	2.18	916.2	1.165	1.27
	Three-group series					
Antequera (1777)	857.0	1.237	1.45	1,067.0	1.052	0.99
Oaxaca (1777)	523.6	3.540	6.77	610.9	1.876	3.07
Puebla (1777)	590.2	1.812	3.07	743.0	1.144	1.54
Durango (1777)	662.2	1.668	2.52	835.6	1.127	1.35
Querétaro (1793)	578.1	2.121	3.67	722.8	1.502	2.08
Puebla (1793)	707.9	1.662	2.35	891.3	1.152	1.29
Guanajuato (1793)	663.7	1.690	2.55	837.5	1.183	1.41
So. Hidalgo (1793)	514.0	2.713	5.29	647.1	1.563	2.41
Val. Mexico (1793)	550.8	3.089	5.61	695.0	1.698	2.44

of the ratios and take the mean. We then find the nine, or the sixteen, deviations, depending upon the area, and derive the variance, $\Sigma d^2/n\text{-}1$ for the area. At the end we reconvert the mean of the logarithms and the variance to the corresponding antilogarithms and take the ratio of the latter to the former. Since these ratios are fractions, they are multiplied by 10^3 in order that we may deal with whole numbers. Logarithms are used for the purpose of reducing the wide dispersion of values inherent in the series of direct ratios. The results, for the four-group series and the three-group series, expressed as antilogarithms, are in Table 2.10. For each of the two hypotheses, the important columns is that which gives the ratio:

$$\frac{\text{antilog of variance } x \ 10^3}{\text{antilog of mean log of ratio } x/m}$$

It will be noted with every group and area that the ratio of variance to mean is smaller under hypothesis II than under hypothesis I. The value of t for the three-group series is 2.85, at the 2 percent level of probability. Since a perfect correspondence between observed and expected numbers would give a variance of zero, the smaller the ratio of variance to mean, the closer the approach to identity. Hypothesis II, therefore, gives results which come nearer to the theoretical value than does hypothesis I. Hence, we conclude that the factor of preference operates jointly with random contact so as to produce the observed marital relations. The very crude assumptions underlying hypothesis II obviously provide no more than a partial correction, even though it is in the right direction. An analysis of probably unattainable intricacy would be necessary for an exact simulation of the ideal conditions. Moreover, when we say preference, in this context, we tacitly include a host of secondary factors which in turn determine what the preference shall be.

IV

In concluding this essay it will be of interest to inquire not only into the degree of racial fusion and the possible mediating factors but also into the rate at which amalgamation was proceeding in the last years of the eighteenth century. Although we have consistently operated with those socio-racial groups under which the data are categorized in the contemporary counts, at the same time we may also think in terms of inheritable characters rather than those emphasized as marks of social distinction. Thus, although we retain for purposes of calculation the various racial combinations, EE, EM, etc., we conceive the population to have been segregated into two primary types, pure and mixed or hybrid. Immediately there emerge three (not four) categories of genetic origin, white, black, and red, or españoles, pardos, and indios. In the terminology which we have employed hitherto, only EE, PP, and II can be considered as pure strains. All other combinations are mixed, including the entire series of mestizos. Our problem, therefore, is to investigate the rapidity with which the three primary races were merging to form a composite population.

Qualitatively the composition of this fusion group is enormously complex, for three human subspecies contribute more or less equally to the final product. This fact renders further and detailed analysis extremely difficult although in theoretical models or in well-controlled animal experiments, Mendelian statistics can solve most similar problems. In the present instance the data are entirely inadequate to support the application of such methods. Consequently, we shall regard this fusion group simply as a mixed population which embraces all kinds of interracial crosses—all the mestizos in the sense employed by Aguirre Beltrán. In the long run it has certainly become Euro- Afro- Indo-mestizo, a unique human ethnic compound, found only in Latin America.

We have pointed out previously that all official recognition of racial groups and all record of their occurrence ceased shortly after the War of Independence of 1810–1820. The usable data, therefore, derive only from 1777 and 1793. As a result, we simply do not know the exact racial composition of the Mexican people today, nor is there any method for calculating it with precision. With the samples from 1777 and 1793, we can try to determine rates of fusion at that time, but we cannot be sure what happened thereafter. On the other hand, we can attempt to make projections subsequent to that date and can estimate very approximately what would have happened if all the conditions of 1770–1800 had remained unaltered until the present time. With this fundamental premise, we must include the following assumptions and considerations.

(1) It is assumed that the populations of the regions used as samples remained stable indefinitely, subsequent to the censuses. This means that birth and death rates did not change, at least in such a manner that the numerical relations among racial groups were disturbed.

(2) It is further assumed that the rates of intermarriage among the various racial components remained fixed and that the factors such as propinquity and preference continued to exert a constant influence. Clearly, these assumptions may or may not be justified by the facts, but we have no means for testing them, and we cannot proceed to any type of analysis without them.

(3) It is considered provisionally, subject to later modification, that there occurred no significant movement of population in or out of each sample area. In other words, each racial stock, at the time of enumeration, constituted a fixed reservoir which was being depleted by intermarriage with other groups but which was neither augmented by immigration from other regions or from foreign sources nor diminished by emigration out of the area.

A technical difficulty, which is not an assumption but a disagreeable fact, relates to the omission of Indians from the 1793 reports. We have previously explained that whereas we work with full representation of all racial components in the census of 1777, we can consider only three in that of 1793, españoles, mestizos, and pardos. For the present purpose, we shall omit mestizos, who fall within the broad group of mixed origin and shall confine our attention to españoles and pardos, whom we shall consider pure groups even though both had substantial admixtures of other racial stock. The rates of fusion which can be calculated for these two groups will differ materially from those which would be found if the probably numerous unions with Indians could be included. Nevertheless, if we wish to use the 1793 data at all, we are obliged to accept a substantial tolerance.

The magnitude involved may be tested by deriving the proportion among all españoles, of those españoles who are married intragroup (EE among all E). In 1777, for the four regions, Antequera, Oaxaca (60 parishes), Puebla (50 parishes), Durango (14 parishes), the mean percentage of españoles who married intragroup, according to the complete count, was 73.72. When the Indians and all españoles married to Indians are removed, the mean percentage becomes 77.37. In effect then we follow the marital behavior of those españoles who did not marry Indians. Similarly, for pardos, the percentages are 71.73 and 79.47. Projections based upon the proportions found when Indians are omitted will consistently show values considerably higher than those based upon ethnically complete populations.

In accordance with these facts we have utilized two series of estimates (see Table 2.11). The first includes all racial groups mentioned in the 1777 census. The results, for the four sample areas concerned, are probably the most accurate which we can get. The second includes the same four areas from the 1777 census, but with all Indians and their spouses omitted. To these are added the five areas from that of 1793 which are shown in Table 2.8, parts I to M, making nine in all. For the purpose of making comparisons and for furnishing approximate indicators, the series is useful.

Within the framework of these restrictions and qualifications, we may now postulate that the fusion of racial types during and subsequent to the period 1770–1800, was an exponential function of time. If we use another mode of expression, we may say that the loss from a pure type into the pool of mixed types was always a function of the number of members in the pure type. In its general form, the governing equation is stated :

$$p_1 = p_0^{e^{-kg}}$$

Here, p_0 is the initial population of the pure group (for example, EE) as read from the census record; p_1 is the population remaining in the pure group after a specified time; k is a constant which expresses the rate of loss to the pure group; g is a unit of time.

Time may be expressed as years or decades. However, both these terms lead to very unwieldy exponents. It is simpler to employ the generation as the secular unit. Since the median age for child bearing probably lay between twenty and twenty-five years (we have no direct information on this point), it is not unreasonable to take the generation (g) as embracing 22.5 years.

The constant, k, is determined as follows. At the time of the census there is a set of combinations, each of which contains at least one member who is derived from some particular racial type, say E. In this set there is one combination (EE) in which both partners are of this type, in other words, the pure stock. Then the ratio of those in the pure stock to the total of this type who are in all combinations is a clue to the rate at which, from the starting point, the pure group is being converted to mixed combinations. In practice this ratio may be expressed as a decimal or (x 100) as a percentage. In either case the value is a function of k and represents the number of persons who remain in the pure strain. Conversely, the total of the entire type minus those in the pure group will indicate the proportion who are going into mixed combinations. The latter magnitude is a direct index to the rate at which the conversion of pure to mixed is taking place and may be used as k.

The term p_0 is the initial population of the pure fraction as given by the census and may be retained in the form of the absolute number stated. It is more desirable, however, to place all values on a relative basis. Therefore we let p_0 equal 1.0 and apply directly the indicated ratio. With g known or assumed, the equation can be solved for p_1, which will then represent the population of the pure fraction after exposure to attrition for the specified number of generations.

We illustrate the application of the method with the españoles in Antequera in 1777. According to the census there were 725 couples or 1,450 persons in the combination EE, that is, the pure type. There were also 541 mixed couples (EM, EP, EI) of whom, of course, 541 individuals were españoles. Hence, the total number in the racial group of E was 1,450 plus 541, or 1,991. The ratio 1,450 to 1,991 is 0.7282, or 72.82 percent. The loss to the pure type is $1.0000 - 0.7282$, or 0.2718. This is k,

Let us assume that g is 5. Then, after 5 generations, or 112.5 years, the remaining persons of pure type will be p_1, where

$$p_1 = 1.0e^{-0.2718 \times 5}$$

The right-hand member of the equation reduces to 0.2569, or 25.69 percent of the original number. In a stationary population this would amount to 25.69 percent of 1,450, or 372 persons in unions of the EE type. After eight generation, or 180 years, the value would be 11.37 percent, or 164 persons in the EE combination. If the population were stable rather than stationary, the absolute values would be different, but the percentages would be the same.

We may desire to know the proportion of the pure type

in the total population after a certain number of generations. If so, we merely calculate the percentage of the pure combination (such as EE) in the total and use it as p_0. In the case described, Antequera in 1777, the EE group constituted 23 percent of the total inhabitants. Then, instead of $p_0 = 1.0$, we substitute $p_0 = 0.2300$ and solve as before. After five generations the surviving EE group is 5.91 percent of the entire population.

Similar procedures may be followed with the other racial types and the other areas. Furthermore, if we wish to estimate the increase in relative size of the consolidated mixed group, it is only necessary to subtract the sum of the pure types from 1.0, or 100 percent. The remainder shows the proportion of the mixed group. For instance, with Antequera in 1777, the sum of EE, PP, and II was 54.76 percent of the total population; consequently, 45.24 percent were mixed. After five generations the latter value would have risen to 85.53 percent, and after eight generations to 93.14 percent. When the Indians are omitted, as is true of the three-group series, the method is identical, with the exception that the total population is taken as the sum of all racial combinations which do not include Indians. The results obtained with both the three-group and the four-group series are shown in Table 2.11 where the values are all expressed as ratios or percentages.

In this table the broad and pronounced trend toward racial amalgamation may be deduced from the experience of the mixed group as seen in the three-group series. At the time of the censuses, and in the nine sample areas, the mean percentage in the total population of this component was 47.22, approximately one-half. The standard deviation is ±14.20; the standard error is ±4.73.

Under the conditions here assumed, a stable population with no migration, the corresponding mean percentage at the end of five generations would have been 77.33 (s.d. ±15.68, s.e. ±5.23), and at eight generations would have been 85.18 (s.d. ±14.90, s.e. ±4.97). This means that in five generations the population would have contained only approximately 25 percent pure whites and blacks, and after eight generations only 15 percent.

The influence of the Indians on changes in racial composition, deliberately ignored in the three-group series, is brought into clear focus by the four-group series. By 1777 the relative number of pure Indian couples in the small city of Antequera

Table 2.11

Rates of racial fusion.

The four-group series contains the racial fractions EE, PP, II, and mixed. The latter category covers all mixtures, including mestizos (MM). In the three-group series, the Indians, in all their racial combinations, have been omitted, in part by deletion (census of 1777), in part by failure to include them in the census (census of 1793).

Column 1 gives the area and the racial group. Column 2 is the percentage of persons shown by the census to be in pure combination (e.g., EE) with respect to those in all combinations (EE in total E). Column 3 is the percentage of persons in pure combination with respect to total population (e.g., EE in the total population). Column 4 is the value of k derived for the expression $p_0^e {}^{kg}$. Column 5a is the percentage of persons in pure combination with respect to those in all combinations (e.g., EE in total E) after 5 generations, and column 5b the percentage with respect to the total population. Columns 6a and 6b repeat columns 5a and 5b, but the time is taken at eight generations.

For the mixed group, column 3 shows the percentage of the mixed group in the total population at the time of the census, calculated by difference : 100 percent minus the sum of the pure groups. Columns 5b and 6b show the percentage of the mixed group as calculated for five and eight generations, respectively.

(1)	(2)	(3)	(4)	(5a)	(5b)	(6a)	(6b)
			Four-group series				
Antequera							
EE	72.82	23.00	0.2718	25.69	5.91	11.37	2.62
PP	50.20	8.16	0.4980	8.29	0.68	1.85	0.15
II	78.07	23.60	0.2193	33.40	7.88	17.31	4.09
Mixed		45.24			85.53		93.14
Durango							
EE	76.15	13.81	0.2385	30.35	4.19	14.84	2.05
PP	74.89	31.93	0.2511	28.48	9.10	13.41	4.28
II	61.06	14.65	0.3894	14.27	2.09	4.48	0.66
Mixed		39.61			84.62		93.01
Oaxaca							
EE	72.52	0.68	0.2748	25.31	0.17	11.10	0.07
PP	91.49	4.59	0.0851	65.53	3.00	50.61	2.32
II	99.44	92.14	0.0056	97.24	89.60	95.63	88.11
Mixed		2.59			7.23		9.50
Puebla							
EE	73.39	3.60	0.2661	26.43	0.95	11.85	0.43
PP	70.34	2.62	0.2966	22.70	0.59	9.32	0.24
II	98.39	79.90	0.0161	92.26	73.72	87.91	70.24
Mixed		13.88			24.74		29.09

Table 2.11 (cont.)

		(1)	(2)	(3)	(4)	(5a)	(5b)	(6a)	(6b)
					Three-group series				
Antequera 1777	EE	75.56	36.45	0.2444	29.46	10.74	14.15	5.16	
	PP	56.67	12.92	0.4333	11.46	1.48	3.13	0.40	
	Mixed		50.63			87.78		94.44	
Durango 1777	EE	79.10	20.75	0.2090	35.17	7.30	18.79	3.90	
	PP	87.77	47.96	0.1223	54.25	26.02	37.58	18.02	
	Mixed		31.29			66.68		78.08	
Oaxaca 1777	EE	78.62	9.98	0.2138	34.34	3.43	18.07	1.80	
	PP	96.23	67.35	0.0377	82.82	55.80	73.97	49.82	
	Mixed		22.67			40.77		48.38	
Puebla 1777	EE	76.23	20.68	0.2377	30.46	6.30	14.93	3.09	
	PP	77.19	14.97	0.2281	31.96	4.78	16.12	2.41	
	Mixed		64.35			88.92		94.50	
Querétaro 1793	EE	82.47	45.82	0.1753	41.62	19.07	24.60	11.27	
	PP	82.73	11.03	0.1727	42.16	4.65	25.12	2.77	
	Mixed		43.15			76.28		85.96	
Puebla 1793	EE	74.83	30.74	0.2517	28.40	8.73	13.35	4.10	
	PP	62.06	7.80	0.3794	15.00	1.17	4.80	0.37	
	Mixed		61.46			90.10		95.53	
Guanajuato 1793	EE	82.79	42.44	0.1721	42.29	17.95	25.24	10.71	
	PP	75.49	18.36	0.2451	29.35	5.39	14.85	2.73	
	Mixed		39.20			76.66		86.56	
S. Hidalgo 1793	EE	77.95	32.73	0.2205	33.20	10.87	17.14	5.61	
	PP	76.22	8.98	0.2378	30.45	2.73	14.92	1.34	
	Mixed		58.29			86.40		93.05	
Val. Mexico 1793	EE	81.02	40.99	0.1898	38.71	15.87	21.90	8.98	
	PP	78.62	5.08	0.2138	34.34	1.74	18.07	0.92	
	Mixed		53.93			82.39		90.10	
Three group series mean	EE	78.73	30.84	0.2238	34.85	11.14	18.69	6.07	
	PP	76.32	21.61	0.2300	36.87	11.53	23.17	8.75	
	Mixed		47.22			77.33		85.18	

and in the bishopric of Durango approximated that of the other racial stocks. The mixed combinations amounted to slightly fewer than the average for the three-group series. In the sixty parishes of rural Oaxaca the proportion of Indians married to Indians (II) was extremely high, 99.44 percent of all Indian casados. In fifty parishes of Puebla, the proportion was nearly as high, 98.39 percent. The mixed combinations in the total population were correspondingly low. As a result of this condition, the subsequent trend was such that under the hypothesis here proposed, by the eighth generation the pure Indian strain would have been maintained at a very high level in rural Oaxaca and Puebla, while it almost disappeared in Antequera and Durango. Although we have little firm data to support the conclusion, observation in the field indicates that this state of affairs actually has been brought to pass.

Confirmatory evidence of a sort may be derived from the 1960 census[20] which shows the number of persons counted as being able to speak only an indigenous language. If we convert these figures to percentage of total population,[21] we get Chihuahua, 0.89, Durango, 0.20, Guanajuato, 0.02, Oaxaca, 17.21, and Puebla, 6.72. The difference between these two sets of states is very clear.

The behavior of the non-Indian group is relatively uniform in both series throughout all sample areas. We may consider the white element and again ignore the effect of immigration. Column 2 of Table 2.11 shows that in the four-group series, the avarage proportion of españoles married to españoles among all españoles was 73.72 percent ±1.66. For the three-group series, the comparable average was 78.73 ±2.92. The difference between the means can be accounted for by the omission of the Indians from the three-group series. Clearly, the degree to which the whites were intermarrying with other racial groups was very similar in all regions and meant that one out of every four españoles was marrying a member of another racial group. The effect of this hybridization after eight generations and in the absence of any recruitment from abroad would have been almost to eliminate the white race in Mexico. According to the four-group series, there would have remained in the total population between 1 and 2 percent of the combination EE, and according to the three-group series approximately

[20] Resumen general, cuadro 14, pp. 263–266.
[21] Ibid., cuadro 1, p. 1 et seq.

6 percent. In rural Oaxaca, if the Indians are included, there would have been only seven pure white married couples left among each 10,000 pairs.

The attrition being suffered by the blacks was comparable to that of the whites, although probably not quite as severe. For the four areas in 1777, the mean proportion of pardos married to pardos among all pardos was 71.73, very close to the paralled value for españoles. However, the variability was greater, for the standard diviation equals 17.00. In the three-group series, the mean proportion of PP unions is 76.32 ± 12,06. With respect to depletion, after eight generations the mean number ot pure black couples in the total population would have been 1.80 percent, according to the four-group series, and 8.75, according to the 3-group series. There is no statistical significance in any of the differences between españoles and pardos indicated by Table 2.11.

If we may summarize briefly this discussion, we may say that the black and white components of the racial complex as provided by our samples from the censuses of 1777 and 1793 were proceeding in an almost identical manner toward extinction of the pure type within no more than ten generations. The same may be said of the Indians in areas where their numbers were substantially equal to those of the other groups (for example, Durango). However, in those regions where the Indians were aggregated in great masses, as in the rural parishes of southern Mexico, they were maintaining their racial identity.

The pure strains were being replaced in the late eighteenth century by a mixed type, which at that time amounted to nearly one-half the total population and which ultimately would have replaced all pure types if the demographic system had remained entirely closed. The process was rapid and would have been fully completed within a few generations in all the towns and in the entirc countryside from the Bajío northward. In the Indian areas to the south, it would have taken far longer to accomplish. This mixed type is of great anthropological and social interest since, as was previously pointed out, it represents the fusion of three racial entities which have been merging more and more closely with each generation.

The almost equal representation by each of the three primary stocks, which is suggested by the data from 1777 and 1793 and which is a consequence of the assumptions under-lying our basic hypothesis, may not present a true picture of

Mexican racial composition in its final form. As we have indicated previously, in order to elucidate the exact composition of the mixed type, we would require a wealth of data which we do not possess, together with an elaborate mathematical treatment beyond the scope of this essay. There are, moreover, a few factors which have been and are important in establishing the nature of Mexican mestization but which could not be predicted by our model based upon the exponential disappearance of pure ethnic types. We may mention three briefly: the Indian reservoir, white immigration, and the vanishing of the Negro as a pure strain.

(1) The Indian reservior is not yet exhausted. Despite a continuous substantial emigration to the coasts, to the north, and to Mexico City, according to the admittedly bad linguistic criterion there are still over 500,000 indigenes living in Oaxaca, Puebla, and Veracruz. These may be regarded as being of pure Indian origin and to have not yet effectively entered the main stream of racial fusion. According to the census of 1950,[22] in these three states 3,166,812 persons, five years or older, spoke only Spanish, 1,134,082 spoke a native language with or without Spanish. The latter group constituted 26.4 percent of the total. This figure is far removed from the 70 to 90 percent of pure Indian casados, among those in the entire population, which would be predicted by the eight generation according to Table 2.11. It does, nevertheless, indicate that the Indian element may still be sufficiently numerous to exert a perceptible influence upon the character of the mixed population.

(2) The extent to which the white component has been reinforced by immigration is difficult to assess although the importance of this source of supply is evident from common knowledge. If immigration is left out of consideration, as we have done in calculating rates of depletion, one must conclude that the white group was about to disappear as a separate entity within the 200 years subsequent to the end of the eighteenth century. A few figures may give some notion of the magnitude of the increment provided by immigration.

We may ignore the rate of the immigration from Europe prior to 1777, which created the pool of white population existing at that time, and direct attention to the following years. Arriaga summarizes the number of foreign born in Mexico according to recent censuses.[23] From the corresponding total

[22]*Resumen general*, cuadro 6, p. 52.
[23]Arriaga, *New Life Tables*, Table XIII–16, p. 188.

populations, we have calculated the percentages. The average is
0.71 percent, a figure which includes the immigrants in Mexico
City and other centers of industry and culture.

Year of Census	No. of Foreign Born (in thousands)	% of Total Pop.
1921	100.8	0.71
1930	159.8	0.97
1940	105.3	0.54
1950	182.3	0.70
1960	223.4	0.64
Mean		0.71

For comparison we may use some data found in the
ramo de Historia.[24] For seven provinces and jurisdictions
(including the province of Guanajuato) are stated the number of
Europeans (that is, immigrants) living in the entity and also
the total population. To these may be added for the jurisdiction
of Guanajuato (the city) the total from Historia[25] and the
number of Europeans actually recorded on the census sheets
themselves.

Entity	%European in Total Pop.
Antequera (city)	1.53
Mexico (prov.)	0.13
Mexico (city)	2.23
Tlaxcala (prov.)	0.09
Mérida (jur.)	0.44
Durango (jur.)	0.73
Guanajuato (prov.)	0.31
Guanajuato (jur.)	0.50
Mean	0.75

The two sets of values, found over a century apart, are
remarkably concordant and justify the conclusion that at any
time since 1770, the population of Mexico has contained, in
round numbers, 0.7 percent of European immigrants. Since in
the late eighteenth century, the white component in the total
population amounted to approximately 20 or 25 percent, the
proportion of European immigrants would have reached 2.5
to 3.5 percent of the pure white group (EE).

[24]Vols. 72, 522, and 523.
[25]Vol. 523, f. 88.

It is possible to modify the basic formula so as to include the increment from abroad, as it arrived per generation and as it in turn declined exponentially. However, the equation would become relatively complex. Furthermore, we have no knowledge how the newcomers were distributed through the country, save that the movement to the urban areas was much heavier than to rural areas. In view of the almost complete lack of information, it is preferable to forego any attempt to calculate exact values and to be contented with the general statement that the percentages shown in Table 2.11 as projections of the probable white population are considerably too low.

(3) The fate of the black component is easier to assess. By the end of the eighteenth century immigration from Africa had ceased. Like the Indians, the Negroes constituted a reservoir subject to attrition but not to renewal. However, they were much fewer in number and were distributed relatively evenly through the country despite local aggregation on the coasts and elsewhere. Hence the data given in Table 2.11 provide a fair representation of their demographic condition. By the eighth generation after the period 1770–1800, the Negro combination (PP) will surely have been reduced to no more than a few percentage points of the total unions in the population. Even among the non-Indians as a whole, their number cannot much exceed the 8 percent indicated by the three-group series in Table 2.11. Indeed, in its treatment of the black ethnic group, our basic model comes reasonably close to predicting the outcome of processes in operation two centuries ago.

Chapter III

Age at Marriage, 1690–1960

The age at which people marry is a factor which, on the one hand, influences the reproductivity of the community and, on the other, is itself modified by numerous social pressures. Clearly, if one assumes a monogamous society with little or no illegal procreation, the number of children per couple will be reduced the later in life they start their reproductive career. Thus, the age at marriage, particularly for females, furnishes a clue to the rate at which the population is increasing or decreasing. If, on the other hand, the formation of reproductive or family units, although monogamous, takes place without formal marriage or involves the creation by men of more than one ménage, the age at which the partners enter such reproductive unions equally will affect the rate at which the population is increasing or decreasing. Unfortunately, such less formal unions characterized by the terms common law marriage, *unión libre,* concubinage, and so forth are almost impossible to trace across long expanses of time because of the lack of records inherent in their very nature whereas marriages, as formal recorded events surrounded by much ceremony and ritual, leave written records.

For Mexico the marriage records are extensive and reach well before the year 1700, but they are almost inaccessible. The investigator is, therefore, forced to be content with a relatively few samples. From the Conquest down to fully 1870 the only source of information is the parish archives. Beginning in the middle sixteenth century, each local priest was required to keep records of all births, deaths, and marriages in his jurisdiction.[1] For every marriage his statement included the previous civil status and usually the age of the participants. In each of the many hundreds of parishes in Mexico there exists

[1] See the discussion in these *Essays,* I, 49–52, and in Borah and Cook, "Marriage and Legitimacy in Mexican Culture," in *California Law Review,* LIV, no. 2 (May 1966), pp. 955–957.

a file of books which record what survives of these vital statistics down to the present year. Survival has been haphazard and the destruction brought by time severe. Nevertheless many parishes in Mexico still have marriage registers of the seventeenth century, and most have a series that begins in the eighteenth century.

In the summer of 1956, with the help of one assistant kindly assigned to us by the Instituto Nacional de Antropología e Historia, we were able to examine and copy numerical values from the books of ten parishes in the Mixteca Alta in the state of Oaxaca. Of these, we obtained usable marriage data from Coixtlahuaca, Tejupan, Yanhuitlán, Teposcolula, Tlaxiaco, Tilantongo, and Teozacoalco. The representation is adequate for the area, and, indeed, there is probably little difference in character between the figures from the Mixteca Alta and from most of rural, Indian Oaxaca.

Limitation of time and resources prevented us from taking notes on all the marriages contained in the parishes mentioned. Furthermore, there were many gaps in the series as now preserved in the parochial archives. We therefore concentrated on several specific periods. The first was from the beginning (about 1690) to 1750. The second was from 1770 to the War of Independence. The third was from the end of that war, at approximately 1820 to 1850. We terminated at this year because the coverage of the records was deteriorating rapidly due to widespread civil disturbance. The fourth period was a relatively small sample from recent times, roughly 1930 to 1950. In all, we obtained from the parish books the ages for 4,675 marriages.

The second major source of information concerning age at marriage consists of the records of the *Registro Civil,* or Civil Register, an agency which, after some years of sporadic existence, began the uninterrupted collection of vital statistics in approximately 1870 and which is still in operation throughout Mexico. The Civil Register records civil marriages, the only ones now legal in Mexico. Each marriage is certificated and one copy of the document filed in the town where the ceremony occurs or in the cabecera of the district or region. Another copy is filed at the end of the year in the state capital, where the records of all births, deaths, and marriages are preserved in bound volumes.[2]

[2]*Ibid.,* pp. 62–65, 967–972, respectively.

These state volumes are open to authorized inspection, and it is relatively simple, even if it is an endlessly tedious task, to copy the ages of the bride and groom from the certificates. Indeed, the labor is so monumental that even though we employed local assistants over a period of several years, we were forced to take samples of only one or two years, at intervals of a decade or more, between 1870 and 1960. Furthermore, it was necessary to limit operations to two restricted regions. The first was northern and western Oaxaca, specifically the ex-districts of Coixtlahuaca, Teposcolula, Tlaxiaco, and Nochixtlán in the Mixteca Alta, and Putla, Juquila, Jamiltepec, Silacayoa-pan, and Zimatlán in the Mixteca Baja, the coast, and the central valleys. The population of these districts has been and still remains essentially Indian and rural. The second region was the city of Guadalajara, which was selected as an example of the urban, non-Indian environment. For the Oaxaca districts we have 15,268 marriages; for Guadalajara 17,427.

The primary objective of this study has been to compare age at marriage for both sexes, with respect to regional or environmental differences and to possible long-term, secular trends. Thus, there might be reflected to some extent variations in reproductive pattern, which in turn might be of importance in the population dynamics of colonial and republican Mexico. However, from the nature of the original sources and from the modifying factors to be described shortly, it will be evident that elaborate statistical treatment is useless and that the analysis of the numerical samples must be kept at a level of extreme simplicity.

If the frequency of marriage is plotted with age of female on the ordinate and that of male on the abscissa, a scatter diagram is obtained. From the row and column totals the frequency distribution with age of females and males, respectively, may be read off or plotted as a simple curve. Two or more samples of either sex, or both sexes jointly, may then be compared.

Any distribution curve of age at marriage is certain to be highly skewed to the left, for the marriage rate rises steeply from zero at puberty to a maximum, and then declines gradually to late middle or old age. Under these circumstances the mean of the entire range becomes of dubious statistical validity. It is also of reduced importance demographically, for we are most concerned with the youthful phase and care little about the reproductively poor late marriages.

There are three reasonably good substitutes for a general mean age, each of which can be used as an index to, or an indicator of, the young, actively procreating component. The first is a division of the distribution into quartiles, with special emphasis on the first and second interquartile points (the latter is, of course, the median). The second is the mean of the males or females under the age of twenty-five years. Here, the later marriages are arbitrarily excluded and attention is focused on those which are predominantly, even if not exclusively, first marriages and which are of major significance for the production of offspring. Moreover, the limits of fourteen or sixteen to twenty-four years define a distribution which is sufficiently close to normal to justify the use of the mean.

The third device is merely to calculate the percentage of persons marrying under age sixteen, age eighteen, and age twenty. These figures show clearly the extent to which the population is resorting to extremely young marriages. Other, similar methods for expressing the relative youthfulness of the marriage system are, to be sure, available. Those mentioned, however, are adequate, individually, or better in combination, to define the pattern with sufficient precision for our purposes.

With the data which we have at our disposal, certain factors are unavoidably present which not only render futile any intricate statistical analysis but even cast doubt upon the results obtained by very simple procedures.

(1) The parish books in the bishopric of Oaxaca, from their beginning down to at least 1850, very frequently recorded the civil status but not the age of the conjugal pair. Some individual priests, indeed, never mentioned age but stated merely that the person involved had been unmarried or was widowed. For instance, in our parish sample covering the period 1690–1750, there are 1,602 marriages, and, of course, 1,602 men and 1,602 women. Of these, twenty-four are listed as *solteros* marrying solteras, and 249 as *viudos* marrying viudas. Aside from gaining insight into the extent of widowhood in the eighteenth century, little can be learned of the older generation from these records, although we can still evaluate the position of the younger component.

In some cases the book records the age with the civil status. Thus, in the sample which runs from 1820 to 1850, ages are shown for 63 widowers and 39 widows. The means of age are, respectively, 36.8 and 30.0 years. With males there is one case of a person under the age of 25; with females there are 9 cases. If these figures are representative, and they probably do not deviate widely from the usual condition, the third indicator, percentages of each sex who married under 20 years of age, will not be affected, for the widows and most of the solteros will simply go into the undifferentiated residue over 19 years old. The second indicator, mean age under 25, will not be seriously influenced with the males but will be subject to some error with the females due to the noninclusion of the solteras and viudas who were between 20 and 25 years old. The first indicator, the interquartile points, will be distorted only to a minor extent since the first interquartile lies below 21 for males and 18 for females. The second interquartile is approximately two years older.

On the whole, the error referable to the omission of ages of older people, although its existence must be recognized, is not sufficient to justify discarding the entire series of parish reports.

(2) The phenomenon known as heaping has been observed in many censuses and classifications according to age. It may be defined as the tendency to assign people to some as opposed to other age categories, usually in terms of specific years, such as 20, 30, 40, etc. Heaping is found in the parish records of Oaxaca and in those of the Civil Register. Of special concern here is the uniform preference for the ages 15, 18, and 20, as compared with 17, 19, 21, etc. As an extreme case we may cite the females in the parishes of Oaxaca in 1690–1750.

Age	No. of Persons
15	336
16	143
17	49
18	145
19	24
20	60
21	1

In the Civil Register, for females in the same area in 1871–1874, we find these values.

Age	No. of Persons
17	269
18	302
19	165
20	216
21	65

The values of all our indices are certain to be displaced by an appreciable amount. The interquartile points will suffer the most. There is, however, no practical method for compensation, except perhaps to draw a smoothed curve through the indicated points and take off readings for each year. But other errors would be introduced which would offset those eliminated. We do the best we can with the figures as they are presented in the records.

(3) Probably the most serious defect of the marriage data with which we have to work is the fact that in the Civil Register and, indeed, in all records since 1870 we are not getting the behavior of the whole population. Briefly, the reason lies in the interaction of Mexican law and custom as they have existed since the reform of the mid-nineteenth century.

Prior to this epoch all marriages were performed by the clergy, and any other type of union was illegitimate. By 1870 there had been established the institution of civil marriage, whereby a couple must be joined in matrimony by the civil authority with no necessary approval by the Church. However, the Church for decades refused to concede the right of the state and has continued to regard only ceremonies performed by the priest as morally, if not legally, valid. As a result, many Mexican are united by civil ceremony alone; many others repudiate the authority of the state and are married only by the Church; still others resort to both forms with two ceremonies.

Even greater confusion has been generated by the increasing prevalence of *unión libre,* a phrase meaning literally free union, and most closely analogous to the Anglo-Saxon common law marriage. The man and woman concerned merely agree between themselves to live together in an established household and raise their children. We have discussed this entire question at length in a paper that need not be repeated here.[3]

In so far as the marital customs pertain to the records covering age, it is clear that in the parish books for the interval since 1870 are found only the religious marriage whereas in the Civil Register are found only the civil marriages. The civil and religious records may overlap and duplicate to an unknown extent while the thousands of agreements to live in unión libre are not put on record at all. What this means numerically can be judged by the figures cited in the 1960 census.[4] In all

[3]*Ibid.,* pp. 971–982, 996–1002, respectively.
[4]*Resumen general,* cuadro 9, p. 112.

Mexico, with both sexes, we find the following separation of persons.

Married	
Civil ceremony only	2,020,812
Religious ceremony	1,138,024
Civil and religious	6,678.940
Total	9,837,776=84.1%
In unión libre	1,852,184=15.9%

The crucial significance of these modes of marriage for the present study is that different elements of the total population have tended to concentrate in one mode as opposed to another. Many persons who adhere strongly to the Catholic faith marry in the Church and refuse to participate in a civil ceremony. On the contrary, many with the anti-clerical sentiments marry only with civil sanction. Apart from such religious and political divergence, however, the socio-economic distinction overrides all others. To be married by either civil or religious ritual costs money and often requires extended travel. As a result of this simple fact, many of the poorer people both in the rural areas and in the slums of the cities, prefer unión libre, an expedient which demands no expense and no contact with officialdom, whether of the Church or of the local government.

Since, in general, the class which is less fortunate economically tends to start reproductive life earlier than those who are better situated in the community, one would expect the age at which unions are undertaken to be younger among the former than among the latter category. In other words, our records since 1870 from parish priests and civil authorities represent only the upper stratum of the population and one which is selected on the basis of social standing and economic advancement. Conversely, unión libre is found predominantly at the bottom of the ladder. There is no cure or correction which we can offer for this bias because the factors involved are too complex and because we have no exact knowledge whatever concerning the age at which people enter into unión libre.

In view of these facts several conclusions are mandatory.

(1) Data for age at marriage from a single source, since 1870, can under no circumstances be accepted as showing the

true value for even a restricted community, to say nothing of the entire country.

(2) Geographical comparisons which are based upon sets of data from different types of source cannot be regarded as valid. On the other hand, comparisons based upon the same source, that is, Civil Register or parish records, for different areas may be accepted, within the limits imposed by the source.

(3) Temporal or secular trends are valid if the data are all drawn from the same source.

(4) No data whatever regarding age at marriage exist for the group in unión libre.

Application of these principles means that we can do certain things.

(1) We can examine the secular trend of our indices for the parish records of Oaxaca, for the Civil Register of Oaxaca, and for that of Guadalajara.

(2) We can compare directly the average values of the indices for the two sets of civil registration.

(3) We can make direct comparisons within a single system, for example, between ethnic groups if they are separately recorded.

The results which we present here must be evaluated in the light of all the considerations just advanced.

The indices described previously, as calculated for all areas and time periods sampled, are shown in Table 3.1. A question arises with respect to the reliability of the individual values and the significance of small numerical differences among them. For the estimate of the significance of difference between two single values of the interquartile points and of the percentages below a specified age, there is no uncomplicated, workable method. For two values of the mean age below 25 years, one could use the critical ratio of the means, or t, were it not that the number of cases, which run into the hundreds and thousands, render such a procedure futile. The values of t become so colossal as to be absurd. On the other hand, for certain purposes it is possible to adapt the ordinary chi square technique.

In order to demonstrate this method we may use the data for Oaxaca at or about 1950. There are two sets of reports: one from the parish records which includes samples taken from the years 1930 to 1950, the other from the Civil Register for the same general area in the years 1951 to 1954. The two sets are not identical in time or place but are as close as the documents permit.

Table 3.1

Age at marriage.

A. Indices for the records from seven parishes in the northern part of the
bishopric of Oaxaca

Date and Sex	First Inter-quartile	Second Inter-quartile	Mean Age Below 25	% Below 16	% Below 18	% Below 20
1690–1750						
Male	18.33	20.51	18.41	11.7	20.0	43.9
Female	14.97	16.20	15.49	48.2	60.3	70.8
1820–1850						
Male	18.60	20.62	18.92	4.1	13.0	39.7
Female	15.79	18.18	16.64	28.3	47.1	65.1
1930–1950						
Male	20.34	22.26	20.46	0.0	3.4	18.9
Female	16.46	18.29	17.52	17.6	45.2	68.5

Value of *r* for above
sequences

Male	+0.907	+0.881	+0.953	+0.989	−0.993
Female	+0.999	+0.900	+0.999	−0.989	−0.928

Comparison of gente de razón and indios in Tlaxiaco and Teposcolula,
1750 to 1820. The records were kept separately.

	First Inter-quartile	Second Inter-quartile	Mean Age Below 25	% Below 16	% Below 18	% Below 20
Gente de razón						
Male	20.64	23.94	20.64	0.2	3.3	17.8
Female	17.94	20.21	18.63	5.7	25.7	48.4
Indios						
Male	16.56	18.88	17.09	24.7	37.2	55.5
Female	14.04	15.43	14.46	58.3	67.2	70.8

B. Indices for samples from the civil registers of nine districts in Oaxaca.

Date and Sex	First Inter-quartile	Second Inter-quartile	Mean Age Below 25	% Below 16	% Below 18	% Below 20
1871–1874						
Male	18.71	20.91	19.41	3.6	15.9	36.9
Female	15.81	17.74	17.14	28.6	52.7	70.9
1888–1894						
Male	19.24	21.62	19.72	3.0	13.7	31.6
Female	16.36	18.42	17.71	20.0	44.1	66.5

Table 3.1 (cont.)

B. Indices for samples from the civil registers of nine districts in Oaxaca (*cont.*)

Date and Sex	First Inter- quartile	Second Inter- quartile	Mean Age Below 25	% Below 16	% Below 18	% Below 20
1905–1912						
Male	19.94	22.49	20.14	1.9	9.4	25.4
Female	16.51	18.85	18.04	18.9	39.0	59.3
1921–1924						
Male	20.88	23.47	20.86	0.2	4.3	15.4
Female	17.57	19.69	18.71	8.7	29.2	52.6
1937–1941						
Male	20.56	23.34	20.48	0.5	5.8	18.8
Female	16.63	18.66	17.94	15.3	40.1	62.0
1951–1954						
Male	21.38	23.70	21.20	0.1	1.3	11.6
Female	17.21	18.99	18.40	11.1	34.6	58.6
Value of *r* for above sequences						
Male	+0.960	+0.956	+0.934	−0.945	−0.961	
Female	+0.758	+0.663	+0.758	−0.847	−0.756	

C. Indices for samples from the Civil Register of the city and municipio of Guadalajara, Jalisco.

Date and Sex	First Inter- quartile	Second Inter- quartile	Mean Age Below 25	% Below 16	% Below 18	% Below 20
1875–1876						
Male	21.95	25.39	20.95	0.3	2.5	11.3
Female	17.96	21.10	18.75	8.6	25.3	43.7
1885–1886						
Male	22.10	25.75	20.93	0.3	1.8	10.7
Female	17.81	21.20	18.67	8.1	26.8	42.8
1895–1896						
Male	21.93	25.55	21.01	0.2	1.4	10.3
Female	18.07	21.61	18.93	6.9	24.3	39.7

Table 3.1 (cont.)

C. Indices for samples from the civil registers of nine districts in Oaxaca (*cont.*)

Date and Sex	First Inter- quartile	Second Inter- quartile	Mean Age Below 25	% Below 16	% Below 18	% Below 20
1905						
Male	21.88	25.38	20.98	0.0	1.6	11.3
Female	18.16	21.13	19.05	6.0	23.1	42.7
1915						
Male	22.51	25.89	21.24	0.1	1.6	8.8
Female	18.24	21.52	19.17	6.4	22.6	39.8
1925						
Male	22.71	26.00	21.46	0.1	1.2	7.0
Female	18.33	21.64	19.41	5.2	21.5	38.0
1935						
Male	23.71	26.92	21.87	0.0	0.6	4.5
Female	18.86	22.29	19.77	4.0	15.9	33.6
1945						
Male	24.45	28.68	22.32	0.0	0.1	1.5
Female	20.44	23.44	20.23	2.4	9.8	22.4
1955						
Male	24.54	28.88	21.68	0.0	1.9	4.8
Female	20.85	24.00	21.26	2.6	9.6	21.1
Value of *r* for above sequences						
Male	+0.915	+0.863	+0.864	−0.859	−0.585	
Female	+0.864	+0.875	+0.949	−0.969	−0.925	

For each set of marriages there are numerical values to be found in Table 3.1 for two sexes and six indicators, a total of twelve items. We observe whether, item for item, one set was greater or smaller than the other. An adjustment, however, is necessary. If the values of one set for interquartiles and mean age below 25 exceed the values of the other set, the reverse should hold for the percentages below specified ages. In order to make the direction uniform in all cases, we change the sign governing the percentages from plus to minus, or vice versa. We now have a consistent array based upon two attributes, greater or smaller.

If the two groups of people who provided the marriage indices behaved in an identical manner, the differences between each pair of items should be determined by random sampling alone, and there should be for either group six greater and six smaller indices. In the instance at hand, however, the civil marriages are greater than the religious group with respect to eleven items and smaller with respect to one item (percent below 16, for males, with the sign reversed). Hence the observed division is eleven and one, instead of the expected six and six. A brief calculation shows the adjusted chi square to equal 6.96. For 1 degree of freedom this value is close to the 1 percent level of probability.

This is definitely significant and may be taken to imply that in these samples, subject to all the modifying influence which we have pointed out, the age of persons marrying in the Church is greater than that of those marrying by civil ceremony. We note, however, that this method tells us only that a difference exists. It does not express the magnitude of this difference.

The series of indices in part A of Table 3.1 are derived from the parish records already mentioned. As we were able to obtain them, they fell into four groups. The first is that covering the period from the earliest found, *ca.* 1690 to *ca.* 1750. A narrower delimitation of time was impossible because of the relatively small number of marriages per year per parish. Furthermore, we expect little, if any, change to take place in marriage behavior within a fifty-year interval. We have 1,602 cases.

The second group falls in the period 1750 to 1820, mostly after 1770. These figures come from the district capitals Tlaxiaco and Teposcolula. They are sharply set apart in the parish books, according to ethnic origin, gente de razón or indios, two castes which were separated by a wide social gap. It is not feasible to combine the two sets of data, for the result would be unrepresentative of the community, but a comparison is of interest. In the samples there are 478 marriages of gente de razón and 223 of indios.

The table shows that for both sexes, the interquartile points and the mean age below 25 years are greater with the gente de razón whereas all the percentages are smaller. With the signs of the latter items reversed, the difference is completely uniform, and the chi square equals 10.08, a highly significant figure. Moreover, inspection of the table shows that the differences are consistently of considerable magnitude. It is clear, therefore, that the Spaniards and mestizos were marrying much later than were the Indians, a distinction undoubtedly associated with their respective social and economic status.

The third group embraces marriages between 1820 and 1850 while the fourth group includes a random sample taken from the books of Tejupan, Teposcolula, and Teozacoalco during the years 1930 to 1950. If we disregard the sample from 1750–1820, we have three widely separated periods in the history of the region : the first half of the eighteenth, the nineteenth, and the twentieth centuries. It would be highly desirable to determine whether there is any detectable and consistent trend in our indicators over this interval of more than 200 years.

Examination of part A of Table 3.1 gives the definite impression that there occurred with both sexes a substantial increase in the value of the interquartile points and the mean age under 25, together with a sharp reduction in the percentages of those marrying under the ages of 16, 18, and 20. This impression may be in some degree confirmed by the use of the coefficient r.

This coefficient is used here merely as a convenient mode of expressing any association which can be found between elapsed time and age at marriage. There is no implication of any causal relationship between the two variables. For time we use the midpoint of each period and call that falling at approximately 1720 equal to zero. The that falling at 1835 is 115, and that falling at 1950 is 220. The dependent variable is expressed as the numerical value of each indicator for each sex. There will thus be twelve corresponding values for r, which we have reduced to ten by omitting the percentage of persons below twenty years of age. These are shown in Table 3.1, part A.

It is evident that a single value for r, calculated for three cases, or 2 degrees of freedom, is a very tenuous statistical entity, for a magnitude of 0.95 is necessary to reach the 5 percent level of probability, and 0.99 to reach that of 1 percent. Yet, of the ten values shown in the table, five are at 0.99, or very close to it, four of the others are at 0.90 or above, and the tenth is 0.88. A very strong presumption exists, therefore, that some degree of increase in age at marriage by religious ceremony has occurred in rural northern Oaxaca throughout the past three centuries.

One particularly surprising fact which emerges in the

tabulation of the parochial marriages is the extremely early age at which the females have been, and apparently still are marrying. The first interquartile point for 1690–1750 was at 14.97 or, let us say, just fifteen years of age. This means that in one-quarter of all marriages the bride was under fifteen years old. Actually, out of the 1,602 women, 24 are recorded as at the age of twelve, 129 at thirteen, and 254 at fourteen. Since the age of puberty itself is close to twelve years, it is clear that the population was being pushed almost to the limit of its procreative capacity.

By 1820–1850 the first interquartile point had risen nearly a full year, to 15.79. There was thus at least moderate mitigation of pressure during the intervening century. And this mitigation, let it be noted, involved the entire population since at this time all marriages were sanctified by the Church. The further increase to 16.46 in 1930–1950 may be due in part to a continuation of this process and in part to the social factors which more recently have determined the type of marriage.

Table 3.1, part B, shows the civil marriages in northern and western Oaxaca since the introduction of the Civil Register. The only direct comparison possible between the two series, civil and ecclesiastical, is that already discussed, between the civil registrations of 1951–1954 and the parish records of 1930–1950. It will be remembered that the civil series indicated a somewhat greater age at marriage than did the religious series.

Another pertinent question, however, is whether the civil registrations give any suggestion of a secular trend since their beginning. Visual inspection shows an apparent aging which is fairly consistent throughout, except for an occasional reversal of direction. Again there may be applied the derivation of the correlation coefficient, particularly since there are six points on the time scale, instead of the three employed in the previous instance. The ten values of r are given in part B. With 5 degrees of freedom, the 5 percent level of probability lies at 0.754 and the 1 percent level at 0.874. We obtain five values above 0.874, four at or above 0.754, and one at 0.663. The trend toward greater ages is therefore reasonably well established even though it reverses occasionally from one decade to another.

Our third set of data comes from the Civil Register of the city of Guadalajara. After Mexico City, Guadalajara has been for decades, the most highly urbanized community in the country. It has been the seat of administration for the north and west since the sixteenth century and has always been the home of a relatively well-to-do Spanish and mestizo group. Hence we should anticipate that its Civil Register would show a mature level of age at marriage. This, indeed, seems to be true when we examine the figures in part C.

A broad comparison is possible between the data for civil marriage in Guadalajara and those in rural Oaxaca if we calculate the value of t for each sex and each indicator. For example, from part B the mean of the first interquartile points for males at six dates in Oaxaca is 20.12. The corresponding mean of the nine points in Guadalajara at nine dates (part C) is 22.86. The value of t for the two means is 4.90. With 13 degrees of freedom, the 1 percent level of probability is at 3.012. The significance of 4.90 is consequently quite high. If we repeat with the other eleven items, we get for the entire series the following values :

Males : 4.90, 5.35, 6.39, 2.90, 3.75, 4.24
Females : 4.09, 7.74, 6.50, 4.61, 5.33, 6.21

There can be no doubt that the age at marriage of those using the civil ceremony has been consistently higher in Guadalajara than in Oaxaca. The time span is the same, and the type of ceremony identical. The difference is probably due to a combination of factors : ethnic distinction, for Guadalajara contains largely non-Indians as opposed to the Oaxaca districts which are still primarily Indian; the better economic circumstances of a large proportion of dwellers in Guadalajara; and the progressive, urban environment of the capital of Jalisco as compared with the conservative atmosphere of the Oaxaca countryside. It is regrettable that we do not have a broader spectrum of samples from Mexico as a whole.

A secular trend can be demonstrated with the indicators from Guadalajara by means of the correlation coefficients. With 8 degrees of freedom a coefficient of 0.632 is at the 5 percent level of probability, and of 0.765 at the 1 percent level. Here (part C) we find for nine cases out of ten, values of r far exceeding 0.765, with one low value, 0.585. The significance is thus adequately established. The increase in age parallels that seen during the same years in Oaxaca. The inference is thus warranted that those who participated in civil marriages show an increasing age during the past century. This finding is consistent with that obtained from the Oaxaca parish records.

The conclusion can be only tentative that there has been a universal increase in age at marriage in Mexico. Our samples are highly restricted with respect to region studied and are subject to the limitations imposed by modern Mexican marriage laws and customs. Whether these factors invalidate any judgement resting upon the data here presented will have to be a matter of individual opinion. This much may be said : As far as they go, these data indicate a slow, steady rise in age at marriage since the early eighteenth century and are not contradicted by any instance of a significant diminution in that age. At this point the case must rest.

If we assume that in fact an increase has occurred, we still cannot maintain that a fall in the number of young people resulted. It must be borne in mind that even though the useful reproductive period in women was cut by one or two years, the drop in death rate permitted relatively more children to survive to puberty and in this manner compensated for the reduction in the total number born. In other words, from the standpoint of population dynamics, age at marriage, although an important factor, must be considered jointly with other demographic variables. From the standpoint of social institutions it may be studied for its own sake.

Chapter IV

Crude Birth Rates in Mexico, 1700–1965

In their classic discussion of vital statistics rates in the United States, Linder and Grove make the following comments: "The crude birth rate is the most frequently used, overall measure of the reproduction of a population," and "The crude birth rate is a number that indicates the proportional contribution or addition made to the total population each year by live births. For certain purposes this may be exactly what is desired."[1] The authors also point out carefully that "Crude rates show the broad changing picture of mortality and natality; specific rates must be used for the accurate study of detail."[2]

In studying population trends of late colonial and early republican Mexico, specific rates cannot be calculated from and accurate detail cannot be found in the very rough data which are available to us. Certainly, not until the national censuses began at the turn of the twentieth century and the civil registration of births reached a more or less satisfactory status after the 1910–1920 revolution can modern demographic techniques be profitably applied. For the antecedent period, however, it is possible to assemble a fairly substantial body of censuses, pseudo-censuses, and counts, together with birth records derived from parish books and early civil registration. From these, approximate values for birth rates, or rather perhaps birth ratios, may be calculated. No one of these will have much claim to accuracy, but with a large number of them we may obtain a reasonable idea concerning the level of reproductivity through more than two centuries.

We begin with an examination of a restricted area, the Mixteca Alta, in north-central Oaxaca. This selection is made not because the Mixteca Alta presents any outstanding advan-

[1]*Techniques of Vital Statistics*, pp. 54–55.
[2]p. 3.

tages compared with other parts of Mexico but because we possess for it data from parish records of births, as well as documentary evidence of the population extending back to the seventeenth century. Our data relative to this area may be organized conveniently, in eight groups, each representing a period, or a point, in the history of the region for which a substantial body of information exists. The first four of these groups include figures obtained from local documents; the last four are based upon selected state or national censuses of the population and upon copies of civil registrations, stored in the state archive, for records of birth.

The first four groups extend over the interval from approximately 1630 to 1855. Here will be found data on populations and births (actually baptisms) pertaining to isolated entities according to their appearance in the relevant documents, towns, parishes, or other units. Since they are thus scattered both temporally and spatially, they have been aggregated in a few major periods of time. Because a given entity may appear more than once at different years within the same period and since some entities may be included in others, such as a town within a parish, no totals can be calculated. On the other hand, the individual values for births per 1,000 population may be averaged. Thus we derive mean values for the period 1630 to 1720, that of 1740 to 1800, and that of 1820 to 1835. The group designated 1803–1804 is based upon a single local account.

The populations were obtained, many of them by conversion from tributaries or families, from a large number of documents. These are described in detail in a previous work on the Mixteca Alta.[3] The data on births are baptisms as they were recorded in the books of ten parishes that we were able to examine in the summer of 1956. We have used B/1,000 to express baptisms and births per 1,000 population without any attempt to adjust for differences between the two categories. In general, recorded baptisms should always be fewer than births because of the impossibility of baptizing stillborn infants and those dying before the priest could make his rounds in a large rural parish that had to be divided into circuits or *rumbos*. (Emergency baptisms by laymen would not be recorded.) The discrepancy between births and baptisms at a minimum might be from 10 to 20 percent. On the other hand, in Mexico

---

[3]Cook and Borah, *The Population of the Mixteca Alta, 1520–1960* (IA : 50), *passim* but especially pp. 22–59 and accompanying tables.

this discrepancy is partly or wholly cancelled out by the fact that the births in the Civil Register fail to include a proportion of live births and a very substantial proportion of stillbirths and deaths in the first few days of life. Despite very great improvement in recording in recent decades, there is still a substantial proportion of omission, which varies very much by state and is especially high in Oaxaca.[4] Therefore, one must balance the discrepancy between births and baptisms, counterweighted in part by the fact that until the middle of the nineteenth century the Church was able to insist that the entire living population of the Mixteca Alta present itself or be presented for baptism and marriage, against the failures of the Civil Register. Our choice has been to treat recorded baptisms and births without attempts at adjustment.

In our tables, it is understood that the population and baptisms for each listed entity refer to the same year or very close to it. The necessity for getting pairs of corresponding figures accounts for the relatively few authentic cases which we can supply in the period prior to 1855.

The first five groups have been exhibited in full in Table 4.1. Here are all the parish data. The fifth group has also been included, although the births are taken from the Civil Register and the population from a state census. The reason is that reports of these small towns, both clerical and civil, have never been published and are not available to most students. The populations and birth registrations since 1895 are either published or on file in the Oaxaca state archive. The last three groups are derived from the national censuses of 1900, 1910, 1921, and 1950. From these, as well as from the state census of 1882, have been extracted the populations of the individual municipalities in the districts, or ex-districts of Coixtlahuaca, Nochixtlán, Teposcolula, and Tlaxiaco. These populations are as reliable as can be obtained. The births from the Civil Register are subject to certain question.

The first problem is that of date. We were not able to get runs from all the districts for years that corresponded precise-

---

[4]See Vol. I, pp. 50–52, of these *Essays*; see also the comment by Hollingsworth, *Historical Demography*, pp. 183–184. In the large Mexican rural parishes of the colonial period and even today, the priest may not be able to visit towns in his parish for weeks. All the parishes in the Mixteca Alta were large and divided into rumbos or circuits. On the failure even today to record stillbirths and infant deaths shortly after birth, see Cordero, "La subestimación de la mortalidad infantil en México," in *Demografía y economía*, II, no. 1 (or no. 4 in count by numbers) (1968), 44–62. The state of Oaxaca has a notably high proportion of such omissions.

Table 4.1

Baptisms or births per 1,000 population (B/1,000) in the Mixteca Alta.

A. Seventeenth century to 1720.[a]

Place	Status	Date	Datum Tribs.	Total Pop.	Average Annual Baptisms	B/1,000
Coixtlahuaca	Parish	1661	605	1,949	87	44.6
Tequixtepec	Town	1661	104	335	16	47.7
Tejupan	Town	1640	168	511	29	56.7
Tejupan	Town	1661	186	599	21	35.1
S. Juan Teposcolula	Town	1680	171	575	23	40.0
Teposcolula	Parish	1661	561	1,807	94	52.0
Tlaxiaco	Town	1661	690	2,221	65	29.2
Ixcatlán	Town	1629	76	228	10	43.9
Tequixtepec	Town	1636	84	255	16	62.7
Tamazola	Town	1671	54	178	5	28.1
Nundiche	Town	1703	32	113	4.5	39.8
Yosotiche	Town	1703	34	120	6.5	54.2
Coixtlahuaca	Town	1715	566	2,037	104	51.1
Mean						45.00
S.D.						±10.47
S.E.						± 2.90

[a] The conversion factor from tributaries to population is by interpolation on the graph for the old system (see Vol. I of these *Essays*).

B. 1740–1800[a]

Place	Status	Date	Datum Tribs.	Total Pop.	Average Annual Baptisms	B/1,000
Coixtlahuaca	Town	1742	604f	2,718	141	51.9
Tequixtepec	Town	1742	88f	396	19	47.9
Ixcatlán	Town	1742	83f	373	13	34.8
Tejupan	Town	1742	192f	865	44	50.9
Soyaltepec	Town	1742	74f	333	24	72.0
Soyaltepec	Town	1742	187t	748	24	32.1
Tonaltepec	Town	1742	64f	288	21	72.8
Soyaltepec	Rumbo	1742	203t	812	37	45.6
Soyaltepec	Rumbo	1742	180f	810	37	45.7
Nochixtlán	Parish	1742	309f	1,390	101	72.6
Teposcolula	Parish	1742	975f	4,388	237	54.0
Tilantongo	Town	1742	102f	459	24	52.3
Sta. Cr. Mitlatongo	Town	1742	58f	261	11	42.2
Stgo. Mitlatongo	Town	1742	48f	216	9	41.7
Jaltepec	Parish	1742	112f	504	34	67.5

Table 4.1 (cont.)

B. 1740–1800 (*cont.*)

Place	Status	Date	Datum Tribs.	Total Pop.	Average Annual Baptisms	B/1,000
Tlaxiaco	Town	1742	888f	3,996	207	51.8
Cuquila	Town	1742	76f	342	16	46.8
Ocotepec Nundaco	Town	1742	216f	472	17	36.0
Yutanduchi	Town	1742	63f	282	18	63.9
Teozacoalco	Parish	1742	297f	1,337	86	64.3
Tamazola	Town	1742	78f	351	9	25.7
Cahuacuá	Town	1774	80t	339	25	73.7
Sindihui	Town	1774	80t	339	22	64.8
Zapotitlán	Town	1774	80t	339	18	53.1
Teposcolula	Town	1782	947t	4,110	197	47.9
Yolomécatl	Town	1782	150t	651	43	66.0
Tilantongo	Town	1791	124f	556	40	71.8
Jaltepec	Parish	1791	192f	865	34	39.3
Jaltepec	Town	1791	68f	306	14	45.7
Nuxaá	Town	1791	65f	292	13	44.5
Yuta	Town	1791	43f	194	7	36.0
Tamazola	Town	1791	104f	468	21	44.8
Soyaltepec	Town	1796	155t	693	24	34.6
Mean						51.35
S.D.						±13.49
S.E.						± 2.35

[a] The datum is indicated by the letter t for tributaries and the letter f for families. The conversion factor from tributaries to population is by interpolation on the graph for the new system (see Vol. I of these *Essays*). The data for 1742 are derived from the *Theatro americano* by Villaseñor y Sanchez. The factor for families is 4.5.

C. 1803–1804 [a]

Place	Status	Total Pop.	Average Annual Baptisms	B/1,000
Yodocono	Town	522	28.3	54.2
Jaltepec + Anuma	Towns	511	24.3	47.5
Nuxaá + Nuxaño	Towns	421	19.0	45.2
Zahuatlán	Town	222	11.0	49.6
Tlaxiaco (gente de razón)	Parish	1,850	69.3	37.4
Tlaxiaco (indios)	Town	1,250	59.5	47.5
Atoyaquillo	Rumbo	1,165	58.0	49.7
Nduaxico	Rumbo	2,275	124.0	54.5
Huamelulpan	Town	550	19.3	35.2

Table 4.1 (cont.)

C. 1803–1804ᵃ (cont.)

Place	Status	Total Pop.	Average Annual Baptisms	B/1,000
Nuyoó	Town	625	26.7	42.8
Yucuhite	Town	425	20.3	47.8
Cuquila	Town	550	21.8	39.5
Cuquila	Rumbo	1,595	73.0	45.7
Coixtlahuaca	Town	1,025	44.0	42.8
Tepelmeme	Rumbo	2,790	103.0	37.0
Ixcatlán	Town	374	16.8	45.0
Tequixtepec	Town	601	13.7	22.6
Coixtlahuaca	Parish	6,614	275.3	41.6
Tamazulapan	Town	1,426	85.0	59.6
Tulancingo	Town	711	33.0	46.3
Tejupan	Town	1,893	58.0	30.6
Soyaltepec	Town	863	38.7	44.9
Tonaltepec	Town	455	29.7	65.3
Tejupan	Parish	3,211	128.0	39.9
Yanhuitlán	Rumbo	2,704	125.0	46.3
Topiltepec	Rumbo	468	29.7	64.6
Tiltepec	Rumbo	541	26.0	48.0
Sayultepec	Rumbo	1,222	48.0	39.3
Yanhuitlán	Parish	5,138	250.0	48.7
Nochixtlán	Parish	4,268	213.8	50.0
Teposcolula	Parish	5,482	251.0	46.7
Tilantongo	Parish	2,146	121.0	56.5
Tilantongo	Town	513	34.0	66.4
Nuxaño	Town	249	11.0	44.0
Tidaá	Town	478	26.0	54.4
Sta. Cr. Mitlatongo	Town	197	11.0	55.8
Stgo. Mitlatongo	Town	187	10.7	57.5
Teozacoalco	Town	221	13.7	62.0
Cahuacuá	Town	657	26.0	39.5
Piedras	Town	320	13.0	40.7
Sindihui	Town	663	27.0	40.8
Yuta	Town	130	6.3	48.6
Yutanduchi	Town	654	24.3	37.2
Zapotitlán	Town	496	21.7	43.8
Tamazola	Town	498	22.7	45.7
Mean				46.86
S.D.				±9.00
S.E.				±1.34

ᵃThe populations are directly from censuses.

Table 4.1 (cont.)

D. 1820–1855.[a]

Place	Status	Year	Total Pop.	Average Annual Baptisms	B/1,000
S. Juan Teposcolula	Town	1821	465	22.8	49.0
Yolomécatl	Town	1821	1,031	45.3	43.9
Ticú	Rumbo	1821	1,010	48.0	48.3
Nuxaño	Town	1821	232	12.0	51.8
Tidaá	Town	1821	497	29.0	58.5
Tejupan	Town	1823	1,586	70.3	44.3
Coixtlahuaca	Town	1826	1,125	65.0	57.7
Tepeleme	Rumbo	1826	3,226	116.5	36.2
Ixcatlán	Town	1826	395	18.0	45.6
Coixtlahuaca	Parish	1826	7,040	295.3	42.0
Tamazulapan	Town	1826	1,459	84.5	57.8
Tulancingo	Town	1826	771	37.5	48.5
Soyaltepec	Town	1826	471	35.0	74.2
Tonaltepec	Town	1826	580	33.0	56.9
Tejupan	Parish	1826	1,912	138.3	72.3
Yanhuitlán	Parish	1826	4,772	243.0	51.0
Nochixtlán	Parish	1826	3,984	213.8	53.6
S. Juan Teposcolula	Town	1826	419	22.8	49.0
Yolomécatl	Town	1826	925	45.3	48.8
Yucunama	Rumbo	1826	650	29.5	45.5
Ticú	Rumbo	1826	846	48.8	57.8
Tixá	Rumbo	1826	855	45.8	53.4
Teposcolula	Parish	1826	4,900	253.0	51.7
Tlaxiaco	Town	1826	2,621	121.3	48.0
Teozacoalco	Town	1826	296	15.0	50.7
Cahuacuá	Town	1826	528	24.0	45.5
Sindihui	Town	1826	404	25.0	62.0
Yuta	Town	1826	184	8.0	43.4
Yutanduchi	Town	1826	567	25.0	43.8
Tamazola	Town	1826	388	23.3	57.8
Soyaltepec	Town	1827	439	35.0	79.7
Tonaltepec	Town	1827	572	33.0	57.7
Tejupan	Parish	1827	2,597	138.3	53.3
Tlaxiaco	Town	1831	2,364	121.3	51.3
Tejupan	Town	1832	1,141	70.3	61.5
Coixtlahuaca	Town	1834	1,416	65.0	46.0
Tlaxiaco	Town	1847	2,926	182.5	62.7
Tepelmeme	Rumbo	1855	4,520	212.0	46.9
Coixtlahuaca	Parish	1855	8,387	303.0	36.2
Mean					52.41
S.D.					±9.37
S.E.					±1.50

[a]The populations are directly from censuses.

Table 4.1 (cont.)

E. About 1882[a]

Place	Total Pop.	Av. Annual Births	B/1,000
Coixtlahuaca	2,366	131.8	55.6
Concepción Buenavista	633	29.7	47.0
Nativitas	1,303	74.4	57.1
Magdalena Jicotlán	621	31.5	50.6
Tepelmeme	1,691	80.4	47.5
Tequixtepec	1,070	56.0	52.3
Tlacotepec Plumas	939	50.7	54.0
San Antonio Abad	263	15.3	58.1
Suchixtlahuaca	841	36.7	43.7
San Francisco Teopan	436	22.4	51.4
Tepetlapan	350	19.5	55.6
Otla	361	18.1	50.2
Tlapiltepec	939	57.2	61.0
Astatla	410	17.1	41.7
Tulancingo	1,280	58.4	45.1
Sta. Catarina Ocotlán	509	28.6	56.3
Calpulapan	132	6.9	52.3
Ihuitlán Plumas	538	32.2	60.0
Nochixtlán *et al.*	5,794	277.0	48.0
Apasco	862	46.9	54.4
Cántaros *et al.*	787	38.0	48.4
Chicahua	931	24.3	26.1
Chindua	598	39.3	66.4
Chachoapan *et al.*	971	52.4	54.4
Diuxi	601	28.9	48.3
Etlatongo	770	43.7	56.8
Huautla	308	18.1	58.7
Huautlilla	817	41.4	50.8
Jaltepetongo	823	46.9	57.0
Jaltepec *et al.*	1,735	67.2	62.8
Nuxaá	613	32.2	52.6
Nuxaño *et al.*	388	19.8	51.1
Nuxino	458	16.8	36.8
Yodocono	1,479	83.3	56.3
Yanhuitlán	2,071	87.5	42.3
Yutanduche	945	38.7	40.9
Yucuhite *et al.*	932	44.9	48.2
Sta. Inez del Río	755	40.5	53.8
Sayultepec *et al.*	799	35.7	44.6
Sindihui	847	38.5	44.0
Sinaxtla	809	38.9	48.3
Piedras	727	33.3	45.7
Teozacoalco	667	19.7	29.5
Tamazola *et al.*	874	34.4	39.4
Tecomatlán	632	32.9	52.1
Tidaá	1,082	59.4	54.9

Table 4.1 (cont.)

E. About 1882 (cont.)

Place	Total Pop.	Av. Annual Births	B/1,000
Tillo et al.	745	35.3	47.5
Tilantongo	910	76.1	83.7
Zahuatlán	598	31.3	52.3
Teposcolula et al.	3,953	153.7	39.0
Tamazulapan	3,565	134.4	37.7
Acutla	738	31.3	41.9
Soyaltepec et al.	1,633	75.2	46.0
Chilapa et al.	4,428	200.5	45.3
Lagunas	954	45.9	48.1
Nopala	487	18.7	38.4
Nejapilla	442	19.1	43.4
Nduayaco et al.	1,241	55.6	49.8
Nuñú	1,242	61.3	49.3
Nicunanduta	594	28.0	49.7
Yolomécatl	1,662	70.9	42.6
Yucunama	593	22.7	38.2
Tejupan	2,652	90.5	34.1
Tlatayapan	590	29.8	50.6
Tonaltepec	1,960	69.4	35.4
Topiltepec et al.	770	36.1	47.0
S. Juan Teposcolula et al.	1,112	55.9	50.0
Mean			48.99
S.D.			±8.86
S.E.			±1.08

[a] The populations are taken directly from the census of 1882. The births are the annual average of the civil registrations for the years 1871–1874 and 1888–1892 in the districts of Coixtlahuaca, Nochixtlan, and Teposcolula. The territorial entities are single towns, except where groups are indicated by the expression et al.

ly with those in which the censuses were taken. Consequently, there is certain to be some displacement of the mean values of births per 1,000 persons. In particular group 5 (part E) is based upon a census taken in 1882[5] whereas the registrations are from the years 1871–1874 and from 1888–1892. The nine annual values of total births for these two sets of years were averaged and probably approximate the births which occurred in 1882. The match, however, cannot be exact.

For the first years of the twentieth century the Civil Register dates are 1905–1908. These fit neither the census of

[5] The results are published in Martínez Gracida, Coleccion de "Cuadros sinópticos" de . . . Oaxaca.

1900 nor that of 1910. In order to come as close as possible, we averaged for each town the populations according to both censuses. Thus, we approached the probable value for the half-way point, 1905. The civil registrations for the group at 1921 were taken from the years 1921–1924. The correspondence is fairly close but by no means perfect. In a similar manner the 1950 census was matched by births in the years 1951–1954.

The second problem is that of incomplete registration. Although the parish records include virtually all baptisms, these were less than the births. The Civil Register is also known to have been defective, particularly in the first years after its introduction. The state and district totals for Mexico as a whole as they appear in the official documents from about 1860 to the 1910 revolution are subject to serious criticism. For Oaxaca, the local registers tend to be more complete in detail than the totals calculated in the central bureaus. The reason seems to be that although the births were actually recorded in the municipios, the town officers were likely to be very remiss in communicating the figures to the state capitals. At best, however, we have to allow for an undercount of births. The result, it should be emphasized, would be to reduce the ratio of births to population and thus produce too low values for apparent crude birth rates.

When one examines Table 4.1 he observes immediately a considerable variation in the values of B/1,000 in the individual entities. The extent of this variation is expressed for each of the eight groups in Table 4.2 as the standard deviation of the mean. The latter values, when converted to the corresponding coefficients of variation extend from approximately 18 to 33 percent of the mean. The high range is referable to error in recording and counting but even more to local and usually random fluctuation in the number of births in a small community. Perhaps a better criterion is the standard error of the mean, which is relatively small : 2 to 6 percent. Here is the advantage of using a large number of cases, 475 in all, for the disturbing factors tend to cancel out, leaving the average relatively stable.

Attention may now be directed to the eight mean values for crude birth to population ratio which are given in Table 4.2. One is impressed first by the fact that they fall closely within the range of forty-five to fifty births per 1,000 people. This is a high level of natality and is characteristic of many pre-industrial cultures which also show a high mortality. A

Table 4.2

Summary of birth rate data for the Mixteca Alta. There are eight groups
of reports from separate territorial units. The first five are from parish books
and other local sources. They have been shown in detail in Table 4.1. The last
three are for municipalities as given in the censuses of 1900–1910, 1921, and
1950. For a full explanation see text.

Group	No of Territorial Units	Mean Value of B/1,000	S.D.	S.E.
17th century to 1720	13	45.00	10.47	2.90
1740–1800	33	51.35	13.49	2.35
1803–1804	45	46.86	9.00	1.34
1820–1855	39	52.41	9.37	1.50
Census 1882	67	48.99	8.86	1.08
Census 1900–1910	110	46.35	12.85	1.22
Census 1921	70	47.53	15.67	1.87
Census 1950	98	44.12	8.38	0.85

second striking feature of this array is its uniformity throughout
nearly 300 years. We could detect, to be sure, only broad
trends and emphatic changes in such a set of values, for minor
fluctuations would be completely obscured. Even the effects of
epidemics and revolutions cannot be noticed. Nevertheless,
there is no major movement in the birth rate.

The uniformity may be tested in various ways. For
example, the average of the means for the eight groups is 47.85.
The standard deviation is 2.927, or 6.1 percent of the mean.
The standard error is 1.035, or only 2.2 percent of the mean.
A slight reduction in the three groups since 1882 seems to be
present. This possibility may be tested by taking the means of the
first five items and of the last three. The means are 48.92 and
46.00. The value of t is 1.48, quite without significance for the
existing degrees of freedom. Furthermore, if there is any
falling off in the crude birth ratio, it can be accounted for very
reasonably by the deficiencies in civil registration as opposed to
parochial baptism records. Our conclusion must be, therefore,
that the data from the Mixteca Alta show for that area a high
level of natality which has been maintained at a very constant
value down to present times.

When we leave the Mixteca Alta, we find that the documents from the various states are the most useful. These begin

after the War of Independence at about 1820 and continue until the introduction of truly national censuses in 1895. Before discussing them in detail, however, it is desirable to mention the work of Alexander von Humboldt, which was based upon the Revillagigedo census of 1793 and parish data furnished by the Archbishop of Mexico. Humboldt comments upon the rapid increase in the Mexican population, which, he notes, exceeds 1 percent per year. As an example, he mentions several towns in the area near Guanajuato which have average annual births (baptisms) of 4,000. The population of these places is from 55,000 to 60,000, say, about 57,500. Then the birth ratio is 69.6. In Mexico City there are, as an eight-year average, 5,930 births in a population which he puts at 130,000. The ratio is 45.6. For Queretaro in 1793 he gives 5,064 births and 69,000 persons, a ratio of 73.4. Regarding Mexico as a whole he says that "en años benignos" (in favorable years) there are probably 374,000 births. His value for the total population is 5,764,731. The birth ratio then would be 64.9 births per 1,000 inhabitants.[6]

These are very high values. Nevertheless, we know from other data that the population of New Spain was increasing rapidly at the close of the eighteenth century. Furthermore, Humboldt was a man of recognized competence, with access to the best data of his day, whose work has been accepted as authoritative by all students since his time. It follows that when he puts the birth ratio at more than 60 per 1,000 persons, even though in "años benignos," his word must be given serious consideration.

We divide the nineteenth century into two phases. The first, from 1820 to 1855, encompasses the period from the close of the War of Independence to the beginning of the social disturbances of the mid-century. It is characterized demographically by numerous and serious attempts on the part of state officials to make counts or relatively close estimates of the local populations, an attempt which was strongly reinforced by the efforts of Mexican scholars to subject the contemporary data to

[6]"Tablas geográfico-políticas del reino de la Nueva-España [en el año de 1803] que manifiestan su superfice, población, agricultura, fábricas, comercio, minas, rentas y fuerza militar. . . presentadas al señor virey del mismo reino en enero de 1804," in SMGEB, 2a ép., I (1869), pp. 636–638. This is apparently a first working of data. In revised form the data and comments were incorporated in the *Essai politique sur le royaume de la Nouvelle-Espagne*, I, 324–340, especially 339–340 (*liv*. II, *ch*. IV). Humboldt found that the population, except for natural disasters, should double every nineteen years, a rate of increase very close to that of the present time.

careful analysis. During these thirty-five years the births could
be quite accurately determined from the clerical or parish
records. Consequently, the birth ratios, within the limits imposed
by a rather primitive system of enumeration, are definitely
reliable.

We have assembled the available published data for this
period in Table 4.3. In the former are placed the total values
according to states, twenty-seven items from nine states. In the
latter are values pertaining to secondary political divisions,
the districts, partidos, cantons, and the like, which operated
up to the Revolution of 1910. There are 116 of these which we
have found and could include.

Table 4.3

Births per thousand population (B/1,000).

A. As reported for certain states of the Republic of Mexico, 1820–1860.

State	Year	Total Pop.	Year	Average Annual Births	B/1,000
Chihuahua[a]	1833	139,081	1833	6,533	46.9
Durange (state)[b]	1831	140,769	1831	6,397	45.4
Durango (city)[c]	1849	24,860	1849	1,580	63.5
Guanajuato[d]	1825	382,829	1825	23,809	62.2
Guanajuato[e]	1850	732,416	1850	37,633	51.4
Jalisco[f]	1830	656,600	1830	31,091	47.3
Jalisco[f]	1831	656,600	1831	31,990	48.7
Jalisco[g]	1839	508,695	1834–1838	24,563	48.3
Jalisco[h]	1848	496,241	1848	21,368	43.1
Mexico[i]	1835	970,472	1835	45,805	47.2
Mexico[j]	1834	1,092,472	1834	49,882	45.7
Michoacan[k]	1826–1829	422,472	1826–1829	21,590	51.1
Oaxaca[l]	1831	485,014	1831	26,719	55.1
	1833	471,172	1833	23,399	49.7
	1834	457,330	1834	31,569	47.2
	1839	501,552	1839	24,959	47.8
	1848	525,101	1848	31,455	60.0
	1851	523,846	1851	30,290	58.0
	1855	528,218	1855	27,648	52.5
	1857	531,502	1857	28,756	54.2

Table 4.3 (cont.)

State	Year	Total Pop.	Year	Average Annual Births	B/1,000
Querétaro[m]	1822–1826	105,460	1822–1826	7,531	71.0
	1827–1831	114,427	1827–1831	8,054	70.4
	1832–1836	131,110	1832–1836	8,123	62.0
	1837–1841	154,893	1837–1841	8,197	44.6
	1842–1844	174,774	1842–1844	8,789	50.3
	1843	174,788	1843	9,187	52.6
Tabasco[n]	1831	54,499	1830	1,830	44.0
Mean					52.60
S.D.					±7.77
S.E.					±1.49

[a]Population and baptisms from "Ensayo estadístico sobre el estado de Chihuahua, parte tercera," *SMGEB*, la ép., V(1857), 274.
[b]Population and baptisms from Escudero, *Noticias estadísticas del estado de Durango*, pp. 28–35. The population for 1831 was taken from Lucas Alamán. The baptisms for 1831 were calculated by Escudero from those of 1848–1849.
[c]Population and baptisms from José Fernando Ramírez, "Noticias históricas de Durango (1848–1849)," in *SMGEB*, la ép., V(1857), 56.
[d]Governor's *Memoria* of 1824–1825, signed by Juan de Grandy 1 January 1826. Population from the "Plan que manifiesta el Censo General"; births from Table 1. According to the statements in the table, twelve places reported births only from January to September, four places from January to June. If these are pro-rated to the full year, the total births are even greater and the value of B/1,000 is still higher. It is probable that the population is also much underestimated. Compare its value with that for 1850 in this same table.
[e]Governor's *Memoria* of 1851, signed by Pantaleón Espinosa 31 December 1851, Table 18.
[f]Banda, *Estadística de Jalisco*, pp. 45, 47, 83. Baptisms were taken by Banda from the parish records.
[g]*Ibid.*, pp. 37–38, 57–81. Six cantons only.
[h]*Ibid.*, pp. 38, 83. Six cantons only.
[i]Governor's *Memoria* of 1834–1835, signed by Luis Varela 30 March 1835, Tables 2 and 3. The births are given for only nine out of eleven prefectures.
[j]Governor's *Memoria* of 1833–1834, signed by Isidro R. Gondra 26 March 1834, Tables 2 and 3. The births are given for only nine out of eleven prefectures. The total is that of all eleven prefectures.
[k]Governor's *Memoria* of 1829, as quoted in "Apuntes para... estado de Michoacán," in *SMGEB*, la ép., I(3rd ed., 1861), 162.
[l]Governor's *Memoria* of 1858, document 11. The population throughout this period was estimated. The basis was the number of births and deaths recorded parochially. They are probably more or less close to the truth.
[m]Raso, *Notas estadísticas del departmento de Querétaro*. Most of the data are from the table on p. 100. For the periods 1822–1826, 1827–1831, 1832–1836, 1837–1841, and 1842–1844, the annual figures given by Raso have been averaged for both population and births. The annual values for population as given in the table by Raso are, of course, his estimates based upon calculation and interpolation between the censuses of 1822 and 1844. The additional figures for 1843 are from his table on p. 112. The births from one parish out of nineteen are missing.
[n]Mestre Ghigliazzi, *Documentos y datos para la historia de Tabasco*, I, 472, 474. The births from one parish out of nine are missing.

Table 4.3 (cont.)

B. as reported for districts, partidos, cantons, and similar territorial entities
for the period 1820–1860.

Area	Year	Total Pop	Year	Average Annual Births	B/1,000
Chihuahua[a]	1833		1833		
Aldama		13,362		246	18.0
Allende		12,412		590	47.5
Balleza		14,716		509	34.6
Batopilas		15,537		712	45.8
Chihuahua		18,322		1,174	64.0
Concepción		11,799		589	49.9
Cusihuiriáchic		13,243		857	64.8
Galeana		7,774		332	42.7
Hidalgo		9,609		438	45.6
Jiménez		7,592		391	51.5
Paso		6,053		364	60.2
Rosales		8,410		259	30.8
Guanajuato[b]	1825		1825		
Guanajuato		33,488		2,595	77.5
Silao		16,694		1,820	109.0
Irapuato		16,054		1,174	73.2
León		42,201		3,357	79.6
Piedragorda		12,485		911	73.1
Pénjamo		20,941		976	46.5
Valle de Santiago		14,677		838	57.1
Salamanca		15,053		897	59.6
Celaya		9,571		956	99.8
Apaseo		15,668		830	53.0
Chamacuero		4,482		327	73.1
Jerécuaro		10,252		628	61.2
Santa Cruz		9,007		506	56.2
Neutla[c]		2,565		169	65.9
S. Miguel Octopan		1,518		52	34.2
Amoles		4,912		298	60.6
S. Juan de la Vega		2,562		164	64.0
Rincón de Tamayo		1,263		103	81.6
Huage[c]		2,002		157	78.4
Acámbaro		8,292		342	41.3
Salvatierra		16,284		1,231	75.6
Yuriria		28,167		1,123	39.8
S. Miguel Grande		29,092		1,748	60.2
Hidalgo		21,710		706	32.5
S. Luis de la Paz		11,167		882	79.3
Xichú		7,469		421	56.3
Casas Viejas		8,850		760	85.8
S. Felipe		19,693		1,026	52.1

Table 4.3 (cont.)

Area	Year	Total Pop	Year	Average Annual Births	B/1,000
Guanajuato[d]	1850		1850		
Guanajuato		49,827		4,007	80.5
Silao		38,922		2,373	61.0
Irapuato		34,213		1,911	55.8
Salamanca		31,033		1,272	41.0
Valle de Santiago		35,014		1,152	32.9
Celaya		39,432		2,437	61.8
Salvatierra		29,329		1,859	63.3
Acámbaro		12,195		571	46.8
Yuriria		43,448		1,097	25.2
Jerécuaro		18,256		878	48.1
Apaseo		16,433		1,044	63.5
Santa Cruz		14,540		772	53.1
Chamacuero		10,538		639	60.6
Allende		37,308		1,872	50.2
Hidalgo		32,381		1,887	58.3
San Felipe		53,376		2,805	52.6
León		79,648		4,314	54.2
Pénjamo		54,441		2,197	40.3
Piedragorda		24,501		767	31.3
S. Luis de la Paz		51,658		2,249	43.5
S. José de Iturbide		25,923		1,531	59.1
Jalisco[e]	1830		1830		
Guadalajara		119,000		6,250	52.5
Lagos		112,000		6,012	53.7
La Barca		96,000		4,762	49.6
Sayula[f]		104,000		3,658	35.3
Etzatlán		76,000		3,538	46.5
Autlán		44,000		2,010	45.7
Tepic		66,000		2,761	41.8
Colotlán[f]		39,600		2,100	53.0
Jalisco[e]	1830		1831		
Guadalajara		119,000		5,354	45.0
Lagos		112,000		6,556	58.7
La Barca		96,000		5,122	53.3
Sayula		104,000		5,735	55.1
Etzatlán		76,000		3,685	48.5
Autlan		44,000		2,017	45.8
Tepic		66,000		1,709	25.9
Colotlán		39,600		1,812	45.7
Jalisco[e]	1839		1834–1838		
Guadalajara		125,030			
Lagos		142,146		6,179	43.4
La Barca		98,096		5,137	52.4

Table 4.3 (cont.)

Area	Year	Total Pop	Year	Average Annual Births	B/1,000
Sayula		110,278		5,977	54.2
Etzatlán		82,287			
Autlán		51,184		2,473	48.3
Tepic		62,620		2,399	38.3
Colotlán		44,371		2,398	53.6
Jalisco[e]	1848		1848		
Guadalajara		126,103			
Lagos		152,117			
La Barca		112,925		5,308	47.0
Sayula		144,717		6,452	44.6
Etzatlán		73,169		3,166	43.3
Autlán		56,649		2,634	46.5
Tepic		65,727		1,548	25.1
Colotlán		43,054		2,260	52.4
Mexico[g]	1834		1833		
Cuernavaca		94,416		5,190	55.0
Este de México		137,750		5,137	37.4
Huejutla		81,096		3,559	43.9
Oeste de México		111,353		5,557	49.9
Sultepec		71,039		2,891	40.7
Toluca		212,584		9,417	44.3
Taxco		87,941		3,952	45.0
Tulancingo		101,509		4,710	46.4
Tula		194,625		9,449	48.6
Mexico[h]	1835		1834		
Acapulco		19,856		843	42.4
Cuernavaca		84,478		3,323	39.3
Este de México		177,071		3,444	19.5
Oeste de México		93,000		5,195	55.9
Sultepec		63,267		2,518	39.9
Taxco		78,770		4,430	56.2
Toluca		192,452		11,027	57.3
Tula		173,529		10,222	58.9
Tulancingo		88,049		4,803	54.6
Veracruz[i]	1831		1830		
Orizaba[j]		46,991		2,462	52.4
Córdoba[k]		24,521		1,465	59.7
Cosamaloapan[l]		9,823		593	60.4
Acayucan[m]		40,343		2,877	71.4
Jalacingo[n]		15,862		1,180	74.4
Cosamaloapan[o]	1836	9,348	1836	528	56.5
Córdoba[p]	1840	21,088	1836	1,156	54.4
Tuxpan[q]	1849	17,801	1844–1849	996	55.9

Table 4.3 (cont.)

Area	Year	Total Pop	Year	Average Annual Births	B/1,000
Chicontepec[r]	1849	23,442	1846–1849	1,371	58.4
Mean of 116 items					53.01
S.D.					±14.88
S.E.					±1.38

[a]"Ensayo estadistico sobre el estado de Chihuahua, parte tercera," in SMGEB, 1a ép., V(1857), 274.
[b]Governor's Memoria of 1824–1825. See note to part A.
[c]The population for 1825 in the text appears erroneous. The value given for 1823 is used instead.
[d]Governor's Memoria of 1854, Table 18.
[e]Banda, pp. 45, 47, 83.
[f]Banda gives baptisms for only one-half a year for Sayula and Colotlán. His figures have been doubled in this table.
[g]Governor's Memoria of 1833–34. See note k to part A.
[h]Governor's Memoria of 1834–1835. See note j to part A.
[i]Governor's Memoria of 1831–1832, entitled Estadistica del estado de Veracruz, in three parts. The pages are noted under the individual cantons, notes j to below.
[j]Ibid., pt. 2, pp. 1–28.
[k]Ibid., pt. 2, pp. 30ff.
[l]Ibid., pt. 2, pp. 43ff.
[m]Ibid., pt. 3, pp. 57–58.
[n]Ibid., pt. 3, pp. 105–107.
[o]SMGEB, 1a ép., V(1857), table opposite p. 111.
[p]"Estadistica del partido de Cordoba," SMGEB, 1a ép., IV(1854), 79–110. Births for all municipalidades are given except for the city of Córdoba. The figures given here are the totals of the other entities.
[q]"Noticias estadisticas sobre el departmento de Tuxpan," in SMGEB, 1a ép., IV(1854), Tables 3 and 4 in series following p. 278. The figure for births is the mean of five years from 1844 to 1849.
[r]Ibid., Tables 24 and 26. Births are the mean of four years.

The mean number of births per 1,000 population in part A of Table 4.3 is 52.60 with the standard deviation equal to ± 7.77, and the standard error equal to ±1.49. The comparable mean value in part B is 53.01, with a standard deviation of ±14.88, and a standard error of ±1.38. The variability is considerable, as might be expected from the sources at our disposal, but the low standard errors and the large sample size suggest that a birth ratio in the range of approximately fifty to fifty-five was indeed characteristic of the first half of the nineteenth century.

The second phase covers the three decades from 1860 to 1890. During this period we continue to rely upon state and local enumerations of population. However, the basis for estimating births has changed. No longer did the administrative officials depend upon the baptisms recorded by parish priests, but they were obliged to utilize the newly established Civil Register. This system was completely foreign to the mass of the people, who for generations had relied upon the Church in all matters pertaining to birth and death. The city and country dwellers alike simply ignored the law and refused to register newly born infants. As a result the recording of births was for a long time extremely inadequate. The problem is subject to extended discussion, which cannot be undertaken here. The expected result however, would be a marked fall in the apparent value of the birth rate since the numerator of the ratio would be spuriously reduced. The actual effect is seen in part A of Table 4.4 for states and in part B for subordinate entities.

Part A, with over forty reports, shows the mean births per 1,000 population to be 35.35 with a standard deviation equal to ±14.21 and a standard error equal to ±2.19. Part B shows mean births per 1,000 people to be 34.16 with a standard deviation of ±19.05. The individual values of items fluctuate wildly from 0.3 to 137.6. It is only the large number of items

Table 4.4

Births per thousand population (B/1,000).

A. As reported for certain states of the Republic of Mexico, 1860–1890.

State	Year	Total Pop.	Year	Average Annual Births	B/1,000
Coahuila[a]	1869	93,150	1869	1,686	18.1
Coahuila[b]	1886	148,288	1886	5,449	36.7
Colima[c]	1888	63,873	1888	1,594	24.9
Guanajuato[d]	1869	729,988	1871–1873	20,040	27.5
Guanajuato[e]	1881	968,113	1881	21,047	21.7
Guanajuato[f]	1890	1,007,116	1889	24,078	23.9
Guerrero[g]	1869	271,534	1869–1870	10,991	40.4
Guerrero[h]	1871	301,080	1870	15,756	52.3
Guerrero[i]	1885	329,235	1885	13,729	41.8
Guerrero[j]	1887	329,235	1886	13,323	40.4
Guerrero[k]	1889	339,135	1889	11,725	34.6
Jalisco[l]	1885	1,152,084	1885	44,791	38.9

Table 4.4 (cont.)

State	Year	Total Pop.	Year	Average Annual Births	B/1,000
Mexico[m]	1870	650,663	1870	19,399	29.8
Mexico[n]	1886	798,480	1886	22,770	28.5
Morelos[o]	1885	142,350	1886	7,666	53.9
Morelos[p]	1887	102,367	1887	3,983	38.9
Morelos[p]	1888	101,695	1888	4,105	40.3
Morelos[p]	1889	100,842	1889	3,916	38.8
Nuevo León[q]	1889	270,852	1887–1889	8,956	33.1
Nuevo León[r]	1891	271,987	1890	9,575	35.2
Oaxaca[s]	1861	507,108	1859–1861	25,100	49.5
Oaxaca[t]	1869	516,494	1868–1869	31,604	61.2
Oaxaca[u]	1881	747,724	1881	30,364	40.2
Querétaro[v]	1868	167,768	1870	12,085	72.1
Querétaro[w]	1872	182,435	1872	12,280	67.3
San Luis Potosi[x]	1873	443,556	1873	16,000	36.0
Sinaloa[y]	1869	162,298	1869	2,450	15.1
Sinaloa[z]	1881	201,118	1881	2,804	13.1
Sonora[aa]	1870	108,965	1870	2,297	21.1
Sonora[bb]	1889	154,532	1888	2,014	13.0
Tabasco[cc]	1890	120,000	1887–1890	3,972	33.1
Tamaulipas[dd]	1888	188,297	1888	4,650	24.7
Tlaxacala[ee]	1886	154,871	1886	6,368	41.2
Veracruz[ff]	1868	437,507	1868	3,614	8.3
Veracruz[ff]	1868	437,507	1869	5,519	12.6
Veracruz[gg]	1885	621,476	1885	18,561	29.9
Veracruz[gg]	1885	621,476	1886	24,052	38.7
Veracruz[hh]	1888	641,824	1888	25,040	39.1
Veracruz[hh]	1888	641,824	1889	22,880	35.7
Veracruz[ii]	1890	645,122	1890	22,850	35.4
Zacatecas[jj]	1868	397,945	1869	19,082	47.2
Zacatecas[jj]	1868	397,945	1870	19,585	49.2
Mean					35.35
S.D.					±14.21
S.E.					± 2.19

Notes to Table 4.4 (cont.)

*a*Population from *La Republica Mexicana. Coahuila. Reseña geografica y estadística,* p. 24, which cites the governor's *Memoria* of 1869. Births are from the governor's *Memoria* of 1869, Table 7. The period is from 1 January to 31 October 1869, and the values have been prorated to a full year. The births, like all of those for the decades 1860–1890, were taken from the Civil Register of the state. In this instance, out of 26 *municipalidades* in Coahuila, 12 reported 10 births or less, and of these, 6 reported no births.
*b*Population is from Portillo, *Anuario coahuilense para* 1886, p. 288. The births are from the governor's *Memoria* of 1886–1888, Table 10. There were 12,268 births from 15 February 1886 to 30 April 1888, that is, approximately twenty-seven months. The annual average is 5,449.
c There is no published population for Colima in 1889. We have taken the mean of six estimates as follows:
1857. 61,243 from Mexico. Secretariá de Fomento, Colonización e Industria, *Memoria,* 1853–1857, app., sec. IX on population by Orozco y Berra.
1871. 65,827 from Almada, *Diccionario de...Colima,* article *censos,* p. 37.
1877. 65,827 from Mexico. Secretariá de Economía, Dirección General de Estadística, *Estadísticas sociales del Porfiriato,* Table 1, p. 7.
1893. 69,549 from Mexico. Secretariá de Comercio e Industria, *Anuario estadístico,* 1893, p. 26.
1895. 55,677 from *ibid.,* 1895, p. 31.
1900. 65,115 from *ibid.,* 1901, p. 73, citing the national census of 1900.
Births are given in the series of governor's Memorias of 1887–1888, 1888–1889, and 1889–1890. Three totals are shown. These we have averaged for the value (1,594).
*d*Populations from governor's *Memoria* of 1873–1875, Table 4; births from Table 5.
*e*Population from Mexico. Secretariá de Economía, Dirección Nacional de Estadística, *Estadísticas sociales del Porfiriato,* Table 1, p. 7. Births are from the governor's *Memoria* of 1880–1882, Table 1.
*f*Population from Velasco. *Geografia...de la República Mexicana,* V(Guanajuato), 250; births from the governor's *Memoria* for 1889–1890, Table 14.
g Governor's *Memoria* for 1869–1870, documents 1 and 4.
h Ibid., 1871–1872, document 8.
i Ibid., 1885–1886, pp. 203–205.
j Ibid., 1887–1888, document 25, pp. 156–158.
k Ibid., 1888–1889, anexo 30.
l Barcena, *Ensayo estadístico del estado de Jalisco,* pp. 27–33, gives both population and births in 1885.
*m*Governor's *Memoria* for 1870–1871, Tables 1 and 4.
n Ibid., 1886–1887, Tables 1 and 4.
o Governor's *Memoria* for 1886, Table 2.
p Ibid., 1890. The table is under the title "Censo de población del estado de Morelos... en los años 1887, 1888 y 1889." The districts of Jonacatepec and Juárez are missing. The totals are based upon the other four districts.
q Governor's *Memoria* for 1887–1889, *resumen,* pp. 155–156.
r Ibid., 1889–1891 document 6, anexo 1 and anexo 5.
s Governor's *Memoria* for 1861, document 12. The births for Etla and Pochutla are missing; births are missing for Tuxtepec as well as the population. The totals include the other districts.
t Ibid., 1869, document 2.
u Ibid., 1881, document 1.
v Septién y Villaseñor, *Memoria estadística del estado de Querétaro,* p. 289.
w Ibid., p. 290.
x Macías Valadez, *Apuntes geograficas y estadísticas sobre el estado de San Luis Potosí,* pp. 124–129. The partido of Tamazunchale did not report births. Its population has been deducted from the state total. All births are given for sixteen months. They have been adjusted in the table.
*y*Governor's *Memoria* for 1869, Tables 4 and 6.
z Ibid., 1881 Tables 16 and 17.
aa The population is from Pérez Hernández, *Compendio de la geografia del estado de Sonora,* p. 73. The Indian population (Yaquis, Opatas, and Mayos) is omitted. Their total, according to Pérez Hernández, was 22,500. The births are from the governor's Memoria for 1870, as published in *SMGEB,* 2a ép., II(1870), 708.

Notes to Table 4.4 (cont.)

ᵇᵇ The population is from Sonora (state), División territorial y censo del estado de Sonora, pp. 55–59. Births are from the governor's Informe for 1888–1889, table at the end of the report. The data refer to the year 1888.
ᶜᶜ Governor's Memoria for 1887–1890, p. 51. Births are the mean of the years 1887–1888, 1888–1889, and 1889–1890.
ᵈᵈ Governor's Memoria for 1888, document 12.
ᵉᵉ Governor's Memoria for 1886–1887, pp. 10–12.
ᶠᶠ Population from governor's Memoria for 1868–1869, Table 25; births are for 1868 from Table 27. Births for 1869 from ibid., 1869–1870, Table 26.
ᵍᵍ Population in 1885 from governor's Memoria for 1885–1886, Table 51; births in 1885 from Table 56. Births in 1886 are from ibid., Table 57 for the first six months and from ibid., 1886–1888, Table 16, for the second half of the year.
ʰʰ Ibid., 1888–1890; population in 1888 on p. 232; births in 1888 and in 1889 on p. 263.
ⁱⁱ Ibid., 1890; population in 1890 on p. 232; births in 1890 on p. 262. Only the first-half year is given. For our table this figure is multiplied by 2.
ʲʲ Population from governor's Memoria for 1869–1870, Table 9; births are from ibid., 1870–1871, Tables 2 and 3.

Table 4.4 (cont.)

B. As reported for districts, partidos, cantons, and similar territorial entities for the period 1860–1890.

Area	Year	Total Pop.	Year	Average Annual Births	B/1,000
Guanajuatoᵃ	1869		1873–1875		
Guanajuato		69,682		1,136	16.3
Silao		46,090		1,464	31.8
Irapuato		46,266		1,418	30.6
Salamanca		47,109		2,368	49.7
Pénjamo		27,966		2,074	74.2
León		119,380		1,560	13.1
Celaya		46,815		351	7.5
Santa Cruz		34,104		1,444	42.2
Salvatierra		60,700		1,879	30.9
Jerécuaro		33,353		1,469	44.0
San Miguel Allende		36,911		174	4.7
Dolores Hidalgo		56,663		1,390	24.5
San Felipe		40,944		1,995	48.7
San Luis de la Paz		23,820		991	41.6
Inturbide		40,185		925	23.0
Guanajuatoᵇ	1881		1881		
Guanajuato		106,968		894	8.3
Silao		54,078		420	7.8
Salamanca		71,320		2,487	34.9
Irapuato		68,746		1,189	17.3
Pénjamo		55,290		2,256	40.8
León		70,022		251	3.6
San Fco. del Rincón		47,020		868	18.5
Celaya		64,166		1,187	18.5

Table 4.4 (cont.)

State	Year	Total Pop.	Year	Average Annual Births	B/1,000
Chamacuero		45,479		1,808	39.8
Salvatierra		89,215		1,949	21.8
Jerécuaro		45,652		1,125	24.6
Allende		49,703		798	16.0
Dolores Hidalgo		65,568		1,848	28.2
San Felipe		57,907		1,617	27.9
San Luis de la Paz		29,466		867	29.5
Inturbide		47,513		1,483	31.2
Guanajuato[c]	1889		1889		
Allende		58,339		1,124	19.3
Hidalgo		47,286		1,371	29.0
San Diego Unión		19,726		853	43.2
San Felipe		51,590		1,689	32.7
Ocampo		7,855		618	78.7
Celaya		42,216		777	18.4
Acámbaro		26,089		902	34.6
Apaseo		26,373		700	26.6
Comonfort		15,257		404	26.5
Cortazar		15,448		751	48.6
Jerécuaro		21,907		710	32.4
Moroleón		11,571		76	6.6
Salvatierra		41,873		855	20.4
Santa Cruz		15,736		775	49.3
Tarimaro		9,554		253	26.5
Yuriria		32,770		808	24.7
Guanajuato		93,042		433	4.6
Abasolo		27,961		765	27.3
Irapuato		42,698		463	10.8
La Luz		13,926		681	48.9
Pénjamo		54,293		1,756	32.4
Romita		16,486		435	25.9
Salamanca		32,309		515	15.9
Silao		37,342		614	16.4
Valle de Santiago		36,274		1,507	41.6
León		77,018		904	11.7
Piedra Gorda		17,205		290	16.8
San Fco. del Rincón		20,309		182	9.0
Purísima del Rincón		10,072		362	36.1
San Luis de la Paz		23,201		811	34.9
Iturbide		30,482		737	24.2
Victoria		21,314		751	35.2
Guerrero[d]	1889		1889		
Bravos		25,000		468	18.3
Guerrero		19,743		913	46.3
Hidalgo		22,869		841	36.7

Table 4.4 (cont.)

State	Year	Total Pop.	Year	Average Annual Births	B/1,000
Alarcón		23,330		803	34.4
Aldama		34,035		1,380	40.5
Alvarez		33,167		1,240	37.4
Zaragoza		13,890		791	57.0
Morelos		32,239		1,790	53.1
Allende		18,464		221	11.9
Abasolo		21,475		596	27.8
Tabares		24,951		817	32.8
Galeana		16,186		585	36.1
La Unión		51,091		1,360	26.6
Jalisco[e]	1885		1885		
Guadalajara		225,431		9,941	44.1
Lagos		109,472		4,800	43.9
La Barca		166,141		6,623	39.9
Sayula		91,244		4,022	44.1
Ameca		78,294		2,421	30.9
Autlán		59,098		2,112	35.7
Colotlán		60,067		2,633	43.9
Ciudad Guzmán		144,913		4,200	29.0
Mascota		49,959		1,660	33.2
Teocaltiche		100,576		3,931	39.1
Tequila		66,889		2,448	36.6
Mexico[f]	1870		1870		
Toluca		77,566		2,901	37.4
Ixtlahuaca		58,475		3,390	57.9
Tenango		49,559		1,050	21.2
Chalco		47,184		1,062	22.5
Jilotepec		44,495		1,551	34.8
Texcoco		42,881		415	9.7
Lerma		39,996		1,118	27.9
Tlalnepantla		38,298		907	23.7
Sultepec		36,927		1,102	29.8
Villa del Valle		35,242		1,307	37.1
Temascaltepec		33,495		507	15.1
Tenancingo		33,282		1,056	31.7
Otumba		32,075		557	17.4
Cuautitlán		31,622		1,038	32.8
Zumpango		27,490		661	24.0
Zacualpan		22,076		777	35.2
Mexico[g]	1886		1886		
Toluca		95,702		3,113	32.6
Cuautitlán		33,716		952	28.2
Chalco		60,095		1,310	21.8
Ixtlahuaca		75,352		2,740	36.4

Table 4.4 (cont.)

State	Year	Total Pop.	Year	Average Annual Births	B/1,000
Jilotepec		57,174		689	12.0
Lerma		48,134		1,948	40.4
Morelos		31,355		620	19.8
Sultepec		55,553		1,843	33.2
Temascaltepec		39,634		662	16.7
Tenango		63,085		1,509	23.9
Tenancingo		58,678		1,519	26.3
Texcoco		53,339		2,023	38.0
Tlalnepantla		53,946		1,382	25.6
Valle de Bravo		44,760		1,854	41.2
Zumpango		22,957		606	21.7
Morelos[h]	1885		1885		
Cuernavaca		37,484		2,429	64.8
Yautepec		19,262		687	35.6
Morelos		25,381		1,135	44.7
Jonacatepec		22,835		1,400	61.3
Tetecala		20,853		1,411	67.7
Jojutla		16,535		604	36.6
Morelos[i]	1887		1887		
Cuernavaca		36,521		1,286	35.2
Yautepec		19,561		767	38.7
Morelos		24,802		1,098	44.2
Tetecala		21,483		832	38.7
Morelos[j]	1888		1888		
Cuernavaca		36,121		1,299	35.9
Yautepec		19,401		781	40.2
Morelos		24,842		1,156	46.5
Tetecala		21,331		869	40.7
Morelos[i]	1889		1889		
Cuernavaca		35,919		1,279	35.6
Yautepec		19,121		600	31.4
Morelos		24,661		1,136	46.1
Tetecala		21,141		901	42.6
Oaxaca[j]	1861		1861		
Centro		41,148		2,868	69.7
Zimatlán		33,681		1,880	55.8
Tlacolula		27,471		1,051	38.3
Yautepec		17,936		598	33.4
Villa Alta		32,492		1,129	34.7
Villa Juárez		19,345		844	43.6
Choapan		10,345		401	38.7
Teotitlán del Camino		20,532		861	41.9

Table 4.4 (cont.)

State	Year	Total Pop.	Year	Average Annual Births	B/1,000
Cuicatlán		13,515		558	41.2
Teposcolula		20,605		1,219	58.2
Tlaxiaco		33,952		2,045	60.2
Nochixtlán		24,528		1,131	46.1
Coixtlahuaca		10,873		470	43.2
Huajuapan		34,814		1,687	48.4
Silacayoapan		28,838		1,542	56.9
Jamiltepec		24,622		1,154	46.8
Juquila		8,992		634	70.5
Ejutla		13,394		846	63.2
Ocotlán		22,225		1,243	55.9
Miahuatlán		28,220		1,096	38.8
Tehuantepec		20,029		1,157	57.7
Juchitán		19,551		1,115	57.1
Oaxaca^k	1869		1869		
Centro		43,768		3,094	70.7
Etla		15,687		1,823	106.3
Teotitlan		21,620		1,504	69.7
Cuicatlán		14,780		525	35.6
Nochixtlán		22,827		1,512	66.3
Teposcolula		18,820		1,068	62.0
Tlaxiaco		37,598		1,921	51.1
Huajuapan		33,846		1,397	41.3
Silacayoapan		19,071		1,066	60.6
Coixtlahuaca		9,316		1,283	137.6
Juxtlahuaca		7,901		723	91.5
Villa Alvarez		22,966		1,406	61.3
Ocotlán		23,982		1,194	50.0
Ejutla		13,738		876	63.7
Miahuatlán		28,708		2,503	87.2
Pochutla		9,679		457	47.3
Juquila		12,987		580	44.7
Jamiltepec		21,782		1,455	67.3
Villa Juárez		17,503		712	40.7
Tuxtepec		17,346		902	52.0
Villa Alta		16,072		1,532	95.4
Choapan		10,034		940	93.8
Tlacolula		25,714		1,539	59.8
Yautepec		14,807		456	30.8
Tehuantepec		16,619		596	35.8
Juchitán		19,323		540	27.9
Oaxaca^l	1881		1881		
Centro		60,206		2,856	47.5
Coixtlahuaca		15,033		743	49.4
Cuicatlán		17,426		785	45.0

Table 4.4 (cont.)

State	Year	Total Pop.	Year	Average Annual Births	B/1,000
Choapan		11,007		497	45.1
Ejutla		22,138		1,047	47.3
Etla		24,100		991	41.1
Huajuapan		37,939		1,224	32.2
Jamiltepec		37,814		1,609	42.6
Juchitán		28,933		1,180	41.8
Juquila		16,869		656	38.9
Juxtlahuaca		15,781		490	31.1
Miahuatlán		36,231		1,569	43.5
Nochixtlán		35,071		1,610	45.9
Ocotlán		29,429		1,055	35.8
Pochutla		12,142		575	47.4
Silacayoapan		25,980		1,125	43.3
Teotitlán		26,839		912	34.0
Tehuantepec		23,641		894	37.8
Teposcolula		31,836		1,411	45.7
Tuxtepec		20,738		966	46.5
Tlacolula		37,696		1,669	44.2
Tlaxiaco		46,484		2,029	43.7
Villa Alta		44,229		1,507	34.1
Villa Álvarez		41,233		1,281	31.0
Villa Juárez		25,614		1,008	39.3
Yautepec		22,254		665	29.9
San Luis Potosí[m]	1873		1873		
San Luis Potosí		116,712		4,007	34.3
Salinas		9,576		134	14.0
Venado		31,792		1,561	49.2
Catorce		47,642		2,332	49.0
Guadalcázar		33,151		1,222	36.8
Cerritos		25,626		830	32.0
Río Verde		38,138		1,540	40.4
Maíz		29,143		914	31.3
Hidalgo		33,405		1,126	33.7
Valles		8,454		319	37.8
Tancanhuitz		24,719		515	20.8
Sinaloa[n]	1869		1869		
Mazatlán		26,298		588	22.4
Rosario		15,387		408	26.5
Concordia		10,676		194	18.1
San Ignacio		8,248		154	18.7
Cosala		13,322		226	17.0
Culiacán		29,093		30	1.0
Mocorito		12,679		232	18.3
Sinaloa		23,157		50	2.2
Fuerte		23,468		568	24.2

Table 4.4 (cont.)

State	Year	Total Pop.	Year	Average Annual Births	B/1,000
Sinaloa[o]	1881		1881		
Mazatlán		30,630		430	14.0
Rosario		18,568		506	27.3
Concordia		12,929		364	28.1
San Ignacio		9,570		150	15.7
Cosala		18,378		184	10.0
Culiacán		38,340		320	8.3
Mocorito		17,030		430	25.3
Sinaloa		27,746		58	2.1
Fuerte		27,927		362	13.0
Sonora[p]	1870		1870		
Ures		18,342		344	18.8
Hermosillo		19,879		319	16.1
Guaymas		14,967		84	5.6
Álamos		22,325		689	30.8
Sahuaripa		8,016		145	18.1
Moctezuma		9,421		314	33.3
Arizpe		6,583		111	16.9
Magdalena		3,940		50	12.7
Altar		5,492		241	44.4
Sonora[q]	1889		1888		
Hermosillo		21,657		126	5.8
Guaymas		11,930		40	3.4
Ures		26,714		404	15.1
Álamos		38,432		428	11.1
Arizpe		11,213		35	3.1
Sahuaripa		11,470		146	12.7
Moctezuma		11,063		164	14.8
Magdalena		10,232		324	31.7
Altar		11,821		347	29.4
Tlaxcala[r]	1886		1886		
Hidalgo		35,482		1,134	31.9
Juárez		34,666		1,742	50.3
Zaragoza		31,974		1,470	46.0
Morelos		19,235		539	28.0
Ocampo		17,505		872	49.8
Barrón-Escandón		16,009		611	38.1
Veracruz[s]	1868		1868		
Acayucan		16,559		21	1.3
Chicontepec		31,177		89	2.8
Coatepec		25,194		96	3.8
Córdoba		31,983		54	1.7
Cosamaloapan		15,557		95	6.1

Table 4.4 (cont.)

State	Year	Total Pop.	Year	Average Annual Births	B/1.000
Huatusco		13,522		59	4.4
Jalapa		46,735		176	3.8
Jalacingo		30.266		100	3.3
Minatitlán		12.583		65	5.2
Misantla		6.912		56	8.1
Orizaba		45.601		153	3.3
Papantla		15.609		86	5.5
Tampico		23.468		1,046	44.6
Tantoyuca		22.123		463	20.9
Tuxpan		26,166		468	17.9
Tuxtlas		21,345		7	0.3
Zongolica		14,793		104	7.0
Veracruz		41,914		480	11.4
Veracruz[1]	1868		1869		
Acayucan				73	4.4
Chicontepec				872	28.6
Coatepec				144	5.7
Córdoba		AS		209	6.5
Cosamaloapan				230	14.8
Huatusco				159	12.5
Jalapa				433	9.3
Jalacingo				104	3.4
Minatitlán		ABOVE		279	22.1
Misantla				46	6.7
Orizaba				734	16.1
Papantla				114	7.3
Tampico				677	28.8
Tantoyuca				690	31.2
Tuxpan				174	6.7
Tuxtlas				101	4.7
Zongolica				130	8.8
Veracruz				330	7.9
Veracruz[u]	1885		1885		
Veracruz		67,373		2,115	31.4
Jalapa		57,128		1,087	19.0
Orizaba		53,879		1,561	29.0
Chicontepec		47,461		1,517	32.0
Jalacingo		41,992		1,713	40.8
Córdoba		41,877		2,323	55.5
Tantoyuca		35,941		1,008	28.0
Coatepec		34,009		1,442	42.4
Tuxpan		33,935		529	15.6
Ozuluama		31,254		1,133	36.2
Tuxtla		29,942		522	17.4
Papantla		29,012		834	28.7

Table 4.4 (cont.)

State	Year	Total Pop.	Year	Average Annual Births	B/1,000
Acayucan		23,119		635	27.4
Cosamaloapan		21,693		502	23.2
Zongolica		21,444		582	27.1
Huatusco		21,056		460	21.8
Minatitlán		18,482		520	28.1
Misantla		11,789		78	6.6
Veracruz[a]	1885		1886		
Veracruz				2,631	39.1
Jalapa				1,989	34.8
Orizaba				1,900	35.2
Chicontepec		AS		1,473	31.0
Jalacingo				2,163	51.5
Córdoba				1,947	46.5
Tantoyuca				1,108	30.8
Coatepec				1,704	50.5
Tuxpan		ABOVE		1,267	37.3
Ozuluama				1,137	36.4
Tuxtla				1,397	46.7
Papantla				1,111	38.6
Acayucan				937	40.5
Cosamaloapan				557	25.7
Zongolica				713	33.2
Huatusco				774	36.7
Minatitlán				728	39.4
Misantla				516	43.7
Zacatecas[a]	1868		1869		
Zacatecas		68,655		2,816	41.0
Fresnillo		55,157		2,089	37.9
Sombrerete		35,745		1,987	55.5
Nieves		28,291		1,478	52.2
Mazapil		7,951		569	71.6
Ciudad García		44,123		2,223	50.4
Pinos		38,846		2,015	51.9
Villanueva		40,893		1,714	41.9
Sánchez Román		27,811		1,519	54.6
Juchipila		18,106		952	52.6
Nochistlán		20,022		1,042	52.1
Ojo Caliente		12,345		678	55.0
Zacatecas	1868		1870		
Zacatecas				3,071	44.7
Fresnillo				2,430	44.1
Sombrerete				2,050	57.3
Nieves		AS		1,440	50.9
Mazapil				723	91.0

Table 4.4 (cont.)

State	Year	Total Pop.	Year	Average Annual Births	B/1,000
Ciudad García				2,177	49.3
Pinos				2,001	51.5
Villanueva		ABOVE		1,623	39.7
Sánchez Román				1,523	54.7
Juchipila				979	54.0
Nochistlán				885	44.3
Ojo Caliente				683	55.4
Mean					34.16
S.D.					±19.05
S.E.					± 1.01

[a]Population in 1869 from the governor's Memoria of 1873–1875, Table 4. The areas are electoral districts. Births are from ibid., Table 5. The poblaciones of this table have been cross-correlated with the electoral districts of Table 4. The births are given for two years; accordingly, one-half of these values have been used here.
[b]Population in 1881 from ibid., 1880–1882, Table 5, by electoral districts. Births are from ibid., Table 1. Juzgados are cross-correlated with electoral districts. Births are given for 1881 only.
[c]Population is from Velasco, Geografía y estadística de la República Mexicana, V, 61–249. Births are from the governor's Mémoria of 1889–1890, Table 13. Juzgados are cross-correlated with partidos. Births are given for 1889 only.
[d]Governor's Memoria of 1888–1889, anexo 21, under the title, "Noticia estadística y geográfica del estado de Guerrero."
[e]Bárcena, Ensayo estadístico del estado del Jalisco, pp. 27–33. Both population and births are shown for 1885.
[f]Governor's Memoria of 1870–1871, Tables 1 and 4.
[g]Ibid., 1886–1887, Tables 1 and 4.
[h]Governor's Memoria of 1886, Table 2.
[i]Ibid., 1890. The table is under the title "Censo de población del estado de Morelos... en los años 1887, 1888 y 1889." The districts of Jonacatepec and Juárez are missing.
[j]Governor's Memoria of 1861, document 12. Births are given for 1859, 1860, and the first-half of 1861.
[k]Ibid., 1869, document 2.
[l]Ibid., 1881, document 1.
[m]Macías Valadez, Apuntes geograficas y estadisticas sobre el estado de San Luis Potosí, pp. 124–129. The partido of Tamazunchale has been omitted since it did not report births. All births are given for sixteen months; they have been adjusted in our table.
[n]Governor's Memoria of 1869, Tables 4 and 6.
[o]Ibid., 1881, Tables 16 and 17.
[p]Population is from Pérez Herández, Compendio de la geografica del estado de Sonora, p. 73. The Indian population—22,500 according to the author—is omitted. Births are from the governor's Memoria for 1870 as published in SMGEB, 2a ép., II(1870), 708.
[q]Population is from Sonora (state), División territorial, pp. 55–59; births are from the governor's Informe for 1888–1889, the table at the end of the report. The data are for 1888.
[r]Governor's Memoria of 1886–1887, pp. 10–12.
[s]Population from the governor's Memoria of 1868–1869, Table 25; births from Table 27.
[t]Population from the governor's Memoria of 1868–1869, Table 25; births from ibid., 1869–1870, Table 26.

^aPopulation in 1885 from *ibid.*, 1885–1886, Table 51; births from *ibid.*, Table 56.
^bPopulation in 1885 from *ibid.*, Table 51. Births in 1886 are from *ibid.*, Table 57 for the first half year and from *ibid.*, 1886–1888, Table 16, for the second half year.
^cPopulation from the governor's *Memoria* of 1869–1870, Table 9; births from *ibid.*, 1870–1871, Tables 2 and 3.

which keep the standard error down to ±1.01. The only possible explanation for these extreme discrepancies is the complete futility of the registration system. The very low values are due to wholesale failures to report births; the very high ones are referable to the occasional appearance of records which had accumulated for long periods prior to submission to the administrative center.

By 1890 the routine of registration had become established even though the machinery operated ineffectively. At this time, also, the federal government began to take national censuses. The first was in 1895, the second in 1900, the third in 1910. During these years Antonio Peñafiel organized the Departmento de Estadística Nacionál and published a series of annual reviews which included much demographic data.[7] Table 4.5 shows the birth ratios for this period. Among the states the dispersion of values is less than in the previous decades, but the means are still low, in the range of 30 to 35 births per 1,000 population. It is clear that although the censuses had improved markedly, birth registration was still defective.

Table 4.5
Births per thousand population (B/1,000) in the states of Mexico for the year 1895, 1900, and 1905.

State	B/1,000		
	1895	1900	1905
Aguascalientes	14.81	22.24	59.30
Baja California	33.47	38.91	18.74
Campeche	40.10	38.03	37.22
Coahuila	22.81	25.83	30.97
Colima	37.63	27.11	28.48
Chiapas	—	30.33	31.72
Chihuahua	—	32.53	25.63
Distrito Federal	7.80	54.35	25.23
Durango	21.80	28.47	60.37

[7]More recently republished in Mexico. Secretaría de Economía, Dirección General de Estadística, *Estadísticas sociales del Porfiriato*, Table 44, p. 156.

Table 4.5 (cont.)

State	B/1,000		
	1895	1900	1905
Guanajuato	24.38	25.98	—
Guerrero	40.67	40.87	36.06
Hidalgo	23.21	26.11	22.96
Jalisco	44.33	45.71	46.99
Mexico	24.17	37.64	31.49
Michoacán	25.91	47.68	28.79
Morelos	32.33	39.71	43.31
Nuevo León	40.42	39.28	38.82
Oaxaca	39.38	40.18	38.98
Puebla	26.70	24.99	34.22
Querétaro	20.71	17.49	19.56
San Luis Potosí	27.92	39.52	37.47
Sinaloa	33.02	29.98	28.15
Sonora	8.98	26.25	19.61
Tabasco	43.85	68.31	43.23
Tamaulipas	19.42	24.96	24.62
Tepic	25.40	57.44	31.67
Tlaxcala	42.49	39.83	34.71
Veracruz	36.21	27.95	27.27
Yucatán	54.98	51.26	50.32
Zacatecas	46.38	47.79	47.82
Mean	30.33	36.56	34.61
S.D.	±11.58	±10.82	±10.95
S.E.	±2.19	±1.98	±2.03

Source: Mexico. Secretaría de Economía, Dirección General de Estadística, Estadísticas sociales del Porfiriato, Table 44, p. 156.

After the Revolution of 1910–1920, national censuses were resumed in 1921, followed by decennial counts beginning in 1930. In 1931 the birth ratios for Mexico were published for the years 1924 to 1929 and are shown in Table 4.6. It is noteworthy that from 1924 to 1928 inclusive the values were low and in the same range as for 1895 to 1905. In 1929 the figure jumped to 42.19. The explanation offered by the Mexican statisticians is highly illuminating and deserves to be quoted (see also notes to Table 4.6): "Reported births, infant mortality, and the natural increase of the population are closer to reality than in previous years because of government regulations which insist upon and facilitate registration of births." [Our translation.]

Table 4.6

Births per thousand population (B/1,000) in the Mexican
Republic during the year 1924–1929 inclusive.

Year	B/1,000	Year	B/1,000
1924	31.52	1927	32.35
1925	34.30	1928	34.58
1926	32.73	1929	42.19

Source: From the table "Movimiento de Poblacion (1924 a 1929)," in
Estadística nacional, revista mensual, VII, no. 108 (October 1931),
485. Note 2 to the table referring to 1929 reads as follows: "La
natalidad, mortalidad infantil y crecimiento natural de la población,
deben considerase más aproximados a la realidad que en los
años anteriores, como consequencia de las disposiciones guberna-
tivas que exigen y facilitan la inscripción de los nacidos."

It is very obvious that the true birth rate was at least
40 per 1,000 and probably higher. How much higher is shown
clearly for the individual states in Table 4.7 and for the country
as a whole in Table 4.8. The range for the last thirty years has
remained without significant change at 43 to 48 births per
1,000 population.

The chief conclusion to be drawn from this study of
gross birth rates is that the change in natality in Mexico has
been very moderate during the past 200 years, if it can be
demonstrated at all. We may tentatively accept Humboldt's
values of above 60 per 1,000 in Guanajuato and Querétaro
and definitely accept the data for 1820–1850 at 52 to 53 births
per 1,000. Then, if we disregard the faulty records of the period
between 1860 and 1920, we have clear evidence of a plateau
from 1920 to 1965 at close to 45 per 1,000. On the other hand,
in the Mixteca Alta, which is, to be sure, a restricted region,
there is no indication of any significant decline between 1700
and 1950.

As a sort of yardstick to measure the magnitude of
changes in Mexico, we may cite those which have occurred in
the United States since 1910. According to the *Statistical
Abstract of the United States* for 1968,[8] the crude birth rate in
1910 was 30.1 per 1,000 population. In 1920 it was 27.7; in
1930, 21.3; in 1940, 19.4; in 1950, 24.1; in 1960, 23.7; and in

[8]P. 47, Table 53.

Table 4.7

Births per thousand population (B/1,000) in the states of Mexico
for the years 1940, 1950, and 1960.

State	B/1.000		
	1940[a]	1950[b]	1960[c]
Aguascalientes	48.3	51.0	53.3
Baja California. Norte	45.9	48.2	48.3
Baja California. Sur	41.4	44.8	42.4
Campeche	48.7	48.1	48.0
Coahuila	61.4	49.4	49.3
Colima	42.1	49.1	48.5
Chiapas	36.7	39.5	40.2
Chihuahua	47.8	42.6	45.0
Distrito Federal	33.6	38.4	43.4
Durango	49.0	47.6	49.0
Guanajuato	55.5	49.7	47.4
Guerrero	40.7	46.1	49.3
Hidalgo	39.3	44.1	46.1
Jalisco	44.8	47.5	45.4
Mexico	47.0	47.4	47.9
Michoacán	43.9	48.0	48.1
Morelos	46.0	44.5	49.7
Nayarit	42.2	49 4	50.0
Nuevo León	43.7	43.7	47.2
Oaxaca	41.5	41.8	43.7
Puebla	44.5	43.6	46.6
Querétaro	46.3	48.2	51.5
Quintana Roo	35.7	44.0	32.5
San Luis Potosí	51.9	49.2	52.8
Sinaloa	36.6	48.5	49.0
Sonora	50.6	50.4	51.2
Tabasco	38.4	43.8	47.0
Tamaulipas	35.4	42.8	42.5
Tlaxcala	53.7	51.5	51.2
Veracruz	32.3	46.8	37.3
Yucatán	46.0	45.1	45.9
Zacatecas	53.5	55.9	54.4
Mean	44.5	46.6	47.0
S.D.	±6.72	±3.67	±4.58
S.E.	±1.19	±0.65	±0.81

[a]From *Anuario estadístico*, 1941, p. 167, Table 80.
[b]From *Anuario estadístico*, 1951–1952, pp. 135, Table 48.
[c]From *Anuario estadístico*, 1960–1961, pp. 45–46, Table 3.5.

Table 4.8

Births per thousand population (B/1,000) in the Mexican
Republic in a series of years between 1938 and 1965.

Year	B/1,000	Year	B/1,000	Year	B/1,000
1938	43.9	1949	45.2	1960	46.0
1939	45.0	1950	45.5	1961	45.3
1940	43.5	1951	44.6	1963	44.1
1941	41.4	1958	44.8	1964	44.8
1948	45.2	1959	47.7	1965	44.2

Source : Those for our Table 4.7 plus the *Anuario estadistico,* 1964–1965,
pp. 61–66, Tables 3.2 and 3.3.

1967, 17.8. There is no suggestion whatever that wide swings of
this nature have been observed in Mexico, apart from the
artifacts caused by faulty enumerations and inadequate registration. If there has been any movement at all in the true value
of the crude birth rate, it has taken the form of an almost im-
perceptible but steady decline since the latter half of the eighteenth century.

Chapter V

Fertility and Similar Ratios in Mexico, 1777–1960

The crude birth rate may be expressed as the ratio of live births per unit time to total population. However, since the latter includes a large body of individuals who could not under any circumstances bear children, that is, all males and all females below and above the reproductive age, it is preferable to restrict the population at risk to reproductive women. This restriction would yield the ratio of live births to females between the conventional ages of 15 and 44, or 15 and 49 years. If registration or similar data for births do not exist, and only a census is available, the births may be replaced by the number of very young children, usually those aged 0–4 years. This is the fertility ratio. It may be written in various ways. Here we shall divide the number of children by that of the reproductive females and multiply by 1,000. The result is, in fact, the number of children in the population per 1,000 females of reproductive age.

This calculation may be performed with each of the Mexican national censuses since 1895 and may be treated by standard statistical techniques although most writers on Mexican population have preferred to employ the registrations of actual births rather than resort to an indirect method such as the fertility ratio. Nevertheless, if it be desired to compare the contemporary period with colonial Mexico, a very simple approach is required because prior to the War of Independence it is not, in general, possible to match birth records with head counts. For this purpose some type of fertility ratio is eminently suitable. We say "some type" because in order to make use of all the available records from the late eighteenth century, it is necessary upon occasion to depart from the strict definition of the term and to make certain modifications in the structure of the ratio.

Our earliest figures are from the census of 1777. We know of no parish records or other enumerations previous to that date which permit the establishment of a complete age distribution. For the children we use the conventional group 0–4 years inclusive. For the adult females the lower limit is 15 years, but the upper limit is not clearly fixed. Therefore, it is advisable to employ two ages for the termination of the reproductive period, 44 and 49. However, in the colonial censuses there was conspicuous heaping, that is, in this instance, a strong tendency to report the age of women as an even 50 years rather than an exact 46, 47, etc. As a result, to cut off the total at a stated 49 means the omission of all those who were actually 46, 47, 48, and 49 but who were recorded as 50 years of age. In order to compensate in part for this error we may add to those listed as 49, one-half of those listed as 50 years. This correction requires the construction of three ratios instead of two, as seen in Table 5.1. With the present-day censuses, however, the correction is unnecessary and is omitted.

The parish counts for the census of 1777 extant in the AGI include a total of 91 from which can be obtained precise figures for the two groups just discussed, children 0–4 years of age and females 15 to 44 or 49. Of these, 60 come from the bishopric of Oaxaca, 11 from that of Puebla, and 20 from that of Durango. The variation in the value of the ratios from parish to parish is great and that among the bishoprics is considerable although without particular significance. Consequently, we derive the means for the 91 parishes collectively as shown in Table 5.1. It will be noted that for children under 5 years of age and women aged 15 to 44, 15 to 49, and 15 to 49 plus 1/2 of those 50, the respective means are 753, 701, and 691 children per 1,000 females. The standard deviations are ±153.0, ±143.4 and ±139.8, and when expressed as a percentage of the corresponding mean (the coefficient of variation, c.v.), they are almost identical for the three categories of female age at 20.2–20.5.

In addition to the parish counts of 1777 there is a series of summaries in the ramo de Historia of the AGN,[1] dating from the Revillagigedo census of 1789–1794. In many of these summaries the population is grouped according to sex and age. The age categories do not conform to the modern system of 5-or 10-year intervals. The youngest children are listed as 0–7 years, then come the periods 7–16, 16–25, 25–40, 40–50 and over

[1]Vols. 522 and 523.

Table 5.1

Fertility ratios from parishes reported in the 1777 census. Column 1
shows the number of children under 5 years per 1,000 females aged 15 to 44 years.
Column 2 shows children under 5 years per 1,000 females aged 15 to 49 years.
Column 3 shows children under 5 years per 1,000 females aged 15 to 49 years
plus one-half of the females reported as being 50 years of age.

Parish	(1)	(2)	(3)
Bishopric Oaxaca			
Apoala	1,148	1,065	1,008
Nochixtlán	990	936	927
Chilapa	976	870	853
Achiutla	768	725	699
Chicahuaxtla	1,097	1,045	1,038
Yolotepec	1,045	992	962
Itundujía	939	882	856
Elotepec	602	574	560
Teojomulco	816	760	755
Teotitlán del Camino	670	636	625
Tuxtla	892	824	813
Jalapa	619	567	563
Huajolotitlán	930	867	848
Zimatlán	1,139	1,058	1,030
Mitla	872	809	804
Acayucan	606	557	554
Teotitlán del Valle	805	746	740
Ejutla	809	756	754
Ometepec	799	763	749
Yalalag	724	658	652
San Agustín Mixtepec	800	743	740
Santa Cruz Mixtepec	853	806	797
Ixtlán	686	638	634
San Francisco del Mar	731	679	676
Zagache	633	599	590
Loxicha	781	758	755
Quetzaltepec	673	626	625
Pinotepa del Rey	717	690	690
Ayoquesco	532	492	485
Lachixío	726	678	675
Pinotepa de Don Luis	838	807	807
Tututepec	733	688	686
Juquila	678	654	647
Amuzgos	1,040	954	946
Totontepec	590	551	546
Talistaca	726	670	667
Cuilapan	703	663	647
Lapaguía	782	731	727
Yaeé	668	591	588
Tepetolutla	781	740	730
Betaza	651	607	603

Table 5.1 (cont.)

Parish	(1)	(2)	(3)
Los Cortijos	618	586	584
Santa Catarina Minas	873	828	806
Zautla	893	830	825
Tlacoazintepec	583	540	535
Quiatoni	753	706	701
Yolox	796	753	751
Chichicastepec	794	739	729
Ozolotepec	754	687	683
Chicomezúchil	710	645	638
Amatlán	790	708	704
Miahuatlán	748	700	694
Tanetze	787	739	734
Atoyac	866	824	824
Ecatepec	722	668	668
Coatlán	728	690	686
Zanatepec	995	904	896
Jalatlaco	846	792	790
Villa de Oaxaca	768	711	707
Antequera	471	442	427
Mean	784	732	724
S.D.	± 143.5	±133.5	±129.0
S.E.	±18.5	±17.2	± 16.7

Bishopric Puebla

Amatlán de los Reyes	546	529	520
Apizaco	830	765	760
Ixtacamaxtitlan	629	579	572
Piaxtla	674	636	624
Huaquechula	762	704	687
Teotlalco	813	782	769
Tlalixcoyan	835	577	569
Cosamaloapan	619	600	593
Actopan	759	737	722
Atzacán	513	484	482
Apasapa	591	548	529
Mean	688	631	621
S.D.	±111.4	±96.6	±96.1
S.E.	±33.6	±29.1	±28.7

Bishopric Durango

Cuencamé	693	644	630
Valle de Suchil	682	640	634
Santa Bárbara	518	505	492
San Bartolomé	599	576	570
Cuatro Pueblos	712	651	643

Table 5.1 (cont.)

Parish	(1)	(2)	(3)
Parral	805	745	722
Maloya	564	513	506
San José Barrios	610	497	494
San Pedro Gallo	565	520	520
Zape	890	847	827
San Sebastián	513	483	474
Rosario	459	422	415
Bodiraguato	642	624	617
Tepehuanes	898	830	820
Bocos y Torrión	875	844	830
Chalchihuites	464	435	413
Culiacán	550	523	512
San Francisco Borja	826	794	775
Matachic	903	834	807
Norogachic	1,109	968	934
Mean	694	645	632
S.D.	±173.8	±159.6	±153.7
S.E.	±38.9	±35.7	±34.4
Total of 91 *parishes*			
Mean	753	701	691
S.D.	±153.0	±143.4	±139.8
S.E.	±15.9	±14.9	±14.6
C.V.	20.3	20.5	20.2

50. With the women it is easy to combine the ages from 16 to 50, but the children present a problem because we wish to eliminate those 5 and 6 years old, leaving the group 0–4 years. However, it is possible to arrive at a fair approximation.

We have the year-by-year age distribution for 60 parishes in Oaxaca from the census of 1777. There were 33,207 persons recorded as being 0–4 years of age and 45,897 who were 0–7 years of age. The ratio of the former to the latter group is 0.724. As a check on the method, the same procedure is possible for a contemporary census, for example that of 1960.[2] The ratio here is 0.715. The closeness of the figures may be fortuitous, but we shall not be far from the truth if we use 72 percent of the age group 0–7 in the Historia counts as corresponding to the group 0–4 in the parish counts of 1777.

There are only ten jurisdictions and provinces which can be treated in this manner, and these show a wide range of

[2]*Resumen general,* cuadro 7, p. 70 *et seq.*

values (see Table 5.2). Hence a mean is of little significance and is omitted. At the same time it is of interest to note the low ratios for Oaxaca and Mexico cities. The explanation probably lies in the migration of young women to the urban centers. Such an hypothesis is supported by the much higher ratios found in the jurisdiction of Antequera and the province of Mexico, both of which embraced substantial rural areas in addition to the cities.

Table 5.2

Ratio of 72 percent of children under 7 years of age to women aged 16 to 50; data from the census of 1793, summarized in the ramo de Historia

Region	Ratio: Children Females	Source
Oaxaca (city)	468	H : 522;259
Antequera (juris.)	629	H : 522;259
Mexico (city)	373	H : 523;145
Mexico (prov.)	656	H : 523;145
Tlaxcala (prov.)	606	H : 523;113
Guanajuato (prov.)	698	H : 523;76
Nuevo México (prov.)	787	H : 522;246
Durango (juris.)	500	H : 522;269
Antigua Calif. (prov.)	637	H : 522;267
Mérida (juris.)	945	H : 522;257

The calculation of fertility ratios for the period since 1895 is relatively simple. Each of the series of decennial censuses shows the distribution of the population by age and sex for the entire country and for each state separately. The only difficulty is the purely technical adjustment made at the 1930 census whereby the age groups were counted according to years completed by the individual instead of counting to the last birthdays. For example, under the old system, dating back to colonial times, the group 16–45 included those persons who had passed their sixteenth birthday to those who had just attained their forty-fifth birthday. Under the new system they would be designated 15–44, that is, those who had completed fifteen years to those who had completed their forty-fourth year. Clearly the same age group is indicated by both systems.

In Table 5.3, part A are given the ratios of children to reproductive females for the total population of Mexico at each

Table 5.3

Ratio of children 0–4 years of age to reproductive women, from the censuses of 1900 to 1960. In the censuses of 1900 and 1910, the women extend from 15 to 44 and 15 to 49 years of age. In 1921 and thereafter, the range is from 16 to 45 and 16 to 50 years.

A. Mexico, total population

Date	Ratio children 0–4/ females 15–44 or 16–45	Ratio children 0–4/ females 15–49 or 16–50	Source in Mexican Censuses
1900	730	661	*Res.* 1930, p. 45, cuadro 17
1910	741	675	*Ibid.*
1921	526	488	*Res.* 1930, p. 47, cuadro 19
1930	621	576	*Ibid.*
1940	630	580	*Res.* 1940, table, p. 1ff.
1950	693	625	*Res.* 1950, pp. 28–33
1960	788	726	*Res.* 1960, pp. 70ff.

B. Mexico by states

State	*Ratio : Children 0–4/Females*					
	1910		1930		1940	
	15–44	15–49	16–45	16–50	16–45	16–50
Aguascalientes	621	558	578	530	550	506
Baja Calif.-Norte			666	621	623	573
Baja Calif.-Sur	745	688	801	726	642	590
Campeche	624	578	640	595	593	551
Coahuila	677	620	611	565	657	604
Colima	781	705	447	415	521	480
Chiapas	865	789	707	666	742	690
Chihuahua	781	705	658	610	690	636
Distrito Federal	481	441	418	387	425	391
Durango	764	697	677	626	723	665
Guanajuato	738	657	663	611	675	593
Guerrero	851	778	653	611	663	613
Hidalgo	872	795	696	645	694	632
Jalisco	649	589	532	490	580	532
Mexico	814	736	719	660	698	630
Michoacán	697	634	620	575	644	592
Morelos	705	637	672	623	620	565
Nayarit (Tepic)	635	578	520	480	594	551
Nuevo León	752	687	584	540	632	581
Oaxaca	779	718	611	567	641	588
Puebla	759	688	651	600	644	589

Table 5.3 (cont.)

B. Mexico by states (*cont.*)

State	Ratio : Children 0–4/Females					
	1910		1930		1940	
	15–44	15–49	16–45	16–50	16–45	16–50
Querétaro	778	701	656	604	642	591
Quintana Roo	741	697	669	633	780	734
San Luis Potosí	800	717	703	660	720	663
Sinaloa	600	548	560	519	661	610
Sonora	710	653	582	540	602	537
Tabasco	900	834	818	770	864	800
Tamaulipas	793	728	596	554	615	572
Tlaxcala	822	742	739	675	717	653
Veracruz	849	782	668	625	660	612
Yucatán	649	594	529	492	583	533
Zacatecas	772	692	719	663	726	670
Mean	735	670	636	590	641	598
S.D.	±97.5	±89.5	±88.8	±80.6	±80.4	±74.5
S.E.	±17.5	±16.1	±15.7	±14.2	±14.2	±13.2
C.V.	13.3	13.4	14.0	13.7	12.5	12.4

	1950		1960	
	16–45	16–50	16–46	16–50
Aguascalientes	713	648	836	764
Baja Calif.-Norte	721	663	893	825
Baja Calif.-Sur	737	675	877	808
Campeche	687	634	774	718
Coahuila	695	635	794	729
Colima	698	640	841	773
Chiapas	765	711	805	754
Chihuahua	686	631	825	761
Distrito Federal	538	492	689	633
Durango	734	672	873	805
Guanajuato	724	660	848	781
Guerrero	698	645	768	715
Hidalgo	757	691	806	741
Jalisco	680	621	797	729
Mexico	749	678	856	788
Michoacán	708	650	820	756
Morelos	660	599	795	736
Nayarit	710	649	842	771
Nuevo León	646	592	739	679
Oaxaca	656	595	728	671
Puebla	694	632	787	722
Querétaro	740	641	860	779

Table 5.3 (cont.)

B. Mexico by state (cont.)

	1950		1960	
	16–45	16–50	16–46	16–50
Quintana Roo	914	852	965	908
San Luis Potosí	734	671	843	779
Sinaloa	730	675	834	773
Sonora	666	614	823	761
Tabasco	816	750	896	832
Tamaulipas	662	606	802	706
Tlaxcala	757	686	882	806
Veracruz	703	648	757	702
Yucatán	690	627	689	629
Zacatecas	780	717	907	837
Mean	714	654	820	755
S.D.	±61.2	±58.2	±61.4	±59.0
S.E.	±10.8	±10.3	±10.9	±10.4
C.V.	8.6	8.9	7.5	7.8

of the seven censuses between 1900 and 1960. Table 5.3, part B, shows similar ratios state by state for five of these censuses: 1910, 1930, 1940, 1950, and 1960. Certain features of these tabulations are worth brief comment.

The average number of children per 1,000 reproductive females as shown by the 1777 census is 753 for women 15–44 years old and 701 for women 15–49 years of age. The adjusted values obtained from the ramo de Historia for the 1793 census, if we omit Mexico City, give a range of 468 to 945 for women 16–50. For the total population of Mexico between 1900 and 1960 the comparable range with women 16–45 was 526 to 788 and for women 16–50, 488–726. Even though these are relatively crude figures, they should bring to light any significant change in the fertility pattern during an interval of nearly two centuries. No such change can be inferred from the data here presented.

It is apparent that the child-female ratios were relatively high prior to the Revolution of 1910 and that they fell sharply thereafter. From the low point in 1921, however, the rise was consistent until at 1950 and 1960 the previous level was reached or even exceeded. Two possible reasons may be suggested to account for this phenomenon. The first is the collapse of the statistical machinery during the Revolution. After the restoration of order when the fourth census was taken, the coverage was very poor, particularly in the more remote rural districts and in Mexico City. Improvement began immediately, and by 1960 the reporting was reasonably accurate. The second possible cause was the declining death rate, notably that of infants. The effect of this factor would be a rise in the apparent value of the fertility ratio even though no more live births actually occurred per female.

The improvement in census-taking procedures is manifested by the increase in the stability of the regional values of the ratios between the end of the colonial period and the present day. For the 91 parishes in 1777, the standard deviation of the ratios, expressed as a percentage of the mean, the coefficient of variation, was close to 20 percent. For the 31 states in 1910 it was down to 13.3–13.9, and for the 32 states in 1960 it had reached an all-time low of 7.5–7.8. Some, but not all, of the residual variability can be accounted for by the factor of internal migration, immigration to the large cities and to the Federal District, and emigration from the rural southern states. A careful study of the data from the 1960 census would no doubt elucidate the factors responsible for variation, but such a study is beyond the scope of the present essay.

Apart from the parish records already cited from 1777, together with a few summaries from the census of 1793, all of which specify usable age groups for both children and adult females, there exists a long series of summaries and compilations from the military census of 1793 and from the Matrícula de Tributaries of 1805. These tabulations, however, do not state in exact years but instead show groups or verbal categories based upon civil status or status within the tribute system. A precise fertility ratio such as we have been discussing previously is obviously impossible to calculate. The question of interest is whether any substitute can be found which will give some idea of the relation between young children and adult females and which can be used to compare the twentieth century censuses with those of the eighteenth century or even earlier.

Most of the reports of this type are scattered through the volumes of the ramo de Padrones of the AGN; a few are in the ramo de Historia.[3] The form is standardized; the population is first split according to sex, then divided according to a combination of age and civil status: niños, solteros, casados, viudos. For children we may then use the niños of both sexes, a group

[3]Vols. 72 and 73.

which runs to the age of puberty, about 14–15 for males and
12–13 for females. For reproductive women we have to take the
sum of solteras, casadas, and viudas. We get a child-woman
ratio, or the number of children of all ages up to puberty, per
1,000 women over the age of 15. Admittedly, this is the crudest
sort of formulation of its type and would not be considered
were anything else available.

The census of 1793, as reported in Padrones and Historia,
segregates the population according to race. Therefore, in
Table 5.4, part A, we give the child-woman ratios for the
Spanish-mestizo component, the gente de razón. In part B
are 49 entities with ratios for pardos. In part C are the few cases
(8 in all) which cover the Indians. The respective mean values of
the ratios are 1,177, 1,482, and 1,234.

The Matrícula of 1805 was a careful count of the entire
tributary class, including Indians and those blacks who were
held for tribute—negros y mulatos libres. The Indians were
divided into two groups, the sedentary population, or indios de
pueblo, and those who moved about, the laboríos y vagos.
We consolidate the two classes since we are interested in the
Indians only as an ethnic unit.

The number of children is read directly from the column
in the document headed "niños y niñas," and there is no reason
to believe that the age range differed significantly from that of
the niños in the summaries of Padrones or Historia. The adult
women include several of the stated categories. First are the
"viudas y solteras," second a number equal to that shown for
"casados con sus iguales," in other words, the wives of these
casados. Third, we have the wives of the "casados sin edad"
(married men under 18), and fourth the "mujeres de los casados
con otra casta" (wives of men married outside their race). The
sum of these four classes corresponds to the solteras, casadas,
and viudas of the 1793 census.

In the summary by provinces of the Matrícula eleven
provinces are listed. The ratios of children to women are given
here in Table 5.4, parts D and E, for Indians and for negros y
mulatos libres, respectively. The mean ratios are 1,365 and
1,601.

At first glance the five means derived from the data in
Table 5.4 appear to differ depending upon the racial group
concerned. The gente de razón with 66 cases gives 1,177; the
two sets of ratios for indios show 1,234 and 1,365. The pardos

Table 5.4

Ratio of children to adult women, expressed as number of children per 1,000 women, for various racial groups, as found in documents of the late eighteenth century. The sources are the ramo de Padrones (P) and the ramo de Historia with their respective vol. and p. no., both reporting results of the 1793 census and the Matrícula of 1805.

A. *Gente de razón*

Entity	Type of Entity	Ratio: Children/ Women	Source
Aguascalientes	Jurisdiction	867	P : 5;1
Oaxaca	City	840	P : 13;292
Colima	Partido	1,072	P : 11;668
Motines	Jurisdiction	1,210	P : 21;321
Amula	Partido	1,120	H : 72;202
Autlán	Partido	1,172	H : 73;127
Ahuacatlán	Partido	899	P : 14;188
Tulancingo	Jurisdiction	1,250	P : 1;338
Ixmiquilpan	Jurisdiction	1,161	P : 2;90
Pachuca	City	1,247	P : 2;211
Coatepec-Chalco	Pueblo	1,233	P : 3;24
Actopan	Jurisdiction	1,412	P : 3;95
Tehuacán	City	911	P : 3;318
Huejutla	Pueblo	1,350	P : 3;406
Cuautitlán	Jurisdiction	1,282	P : 4;241
Ápam	Pueblo	1,183	P : 4;369
Coyoacán	Jurisdiction	1,011	P : 6;115
Tacuba	Jurisdiction	1,281	P : 6;299
San Cristóbal	Jurisdiction	1,450	P : 6;361
Tula	Jurisdiction	1,140	P : 7;406
Cuautla Amilpas	Jurisdiction	937	P : 8;107
San Juan de los Llanos	Jurisdiction	1,089	P : 8;229
Chicontepec	Pueblo	1,411	P : 12;25
Charo	Villa	1,024	P : 12;43
Huamelula	Pueblo	1,113	P : 12;65
Tochimilco	Pueblo	1,012	P : 12;112
Querétaro	Intendencia	944	P : 12;141
Otumba	Jurisdiction	1,332	P : 12;203
Lerma	City	1,311	P : 12;244
Cuitzeo	Jurisdiction	1,334	P : 16;66
Chilapa	Jurisdiction	1,206	P : 16;194
Acapulco	Jurisdiction	1,109	P : 16;244
Tixtla	Jurisdiction	1,235	P : 17;26
Tetepango	Jurisdiction	1,586	P : 18;101
Tamiahua	Jurisdiction	1,092	P : 18;184
Tamapache	Pueblo	1,200	P : 18;178
Ihualapa	Jurisdiction	1,528	P : 18;230
Teotihuacán	Jurisdiction	1,165	P : 18;341
Orizaba	Villa	792	P : 19;325

Table 5.4 (cont.)

A. Gente de razón (cont.)

Entity	Type of Entity	Ratio: Children/ Women	Source
Zempoala	Jurisdiction	1,268	P:20;33
Jalapa	Pueblo	1,028	P:20;245
Tlapa	Pueblo	1,555	P:21;52
Toluca	City	972	P:21;260
Tlaxcala	City	1,291	P:22;403
Acámbaro	Pueblo	909	P:23;217
Atlixco	Jurisdiction	1,222	P:25;85
Huejotzingo	Jurisdiction	1,276	P:27;141
Izúcar	Pueblo	1,297	P:28;84
Chietla	Pueblo	1,338	P:28;184
San Felipe	Villa	1,094	P:34;253
San Juan del Río	Jurisdiction	1,148	P:35;587
Tepeaca	Partido	1,522	P:38;541
Pénjamo	Pueblo	1,127	P:41;294
Texcoco	Jurisdiction	1,031	P:43;153
Zumpango	Jurisdiction	1,365	H:72;165
Xochimilco	Jurisdiction	1,169	P:29;3
Jicayán	Province	1,770	H:72;197
Jiquilpan	Jurisdiction	2,453	H:73;507
Yucatán	Province	1,159	H:523;9
Dolores	Jurisdiction	878	P:24;114
Celaya	City	982	P:26;926
Silao	Jurisdiction	1,026	P:42;327
San Miguel el Grande	Jurisdiction	882	P:36;264
Irapuato	Jurisdiction	927	P:37;448
Guanajuato	City	629	P:30;839
Puebla	Jurisdiction	645	H:73;122
Mean		1,177	

B. Pardos

Entity	Type of Entity	Ratio: Children/ Women	Source
Aguascalientes	Jurisdiction	1,558	P:5;1
Oaxaca	City	851	P:13;292
Motines	Jurisdiction	1,593	P:21;364
Ahuacatlán	Partido	1,236	H:523;75
Tulancingo	Jurisdiction	1,218	P:1;375
Pachuca	City	1,385	P:2;259
Tehuacán	City	1,377	P:3;318
Huejutla	Pueblo	1,596	P:3;406

Table 5.4 (cont.)

B. Pardos (cont.)

Entity	Type of Entity	Ratio: Children/ Women	Source
Cuautitlán	Jurisdiction	1,976	P : 4 ; 241
Apam	Pueblo	1,497	P : 4 ; 398
Coyoacán	Jurisdiction	1,830	P : 6 ; 143
Tacuba	Jurisdiction	1,345	P : 6 ; 314
Valle San Francisco	Pueblo	1,591	H : 72 ; 65
Tula	Jurisdiction	1,515	P : 7 ; 406
Cuautla Amilpas	Jurisdiction	1,101	P : 8 ; 264
Chicontepec	Pueblo	1,624	P : 12 ; 32
Huamelula	Pueblo	1,465	P : 12 ; 75
Querétaro	Intendencia	1,168	P : 12 ; 141
Otumba	Jurisdiction	1,324	P : 12 ; 202
Cuitzeo	Jurisdiction	1,597	P : 16 ; 106
Chilapa	Jurisdiction	2,096	P : 16 ; 212
Acapulco	Jurisdiction	1,385	P : 16 ; 429
Tixtla	Jurisdiction	1,531	P : 17 ; 182
Tetepango	Jurisdiction	1,499	P : 18 ; 101
Tamiahua	Jurisdiction	1,057	P : 18 ; 124
Tamapache	Pueblo	1,422	P : 18 ; 178
Ihualapa	Jurisdiction	2,114	P : 18 ; 232
Teotihuacán	Jurisdiction	1,181	P : 18 ; 351
Orizaba	Villa	882	P : 19 ; 425
Zempoala	Jurisdiction	1,716	P : 20 ; 57
Jalapa	Pueblo	1,190	P : 20 ; 337
Tlapa	Pueblo	1,728	P : 21 ; 94
Toluca	City	1,016	P : 21 ; 263
Tlaxacala	City	1,788	P : 22 ; 405
Acámbaro	Pueblo	1,379	P : 23 ; 341
Atlixco	Jurisdiction	1,238	P : 25 ; 87, 99, 105
Huejotzingo	Jurisdiction	1,850	P : 27 ; 143, 45, 149
Izúcar	Pueblo	1,950	P : 28 ; 86, 97, 135
Chietla	Pueblo	1,674	P : 28 ; 186
San Juan del Río	Jurisdiction	1,879	P : 35 ; 671
Tepeaca	Partido	2,220	P : 38 ; 569
Ostotipac	Partido	1,366	H : 73 ; 125
Jicayán	Province	2,067	H : 72 ; 197
Jiquilpan	Jurisdiction	1,931	H : 73 ; 507
Yucatán	Province	1,590	H : 523 ; 9
Celaya	City	1,346	P : 26 ; 1175
Irapuato	Jurisdiction	1,197	P : 37 ; 601
Guanajuato	City	992	P : 33 ; 672
Puebla	Jurisdiction	543	H : 73 ; 122
Mean		1,482	

Table 5.4 (cont.)

C. Indios

Entity	Type of Entity	Ratio: Children/ Women	Source
Oaxaca	City	1,045	P:13;292
Querétaro	Intendencia	1,056	P:12;141
Xochimilco	Jurisdiction	1,122	P:29;3
Jicayán	Province	1,686	H:72;197
Jiquilpan	Jurisdiction	1,191	H:73;507
Jalapa	Jurisdiction	1,345	H:72;239
Yucatán	Province	1,443	H:523;9
Puebla	Jurisdiction	987	H:73;122
Mean		1,234	

D. Indios from the Matricula of 1805

Province	Ratio; Children/ Women	Province	Ratio; Children/ Women
Mexico	1,244	S.L. Potosí	1,375
Puebla	1,297	Guadalajara	1,195
Veracruz	1,382	Zacatecas	1,463
Oaxaca	1,356	Arizpe	1,658
Valladolid	1,039	Mérida	1,387
Guanajuato	1,614	Mean	1,365

E. Negros y mulatos libres from the Matricula

Province	Ratio; Children/ Women	Province	Ratio: Children/ Women
Mexico	1,410	S.L. Potosí	1,676
Pubela	1,486	Guadalajara	1,381
Veracruz	1,414	Zacatecas	1,496
Oaxaca	1,834	Arizpe	1,511
Valladolid	1,470	Mérida	1,928
Guanajuato	2,001	Mean	1,601

and negros y mulatos libres are highest, 1,482 and 1,601. Are these differences real, or are they only random results, dependent upon the operation of unknown but irrelevant factors? We can apply only a simple test. An analysis of variance with the five groups yields for F, 10.35. If the two sets of Indians and the two sets of pardos are consolidated, the value of F for the resulting three groups is 19.47. Both these values of F are highly significant. There can be no doubt, therefore, that a racial difference existed, but regarding the mediating factors, these data give us no further enlightenment.

The censuses of the twentieth century contain full tabulations of the population according to age. These have already been considered. For comparison with the verbal categories of the late eighteenth century, there remains only the classification by civil status. From 1900 through 1960 the younger fraction of both sexes was consolidated under the heading "menores de edad" (minores), and these may be regarded as equivalent to the niños of the earlier documents. In 1960 this group was omitted completely. Consequently, this census is for the present purpose best left out of consideration. The females can be determined by taking the total of the various adult groups, solteras, viudas, and casadas by several types of ceremony. The results of these operations are shown in Table 5.5.

The figures extend from 1,026 to 1,313 menores de edad per 1,000 adult females and fall within the range found for niños per 1,000 females in 1790–1805. One can conclude, therefore, that in so far as these ratios have any validity, they show no clear change in child-woman relationship in Mexico during a span of nearly two centuries.

Table 5.5

The ratio of children to adult women as found
in seven present-day censuses.

Date	Ratio: Children/ Women	Source in Mexican Censuses
1900	1,026	*Res.*, 1930, p. 50, cuadro 21
1910	1,072	*Ibid.*
1921	1,166	*Ibid.*
1930	1,198	*Ibid.*
1940	1,296	*Res.*, 1940, table, p. 1ff.
1950	1,313	*Res.*, 1950, p. 48, cuadro 4

Chapter VI

Mortality in Mexico Prior to 1850

Chapters IV and V have shown that natality in Mexico throughout its history from the conquest to the present has been high and that if a decline has occurred, it has been very slight. On the other hand, it is common knowledge that Mexico, together with all its Latin-American neighbors, has witnessed a profound fall in the death rate. The full force of this reduction has been felt only since 1900, or even since 1920. Consequently, a study of the phenomenon will necessarily require analysis of the Civil Register, which since approximately 1870 has been the primary and almost the only available source of data concerning mortality. The death records are more nearly complete than the birth records and provide information concerning age and cause of death. It follows that the century from 1870 to 1970 must be treated quite independently of the remainder of Mexican history, and we shall leave it for separate consideration.

A problem of broad demographic interest relates to the date at which the modern decline in mortality began. In Europe a perceptible drop in death rates can be detected as far back as the late eighteenth century, and clear evidence of the trend is apparent in several countries by the early nineteenth century. In Latin America, and specifically in Mexico, we should look for indications of a change by the middle of the nineteenth century. Consequently, it is desirable to examine mortality data for the period prior to 1850.

The possible sources of knowledge are those described for natality. Before the War of Independence there exist only the parish archives, in which deaths as well as births (that is, baptisms) and marriages were recorded. In addition, there are a few summaries from the 1793 census in the ramo de Padrones in the AGN. After 1820 the files of state documents, particularly the memorias of the governors, provide a good deal of information derived from reports by parish priests until the period

1850–1860, at which time the clerical records cease to be of value. Finally, there is the excellent compilation of Longinos Banda embracing the half-century from 1801 to 1855, which he extracted from the church records of Jalisco, but unfortunately it covers only that state.

The parish books which we examined in 1956 in the Mixteca Alta give total number of deaths by year for each town and for a great many years. Included also are a number of files which cover entire parishes. We were able to excerpt some but not all of these.

It is not feasible to attempt the calculation of crude death rates, first, because the number of cases in which an exact correspondence could be secured between deaths in a certain year and the population of the entity in that year is very limited and, second, because the number of deaths in any short period of time was subject to wide fluctuation. These restrictions hold for the parish records of the Mixteca Alta and in even greater measure for the other three principal sources. We are therefore obliged to adopt a substitute procedure, one which entails the comparison of deaths not with total population but with births during an identical but limited period of time, five years where possible, one year if necessary. As a check on the validity of the birth reports and because the appropriate data are frequently and readily available, we have calculated the relation of births to marriages as well as to deaths.

As a preliminary study of the clerical records from the Mixteca Alta, we compared the relative variability or its converse, the stability of the births and deaths in that region. To do this we first examined our transcripts of the books in the ten parishes visited and selected runs or consecutive series of at least 20 annual totals of births in each political or clerical entity listed : towns, rumbos, and whole parishes. There were 45 such entities and 96 series of from 20 to 50 years of annual birth totals. Then, with each series, we calculated the mean number of births per year, together with its standard deviation. We expressed the latter as the coefficient of variation, that is, the standard deviation written as a percentage of the mean. Finally, we averaged the means of the 96 series, and those of the corresponding coefficients of variation. As a result, we found that the 96 series had an average of 26.9 births per year, and a mean C.V. of 30.3. In other words, the average standard deviation of a 20–50-year series of births was 30.3 percent of the mean.

When we proceeded in a similar manner with 56 sequences of deaths, we found the average number of deaths per year to be 18.7 and the average coefficient of variation to be 96.9.

When expressed in this form the variability of numbers of deaths per year is more than three times that of the births. Therefore, it is reasonable to compare regions and time intervals by relating the deaths which occurred to the births instead of to the existing population, which, indeed, in most cases is unknown. This is most easily done for any specific place and time by taking the numerical ratio of births to deaths.

The cause of the high variability in numbers of deaths per year is not far to seek. Except for long-term trends, births and marriages in a more or less unsophisticated society such as that of colonial Mexico tend to follow the population closely. They are, of course, subject to local conditions and to errors in recording, but within these limits they are relatively stable. Deaths, however, are subject to changes in the pattern of public health and are particularly influenced by epidemics. Repeatedly, in all the death records up to the nineteenth century, a town or parish shows a series of low annual death totals, representing old age and endemic maladies. Then, without warning, comes an enormous jump in the number during one or two years. This explosion is usually followed by a return to the former low level. These wide and rapid shifts within a year's time results in extreme statistical variability.

For the Mixteca Alta the results are consolidated in Table 6.1. Here are shown three ratios: births (baptisms) to marriages, births (baptisms) to deaths, and child deaths to total deaths. For each ratio the records were divided into fifty-year periods, and the individual items from town or parish were assembled for each half-century between 1651 and 1850. Then, within each half-century, the corresponding births and marriages, or births and deaths, when they were present in the record, were totalled by five-year periods, beginning with 1651–1655, 1656–1660, etc. In a few cases it was necessary to reduce the interval to four years or extend it to six in order to utilize all the figures possible. To illustrate our procedure, to arrive at the ratio of births to marriages during the half-century 1651–1700, there were twenty-one cases, for each of which, at the same locality and in the same five-year periods between 1651 and 1700, we could get a total of both births and marriages. We took the ratio of the totals in each of the twenty-one cases

Table 6.1

Ratio of births (baptisms) and deaths in ten parishes
of the Mixteca Alta between 1651 and 1850.

Date	No. of Cases	Mean	S.D.	S.E.
		Ratio : Births/Marriages		
1651–1700	21	4.37	1.172	0.156
1701–1750	123	4.37	1.445	0.130
1751–1800	226	5.10	1.840	0.122
1801–1850	179	4.66	1.630	0.122

Values of t for pairs of periods :
    1651–1700 : 1701–1750=0.00
    1701–1750 : 1751–1800=3.77
    1751–1800 : 1801–1850=2.49

Date	No. of Cases	Mean	S.D.	S.E.
		Ratio : Births/Deaths		
1651–1700	32	2.36	1.587	0.281
1701–1750	45	2.03	1.050	0.157
1751–1800	73	1.91	1.815	0.212
1801–1850	104	1.61	0.775	0.076

Values of t for pairs of periods :
    1651–1700 : 1701–1750=1.10
    1701–1750 : 1751–1800=0.40
    1751–1800 : 1801–1850=1.40

Date	No. of Cases	Mean	S.D.	S.E.
		Ratio : Child Deaths/Total Deaths		
1651–1700	21	0.53	0.136	0.030
1701–1750	30	0.60	0.142	0.026
1751–1800	20	0.51	0.135	0.030
1801–1850	33	0.53	0.107	0.019

Values of t for pairs of periods :
    1651–1700 : 1701–1750=1.76
    1701–1750 : 1751–1800=2.24
    1751–1800 : 1801–1850=0.60

and then calculated the mean, the standard deviation, and the
standard error. The same procedure was adopted for the ratio
of births to deaths and for that of child deaths to total deaths.
With regard to the latter ratio an explanation is necessary.
In some of the parish books, part of the time the priest entered

the actual age of the deceased. In others he distinguished only between *párvulos* and *adultos*. In still others there is no differentiation. We can use the segregation of párvulos because quite uniformly this term was applied to the pre-pubertal group—the females below thirteen and the males below fifteen years of age. These limits may then be applied to the records which state the actual age at death. It will be noted in Table 6.1 that we found a total of 104 cases in which children could be thus set apart from adults.

The mean values obtained, 0.5 to 0.6, are of interest per se. However, they cannot be compared with the other tabulations for two reasons. First, the state reports in our possession so rarely indicate the number of child or infant deaths that as a whole they are useless for this purpose. Second, the age breakdown, where given by Banda, runs from 0 to 9 years inclusive. Since the Mixteca figures must apply to those aged 0 to 13 or 0 to 15, the two sets of data are not comparable numerically without extraordinary adjustment and correction.

If we now revert to the ratio of births to marriages, we see that the mean values of ratios for the half-century periods differ by perceptible amounts. The statistical significance of these differences is shown by the values of t calculated according to consecutive pairs of periods. The high value of 5.10 for the interval 1751–1800 appears to vary significantly from that for the period preceding and that for the one following. Although it must be remembered that the contributing entities were not always the same and the selection therefore subject to local influence, nevertheless, there may have been a real increase between 1751 and 1800 of births relative to marriages. If so, we have no explanation to offer.

The ratio of births to deaths shows consistently lower values than does the ratio of births to marriages. This finding is to be anticipated since we know that the population was increasing throughout the entire two centuries concerned. The most interesting feature of the tabulation, however, is the uniform decline in the ratio from 2.36 to 1.61. The magnitude of the change is not great, and the values for t for consecutive periods are of no significance. On the other hand, the change from 2.36 to 1.61 is definitely significant, for the value of t for the two half-century periods 1651–1700 and 1801–1850 is 3.61.

The meaning of this movement is difficult to appreciate.

Part of it may be due to the manner of sampling, as is probably true of the fluctuations in birth to marriage ratio, but the consistent fall of the birth to death ratio cannot be thus explained completely and may represent a real phenomenon. If so, it indicates a rise in mortality with reference to natality, for the denominator is increasing at the expense of the numerator. However, there is no other evidence of which we are aware for a steady increase in mortality over so long a period. Indeed it is well-established that the total population of this area, the Mixteca Alta, was consistently rising from the seventeenth to the nineteenth century.

Whether or not we are dealing with an artifact produced by the mode of accumulating data or with an actual change in the birth to death ratio, it is certainly clear that the mortality was not diminishing. This is the point with which we are most acutely concerned, for it enables us to conclude with reasonable confidence that the modern decrease in mortality rate had not made itself manifest in the Mixteca Alta prior to 1850. In so far as the parish records are valid, they indicate that the trend, if there was any, took the opposite direction.

Table 6.2 gives the same ratios as are in Table 6.1. It contains the figures for twenty-one localities which are listed in various volumes of the ramo de Padrones. In this series there

Table 6.2

Ratio of births and deaths as reported for 21 localities in the ramo de Padrones from the census of 1739. The duration of the periods involved is not stated but includes at least one full year.

Locality	Ratio: Births/ Marriages	Ratio: Births/ Deaths	Ratio: Child/ Total Deaths	Padrones (vol.)
Coatepec de los Costales	3.97	1.15	0.65	10
Apaxtla	3.52	0.91	0.54	10
Ixcateopan	4.19	1.09	0.56	9
Ixtapa	4.32	0.97	0.61	9
Alahuixtlán	3.81	0.99	0.48	9
Zacualpan, 1791–1796	3.85	1.38	0.55	51
Zacualpan, 1797–1801	3.72	1.40	0.43	51
Ixmiquilpan	5.45	2.21	0.34	44
Salvatierra (city)	3.03	3.12	0.23	45
Ecatepec	6.20	0.78	0.39	47
Jonacahuacán	5.85	1.78	0.34	47

Table 6.2 (cont.)

Locality	Ratio: Births/ Marriages	Ratio: Births/ Deaths	Ratio: Child/ Total Deaths	Padrones (vol.)
Apetatitlán	6.14	1.37	0.52	48
San Dionisio Huamantla	4.94	1.23	0.54	48
San Luis Huamantla	5.98	1.33	0.59	48
Tetla	6.47	1.31	0.84	48
Tlaxcala (city)	4.51	0.96	0.48	48
Zumpantepec	5.00	1.37	0.62	48
Ixtenco	9.29	1.30	0.50	48
Texcaltitlán	5.53	1.14	0.62	49
Minas del Cardonal	5.26	1.28	0.56	50
Chilcuautla	4.24	1.05	0.47	50
Mean	5.01	1.34	0.52	
S.D.	±1.405	±0.508	±0.130	
S.E.	±0.307	±0.111	±0.028	

occurs occasionally a very brief summary for a certain locality stating total births, total marriages, child and adult deaths. It is probable that with the exception of Zacualpan, each one covers a single year. The means of the ratio of births to marriages and of that for child to total deaths are very close to those shown in Table 6.1 for the Mixteca Alta. The ratio of births to total deaths is low, 1.34, as compared with 1.91 in the Mixteca. The most acceptable explanation for this discrepancy is that the census of *ca.* 1793, which was the basis for the reports in Padrones, was taken in the year of an epidemic, perhaps smallpox, which ravaged central Mexico during the 1790s. At any rate, here is a good example of the danger of using death records for only a short interval of time.

Table 6.3 rests upon a much broader foundation than Table 6.2. Here are listed the ratios for over one hundred localities in eleven states, well-distributed throughout Mexico, and covering the period between 1820 and 1850. Most of the entities are partidos or districts, but there are several series of municipalities and a few states entire. Except for Durango, most of the localities provide figures for births, marriages, and deaths, but with no segregation of children. During these three decades the state authorities were still depending upon the clergy.

Table 6.3

Ratios of births and deaths as reported in state censuses and other documents for the period 1810–1850. The time periods and the type of locality vary and are indicated in the first two columns.

Date	Locality	Ratio: Births/ Marriages	Ratio: Births/ Deaths	Source
1833	Chihuahua (state)			
	Aldama (partido)	13.68	2.43	Pedro García Conde,
	Allende	6.09	2.85	"Ensayo estadístico,"
	Belleza	7.27	3.51	*SMGEB* 1a ép., V
	Batopilas	3.31	2.39	(1857), 274
	Chihuahua	7.52	2.09	
	Concepción	3.64	2.04	
	Cusihuiriáchic	6.08	2.79	
	Galeana	3.86	3.19	
	Hidalgo	10.20	1.55	
	Jiménez	7.67	3.18	
	Paso	5.28	1.75	
	Rosales	7.00	4.39	
1842–1846	Colima (city)	5.99	1.19	*Ensayo estad. de Coli-*
1846	Almoloya (villa)	4.13	1.42	*ma*, pp. 26–28
1843–1849	Durango (city)	6.06	1.10	José F. Ramírez, "No-
1848–1849	Durango (state)			ticias historicas,"
	Durango (partido)		1.12	*SMGEB*, 1a ép., V
	Nombre de Dios		1.96	(1857), 55; Escudero,
	San Juan del Río		2.30	*Noticias*, p. 34, from
	Mezquital		2.36	Gov., Mem., 1848–
	San Dimas		0.81	1849
	Papasquiaro		1.94	
	El Oro		1.91	
	Indé		4.58	
	Cuencamé		1.81	
	Mapimí		0.79	
	Nazas		2.32	
1825–1829	Guanajuato (state)		1.49	José G. Romero, "No-
1830–1833	"		0.78	ticias," *SMGEB*, 1a
1825	"		.	ép., IX (1862),93;Gov.,
	Guanajuato (munic.)	3.64	0.72	*Mem.* 1824–1825,
	Celaya	4.29	0.82	Table 1
	Acámbaro	3.45	0.68	
	León	4.28	0.93	
	Silao	2.75	1.07	
	Apaseo	3.06	0.89	
	San Felipe	4.77	1.45	
	San Luis de la Paz	3.85	1.75	
	Casas Viejas	3.73	2.20	

Table 6.3 (cont.)

Date	Locality	Ratio : Births/ Marriages	Ratio : Births/ Deaths	Source
	Chamacuero	3.48	3.55	
	Salvatierra	4.13	1.21	
	Piedra Gorda	2.21	1.07	
	Irapuato	2.65	2.60	
	Yuriria	3.58	2.85	
	Valle de Santiago	4.13	1.55	
	Amoles	2.76	2.63	
	Jerécuaro	3.63	1.49	
	Huaje	2.91	1.75	
	Neutla	2.45	1.22	
	Rincón	3.43	3.67	
	San Juan de la Vega	1.88	2.00	
	Santa Cruz	3.89	1.16	
	Xichú	5.85	2.28	
	Salamanca	3.86	2.29	
	San Miguel Grande	2.98	1.94	
	Hidalgo	2.12	1.61	
	Pénjamo	3.37	2.86	
	San Miguel Octopan	4.17	1.75	
1825	Tulancingo (district)	2.08	1.49	Mexico (state), Gob.,
1833	Mexico (state)			*Ensayo,* cuadro 3
	Cuernavaca (prefec-			Gov. *Mem.* 1833–
	ture)	5.42	0.35	1834, cuadro 4
	Este	6.46	0.67	
	Huejutla	4.27	0.55	
	Oeste	6.92	0.80	
	Sultepec	4.88	0.61	
	Toluca	5.59	0.85	
	Tasco		0.64	
	Tulancingo	7.75	1.13	
	Tula	5.76	1.08	
1834	Acapulco	2.29	1.05	Gov., *Mem.* 1834–1835,
	Cuernavaca	3.41	1.21	cuadro 3
	Este	2.18	1.60	
	Oeste	3.85	1.68	
	Sultepec	3.46	2.18	
	Tasco	3.05	2.09	
	Toluca	4.18	2.00	
	Tula	4.80	2.16	
	Tulancingo	5.38	2.05	
1826–1828	Michoacán (state)			Ignacio Piquero,
	Norte (district)	4.81	2.10	"Apuntes," *SMGEB,*
	Oriente	3.48	1.71	1a ép., I(3rd ed., 1861),
	Sur	3.39	1.28	162
	Poniente	5.66	2.43	

Table 6.3 (cont.)

Date	Locality	Ratio : Births/ Marriages	Ratio : Births/ Deaths	Source
1842	Norte	7.28	2.08	Ibid., I, 163
	Sur	4.58	1.35	
	Oriente	4.57	1.79	
1849	Morelos (state)			Gov., Mem. 1850,
	Cuernavaca (district)	3.73	1.34	cuadro 2
	Morelos	4.41	1.61	
	Yautepec	2.79	1.27	
	Jonacatepec	4.87	1.54	
	Tetecala	3.97	1.20	
1829	Puebla (state)			Gov., Mem. 1829–
	Atlixco (partido)	5.06	1.89	1830, cuadro 1
	Chiautla	3.01	1.48	
	Huauchinango	4.51	2.38	
	Matamoros	2.49	1.22	
	Puebla	7.08	1.12	
	Tlapa	4.35	1.91	
	Tuxpan	4.66	2.62	
	Tepeji	4.42	1.83	
1822–1826	Querétaro (state)			Raso, p. 99
	Querétaro (munic.)	5.74	1.50	
	San Juan	4.45	1.43	
	Amealco	3.64	1.83	
	Tolimán	4.20	1.89	
	Jalpan	3.50	2.00	
	Cadereyta	4.53	2.54	
1822–1826	Querétaro (state)	4.67	1.66	Raso, p. 101
1827–1831	"	5.54	1.96	
1832–1836	"	4.98	1.93	
1837–1841	"	5.14	1.96	
1842–1844	"	4.72	2.38	
1844	"	4.80	2.40	Raso, p. 112
1845	"	6.10	2.33	Estad. del dept., p. 6
1830	Tabasco (state)			Mestre Ghigliazzi,
	San Juan Bautista			I, 472
	(parish)	8.65	1.82	
	Nacajuca	4.36	0.97	
	Tacotalpa	12.37	2.16	
	Teapa	2.54	1.11	
	Jalapa	6.16	2.70	
	Macuspana	5.54	1.25	
	Cunduacán	7.62	1.53	
	Jalpa	4.83	1.13	

Table 6.3 (cont.)

Date	Locality	Ratio : Births/ Marriages	Ratio : Births/ Deaths	Source
1816–1849	Veracruz (state, by canton)			Each canton is total of
1830	Orozaba		0.88	towns in *Estad. del esta-*
1830	Córdoba		0.95	*do, passim.*
1830	Cosamaloapan		1.21	
1825–1830	Acayucan		1.57	
1816–1820	Acayucan		1.17	
1824–1828	Acayucan		3.06	
1830	Acayucan	4.41	1.27	
1830	San Andrés Tuxtla	7.70	1.39	
1830	Huimanguillo	5.08	2.08	
1830	Jalacingo	4.80	1.22	
1844–1849	Tuxpan	5.27	1.56	M. Ramírez, (1854),
1846–1849	Chicontepec	4.64	1.66	"Estadadistica," *SMG-*
1836	Cosamaloapan		1.70	*EB,* 1*a* ép., IV(1854),
1836	Córdoba		2.05	cuadros 4 and 25; *Ibid.,* table opp. p. 111; *Ibid.,* pp. 73 ff.
All localities				
Number		108	130	
Mean		4.74	1.76	
S.D.		±1.296	±0.753	
S.E.		±0.125	±0.066	

There are 108 values for the ratio of births to marriages. The mean is 4.74, quite close to the mean of 4.66 (Table 6.1) obtained for the Mixteca Alta. For the ratio of births to deaths we have 130 cases, with a mean of 1.76. This value lies slightly above that of 1.61 (Table 6.1) found for the Mixteca. The value of *t* for the two means (see Table 6.5) is 1.49, of no significance.

Table 6.4 lists the ratios provided by the birth and death figures in the book by Longinos Banda (1873) for the state of Jalisco. Banda used clerical records exclusively. The localities are mostly parishes and municipalities, organized according to canton, together with a number of ratios for the entire cantons themselves. The time span extends from 1800 to 1855. The mean ratio of births to marriages, with 86 cases, is 5.34, for ratio of births to deaths, with 186 cases is 1.87. The former is high; the latter is not far from that obtained with the parish records of the Mixteca Alta, 1.61.

Table 6.4

Ratios of births and deaths in the state of Jalisco from 1801 to 1855 as reported by Longinos Banda. Banda derived his figures from clerical records, as did the state government up to the decade 1850–1860.

A. Parishes and towns				
Date	*Local Entity*	*Ratio :* *Births/* *Marriages*	*Ratio :* *Births/* *Deaths*	*Ratio :* *Children 0–9/* *Deaths Total* *Pop.*
	Guadalajara (canton)			
1801–1805	Mejicalcingo	5.33	1.95	0.54
1806–1810	,,	4.23	2.08	0.36
1811–1815	,,	3.44	1.14	0.59
1816–1820	,,	4.78	1.77	0.42
1821–1825	,,	4.55	1.17	0.43
1826–1830	,,	4.22	1.04	0.51
1831–1835	,,	4.90	0.98	0.44
1836–1840	,,	6.51	1.25	0.52
1841–1845	,,	7.00	1.31	0.53
1846–1850	,,	6.01	1.00	0.50
1851–1854	,,	7.75	0.89	0.58
1811–1820	Zapopan	3.36		
1831–1840	,,	3.20		
1841–1850	,,	4.85		
1851–1854	,,	3.39		
1823–1827	Tlajomulco		1.76	
1828–1832	,,		1.72	
1833–1837	,,		1.70	
1845–1850	Tala	3.58	2.16	0.23
1851–1854	,,	3.09	3.17	0.20
1852–1856	Guadalajara (city)	5.31	1.03	
1852–1856	San Pedro	5.08	1.57	
1852–1856	Tonalá	4.13	1.47	
	Lagos (canton)			
1834–1838	San Miguel	5.67	2.26	
	San Juan		1.93	
	Encarnación		1.82	
	Lagos		1.24	
	Adobes		2.65	
	Talpa		1.51	
	Teocaltiche		1.22	
	Mexticacán		1.69	
	Paso de Sotos		1.97	
	La Barca (canton)			
1834–1838	La Barca		2.46	
	Atotonilco		1.55	
	Ayo el Chico		1.28	

Table 6.4 (cont.)

A. Parishes and towns (*cont.*)

Date	Local Entity	Ratio: Births/ Marriages	Ratio: Births/ Deaths	Ratio: Children 0–9/ Deaths Total Pop.
	La Barca (*cont'd.*)			
	Portezuelo		2.31	
	Jamay		0.98	
	Ocotlán		2.38	
	Poncitlán		1.75	
	Tototlán		1.99	
	Zapotlán del Rey		1.57	
	Tepatitlán		1.97	
	Acatic		1.93	
	Arandas		1.91	
	Cañadas		2.10	
	Jesus María		2.07	
	Sayula (canton)			
1834–1838	Sayula		1.49	
	Amacueca		1.53	
	Zacoalco		2.16	
	Tizapán		2.54	
	Teocuitatlán		2.35	
	Atoyac		2.07	
	Tapalpa		3.31	
	Chiquilistlán		2.02	
	San Gabriel		2.43	
	Tuxcacuesco		3.08	
	Zapotitlán		3.49	
	Tolimán		3.11	
	Totzín		1.19	
	Teutlán		1.85	
	Mazatlán		2.79	
	Tetapán		1.66	
	Copala		2.86	
	Tonaya		1.17	
	Zapotlán		2.41	
	Zapotiltic		3.04	
	Tuxpan		1.95	
	Tonila		2.69	
	Tamazula		2.01	
	Tecaltitlán		2.47	
	Pihuamo		3.18	
	Jilotlán		2.32	
	Quitupan		1.39	
	Atemajac		3.50	
1849–1854	Sayula	5.45	1.49	0.39
1845–1849	Zapotlán	4.92	1.55	0.50
1850–1854	,,	3.26	1.22	0.33

Table 6.2 (cont.)

A. Parishes and towns (cont.)

Date	Local Entity	Ratio: Births/ Marriages	Ratio: Births/ Deaths	Ratio: Children 0–9/ Deaths Total Pop.
1845–1849	San Sebastián		1.46	0.59
1850–1854	"		1.25	0.41
1802–1806	Santa Ana	7.20	2.13	
1807–1811	"	4.37	1.57	
1812–1816	"	4.16	1.42	
1817–1821	"	6.08	3.20	
1822–1826	"	6.31	2.45	
1827–1831	"	6.17		
1832–1836	"	8.26	2.62	
1837–1841	"	9.62	2.52	
1842–1846	"	9.60	3.22	
1847–1851	"	7.48	0.73	
1852–1853	"	5.47	1.22	
1801–1805	Teocuitatlán	5.16	3.78	0.68
1806–1810	"	5.37	2.08	0.53
1811–1815	"	4.22	1.83	0.40
1816–1820	"	3.86	1.46	0.50
1821–1825	"	4.48	2.20	0.42
1826–1830	"	4.12	2.46	0.40
1831–1835	"	5.27	1.91	0.33
1836–1840	"	5.27	2.46	0.33
1841–1845	"	5.25	1.79	0.36
1846–1850	"	5.05	1.39	0.25
1851–1854	"	3.87	1.55	0.29
	Etzatlán (canton)			
1843–1847	Tequila	6.04	3.66	0.47
	Amatitán	8.90		0.42
1845–1849	Magdalena	5.36	1.74	0.46
1850–1854	"	3.82	1.38	0.50
	Autlán (canton)			
1834–1838	Autlán		1.94	
	Purificación		1.68	
	Cuautitlán		3.33	
	Amula		1.45	
	Ejutla		2.86	
	Tala		2.20	
	Tenamastlán		2.38	
	Mascota		2.06	
	Talpa		2.17	
	Tomatlán		1.70	
	San Sebastián		2.28	

Table 6.4 (cont.)

A. Parishes and towns (*cont.*)

Date	Local Entity	Ratio : Births/ Marriages	Ratio : Births/ Deaths	Ratio : Children 0–9/ Deaths Total Pop.
	Tepic (canton)			
1834–1838	Tepic		1.13	
	Compostela		1.76	
	Jalisco		2.84	
	Acaponeta		1.79	
	Santiago		1.27	
	Rosa Morada		1.61	
	Ahuacatlán		2.49	
	Ixtlán		2.12	
	Jala		2.66	
	San Pedro Lagunillas		0.73	
	Santa María del Oro		1.93	
	Colotlán (canton)			
1834–1838	Colotlán		1.76	
	Santa María de los Ángeles		1.76	
	Tlalcosahua		3.17	
	Huejúcar		3.15	
	Mexquitic		2.37	
	Huejuquilla		2.68	
	Teul		1.25	
	Bolaños		1.74	
	Chimaltitán		0.81	
	San Martín		1.58	
	Totatiche		2.81	
1854	Colotlán		1.89	
	Santa María		1.70	
	Huejúcar		2.06	
	Mexquitic		1.45	
	Huejuquilla		2.55	
	Teul		1.88	
	Bolaños		1.07	
	Chimaltitán		1.69	
	Totatiche		2.05	
	Guadalajara (canton)			
1852–1856	Sagrario	5.48	1.25	
	Analco	5.47	1.00	
	Mejicalcingo	6.80	0.93	
	Santuario	4.68	0.87	
	Jesús	5.72	1.33	
	San Pedro	5.08	1.57	
	Tonalá	4.13	1.46	

Table 6.4 (cont.)

A. Parishes and towns (*cont.*)

Date	Local Entity	Ratio : Births/ Marriages	Ratio : Births/ Deaths	Ratio : Children 0–9/ Deaths Total Pop.
	Guadalajara (*cont'd.*)			
	Zapopan	4.53	1.88	
	Tlajomulco	3.29	1.22	
	Acatlan	5.19	1.25	
	Tala	3.66	1.10	
	Etzatlán	4.71	2.53	

B. Cantons

Date	Canton	Ratio : Births/ Marriages	Ratio : Births/ Deaths	Ratio : Children 0–9/ Deaths Total Pop.
1830	Guadalajara	5.32	0.89	
1831	”	4.89	1.53	
1847	”	6.55	1.84	
1848	”	3.68	1.47	
1830	Lagos	8.24	1.12	
1831	”	6.26	2.57	
1830	La Barca	8.13	1.09	
1831	”	5.03	1.77	
1848	”	3.57	1.69	
1830	Sayula		0.95	
1831	”		1.32	
1834	”		2.28	
1835	”		2.55	
1836	”		2.26	
1837	”		2.10	
1838	”		2.22	
1847	”		1.84	
1848	”		1.57	
1830	Etzatlán	8.58	1.82	
1831	”	5.62	1.71	
1847	”	6.54	1.45	
1848	”	3.79	1.30	
1830	Autlán	4.32	2.20	
1831	”	4.67	1.01	
1847	”	3.01	0.93	
1848	”	4.35	1.59	
1830	Tepic	8.11	1.55	
1831	”	4.22	0.57	
1847	”	7.90	0.89	
1830	Colotlán	6.44	2.36	

Table 6.4 (cont.)

B. Cantons (*cont.*)

Date	Canton	Ratio: Births/ Marriages	Ratio: Births/ Deaths	Ratio: Children 0–9/ Deaths Total Pop.
1831	Colotlán	6.10	1.10	
1847	,,	6.10	2.16	
1848	,,	4.67	1.18	
All localities				
Number		86	186	
Mean		5.34	1.87	
S.D.		±1.596	±0.670	
S.E.		±0.172	±0.049	

A comparison of the four sources of data is provided in Table 6.5. For periods which are approximately contemporaneous we have tabulated the values of *t* derived from the ratios of births to marriages and of births to deaths. The only difference of notable significance among the Mixteca Alta, central Mexico from the ramo de Padrones, central Mexico from the state reports, and Jalisco as recorded by Banda is that between the Mixteca Alta and Jalisco in the half-century 1801–1850. Both values of *t* (3.38 and 2.98) are at or beyond the one percent level of probability. However, the two regions in the early nineteenth century differed so widely in geography, economic status, and social background that some disparity in birth and death performance is not to be regarded as surprising.

If we consider the tabulations as a whole, we observe numerous small differences in birth to death ratios which occur in both place and time. Much of the variation is referable to the uneven sampling made necessary by the erratic availability of the records. Some of it is probably due to real distinctions in births and particularly deaths. However, two features of the data deserve to be stressed. In the first place, the differences which appear in the mean values given by the tables are all minor, for they come barely, or not at all, within the range of statistical significance. It is likely that if we had a hundred times as many figures the small deviations would still persist. In the second place, there is no pronounced trend toward either an

Table 6.5

Critical ratios (*t*) of pairs of means shown in the preceding tables for
the ratios of births to marriages and for births to deaths in the regions and at the
dates indicated. For the means, standard deviations, and standard errors refer
to Tables 6.1 to 6.4.

Date	Region	Type of Entity	t for Ratio: Births/ Marriages	t for Ratio: Births/ Deaths
1751–1800	Mixteca Alta[a]	Towns		
1793	Central Mexico[b]	Towns and partidos	0.22	1.40
1801–1850	Mixteca Alta[a]	Towns		
1801–1850	Central Mexico[c]	Towns and partidos	0.36	1.49
1801–1850	Mixteca Alta[a]	Towns		
1801–1855	Jalisco[d]	Parishes and cantons	3.38	2.98
1801–1850	Central Mexico[c]	Towns and partidos		
1801–1855	Jalisco[a]	Parishes and cantons	2.45	0.73
1801–1850	Central Mexico[c]	Towns and partidos		
1959–1960	Mexico entire	States		16.86

[a] From parish records.
[b] From ramo de Padrones.
[c] From state reports.
[d] From Bando.

increase or a decrease of mortality, in so far as such a trend can
be detected by the use of natality figures rather than of total
populations. Indeed, if there is any movement at all which can
be detected, it is in the direction of an increase in relative number
of deaths.

By way of contrast, and for the sake of emphasis, we
submit Table 6.6, which shows the birth to death ratios for the
thirty-two Mexican states in 1959–1960, as calculated from the
births and deaths given by the *Compendio estadístico,* 1960.
Marriages cannot be utilized because the Civil Register cannot
record unión libre. The mean of the state birth to death ratios

Table 6.6

Ratio of births to deaths in 32 states of Mexico for the years 1959–1960.

State	Ratio: Births/Deaths
Aguascalientes	4.53
Baja California-Norte	5.87
Baja California-Sur	5.25
Campeche	4.96
Coahuila	4.51
Colima	3.60
Chiapas	3.37
Chihuahua	4.50
Distrito Federal	4.24
Durango	5.36
Guanajuato	3.64
Guerrero	4.88
Hidalgo	3.26
Jalisco	4.05
Mexico	3.16
Michoacán	4.93
Morelos	4.72
Nayarit	4.65
Nuevo León	5.50
Oaxaca	2.60
Puebla	2.77
Querétaro	3.65
Quintana Roo	6.38
San Luis Potosí	4.12
Sinaloa	5.46
Sonora	5.03
Tabasco	4.80
Tamaulipas	5.07
Tlaxcala	3.28
Veracruz	3.62
Yucatan	3.65
Zacatecas	4.88
All 32 states	
Mean	4.39
S.D.	±0.926
S.E.	±0.164
Mexico, total population	
Mean	3.96

Source: *Compendio Estadístico*, 1960, Dirección General de Estadística, Mexico City, Table 11, pp. 16–17.

was 4.39, and if we employ the total population of Mexico, it was 3.96. These values are to be compared with those for

1801 to 1850 : 1.61 in the Mixteca Alta (Table 6.1), 1.76 in eleven states of central Mexico (Table 6.3), 1.87 in Jalisco (Table 6.4). The value of t between the 130 localities in the eleven states from 1801 to 1850 and the 32 entire states in 1959 and 1960 is 16.86. These figures give some idea of the enormous downward movement in mortality since the middle of the nineteenth century and demonstrate the triviality of the differences we encounter prior to that time. The data which we have presented are far from adequate in a highly sophisticated sense, but to the extent of their validity, they indicate no change in mortality status in colonial and republican Mexico before the middle of the nineteenth century.

Chapter VII

Mortality Patterns in Mexico Since 1860 : Age at Death

The death rate in Mexico, which has declined sharply since 1860, and especially since 1920, has been stated in numerical terms by the statistical reports of the Mexican government and has been discussed by many demographers. Among these may be mentioned Gilberto Loyo, *La población de Mexico, estado actual y tendencias*; Raúl Benítez Zenteno, *Análisis demográfico de México*; Julio Durán Ochoa, *Población*; Eduardo E. Arriaga, *New Life Tables for Latin American Populations in the Nineteenth and Twentieth Centuries,* and particularly *Mortality Decline and Its Demographic Effects in Latin America.* We have no intention of recapitulating these works here. What we would like to do is to describe certain aspects of the improvement in public health in so far as they relate to restricted portions of Mexico in which we are interested. In so doing we would emphasize some of the environmental, or ecological, factors involved.

In the late 1950s we were able to secure access to the files of the Civil Register of births, marriages, and deaths in two states, Jalisco and Oaxaca. It was immediately evident that here was (as it still is) a vast source of largely unexploited information concerning vital statistics in Mexico, extending from approximately 1870 to the present. We therefore undertook to abstract as much data as was possible for us under the circumstances.

We appreciated and keenly regretted the fact that with the Civil Register alone we could not compute death rates, even of the crudest sort, because we lacked the corresponding censuses. It is true that for the period since 1900 they are available on a national and state scale. However, for the years from 1870 to 1900 there are none upon which we could rely. Furthermore, for the entire century from 1860 to 1960 there are no counts to which we had access for the specific municipalities in Jalisco and the ex-districts in Oaxaca for the dates which we were able to utilize from the Civil Register. Nevertheless, a great deal can be learned concerning the history of mortality from the death records alone.

Since the death certificate always states the age and sex of the decedent, it is possible to employ the method of proportion to calculate the distribution of deaths by age. At the same time we can tabulate the level of survivorship according to age, as well as the relative age specific mortality. With these data, comparisons can be made in time and in locality. The certificate also contains the cause of death. Although, as will be pointed out later, the causes as written are quite unreliable, the trends in the major sources of disease can be traced and can be compared at different times and places.

There are in Mexico thirty-two states and other federal entities, in the capital of each of which is preserved a file of birth, marriage, and death certificates dating from the inception of the system and derived from each of the local municipal entities. If complete, the file of a large state such as Jalisco would contain many thousands of bound volumes, each holding several hundred certificates, and the total recorded deaths would reach many millions. For our purposes it was necessary to secure a sample, but as large a sample as our resources would permit.

We were able to collect data in the state files at Guadalajara, Jalisco, and at Oaxaca City, Oaxaca. In each case, after having decided which years and localities should be excerpted, we employed local persons to copy the essential information. They went consecutively from one death certificate to another and listed in tabular form, for each year and locality, the sex, age, and cause of death as written on the certificate. The tabulated sheets were then sent to us in Berkeley. The three parameters, sex, age, and cause, were then coded for further analysis by computer. With the codes, cards were punched, which ultimately were processed. The results take the form of extensive printed tables. In this way we were able to handle over 600,000 cards, which represented an equal number of deaths. The entire operation consumed more than ten years.

Sampling presented numerous problems. In the first place, it was obvious that we could not include more than two states in our study. Jalisco and Oaxaca were selected because

our previous experience had been in these areas and because
they represented, respectively, one of the newer, more progressive and one of the older, more conservative states. Moreover,
both extend from the coast to the plateau with a full spectrum
of climate.

In the second place, we could not utilize all the local
entities in either state. In 1960, Jalisco, contained 124 municipalities, including the city of Guadalajara. We first segregated the
deaths in the city which occurred in the years 1860, 1870, etc.,
to 1960. There were 61,531 of these. Then we selected sixteen
municipalities from the coast, practically all there are, and
recorded the deaths from the years of even decades. We began
with 1880, for the records of preceding years were either defective
or missing. With many of the smaller units we extended the
time a year or two past the decennial year. The year 1910 and
the decade 1910–1919 were omitted. During the revolution the
small town records were so poorly kept that they are useless
for statistical analysis.

Inland from the coast we established an intermediate
area which embraces the escarpment of the plateau up to the
level of Lake Chapala and the towns directly northeast of
Guadalajara. In this portion of the state we selected twenty
municipalities and had data excerpted for the same dates
as were mentioned for the coast, 1880 through 1960, with the
exception of 1910. The third region was on the plateau, beginning
with Tepatitlán and Pontitlán and thence extending northeast-
ward as far as Colotlán and Teocaltiche. The same dates were
used, with eleven municipalities. The list of towns included in
all these regions will be found appendix B.

The total deaths in our sample of the state of Jalisco
include those occurring in Guadalajara. However, since this
great city is so distinct in almost every respect from the remainder
of the state, in treating the data and in making comparisons, we
have established it as an independent entity. The rest of the
sample from the state, which we call rural Jalisco, may be
compared with our Oaxaca sample, which contains no large
cities. Rural Jalisco, to be sure, includes the intermediate
area, as previously delineated. However, for the purpose of
comparing deaths in the low, coastal region with those of the
high, interior altitudes, it is better to omit the intermediate
territory and to set opposite each other the data for the coast
and for the plateau. This procedure has been adopted uniformly
in constructing the tables.

According to the census of 1960 there were 571 municipalities in the state of Oaxaca. Prior to the Revolution of 1910–1920 they were grouped into some twenty-five or thirty districts. These were abolished as administrative entities during the Revolution, but due to the multitude of small municipal governments, they are still employed for archival convenience as ex-districts. In the archive of the Civil Register the volumes are bound and organized according to ex-districts and hence we use them here for territorial division.

The Oaxaca archive has suffered physical damage and clerical neglect over many years, resulting in the loss of numerous volumes. Indeed, it is almost impossible to get a complete series for any ex-district. For this reason and others, we have not been able to make a secular division which depended upon even decades, as we did in Jalisco. As a substitute we selected six short periods of years, as widely spaced as the facilities of the archive permitted. The earliest was approximately 1871–1875. A glance at appendix B, which also lists all the ex-districts that we covered, will show that actually the periods extended over various intervals of three to five years within the limits mentioned. Since a variation of one or two years is of no statistical significance, we permitted a similar tolerance to characterize the other five periods. It was not possible to get a sequence of significance subsequent to 1954. These reports were being copied during the mid-1960s, and at that time it would have been neither feasible nor diplomatic to use the books covering that decade.

It will also be observed in appendix B that only one ex-district in the Mixteca Baja dates as far back as 1871. This is Silacayoapan. The data for Putla begin in 1907 and those for Juxtlahuaca only in 1938. The district of Putla was not formed until near the end of the Díaz regime, and, in any event, no death records are available from either ex-district for the earlier years.

For the purpose of tabulation and particularly of constructing tables, it is necessary to establish a central year for each of the six periods. With Jalisco the years ending in zero are appropriate, for it was possible to get the records of these exact years, or very close to them. With Oaxaca it was necessary to establish arbitrarily a point which most closely fell at the center of each period. Those which we have used are as follows :

1871–1875 :	1872	1920–1924 :	1922
1888–1892 :	1890	1936–1942 :	1940
1905–1908 :	1907	1948–1954 :	1952

For the formulation of the data by computer it was clear from the outset that practical considerations would dictate a great deal of consolidation. Consequently, we established the series of regions to which we adhered throughout. With Jalisco we combined the records of the municipalities so as to form the three geographical territories previously mentioned : the coast, the intermediate area, and the plateau. Then we combined the three regions in order to obtain the sum for rural Jalisco. Guadalajara was retained in a separate category but may be added to rural Jalisco to complete the coverage of the entire state. There are therefore six sets of computer tables for Jalisco.

With Oaxaca we tabulated each of the twelve ex-districts. Subsequently, however, we determined that these entities are actually too small. The data are subject to so much local variation that the differences among them become nonsignificant. In order to avoid this difficulty we combined the ex-districts into four larger areas as shown in appendix B : the coast, the valley of Oaxaca, the Mixteca Baja, and the Mixteca Alta. The final step was to combine the four regions and thus obtain the total for the western half of the state. Therefore, when we disregard the individual ex-districts, we have five sets of computer tables. When we wish to compare directly the coast and the plateau, we ignore the intermediate regions, the valley of Oaxaca and the Mixteca Baja, and use only the values found for the coastal area and the Mixteca Alta.

Although the death records contain the exact age of each individual, we found it desirable to present the data in the form of age groups. The presentation of all ages, year by year, would render tabulation, even with a computer, exceedingly cumbersome and onerous. Another reason is that in the younger age range the number of deaths per year of age in our samples becomes too small for adequate statistical treatment. Finally, in the period subsequent to age 30, the earlier records show such a marked tendency to aggregate ages at 40, 50, 60, etc., that they destroy the usefulness of a formulation according to single years.

For certain purposes we have segregated the year of birth (zero years), leaving the interval 1–4 to complete the first five-year period. As a rule, however, the entire period 0–4 years is included as a complete unit. We then have employed the periods 5–9, 10–14, 15–19, and 20–24. Thereafter, ten-year periods are adequate : 25–34, 35–44, 45–54, 55–64, 65–74, 75–84, and 85 years and over. We divide at the middle of each decade in order to avoid as far as possible the heaping effect just mentioned.

The records show, and the cards were punched with the code for, the sex of each decedent. The separation of all tables according to sex, together with those in which the sexes were combined, would have tripled the volume of computer output. Such an increase would have carried the task beyond the limit of our resources and of those who generously contributed to the burden of cost. This restriction was unfortunate but decisive. We regret most heartily the lack of sex distinctions in the analysis of the distributions of age at death. We readily concede the absurdity of reporting for both sexes the number of deaths at childbirth. On the other hand, we have been forced to yield to the exigencies of material support and base our findings upon the consolidation of male and female.

The results, as printed from the computer, are embodied in nearly a hundred numerical tables which are concerned with age alone and which omit those dealing with the individual ex-districts of Oaxaca. To publish these tables without abridgement would require an inordinate outlay of labor and expense. An even more compelling consideration for abridgment is the extreme difficulty which would confront a reader in trying to assimilate such a mass of numbers, make comparisons, and discover trends. Consequently, we have recast the data and have converted it to other forms.

First, we have transcribed seven of the computer tables directly (Table 7.1, parts A to G). These show the absolute numbers of deaths in our samples for (A) rural Jalisco, (B) western Oaxaca entire, (C) Guadalajara, (D) the coast of Jalisco, (E) the plateau region of Jalisco, (F) the three coastal ex-districts of Oaxaca, and (G) the four ex-districts of the Mixteca Alta. Second, we have constructed 52 abridged life tables for the same areas at the series of dates from 1860 to 1960 (not published here). Third, we give approximately twenty tables which summarize certain portions of the life tables, and which are discussed in the following paragraphs (Tables 7.2 to 7.21 inclusive). Copies of the computer output without alteration are preserved on file at the Bancroft Library in Berkeley. They may be inspected by any one who so desires.

There are several procedures which may be adopted for the analysis of a body of death records in the absence of censuses or other accurate information concerning total population. The simplest of these is the distribution of deaths according to the age of the decedents, a method suitable for a rough exposition of comparisons and broad trends. The initial formulation is in absolute numbers, such as is given in tables 7.1.

In part A is displayed the number of deaths in our sample from rural Jalisco for each age group in each of eight decades. In part B similar figures are given for Oaxaca, and in part C for Guadalajara. The other four tables show the distribution of deaths according to age for the geographical zones in which we are interested, the coastal areas of Jalisco (part D) and Oaxaca (part F) and the corresponding areas in the highlands (parts E and G).

Probably a more illuminating method of presenting the data is to use relative instead of absolute values. For this purpose the number of deaths in each age group is converted to the proportion it bears to the total deaths, expressed as a percentage. As an example, we find that the deaths in age group 0–4 in rural Jalisco, at the year 1880, amounted to 19,840 out of the total of 37,984, or 52.2 percent. In Figure 7.1, we depict graphically the percentages in the successive age groups of rural Jalisco in the year 1880 and in the year 1960. The individual points fall with considerable irregularity, but this defect is inherent in the records of the Civil Register and is also referable to the relatively small size of the sample. Nevertheless, the general features of the graph, the steep drop in percentage following birth, the subsequent rise and final decline, and the displacement of the mode toward older age groups in the later time period, are all unmistakable. Similar comment applies to Figures 7.2 and 7.3 which show, respectively, the percentage distribution of age at death in Oaxaca and Guadalajara.

It is clear that such a distribution is characteristic of the population as it existed at the date of record. It does not, and cannot, take into account the experience of the various age groups as they have progressed through life up to the time of their demise. There may have been gross fluctuations in natality and mortality which would be reflected in the absolute and relative number of any age. Since we have no precise knowledge of these perturbations and thus cannot introduce them into our calculations, we make the broad assumption that they did

Table 7.1

Number of deaths for each age group for each period.

A. Rural Jalisco

Age group	1880	1890	1900	1920	1930	1940	1950	1960
0	6,562	7,984	9,132	7,530	7,614	6,228	5,867	7,575
1–4	13,278	15,203	12,987	11,254	11,245	10,766	7,346	6,500
0–4	19,840	23,187	22,119	18,784	19,329	16,994	13,213	14,075
5–9	2,450	3,195	2,565	1,866	1,839	1,389	865	710
10–14	737	1,106	858	683	643	483	329	307
15–19	876	1,277	1,053	911	901	701	389	434
20–24	1,315	1,653	1,405	1,129	1,194	850	503	490
25–34	2,999	4,349	3,132	2,277	2,423	1,712	1,027	1,116
35–44	2,776	3,997	3,306	2,286	2,383	1,715	1,224	1,289
45–54	2,418	4,184	3,167	2,128	2,395	1,675	1,202	1,451
55–64	2,252	4,314	3,476	2,304	2,533	2,103	1,414	1,951
65–74	1,152	2,082	2,372	1,948	2,445	2,197	1,828	2,298
75–84	763	1,179	1,561	1,362	1,899	1,699	1,556	2,118
85+	406	617	795	770	1,077	1,196	1,150	1,606
Total	37,984	51,140	45,809	36,448	39,061	32,714	24,700	27,845

B. Oaxaca

Age Group	1872	1890	1907	1922	1940	1952
0	5,957	11,146	12,256	8,977	5,134	11,226
1–4	9,005	13,445	14,479	9,034	6,043	12,932
0–4	14,962	24,591	26,735	18,011	11,177	24,158
5–9	2,826	3,494	3,543	2,578	1,360	2,946
10–14	730	1,401	1,410	1,285	527	1,134
15–19	722	1,594	2,287	1,414	621	1,406
20–24	926	1,974	2,489	1,775	782	1,745
25–34	2,068	4,414	5,525	3,713	2,021	3,559
35–44	1,676	4,285	5,048	3,241	1,960	3,837
45–54	1,226	3,644	4,422	2,681	1,560	3,847
55–64	1,164	4,012	4,896	2,607	1,722	4,089
65–74	827	2,115	2,615	1,478	1,344	3,442
75–84	399	782	1,142	729	719	2,001
85+	106	295	413	308	380	1,113
Total	27,632	52,601	60,525	39,820	24,173	53,277

Table 7.1 (cont.)

C. Guadalajara

Age Group	1860	1870	1880	1890	1900
0	115	404	268	485	306
1–4	365	938	1,070	1,063	1,536
0–4	480	1,342	1,338	1,548	1,842
5–9	53	87	155	123	205
10–14	16	49	46	43	55
15–19	21	97	75	74	88
20–24	37	172	120	123	151
25–34	62	366	326	301	358
35–44	63	321	354	296	322
45–54	52	308	383	285	402
55–64	63	264	291	269	323
65–74	36	146	160	151	240
75–84	13	67	98	84	152
85+	9	24	32	31	66
Total	905	3,243	3,378	3,328	4,204

C. Guadalajara (*cont.*)

Age Group	1920	1930	1940	1950	1960
0	433	514	645	671	4,964
1–4	1,685	1,747	1,786	1,236	4,035
0–4	2,118	2,261	2,431	1,907	8,999
5–9	182	185	141	105	427
10–14	73	82	79	51	266
15 19	127	135	137	78	347
20–24	204	235	199	99	426
25–34	384	431	439	280	941
35–44	496	464	495	308	1,249
45–54	429	473	504	354	1,402
55–64	390	458	535	379	1,921
65–74	328	440	482	433	1,947
75–84	231	274	353	308	1,802
85+	151	173	257	181	1,195
Total	5,113	5,611	6,052	4,483	20,922

Table 7.1 (cont.)

D. Jalisco, coast

Age Group	1880	1890	1900	1920	1930	1940	1950	1960
0	709	945	1,195	950	1,004	844	835	938
1–4	1,671	1,645	1,516	1,460	1,618	1,553	1,372	921
0–4	2,380	2,590	2,711	2,410	2,622	2,397	2,207	1,859
5–9	440	443	333	301	308	190	172	115
10–14	152	197	130	122	109	83	52	53
15–19	211	260	178	191	152	129	66	80
20–24	266	364	284	248	241	152	112	99
25–34	689	877	593	448	478	358	231	192
35–44	574	727	656	443	492	296	252	209
45–54	346	666	553	378	442	291	211	192
55–64	321	545	509	329	421	336	235	250
65–74	179	280	327	237	327	307	280	311
75–84	84	160	213	161	239	223	265	259
85+	54	85	118	88	125	183	191	239
Total	5,696	7,194	6,605	5,356	5,956	4,945	4,274	3,858

E. Jalisco, plateau

Age Group	1880	1890	1900	1920	1930	1940	1950	1960
0	2,918	3,392	3,816	2,436	2,841	2,256	2,035	2,536
1–4	5,876	7,335	6,175	4,349	4,764	4,429	2,663	2,149
0–4	8,794	10,727	9,991	6,785	7,605	6,685	4,698	4,685
5–9	894	1,293	1,014	668	665	528	304	233
10–14	272	423	326	221	241	190	127	94
15–19	308	498	357	336	334	241	142	155
20–24	532	653	490	347	375	271	178	150
25–34	1,022	1,691	1,054	699	806	526	295	359
35–44	982	1,618	1,091	730	757	534	379	379
45–54	902	1,675	1,144	692	787	496	382	495
55–64	832	1,955	1,379	828	980	805	489	648
65–74	468	998	978	742	968	877	667	803
75–84	332	520	681	549	781	660	582	773
85+	180	252	311	260	407	423	416	540
Total	15,518	22,303	18,816	12,857	14,706	12,236	8,659	9,314

Table 7.1 (cont.)

F. Oaxaca, coast

Age Group	1872	1890	1907	1922	1940	1952
0	1,036	1,997	1,868	1,931	968	2,601
1–4	1,559	2,560	2,255	2,388	1,089	2,888
0–4	2,595	4,557	4,123	4,319	2,057	5,489
5–9	492	963	738	926	357	823
10–14	135	398	315	478	162	367
15–19	223	485	460	476	186	469
20–24	332	564	617	580	245	643
25–34	792	1,435	1,482	1,459	656	1,330
35–44	615	1,311	1,258	1,202	586	1,308
45–54	394	943	951	861	401	1,080
55–64	245	847	838	756	386	961
65–74	127	326	348	318	202	565
75–84	57	104	102	126	122	337
85+	11	41	41	54	52	164
Total	6,018	11,974	11,273	11,555	5,412	13,536

G. Oaxaca, Mixteca Alta

Age Group	1872	1890	1907	1922	1940	1952
0	2,706	4,807	4,770	2,691	1,431	3,593
1–4	4,082	6,150	5,676	2,551	1,504	4,738
0–4	6,788	10,957	10,446	5,242	2,935	8,331
5–9	1,105	1,364	1,103	522	325	981
10–14	265	559	481	263	110	326
15–19	216	625	1,040	259	120	358
20–24	268	769	857	358	131	396
25–34	480	1,521	1,663	601	292	746
35–44	438	1,564	1,601	556	322	928
45–54	364	1,403	1,446	523	260	1,050
55–64	388	1,737	1,768	618	355	1,253
65–74	355	1,008	1,127	444	352	1,199
75–84	178	394	472	219	175	645
85+	49	151	175	78	105	367
Total	10,894	22,052	22,179	9,683	5,482	16,580

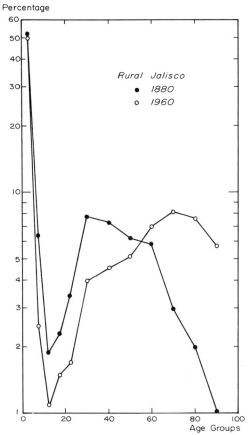

Percentage

Figure 7.1.   Distribution of deaths according to age in rural Jalisco.

not exist. The population is considered to have been *stable,* that is, the birth and death rate affecting the population were constant. We go even further. Although we know that the population was actually increasing, we assume that it maintained a fixed level, or was *stationary.* Thus we can get a series of patterns, each depicting the momentary condition of the population at a corresponding series of dates. Only in this way can we utilize the death records from the Civil Register in the absence of reliable censuses.

These distributions conform to the well-recognized reduction of mortality in Mexico which has been in progress for a century and to the postponement of death to consistently greater ages. In view of these facts, and also in view of the significant fall in proportion of deaths occurring in the 5–9 year age group, one would expect a marked diminution in the relative

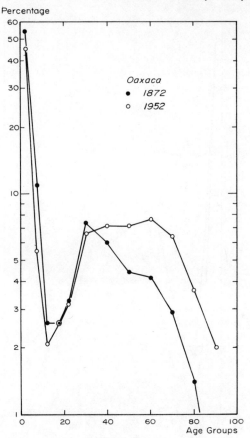

Figure 7.2.   Distribution of deaths according to age in Oaxaca.

number of deaths in the 0–4 year age group, the infants and small children. Such a displacement does not manifest itself (see figures 7.1 to 7.3). Consequently, the reports in the Civil Register for this age category become suspect.

It is now generally admitted that from the inception of civil registry in Mexico down to 1950, 1960, and perhaps 1970, the registration of infant deaths was very defective. Particularly at the lower economic level, in both city and country, stillbirths and perinatal deaths were apt to occur unnoticed by authorities. The corpses were buried or otherwise disposed of without notification of the civil authorities, or on many occasions even the parish priest. Particularly if the child died before baptism, and this event occurred frequently in the more remote areas, nothing was ever said. Because of the extreme preoccupation of the priest with his large parish and manifold duties, the usually

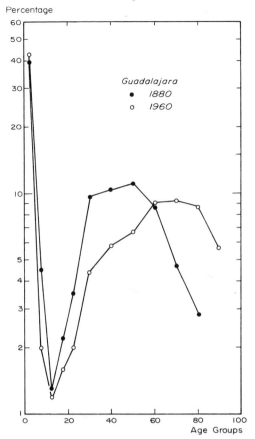

Figure 7.3.   Distribution of deaths according to age in Guadalajara.

long and tedious trip to the center of civil authority, and an innate suspicion of all things official, deaths even to the age of one or two years went unreported.

This state of affairs was largely ignored until interest on the part of public health workers caused an official reaction which resulted in considerable improvement. This attention to the problem is reflected in several recent studies, one of the results of which has been to emphasize the real magnitude of the under-registration in the infant category. Among these should especially be noted the two studies by Eduardo Arriaga and the one by Eduardo Cordero. These authors have not only described and discussed underregistration but have also elaborated highly sophisticated methods for correcting the deficiency in the registration records since approximately 1930.

When one examines the crude death rates for the Mexican

states, as published by the Dirección General de Estadística, he is certain to be impressed by their variability from state to state. As a base line we may use the reports from our own states for 1960, according to the *Stastical Abstract of the United States* for 1968.[1] If Alaska and Hawaii are omitted, the remaining forty-eight states plus the District of Columbia gave an average crude death rate of 9.48 deaths per 1,000. The standard deviation is 1.05, and the coefficient of variation is 11.07. The comparable values for the thirty-two states of Mexico[2] are a mean of 9.26 deaths per 1,000 in the year 1968, and a c.v. of 23.19. Meanwhile the c.v. for infant mortality in the same year is 29.09 whereas that for natality is 11.55.

Cordero has assembled the data for the Mexican states in 1950, 1960, and 1965. He has then recalculated, state by state, the probability of death (q_0 in a life table) for the age group 0–4 years and compared his value with that given officially. His final result is an expression called the "percentage of omission," obtained by subtracting the official q_0 from the calculated q_0 and dividing by the latter (Tables 7 to 9 in his study). If, for the data of 1950, we disregard three states for which the official value for q_0 was greater than that calculated by Cordero and estimate the variability of the remaining twenty-nine states we get a mean "percentage of omission" of 30.49 with the c.v. equal to 49.39. This is a very high value and establishes a great difference among the Mexican states with respect to the technique of securing registration of infant deaths. The variability was still considerable in 1965 although according to Cordero's analysis, the "percentage of omission" at the national level fell from 34.9 in 1950 to 16.3 in 1960 and 15.7 in 1965.

The two states in which we are particularly interested, Jalisco and Oaxaca, showed a very wide disparity. Cordero gives for Jalisco a percentage of omission of 10.3 in 1950 but none at all in 1960 and 1965. On the other hand, Oaxaca had 55.0 in 1950, 52.2 in 1960, and 60.1 in 1965, consistently the highest values of any state. No one could possibly make a comparison between these two states with respect to infant deaths on the basis of the official reports in the Civil Register. For our specific samples we have no computations such as those developed by Arriaga and Cordero. However, since our samples embrace a substantial fraction of each state, the statewide findings may be applied in principle.

[1]P. 56, Table 70.
[2]*Anuario estadístico compendiado,* 1968, cuadro 3.5, pp. 29–32.

It is very evident that our records from the Civil Registers of Jalisco and Oaxaca suffer seriously from the effect of under-registration. Our problem is what to do about it. One possibility is to attempt the application of the adjustments worked out by Arriaga and Cordero. It is doubtful whether this course would be feasible, for the corrections depend upon the use of other data beyond simple age at death, which we do not have available in our samples. In particular, we have no direct census enumerations of the type which can be utilized on the scale of the nation or of complete states. Some other procedure appears preferable. The simplest and most direct alternative is to delete the age group 0–4 years entirely and work with the more mature child and adult population. This expedient is especially justified since we are attempting primarily to make comparisons and study trends, not to analyze the population in detail. We shall, therefore, proceed by omitting from our calculations the group where age at death fell between 0 and 4 years inclusive.

The remainder of the population can be treated most effectively by application of the life table method, particularly if the concept of stable or stationary populations be admitted as a working hypothesis for the purpose of making comparisons and of demonstrating secular trends. The first step is to recast the mortality data for the seven areas which we wish to compare at series of dates ranging from 1860 to 1960. For each region and date we have the total number of deaths. In each case the recorded deaths to persons 0–4 years of age are excluded, leaving a balance for use. For instance, we have for rural Jalisco, in 1880, a total of 37,984 deaths, of which 19,840 occurred to infants and children under five-years old. The others, 18,144 in all were distributed among ages 5 years to 85 years and over. This figure, 18,144 then becomes the base from which the calculation starts, and we set 18,144 as equivalent to 100,000 who enter the life table in column l_x. Then we complete columns d_x and l_x. There were 2,450 who died in the group 5–9 years. Prorated to 100,000, this figures becomes 13,503, in column d_x, and similarly for the other age groups. Column l_x is built up by subtracting the deaths in each age group from the number who entered the group. Accordingly 100,000 minus 13,503, or 86,497, entered the group 10–14 years; and so on.

The life table thus constructed is truncated because it begins only with the age of 5 years. It is also abridged, drastically so after the age of 25. Furthermore, the fact that we have no information concerning the exact age at death for those over 85 years makes it impossible to ascertain the precise values for the last row in the table, age 85 plus, except that the probability of death, q_x, must be 1.0. As a purely empirical procedure, and one which undoubtedly introduces a small error, we have considered that the average age at death of this group was 90 years, 5 years after the initial age of 85. In spite of these shortcomings, the tables permit comparison of the mortality pattern among areas and temporal periods.

The completion of each table is straightforward once columns d_x and 1_x are established. We use almost exclusively columns q_x and e_x. Column q_x, the probability of death, is found by dividing each value in column d_x by the corresponding figure in column 1_x. Column e_x, the expectation of life at age x, is calculated by introducing two other columns, L_x and T_x. The details of the method are irrelevant to the present discussion. Two points should be observed, however. First, q_x, the probability of death, is equivalent to the age specific death rate in a living census population. For each age group it is unique and is independent of the mortality in both younger and older groups. Second, e_x, the expectation of life at age x, is an expression of future conditions, that is, of mortality in all years subsequent to x. Consequently, it is dependent upon the mortality pattern of all older age groups. At the same time it is independent of mortality in younger groups. It follows that the best criterion of survivorship is the value of e_x for the age at which the individuals enter the youngest group. This is at birth for usual population. In our case it is at five years of age because we have disregarded all persons younger, living and dead. The values of e_x for later age groups may be employed, and we have used them for certain purposes, but the older the group the less the significance in making comparisons.

Our initial comparison, and one which may serve as a model for all others, is that between our samples from rural Jalisco and those from western Oaxaca. It has already been pointed out that during the past several decades the two states have differed widely with respect to the registration of infant births and deaths. After we exclude these, there remains the question whether there persists a disparity in the adolescent and adult mortality patterns. Our first test, which we shall designate No. 1A, is made by means of the probability of death in equivalent age groups (q_x in the life table) at the same points in time in the two states. This test, in turn, requires several procedural devices which must be described.

One of these relates to the calendar periods covered by the respective data from Jalisco and from Oaxaca. The central points in time for the Jalisco samples are 1880, 1890 etc., to 1960. Those for Oaxaca are 1872, 1890, 1907, 1922, 1940, and 1952. Only two of these, 1890 and 1940, coincide with the years for Jalisco; yet we wish to compare the two regions as they existed at the same dates. The most practical solution, even if it involves considerable uncertainty, is graphic interpolation. We plot on coordinate paper the q_x values for Oaxaca, following each age group through the six known points from 1872 to 1952. (See Figure 7.4.). Then we connect the consecutive pairs of points within each age group and finally read off from the graph the probable values for 1880, 1900, etc. Short extrapolations have to be made for 1870 and 1920, and one of eight years for 1960. With large scale plots (not the one shown in Figure 7.4) the accuracy of reading is good to three significant digits, quite adequate for the purpose. It is obvious that the real values of q_x for the interpolated dates may have been different from those

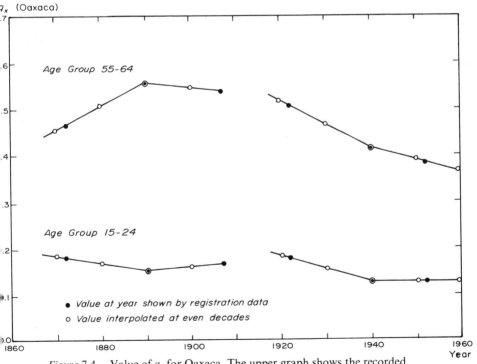

Figure 7.4.   Value of q_x for Oaxaca. The upper graph shows the recorded points for the age group 55–64; the lower for the age group 15–24.

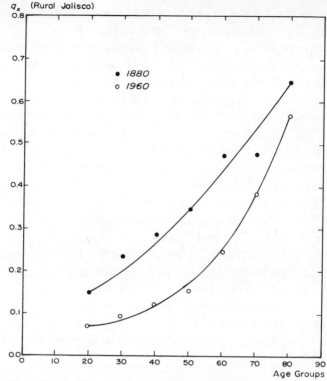

q_x (Rural Jalisco)

Figure 7.5.   Values of q_x for rural Jalisco plotted against age on paper with direct rectangular coordinates.

derived graphically. Nevertheless, they will be in the same range and will represent the best guess possible. It will be noted, of course, that this method need not be used for internal comparisons within either Jalisco or Oaxaca, nor for comparisons between Jalisco and Guadalajara.

Another device has been employed when we deal with values of q_x which occur in sets according to consecutive age groups at the same date. These values tend to follow a curvilinear course, such as is shown for Jalisco in 1880 and 1960 in Figure 7.5. In order to obtain averages and to calculate regression coefficients (see discussion below), it is desirable that the points be ordered as nearly as possible in a straight line. Some improvement may be obtained by using the logarithms rather than the direct numbers, an improvement which is demonstrated by the 1880 and 1960 data for Jalisco when plotted on semilog paper (Figure 7.6). The use of logarithms, instead of the original numbers, does not adversely affect any comparisons which we might wish to make.

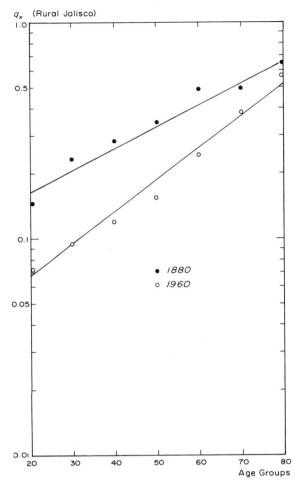

Figure 7.6.   Values of q_x for rural Jalisco. The same points as in Figure 7.5 but plotted on semilog paper.

For the test No. 1A between Jalisco and Oaxaca, we determined the mean value of log q_x for seven age groups in each region and at each date, 1880, 1890, etc. This mean value of q_x for a set of seven consecutive age groups has little theoretical significance. Each q_x value itself represents the mean of the ten years included in the group. Furthermore, the set is restricted to the adolescent and adult years from 15 to 85. Nevertheless, we obtain an *index* number, an *indicator* of the relative level of mortality characteristic of the specified time and place, which can then be compared with some other time or locality. Hence, it serves as a purely empirical guide.

In Table 7.2, part A, are shown the mean values of log q_x

Table 7.2

Rural Jalisco and western Oaxaca

The mean value of log q_x was determined for each set of seven age groups from 15 to 24 years to 75 to 84 years inclusive in each region and at each date.

A. These means are tabulated, and the value of t is determined for the differences between the respective means.

B. For each date and in each region, the regression coefficient, b, of each set of age groups is calculated and tabulated. The value of t is determined for the differences between the b's in each pair. Each value of b has been multiplied by 100 in order to move the decimal point two places to the left.

In part A the values and means of log q_x are all positive. The differences and the mean difference are also positive. The figures for Jalisco are subtracted from those of Oaxaca. In part B, the values for b are also all positive. The differences with one exception and the mean difference are also positive. Here the values for Oaxaca are subtracted from those for Jalisco. Negative values carry minus signs but positive values are unmarked.

A. Mean value of log q_x for each date and each region

Date	Jalisco	Oaxaca	Difference
1880	1.534	1.573	0.039
1890	1.514	1.564	0.050
1900	1.468	1.563	0.095
1920	1.449	1.567	0.118
1930	1.413	1.525	0.112
1940	1.364	1.491	0.127
1950	1.290	1.459	0.169
1960	1.260	1.427	0.167
Mean	1.412	1.521	
Mean difference			0.109
$t=2.44$			

B. Value of b for each date and each region

Date	Jalisco	Oaxaca	Difference
1880	1.011	1.068	−0.057
1890	1.189	1.158	0.031
1900	1.213	1.128	0.095
1920	1.139	0.918	0.221
1930	1.176	1.039	0.137
1940	1.215	1.034	0.181
1950	1.332	1.204	0.128
1960	1.509	1.271	0.238
Mean	1.223	1.103	
Mean difference			0.120
$t=2.09$			

for Jalisco and Oaxaca at eight dates from 1880 to 1960. It will be observed that at each date the value of $\log q_x$ for Oaxaca is higher than that for Jalisco. The conclusion would therefore be that at all ages between 15 and 85 the average probability of death has been greater in the former state than in the latter. The validity of such a conclusion may be tested by calculating the value of t for the differences between the two states at the series of consecutive dates. The mean for Jalisco is 1.412 (see Table 7.2, part A), for Oaxaca 1.521. The mean or average difference between the paired values is 0.109, in favor of Oaxaca. The critical ratio of the means (that is, t) is calculated by the simple formula:

$$t = \frac{\text{mean difference}}{\text{standard error of the difference}}$$

Here its value is 2.44. With 7 degrees of freedom, this figure is slightly beyond the 5 percent level of probability. (The 5 percent level is at 2.365.) The difference is thus moderately but not highly significant.

The test which we designated No. 1B uses the same sets of values for q_x, but in this case we examine not the mean but the trend in each set from the youngest to the oldest age group. The probability of death is, of course, always least in the group 15–24 years of age. (We are omitting the infants and young children). It is greatest in the group 75–84, and all sets converge to the value 1.0 in the group 85 and older. Consequently, the mortality status of the adult population is described by the separation between youngest and oldest, for if q_x for the group 15–24 years is small, the range between it and 1.0 will be relatively great, and vice versa. At the same time, the rapidity or rate of change in q_x while progressing from a low value at 15–24 years to the maximum at 75–84 years will be greater the lower the starting point at 15 years. This relationship is clearly displayed in Figure 7.6 where the age group sets of q_x for rural Jalisco in 1880 and 1960 have been plotted on semilog paper.

What we need now is a method for expressing numerically the rate at which probability of death changes with age. Graphic methods are possible, but the simplest procedure is to employ the regression coefficient, usually designated b. The value of q_x in each age group increases from young to old in each age group in a more or less linear fashion, often, however, with considerable fluctuation. Hence, the regression coefficient, which should be applied only to strictly linear relationships, will be to some extent inaccurate. On the other hand, it furnishes the closest measure which we can obtain for the trend or slope of the q_x values. As such it may be used as an index to relative mortality. Since we are working with only a segment of the line representing the progression from birth to death, we are not interested in the point of origin at the zero ordinate. We consider only the average slope, which may be calculated by the formula $b = \dfrac{(dx)\,(dy)}{dx^2}$, where dx and dy are the deviations from the respective means of x and y. Here, x is the age (that is, the central years of the consecutive age groups) and y is the value of q_x.

In Table 7.2, part B, are given the figures representing b for rural Jalisco and Oaxaca at each of the eight dates previously specified. At all of these except 1880, b in Jalisco exceeded b in Oaxaca, a finding which implies that the probability of death in the younger, age groups with respect to the older age groups, was less in the former state than in the latter. The value of t is 2.09, between the 5 and the 10 percent levels of statistical probability and, hence, of only marginal significance. Nevertheless, the direction of difference agrees with that suggested by the preceding test, No. 1A.

For the test which we designate No. 2, we proceed somewhat differently, although we utilize the same values for q_x. Here they are not put in logarithmic form but are used directly as given in the life tables. Instead of averaging the set corresponding to each series of consecutive age groups, we get with each age group the mean value of q_x for the set of successive dates. With Jalisco, and with Oaxaca by graphic interpolation, there are eight of these. They fall on even decades from 1880 to 1960, with the omission of 1910. For instance, with Jalisco and with Oaxaca, using the age group 15–24 years, we average the eight values of q_x and get for the former 0.1146 and for the latter 0.1496. The difference between these means is 0.0350, and the value of t for this difference is 7.60, highly significant. The same procedure is adopted with the other six age groups, and the results are shown in Table 7.3, part A. From this table it is clear that for each age group throughout the time span indicated, the mean value of q_x is greater in Oaxaca than in rural Jalisco, and the differences are of consi-

Table 7.3

Rural Jalisco and western Oaxaca.

Values of q_x for Jalisco are from life tables, direct figures, not logarithms. The same for Oaxaca at 1890 and 1940. At other dates by graphic interpolation. For Jalisco and for Oaxaca the mean value of q_x was calculated for each age group at the dates 1880 to 1960, eight dates in all. There were seven age groups 10 years apart, from 15 to 84 years of age. The mean values of q_x are tabulated with their differences for the two states, together with the value of t for the mean difference. (All numbers are positive. Values for Jalisco are subtracted from those for Oaxaca.)

	Mean value of q_x at 8 dates for each age group			
Age Group	*Jalisco*	*Oaxaca*	*Mean Difference*	*t*
15–24	0.1146	0.1496	0.0350	7.60
25–34	0.1625	0.2182	0.0557	7.41
35–44	0.1975	0.2606	0.0631	8.09
45–54	0.2451	0.3078	0.0627	3.80
55–64	0.3570	0.4705	0.1135	5.08
65–74	0.4635	0.5682	0.1047	7.12
75–84	0.6222	0.6929	0.0707	11.26

derable magnitude. The results of this test, therefore, coincide in principle with those of the previous tests.

The tests which we designate No. 3 and No. 4 employ e_x instead of q_x. The expectation of life, e_x, is derived from the same basic data as q_x, and the two magnitudes are, therefore, to a considerable degree interdependent. However, e_x is in a sense the inverse of q_x, for as the probability of death, q_x, increases, the expectation of life, e_x, diminishes. Hence, a population with a high mortality rate should demonstrate a relatively low expectation of life.

The No. 3 simulates test No. 1, with certain differences. We determine the values of e_x in 1880, 1890, etc., for Oaxaca by graphic interpolation, as previously. However, we use the direct values, not the logarithms. The reason for this choice is that when the values of e_x for most sets of age groups are plotted, the trend is somewhat curvilinear, regardless of whether the coordinates are rectangular or semilogarithmic. Since we must endure some departure from strict linearity in any case, there is no advantage in the conversion of the direct values to logarithms. Another distinction is that with e_x the age group can be expressed only as its first year, for a specific expectation of life is not a continuous function which extends throughout the ten years of an age group and which can be easily averaged, as is true with q_x. Rather, it is an instantaneous function, applicable only to the beginning of the age interval. Its value changes, to be sure, throughout the interval, but we have no means for estimating it until the beginning of the next interval is reached.

We calculated the mean values of e_x for each set of age groups but did not compare pairs of these means as we did in test No. 1A (see Table 7.2, part A, for test No. 1A). The reason for not doing so is that e_x is a cumulative magnitude, expressing the mortality experience of all older age groups, and is not characteristic solely of the particular age group for which it is calculated. On the other hand, the trend of e_x from young to old can be profitably employed. This trend is expressed as the regression coefficient, b, as in test No. 1B. With e_x, however, the trend is from the larger to the smaller numbers and, hence, carries a minus sign. For each date, therefore, we calculated b, in rural Jalisco and in Oaxaca. The values are tabulated and will be found in Table 7.4, together with the differences between b's for the two regions. The critical ratio of the mean difference, t, is 4.38, highly significant. Test No. 3, consequently, as it should, confirms the results of test No. 1B in that the slopes are steeper and the trends more intense in Jalisco than in Oaxaca. Indeed, it surpasses the preceding test in statistical significance.

Test No. 4A simulates test No. 2. The values of e_x for each age group separately are averaged over the period 1880 to 1960, and the means are compared for the two states. It will be noted that these mean values of e_x are referred in the table to the first year of the respective age group and that the group 5–14 years is included. (see Table 7.5.) The differences between Jalisco and Oaxaca are of considerable magnitude for each year of age given from 5 to 75 and are highly significant statistically. The values for Jalisco at all ages exceed those for Oaxaca. This finding is consistent with that shown in test No. 2, Table 7.3, in which the level of q_x was lower in Jalisco than in Oaxaca. It will also be noted that the mean differences diminish with increasing age even though they remain very significant. This reduction is of course referable to the fact that the values for e_x steadily diminish from a maximum at five years to a minimum in old age. With the data from the two states, however, the mean difference for 75 years, despite its small size in absolute terms, still shows a high value for t.

Table 7.4

Rural Jalisco and western Oaxaca.

Values of e_x for Jalisco are from life tables (direct figures, not logarithms);
the same for Oaxaca at 1890 and 1940; at other dates by graphic interpolation.
For each set of seven age groups (from 15 years to 84 years), the regression
coefficient, b, was calculated at each date in each of the two regions. The values
of b were tabulated, and the value of t was determined for the mean difference
between b's in each regional pair. (Oaxaca is subtracted from Jalisco.)

Value of b for each set of age groups at each date and each region

Date	*Jalisco*	*Oaxaca*	*Difference*
1880	− 0.3553	−0.3598	0.0045
1890	− 0.3889	−0.3746	−0.0143
1900	− 0.4353	−0.3891	−0.0462
1920	− 0.4472	−0.3357	−0.1115
1930	− 0.4798	−0.3793	−0.1005
1940	− 0.5190	−0.4070	−0.1120
1950	− 0.5712	−0.4439	−0.1273
1960	− 0.6052	−0.4813	−0.1239
Mean	−0.4752	−0.3964	
Mean difference			−0.0788
$t = 4.38$			

If we consider the life tables constructed for rural Jalisco
and western Oaxaca, as tested by the methods just described,
we find a strong, consistent contrast. The probability of death
among adults, not infants, has been higher, and the expectation
of life beyond the age of five years has been lower in the latter
state. The investigations of Cordero and others have demonstrated that registration of infant deaths in Oaxaca has always been
extremely deficient. Nevertheless, when we delete the infant
category entirely, we find a poorer mortality performance in
rural Oaxaca than in rural Jalisco. The causes must lie deeper
than mere unwillingness to cooperate in recording vital statistics.

Our data for Guadalajara extend from 1860 to 1960, with
the exception of 1910. It is possible, therefore, to compare the
city with the rural areas of Jalisco at eight dates, beginning with
1880. This comparison is of interest because one might anticipate
a pattern of survival and mortality in the large urban center

Table 7.5

Rural Jalisco and western Oaxaca.

Values of e_x for Jalisco are from life tables; the same for Oaxaca at 1890 and 1940; at other dates by graphic interpolation.

For Jalisco and for Oaxaca is calculated the mean value of e_x for the first year of each age group from 5 to 84 years of age, at the dates 1880 to 1960, a set of eight dates in all. There are eight age groups.

The mean values of e_x and their differences have been tabulated. For each age group the mean difference at the eight dates is shown, together with the value of t for each difference in means. (The means for Oaxaca have been subtracted from those for Jalisco.)

	Mean value of e_x at 8 dates for each age group			
First Year of Age Group	*Jalisco*	*Oaxaca*	*Mean Difference*	*t*
5	41.80	35.38	6.42	7.07
15	37.26	31.73	5.53	5.87
25	31.29	26.21	5.08	5.73
35	26.17	21.79	4.38	5.55
45	21.08	17.61	3.47	5.36
55	16.22	13.20	3.02	7.93
65	12.45	10.42	2.03	34.88
75	8.78	8.06	0.72	13.43

which would differ strongly from that characteristic of the countryside. In order to examine this possibility we tested the levels of q_x and e_x of the appropriate life tables by the same methods which we employed to differentiate between Jalisco and Oaxaca.

In test No. 1A the mean value of log q_x in each set of age groups from 15 years to 84 years is determined for each entity, rural Jalisco and Guadalajara, at each available date. The means at Guadalajara in 1860 and 1870 are recorded in Table 7.6, part A, but are not used for comparison. Those from 1880 to 1960 inclusive are paired with the corresponding figures for Jalisco, which are taken from Table 7.2, part A. The average difference for all dates is very small and of poor significance statistically. In so far as any conclusion can be drawn, it is that the probability of death has been slightly higher in the city than in the state at large.

Test No. 1B employs the regression coefficient, b, for

Table 7.6

Rural Jalisco and Guadalajara

The procedure is the same as for Table 7.2. The data for Jalisco are taken from that table; for Guadalajara the figures are calculated from life tables. In part A, the logarithms of q_x are used. The values of b have been multiplied by 100 and are all positive. (In both parts the values for Jalisco are subtracted from those of Guadalajara.)

A. Mean value of log q_x for each date and for each entity.

Date	Jalisco	Guadalajara	Difference
1860		1.531	
1870		1.529	
1880	1.534	1.524	−0.010
1890	1.514	1.528	0.014
1900	1.468	1.483	0.015
1920	1.449	1.445	−0.004
1930	1.413	1.431	0.018
1940	1.364	1.388	0.024
1950	1.290	1.346	0.056
1960	1.260	1.280	0.020
Mean	1.412	1.428	
Mean difference			0.016
$t = 1.72$			

B. Value of b for each date and each entity

Date	Jalisco	Guadalajara	Difference
1860		1.042	
1870		1.220	
1880	1.011	1.327	0.316
1890	1.189	1.238	0.049
1900	1.213	1.256	0.043
1920	1.139	1.136	−0.003
1930	1.176	1.191	0.015
1940	1.215	1.255	0.040
1950	1.332	1.508	0.176
1960	1.509	1.586	0.077
Mean	1.223	1.312	
Mean difference			0.089
$t = 1.77$			

Essays in Population History

the same sets of groups at the same dates. The average of b for Guadalajara (see Table 7.6, part B) is slightly higher than for rural Jalisco, a result which contradicts that obtained with test No. 1A. It will be remembered that with q_x the steeper the slope of the line, or the greater the value of b, the smaller is the probability of death at the early ages. However, in both tests the value of t for the mean difference is too small to be given serious weight.

In test No. 2, for which the results are in Table 7.7, the values of q_x are segregated according to age group and averaged in sets of dates from 1880 to 1960. Thus, for Jalisco (see also Table 7.3) and for Guadalajara, the mean value of q_x is calculated for each age group as the average of eight dates. The difference between the two means for each age group is found by subtracting the value for Guadalajara from that for Jalisco, and the value of t is determined for the difference. The differences are higher in Jalisco with age groups 15–24 and 25–34, higher in Guadalajara with the older groups, but, again, the significance of several differences is very low. On the whole, the results are too equivocal to warrant the formation of any conclusions.

Table 7.7

Rural Jalisco and Guadalajara

The value for Jalisco are taken from Table 7.3; those for Guadalajara from life tables.

As in Table 7.3, there is calculated for Jalisco and for Guadalajara, the mean value of q_x for each age group, between 15 and 84 years of age, at the dates 1880 to 1960. There are eight dates in all and seven age groups.

The mean values for q_x and their differences are tabulated, together with their differences. For each age group is shown the mean difference at each of the eight dates and the value of t for each mean difference. (The figures for Guadalajara are subtracted from those of Jalisco.)

	Mean value of q_x at 8 dates for each age group			
Age Group	*Jalisco*	*Guadalajara*	*Difference*	*t*
15–24	0.1146	0.1029	0.0117	2.56
25–34	0.1625	0.1599	0.0026	0.43
35–44	0.1975	0.2091	−0.0116	1.89
45–54	0.2451	0.2807	−0.0356	5.46
55–64	0.3570	0.3756	−0.0186	1.50
65–74	0.4635	0.4884	−0.0249	3.08
75–84	0.6222	0.6511	−0.0289	1.68

Test No. 3 employs the expectation of life, e_x, with the figures for Jalisco taken from Table 7.4, those for Guadalajara from life tables. As in the previous instance we use the regression coefficient, b, for the respective sets of age groups between 15 and 84 years of age, as they were calculated at each of the eight dates, 1880 to 1960. With e_x the coefficients are negative since all sets of age groups diminish to a common level at extreme old age. The data shown in Table 7.8 make it clear that the differences in values of b for Jalisco and Guadalajara are too small and too variable to be of significance. The mean difference for the eight dates is less than 2 percent of either mean, and t reaches only 0.98.

Test No. 4 utilizes the procedure described for Table 7.5. The mean value of e_x was calculated for the set of eight dates in each entity and for the first year of each age group, beginning with 5 years. The results are given in Table 7.9 and include the value of t for each mean difference. Here, as previously, the

Table 7.8

Rural Jalisco and Guadalajara.

The values of e_x for Jalisco are taken from Table 7.4; those for Guadalajara are from life tables.

The regression coefficient produced by each set of age groups has been calculated for each date from 1880 to 1960 in each entity. These values of b have been tabulated according to date, and t is determined for the mean difference between the values of b for each pair. (All values of b are negative; those for Guadalajara are subtracted from those for Jalisco.)

Value of b for each set of age groups at each date and region			
Date	*Jalisco*	*Guadalajara*	*Difference*
1880	−0.3553	−0.3940	0.0387
1890	−0.3889	−0.3920	0.0031
1900	−0.4353	−0.4318	−0.0035
1920	−0.4472	−0.4324	−0.0148
1930	−0.4798	−0.4615	−0.0183
1940	−0.5190	−0.4868	−0.0322
1950	−0.5712	−0.5428	−0.0284
1960	−0.6052	−0.5990	−0.0062
Mean	−0.4752	−0.4675	
Mean difference			−0.0077
$t=0.98$			

Table 7.9

Rural Jalisco and Guadalajara.

The values of e_x for Jalisco are taken from Table 7.5; those for Guadalajara are from life tables.

For Jalisco and for Guadalajara the mean value of e_x is calculated for the first year of each age group at the dates 1880 to 1960. There are eight dates in all, and eight age groups from 5 to 75 years inclusive.

The mean values of e_x and their differences are tabulated. For each age group is shown the difference between the means at each of the eight dates, together with the value of t for each difference between means. Finally, the eight mean differences are averaged and the critical ratio of the average difference is determined. (The mean of Guadalajara is subtracted from that of Jalisco.)

Mean value of e_x at 8 dates for each age group

First Year of Age Group	Jalisco	Guadalajara	Difference	t
5	41.80	43.37	−1.57	3.52
15	37.26	36.88	0.38	1.26
25	31.29	30.19	1.10	3.28
35	26.17	24.79	1.38	6.10
45	21.08	19.94	1.14	3.91
55	16.22	15.57	0.65	2.77
65	12.45	11.93	0.52	2.78
75	8.78	8.49	0.29	1.73

Ave. mean difference   0.49
$t = 1.51$

mean differences are small and the values of t are erratic. In order to test further the validity of the differences, we obtained their average and determined the critical ratio of that average. Its value is 1.51, of very little, if any, significance.

In none of these tests have we been able to show that the life tables derived from the mortality records of rural Jalisco differed in any clear manner or to any profound extent from those constructed for Guadalajara. Indeed, the similarity between the two entities is as striking as the divergence between the two rural areas in Jalisco and Oaxaca. We must, therefore, conclude that no urban-rural distinction can be found with our present data from the state of Jalisco.

The contrast between the coastal and highland areas of Jalisco and Oaxaca is subjected to the same tests as those which have been described for rural Jalisco and western Oaxaca.

These are arranged in two series, one for each of the two states, respectively. Each series consists of four parts, corresponding to the four tests, two of which utilize the probability of death, q_x, and two of which utilize the expectation of life, e_x. There is no problem with respect to dates because for each date there is in all cases a coast-highland pair which may serve as a basis for comparison. The procedures have already been outlined, and further detail is supplied with each table. We may consider first Jalisco.

The coastal area of Jalisco embraces the municipalities listed in Appendix B; our sample for the plateau is also listed in that appendix. The two are separated by a broad intermediate zone, the mortality data for which are not included in the present calculations. Table 7.10, part A, shows the mean value of log q_x in seven age groups at each of eight dates in the two regions. In all instances the value for the coast exceeds that for the plateau. The mean difference is highly significant, for t equals 15.68. This result is confirmed by the figures in Table 7.10, part B. The value of b for the same sets of age groups is greater for the plateau at all dates except 1880, with t for the mean difference equaling 4.33.

That the probability of death has been higher on the coast than on the plateau is also attested by the figures in Table 7.11. Here is shown the mean value of q_x in each set of eight dates for the individual groups from 15 to 84 years of age. In each group from 15 to 24 years to that 45 to 54 years, the difference between the means of the coast and the plateau is highly significant. In the older groups the differences are smaller and of lower significance.

This distinction is of interest because it indicates, first, that the difference in mortality between the two areas was concentrated in the younger segment of the adult population and, second, that the difference between the climatic and altitudinal zones of coast and highland varied qualitatively from that between the political areas Jalisco and Oaxaca. Table 7.3, which gives the mean values of q_x for the two states segregated according to age group, gives no indication of a reduction in mean difference with age. The conclusion must be that the factors controlling mortality at the state level must have been different from those operating with respect to ecological zones. Regarding the nature of these factors we can only hazard the guess that in the latter instance they involve health conditions, disease vectors,

Table 7.10

Jalisco : Coast versus plateau.

Values of q_x for both coast and plateau were taken from the corresponding life tables. As in Tables 7.2 and 7.6 the logarithms were used in calculating the means of q_x in part A, below.

In part A for each date the mean of log q_x was calculated for the set of seven age groups in each region. These means were tabulated and the value of t was determined for the difference between the two series of means. For the difference, the figure for the coast was subtracted from that of the plateau.

In part B for each date and for each region the regression coefficient, b, was calculated in each set of age groups and multiplied by 100 in order to move the decimal point. The values of b were tabulated and t determined for the difference between the b's in each pair. (For the difference the value for the coast was subtracted from that of the plateau.)

A. Mean value of log q_x for each date and region

Date	Coast	Plateau	Difference
1880	1.583	1.513	−0.070
1890	1.557	1.503	−0.054
1900	1.503	1.441	−0.062
1920	1.516	1.429	−0.087
1930	1.473	1.386	−0.087
1940	1.403	1.334	−0.069
1950	1.336	1.276	−0.060
1960	1.296	1.217	−0.079
Mean	1.458	1.387	
Mean difference			−0.071
$t = 15.68$			

B. Value of b for the set of age groups at each date in each region

Date	Coast	Plateau	Difference
1880	1.031	1.023	−0.008
1890	0.979	1.268	0.289
1900	1.085	1.316	0.231
1920	0.927	1.204	0.277
1930	1.091	1.262	0.171
1940	1.051	1.331	0.280
1950	1.198	1.408	0.210
1960	1.181	1.772	0.591
Mean	1.068	1.323	
Mean difference			0.255
$t = 4.33$			

Table 7.11

Jalisco : Coast versus plateau.

Value of q_x for coast and plateau are from the life tables.
For the coast and for the plateau the mean value of q_x for the set of eight dates between 1880 and 1960 was calculated for each age group. There are seven age groups, consisting of ten years each, from 15 to 24 years to 75 to 84 years.
The mean values of q_x and their differences are tabulated. For each age group is shown the mean difference between the two sets of eight dates, together with the value of t for each mean difference. (For the difference the value for the plateau is subtracted from that for the coast.)

Age Group	Mean value of q_x at 8 dates for each age group			
	Coast	Plateau	Mean Difference	t
15–24	0.1368	0.1118	0.0250	5.95
25–34	0.2010	0.1469	0.0541	7.83
35–44	0.2438	0.1776	0.0662	7.80
45–54	0.2759	0.2222	0.0535	4.72
55–64	0.3786	0.3511	0.0275	2.84
65–74	0.4689	0.4616	0.0073	0.56
75–84	0.6073	0.6408	−0.0335	3.83

and biological determinants whereas in the former they have been social, economic, and political in nature.

If we return now to consideration of the series of tests, we find that Table 7.12 shows for e_x higher values of b at each date in the set of age groups from the plateau. Since the value of b is directly proportional to the expected length of life, this result runs parallel to that obtained with q_x (see Table 7.10, part B) where the value of b is inversely proportional to the probability of death throughout the set of age groups.

Table 7.13 gives for e_x the figures analogous to those for q_x in Table 7.11. The mean values of e_x for the sets of eight dates are arranged according to age group, and t for each mean difference is calculated. Clearly, there is a progressive reduction in mean difference as the group age advances, even reaching a reversal of direction past the age of sixty-five. This phenomenon is referable in part to the inevitable reduction in expectation of life which accompanies aging with consequent decrease in differences of e_x and deterioration of statistical reliability. It may also in part be associated with the higher level of survivorship manifested by the younger component of the popula-

Table 7.12

Jalisco : Coast versus plateau.

Values of e_x for the coast and the plateau are from the life tables.
The value of the regression coefficient, b, was calculated with each set of
age groups from 15 to 84 years of age for each region at each date. There were
eight dates, from 1880 to 1960. The values of b are tabulated, and the critical
ratio, t, is determined for the difference between b's in each pair. (For the difference the value for the coast is subtracted from that for the plateau.)

Value of b in each set of age groups at each date and in each region

Date	Coast	Plateau	Difference
1880	−0.2588	−0.3674	−0.1086
1890	−0.3264	−0.4142	−0.0878
1900	−0.3846	−0.4693	−0.0847
1920	−0.3700	−0.4795	−0.1095
1930	−0.4185	−0.5152	−0.0967
1940	−0.4650	−0.5643	−0.0993
1950	−0.5295	−0.5985	−0.0690
1960	−0.5640	−0.6226	−0.0586
Mean	0.4146	0.5039	
Mean difference			−0.0893
$t = 13.87$			

tion on the plateau, behavior upon which comment has been
made above.

Regardless of what explanation is offered for these
anomalies, there can be little question, as a result of the procedures illustrated in Tables 7.10 to 7.13, that the two geographical
zones in Jalisco have demonstrated diverse patterns of mortality
during the past century. Furthermore, it may be deduced from
these data that at least among the younger and middle-aged
adults, there has been less mortality and, therefore, expectation
of longer life on the highland plateau than along the low-lying
coastal plain.

The coastal and highland areas of Oaxaca from which
our samples are drawn have been described in terms of ex-
districts. What we designate as the coast consists of the former
districts of Juquila, Jumiltepec, and Pochutla. The highland or
plateau area embraces the territory known as the Mixteca Alta,

Table 7.13

Jalisco : Coast versus plateau.

Values of e_x for the coast and the plateau are from the life tables. The mean value of e_x was calculated at the first year of each age group from 5 to 75 years at the dates 1860 to 1960. There are eight dates in each set and eight sets, corresponding to the eight age groups.

The mean values of e_x and their differences are tabulated, one pair for each age group, together with the value of t for each difference in means. Finally, the mean differences for the eight age groups are averaged and the value of t determined. (For the difference the value for the coast is subtracted from that of the plateau.)

Mean value of e_x at 8 dates for each age group

First Year of Age Group	Coast	Plateau	Mean Difference	t
5	39.36	42.73	3.37	11.29
15	34.30	38.50	4.20	13.87
25	28.71	32.57	3.86	10.98
35	24.40	27.14	2.76	7.31
45	20.34	21.74	1.40	4.12
55	15.93	16.33	0.40	1.62
65	12.42	12.34	−0.08	0.43
75	8.92	8.59	−0.34	3.93

Ave. mean difference   1.95
$t = 3.32$

the ex-districts of Coixtlahuaca, Nochixtlan, Teposcolula, and Tlaxiaco. Within this region the climate is uniformly cool, the rainfall light, and the altitude with a range of about 1,500 to 2,500 meters. Ecologically, the coastal and highland areas of Oaxaca closely resemble those we have examined in Jalisco.

The mortality data for the Oaxaca coast and highland are given in Table 7.14 to 7.17 inclusive. The treatment with respect to the life table parameters q_x and e_x is almost identical with that employed with Jalisco, with one exception. There are six dates instead of eight, 1872, 1890, 1907, 1922, 1940, and 1952. No attempt is made to estimate values for 1880, 1900, etc., by graphic interpolation. Such a device is unnecessary because within Oaxaca comparisons can be limited to those dates for which we have figures from both the coast and the Mixteca Alta.

Table 7.14 tells us that the mean value of log q_x in each set of age groups was higher at all six dates on the coast than in the interior whereas the value of b was lower. According to Table 7.16, the value of b with e_x for each set of age groups was consistently higher in the Mixteca Alta. From Tables 7.15 and 7.17 we learn that for each age group the mean value of q_x in each of dates was higher on the coast than in the Mixteca Alta whereas the mean value of e_x was lower. We also learn that the magnitude of the mean difference in q_x and e_x diminished with increasing age, just as it did in Jalisco, although the effect is not so pronounced as in the latter state.

All these results point to an amazing similarity in the respective mortality patterns shown by the coast as opposed to the highland zones in both states. In each case, as indicated by statistically valid criteria, the probability of death, particularly among those persons of ages between 15 and 54, has been higher on the coast than on the plateau. Correspondingly, the expectation of life among the older children and the young adults has been much lower. We are clearly dealing with a biomedical phenomenon of significance which extends beyond the restricted areas studied here.

The contrast between the lowland and the highland in the New World has been manifest since the discovery by Europeans. Prior to this event there is much reason to believe that the coasts of North and South America were heavily populated, at least as heavily as the habitat at higher elevation. There is no indication of poorer demographic conditions in the low country. Yet when the white man arrived, the coasts were the first and most severely affected. In some instances the depletion was so rapid that almost all record of former occupancy was lost after no more than a decade. Furthermore, after the initial shock subsided the coasts were the slowest to recover. In Nueva Galicia, for example, the regions of Purificación and Banderas were totally denuded of inhabitants and recovered only two or three centuries later through migration from the interior. A simple explanation is the greater virulence in the low, hot, humid zone of introduced diseases; yet with the exception of malaria, all these were active throughout the country. It is clear that for native and even mixed populations, the physical environment has been a decisive factor in the determination of demographic characteristics.

We may now consider changes which have occurred

during the course of time rather than differences across geographical boundaries. The consistent amelioration of health conditions and the steady increase in the population of Mexico since the mid-nineteenth century are reflected in the data derived from the abridged life tables which we have constructed for

Table 7.14

Oaxaca : Coast versus Mixteca Alta.

Values of q_x in both regions for the years 1872, 1890, 1907, 1922, 1940, and 1952 were taken from the corresponding life tables. As in Tables 7.2, 7.6, and 7.10 the logarithms were used in calculating the means of q_x in part A, below.

For parts A and B the respective procedure was the same as in Table 7.10, to which reference is made. (In both parts for differences the figure for the coast was subtracted from that for the Mixteca Alta.)

A. Mean value of log q_x for each date and each region

Date	Coast	Mixteca Alta	Difference
1872	1.663	1.526	−0.137
1890	1.626	1.534	−0.092
1907	1.628	1.541	−0.087
1922	1.620	1.517	−0.103
1940	1.566	1.429	−0.137
1952	1.545	1.402	−0.143
Mean	1.608	1.492	
Mean difference			−0.116
$t = 11.23$			

B. Value of b for each date and each region

Date	Coast	Mixteca Alta	Difference
1872	0.809	1.095	0.286
1890	1.027	1.213	0.186
1907	1.017	1.100	0.083
1922	0.937	1.127	0.190
1940	0.984	1.252	0.268
1952	0.991	1.406	0.415
Mean	0.961	1.198	
Mean difference			0.237
$t = 5.06$			

Table 7.15

Oaxaca : Coast versus Mixteca Alta.

Values of q_x in both regions were taken from the life tables.

The mean values of q_x and their differences are tabulated for each age group at the set of dates from 1872 to 1952. The procedure is the same as in Table 7.11. (For the differences the figure for the Mixteca Alta is subtracted from that for the coast.)

Mean value of q_x at 6 dates for each age group

Age Group	Coast	Mixteca Alta	Mean Difference	t
15–24	0.1740	0.1521	0.0219	2.57
25–34	0.2908	0.1809	0.1099	15.12
35–44	0.3568	0.2240	0.1328	14.09
45–54	0.4010	0.2635	0.1375	10.76
55–64	0.5689	0.4339	0.1350	20.17
65–74	0.6263	0.5988	0.0275	1.86
75–84	0.7235	0.7060	0.0175	0.99

Table 7.16

Oaxaca : Coast versus Mixteca Alta.

Values of e_x for the coast and Mixteca Alta are from the life tables.

The value of the regression coefficient, b, was calculated in each set of age groups from 15 to 84 years of age for each region at each date. There are six dates, from 1872 to 1952. The values of b are tabulated and the critical ratio, t, is determined for the difference between b's in each pair. (For the differences the values for the coast are subtracted from those for the Mixteca Alta.)

Value of b for each set of age groups at each date and in each region

Date	Coast	Mixteca Alta	Difference
1872	−0.2664	−0.3972	−0.1308
1890	−0.3043	−0.4078	−0.1035
1907	−0.2800	−0.3990	−0.1190
1922	−0.2930	−0.4188	−0.1258
1940	−0.3283	−0.4780	−0.1497
1952	−0.3515	−0.5095	−0.1580
Mean	−0.3039	−0.4350	
Mean difference			−0.1311
$t = 16.02$			

Table 1.17

Oaxaca : Coast versus Mixteca Alta.

Values of e_x for coast and Mixteca Alta are from the life tables.
The mean value of e_x was calculated for coast and for the Mixteca Alta at the first year of each age group from 5 to 75 years at the dates 1872 to 1952. There are six dates in each set and eight sets. corresponding to the eight age groups.

The mean values of e_x and their differences are tabulated, one pair for each age group. together with the value of t for each difference in means. Finally, the mean differences for the eight age groups are averaged and the value of t determined. (For the differences the value for the coast is subtracted from that for Mixteca Alta.)

Mean value of e_x at 6 dates for each age group			
First Year of Age Group	*Coast*	*Mixteca Alta*	*Mean Difference*	*t*
5	31.27	35.79	4.52	4.53
15	26.77	33.28	6.51	10.02
25	21.24	28.24	7.00	16.10
35	17.84	23.30	5.46	19.19
45	14.88	18.78	3.90	12.94
55	11.43	13.65	2.22	16.98
65	9.79	10.15	0.36	2.74
75	7.77	7.94	0.17	1.04

Average mean difference   3.80
       $t=4.09$

rural Jalisco and Oaxaca. Most conspicuous is the decline in the mean value of q_x, the probability of death, seen in Table 7.2, part A, Table 7.10, and Table 7.14, together with the parallel rise in the value of b, recorded in the same tables. Since b is an index to the rate of change in q_x as we progress through the age groups at each date, an increase in its magnitude with calendar time may be taken as widening of the gap between the low probability of death in the young component and the inevitable decease of all members of the most aged group. An increase in the cofficient b, therefore, may be regarded as an improvement in the mortality status.

Another simpler and, perhaps, more convincing criterion is the expectation of life, represented by the column e_x in the life table. In the present instance we may examine e_x for the first year of each ten-year age group in rural Jalisco, Guadalajara, and Oaxaca, respectively, as the value moved from the earliest to the latest year of our samples. The time limits vary in the three entities : in rural Jalisco from 1880 to 1960, in Guadalajara from 1860 to 1960, and in Oaxaca from 1872 to 1952. The mean values of e_x would be of little use, for we wish to determine the trend or rate of change. The change, of course, takes the form of an increase in e_x, the expectation of life. For this purpose the regression coefficient, b, is well adapted since it expresses the steepness of the slope of the line described by e_x as this factor progresses from the beginning to the end of the time interval.

The pattern developed in the three entities is shown graphically for e_x at five years of age in Figure 7.7. The consistent increase is unmistakable, but certain other features are also noteworthy. It is clear that each set of points does not fall with precision upon a straight line. Part of the deviations are referable to error inherent in the sampling, particularly in the early years and in Oaxaca. Part can be explained if it is assumed

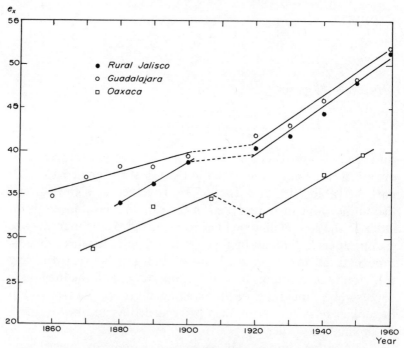

Figure 7.7   Values of e_x at 5 years of age for rural Jalisco, Guadalajara, and Oaxaca throughout the time span covered by our samples. The lines represent trends as estimated by eye.

that the increase actually was not linear but slightly curved. This effect is visible in Jalisco and Oaxaca in the decades since 1920. However, the greatest disturbance was caused by the Revolution of 1910–1920. All three entities display a discontinuity, very slight in Guadalajara, moderate in rural Jalisco, sufficiently great in Oaxaca to produce a fall in e_x between 1907 and 1922. There can be no doubt that we here witness a side effect of the demographic disruption which occurred as a result of the civil war and the social upheaval. In addition to the sharp break, we note that the slope of the lines differs in the later from the earlier period. It is uniformly steeper. The implication is that the improvement in expectation of life at five years of age was proceeding at a moderate rate prior to the Revolution but accelerated considerably thereafter.

This possibility is tested by the data in Table 7.18. Here we calculate the regression coefficient, b, of e_x in each entity both before and after the Revolution and compare its magnitude during each of the two temporal intervals. In order to increase the number of cases, we have performed this operation with the first year of each age group from that 5–14 years to that 55–64 years. Subsequent to 65 years the changes in e_x with calendar time become too small and too confused to warrant any numerical analysis. In constructing Table 7.18, we recognized that the value of b is calculated for Jalisco and Oaxaca prior to 1910 and for Oaxaca after 1920 upon the basis of only three points. Unless these points fall very closely on a straight line, the calculated value of b is likely to be grossly inaccurate, and even if the graph is perfectly linear, the statistical validity is relatively low. Nevertheless, if enough cases can be secured and if the direction of change is predominantly or exclusively uniform, the overall trend can be accepted with confidence. The values of t for 5 degrees of freedom, which range from 4.8 in Guadalajara to 9.5 in Oaxaca (see Table 7.18) are sufficient evidence that the increase in expectation of life was much more rapid after the Revolution than it had been previous to it.

It is probable that the accelerating improvement in demographic position would have occurred in Oaxaca and Jalisco, as in all of Mexico, had there been no Revolution because of other factors such as the development of preventive medicine and modernization of economic life. Yet the years of internal struggle were able to diminish, if not to nullify, temporarily the influence of changing social environment. The demo-

Table 7.18

Rural Jalisco, Oaxaca, and Guadalajara :
Value of *b*, pre-1910 and post-1919 for each age group in three entities.

Values of e_x were taken for rural Jalisco, Oaxaca, and Guadalajara directly from the life tables at the dates there specified. These values were segregated according to pre- and post-revolutionary time : *pre*-1910 and *post*-1919.

For each entity we calculated the trend, *b*, for e_x in each of the two time intervals. The value of *b* was calculated for e_x in the first year of each of six age groups from 5 years to 55 years inclusive.

For each entity the pre- and post-revolutionary values of *b* are tabulated for each age group and are compared within each age group. Finally, *t* was calculated for the pre- and post-revolutionary values for each entity. (For differences the pre-1910 value is subtracted from the post-1919 value.)

A. Jalisco

First Year *of Age Group*	*Pre*-1910	*Post*-1919	*Difference*
5	0.2530	0.2948	0.0598
15	0.2040	0.2565	0.0525
25	0.1955	0.2187	0.0232
35	0.1440	0.1685	0.0245
45	0.1020	0.1362	0.0342
55	0.0530	0.0882	0.0352
Mean	0.1556	0.1938	
Mean difference			0.0382
t=6.29			

B. Oaxaca

First Year *of Age Group*	*Pre*-1910	*Post*-1919	*Difference*
5	0.1703	0.2358	0.0655
15	0.1147	0.2214	0.1067
25	0.0414	0.1952	0.1538
35	0.0097	0.1451	0.1354
45	−0.0191	0.1089	0.1280
55	−0.0294	0.0883	0.1177
Mean	0.0479	0.1658	
Mean difference			0.1179
t=9.54			

Table 7.18 (cont.)

C. Guadalajara			
First Year of Age Group	Pre-1910	Post-1919	Difference
5	0.1031	0.2529	0.1498
15	0.1007	0.2299	0.1292
25	0.0290	0.1905	0.1615
35	0.0337	0.1550	0.1213
45	0.0182	0.0984	0.0802
55	0.0394	0.0506	0.0112
Mean	0.0540	0.1629	
Mean difference			0.1089
t = 4.80			

graphic effects in Guadalajara were barely perceptible, and Guadalajara suffered physically to a very minor degree. On the other hand, in rural Oaxaca, where devastation and economic dislocation were severe, the demographic improvement, relatively slow in any event, was put back twenty or thirty years. Thus, we observe the consequence of war and violence in a relatively unsophisticated society.

It is difficult to determine the point of origin of these changes. As a whole, they seem to have been under way at the time of our earliest records. A direct approach is to examine the numerical values found in the computer tables or the life tables and determine the direction of movement during the first recorded time interval in each region. To do this a simple procedure is to tabulate for rural Jalisco and Oaxaca, their respective coastal and highland zones, and the city of Guadalajara, the overall change from the earliest to the latest date in each age group for each of the two parameters from the life tables, q_x and e_x. Then we may note the direction of change from the earliest date to the one next following and decide whether it conforms to the long-term trend. If there was no net increase or decrease during the first time interval or if many individual age groups showed a change contrary to the subsequent movement, we would conclude that the major swing had not yet been initiated. On the other hand, if the direction during the first recorded interval corresponded to that of the long term, we could conclude that the latter had already begun at the time of the earliest records of the Civil Register.

One case, to be sure, is totally inadequate. However, the seven areas mentioned above provide eight usable age groups from 5–9 years to 55–64 years, and two criteria, q_x and e_x. There are, therefore, $7 \times 8 \times 2$, or 112 possible comparisons. If the movement was wholly random during the first interval, there should be 56 cases in each direction, increase or decrease. Actually, in 81 cases the direction of change in the first interval is the same as that in the long term while 31 cases show the reverse direction. The chi square value for the observed distribution is 21.44, far beyond the 1 percent level of probability. There is a fair likelihood, therefore, that the increase of age at which death occurred was already operative at the period 1860–1880.

At first glance it is not easy to reconcile these findings with the facts brought out in a previous chapter, which pointed to no improvement in mortality prior to 1850. However, certain considerations are pertinent. In the first place, we cannot tell from the record of the Civil Register how long antecedent to our first dates, 1860 for Guadalajara or 1880 for rural Jalisco, the redistribution of age at death began. In second place, the types of data from before 1850 do not correspond with those which can be derived from the Civil Register and, therefore, cannot be directly compared. Moreover, the pre-1850 figures are in general less precise and less likely to manifest small changes in time than those obtained from later sources.

The single exception to these statements which has come to our attention is the collection of parish data assembled by Longinos Banda for Jalisco in the period 1801 to 1854. For certain parishes Banda gives a breakdown of deaths according to age and to calendar year. We have no information concerning the way in which this formulation was accomplished, but the results as they stand are interesting. There are seven parishes for which deaths are listed by age and year. The first is Mejicalcingo, one of the metropolitan parishes of Guadalajara. The others are all rural : Tala, Sayula, Zapotlán, San Sebastián, Magdalena, and Teocuitatlán. The records for Mejicalcingo and Teocuitatlán are continuous from 1801 to 1854; those for the others for varying periods between 1845 and 1854. In all of them the age groups extend from 0 to 10 years, from 11 to 20, and so forth to the group 90 to 100 years. The total numbers will be found in Table 7.19.

One reasonable method for the comparison of mortality

Table 7.19

Deaths occurring in seven Jalisco parishes at the dates indicated, as given by Longinos Banda. The numbers are the totals of the annual values between the dates shown.

Age Group	Mejicalcingo 1801–1854	Sayula 1849–1854	Zapotlán 1845–1854	Teocuitatlán 1801–1854	Tala 1845–1854	San Sebastián 1845–1854	Magdalena 1845–1854	Total
0–10	7,271	774	2,155	3,614	264	846	431	15,355
11–20	999	176	742	271	209	272	72	2,741
21–30	1,462	243	879	991	139	158	103	3,975
31–40	1,820	248	450	1,638	84	113	90	4,443
41–50	1,463	176	344	1,632	88	94	82	3,879
51–60	1,096	174	311	1,133	91	80	77	2,962
61–70	509	109	222	262	93	49	42	1,286
71–80	277	66	105	64	80	31	24	647
81–90	123	28	66	9	66	21	9	322
91–100	33	12	45	4	62	20	2	178
Total	15,053	2,006	5,319	9,618	1,176	1,684	932	35,788

in the parishes of Banda with the Civil Register samples would be to construct abridged life tables for the parishes and determine the expectation of life, e_x, at the youngest age available. It is possible to do this if we utilize only the data derived from the decade 1845–1854 and if we exclude the age group 0–10 years. The exclusion is necessary in order to conform to the procedure adopted with the records for rural Jalisco and Guadalajara. Moreover, there is strong reason to believe that the number of infant deaths reported by the priests in the mid-nineteenth century was little more complete than that found in the Civil Register.

We have accordingly constructed abridged life tables for each of the seven parishes, crude as they may be, with the small size of the samples and the obvious distortion of the age distributions. We also have the table for the combined parishes. The values of e_x at the ages of 10 and of 20 years, which may be directly compared with those found in the life tables of rural Jalisco and Guadalajara, are summarized in Table 7.20. Despite the wide variation shown by the seven individual parish estimates of e_x, both the mean values and that obtained from the consolidated total deaths appear to be somewhat lower than the life expectancies calculated for Guadalajara in the years 1860–1880 and for Jalisco in 1880. The only clear exception is the figure for the coast of Jalisco in 1880, which has been demonstrated to have shown a mortality higher than the state average. Those results are by no means completely convincing, but they do create the presumption that the expectation of life in at least seven parishes in the decade 1845–1854 was less than in much same area twenty or thirty years later.

This presumption may be tested by deriving the value of t between the mean of Banda's seven parishes for e_x at 10 years of age (29.75) and the mean value of Guadalajara in 1860, 1870, and 1880, plus Jalisco entire and the Jalisco plateau in 1880 (34.59). The coast may be omitted because it contributed no data to the tables of Banda. The value of t is 2.94, which lies between the 1 and 2 percent levels of probability.

Another indicator which may be applied at the present juncture is the mean age at death, as calculated from the computer tables for Jalisco and Guadalajara, as well as from the parish figures supplied by Banda. Mean age at death possesses little significance as a guide to the processes and movements underlying mortality data, for it establishes only a single point on the

Table 7.20

Comparative values of expectation of life (e_x) at ages 10 and 20 years in various portions of Jalisco, 1800 to 1880.

Area	Date	e_x at 10 years	e_x at 20 years
Parishes from Banda			
Mejicalcingo	1801–1854	29.36	23.33
Teocuitatlán	"	30.79	22.03
Mejicalcingo	1845–1854	29.41	22.86
Tala	"	36.13	35.40
Sayula	1849–1854	30.81	25.13
Zapotlán	1845–1854	25.93	22.25
San Sebastián	"	25.56	25.45
Teocuitatlán	"	30.03	21.40
Magdalena	"	30.34	27.93
Mean of the above *7 parishes*	1845–1854	29.75	25.78
Consolidated deaths *in the above* *7 parishes*	1845–1854	29.01	23.88
Civil registration			
Guadalajara	1860	34.45	27.65
"	1870	33.54	25.96
"	1880	36.18	28.28
Rural Jalisco (total)	1880	33.95	27.20
" (coast)	"	30.29	23.88
" (plateau)	"	34.82	28.09

age scale and tells nothing concerning the distribution of ages above and below the mean value. Thus, a rise in the mean can result from either a reduction of deaths among the young or an increase among the old. Nevertheless, a change in the mean has utility as a signal that some alteration has taken place in the mortality structure, even if we do not know what it is.

For the present purpose we cannot employ the mean age at death of the entire population because we are obliged to omit consideration of the infants and young children, a difficulty which has been discussed previously. As a result, it is necessary to delete from Banda's tables the entire age group from 0 to 10 years, and in order to keep the calculation consistent, the groups 0–4 and 5–9 years must be omitted from our records of Jalisco and Guadalajara. We then emerge, in both cases, with the mean age at death of those who died at 10 years or older, essentially the adult population. The values, naturally, are much higher than would be found if the infants and children were included.

The essential data are summarized in Table 7.21. The mean age at death of those 10 years or older in the seven parishes recorded by Banda for the years 1845–1854 varies between rather wide limits, 35.57 and 46.12, with an average of 39.77. If the deaths are consolidated so as to give a single mean age, the value is slightly less, 39.01. Meanwhile, the value for Guadalajara in 1860, 1870 and 1880 is, respectively, 44.03, 43.13, and

Table 7.21
Mean age at death of those who died at the age of 10 years and older.

Area	Date	Mean Age at Death
Parishes from Banda		
Mejicalcingo	1801–1854	39.37
Teocuitatlán	,,	40.79
Mejicalcingo	1845–1854	39.43
Tala	,,	46.12
Sayula	1849–1854	40.94
Zapotlán	1845–1854	35.91
San Sebastián	,,	35.57
Teocuitatlán	,,	40.02
Magdalena	,,	40.35
Mean of the above 7 parishes	1845–1854	39.77
Consolidated deaths in the above 7 parishes	1845–1854	39 01
Civil registration		
Guadalajara	1860	44.03
,,	1870	43.13
,,	1880	45.75
Rural Jalisco (total)	1880	43.52
,, (coast)	,,	33.92
,, (plateau)	,,	44.40
,, (intermediate)	,,	44.27

45.75, notably higher. In rural Jalisco entire in 1880 the mean is
43.52. For the subordinate areas, the coast is very low, 33.92,
but none of Banda's parishes lay on the coast. The plateau
region at the same time shows 44.40, and the intermediate
zone, which contains most if not all of Banda's parishes, shows
44.27. We can obtain a rough estimate of the significance of
the difference if we calculate t for the mean age in the seven
parishes of Banda as opposed to five later values. These include
the three for Guadalajara plus the intermediate and plateau
zones of Jalisco. The coast of Jalisco is omitted because it is
outside the area. The value of t is 2.78, which is very close to the
2 percent level of probability.

The three bits of evidence which we have adduced agree
in suggesting that in Jalisco the mortality was greater during the
decade 1845–1854 than it was in the period 1860–1880. The
improvement, therefore, must have been initiated by 1845.
For Oaxaca we cannot reach dates prior to 1872 with our present
data. However, we know that although some change was in
progress at and after that date, we have no idea when it may
have started. Furthermore, the trend was very slight and did
not accelerate significantly until after the Revolution.

We cannot trace the movement of either e_x or the mean
age at death in Jalisco with Banda's compilation prior to 1845.
There are only two parishes for which he gives an age breakdown
from 1801 to 1854: Mejicalcingo and Teocuitatlán. For the
earlier decades the numerical values are too small and scattered
to be of real use. However, the level of e_x and the mean age at
death based upon the whole run of each parish is very close to
that exhibited by the ultimate decade, 1845–1854, alone. There
is, therefore, no evidence which indicates change before 1845.
It is our conclusion that the decrease in probability of death
and the increase in expectation of life which is at its maximum
today must have begun somewhere in the middle of the nineteenth century, probably about 1840–1850 in Jalisco, perhaps
at other dates in other areas.

A final comment may be permitted. From the low point
following the conquest of Mexico, at about 1610, the population
increased with only temporary setbacks through the eighteenth
century and well into the nineteenth century. During this
entire period the regime was one of a very high birth rate,
associated with an almost equally high death rate. Probably the
birth rate declined very little while the death rate, at least during

certain intervals such as the late eighteenth century, may have moderated somewhat. From 1840 or 1850 onward, however, whereas the birth rate remained at its customary high level, the death rate began a definitive decline, slowly at first, more rapidly in recent times. The population, therefore, underwent an increasing augmentation which has carried it to its present-day level, such that the country is now operating on the basis of a high birth rate and a very low death rate. Contemporary demographers, such as Arriaga, see no end in the near future, nor do they dare to predict the outcome.

Chapter VIII

Mortality Patterns in Mexico Since 1860 : Cause of Death

The determination of the cause of death and its statement in no more than a word or short phrase on a certificate have been sources of perplexity and worry to physicians and public health officers since the inception of the registration system nearly two centuries ago. The fundamental difficulty lies in the fact that very frequently there is no single factor which causes the death of an individual. In the last resort, perhaps, the universal cause is the failure of the heart beat. But, in a particular case, what induced the heart to stop? One might say that it was acute anoxia produced by cessation of breathing. But what caused respiration to cease? Possibly because the person drowned. If so, was the cause of death cardiac arrest, respiratory failure, or accident? The semantic problem here is enormous and, indeed, probably insoluble, even by the most sophisticated present-day pathologists.

We do not intend to pursue the discussion of theory. It is, however, necessary to appreciate what obstacles not only laymen but also professionally trained officials encounter when they try to give an intelligent answer to the question: What caused a certain death? The problem becomes even more acute when we deal with a rural, relatively uneducated group of communities, such as have existed in Mexico throughout its history. Until the past two or three decades, outside of the larger cities, there have been no persons whatever who were trained in medicine or who were familiar with exact medical terminology. Consequently, death certificates had to be filled out by civil officials who were as ignorant as any of their fellow citizens. Moreover, only rarely did even these officials have any first-hand acquaintance with the circumstances of death. They were obliged to take the word of the next-of-kin, who in turn may have had only the haziest notion of the actual cause of the decease. As a result we are confronted with an amazing conglomeration of guesses, and the miracle is that the truth was attained as often as it was.

Our preliminary task was twofold. In the first place, the expressions used on the certificates were partly from the ordinary vocabulary of the people, partly semi- or pseudotechnical, and only occasionally accurate and professional. These had to be translated not only into the English language but also into reasonable contemporary medical terminology. This work is embodied in a concordance of nearly 2,000 separate items. Rather than reproduce so cumbersome a document here, we have placed a copy on file in the Bancroft Library, together with the sheets of transcript prepared in Mexico, the four rolls of magnetic tape abstracting the data for computer analysis, and a copy of the computer print-outs.

The second phase of the preliminary organization was so to classify the causes that they could be coded for computer analysis. This meant, in turn, that categories had to be established which would make sense medically. For this purpose we had recourse to the international scheme for classification of causes of death. For many years and in response to obvious need for such a work in all countries, the World Health Organization in Geneva has issued at intervals a publication in several volumes entitled *Manual of International Statistical Classification of Diseases, Injuries, and Causes of Death*. We used that portion entitled *International Classification of Diseases*, vol. 1, 7th rev., 1955, issued at Geneva, 1957.

The system elaborated in this compilation is enormously complex. For our purposes it was necessary to simplify it greatly. We were obliged to omit many categories entirely and to retain only those which appeared to conform to our records. In broad subdivisions, however, we follow the numbering system stated in the *Manual*. There are ten principal groups of causes, some of which we have modified considerably to fit our needs. Each group is coded in the *Manual* according to a numerical system which uses for each main group a three-digit number, beginning with 000, followed by 100, 200, etc., up to 900. The first digit, therefore, specifies the broad type of cause. Then a tenfold division runs according to the second digit: 000, 010, 020, . . . 090. If desirable another tenfold division can be introduced by means of the third digit: 001, 002, 003, . . . etc.

Thus, it is theoretically possible to obtain 1,000 key numbers for as many causes of death. These numbers may be transferred easily to punch cards for computer analysis.

As we suggested, it was necessary to modify the international system to suit our requirements. This meant, first, that the total number of items was drastically reduced and, second, that certain types of category had to be substituted in even the main groups. The numbers, as we used them, are listed *in extenso* in Appendix C. Here we explain our use of primary divisions.

000 This group includes the relatively well-identified infective diseases, together with "fever" *(fiebre)* unspecified as to nature. This aggregate, which up until recently accounted for more than one-half the deaths in Mexico, is based upon a quite well-developed knowledge. The people at large recognized the symptoms of and correctly diagnosed most of the common epidemic ailments.

100 Here are the neoplasms, a difficult group. Clearly manifest tumors, and terminal cancer were well known, although many internal malignancies probably went unobserved.

200 We lump together a series of unrelated ailments, referable to endocrine, metabolic, and nutritional disfunction. The complete list (Appendix C) gives an idea of the conditions reported by name on the death certificates. Many of the terms are antiquated and show only the most conspicuous symptom displayed by the decedent rather than the true cause of death. Furthermore, it is often impossible to distinguish between this and the following group with respect to allocation of the cause of death.

300 Here is a catchall for a vast array of internal maladies. The common characteristic, and the one which justifies the use of the category, is the fact that in almost every case the certificate mentions only the organ system which appeared to be involved in the demise. In many instances there is no indication whether the ailment was of organic origin or was due to an infection. Indeed, the reporter probably did not know the exact source of the disease. In many other instances the allocation to the organ system is probably wrong—again due to ignorance and the total lack of any competent diagnostician. This problem is particularly acute in relation to the liver, kidney, and bladder. In still other instance the diagnosis is incomprehensible, as in the case of mental disorders, where the only apparent cause of death was a highly disordered personality.

As a result of these circumstances this group is and unavoidably must be an *ad hoc* assemblage of causes based frankly upon the descriptions written by those who reported the deaths. Nevertheless, the majority of the items undoubtedly reflect organic disturbances localized as mentioned on the certificates. Although the type and cause of the disturbance may remain unknown, the immediate condition preceding decease is usually closely identified. Moreover, it should be noted that clear cases of infection, such as enteritis and dysentery, were as a rule recognized and reported in the correct category, rather than being merely allocated to an organ system. We may also emphasize that diagnosis has so improved during the past generation that the specified causes of death due to internal pathology are far more accurately reported since 1940 than they ever were previously.

400   Here are all the difficulties attending childbirth, in so far as they pertain to the mother. There is little difficulty in recognizing these causes, and the group is quite reliable as shown on the certificates.

500   These causes involve the child at the time of birth. They include all sorts of conditions: still birth, congenital defects, perinatal infections, and many others. The single feature characteristic of all of them is the fact that the infant died as a result of some condition associated with fetal life, with parturition, or with the immediate sequelae of these events.

600   This group includes all deaths which were ascribed by the relatives and friends to old age. If any disease or organic ailment was known to be responsible, the death would be classified under one of the other principal categories. If no obvious malfunction or disease was present, if the victim was advanced in years, and if there was evidence of either physical or mental senility, the family and the authorities simply surrendered any pretense of diagnosis and inscribed the cause as old age. And, from the practical point of view, unless one insists upon a pedantic application of pathological expertise, the cause was correctly stated.

700   This group embraces all external causes. They are utterly evident and almost impossible to report falsely, such as accident, homicide, suicide, or animal bites.

800   This group we segregate as a separate entity in order to account for the numerous deaths, the causes of which

are impossible to classify because they are excessively generalized and vague. Such terms as inflammation, pain, exhaustion, and even abscess and gangrene may actually denote almost any of the preceding groups of causes and may be of either bacterial or intrinsic organic origin. It is true that with the increase of medical knowledge this category has markedly diminished in importance. Nevertheless, in the reports prior to 1920, ambiguous causes account for up to 10 percent of the total and even today may reach 3 to 4 percent.

900   Here are the certificates upon which the cause is stated as unknown or which themselves are illegible or completely unintelligible. Although they must be placed in a separate category, their number is not great, scarcely 0.1 percent of the total.

Although we established these ten groups of causes for computer analysis, we have since found that considerable rearrangement and consolidation are desirable. In order to detect secular trends and regional differences, we need the broadest criteria and the largest samples which can be obtained. For working purposes, therefore, we have reduced the ten major groups to six. The infective, febrile diseases (000) constitute a relatively clearcut, natural unit and represent a type of malady which could be recognized and in most cases diagnosed with precision by the population generally. On the contrary, the internal organic, biochemical, and endocrine disturbances were obscure and frequently far beyond the diagnostic ability of even the physicians of the earlier decades. These types of ailment are found throughout number groups 100, 200, and 300. To them may be added 600, for death due to old age is almost invariably associated, in reality, with some direct or remote organic malfunction. Hence, for the purpose of examination we consolidate the four groups into a single category of organic causes. We designate it by the four numbers 100, 200, 300, 600 and refer to it as the consolidated group of death causes.

The other groups remain distinct. Group 400 applies only to women in association with childbirth; group 500 concerns only infants at or near the time of birth. No serious error of diagnosis is likely to be involved. The same consideration applies even more strongly to group 700. Violent death would hardly be mistaken by anyone who was entrusted with the completion of death certificates.

The final groups, 800 and 900, constitute something of a problem. They comprise an appreciable fraction of the total deaths. Yet, usually, they do not specify the cause with sufficient clarity to justify allocation to any of the recognized categories. For many purposes it is probably better to disregard them completely and calculate numbers and proportions upon the basis of deaths clearly attributable to some disease or internal disorder. At the same time the person concerned undoubtedly did die and hence should be counted among the decedents. The result is that in some of the tables and graphs, we have had to present the data both with and without the undetermined cause.

As an additional criterion, and one of interest in itself, we select six important and well-recognized epidemic or infective diseases. We select them both because they are numerically of great significance and because they carry strong implications for social welfare and public health. They are dysentery, whooping cough, measles, smallpox, malaria and pneumonia. The first and last, determined as they were by very unsophisticated persons, may well and probably do include several secondary pathological entities. Dysentery may be amoebic or bacillary. Pneumonia, so stated, may embrace much influenza. Nevertheless, they are sufficiently distinct and numerically important to warrant inclusion. To them we add, for the record, the group 095, the unidentifiable fever which was so commonly written on the death certificates. Probably some of the six important diseases just mentioned were actually included with the unidentified group in the reports of 1860 to 1900, but we have no way of determining their number.

In Table 8.1, part A, is shown the percentage of all deaths ascribed in the records to group 000, to the consolidated group 100, 200, 300, 600, to the separate groups 400, 500, and 700, and, finally, to the combined groups 800 and 900. In Table 8.1, part B, these values are recalculated after the unidentified causes (groups 800 and 900) have been excluded. The three principal areas, rural Jalisco, Oaxaca, and Guadalajara have been kept separate from each other. Some of the data from part B are shown in graphic form in Figure 8.1, specifically the points representing the values for the infective diseases (group 000) and those for the internal organic ailments (consolidated group 100, 200, 300, 600).

Inspection of the graph and the tables immediately

Table 8.1

Percentage of each major cause of death with all age groups. All causes are included. The groups are as follows. 000, infective. epidemic, febrile diseases; 100, neoplasms, combined with 200, biochemical disturbances, 300, internal organic disfunction, and 600, old age; 400, maternal accidents of pregnancy and parturition; 500, perinatal death and congenital difficulties; 800 and 900, the cause of death either unidentifiable from the certificates or completely unknown. In part B the groups are the same except that group 800 and 900 has been omitted. and the remaining groups adjusted to conform with the total deaths after the removal of the group mentioned.

		A.				
		Group				
Date	000	100 200 300 600	400	500	700	800 900
Jalisco						
1880	65.0	12.3	1.9	7.1	3.1	10.1
1890	68.2	13.7	1.5	6.4	2.8	6.8
1900	63.9	16.5	1.6	10.0	3.6	3.9
1920	61.3	16.7	1.6	11.0	5.1	3.9
1930	60.2	18.3	1.5	9.7	4.9	4.8
1940	58.1	21.0	1.2	9.7	5.6	4.0
1950	47.9	26.4	1.0	12.2	6.9	5.2
1960	39.5	35.3	1.6	13.3	6.0	3.7
Oaxaca						
1872	73.3	16.4	1.0	0.1	1.8	6.8
1890	72.5	20.5	1.1	1.1	1.6	2.7
1907	73.7	17.0	0.8	3.9	2.2	2.1
1922	73.5	15.4	0.8	3.4	4.0	2.5
1940	71.6	17.0	0.9	2.7	4.3	2.9
1952	70.0	15.5	0.7	1.5	5.1	6.7
Guadalajara						
1860	60.6	13.3	1.2	12.7	1.9	9.9
1870	54.1	18.5	0.9	12.4	6.5	7.2
1880	67.5	16.2	0.5	7.9	2.9	4.5
1890	58.3	19.3	0.6	14.5	2.8	4.0
1900	65.4	16.4	0.9	7.4	3.2	2.0
1920	57.9	27.4	0.7	8.6	4.1	1.0
1930	53.6	31.2	0.8	7.7	5.3	0.9
1940	47.4	36.2	0.7	9.4	4.6	1.2
1950	32.5	41.4	0.2	8.3	10.1	7.0
1960	33.4	45.5	0.7	11.0	5.9	3.1

Table 8.1 (cont.)

			B.		
			Group		
Date	000	100 300 300 600	400	500	700
Jalisco					
1880	72.3	13.7	2.1	7.9	3.4
1890	73.2	14.7	1.6	6.9	3.0
1900	66.5	17.2	1.7	10.4	3.7
1920	63.8	17.4	1.7	11.5	5.3
1930	63.3	19.2	1.6	10.2	5.1
1940	60.5	21.9	1.3	10.1	5.8
1950	50.6	27.9	1.1	12.9	7.3
1960	41.0	36.7	1.7	13.8	6.2
Oaxaca					
1872	78.6	17.6	1.1	0.1	1.9
1890	75.0	21.2	1.1	1.2	1.6
1907	75.2	17.4	0.8	4.0	2.3
1922	75.4	15.8	0.8	3.5	4.1
1940	73.7	17.5	0.9	2.8	4.4
1952	75.0	16.6	0.8	1.6	5.4
Guadalajara					
1860	67.3	14.6	1.3	14.1	2.1
1870	58.4	19.9	1.0	13.4	7.0
1880	70.7	17.0	0.5	8.3	3.0
1890	60.8	19.9	0.6	15.1	2.9
1900	69.8	17.5	1.0	7.9	3.4
1920	64.4	27.7	0.7	8.7	4.1
1930	54.2	31.5	0.8	7.8	5.4
1940	48.0	36.6	0.7	9.5	4.7
1950	35.0	44.5	0.2	8.9	10.9
1960	34.5	47.0	0.7	11.3	6.1

brings to light two conspicuous features : (1) the secular change in distribution of cause of death is clearly evident; and (2) the two states of Jalisco and Oaxaca differ sharply in the pattern of causes.

In rural Jalisco, and to a somewhat greater extent in Guadalajara, the infective, epidemic diseases have undergone a substantial decline in relative significance as a cause of mortality while the endemic, organic types of disfunction, such as

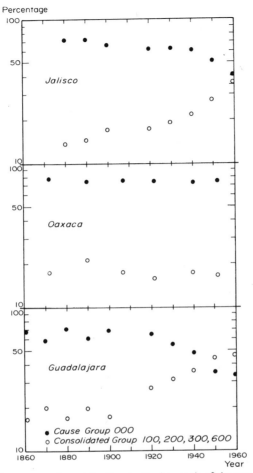

Percentage

Figure 8.1.   Percentage of total deaths ascribed to each of the two major causes. adjusted for removal of unidentified causes. groups 800 and 900.

cancer, cardiovascular renal failure, and pure old age, have correspondingly increased. This phenomenon has, of course, been observed almost universally as a consequence of improvement in sanitation, hygiene, and preventive medicine throughout the world, and its appearance here is not surprising.

The other groups follow a more or less expected course. The unidentified causes diminish in a rather consistent manner from the earliest to the latest date. Such a reduction is referable, of course, to a steady improvement in diagnostic techniques as well as in public education and dissemination of medical knowledge not only among professionals but also among laymen. The deaths ascribed to the events of pregnancy and childbirth do not change in a clearly consistent manner in Jalisco and Guadalajara whereas those due to external causes have undergone a definite increase. It must be remembered that these effects are relative and indicate only the proportion assignable to each type of cause with respect to all deaths. The actual mortality rate is well understood to have fallen greatly in all categories, except perhaps group 700, the external causes. Traffic and industrial accidents, together with homicide, have not been mitigated by progress in hygiene and medicine.

We may revert for further discussion to the two major categories of cause, infective diseases and organic failure. The former has undergone relative, as well as absolute, reduction. The latter show a relative, although probably not an absolute, increase. These changes have been proceeding since approximately the time of the earliest record in the Civil Register. In order to describe more fully the course of these events, we may utilize certain subsidiary devices.

One method is to take the ratio of the number of deaths due to infective diseases to that of deaths from organic disfunction, that is that of group 000 to that of consolidated group 100, 200, 300, 600. This procedure amplifies and clarifies the reciprocal relationship between the two types. The values of the ratio as seen in Jalisco and Guadalajara (see Table 8.2) show a continuous and sharp decline since the period 1860–1880, which is presented in an even more conspicuous form by the graphs in Figure 8.2.

Another method is to study the secular rate of change in the percentage values for group 000 and group 100, 200, 300, 600, which are given in Table 8.1, part B. This change may be expressed in terms of the slope of the lines in Figure 8.1, specifically the sign and magnitude of the constant which describes that slope. This method was used in Chapter VII which dealt with distribution of age at death. Although we use the formula for the regression of the percentage upon time, the coefficient b, as here employed, must be regarded as simply a rough index to the trend of the line.

Examination of the table, as well as of Figure 8.1, makes it clear that the change in type of cause of death, as seen in rural Jalisco and Guadalajara, was not perfectly linear but rather began very slowly and later accelerated. Consequently, although it is possible, if necessary, to calculate a coefficient for the entire time up to 1960, it is preferable to break the whole trend

Table 8.2

Ratio of deaths in group 000 to that in consolidated group 100, 200, 300, 600. Absolute numbers rather than percentages are used.

Date	Ratio
Jalisco	
1880	5.28
1890	4.98
1900	3.87
1920	3.67
1930	3.29
1940	2.77
1950	1.81
1960	1.12
Oaxaca	
1872	4.47
1890	3.53
1907	4.33
1922	4.77
1940	4.21
1952	4.52
Guadalajara	
1860	4.56
1870	2.93
1880	4.17
1890	3.02
1900	3.99
1920	2.11
1930	1.72
1940	1.31
1950	0.79
1960	0.73

into stages. This may be done in a crude fashion for these areas by using twenty-year segments. Thus, for rural Jalisco we get a coefficient for the first twenty years, 1880–1900, then one for the interval 1920–1940, and finally one for 1940–1960. With Guadalajara, four stages may be obtained. When for each stage a value of b is calculated, we get the result seen in Table 8.3.

The precision, obviously, is poor, and the values of b should not be accorded significance beyond the first digit after the decimal point. The error will certainly be of at least plus or minus one unit. Thus, -0.410 should be regarded as

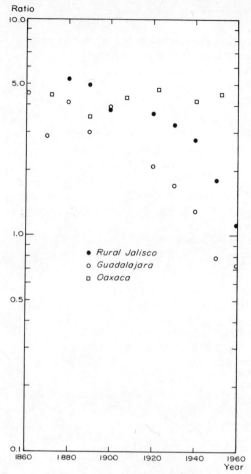

Figure 8.2.   Ratio of numbers dying from cause 000 to those dying from consolidated causes 100, 200, 300, 600.

meaning any value between −0.3 and −0.5. Nevertheless, the
movement is clear, toward progressively higher values from
ca. 1880 to 1960. Group 000 carries a minus sign, indicating
a decrease, and the consolidated group a plus sign, indicating
an increase.

There is no doubt that the change was slow at first,
although both rural Jalisco and Guadalajara demonstrate
a clearly perceptible shift in the distribution of death causes
between 1880 and 1900. When the redistribution started is
difficult to determine. It was probably before 1880 because
in spite of the small plus for *b* in Guadalajara between 1860 and
1880, the other indicators suggest a slight movement during

Table 8.3

Values of *b* for short time intervals. Based upon the percentage of each cause group (000 and 100,200,300,600) at all ages, adjusted for the removal of group 800,900. (See Table 8.1, part B) For each time interval the mean percentage value is equated to 100.

	Group 000	Group 100,200,300,600	Ratio : Group 000/ Group 100, etc.
Jalisco			
1880–1900	−0.410	1.150	−1.495
1920–1940	−0.260	1.150	−1.375
1940–1960	−1.965	2.565	−4.345
Oaxaca			
1872–1907	−0.098	0.071	−0.170
1922–1952	−0.029	0.292	−0.075
Guadalajara			
1860–1880	0.265	0.695	−0.500
1880–1900	−0.070	0.140	−0.290
1920–1940	−1.480	1.395	−2.340
1940–1960	−1.720	1.330	−3.085

that period. There may have been a halt and perhaps an unimportant retrogression during the revolutionary decade of 1910–1920 in rural Jalisco, although the hostilities appear to have exerted little effect in the city. Since 1920 the shift away from the infectious diseases has become more and more pronounced until at the present they account for no more than one-half of their proportionate mortality a century ago. The redistribution of cause resembles that of age at death in that it seems to have been initiated, at least in Jalisco, somewhere near the middle of the nineteenth century.

Further detail with respect to this trend is provided by the individual diseases which are most commonly involved and which have already been mentioned. Table 8.4 gives the proportions in which they have appeared among all reported deaths. In rural Jalisco and Guadalajara some have demonstrated a significant decrease, among which the most notable example is smallpox. This malady, which probably has been the cause of more deaths in Mexico than any other of the epidemic type, has been on the decline in absolute terms since the introduction

Table 8.4

Specific diseases of the infective, febrile type. Percentage of all reported deaths. 010, dysentery; 050, whooping cough; 055, measles; 060, smallpox; 065, malaria; 085, pneumonia; 095, fever, not further identified.

A. Jalisco

Disease	1880	1890	1900	1920	1930	1940	1950	1960
010	18.0	22.1	23.1	21.4	24.0	25.7	22.7	16.7
050	3.5	3.0	2.8	3.0	3.0	2.1	0.9	0.7
055	1.9	1.1	1.1	2.9	2.6	2.1	1.1	0.8
060	10.5	6.9	4.7	4.8	1.0	0.3	0.0	0.1
065	1.7	2.9	2.4	2.2	2.9	2.2	0.7	0.1
085	8.8	14.0	16.5	13.7	13.2	13.6	13.1	14.8
095	18.7	15.2	9.0	9.0	7.8	5.4	4.3	2.4

B. Oaxaca

Disease	1872	1890	1907	1922	1940	1952
010	10.1	14.0	20.2	18.4	24.5	21.6
050	8.6	10.2	9.8	9.5	6.5	7.1
055	1.5	1.3	2.5	2.0	5.1	3.2
060	25.3	12.0	3.5	7.1	0.1	0.0
065	8.7	14.0	18.2	17.1	14.7	18.5
085	2.4	2.8	4.3	4.6	3.9	2.8
095	11.8	5.2	1.3	1.9	2.7	4.2

C. Guadalajara

Disease	1860	1870	1880	1890	1900	1920	1930	1940	1950	1960
010	31.0	25.7	28.9	20.0	37.5	30.1	29.2	23.6	11.0	12.4
050	2.4	0.6	0.3	1.0	0.2	0.6	0.1	0.7	0.2	0.2
055	0.0	0.3	2.2	4.7	0.9	2.0	0.4	0.1	0.8	0.4
060	2.7	0.3	3.2	0.1	0.1	1.3	0.8	0.1	0.0	0.0
065	1.2	1.1	2.0	1.2	1.5	0.6	0.7	0.4	1.0	0.0
085	8.0	12.9	18.9	22.5	14.8	13.7	13.6	12.7	14.3	14.1
095	14.3	6.6	6.3	2.5	0.2	0.3	0.0	0.0	0.0	0.1

of vaccination in the early nineteenth century. Relative to other causes it was diminishing in rural Jalisco at a rapid rate in the decade 1880–1890 although it was still at a quite high level of incidence. By 1940 it had practically disappeared, as a result of the consistent program of vaccination undertaken by the Mexican federal and state authorities. Meanwhile, in the city of Guadalajara it had already declined almost to disappearance (2 to 3 percent of the total deaths) by the year 1880. Thereafter, its influence has been minimal. The better record of the city is referable to tighter control and superior medical facilities.

Other maladies which had declined, in relative terms as well as absolute, by the year 1960, were whooping cough, measles, and malaria. It is notable that the first two, the preeminently child diseases, remained constant, if we ignore sampling fluctuations and occasional epidemics, until after the Revolution, when they definitely began to decline. The third, malaria, still exacted a toll of 2 to 3 percent of total deaths in the rural areas until after 1940, after which date the effect of the campaign against *paludismo* became very evident. The disease was never very serious in the city of Guadalajara.

Dysenteries and respiratory infections included under the name of pneumonia have not only remained relatively unchanged but have maintained a very high level of attack. This behavior is due in part to the statistical fact that the drastic decline of smallpox and certain other contagions has shifted the balance in proportionate status to diseases which have diminished less rapidly, among which are those mentioned, dysentery and pneumonia. It is also referable to the fact that slower progress has been made in reducing the absolute incidence of the latter. There is only a suggestion that since 1950 the trend has taken a definite turn downward. Thus, in rural Jalisco the percentage of deaths attributable to gastro-intestinal infections dropped from 22.72 in 1950 to 16.70 in 1960. A similar, and perhaps earlier break occurred in Guadalajara.

If we summarize briefly, we may say that in both rural and urban Jalisco since about 1860, there has been evident an accelerating reduction in the proportion of deaths due to infective, febrile diseases, both as a group and individually, with concomitant increase in proportion on the part of internal, organic disfunction and failure. These changes are associated with the broad program of improvement in preventive medicine and sanitation which was initiated modestly during the days of Juárez and Díaz and perhaps their predecessors and has reached countrywide coverage in recent decades.

When we come to Oaxaca, we find a very different picture. Examination of Table 8.1 discovers only a very small reduction in the percentage for group 000 and an increase for the consolidated group 100, 200, 300, 600. The graph in Figure

8.1 likewise suggests no clear-cut change in either component. The series of six ratios in Table 8.2 and the corresponding series of points in Figure 8.2 both indicate no variations other than those produced by sampling error and local epidemic fluctuations. The values of b given in Table 8.3 for the two available stages, 1872–1907 and 1922–1952, are consistent in sign : minus for contagious disease and the ratio, plus for organic ailments. However, the magnitude of b in all six cases is small, less than 0.3, and reaches only the margin of significance. The conclusion must be, therefore, that the redistribution of causes of death in Oaxaca was very slight, if it was present at all, between 1872 and 1952.

The data for individual diseases, given in Table 8.4, are also of interest. Smallpox underwent a great reduction, from 25.30 percent of total deaths in 1872 to practical extinction in 1952. Meanwhile the relative incidence of dysenteries almost doubled, as did that of malaria. It is noteworthy that the latter disease, which in Jalisco was much reduced by 1950, up to that time in Oaxaca was not at all affected by the antimalaria campaign. In contrast, whooping cough, measles, and pneumonia remained at a substantially constant level throughout the entire period. These findings tend to confirm the conclusion that apart from the relief from smallpox provided by extensive vaccination, little alteration was made in the pattern of death causation prior to 1952. What may have happened recently, we do not know.

Not only does Oaxaca deviate from the Jalisco model in that there is little if any change in distribution pattern but the major groups also differ in magnitude. Very conspicuous is the fact that the percentage of group 000 in the total deaths has remained close to 75 in Oaxaca whereas it has declined from approximately 73 to 41 in Jalisco (see Table 8.1, part B). Also puzzling is the difference in the percentage of deaths at or near birth (group 500). In Jalisco the average of this cause at eight dates is 10.5; in Oaxaca at six dates the average is 2.2, a fivefold difference. Perinatal death is a quite stable magnitude under conditions of substantially the same methods of medical procedure, such as existed in Jalisco and Oaxaca.

We noticed in the examination of distribution of age at death (Chapter VII) that Oaxaca lagged far behind Jalisco with respect to the degree of progress made since the middle of the nineteenth century. This lag appears even more pronounced when we consider the data pertaining to redistribution of causes of death. The reason for such a wide disparity must stem, at least partially, from the fact that the two states are widely separated geographically and have been subject to different influences culturally and politically. Tradition, custom, and administrative policy have been by no means identical and may have determined to a considerable extent not only the dissemination but also the character of medical knowledge. A case in point is the inclusion of many stillbirths in Jalisco and the evident neglect of this category in Oaxaca. A clue to the distinction lies in the words *al nacer* (at birth), a term applied very often to stillbirth. It occurs with great frequency in the records of the Civil Register in Jalisco, rarely in Oaxaca. The inference, therefore, must be that stillbirths were often reported in this way in Jalisco but were not reported in Oaxaca, at least under the phrase *al nacer*. It follows that the difference was referable to the system of recording not to the actual birth performance. The effect is appreciable, for the inclusion of stillbirths to the extent of 5 to 8 percent of the total deaths in Jalisco correspondingly reduces the proportion of the other causes and results in their showing an apparently lower level than in Oaxaca, where the perinatal deaths *in toto* run on the average at only approximately 2 percent of all deaths.

Another source of difference may have been the degree of progress in public health and preventive medicine which characterized the two states, for there can be no question that Jalisco has been more advanced in this field than has Oaxaca. Jalisco has always been able to follow the lead and draw upon the resources of Guadalajara, the second city in Mexico in size and the intellectual and cultural center of the west and the northwest. In it there has been established for more than three centuries a group of citizens active in the pursuit of practicing medicine and public health. Oaxaca has never possessed these advantages.

We have studied at length the question whether the pattern of distribution of causes of death was significantly different in the low, coastal areas from that characteristic of the high plateau. Most informed opinion holds that the coasts suffer from fevers, endoparasitism, and gastro-intestinal infections more heavily than the dry, cool interior. On the other hand, the latter zone is considered to be more prone to respiratory infections such as tuberculosis and pneumonia.

A factor completely apart from bioclimatic influence, however, was operative in the areas and during the years which are covered by this study. We refer to the universal tendency toward improvement in health status, supported by specific therapeutic procedures which were confined to no particular geographic region. This factor would tend to mitigate or obliterate a causative agent wherever it occurred and, therefore, would blur or erase any distinction based upon the environment. The more effective the preventive measure, the sooner and more completely would the cause of mortality be removed from all areas.

When we tabulate and graph the proportionate distribution of cause of death for the coastal and plateau portions

Table 8.5

Percentage of each major cause of death with all age groups. Death causes omit group 800, 900, as in Table 8.1, part B, with the remaining groups adjusted accordingly.

		A. Jalisco			
		Group			
Date	000	100 200 300 600	400	500	700
Coast					
1800	75.0	11.8	2.2	5.8	4.8
1890	72.9	11.2	2.0	8.4	5.0
1900	64.7	13.6	2.1	12.7	6.5
1920	63.0	14.1	2.3	11.9	8.0
1930	64.0	15.5	2.4	10.5	7.0
1940	61.4	19.1	1.6	9.5	8.0
1950	48.7	27.0	1.7	11.1	7.1
1960	40.0	29.1	3.9	13.5	8.8
Plateau					
1880	67.0	17.9	2.4	9.1	2.9
1890	71.2	18.7	1.5	5.8	2.4
1900	65.5	19.5	1.5	10.3	2.7
1920	64.9	19.2	1.7	10.0	4.5
1930	63.1	21.1	1.6	9.0	4.5
1940	62.6	21.0	1.3	9.8	4.7
1950	51.6	26.1	1.0	14.2	6.6
1960	41.8	37.3	1.4	12.7	6.4

Table 8.5 (cont.)

		B. Oaxaca			
		Group			
Date	000	100 200 300 600	400	500	700
Coast					
1872	76.0	19.1	1.5	0.2	2.6
1890	78.3	17.1	1.5	0.1	2.7
1907	76.9	13.2	1.1	5.3	3.1
1922	75.5	13.6	1.1	4.0	5.3
1940	71.0	13.3	1.5	4.6	4.5
1952	73.9	12.3	1.4	1.8	10.0
Plateau (Mixteca Alta)					
1872	84.1	13.4	0.9	0.0	1.1
1890	75.7	20.8	0.9	0.7	1.4
1907	70.3	22.3	0.6	4.4	1.8
1922	73.3	20.0	0.4	2.9	1.3
1940	70.0	24.7	0.6	2.0	2.1
1952	82.4	13.7	0.6	0.5	1.9

of Jalisco, we find that the relation between the two zones deviates widely from the relation between them in Oaxaca. In other words, the mortality patterns of the coast and plateau in Jalisco differ profoundly from the comparable pattern found in Oaxaca.

For Jalisco we have placed the data in table 8.5, part A. We show, for all age groups, the percentage of deaths referable to each major cause, after having removed the deaths unidentifiable as to cause. As in table 8.1, we utilize five categories : infective disease (group 000), organic failure (consolidated group 100, 200, 300, 600), accidents of pregnancy and parturition (group 400), perinatal deaths (group 500), and external events (group 700). The percentage values are given in two series, one for the coast, the other for the plateau. The intermediate area is omitted. These values are shown in graphic form in Figure 8.3. As a further indicator we have employed the ratio of the group 000 to the consolidated group 100, 200, 300, 600 according to the absolute numbers contained in the records and found in the computer print-out.

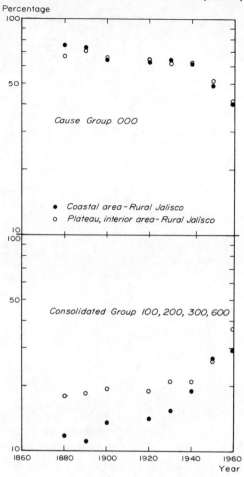

Figure 8.3.   Rural Jalisco : Percentage of total deaths, adjusted for removal of
unidentified causes, groups 800 and 900.

From Table 8.5, part A, and Figure 8.3, it is clear that
the proportion of infective diseases on both the coast and
plateau in Jalisco fell steadily and with accelerating velocity
from the beginning of the record to 1960. At the same time,
the organic ailments increased. The course of the change was
almost identical in the two areas in so far as group 000 is concerned. However, the consolidated groups 100, 200, 300, 600 in
the two zones were by no means identical. On the coast the
proportion of these disfunctions, adjusted for unidentifiable
causes, was approximately 12.2 percent from 1880 to 1900
whereas on the plateau it was close to 18.7 percent. However,
after the Revolutionary era this difference disappeared. The

values for the two areas approached each other until in the period 1940–1960, they averaged, respectively, 25.1 and 28.1 percent. The ratios of the group 000 to the consolidated group tell the same story, as is clear from Table 8.6 and Figures 8.4 and 8.5. The averages for the ratio in coast and plateau in 1880–1900 were, respectively, 5.75 and 3.60; in 1940–1960 they were 2.05 and 2.01. The other three groups of causes, 400, 500, and 700, show slight differences between coast and plateau but none of serious significance. This condition is to be expected for deaths referable to childbirth or to external causes such as accident and homicide, for they are not conditioned by physical environmental factors, particularly when the political and social circumstances are widely uniform.

From these results may be deduced that in the nineteenth century, and through the Revolution, there was a definite difference between the coast of Jalisco and the high interior with respect to the distribution of disease types. This distinction was manifested in a relatively higher incidence of organic failure on the plateau when compared with epidemic disease.

Table 8.6

Ratio of deaths in group 000 to those in consolidated group 100, 200, 300, 600, as in Table 8.2.

Date	Ratio	
Jalisco	*Coast*	*Plateau*
1880	6.27	3.68
1890	6.42	3.78
1900	4.57	3.35
1920	4.38	3.38
1930	4.08	2.97
1940	3.18	2.94
1950	1.79	1.97
1960	1.19	1.12
Oaxaca	*Coast*	*Plateau*
1872	3.94	6.18
1890	4.53	3.80
1907	5.78	3.13
1922	5.45	3.65
1940	5.12	2.82
1952	5.92	5.92

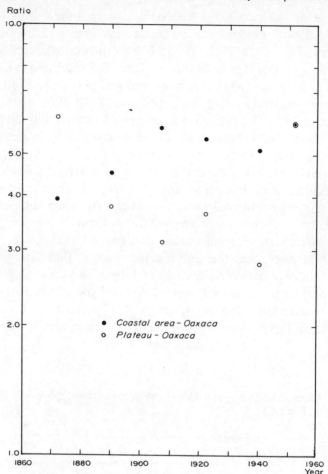

Figure 8.4.   Oaxaca: Percentage of total deaths, adjusted for removal of
unidentified causes, groups 800 and 900.

Further points of interest are brought out in Table 8.7,
part A. Here are recorded the percentage of all deaths which
were ascribed in our sample of the Civil Register of Jalisco
to groups 010 (dysentery, enteritis, etc.), 060 (smallpox), 065
(malaria), 085 (pneumonia), and 095 (unidentified fever).
In the early reports 095 assumes a very large proportion:
20 to 30 percent on the coast and 11 to 12 percent on the plateau.
One may well inquire what was the nature of the fever which
could not be further identified and which did not carry the
symptoms of well-known ailments such as measles or smallpox.
One reasonable suggestion is that in part this category should
have been reported as malaria. Prior to 1900–1910 many types

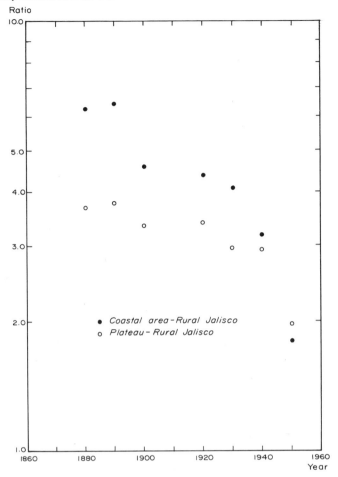

Figure 8.5.   Rural Jalisco : Ratio of numbers dying from cause 000 to those dying
from consolidated causes 100, 200, 300, 600.

of chronic, intermittent fevers of malarial origin were not
recognized as a pathological entity but were simply classed
as fever, particularly by the population at large. Obviously,
this explanation will not cover all cases, for from 2 to 5 percent
of febrile infections were still undiagnosed as late as 1960.
Nevertheless, if no more than a substantial fraction of the
cases actually were malarial, they should be added to the low
values for these early years on both coast and plateau and
would account for the apparent increase in malaria between
1880 and 1930.

Malaria, so stated, seems to have shown a somewhat
greater incidence on the coast than on the plateau, a situation

Table 8.7

Specific diseases of the infective, febrile type. Percentage of all reported deaths. 010, dysentery; 060, smallpox; 065. malaria; 085, pneumonia; 095, fever. not further identified.

A. Jalisco

Disease	1880	1890	1900	1920	1930	1940	1950	1960
Coast								
010	14.3	13.7	14.5	15.2	18.0	17.3	19.8	13.2
060	9.7	6.8	2.1	6.2	0.2	0.1	0.1	0.2
065	1.5	3.6	4.4	3.2	7.1	5.7	1.9	0.1
085	9.1	17.4	19.6	14.9	15.2	13.9	11.7	14.0
095	30.5	21.0	14.4	12.7	11.9	8.5	7.0	4.5
Plateau								
010	18.0	27.6	28.6	26.6	26.6	31.9	27.5	19.3
060	11.3	4.6	3.8	5.0	1.1	0.4	0.0	0.0
065	2.0	3.2	2.0	2.5	2.5	1.6	0.3	0.1
085	5.9	8.7	10.6	9.5	9.4	12.5	11.5	13.8
095	11.6	12.6	7.6	5.6	6.1	3.4	3.0	2.0

B. Oaxaca

Disease	1872	1890	1907	1922	1940	1952
Coast						
010	6.9	7.7	10.5	8.9	14.0	12.9
060	14.7	11.5	0.5	9.3	0.0	0.0
065	18.8	24.2	44.0	28.5	22.6	31.5
085	1.5	1.5	1.1	1.6	3.7	2.5
095	18.9	15.4	0.7	3.0	4.9	6.4
Plateau (Mixteca Alta)						
010	10.1	13.6	14.4	14.1	19.8	23.3
060	29.1	11.7	2.6	7.5	0.4	0.1
065	6.1	9.3	9.4	8.3	8.0	14.7
085	2.1	2.9	2.4	4.2	6.6	5.3
095	12.0	2.6	2.1	2.8	5.1	6.1

which is universally observed in such areas and which is referable to the distribution of the mosquito. The precipitous decline in the incidence of the disease which is evident after 1930 is, of course, due to the intensive anti-malarial campaign mounted by the federal government in recent years.

The steady decline of smallpox is manifest in both

zones, with no essential quantitative difference between them. The general use of vaccination and its consistent application have exerted the same influence regardless of other factors and have contributed heavily to the similarity which now appears to exist between the mortality pattern on the coast and in the interior. The other infections, gastro-intestinal and respiratory, underwent a relative increase during the period when smallpox and malaria were being reduced. Now that these two sources of mortality have been stabilized at a very low level throughout the state, the other sources are again diminishing proportionally to all recorded deaths. It seems evident, therefore, that most of the broad differences between coast and plateau, as well as secular changes in individual diseases, can be ascribed ultimately to the original high incidence of malaria on the coast and its virtual extirpation during the past three decades.

The corresponding data for the coastal three ex-districts of Oaxaca and the four ex-districts from the highland Mixteca Alta are given in Table 8.5, part B, and Tables 8.6, and 8.7, together with Figures 8.4 and 8.6. From the first of these, it is clear that in both regions the reduction in percentage of all deaths in group 000 has been very slight, if, indeed, it has been present at all. At the same time, the consolidated group, 100, 200, 300, 600, either failed to change or diminished slightly. It showed no sign of relative increase, as it did in both coastal and plateau areas of Jalisco. A similar lack of any well-defined trend is also manifest in the ratios of the first of these groups to the second. (See Figure 8.6). In other words, in so far as epidemic as opposed to organic disease is concerned, there was no pronounced movement of any kind in either the coastal or inland samples from Oaxaca between 1870 and 1950. This complete failure to alter the distribution of causes of death is consistent with what we have observed with the state as a whole, not only in regard to cause of mortality but also with respect to distribution of age at death.

The behavior of certain specific diseases does resemble that noticed in Jalisco. The response to vaccination programs was very similar, probably because the effort was national in scope and affected all regions in more or less the same way. Both on the coast of Oaxaca and in the Mixteca Alta the mortality due to smallpox fell to nearly zero between 1930 and 1950, although the proportion of deaths from this cause had been

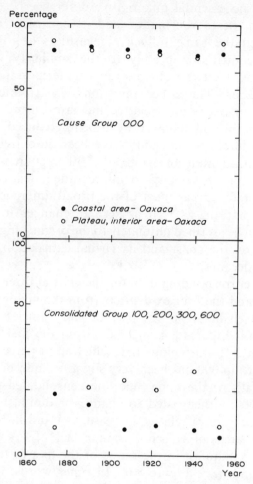

Figure 8.6.   Oaxaca : Ratio of numbers dying from cause 000 to those dying
from consolidated causes 100, 200, 300, 600.

much higher than in Jalisco, particularly on the plateau (the
Mixteca Alta).

Malaria prior to the Revolution had been particularly
virulent on the coast of Oaxaca. If we concede that many of the
cases of fever were actually malaria, this disease alone accounted
for one-third to one-half of the total deaths in the area whereas
its relative importance on the plateau was far less. Another
interesting feature of malaria is the fact that by 1950 it had
not been significantly reduced in its relative lethal effect. In
both coastal and interior areas the percentage of death attributed
to it remained very high and on the plateau may even have

increased. Since 1930 the diagnosis of malaria has been adequate, and there is no reason to doubt the validity of the values shown in Table 8.7. Evidently the efforts of the public health authorities have been much less effective in Oaxaca than in Jalisco.

On the whole, therefore, and by all criteria, the pattern of death causes, like that of age distribution, had not essentially altered in Oaxaca at the date of the last record sample in approximately 1952. Whether it has done so since then, we cannot at present determine.

Appendix A.

Individual Parishes Used from the Census of 1777.

Central plateau : eastern section. Area C.

Parish	Total Pop.	Indian	Non-Indian	Españoles	Mestizos	Pardos
Apizaco	2,523	1,651	872	93	750	29
Ixtacamaxtitlán	4,295	3,242	1,053	100	936	17
Huauquechula	5,638	4,495	1,143	172	790	181
Tecamachalco	4,190	1,843	2,347	1,100	1,136	111
Tepeyahualco	1,776	1,288	488	229	248	11
Zompochtepec	4,527	3,929	598	259	300	39
Eloxochitlán	2,911	2,883	28	23	4	1
Tepetzintla	1,724	1,703	21	11	10	0
Atlequizayan	2,136	2,130	6	2	4	0
Tenango	1,583	1,414	169	51	118	0
Cuatinchán	1,405	1,110	295	38	256	1
Teopantlán	2,186	1,827	359	55	71	233
Tepanco	3,048	2,971	77	23	37	17
S. Pablo del Monte	5,539	5,429	110	78	21	11
Naupan	2,224	2,217	7	4	3	0
Necoxtla	1,769	1,760	9	7	1	1
Nopalucan	2,920	1,636	1,284	449	760	75
Tzicatlacoyan	1,072	799	273	64	183	26
Xochitlán	1,309	1,024	285	184	77	24
Yahualtepec	2,161	1,822	339	71	259	9
Tlacuilotepec	1,900	1,820	80	21	59	0
Sta. María Chiapa	1,453	1,330	123	86	28	9
S. Agustín Palmar	3,289	1,808	1,481	409	945	127
Zapotitlán	2,650	2,597	53	20	33	0
Santos Reyes	2,966	2,760	206	56	131	19
S. Antonio Cañada	2,538	2,423	115	59	4	52
Hueyotlipan	2,030	1,940	90	53	19	18
Acatzingo	6,626	4,202	2,424	357	1,948	119
Acajete	5,279	4,880	399	117	184	98
Amozoc	6,213	3,634	2,579	356	1,868	355
Ahuacatlán	4,626	4,369	257	28	220	9
Chignahuapan	5,447	3,235	2,212	941	1,222	49
Tecali	3,086	2,781	305	95	131	79
Ahuatelco	2,584	2,472	112	0	43	69

Central plateau : eastern section. Area C. (*Cont.*)

Parish	Total Pop.	Indian	Non-Indian	Espa-ñoles	Mesti-zos	Pardos
Atzalan	5,649	4,022	1,627	118	1,509	0
Chapulco	3,135	2,986	149	53	91	5
Chalchicomula	7,875	4,563	3,312	2,509	727	76
Huatlatlauca	3,541	3,378	163	91	62	10
Zacapala	2,228	1,794	434	97	153	184
Coxcatlán	10,039	8,599	1,440	71	489	880
Tlacotepec	4,947	3,982	965	481	441	43
Tlatlauquitepec	7,429	5,541	1,888	446	935	507
Cuapiaxtla	1,900	1,438	462	128	272	62
Tlaxcala	2,197	2,062	135	65	66	4
Tochtepec	2,211	2,114	97	22	75	0
Xochitlán	2,766	2,433	333	198	123	12
Atzitzihuacán	2,035	1,923	112	26	52	34
Totomehuacán	2,662	2,439	223	71	31	121
Ixtenco	1,210	841	369	54	202	113
Tepeaca	5,159	3,470	1,689	899	635	155
Cuauquemecan	2,591	2,386	205	43	142	20
Zozocolco	2,590	2,557	33	3	1	29
52 *parishes*	175,787	141,952	33,835	10,986	18,805	4,044
Tepapayeca	2,494	2,275	219			[a]
Zacapoaxtla	5,887	4,084	1,803			[a]
54 *parishes*	184,168	148,311	35,857			
Huehuetla	2,340	2,340				[b]
Ilamatlán	2,635	2,635				[b]
Quecholac	3,824	3,824				[b]
Coetzala	2,716	2,716				[b]
58 *parishes*	195,683	159,826				

[a] Non-Indian total given but not segregated by racial group.
[b] Only the Indian population given in the report.

Central plateau : eastern section. Area C.

Parish	% Non-Indian in Total Pop	% in Non-Indian Pop.		
		Españoles	Mestizos	Pardos
Apizaco	34.55	10.58	86.09	3.33
Ixtacamaxtitlán	24.53	9.50	88.89	1.61
Huauquechula	20.30	15.05	69.10	15.85

Central plateau : eastern section. Area C. (*Cont.*)

Parish	% Non-Indian in Total Pop	% in Non-Indian Pop.		
		Españoles	*Mestizos*	*Pardos*
Tecamachalco	56.10	46.90	48.37	4.73
Tepeyahualco	27.48	46.95	50.79	2.26
Zompochtepec	13.21	43.30	50.18	6.52
Eloxochitlán	0.96	82.20	14.30	3.50
Tepetzintla	1.22	52.35	47.65	0.00
Atlequizayan	0.28	33.33	66.67	0.00
Tenango	10.68	32.20	67.80	0.00
Cuatinchán	21.00	12.88	86.78	0.34
Teopantlán	16.43	15.30	19.78	64.92
Tepanco	2.52	29.88	48.05	22.07
S. Pablo del Monte	1.99	70.90	19.08	10.02
Naupan	0.31	57.20	42.80	0.00
Necoxtla	0.51	77.76	11.12	11.12
Nopalucan	43.95	35.00	59.20	5.80
Tzicatlacoyan	25.45	23.42	67.05	9.53
Xochitlán	21.78	64.50	27.00	8.50
Yahualtepec	15.70	20.94	76.40	2.66
Tlacuilotepec	4.21	26.25	73.75	0.00
Sta. María Chiapa	8.46	69.90	22.77	7.33
S. Agustín Palmar	45.05	27.61	63.80	8.59
Zapotitlán	2.00	37.73	62.27	0.00
Santos Reyes	6.95	27.20	63.65	9.15
S. Antonio Cañada	4.53	51.30	3.50	45.20
Hueyotlipan	4.43	59.90	21.13	18.97
Acatzingo	36.60	14.74	80.35	4.91
Acajete	7.56	29.33	46.12	24.55
Amozoc	41.52	13.80	72.45	13.75
Ahuacatlán	5.56	10.90	85.60	3.50
Chignahuapan	40.63	42.54	55.30	2.16
Tecali	9.89	31.14	42.95	25.91
Ahuatelco	4.33	0.00	38.40	61.60
Atzalan	28.82	7.26	92.74	0.00
Chapulco	4.75	35.55	61.10	3.35
Chalchicomula	42.10	75.70	21.95	2.35
Huatlatlauca	4.60	55.85	38.05	6.10
Zacapala	19.50	22.34	35.25	42.41
Coxcatlán	14.35	4.93	34.00	61.07
Tlacotepec	19.50	49.85	45.70	4.45
Tlatlauquitepec	25.42	23.62	49.95	26.43
Cuapiaxtla	24.33	27.70	58.90	13.40
Tlaxcala	6.15	48.15	48.90	2.95
Tochtepec	4.39	22.70	77.30	0.00
Xochitlán	12.04	59.40	36.90	3.70
Atzitzihuacán	5.51	23.20	46.42	30.38
Totomehuacán	8.37	31.85	13.90	54.25
Ixtenco	30.50	14.64	54.74	30.62
Tepeaca	32.75	53.26	37.65	9.09

Central plateau : eastern section. Area C. (*Cont.*)

Parish	% Non-Indian in Total Pop	% in Non-Indian Pop.		
		Españoles	*Mestizos*	*Pardos*
Cuauquemecan	7.91	20.96	69.30	9.74
Zozocolco	1.27	9.09	30.30	60.61
52 parishes, mean	16.40	34.79	50.61	14.60
Tepapayeca	8.78			
Zacapoaxtla	30.60			
54 parishes, mean	16.52			

Central plateau : central Veracruz. Area E.

Parish	Total Pop.	Indian	Non- Indian	Espa- ñoles	Mesti- zos	Pardos
Amatlán Reyes	3,034	1,409	1,623	125	129	1,371
Atzacán	1,505	1,379	126	2	119	5
Huatusco	3,205	2,396	809	180	553	76
Quimixtlán	3,364	3,196	168	42	123	3
Misantla	3,526	2,682	844	155	249	440
Perote	2,708	1,034	1,674	374	1,278	22
Naranjal	1,483	881	602	29	121	452
Orizaba	9,929	2,840	7,089	2,424	4,363	302
Ixhuatlán	2,514	2,138	376	105	51	220
Ixhuacán Reyes	3,232	2,772	460	32	428	0
Actopan	1,441	642	799	410	93	296
11 parishes	35,941	21,369	14,572	3,878	7,507	3,187
Jilotepec	2,289	1,741	548			[a]
Totutla	1,811	1,715	96			[a]
13 parishes	40,041	24,825	15,216			
Tonayan	2,176	2,176				[b]
Tequila	4,106	4,106				[b]
Tehuipango	2,160	2,160				[b]
16 parishes	48,483	33,267				

[a] Non-Indian total given but not segregated by racial group.
[b] Only the Indian population given in the report.

Central plateau : central Veracruz. Area E.

Parish	% Non-Indian in Total Pop	% in Non-Indian Pop.		
		Españoles	Mestizos	Pardos
Amatlán	53.35	7.68	7.94	84.38
Atzacán	8.37	1.58	94.45	3.97
Huatusco	25.24	22.26	68.35	9.39
Quimixtlán	5.00	25.00	73.30	1.70
Misantla	23.94	18.37	29.52	52.11
Perote	61.85	22.35	76.40	1.25
Naranjal	40.60	4.82	20.10	75.08
Orizaba	71.40	34.23	61.60	4.17
Ixhuatlán	14.95	27.90	13.55	58.55
Ixhuacán Reyes	14.23	6.96	93.04	0.00
Actopan	55.40	51.30	11.64	37.06
11 parishes, mean	34.05	20.22	49.99	29.79
Jilotepec	23.96			
Totutla	5.30			
13 parishes, mean	31.06			

Central plateau : highland Oaxaca. Area G.

Parish	Total Pop.	Indian	Non-Indian	Españoles	Mestizos	Pardos
Apoala	2,364	2,352	12	10	2	0
Nochixtlán	3,468	3,139	329	38	280	11
Chilapa	2,221	2,007	214	1	213	0
Yolotepec	1,973	1,909	64	13	49	2
Itundujía	1,733	1,674	59	8	47	4
Elotepec	1,899	1,893	6	4	0	2
Teojomulco	1,734	1,552	182	35	75	72
Ecatepec	2,506	2,468	38	13	25	0
Jalapa	9,077	9,052	25	14	5	6
Coatlán	1,968	1,930	38	12	2	24
Jalatlaco	2,378	2,109	269	44	96	129
Villa de Oaxaca	3,147	2,949	198	119	27	52
Zaachila	4,972	4,715	257	165	92	0
Teotitlan del Valle	4,138	4,078	60	20	19	21
S. Agustin Mixtepec	2,092	2,011	81	40	24	17
Ejutla	3,766	3,125	641	121	244	276
Zagache	2,526	2,456	70	33	7	30
Totontepec	2,452	2,408	44	2	42	0

Central plateau : highland Oaxaca. Area G. (*Cont.*)

Parish	Total Pop.	Indian	Non-Indian	Espa-ñoles	Mesti-zos	Pardos
Cuilapan	4,055	3,920	135	29	0	106
Yaeé	3,073	3,065	8	4	4	0
Lachixío	2,604	2,563	41	15	26	0
Ayoquesco	2,674	2,584	90	58	11	21
Ixtlán	3,629	3,590	39	14	20	5
Loxicha	2,095	1,869	226	9	12	205
Quetzaltepec	2,879	2,869	28	5	5	18
Sta. Cruz Mixtepec	1,907	1,660	247	32	80	135
Amatlán	2,181	1,778	403	58	150	195
Miahuatlán	2,987	2,752	235	82	94	59
Betaza	3,114	3,110	4	2	0	2
Sta. Catarina Minas	2,894	2,747	147	69	31	47
Yautla	3,810	3,669	141	52	66	23
Quiatoni	1,857	1,848	9	4	5	0
Ozolotepec	1,972	1,932	40	5	21	14
Chicomezúchil	2,394	2,389	5	3	0	2
Tanetze	3,300	3,271	29	7	20	2
Teotitlán del Camino	3,626	2,912	724	35	270	419
Zimatlán	6,757	5,916	841	186	225	430
Mitla	5,994	5,754	240	23	45	172
Huajolotitlán	2,477	2,310	167	53	97	17
39 *parishes*	120,721	114,335	6,386	1,437	2,431	2,518
Achiutla	3,048	3,046	2			[a]
Chicahuaxtla	1,655	1,652	3			[a]
Yalalag	2,489	2,488	1			[a]
Tlacoatzintepec	1,722	1,721	1			[a]
Yolox	3,152	3,149	3			[a]
Chichicastepec	1,469	1,468	1			[a]
Almoloyas	1,081	1,080	1			[a]
46 *parishes*	135,337	128,939	6,398			
Lapaguía	725	725				[b]
Tepetolutla	2,179	2,179				[b]
48 *parishes*	138,241	131,843				

[a] Non-Indian total given but not segregated by racial group. In all these parishes, the non-Indians consist only of the priest himself, plus occasionally one or two assistants.
[b] Only the Indian population given in the report.

Central plateau : highland Oaxaca. Area G.

Parish	% Non-Indian in Total Pop	% in Non-Indian Pop.		
		Españoles	Mestizos	Pardos
Apoala	0.51	83.33	16.67	0.00
Nochixtlán	9.50	11.55	85.15	3.30
Chilapa	9.65	0.45	99.55	0.00
Yolotepec	3.24	20.34	76.60	3.06
Itundujía	3.41	13.56	79.70	6.74
Elotepec	0.32	66.67	0.00	33.33
Teojomulco	10.51	19.25	41.20	39.55
Ecatepec	1.52	34.20	65.80	0.00
Jalapa	0.28	56.00	20.00	24.00
Coatlán	1.93	31.56	5.26	63.18
Jalatlaco	11.32	15.36	35.67	48.97
Villa de Oaxaca	6.30	60.10	13.63	26.27
Zaachila	5.17	64.20	35.80	0.00
Teotitlán del Valle	1.45	33.33	31.67	35.00
S. Agustín Mixtepec	3.87	49.35	29.62	21.03
Ejutla	17.02	18.88	38.06	43.06
Zagache	2.77	47.15	10.00	42.85
Totontepec	1.80	45.45	54.55	0.00
Cuilapan	3.33	21.46	0.00	78.54
Yaeé	0.26	50.00	50.00	0.00
Lachixío	1.57	36.60	63.40	0.00
Ayoquesco	3.37	64.45	12.22	23.33
Ixtlán	1.08	35.88	51.30	12.82
Loxicha	10.78	3.98	5.31	90.71
Quetzaltepec	0.96	17.85	17.85	64.30
Sta. Cruz Mixtepec	12.95	12.95	32.38	54.67
Amatlán	18.48	14.48	37.23	48.29
Miahuatlán	7.87	34.90	40.00	25.10
Betaza	0.13	50.00	0.00	50.00
Sta. Catarina Minas	5.08	46.95	21.10	31.95
Yautla	3.70	36.85	46.85	16.30
Quiatoni	0.48	44.45	55.55	0.00
Ozolotepec	2.03	12.50	52.50	35.00
Chicomezúchil	0.21	60.00	0.00	40.00
Tanetze	0.88	24.14	69.00	6.86
Teotitlán del Camino	19.90	4.83	37.26	57.91
Zimatlán	12.45	22.13	26.76	51.11
Mitla	4.01	9.58	18.75	71.67
Huajolotitlán	6.75	31.75	59.10	9.15
39 parishes, mean	5.30	33.50	36.80	29.70
Achiutla	0.07			
Chicahuaxtla	0.18			
Yalalag	0.04			
Tlacuatzintepec	0.06			
Yolox	0.10			
Chichicastepec	0.07			
Almoloyas	0.09			
46 parishes, mean	4.51			

Central plateau : Mixteca Baja-Balsas. Area H.

Parish	Total Pop.	Indian	Non-Indian	Espa-ñoles	Mesti-zos	Pardos
Piaxtla	2,866	2,274	592	45	311	236
Teotlaco	1,807	1,465	342	27	188	127
Totoltepec	1,157	1,071	86	76	10	0
Totoltzintla	991	961	31	3	10	18
Tlacotepec	2,167	2,051	116	59	41	16
Tlacozautitlán	1,969	1,943	26	14	7	5
Tonalá	1,954	1,846	108	0	77	31
Zitlala	1,383	1,374	9	7	0	2
Atlemajalcingo	3,505	3,381	124	20	40	64
Alcozauca	1,201	985	216	27	61	128
Huapanapa	1,356	1,318	38	8	0	30
Tequixtepec	2,909	2,732	177	66	·105	6
Tezoatlán	2,009	1,708	301	9	102	190
Tlapatzingo	2,734	2,461	273	16	98	159
Tixtla	6,845	4,772	2,073	326	1,167	580
Igualtepec	3,334	2,756	578	32	208	338
Tehuitzingo	1,348	932	416	39	115	262
Chiautla	4,244	2,820	1,424	163	825	436
Atliztac	2,940	2,914	26	11	15	0
Chila	3,965	3,180	785	85	555	145
Xochihuehuetlán	1,876	1,786	90	20	25	45
Ixcateopan	977	867	110	7	41	62
Chazumba	2,196	2,152	44	3	27	14
Soyatlán	4,642	4,612	30	8	13	9
Huamuxtitlán	3,003	2,620	383	31	215	137
25 parishes	63,379	54,981	8,398	1,102	4,256	3,040
Huajolotitlán	1,952	1,936	16			[a]
26 parishes	65,331	56,917	8,441			
Apango	2,804	2,804				[b]
Metlatonoc	3,216	3,216				[b]
28 parishes	71,351	62,937				

[a]Non-Indian total given but not segregated by racial group.
[b]Only the Indian population given in the report.

Central plateau : Mixteca Baja-Balsas. Area H.

Parish	% Non-Indian in Total Pop	% in Non-Indian Pop.		
		Españoles	Mestizos	Pardos
Piaxtla	20.66	7.60	52.30	40.10
Teotlaco	18.92	7.89	54.95	37.16

Central plateau : Mixteca Baja-Balsas. Area H. (*Cont.*)

Parish	% Non-Indian in Total Pop	% in Non-Indian Pop.		
		Españoles	Mestizos	Pardos
Totoltepec	7.43	88.37	11.63	0.00
Totoltzintla	3.13	9.68	32.30	58.02
Tlacotepec	5.36	50.90	35.35	13.75
Tlacozautitlán	1.32	53.90	26.95	19.15
Tonalá	5.53	0.00	71.30	28.70
Zitlala	0.65	77.80	0.00	22.20
Atlemajalcingo	3.54	16.12	32.24	51.64
Alcozauca	17.98	12.50	28.24	59.26
Huapanapa	2.80	21.05	0.00	78.95
Tequixtepec	6.09	37.30	59.30	3.40
Tezoatlán	14.98	2.99	33.90	63.11
Tlapatzingo	9.98	5.86	35.90	58.24
Tixtla	30.30	11.94	56.35	31.71
Igualtepec	17.34	5.55	36.00	58.45
Tehuitzingo	30.85	9.38	27.65	62.97
Chiautla	33.55	11.45	58.00	30.55
Atliztac	0.88	42.30	57.70	0.00
Chila	19.80	11.83	70.70	17.47
Xochihuehuetlán	4.80	22.22	27.80	49.98
Ixcateopan	11.25	6.36	37.28	56.36
Chazumba	2.00	6.82	61.30	31.88
Soyatlán	0.65	26.67	43.33	30.00
Huamuxtitlán	12.75	8.09	56.10	35.81
25 *parishes, mean*	11.30	22.18	40.26	37.56
Huajolotitlán	0.82			
26 *parishes, mean*	10.90			

Central coasts : Atlantic and Pacific. Areas D and J.

Parish	Total Pop.	Indian	Non- Indian	Espa- ñoles	Mesti- zos	Pardos
Tlalixcoyan	757	54	703	65	0	638
Cosamaloapan	1,135	1,127	8	4	0	4
Apazapan	1,181	1,066	115	27	62	26
Alvarado	1,478	21	1,457	278	47	1,132
S. Pedro Amatlán	1,720	1,672	48	12	3	33
Medellín	1,410	194	1,216	49	51	1,116
Tlacotalpan	3,004	1,308	1,696	220	0	1,476
Tuxpan	1,050	386	664	86	191	387

Central coasts.: Atlantic and Pacific. Areas D and J. (*Cont.*)

Parish	Total Pop.	Indian	Non-Indian	Espa-ñoles	Mesti-zos	Pardos
Acayucan	9,458	6,811	2,647	143	9	2,495
Tuxtla	7,822	6,461	1,361	212	479	670
Chicontepec	5,137	4,853	284	59	88	137
Zanatepec	1,885	1,263	622	5	0	617
Ometepec	3,716	2,667	1,049	64	63	922
Juquila	2,457	2,081	376	40	11	325
Pinotepa del Rey	2,700	2,043	657	52	0	605
Amuzgos	2,236	1,938	298	29	116	153
Tututepec	3,751	3,064	687	44	24	619
Pinotepa de Don Luis	2,693	2,663	30	16	13	1
S. Francisco del Mar	2,423	2,382	41	0	21	20
Atoyac	1,845	1,773	72	18	41	13
Los Cortijos	2,359	0	2,359	50	0	2,309
Cuilutla	1,796	1,090	706	18	24	664
22 parishes	62,013	44,917	17,096	1,491	1,243	14,362

Central coasts : Atlantic and Pacific. Areas D and J.

Parish	% Non-Indian in Total Pop	% in Non-Indian Pop.		
		Españoles	Mestizos	Pardos
Tlalixcoyan	92.90	9.25	0.00	90.75
Cosamaloapan	0.70	50.00	0.00	50.00
Apazapa	9.74	23.48	53.90	22.62
Alvarado	98.70	19.08	3.22	77.70
S. Pedro Amatlán	2.79	25.00	6.25	68.75
Medellín	86.20	4.03	4.19	91.78
Tlacotalpan	56.45	12.97	0.00	87.03
Tuxpan	63.25	12.95	28.76	58.29
Acayucan	28.00	4.86	0.33	94.81
Tuxtla	17.40	15.58	35.18	49.24
Chicontepec	39.30	2.55	3.40	94.05
Zanatepec	33.00	0.80	0.00	99.20
Ometepec	28.25	6.10	6.01	87.89
Juquila	15.31	10.64	2.93	86.43
Pinotepa del Rey	24.34	7.92	0.00	92.08
Amuzgos	13.33	9.73	38.94	51.33
Tututepec	18.31	6.41	3.49	90.10
Pinotepa de Don Luis	1.12	53.33	43.33	3.34
S. Francisco del Mar	1.69	0.00	51.20	48.80
Atoyac	3.90	25.00	57.00	18.00
Los Cortijos	100.00	2.13	0.00	97.87
Cuilutla	39.30	2.55	3.40	94.05
22 parishes, mean	30.69	13.83	15.52	70.65

North : Durango (bishopric), towns, and settlements. Area III E.

Parish	Total Pop.	Indian	Non-Indian	Espa-ñoles	Mesti-zos	Pardos
Cuencamé	5,617	2,649	2,968	613	1,265	1,090
Valle de Suchil	1,905	464	1,441	209	134	1,098
Sta. Barbara	1,106	116	990	532	349	109
Valle de S. Bartolomé	5,738	852	4,886	1,111	3,303	472
Parral	4,223	251	3,972	1,346	781	1,845
S.J.B. Maloya	1,283	745	538	68	16	454
S. José Barrios	596	150	446	104	126	216
S. Pedro Gallo	509	26	483	46	297	140
Zape	2,355	249	2,106	472	281	1,353
S. Sebastián	3,420	564	2,856	901	67	1,888
Rosario	2,729	102	2,627	87	0	2,540
S. Juan Badiraguato	1,665	818	847	225	17	605
Sta. Cat. Tepehuanes	1,490	53	1,437	451	5	981
S. Isidro Torreón	1,548	258	1,290	220	446	624
Sto. Cristo Burgos	773	78	695	332	297	66
S. José Basis	289	88	201	92	8	101
S. Andrés Teul	893	753	140	2	7	131
S. Francisco Borja	2,309	1,908	401	136	140	125
S. Rafael Metachic	885	756	129	42	0	87
Tavaguero	1,110	431	679	338	115	226
Valle de Parras	3,120	773	2,347	237	51	2,059
Chalchihuites	1,291	453	838	330	86	422
Durango City	12,848	1,637	11,211	1,667	319	9,225
Real de Mapimí	1,870	427	1,443	448	440	555
Real de 11,000 Virgenes	3,760	853	2,907	398	2	2,507
Sombrerete	10,515	3,355	7,160	1,951	0	5,209
Cusihuriáchic	3,496	614	2,882	912	859	1,111
Nombre de Dios	2,250	194	2,056	103	27	1,926
Papasquiaro	4,622	1,011	3,611	2,134	7	1,470
Chínipas	450	211	239	86	0	153
30 parishes	84,665	20,839	63,826	15,593	9,445	38,788

North : Durango (bishopric), towns, and settlements. Area III E.

Parish	% Non-Indian in Total Pop	% in Non-Indian Pop.		
		Españoles	Mestizos	Pardos
Cuencamé	52.90	20.66	42.60	36.74
Valle de Suchil	75.65	14.50	9.29	76.21
Sta. Barbara	89.50	53.70	35.25	11.05
Valle de S. Bartolomé	85.10	22.73	67.60	9.67
Parral	94.00	33.90	19.65	46.45
S.J.B. Maloya	41.92	12.63	2.98	84.39

North : Durango (bishopric), towns, and settlements. Area III E. (*Cont.*)

Parish	% Non-Indian in Total Pop	% in Non-Indian Pop.		
		Españoles	Mestizos	Pardos
S. José Barrios	74.80	23.35	28.24	48.41
S. Pedro Gallo	94.90	9.53	61.50	28.97
Zape	89.40	22.42	13.35	64.23
S. Sebastián	83.50	31.60	23.46	44.54
Rosario	96.30	3.31	0.00	96.69
S. Juan Badiraguato	50.85	26.56	2.01	71.43
Sta. Cat. Tepehuanes	96.50	31.38	0.35	68.27
S. Isidro Torreón	83.35	17.05	34.45	48.50
Sto. Cristo Burgos	89.90	47.80	42.70	9.50
S. José Basis	69.55	45.80	3.98	50.22
S. Andrés Teul	15.70	1.43	5.00	93.57
S. Francisco Borja	17.36	33.92	34.90	31.18
S. Rafael Metachic	14.57	32.55	0.00	67.45
Tavaguero	61.15	49.80	16.93	33.27
Valle de Parras	75.30	10.15	2.17	87.68
Chalchihuites	64.90	39.40	10.27	50.33
Durango City	87.30	13.98	3.84	82.18
Real de Mapimí	77.20	31.08	30.50	38.42
Real de 11,000 Vírgenes	77.35	13.70	0.07	86.23
Sombrerete	68.10	27.36	0.00	72.64
Cusihuriáchic	82.50	31.64	29.80	38.56
Nombre de Dios	91.30	5.01	1.32	93.67
Papasquiaro	78.10	59.10	0.19	40.71
Chínipas	53.10	36.00	0.00	64.00
30 *parishes, mean*	71.07	26.74	17.41	55.85

Appendix B.

Towns whose death records have been used.

A. *Towns in Jalisco*

Coastal Zone	*Intermediate Zone*	*Interior Zone (Plateau)*
Autlán	Ameca	Yahualica
Cihuatlán	Sayula	Ojuelos

Appendix B. (*Cont.*)

Coastal Zone	Intermediate Zone	Interior Zone (Plateau)
Purificación	Tlajomulco	Tepatitlán
Mascota	Jocotepec	Arandas
Talpa	Ciudad Guzmán	Poncitlán
Puerto Vallarta	Tequila	Colotlán
El Tuito	Etzatlán	Teocaltiche
Tecolotlán	Tamazula	Lagos de Moreno
Casimiro Castillo	Tecalitlán	San Juan de los Lagos
La Huerta	Zacoalco	Encarnación de Díaz
Ayotitlán	Jilotlán	Atotoniclo el Alto
Cuautitlán	Tuxpan	
El Limón	Cocula	
El Grullo	Acatlán	
Ahuacapán	Ahualulco	
Tequesquitlán	Zapopan	
	Tonalá	
	Chapala	
	Juanacatlán	
	Tlaquepaque	

B. *Ex-districts in Oaxaca. The periods of years shown are inclusive.*

Coast	Intermediate, Mixteca Baja	Intermediate, Central Valley	Plateau, Mixteca Alta
Juquila	*Putla*	*Zimatlán*	*Coixtlahuaca*
1871–1875	1907–1912	1871–1874	1871–1873
1888–1892	1921–1923	1888–1892	1888–1892
1905–1908	1937–1939	1905–1908	1905–1908
1921–1925	1951–1954	1921–1924	1921–1924
1938–1941		1937–1940	1938–1942
1951–1954	*Juxtlahuaca*	1951–1954	1951–1954
Jamiltepec	1938–1939	*Centro*	*Nochixtlán*
	1951–1954		
1871–1875		1871–1874	1871–1874
1888–1892	*Silacayoapan*	1888–1889	1888–1892
1905–1909		1905–1911	1905–1908
1920–1925	1871–1874	1921–1923	1922–1924
1937–1942	1888–1892	1936–1940	1938–1940
1951–1954	1905–1908	1948–1954	1951–1954
	1921–1924		

Appendix B. (*Cont.*)

Coast	Intermediate, Mixteca Baja	Intermediate, Central Valley	Plateau, Mixteca Alta
Pochutla	*Silacayoapan* (cont.)		*Teposcolula*
1871–1875	1939		1872–1874
1888–1892	1951–1954		1888–1892
1905–1908			1905–1908
1920–1923			1921–1924
1938–1943			1938–1942
1951–1954			1951–1954
			Tlaxiaco
			1871–1874
			1888–1892
			1905–1908
			1922–1923
			1939–1940
			1951–1954

Appendix C.
Numbering System Used for Coding Causes of Death.

000

Relatively well-identifiable, infective diseases, including "fever"

005 Tuberculosis
010 Dysentery, diarrhea, gastritis, enteritis, colitis, *"irritación"*
015 Cholera
020 Typhoid and paratyphoid
025 Typhus
030 Meningitis and encephalitis
035 Scarlet fever
040 Erysipelas
045 Diphtheria
050 Whooping cough
055 Measles
060 Smallpox
065 Malaria
070 Yellow fever
075 Syphilis
080
085 Pneumonia
090 Minor, identifiable, febrile diseases
095 "Fever," unspecified as to nature

Appendix C. (*Cont.*)

100

Neoplasms

110	Cancer, stated as such	160	
120	Tumors	170	
130		180	Adenoma
140		190	
150			

200

Endocrine, metabolic, and nutritional ailments

210		260	Arthritis, rheumatism, gout
220	Thyroid, goiter, etc.	270	Dropsy, edema, dehydration
230	Avitaminoses	280	Biochemical disturbances
240	Malnutrition	290	Miscellaneous
250	Diabetes		

300

Organic, infective, or undescribed ailments referred to specific organ systems

310	Mental or personality disorders	360	Liver and gall bladder
320	Central nervous system, perpheral nerves, sense organs	370	Kidney, bladder, and non-reproductive disfunction of genitals
330	Cardiovascular system		
340	Respiratory system, except tuberculosis and pneumonia	380	Blood, anemia, leukemia
350	Gastro-intestinal system, except gastritis, enteritis, colitis	390	Other organs or tissues specifically mentioned

400

Pregnancy, childbirth, puerperium

410	Accidents of parturition	460	
420	Dystocia	470	Puerperal fever
430	Shock	480	Eclampsia
440		490	
450			

500

Perinatal

510	*Al nacer*—an expression repeatedly used to denote death at the time of delivery, no other cause specified	540	Atrepsia
		550	Specific congenital defects
		560	Perinatal infections
		570	Convulsions of various types
520	Specified stillborn or premature	580	
530	Congenital debility or inanition	590	Unspecified as to cause

Appendix C. (*Cont.*)

600

Senility

610   "Old age," "senility," "decrepi-
      tude," etc. (no other categories
      used)

700

External causes

710	Accidents	760	Homicide, by firearm, knife, or blow
720		770	Execution
730	Shock, electric	780	Suicide
740	Animal bites	790	Cause unknown
750	Poison		

800

Ill-defined causes, not possible to classify

810	Inflammation, infection	860	
820	Pain	870	
830	Debility, exhaustion	880	
840	Fevers	890	Miscellaneous, "epidemia," "natural ataque," "atrofia," "caquexia"
850	Abscess, cellulities, gangrene		

900
Cause unknown

910	Stated as unknown cause	930	Cause as stated illegible
920	Cause as stated unintelligible	940	No cause stated

Works Cited

Materials in archives

Spain :

Archivo General de Indias, Seville (AGI) :

Audiencia de Guadalajara :

Legajo 401. Informe de curatos, 1760, report by the Bishop of Guadalajara on population by parish.

Audiencia de Guatemala :

Legajo 128. Tassaciones de los naturales de las provincias de Guathemala y nicaragua y yucatan e pueblos de la villa de Comaiayua q̃ se sacaron por mandado de los señores presidente e oidores del audiencia e chancilleria real de los conffines, 1548–1549, 413ff.

Audiencia de Méjico :

legajo 471. Summary of the reply of the governor of Yucatan, reporting in obedience to real cédula of 11 May 1688 on quotas of Indian tributaries, in letter of 1 May 1689.

798. A series of counts for tribute purposes preserved in the records of a suit over fees, 1715–1755.

1035. Matricula y razon individual de el numᵒ fixo de los Indos Tributarios de Administración y Doctrina, de cada Conuento y Guardianía, en esta Provinçia de San Joseph de Yucathan, assi de los que estan en cada Pueblo debaxo de Campana, como de los que Viuen en las estancias, Sitios y Ranchos..., 28 June 1700, 6ff.

1841. Minuta de los encomenderos desta provyᵃ y la rrenta que cada vno tiene, 1606.

2578–2581, 2589–2591. Portions of 1777 census reports from the bishoprics of Puebla and Oaxaca.

legajo 3168. Report of pastoral inspections by the Bishop of Yucatan, 1736–1737.

Contaduría :

legajos 911A–911B. Cuentas de real hacienda dadas por los oficiales reales de Yucatan, 1540–1650.

920, expediente 1. Matrícula de los pueblos de la provincia de Yucatan con certificaciones de los vicarios : Comprehende no solo los [indios] encomendados si [no] tambien los Negros y Españoles, 1688.

920, expedient 2. Cuaderno de testimonios de certificaciones dadas por los oficiales de Yucatan y alcaldes mayores de sus partidos de las personas que poseían las encomiendas y su producto, 1688.

Indiferente General :

legajos 102, 1736. Portions of the 1777 census for the bishopric of Durango.

107–108. Geographic and demographic reports on New Spain by provincial governors, 1742-1746 (remnants of census of 1742–1746).

Archivo Histórico Nacional, Madrid (AHN) :
Cartas de Indias, caja 2a, no. 21. Letter of Guillén de las Casas, Governor of Yucatan, to the Crown, Mérida 25 March 1582, with appendix, Memoria de los conuentos, vicarias y pu°s que ay en esta gouernacion de yucatan, cocumel y tauasco.

Mexico :

Archivo General de la Nación, Mexico City (AGN) :
Historia :
vols. 72–73, 522–523. Summaries by intendancies and provinces of incomplete censuses taken during the administration of Viceroy Revillagigedo II, 1789–1794.
Padrones :
108 vols. Returns of the military census (counts of non-Indian population), 1791–1793.
Tierras :
vol. 2809, expediente 20. Cuenta y visita del pueblo de Ppencuyut, 1584.

Archivo General del Estado, Guadalajara :
Archivo del Registro Civil.

Archivo del Estado, Oaxaca :
Archivo del Registro Civil.
Parish Archives in the state of Oaxaca (registers of baptisms, marriages, deaths) :
Archibishopric of Oaxaca :
Jaltepec
Nochixtlán
Teozacoalco
Teposcolula
Tilantongo
Tlaxiaco
Yanhuitlán
Bishopric of Huajuapan (Archbishopric of Puebla)
Coixtlahuaca
Tamazulapan
Tejupan

Materials printed or identified primarily by name of author.

Adams, Richard E.W. "Maya Archaeology 1958–1968, a Review," *Latin American Research Review,* IV, no. 2(1969), 3–46.
Aguirre Beltrán, Gonzalo. *La población negra de México,* 1519–1810; *estudio etnohistórico.* Mexico City, 1946.

Almada, Francisco R. *Diccionario de historia, geografia y biografia del estado de Colima*. Colima, 1939.

Anghiera, Pietro Martire d'. *Decadas del Nuevo Mundo*. Transl. Agustín Millares Carlo. Mexico City, 1964–1965. 2 vols.

Arriaga, Eduardo E. *Mortality Decline and Its Demographic Effects in Latin America*. (University of California, Berkeley, Institute of International Studies, Population Monograph Series, no. 6.) Berkeley, 1970.

———. *New Life Tables for Latin American Populations in the Nineteenth and Twentieth Centuries*. (University of California, Berkeley, Institute of International Studies, Population Monograph Series, no. 3.) Berkeley, 1968.

Aznar Barbachano, Tomás, and Juan Carbó. *Memoria sobre la conveniencia utilidad y necesidad de erigir constitucionalmente . . . el antiguo distrito de Campeche*. Mexico City, 1861.

Bancroft, Hubert Howe. *History of Mexico*. San Francisco, 1883–1888. 6 vols.

Banda, Longinos. *Estadística de Jalisco*. Guadalajara, 1873.

Baqueiro, Serapio. *Reseña geográfica, histórica y estadistica del estado de Yucátán desde los primitivos tiempos de la peninsula*. Mexico City, 1881.

Bárcena, Mariano. *Ensayo estadístico del estado de Jalisco*. Mexico City, 1888.

Benítez Zenteno, Raul. *Analisis demográfico de México*. Mexico City, 1961.

Betancourt Pérez, Antonio. *Historia de Yucatan*, vol. 1. Mérida, 1970.

Bolio, Edmundo. *Diccionario histórico, geográfico y biográfico de Yucatán*. Mexico City, 1944.

Borah, Woodrow. "Francisco de Urdiñola's Census of the Spanish Settlements in Nueva Vizcaya, 1604," *Hispanic American Historical Review*, XXXV (1955), 398–402.

———. *New Spain's Century of Depression* (Ibero-Americana : 35). Berkeley and Los Angeles, 1951.

Borah, Woodrow, and Sherburne F. Cook. *The Aboriginal Population of Central Mexico on the Eve of the Spanish Conquest* (Ibero-Americana : 45). Berkeley and Los Angeles, 1963.

———. "Marriage and Legitimacy in Mexican Culture : Mexico and California," *California Law Review*, LIV, no. 2 (May 1966), 946–1008.

———. *The Population of Central Mexico in* 1548 : *An Analysis of the Suma de visitas de pueblos* (Ibero-Americana : 43). Berkeley and Los Angeles, 1960.

Brinckmann, Lutz. *Die Augustinerrelationen Nueva España 1571–1573. Analyse eines Zensusmanuskripts des 16. Jahrhunderts*. (Hamburgischen Museum für Völkerkunde und Vorgeschichte, Beiträge zur mittelamerikanischen Völkerkunde, VIII.) Hamburg, 1969.

Bronson, Bennett. "Roots and Subsistence of the Ancient Maya," *Southwestern Journal of Anthropology*, XXII(1966), 251–279.

Bullard, William R., Jr. "The Maya Settlement Pattern in Northeastern Peten, Guatemala," *American Antiquity*, XXV (1960), 355–372.

———. "Settlement Pattern and Social Structure in the Southern Maya Lowlands During the Classic Period," *International Congress of Americanists*, XXXV, Mexico City, 1962, *Actas y memorias*, I, 279–287.

Camavitto, Dino. *La decadenza delle popolazioni messicane al tempo della conquista*. Rome, 1935.

Cárdenas Valencia, Francisco de. *Relacion historial eclesiastica de la provincia de Yucatán de la Nueva España, escrita el año de* 1639. Mexico City, 1937.

Carmagnani, Marcello. "Demografia e societá. La struttura sociale di due centri minerari del Messico settentrionale (1600–1720)," *Revista storica italiana*, LXXXII(1970), 560–591.

Carrasco, Pedro. "Don Juan Cortés, cacique de Santa Cruz Quiché," *Estudios de cultura maya*, VI(1966), 251–266.

Casas, Fray Bartolomé de las. *Obras escogidas*. Ed. and introd. Juan Pérez de Tudela Bueso. (Biblioteca de autores españoles, vols. 95, 96, 105, 106, 110.) Madrid, 1957–1961. 5 vols.

Chamberlain, Robert S. *The Conquest and Colonization of Yucatan, 1517–1550*. (Carnegie Institution of Washington, Publication no. 582). Washington, D.C., 1948.

———. transl. and ed. *The First Three Voyages to Yucatan and New Spain, According to the* Residencia *of Hernan Cortés*. (University of Miami, Hispanic-American Studies, no. 7.) Coral Gables, 1949.

———. *The Pre-Conquest Tribute and Service System of the Maya as Preparation for the Spanish* Repartimiento-Encomienda *in Yucatan*. (University of Miami, Hispanic-American Studies, no. 10.) Coral Gables, 1951.

———. "Spanish Methods of Conquest and Colonization of Yucatan, 1527–1550. II. The Conquest and Initial Colonization," *Scientific Monthly*, XLIX, no. 4 (whole no. 289) (October 1939), 351–359.

Ciudad Real, Fray Antonio de and Fray Alonso de San Juan. (See *Relacion breve y verdadera de... Fray Alonso Ponce*.)

Cline, Horward F. "Related Studies in Early Ninteenth Century Yucatecan Social History." Microfilm collection of manuscripts on Middle American Cultural Anthropology, no. XXXII, University of Chicago Library, 1950.

Coahuila (state). Gobernadro. *Memoria*, 1869.

Cogolludo, Diego López de. (See López de Cogolludo, Diego.)

Colección de documentos inéditos relativos al descubrimiento, conquista y organización de las antiguas posesiones españolas de América y Oceanía, sacados de los archivos del reino, y muy especialmente del de Indias (DII). Madrid, 1864–1884. 42 vols.

Colección de documentso inéditos relativos al descubrimiento, conquista y organización de las antiguas posesiones españolas de Ultramar (DIU). Madrid, 1885–1932. 25 vols.

Colima (state). Gobernador. *Memoria*, 1887–1888, 1888–1889, 1889–1890.

Cook, Sherburne F. "The Population of Mexico in 1793," *Human Biology*, XIV(1942), 499–515.

Cook, Sherburne F., and Woodrow Borah. *The Indian Population of Central Mexico, 1531–1610* (Ibero-Americana : 44). Berkeley and Los Angeles, 1960.

———. *The Population of the Mixteca Alta, 1520–1960* (Ibero-Americana : 50). Berkeley and Los Angeles, 1968.

Cook, Sherburne F., and Robert F. Heizer. *The Quantitative Approach to the Relation Between Population and Settlement Size*. (University of California, Archaeological Survey, Reports, no. 64.) Berkeley, March 1965.

———. "Relationships Among Houses, Settlement Areas, and Population in Aboriginal California," in *Settlement Archaeology*. Ed. K.C. Chang. Palo Alto, 1968, pp. 79–116.

Cordero, Enrique. "La subestimación de la mortalidad infantil en México," *Demografia y economía*, II no. 1 (or no. 4 in count by numbers) (1968), 44–62.

Cortés. Hernán. *Cartas y documentos*. Introd. Mario Hernández Sánchez-Barba. Mexico City, 1963.

Cowgill, George L. "The End of Classic Maya Culture : A Review of Recent Evidence," *Southwestern Journal of Anthropology*, XX(1964), 145–159.

Cowgill, Ursula M. "An Agricultural Study of the Southern Maya Lowlands," *American Anthropologist*, LXIV(1962), 273–286.

———. "Soil Fertility and the Ancient Maya," Connecticut Academy of Arts and Sciences, New Haven, *Transactions*, XLII(1961), 1–56.

———. "Soil Fertility, Population, and the Ancient Maya," National Academy of Sciences, *Proceedings*, XLVI, no. 8(August 1960), 1009–1011.

Cowgill, Ursula M. and G.E. Hutchinson. "Sex Ratio in Childhood and the Depopulation of the Peten. Guatemala," *Human Biology*, XXV (1963), 90–103.

Denevan, William M. "Aboriginal Drained-Field Cultivation in the Americas," *Science*, CLXIX(14 August 1970), 647–654.

Díaz del Castillo, Bernal. *Historia verdadera de la conquista de la Nueva España*. Ed. Joaquín Ramírez Cabañas. 5th ed. Mexico City, 1960. 2 vols.

Diez de la Calle, Juan. *Memorial y noticias sacras y reales de las Indias Occidentales*. 2nd ed. Mexico City, 1932.

Dumond, Donald E. "Swidden Agriculture and the Rise of Maya Civilization," *Southwestern Journal of Anthropology*, XVII(1961), 301–316.

Durán Ochoa, Julio. *Población*. Mexico City and Buenos Aires, 1955.

Echánove, Policarpo Antonio de. "Cuadro estadistico de Yucatan en 1814," *El Fénix*, Campeche, nos. 21–25, 27–29, 10 February 1849–20 March 1849. (The report was signed by Pedro Bolio and Echánove but was the work of the latter.)

————. "Resumen instructivo de los fondos de medio real de ministros y comunidades de indios de la provincia de Yucatan, en su tesorería principal de Mérida," *El Fénix*, Campeche, no. 33, 10 April 1849. (See comment in previous item.) The report is dated Mérida, 22 April 1813.)

Edwards, Clinton Ralph. "Quintana Roo : Mexico's Empty Quarter." Master's thesis, University of California, Berkeley, 1957.

Ensayo estadístico sobre el territorio de Colima, mandado formar y publicar por la muy ilustre municipalidad de la capital del territorio. Mexico City, 1849.

Escudero, José Agustin de. *Noticias estadísticas del estado de Durango*. Mexico City, 1849.

Fonseca, Fabián de, and Carlos de Urrutia. *Historia general de real hacienda*. Mexico City, 1845–1853. 6 vols.

García Icazbalceta, Joaquín, ed. *Colección de documentos para la historia de México*. Mexico City and Paris, 1858–1866. 2 vols.

Girerol, Manuel. *Expediente de la visita oficial del estado hecha por el C. Lic... vice gobernador constitucional del mismo en cumplimiento del articulo 56 de la constitucion politica de Yucatan*. Mérida, n.d. but 1870.

González Navarro, Moisés. *Raza y tierra. La guerra de castas y el henequén*. Mexico City, 1970.

Gordon, B. Leroy. *Anthropogeography and Rainforest Ecology in Bocas del Toro Province, Panama*. Mimeographed field report, Department of Geography, University of California, Berkeley, 1969.

Guanajuato (state). Gobernador. *Memoria*, 1824–1825, 1851, 1873–1875, 1880–1882, 1889–1890.

Guerrero (state). Gobernador. *Memoria*, 1869–1870, 1871–1872, 1885–1886, 1887–1888, 1888–1889.

Handbook of Middle American Indians. Ed. Robert Wauchope. Austin, 1964–1971. 11 vols. to that date.

Haviland, William A. "A New Population Estimate for Tikal, Guatemala," *American Antiquity*, XXXIV(1969), 429–433.

————. "Stature at Tikal, Guatemala : Implications for Ancient Maya Demography and Social Organization," *American Antiquity*, XXXII(1967), 316–325.

Hester, J.A., Jr. "Natural and Cultural Bases of Ancient Maya Subsistence Economy." Doctoral thesis, University of California, Los Angeles, 1954.

Hollingsworth, T.H. *Historical Demography*. Ithaca, 1969.

Humboldt, Alexander Freiherr von. *Essai politique sur le royaume de la Nouvelle-Espagne*. 2nd ed. Paris, 1811. 5 vols.

Ibero-Americana (IA). (University of California Publications, Berkeley and Los Angeles :

No.
43 Borah, Woodrow, and Sherburne F. Cook. *The Population of Central Mexico in 1548 : An Analysis of the* Suma de visitas de pueblos. 1960.
44 Cook, Sherburne F., and Woodrow Borah. *The Indian Population of Central Mexico, 1531–1610.* 1960.
45 Borah, Woodrow, and Sherburne F. Cook. *The Aboriginal Population of Central Mexico on the Eve of the Spanish Conquest.* 1963.
50 Cook, Sherburne F., and Woodrow Borah. *The Population of the Mixteca Alta, 1520–1960.* 1968.
"Incorporacion a la Real Corona de las encomiendas de la provincia de Yucatan. Distritos de las Reales Cajas de Merida y Campeche," 1785–1786, AGN, *Boletín*, ser. 1, IX(1938), 456–569, 591–675.
Instituto Panamericano de Geografía e Historia. Comisión de Historia. *El mestizaje en la historia de Ibero-America.* Mexico City, 1961. Also published in *Rivista de historia de América,* nos. 53–54(junio-diciembre 1962), 127–218.
Jakeman, Max Wells. "The Maya States of Yucatan, 1441–1545." Doctoral thesis, University of California, Berkeley, 1938.
Landa, Diego de. *Landa's Relación de las Cosas de Yucatan. A Translation Edited with Notes by Alfred M. Tozzer.* (Harvard University, Peabody Museum of American Archaeology and Ethnology, Papers, XVIII.) Cambridge, Mass., 1941; reprinted New York, 1966. (Cited in footnotes as Landa-Tozzer.)
———. *Relacion de las cosas de Yucatan.* Introd. Angel María Garibay. 8th ed. [*sic,* but really 9th]. Mexico City, 1959.
———. *Yucatan Before and After the Conquest, by Friar Diego de Landa, with Other Related Documents, Maps and Illustrations.* Transl. and notes William Gates. Baltimore, 1937.
Lange, Frederick W. "Marine Resources: A Viable Subsistence Alternative for the Prehistoric Lowland Maya," *American Anthropologist,* LXXIII(1971), 619–639.
———. "Una reevaluación de la población del norte de Yucatán en el tiempo del contacto español: 1528," *América indígena,* XXXI, no. 1 (January 1971), 117–139.
Latorre, Germán, ed. *Relaciones geograficas de Indias (contenidas en el Archivo General de Indias de Sevilla). La Hispano-América del siglo XVI : Virreinato de Nueva España. (México—censos de población.)* Seville, 1920.
León, Nicolás. *Las castas del México colonial o Nueva España. Noticias etno-antropológicas.* Mexico City, 1924.
Linder, Forrest E., and Robert D. Grove. *Techniques of Vital Statistics.* (National Office of Vital Statistics, Department of Health, Education, and Welfare; reprint of Chapters I-IV of *Vital Statistics Rates in the United States, 1900–1940,* pp. 1–91). Washington, D.C. 1959.
López de Cogolludo, Diego. *Historia de Yucatan.* 5th ed. Mexico City, 1957. 2 vols. Facsimile of 1st ed. of 1688.
López de Velasco, Juan. *Geografía y descripción universal de las Indias.* Ed. Justo Zaragoza. Madrid, 1894.
Love, Edgar F. "Marriage Patterns of Persons of African Descent in a Colonial Mexico City Parish," *Hispanic American Historical Review,* LI(1971), 79–91.
Loyo, Gilberto. *La población de México. Estado actual y tendencias.* Mexico City, 1960.
Macías Valadez, Francisco. *Apuntes geograficas y estadisticas sobre el estado de San Luis Potosí.* San Luis Potosí, 1898.
Martínez Alomía, Gustavo. *Historiadores de Yucatan.* Campeche, 1906.
Martínez Gracida, Manuel. *Colección de "Cuadros sinópticos" de ... Oaxaca.* Published as an appendix to the *Memoria* of the governor of the state of Oaxaca for 1883.

Martyr, Peter. (See d' Anghiera, Pietro Martire.)
Means, Philip Ainsworth. *History of the Spanish Conquest of Yucatan and of the Itzaes.* (Harvard University, Peabody Museum of American Archaeology and Ethnology, Papers, VII.) Cambridge, Mass., 1917.
Mestre Ghigliazzi, Manuel. *Documentos y datos para la historia de Tabasco.* Mexico City, 1916–1926. 4 vols.
Mexico (state). Gobernador. *Ensayo de una memoria estadística del distrito de Tulancingo.* Mexico City, 1825.
———. *Memoria,* 1833–1834, 1834–1835, 1870–1871, 1886–1887.
Mexico. Archivo General de la Nación. *Boletín.* Mexico City, 1930–1969. 40 vols.
———Dirección General de Estadistica. *Anuario estadistico.* Mexico City, 1893–1969. 33 nos.
———. *Anuario estadístico compendiado,* 1968.
———. Dirección General de Estadística.
Censos generals :
   1895. *Censo general de la Republica Mexicana verificado el 20 de octubre de 1895.* Mexico City, 1897–1899. 31 pts.
   1900. *Censo general de la República Mexicana... verificado en 1900.* Mexico City, 1901–1907. 34 pts.
   1910. *Tercer censo población de los Estados Unidos Mexicanos...* 1910. Mexico City, 1918–1920. 12 pts. in 3 vols.
   1921. *Censo general de habitantes. 30 de noviembre de 1921.* Mexico City, 1925–1928. 30 pts.
   1930. *Quinto censo de población, 15 de mayo 1930.* Mexico City, 1932–1936. 34 pts.
   1940. *6° censo de población,* 1940. Mexico City, 1943–1948. 30 pts.
   1950. *Septimo censo general de población, 6 de junio de 1950.* Mexico City, 1952–1953. 33 pts.
   1960. *VIII censo general de población,* 1960. Mexico City, 1962–1964. 35 pts.
———. *Estadística nacional, revista mensual.* Mexico City, 1925–1931. 8 vols. (año 1–8, números 1–122).
———. *Estadisticas sociales del Porfiriato* 1877–1819. Comp. Moisés González Navarro. Mexico City, 1956.
———. Secretaría de Economía or Secretaría de Comercio e Industria. Dirección General de Estadistica. *See* Mexico. Dirección General de Estadística. (The Dirección General de Estadística has had other names in the past but is here listed under its current one.)
———. Secretaría de Fomento, Colonización e Industria. *Memoria,* 1853–1857.
Miranda, José. *El tributo indigena en la Nueva España durante el siglo XVI.* Mexico City, 1952.
Molina-Hübbe, Richardo. *Las hambres de Yucatan.* Mexico City, 1941.
Molina Solís, Juan Francisco. *Historia de Yucatan desde la independencia hasta la época actual.* Mérida, 1921–1927. 2 vols.
———. *Historia de Yucatan durante la dominacion española.* Mérida, 1904–1913. 3 vols.
———. *Historia del descubrimiento y conquista de Yucatan con una reseña de la historia antigua de esta península.* Mérida, 1896.
Mora, José María Luis. *Obras sueltas de...ciudadano mexicano.* 2nd ed. Mexico City, 1963.
Morelos (state). Gobernador. *Memoria,* 1850, 1886, 1890.
Moreno Navarro, Isidoro. "Un aspecto del mestizaje americano : el problema de la terminología," *Revista española de antropología americana* [*trabajos y conferencias*], IV(1969), 202–217.

Moreno Toscano, Alejandra. *Geografía económica de México (siglo XVI)*. Mexico City, 1968.

Morley, Sylvanus G. *The Ancient Maya*. 3rd ed. Rev. by George W. Brainerd. Stanford, 1956.

Mörner, Magnus, ed. *Race and Class in Latin America*. New York, 1970.

———. *Race Mixture in the History of Latin America*. Boston, 1967.

Navarro y Noriega, Fernando. *Catalogo de los curatos y misiones de la Nueva España*. Mexico City, 1943. (New ed. of work first published in Mexico City, 1813).

———. *Memoria sobre la poblacion del reino de Nueva España*. Mexico City, 1943. (New ed. of work first prepared in 1814).

Nuevo León (state). Gobernador. *Memoria*, 1887–1889, 1889–1891.

Oaxaca (state). Gobernador. *Memoria*, 1858, 1861, 1869, 1881.

Oviedo y Valdés, Gonzalo Fernández de. *Historia general y natural de las Indias*. (Biblioteca de autores españoles, vols. 117–121.) Madrid, 1959. 5 vols.

Pacheco Cruz, Santiago. *Diccionario de etimologias toponimicas mayas*. 2nd ed. Mérida, 1959.

Palafox y Mendoza, Juan de. *Tratados mejicanos*. Ed. and introd. Francisco Sánchez-Castañer. (Biblioteca de autores españoles, vols. 217–218.) Madrid, 1968. 2 vols.

Paso y Troncoso, Francisco del, compiler. *Epistolario de Nueva España, 1505–1818*. Mexico City, 1939–1942. 16 vols. (Cited in text as *ENE*.)

———. *Papeles de Nueva España : Segunda serie, geografía y estadística*. Mexico City, 1905–1906. 6 vols. (Plus appendixes and additional volumes published by Vargas Rea. Mexico City, 1944–1948.)

Pérez Bustamante, Ciriaco, P. Lorenzana, and S. González García. "La población de Nueva España en el siglo XVI," *Boletín de la Biblioteca Menéndez y Pelayo*, año X(1928), 58–73.

Pérez Galaz, Juan de Dios, ed. "Situacion estadistica de Yucatan en 1851," AGN, *Boletín*, ser. 1, XIX(1948–1949), 399–462, 545–622; XX, 127–186, 277–300.

Pérez Hernández, José María. *Compendio de la geografía del estado de Sonora*. Mexico City, 1872.

Ponce, Fray Alonso. (See *Relacion breve y verdadera de . . . Fray Alonso Ponce*.)

Portillo, Esteban L. *Anuario coahuilense para 1886*. Saltillo, 1886.

Puebla (state). Gobernador. *Memoria*, 1829–1830.

Puleston, Dennis E. "An Experimental Approach to the Classic Maya Chultuns," *American Antiquity*, XXXVI(1971), 322–335.

Querétaro (state). Asamblea Departmental. *Estadística del departmento de Querétaro, relativa á la población. Presentada . . . en 19 de mayo de 1846*. Querétaro, 1846.

Raso, José Antonio del. *Notas estadísticas del departmento de Querétaro*. Mexico City, 1848.

Recopilación de leyes de los reynos de las Indias. (See Spain. Laws.)

Reed, Nelson. *The Caste War of Yucatan*. Stanford, 1964.

Reina, Ruben E. "Milpas and Milperos : Implications for Prehistoric Times," *American Anthropologist*, LXIX(1967), 1–20.

Relacion brave y verdadera de algunas cosas de las muchas que sucedieron al padre fray Alonso Ponce en las provincias de la Nueva España. Madrid, 1872. 2 vols. Also published in *Colección de documentos inéditos para la historia de España*, LVII–LVIII.)

Relacion de los conquistadores y pobladores que habia en la provincia de Yucatan, en la ciudad de Mérida, 25 July 1551, a report of Juan de Paredes and Julián Donzel to Lic. Cerrato, President of the Audiencia of Guatemala, *DII*, XIV, 191–220.

Relaciones de Yucatan (*DIU*, XI and XII). Madrid, 1898–1900. 2 vols.

Remesal, Fray Antonio de. *Historia general de las Indias Occidentales y particular de la gobernacion de Chiapa y Guatemala.* Ed. Carmelo Sáenz de Santa María, S.J. (Biblioteca de autores españoles, vols 175, 189.) Madrid, 1964–1966. 2 vols.

La Republica Mexicana. Coahuila. Reseña geografica y estadistica. Paris and Mexico City, 1909.

Ricketson, Oliver G., Jr., and Edith Bayles Ricketson. *Uaxactun, Guatemala. Group E—1926–1931.* (Carnegie Institution of Washington, Publication no. 477.) Washington, D.C., 1937.

Roncal, Joaquin. "The Negro Race in Mexico," *Hispanic American Historical Review*, XXIV(1944), 530–540.

Rosenblat, Angel. *La población indígena y el mestizaje en América.* 3rd ed. Buenos Aires, 1954. 2 vols.

Roukema, E. "A Discovery of Yucatan Prior to 1503," *Imago Mundi*, Stockholm, XIII(1956), 30–38.

Roys, Ralph L. *The Book of Chilam Balam of Chumayel.* 2nd ed., Norman, 1967.

———. *The Indian Background of Colonial Yucatan.* (Carnegie Institution of Washington, Publication no. 548.) Washington, D.C., 1943.

———. *The Political Geography of the Yucatan Maya.* (Carnegie Institution of Washington, Publication no. 613.) Washington, D.C., 1957.

———. *The Titles of Ebtun.* (Carnegie Institution of Washington, Publication no. 505.) Washington, D.C., 1939.

Roys, Ralph L., France V. Scholes, and Eleanor B. Adams. "Census and Inspection of the Town of Pencuyut, Yucatan, in 1583 by Diego García de Palacio, Oidor of the Audiencia of [Mexico]," *Ethnohistory*, VI(1959), 195–225.

———. "Report and Census of the Indians of Cozumel, 1570," *Contributions to American Anthropology and History*, vol. 6. (Carnegie Institution of Washington, Publication no. 523.) Washington, D.C., 1940, pp. 5–30.

Rubio Mañé, Jose Ignacio, ed. *Archivo de la historia de Yucatan, Campeche y Tabasco.* Mexico City, 1942. 3 vols.

Ruz Lhuillier, Alberto. *La costa de Campeche en los tiempos prehispanicos. Prospeccion ceramica y bosquejo historico.* Mexico City, 1969.

Sabloff, J.A., and G. R. Willey, "The Collapse of Maya Civilization in the Southern Lowlands : A Consideration of History and Process," *Southwestern Journal of Anthropology*, XXIII(1967), 311–336.

Salazar, Eduardo, and Prudencio P. Rosado. *Memorias de las secretarías de gobernación y hacienda y de guerra y guardia nacional reductadas por los secretarios . . . y leidas ante la H. legislatura del estado en la sesion del 11 setiembre de 1874.* Campeche, 1874.

Sánchez de Aguilar, Pedro. *Informe contra idolorum cultores del obispado de Yucatan.* 3rd ed. Mérida, 1937.

Sanders, William T. "Cultural Ecology of the Maya Lowlands," *Estudios de cultura maya*, II, 79–121; III, 203–241 (1962–1963).

Sanders, William T., and Barbara J. Price. *Mesoamerica. The Evolution of a Civilization.* New York, 1968.

Sauer, Carl Ortwin. *The Early Spanish Main.* Berkeley and Los Angeles, 1966.

Scholes, France V., ed. *Documentos para la historia de Yucatan.* Mérida, 1963–1938. 3 vols.

Scholes, France V., and Eleanor B. Adams, eds. *Don Diego Quijada, alcalde mayor de Yucatan 1561–1565. Documentos sacados de los archivos de España y publicados.* Mexico City, 1938. 2 vols.

Scholes, France V., Ralph L. Roys, Eleanor B. Adams, and Robert S. Chamberlain. *The Maya Chontal Indians of Acalan-Tixchel. A Contribution to the History of the Yucatan Peninsula.* (Carnegie Institution of Washington, Publication no. 560.) Washington, D.C., 1948.

Septién y Villaseñor José Antonio. *Memoria estadística del estado de Querétaro.* Querétaro, 1875.

Sims, Harold D. "Las clases económicas y la dicotomía criollo-peninsular en Durango, 1827," *Historia mexicana,* XX, no. 4 (no. 80) (abril-junio 1971), 539–562.

Sinaloa (state). Gobernador. *Memoria,* 1869, 1881.

Sociedad Mexicana de Geografía y Estadística. *Boletín.* Mexico City, 1839–1964. 97 vols. (Cited in text as *SMGEB*).

Sonora (state). *Division territorial y censo del estado de Sonora.* Guaymas, 1890.

————. Gobernador. *Informe,* 1888–1889.

Spain. Laws. *Recopilacion de leyes de los reynos de las Indias.* Facsimile of 4th ed. Madrid, 1943. 3 vols.

————. Ministerio de Fomento. *Cartas de Indias.* Madrid, 1877.

Spinden, J.H. "The Population of Ancient America," Smithsonian Institution, Washington, D.C., *Annual Report,* 1929, pp. 451–471.

Steggerda, Morris. *Maya Indians of Yucatan.* (Carnegie Institution of Washington, Publication no. 531.) Washington, D.C., 1941.

Stephens, John L. *Incidents of Travel in Yucatan.* New ed. New York, 1963. 2 vols.

Tabasco (state). Governador. *Memoria,* 1887–1890.

Tamaulipas (state). Gobernador. *Memoria,* 1888.

Tasaciones de los pueblos de la provincia de Yucatán hechas por la Audiencia de Santiago de Guatemala en el mes de febrero de 1549, Paso y Troncoso, *Epistolario de Nueva España,* V, 103–181; VI, 73–107.

Teixidor, Felipe. *Bibliografía yucateca.* Mérida, 1937.

Termer, Franz. "The Density of Population in the Southern and Northern Maya Empires as an Archeological and Geographical Problem," in *The Civilizations of Ancient America. Selected Papers of the XXIXth International Congress of Americanists,* ed. Sol Tax. New York, 1949; published Chicago, 1951, pp. 101–107.

Thompson, J. Eric S. "Estimates of Maya Population: Deranging Factors," *American Antiquity,* XXXIV(1971), 214–216.

————. "The Maya Central Area at the Spanish Conquest and Later: A Problem in Demography (The Huxley Memorial Lecture 1966)," Royal Anthropological Institute of Great Britain and Ireland, *Proceedings,* 1966, pp. 23–37.

————. *Maya History and Religion.* Norman, 1970.

————. *The Rise and Fall of Maya Civilization.* Norman, 1954.

————. "Trade Relations between the Maya Highlands and Lowlands," *Estudios de cultura maya,* IV(1964), 13–49.

Tlaxcala (state). Gobernador. *Memoria,* 1886–1887.

United States. Department of Commerce, Bureau of the Census, Statistical Reports Division. *Statistical Abstract of the United States for 1968.* Washington, D.C., 1968.

Vázquez de Espinosa, Antonio. *Compendio y descripción de las Indias Occidentales.* (Smithsonian Miscellaneous Collections, vol. 108.) Washington, D.C., 1948.

Velasco, Alfonso Luis. *Geografía y estadística de la República Mexicana.* Mexico City, 1889–1895. 12 vols.

Veracruz (state). *Estadística del estado libre y soberano de Veracruz.* Jalapa, 1831–1832.

――――. Gobernador. *Memoria,* 1831–1832, 1868–1869, 1869–1870, 1885–1886, 1888–1890, 1890.

Villa Rojas, Alonso. *The Maya of East Central Quintana Roo.* (Carnegie Institution of Washington, Publication no. 559.) Washington, D.C., 1945.

Wagner, Helmuth O. "Die Besiedlungsdichte Zentralamerikas vor 1492 und die Ursachen des Bevölkerungsschwundes in der frühen Kolonialzeit unter besonderer Berücksichtigung der Halbinsel Yucatán," *Jahrbuch für Geschichte von Staat, Wirtschaft und Gesellschaft Lateinamerikas,* V(1968), 63–103.

――――. "Los pozos prehispanicos en la peninsula de Yucatan." Draft paper, 1971.

――――. "Subsistence Potential and Population Density of the Maya on the Yucatan Peninsula and Causes for the Decline in Population in the Fifteenth Century," International Congress of Americanists, XXXVIII, Stuttgart-Munich, 1968, *Verhandlungen,* I, 179–196.

West, Robert C., Norbert P. Psuty, and Bruce G. Thom. *The Tabasco Lowlands of Southeastern Mexico.* (Louisiana State University, Coastal Studies Institute, Technical Report no. 70, November 30, 1969.) Baton Rouge, 1969.

Wilken, Gene C. "Food-Producing Systems Available to the Ancient Maya," *American Antiquity,* XXXVI(1971), 432–448.

World Health Organization, Geneva. *Manual of International Statistical Classification of Diseases, Injurises, and Causes of Death, Vol. I. International classification of Diseases.* 7th rev., 1955. Geneva, 1957.

Ximénez, Francisco. *Historia de la provincia de San Vicente de Chiapa y Guatemala.* Guatemala City, 1929–1931. 3 vols.

Yucatan. Papeles relativos a la visita del oidor Dr. Diego Garcia de Palacio. Año de 1583, AGN, *Boletín,* ser. 1, XI(1940), 385–482.

Zacatecas (state). Gobernador. *Memoria,* 1869–1870, 1870–1871.

Glossary

Adelantado. A formal title given by royal grant to the leader of an expedition of conquest and held by him thereafter as governor of the conquered area.

Adulto. An adult.

Africanos. Literally Africans, but applied to persons of whole or part-Negro descent.

Animas de confesión. Persons held to confession and communion, that is, adults in religious terms.

Audiencia. In colonial Spanish America, a high court of appeal and the territory of its jurisdiction. In a viceregal capital, the court functioned as viceregal council as well as judicial body; where there was no viceroy, it functioned as governing body for the territory.

Cabecera. Within a district, the seat of administration; within a town, the core settlement and center of authority.

Cabecera de curato. The chief town in a parish.

Caja. A royal treasury.

Casa. House or household.

Casado. A married men; in the plural the term may be applied to all married persons.

Casco. The built-up core of settlement within a town's territory.

Cédula or cédula real. A royal command from the monarch in Spain to the colonial administration or to any person in the colonies.

Confesados, confesantes. People taking part in confession and mass; the term was sometimes used to count Indians of the age of puberty and above.

De administración. Under civil or religious administration in a district or parish.

Delegación. A district within the territory of Quintana Roo, where settlement is too sparse for the standard division into municipios.

Despoblado. Land without people; waste.

Doctrina. An Indian parish administered by friars acting as parish priests; originally a missionary parish.

Donativo gracioso. Legally a voluntary offering by the people to the monarch; in practice compulsory, but given this name because only the Cortes could authorize compulsory direct levies.

Encomendero. A person holding an encomienda.

Encomienda. A grant by the Crown to a private person of the right to the tribute due the Crown from a town or towns.

Europeos. Literally, Europeans; in Spanish America applied to persons born in Europe.

Expediente. A file of papers or docket.

Fanega. A Spanish unit of dry measure, somewhat larger than the U.S. bushel. In colonial Mexico a fanega of maize was 101 U.S. pounds by weight, or 100 Castilian pounds.

Gente menuda. People not counted as full tributaries although they helped to pay the tribute assessed against the town; in particular, unmarried men and women and widows and widowers.

Gente de razón. Literally, people of reason. In its widest usage, the term meant all non-Indians; in a narrower and less frequent usage, it was applied to middle and upper class people of European culture.

Hombres. Men, adult males.

Indios de barrio. Indians living in suburbs of Spanish cities and therefore held to a different rate of tribute from that of Indians living in Indian towns.

Indios de pueblo. Indians living in towns under Indian local administration and paying tribute through the town.

Laboríos. Indian workers on haciendas, without connection with an Indian town; held to a lower rate of tribute.

Laboríos y vagos. Indian laborers attached to Spanish estates and Indians without affiliation to any town or estate.

Legajo. A bundle of documents, especially in an archive.

Memorias. Reports, usually annual.

Naborías, naboríos. Indians working for Spaniards and usually settled close to or within Spanish cities. (For term as used in Hispaniola, see glossary of volume I.)

Negros y mulatos horros. Free Negroes and mulattoes.

Negros y mulatos libres. Free Negroes and mulattoes.

Niños, niñas. Children, often the age group between nursing infants and adolescents.

Obvenciones. In the nineteenth century a head tax on Indian adult males paid in lieu of tithes for the support of the Church.

Oidor. A judge of the audiencia or high court of appeal.

Pardos. People of Negro or part-Negro descent.

Partido. A district.

Párvulos. Children, usually those under age 12–15.

Personas de confesión. People taking part in confession and receiving communion; adults.

Poblezuelos. Small towns.

Principales. Indian nobility.

Ramo. A section in AGN; a division within a legajo or volume in AGI.

Real. A silver coin in colonial and nineteenth century Mexico, worth one-eighth of a peso or of one ounce of silver; worth 12 ½ U.S. cents.

Real cédula. See cédula.

Relación. A report or a description.

Reservados. Indians exempt from tribute.

Rumbo. A subdivision within a parish.

Solteros. Unmarried males; in a wider usage, all unmarried people of both sexes.

Subcaja. A subtreasury.

Subdelegación. A district within an intendancy administered by a subdelegado; often called a partido.

Sujetos. Subordinate villages and settlements within an Indian town.

Sujetos de doctrina. Towns other than the cabecera within a parish.

Tributarios enteros. Full tributaries.

Unión libre. Consensual sexual union; formation of a family group without civil or religious marriage ceremony.

Vecinos. Citizens or residents of a town; householders.

Vicaría. A district administered separate from other parishes but not regarded as yet fully a parish.

Villa. A Spanish city of second rank, below a ciudad but above a pueblo.

Visita. A formal tour of inspection by a government official or a bishop.

Visita de curas. Under administration by secular clergy.

Viudos. Widowers; in a wider sense, both widows and widowers.

Index

Acalán: Mayan state, 2; evidence of Mayan cultivation, 3–4; population at Conquest, 36–38; decimation of population, 47; description of (1525–1530), 36–37

Acalán-Tixchel, tributaries in, 47

Acapulco, non-Indian population, 237

Aguascalientes, non-Indian population, 221

Aguirre Beltrán, Gonzalo: data on racial distribution, 183, 196–199, 226, 238; distortions in data on racial distribution, 185; racial categories of, 188–189, 195, 226, 258; data on racial distribution revised, 199–200

Antequera: number of couples in, 1777, 240; racial amalgamation in, 261–262; high fertility ratios in, 327

Apache tribe, 220

Archbishop of Mexico, 297

Archivo General de Indias, 183, 184, 185, 200, 323

Archivo General de la Nación, 183, 186, 213, 240, 323, 331, 338

Arizona, as ultimate frontier of Mexico, 221

Arriaga, Eduardo: data on European immigration to Mexico, 1921–1960, 267–268; studies in infant mortality, 371, 372, 373; views on low death rate, 408

Asensio, Father Cristobal de, inspection of Pencuyut, 29

Audiencia of Guatemala: jurisdiction over Yucatan, 6; ratified tribute schedules, 8, 40; reviewed tribute system, 9

Audiencia of Mexico: jurisdiction over Yucatan after 1560, 6; appeals for tribute exemptions to, 12; exempted Mexican Indians in Yucatan from tribute, 77; Indian population, 199

Audiencia of Nueva Galicia, Indian population, 199

Augustinian missionaries, data from parish reports, 51, 54

Bacalar, Indian population, 113

Bahía de la Ascensión, flight of fugitive Indians to, 118

Banda, Longinos, source of mortality data, 339, 342, 348, 354, 402–407

Belize, Maya in, 2

Benificios Altos, increase in Indian population, 113

Beneficios Bajos, 86

Bienvenida, Fray Lorenzo de: household and family data for Yucatan, 27, 29, 31; description of Indian towns, 30; estimates of Indian population at Conquest, 30, 33, 35–36; Indian towns listed by, 36

Birth rates. See Natality

Bishop of Guadalajara, report of pastoral inspections by, 185

British Honduras. See Belize

Caja de Mérida, royal treasury in Yucatan, 6

California, Antigua, Baja, or Lower: non-Indian population, 220, 221

California, upper, as ultimate frontier of Mexico, 221

Camino Real Bajo, decrease in Indian population in, 113

Campeche: boundaries of, 1, 2; area of, 2; geography of, 2–3, 176; description of town at Conquest, 31, 32; Spanish villas in, 40; personas de confesión in, 53, 81; tribute counts, 70–72; tributaries to total population ratio, 72; militia in, 80–81; population counts, 80–81, 84, 85, 86; population density, 137, 145; urbanization in, 145, 154, 174, 175; increase in population to 1960, 154

Candelaria River, 2, 36

Cárdenas Valencia, Francisco de, population data for Yucatan, 79–82, 97, 102

Carmen, Isla del, as separate federal territory, 120

Casados, 48, 49, 65

Catálogo de los curatos of 1813, 102, 103

Celaya, non-Indian population, 221

Census(es): national, 121, 122, 130, 288, 297, 317; decennial counts, 130, 318, 327; military, of 1789–1793, 183, 331; Revillagigedo census, 185–186, 297, 323; racial data in, 201, 203–207, 238–251; data on marriage in, 238–251;

birth rate data in, 287, 294; Oaxaca state census, 288; fertility data in, 323, 324, 326, 327; coverage poor after Revolution, 330–331; improvement in procedures, 331; mortality data in, 338, 344. *See also* individual censuses; *Matrícula de Tributarios* of 1805

Census of 1742–1746, racial data in, 183, 184, 200–201, 203–207

Census of 1777: racial data in, 183, 185, 195, 207, 213, 238–239, 240–241, 248–252; demographic reports by parish priests, 185; source for fertility ratios, 323, 326

Census of 1789, 83–84, 92, 213

Census of 1793: racial data in, 195, 213, 238–239, 240–241, 248, 252; mortality data in, 338, 344

Census of 1794–1795: population data in, 92–93, 97, 102–103, 106, 154, 156; territorial divisions in, 145–146, 150, 168–169

Census of 1910: most complete prior to Revolution, 130; territorial divisions in, 146, 150; population data in, 154, 156–157, 165, 169, 174

Census of 1950, data on Indian population in, 267

Census of 1960: population data in, 131, 137, 152, 154, 165, 169, 174; territorial divisions in, 146, 150, 156–157, 146–150; municipalities in Oaxaca, 361

Chalco, population of, 200

Champotón, description of town at Conquest, 31, 32

Chan Santa Cruz, fugitive settlement, 127

Chauaca: household and family data for, 29; description of town (1528), 31–32, 34; tributaries in, 64

Chetumal: area of, 2; Indian population at Conquest, 32, 33; decimated by Montejo expedition, 47; urbanization in, 174

Church records: parish counts, 50–55, 65, 74–75, 80–81, 97, 102–103, 106–107, 111–114, 131, 185; Bishop's *visita* of 1736, 97; continual counts ended after Mexican independence, 121; marriage data in, 270–271, 277; birth data in, 286–288, 295, 297, 323; mortality data in, 338–339, 402–407. *See also* Franciscan missionaries

Civil records: marriage data in, 271–272, 274–277, 283, 284; marriage data incomplete, 275, 355; birth data in, 286, 288, 294–295; introduction of, 304; problems in birth records, 304, 317; mortality data in, 338, 358–359, 401, 425; territorial divisions in, 361; de-

fects in mortality records, 364, 369, 370, 373, 402; mortality data compared to Banda's, 404; causes of death recorded in, 418, 430; stillbirths recorded in, 425

Cochua, decimated after Conquest, 47

Cogolludo, Diego López de: description of religious education of young, 51–52; report on compulsory church attendance for Indians, 68–69; population data by, 102; description of calamities, 115–119 *passim*

Compendo estadístico, 1960, 355

Conil, pre-Conquest population estimates, 32, 33, 34

Convent(s): as territorial unit, 131; size of settlement, 134–136; sphere of influence, 136

Cordero, Eduardo, studies in infant mortality, 371, 372, 373, 383

Córdoba, Hernández de, expedition to Yucatan, 4–5, 38

Cortés, Hernán: expedition to Yucatan, 4–5; expedition to Acalán, 36, 37

Costa, La: heads of families in, 86; return of fugitives to, 118

Cozumel, island of: 34, 49, 54; household and family data for, 28–29; Indian towns in, 34; in census of 1570, 65; disappears from population record after 1639, 113

Cusama, household and family data for, 29

Death rate. *See* Mortality

Demographic materials: tribute lists, 7, 8, 13, 40, 45–50, 55, 70–83 *passim*; public school lists, 83–84; 97; in published form after 1813, 120–121; population counts reviewed, 130–131; sources of data on racial groups, 182–187, 186, 195; sources of marriage data, 270–272; sources of birth data, 286–296 *passim,* 303–304, 317, 318; sources of mortality data, 338–339, 358, 359. *See also* Church records; Civil records

Demographic methods: conversion factors (1543–1813), 48–55; population ratios, 48–55, 204–205; logarithmic formulations, 95–96, 255–257, 376–377, 379, 381, 384, 389; territorial consolidation of data, 103, 362; 4 × 4 and 3 × 3 tables for marital combinations, 241, 248–249; intragroup to extragroup marital ratios, 251–257; projections of racial composition of population, 259–262, 265–269; data collection, marriage records, 271; problems in statistical analysis of marriage records, 272–277; heaping, 274, 323, 362, 363; crude birth rate, 286, 322; fertility ratios,

322, 327, 331–332; births to marriages ratios, 339, 340, 341; mortality ratios, 339, 340, 341; problems in mortality data collection, 340, 344, 359–363; age distribution groups in mortality records, 363; life tables in mortality studies, 363, 372, 373–374, 380, 383, 384, 388, 395, 397, 404; procedures for analysis of death records, 364, 369, 373–374; percentage of omissions in death records, 372; probability of death (q_o) in life table, 372; deletion of ages 0–4 in mortality calculations, 373; expectation of life (e_x), 374, 381–407 passim; probability of death (q_x) 374–397 passim, 401, 402; graphic interpolation, 375–376, 380; classification of causes of death, 410–414; percentage distribution of causes of death, 414, 416, 423–429 passim; graphs of mortality figures, 414, 417, 418, 420, 423, 428, 430, 431; ratios of causes of death, 418, 419, 420

Departmento de Estadística Naciónal, 317

Díaz de Alpuche, Giraldo, 63

Diez de la Calle, Juan: source of racial data, 182; population data for urban centers, 199

Dirección General de Estadística, crude death rates published by, 371–372

Dohot, tributaries in, 63

Donativo gracioso, 19

Donativo list of 1599, population data from, 131

Donzel, Julián, 17

Durango: racial groups in, 205–207, 211–212, 213, 220, 221, 224; number of couples in, 240; fertility ratios for, 323, 325–326, 327

Ecab, 4, 32, 34

Echánove, Policarpo Antonio de, population data by, 83, 84

Encomenderos, 55–65, 77, 119

Encomiendas: as main support of Spaniards, 5; expropriation of by Crown, 12; listed, 97; boundaries not defined, 131

Family. See Household and family data

Fertility ratios: child-female ratios, 322; differences in urban and rural areas, 327; changes over 200 years, 330, 337; differences in racial groups, 332, 336–337; since 1900, 337

Fiscal records. See Tribute counts and assessments

Franciscan missionaries: opposition to tribute assessments, 8, 10, 11; lists of convents and towns, 35–36; report on convents in Yucatan, 52–53; data on Indian population, 65, 68–70, 74–75, 97, 102, 103, 106–107, 113–114; efforts to return fugitives to Spanish control, 118; dominant sect in Yucatan, 177; resettlement of Indians by, 177

Fuenclara, population count of 1742–1746, 183

García Cubas, estimate of population, 127–128

García de Palacio, Dr. Diego: effect of visit to Yucatan, 10, 11; population counts by, 49, 50, 54, 63–65

González, Blas, report on Indian population, 34, 63

Grijalva, Juan de, expedition to Yucatan, 4–5

Guadalajara: marriage data from, 272, 277, 283–284; mortality data from, 359, 360, 383–384, 386–388; causes of death in, 414, 418, 419, 420, 421, 423, 425. See also Jalisco

Guanajuato: non-Indian population, 220, 221, 235, 237; number of couples in, 240; European immigration to, 268; birth rate in, 297, 319

Guatemala, Maya in, 2

Guerrero, non-Indian population, 237

Gutiérrez Picón, Juan, population report by, 34

Hidalgo: racial groups in, 201, 205–207; number of couples in, 240

Household and family data: for pre-Conquest Yucatan, 24–29; multifamily households, 25–30; reported by Bienvenida, 27, 29, 31; ratio of persons to household units, 82; number of families in Mexico (1742–1746), 204; types of marriage, 275–276

Huatulco, non-Indian population, 237

Humboldt, Alexander Von, birth rate data by, 297, 297n, 319

Ichmul, tributaries in, 63

Igualapa, non-Indian population, 237

Indian population: relocation of by Spanish, 9–10; in service to Spanish, 11, 14, 76; size of households, colonial period, 24–25; decimation after Conquest, 30, 36, 37–38, 39, 40, 64–65, 69, 115–116; rebellion of 1545–1547, 55, 64; reported by encomenderos, 55–65, 71; pre-Conquest estimates, 60–61, 180; indios de pueblo (1580–1610), 65–75; required counts at mass, 68–69; counts underestimated, 69–70; estimates, colonial period (1610–1813), 96–114; density and distribution in Yucatan, 107, 113–114, 129–156; movement, 100, 113–

114, 145, 156, 174; effects of disasters
on, 114–120; fugitive settlements in
interior, 116–120, 127–128, 137, 178,
179; survival of pure racial type, 267.
See also Household and family data:
Population; Tributary(ies); Yucatan
Informe de Curatos, 183, 185, 200, 203
Instituto Nacional de Antropología e
Historia, 271
Irapuato, non-Indian population, 221
Isthmus of Tehuantepec, 176, 180, 192,
226
Itzamkanac, description of town, 37

Jicayán, non-Indian population, 237
Jalisco: racial groups in, 203, 235; age
at marriage in, 284; parish records from,
339; mortality data from, 348, 354,
358–408 *passim,* 424; geographical features of, 360; geographical regions in,
362; causes of death in, 414–435 *passim*

Landa, Fray Diego de: description of pre-
Conquest households, 25–27; description of epidemic, 38; report on pre-
Conquest disasters, 40; report on decimation of population after Conquest,
47; report of age at marriage, 51;
work among fugitive Indians in
Yucatan, 117
Lista de las localidades (1960), 156–157
Localidades de la república (1960), 157
López de Velasco, Juan: population data
by, 45; racial distribution data by,
196, 197–198
López Medel, Lic. Tomás, changes in
tribute system by, 9
Luján, Alonso de, population data by,
24, 32

Malaria, incidence of, 431–435 *passim*
Maldonado, Fernando Centeno, campaign to return fugitives, 118
Marriage: age at, reported by Landa,
51; marital patterns of racial groups,
195, 238–241, 248–257; proportion of
intragroup to extragroup, 248–259
passim; sources of data, 270–272; relation to population dynamics of age at,
270, 272; unión libre, 270, 275, 276;
mean age at, 272–273, 274; types of,
275–276; Church-sanctioned, 275–276,
283; socio-economic differences in marital patterns, 276, 281–282, 283, 284
Martyr, Peter, estimate of population at
Conquest, 31
Matrícula de Tributarios of 1805: population data from, 49, 50, 93, 94, 95, 97;
racial data from, 95, 183, 187, 223–226,
235–237, 238; fertility ratios from, 331,
332, 336–337

Maya Indians: pre-Conquest history, 3–4;
different estimates of peak population,
22; household and family data, 24–30;
flight to interior, 116–120; growth of
independent communities, 117. *See also*
Indian population
Mayapán, League of, 4, 40
Mazanahau, pre-Conquest population
estimates, 32, 33
Memoria of 1580, 65, 68, 69
Memoria of 1582, 65, 69, 70, 74, 102, 131,
134–135
Memoria of 1586, 65, 68, 69
Mérida: royal treasury in, 6; Spanish
villas in, 40; tributary population of,
49; population counts in, 70–72; 80;
tributaries to total population ratio,
72; non-Indian population, 80, 85;
capital city of Yucatan, 84–85, 120;
Indian to non-Indian population ratios
for, 84; Indian population, 85, 113;
household and family data for, 86;
growth of city, 145, 154
Mexican Constitution of 1917, 146
Mexican Revolution (1910–1920): 286,
295, 298, 330; demographic effects of,
318, 361, 399, 401; lack of mortality
records during, 360
Mexico City: royal treasury in, influence
on Yucatan, 95; immigration to, 268;
birth rate in, 297; low fertility ratio
for, 327
Mexico: War of Independence, demographic effects of, 120, 187, 258, 322, 338;
federation, 120, 136, 137; geographical
variations in effects of Conquest, 176;
decimation of population after
Conquest, 176, 180, 394; land not
available for fugitives, 178; population
decimation and recovery compared to
Yucatan, 179; population density,
(1519), 180; Spanish population (1521),
180; racial groups in, 195, 199–201,
205–207, 210–213, 220–221, 226, 235–
238; geographical areas in, 192–194,
199; regional differences in population,
205; geographical distribution of racial
groups, 206–207, 210–213; northwest,
as wild Indian country, 220; geographical distribution of tributaries, 235–238;
European immigration to (1921–1960),
267–268; fertility ratios for, 297, 327,
330, 337; population increase (1650–
1850), 342. *See also* Jalisco; Oaxaca
Mexico, province and state of: racial
groups in, 201, 203, 205–207, 221, 224,
235; number of couples in, 240–241;
high fertility ratios for, 327
Michoacán, racial groups in, 206, 221,
235

Minuta de los encomenderos of 1606, 70, 71, 72

Mixteca Alta: non-Indian population, 205; marriage records from, 271, 272; birth rates in, 286–296; mortality data for, 339–343, 354; causes of death in, 433, 434. *See also* Oaxaca

Mixteca Baja, marriage records from, 272. *See also* Oaxaca

Mochi, pre-Conquest population estimates, 32, 34

Montejo, Francisco de: role of in Conquest of Yucatan, 5; expedition of 1528, 34; expedition to Acalán, 37; expedition to Uaymil-Chetumal, 47; expedition to Southern Yucatan, 117

Morelos, non-Indian population, 201

Mortality: decline in death rate, 285, 338, 358, 369; high birth rate coupled with high death rate, 295, 407–408; decline in infant mortality, effect on fertility ratio, 331; sources of data, 338–339, 358, 359; ratios, prior to 1850, 338–357; births to deaths ratios, 340, 341; problems in data collection, 340, 344, 359–363, regional disparities in, 354, 355; underregistration of infant deaths, 370–371, 404; crude death rates for U.S. and Mexico compared, 372; expectation of life (e_x), 374, 381–407 *passim*; probability of death (q_x), 374–397 *passim*, 401, 402; comparison of mortality, Jalisco and Oaxaca, 383; geographical differences in, 388–399, 425–435; differences over course of time, 395–408; changes in after Revolution of 1910–1920, 399–401; mean age at death, 404–405, 406, 407; classification of causes of death, 409–414, 430–431; percentage distribution of causes of death, 414–416; most common epidemic and infective diseases, 414, 421–423, 424, 431–435 *passim*

Nahuatl zone, 1

Narváez, Pánfilo, 38

Natality: baptismal records, 287–288; problem of incomplete registration of births, 287–288, 295; sources of data on birth rates in the Mixteca Alta, 286–296 *passim*; high birth rate coupled with high death rate, 295, 407–408; uniformity of birth rate over 300 years, 296, 319, 321; birth ratios, sources for, 303–304, 317, 318; failure to report births, 317; birth rates, Mexico and U.S. compared, 319, 321; high birth rate coupled with low death rate, 408. *See also* Fertility ratios

Nayarit, non-Indian population, 221

New Mexico, Indian population, 220 221

New Spain: Yucatan as province of, 1; free trade granted, 6; racial groups in, 201–205, 226, 238; total tributary population (1805), 238; population increase in, 297. *See also* Mexico

Noriega y Navarro, Fernando de, 93

Nueva Galicia: non-Indian population, 205; racial groups in, 206; decimation of population in, 394

Oaxaca: census of 1777, 48–49; racial groups in, 205–207, 211–212, 221, 224; number of couples in, 240; survival of pure Indian racial type in, 267; marriage records from, 271, 272, 273–274, 277, 281–285; examination of birth ratios in the Mixteca Alta, 286–296 *passim*; state census, 288; fertility ratios in, 323, 326, 327; population distribution by age (1777), 326; mortality data from, 359–408 *passim*, 424; geographical features of, 360; geographical regions in, 362; underregistration of infant deaths in, 383; climate in, 393; causes of death in, 414–435 *passim*

Obvenciones, 121, 128

Ordinance of Intendants of 1786, 49n, 93

Oviedo y Valdés, Gonzalo Fernandez de, estimates of population by, 30–35 *passim*

Pacheco, Alonso, 30

Pacheco, Gaspar, 30

Pánuco, non-Indian population, 236

Paredes, Juan de, 17

Parish, as territorial unit, 131

Paso y Troncoso, Francisco del, tribute counts of, 40, 45

Paxbolon, Pablo: expedition to interior of Yucatan, 117; cacique of Tixchel, 117, 118

Peñafiel, Antonio, 317

Pencuyut, population of, 28, 29, 49

Petén: region of Guatemala, 2; Indian population (1549), 48; flight of fugitive Indians to, 118

Philip II, 11, 18

Picón, Gutierrez, household and family data by, 29

Population: decimation after Conquest, 62, 137, 177, 179, 394; distribution in cities, 92; trends, 95–96, 120–129, 154–156, 177–179; graph of change, 96; movement, 100, 113–114, 145, 156, 174, 331; density and distribution, 129–156, 326; settlement size, 134–136, 156–176; Mexico and Yucatan compared at Conquest, 176, 177; problems in determining validity of data, 200–201; urban-rural distribution, 221–223; total tributary (1805), 238; effects of physical environment, 394; at low point in 1610, 407. *See also* Indian population; Racial groups; Tributary(ies)

Population categories: tributaries, 8, 10–14, 332; gente menuda, 10; indios de pueblo, 11, 75–76; negros y mulatos horros (pardos), 11, 12, 75; mestizos, 11, 75; naboríos, 11, 76; personas de confesión, 51, 53, 102; children, 51–53, 85, 86, 331, 332; Europeans, 75; non-Indians, 75–76, 188–189, 195, 226; gente de razón, 75, 332; laboríos, 76; Mexican Indians, 76–77; heads of families, 85, 86; school-age children, 85, 86; españoles, 195; age categories, 323, 326, 327, 341–342; casados, 331, 332; solteras, 331, 332; viudas, 331, 332. *See also* Racial groups

Population ratios: tributaries to total population, 47, 48, 50, 61–63, 64, 70, 72, 79, 82, 83, 95, 99, 102; method, 48–55, 204–205; casados to total population, 48, 65; differences between Mexico and Yucatan, 49, 50, 54; personas de confesión to total population, 51, 53–55, 65, 75, 102, 106; children to total population, 53, 54; persons to households, 77, 79, 80–81, 82; Indians to non-Indians, 84–86, 102–103, 128–129; adult/child, 85–86; urban to rural populations, 175; vecinos to total population, 196, 198; non-Indians to total population, 199, 201–207, 211, 214–216; pardos to total tributaries, 211, 212, 224, 237–238, 269; intragroup to extragroup marriages, 251–257; Europeans to total population, 268; births to total population, 297

Public schools, 83–84, 97

Puebla: groups in, 205–207, 211–212, 213, 224, 235, 265; number of couples in, 240; fertility ratios for, 323, 325

Puuc: mountain range in Yucatan, 2; settlement of, 114; fugitive settlements in, 118

Querétaro: non-Indian population, 221, 235, 237; number of couples in, 240; birth rate in, 297, 319

Quijada, Diego, governor of Yucatan, 11

Quintara Roo: area of, 1–2; geography of, 3; as separate federal territory, 120, 130; population density in, 137, 145; increase in population in, 154; urbanization in, 174, 175; flight of Indians to, 178

Racial groups: categories, 11, 75–76,

180, 181, 187–191, 195, 205, 226; not recorded in censuses after 1810, 121–122, 187, 258; in Yucatan, 178–179; interbreeding after Conquest, 180, 181; sources of data, 182–187, 186, 195; categories of Aguirre Beltrán, 188–189, 226; distinctions blurred, 189; socio-economic differences, 190; geographical distribution of, 191–194, 206, 213, 221, 224–225, 227, 235–238; problems in using data, 203–206; marital patterns of, 238–241, 248–257; fusion of, 257–269; exponential disappearance of pure racial types, 260–267; European immigrants, 267–269

Ramo de Historia: general census in, 186; racial data from, 213, 220; data on European immigration from, 268; fertility data from, 323, 326, 330, 331, 332

Ramo de Padrones: population data from, 186; racial data from, 213, 220; source of data on intergroup marriage, 240, 241; fertility data from, 331, 332; mortality data from, 338, 343–344

Relaciones Geográficas of 1579–1582: 5, 7, 18, 34; description of Indian houses in, 24–25; source for geography of Yucatan at Conquest, 45; index to population change in 16th century Yucatan, 55–65; written by encomenderos, 63; definition of tributary in, 63–64; population total in, 68

Repartimiento de mercancias, 117

Revillagigedo census, 185–186, 297, 323

Revolution of 1910–1920, demographic effects of, 318, 361, 399

Roys, Ralph: population study of Yucatan, 23, 130; data on Indian towns, 32, 33, 34, 45, 47, 48; tributaries counted by, 45–46

Sahcabchén, resettlement of returned fugitives in, 118

Salamanca de Bacalar: Spanish villas in, 40; population, 81, 92, 169

Sanders, estimate of population of Yucatan, 48

San Luis Potosí, racial groups in, 224

Sierra Baja, Indian population in, 113

Sinaloa, non-Indian population, 220, 221

Smallpox: epidemic, 38–39; decline in, 432–433, 434

Sonora, non-Indian population, 220, 221

Sopuerta, Fray Hernando de, 65

Spaniards: conquest of Yucatan by, 5; in Yucatan, 5, 76–77, 180; efforts of to return fugitive Indians to towns, 117–120; resettlement of Indians by, 131, 134; area of Yucatan under administra-

tive control of, 139; destruction by, 176;
immigration of, 180; northward advance of, 199. *See also* Population
categories; Tribute system
Statistical Abstract of the United States,
1968, 372

Tabasco: borders with Yucatan, 1–2;
Maya in, 2; branch of royal treasury
in, 6; non-Indian population, 84; geo-
graphy of, 176
Tarahumara tribes, 207
Tarascan territory, non-Indian popula-
tion, 205
Taxation. *See* Tribute counts and assess-
ments
Tehuantepec, 204, 236, 237
Tejupan, marriage data from, 282
Teozacoalco, marriage data from, 282
Tepehuán tribes, 207
Teposcolula, marriage data from, 281, 282
Testimo del donativo of 1599, 70, 72,
97, 102, 103, 106
Theatro americano, 183, 184–185, 200
Tixcacaltuyu, 53
Tixchel, 38, 117
Tizimín, 35, 86
Tlaxcala, racial groups in, 205–207, 220,
221
Tlaxiaco, marriage data from, 281
Toltec conquest, 1
Toltec confederation, 22
Torres, Gaspar de, 46
Tributary(ies): definitions of, 8, 10, 10n26,
10n28, 11–14, 48, 50, 62–64, 188, 226;
conversion from tributaries to total
population, 47; tributaries to total
population ratios, 47, 48, 50, 61–64,
70, 72, 79, 82, 83, 95, 99, 102; fertility
ratios for, 332, 336–337; lists of, 9, 97
Tribute counts and assessments: as demographic source, 7, 8, 13, 40, 45–50, 55,
70–83 *passim,* 93–102 *passim*; first official schedules, 8; objections of Franciscan missionaries to, 8; quotas, 8–9,
10–11, 12, 13, 14, 40, 77, 82, 94; reassessments, 9, 10–11, 14, 93, 94; use of
Church records for, 9n23, 65, 68–69,
74–75; by García de Palacio, 10–11,
49, 50, 63–65; exemptions, 11, 12–13,
14, 76, 77, 95, 237; evasions, 14; by
encomenderos, 55–61; of non-Indians,
76, 77, 79; of naboríos, 82; replaced by
obvenciones, 121; as source of racial
data, 182. *See also Matrícula de Tributarios* of 1805
Tribute system: as basic support of
Spanish, 5; different from pre-Conquest
system, 8; during colonial period, 8–14;
renewed by López Medel (1552–1553),

9; exemptions, 11, 12–13, 14, 76, 95,
237; changes in 17th-18th century,
12–14
Triple Alliance, 1, 192, 193

Uaymil-Chetumal: decimation by Spanish
conquest, 30, 47–48, 61; geography of,
47
Uaymil, pre-Conquest population estimates, 32, 33
Urrutia, Juan de, 64

Valladolid: Spanish settlements in, 5, 40;
Indian population, 46, 72; indoctrina-
tion of Indian children in, 53; non-
Indian population, 80, 86
Vázquez de Espinosa, Antonio: population data by, 70, 74–75, 97, 102, 131,
134–135; racial data by, 182
Veracruz: Spanish landing at, 180; racial
groups in, 210–211, 236–237; survival
of pure Indian racial type in, 267
Villaseñor y Sánchez, José Antonio, 183
184–185, 200
Viudos, marriage data on, 273–274

War of Independence, 1810–1820, demographic effects of, 127, 187, 258, 322,
338
War of the Castes, demographic effects of,
6–7, 121, 126–127, 178
World Health Organization, classification
of causes of death, 410

Yucatan: area of, 1–2; boundaries of, 1–2,
131; geography of, 1–3, 5, 47, 115, 116,
129–130, 176, 177, 179; Mayan history
and culture, 1–4; history of, 1–7; political organization of, 4, 6, 120, 138, 144–
146, 152; League of Mayapán, 4, 40;
particularism in, 6–7, 120; War of the
Castes, demographic effects of, 6–7, 121,
126–127, 178; economic isolation of,
6–7, 176; development of trade in, 6,
178; historical divisions for population
study, 7; population categories in, 8,
10–14, 51–53, 75–76, 79, 85, 86, 128–129,
178; population of at Conquest, 22–40,
48, 177; pre-Conquest population estimates, 22–40, 176; decimation of population after Conquest, 62, 137, 177,
179; Indian rebellion of 1545–1547,
55, 64; Mexican Indians in, 76; population movement in, 100, 114, 145, 156,
174; population density and distribution, 107, 113–114, 129–156; calamities
and fugitivism in, 114–120; raided by
English and French corsairs, 117, 119;
basis for taxation after independence,
121; graph of population (1549–1960),

122; independent native states in, 127, 137; effect of Revolution of 1910–1920, 128; immigration to, 128–129, 178–179; settlement size, 134–136, 156–176; urbanization in, 145, 174, 175; peak population in Toltec period, 176; population history compared to Mexico, 176–179 *passim*; geographical variations in effects of Conquest, 177; Franciscans dominant sect in, 177; little racial fusion in, 178–179. *See also* Household and family

data; Indian population; Tributary(ies); Tribute counts and assessments; Tribute system
Yumpetén, pre-Conquest population estimates, 32–33

Zacatecas, 203
Zacatula, non-Indian population, 236–237;
Zapoteca. *See* Oaxaca
Zapotitlán, 47, 117